# World Myth

### Barry B. Powell
*University of Wisconsin-Madison*

**PEARSON**

Boston   Columbus   Indianapolis   New York   San Francisco   Upper Saddle River
Amsterdam   Cape Town   Dubai   London   Madrid   Milan   Munich   Paris   Montreal   Toronto
Delhi   Mexico City   São Paulo   Sydney   Hong Kong   Seoul   Singapore   Taipei   Tokyo

# Dedication

*This book is for the grands Grace and Spencer,*
*who always sit quietly for a good story*

**Editor in Chief:** Joe Terry
**Editorial Assistant:** Sean Strathy
**Editorial Director:** Joe Opiela
**Senior Marketing Manager:** Joyce Nilsen
**Production Project Manager:** Debbie Ryan
**Creative Art Director:** Jayne Conte
**Cover Designer:** Suzanne Behnke
**Cover Art:** Werner Forman/Art Resource, NY
**Full-Service Project Management:** Chitra Ganesan
**Composition:** PreMediaGlobal
**Printer/Binder/Cover Printer:** STP/RRD/Harrisonburg
**Text Font:** Minion Pro-Regular 10/12

Credits and acknowledgments borrowed from other sources and reproduced, with permission, in this textbook appear on the appropriate page within the text.

**Library of Congress Cataloging-in-Publication Data**
Powell, Barry B.
  World myth / Barry B. Powell.
      p. cm.
  Includes index.
  ISBN-13: 978-0-205-73052-0
  ISBN-10: 0-205-73052-3
1. Mythology.  2. Myth.  I. Title.
  BL312.P69 2013
  201'.3—dc23
                                        2012036295

10 9 8 7 6 5 4 3 2

ISBN 10: 0-205-73052-3
ISBN 13: 978-0-205-73052-0

# CONTENTS

# LIST OF MYTHS BY THEME

## MYTHS OF CREATION

## MYTHS OF DEATH

## MYTHS OF FERTILITY

## MYTHS OF THE VENGEFUL OR TREACHEROUS FEMALE

## MYTHS OF PARADISE

## MYTHS OF THE CULTURE BEARER

## MYTHS OF CANNIBALISM

# LIST OF FIGURES

# LIST OF PERSPECTIVES

# MAPS

# CHARTS

# PREFACE

Most books on myths of the world prefer to choose a large theme, such as "myths of the goddess," "trickster myths," and "creation myths," then find stories that appear to fall into the appropriate category. They do not take into account how such stories were preserved in the first place and pay little attention to the historical and cultural forces that lay behind the myths.

In this book I have preferred to organize the myths by *chronology* and *geography*, beginning at the beginning with stories from ancient Sumer and Egypt, and ending with the stories from Oceania, North America, and Africa collected by anthropologists in the 19th and 20th centuries. In this way the stories that people told, and in some cases still tell, reveal how they thought and what they valued. I append a timeline at the beginning of each chapter to show where the various myths come from and how they relate to other mythical traditions.

I also pay attention to how the myths were recorded, which means that in many cases we must consider systems of writing very different from our own. For not all writing systems are the same, and the functioning of writing determines to a surprising degree the shape of a myth. Such a book, arranged chronologically and geographically, becomes, in a very small way, a "history of the world," showing us how different peoples understood their environment and its challenges.

However, I have provided an alternate table of contents organized by theme for those who wish to pursue a thematic approach to world myth. Of course many myths contain more than one theme, so that several myths will fall into different thematic categories.

Naturally the interpretation of myth is a topic of abiding interest, and I have much to say about interpretation as we work our way through different countries and through historical time. I have reserved the last chapter for a systematic review of the schools of myth interpretation, and some instructors may prefer to begin study with this chapter. Nonetheless, I do place interpretation in the background, believing that we should allow these highly varied stories of diverse origins to stand at the forefront of our interest as a treasure of the human spirit, that we should "let the myths speak for themselves." Speculation about the "meaning" of the stories can be very wide-ranging and, often, reflect one's personal prejudices, so that the interpretive remarks I do make will no doubt form the basis as much for objection as agreement!

I have included many maps in the book, and always where a place on the map is first cited in the text, and in some cases peoples, I place that name in SMALL CAPS. I place in **bold typeface** terms and people of special importance to the study of a particular myth and assemble these items under Key Terms at the end of each chapter. I give the pronunciation of unfamiliar and difficult names the first time these names occur, then repeat this information in the Index, which also serves as a glossary. In the Perspectives, I give information that is tangential to the material in the chapters, showing how various myths have inspired other developments, usually in the modern world.

The English versions of the various myths are always in my own voice, prepared with the assistance of the original texts, commentaries, and earlier translations, except for the ethnographical reports of the late 19th and early 20th centuries of Chapters 13–15. I have adopted this practice: When quoted material first appears in a chapter, I say in a note "cf. etc." to indicate the primary sources of my own English version. Then I say, "see also . . ." to give other publications that I have looked at. In the rare cases that stories are not told in my own voice, I indicate the source by means of a footnote.

I hope that readers and instructors will let me know suggestions for future editions. I can be reached at bbpowell@wisc.edu.

## ACKNOWLEDGMENTS

I want to thank William Aylward for his help with the Roman material. Thanks go to my wife Patricia for her assistance in all matters editorial.

—*BBP*
*Santa Fe, 2012*

CHAPTER

1

# The Nature of Myth

Myth is an attempt to narrate a whole human experience, of which the purpose is too deep, going too deep in the blood and soul, for mental explanation or description.

D. H. LAWRENCE (*British poet, novelist, and essayist, 1885–1930*)

Human beings have told stories from time immemorial, for stories are a natural product of spoken language, an outgrowth of the imaginative power that clearly separates us from our animal cousins. The story is a universal ingredient of human culture, bringing relief from the tedium of everyday labor and reminding listeners of their own values, beliefs, and history. Myths reflect the society that produces them. In turn, they determine the nature of that society. They cannot be separated from the physical, social, and spiritual worlds in which a people live or from a people's history.

This book is concerned with a certain type of story known as *myth*. The term *myth* is hard to define, in part because of the enormous variety of stories gathered from many cultures by ethnographers, anthropologists, and literary historians. Originally, the Greek word *mythos* simply meant "authoritative speech," "story," or "plot," but later writers used the term *myth* in more restricted ways. Some recent authorities, exasperated by the complexity of the phenomena, deny that the term *myth* expresses a coherent concept at all. However, a definition widely agreed on is that myth is *a traditional story with collective importance*. We can accept this definition, but we must consider carefully what it means.

## WHAT IS A MYTH?

To say that a myth is a story is to say, first, that it has a plot, a narrative structure consisting of a beginning, a middle, and an end. In the beginning of a typical story, we are introduced to characters whom we find in a certain situation, usually one involving conflict with other characters, with misfortune, or with themselves. The word *charac-ter* is a Greek word meaning "a stamping tool," hence by extension "a certain mental imprint." Hamlet cannot make up his mind, Macbeth is ambitious, King Lear is blind to the nature of others. Character, as a quality, is the sum of the choices one makes. As an actor in a story, a character embodies a certain pattern of choices.

In the middle of a typical story, the situation grows more complex, and tension and conflict develop. In the end, the tension is somehow resolved. Today we might find an example of this basic structure in the plot common to a thousand novels and feature films: Girl meets boy (the beginning), girl loses boy (the middle), girl finds boy (the end). Plot is an essential feature of myth. Without a beginning, a middle, and an end, there can be no story and hence no myth.

In casual speech we sometimes say that the Greek god Zeus, for example, is a myth. However, strictly speaking, Zeus is not a myth, but a character in myth, in the plotted stories that tell of his exploits. Belief in the existence of a particular god, the observance of a ritual in a god's honor, and religious symbols are not myths, although many commentators admit such confusions.

Like all other stories, myths have characters as well as plots. In myths, the characters may be gods, goddesses, or other supernatural beings, but they may also be human beings or even animals that speak and act in the manner of human beings. Another element of myth is setting. The setting is the time and place in which the action of the story unfolds. Myths are never set in the present or the recent past; the action always takes place in the distant past or in a shadowy time altogether outside human chronology. The setting of myths may be in an actual city, or some location familiar to the audience. In other myths, the setting is an obscure place: the underworld, which no one in the real world ever visited; a high mountain, which may exist but in myth is the home of the gods; or somewhere a very long time ago.

Thus myths have plot, characters, and setting, but a myth is not just any story but a certain kind of story that we describe as *traditional*. Our word *traditional* comes from Latin *trado*, "hand over," and a traditional story is one that has been "handed over" orally from one storyteller to another without the intervention of writing. Then eventually somebody—a scribe or scholar—writes it down.

In societies that do not use writing, stories must be handed on verbally, so tradi-tional tales are the vehicle for transmitting one generation's thought to another. In this way, traditional tales maintain contact with the past (about which little real is known) and pass inherited wisdom on to the future. They explain a society to itself, promul-gating its concerns and values.

From this function derives myth's *collective importance*—myths hold meaning for the group, not just the individual. They describe patterns of behavior that serve as models for members of a society, especially in times of crisis. For example, in Homer's *Iliad* (written down in the 8th century BC), Achilles tries to persuade King Priam of Troy to eat at a time when Priam is heartbroken for his dead son Hector, killed by Achilles. Achilles tells the story of Niobê, a Theban princess: Although Artemis and Apollo had killed her seven sons and seven daughters, still she ate, and so should Priam. Four hundred years later, when he was on trial for his life, the philosopher Socrates defended his insistence on telling the truth in spite of threats against him by recalling the example of Achilles, who was ashamed to live as a coward and chose to die bravely before the walls of Troy.

Because they are traditional, myths are also anonymous. In contrast to such modern forms of storytelling as Leo Tolstoy's *War and Peace*, J. R. R. Tolkien's *Lord of the Rings*, J. D. Salinger's *Catcher in the Rye*, or George Lucas's film *Star Wars*, myths never have identifiable authors. Literary works based on myth may have authors, but not the myths themselves. The Greek dramatist Sophocles wrote a play about Oedipus the king, but the *myth* of Oedipus existed long before, and no one can say who created it.

This anonymity helps us understand why the Greeks, following the lead of the philosopher Plato, eventually came to contrast their word *mythos*, "story" or "myth," with *logos*, "account." The teller of a *logos* takes responsibility for the truth of what is said. A *logos* is a reasoned explanation of something that emphasizes a continuing causal sequence, as in the proofs of plane geometry. We still use the suffix *-logy* to indicate a reasoned inquiry into a topic, as in anthropo*logy*, study of human beings; bio*logy*, study of life forms; or even mytho*logy*, study of myth (although *mythology* often is used as a synonym for *myth*). By contrast, the teller of a *mythos* does not claim personal responsibility for what is said. After all, the teller did not invent the story, but only passed it on.

## PERSPECTIVE 1

## The "Myth of Atlantis"

In his dialogue *Timaeus*, Plato puts into the mouth of the Athenian lawgiver Solon (c. 638–c. 559 BC) an account of Solon's trip to Egypt, where he learned of a utopian* kingdom that once existed on an island in the western seas somewhere beyond the Pillars of Heracles (Gibraltar). The island was larger than Libya and Asia together. A powerful, highly civilized people once lived on this vast island until in a single night earthquake and flood destroyed everything; the continent sank beneath the waves. In another dialogue, the *Critias*, Plato gives a still more detailed account of what he now calls Atlantis ("the realm of Atlas," the Titan thought to support the world).

There is no evidence for this story before Plato, who seems to have modeled it on the story of the Hesperides ("nymphs of the West"), the protectors of a magic tree on an island beyond the Pillars of Heracles. The story is not a myth as we have defined the term, because it is not a traditional tale but an artificial construction devised by Plato to make certain points about ideal government. For a long time *Atlantis* was used as equivalent to a utopian state. Francis Bacon (1561–1626), a philosopher and literary figure during the reign of Queen Elizabeth I, wrote *The New Atlantis* about a utopian world.

The modern search for a real Atlantis buried beneath the Atlantic Sea, or some place else, goes back to 1882, with the publication of *Atlantis: The Antediluvian World*, by one Ignatius Donnelly (1831–1901). Donnelly argued that Plato's description

---

*The word *utopia* = Greek "nowhere," a word coined by Sir Thomas More (1478–1535), an advisor to Henry VIII (who beheaded him), for an imaginary perfect state.

**PERSPECTIVE FIGURE 1**   The caldera in the center of the Cycladic island of Thera. Before the huge explosion c. 1620 BC, the largest known in the geological record, this was solid land. (Mikel Bilbao Gorostiaga / Alamy)

was literally true. On the lost island of Atlantis first appeared human civilization, he thought, which then spread outward over the earth. Stories of the Hebrew Garden of Eden, the heavenly Greek Elysian Fields, and the like are reminiscences of Atlantis, whose kings and queens became the gods and goddesses of the Greeks, Phoenicians, Hindus, and Scandinavians. The original religion of Atlantis was sun-worship, preserved in Egypt and Peru. Remnants from the high civilizations of the so-called Bronze Age are really remnants of the Atlantean civilization, which spread to the mainland, bringing with them stories of the Great Flood.

Recent discoveries that the island of Thera, the southernmost of the Cycladic islands in the Aegean Sea, blew up in an enormous volcanic explosion revived hopes of explaining the origin of Plato's story in prehistory (Perspective Figure 1).

It seemed that the explosion might have caused the collapse of the civilization on Crete about 1450 BC, perhaps the origin of the story of Atlantis. However, in 1991, with the help of the radiocarbon dating of ice-cores from Greenland and evidence of frost events in tree rings, the explosion was shown to have taken place about 1620 BC, far too early to have destroyed the Cretan civilization.

Though not a myth, the same methods used to explain traditional myths have been freely applied to the story of Atlantis. Always at the edge of a definition stand exceptions that do not fit. Scholars emphasize Plato's transitional role as a thinker who stood between the oral world from which myth came and the literate world in which we live today.

During oral transmission, a traditional tale is subject to constant change. Different narrators of a story have different motives and emphasize or embroider on different aspects. The story of Niobê could easily illustrate the dangers of self-assertion (Niobê bragged that she had more children than the mother of Apollo and Artemis), but Achilles uses the story to prove that eating food can lessen grief. Homer describes

Achilles' anguished choice between a short, glorious life and a long, inglorious one, but never presents the choice as between courage and cowardice.

In short, we often find strikingly different versions of the same myth. The poets Homer and Sophocles both report that Oedipus, king of Thebes, killed his father and married his mother, but in Homer's account, Oedipus continues to rule after the truth comes out, whereas in Sophocles' play he pokes pins in his eyes and leaves the city, a wretched wanderer. Neither is the "true" version of the myth, of which the other is a variant. The myth of Oedipus contains *all* the variants.

## TYPES OF MYTH

Modern scholars like to distinguish between several types of myth based on the nature of the principal characters and the function that the story fulfilled for the listener and the teller. **Divine myths** (sometimes called *true myths* or *myths proper*) are stories in which supernatural beings are the main actors. Such stories generally explain why the world, or some aspect of it, is the way it is. **Legends** (or sagas) are stories of the great deeds of human heroes or heroines. Legends narrate the events of the human past. The word comes from Latin *legenda*, "things that should be read," that is, originally, morally uplifting stories about Christian saints. **Folktales** are stories whose actors are ordinary people or animals. Folktales entertain the audience and teach or justify customary patterns of behavior. We will discover that in studying myths of the world folktales are *by far* the predominant type.

The more we learn about myth, the more we discover how difficult it can be to separate one type from another. For example, stories that appear to be legends often incorporate elements of folktales or explain the nature of things, as do divine myths. Such distinctions are nonetheless valuable because they allow us to isolate and study various aspects of myth. Let us look more closely at each type.

### Divine Myth

The supernatural beings who are the principal characters in divine myth are depicted as superior to humans in power and splendor. Sometimes they take on human or animal shape at will. They control awesome forces of nature: thunder, storm, rain, fire, earthquake, or fecundity. When these beings appear in their own form, they can be enormous and of stunning beauty or ugliness. Conflicts among them can take place on an immense scale and involve whole continents, high mountains, and vast seas.

Sometimes the supernatural characters in divine myth are little more than personified abstractions without clearly defined personalities. In other cases, the supernatural beings are gods, goddesses, or demons with well-developed and distinctive personalities of their own. The events of divine myth usually take place in a world before or outside the present order where time and space often have different meanings from those familiar to human beings.

For example, one Greek myth explained how Zeus came to rule the world: He fought against the Titans, an earlier race of gods,[1] defeated them in a terrible battle,

---

[1]With a lower case *god* refers to a system in which there are many divine beings; with an uppercase *God* refers to a monotheistic system.

and established his empire on the ruin of theirs. It would be pointless to ask when these events occurred, even within the context of the story, because they are set in a time before human chronology has meaning. Moreover, many divine myths are set in a place far removed from the familiar world of human beings.

Understandably, many of the gods about whom traditional tales were told were both actors in the stories and objects of veneration in religious cult. Because of this double function of the gods, divine myth is easily confused with religion, but the two must be clearly distinguished. Myths are *traditional stories*; religion is *belief and the course of action that follows from belief. Belief* is best defined as "what you accept (with or without proof) as a basis for action." For example, the Egyptians believed that Amun brought victory in war. Therefore, they built great temples to Amun to persuade him to do just that.

Myths often justify a religious practice or a form of religious behavior, but we can retell a myth, even a myth about divine beings, without engaging in religious behavior. The relationship between myth and religion is complicated, and we will have more to say about it later, but we must remember that myth is *a traditional story with collective importance*, whereas religion is *a set of beliefs that motivates a course of action*.

Divine myths served a function in early cultures analogous to that of theoretical science in our own: They explained why the world is the way it is. Many of these myths tell of the origin and destruction of grand things: the universe, the gods, and ourselves; the relations of gods with one another and with human beings; and the divine origin of such human economic and social institutions as the growing of crops, the cycle of the seasons, the making of wine, and prophecy and oracles. Many divine myths deal with limited matters, such as the origin of local customs and practices.

In more technical language, we can describe such explanatory myths as etiological, from the Greek word *aition*, "cause." A creation myth is an example of an **etiological tale** because it explains the causes that brought the world into existence. The etiological tale expresses a conjecture about the cause of something that existed long before the explanation.

Both divine myth and modern science offer explanations of why the world is the way it is, but they do so in very different ways. Scientific explanations are based on impersonal general laws and statistical probabilities discovered, or at least verified, by repeatable quantitative experiments, whereas mythic explanations, expressed in traditional tales, assume that supernatural beings control the world through the exercise of personal will. Assigning human qualities, especially unpredictability, to the forces that stand behind the world is characteristic of the worldview we find in myth. Thunder is an expression of Thor's anger, not the necessary result of impersonal physical forces. Modern scientists may be puzzled by death from cancer, but they do not blame such death on a divine and irrational agent. The modern world was born from the struggle of scientific thought against traditional explanations for why and how things happen in the world, a struggle by no means concluded today.

## Legend

If divine myth in oral cultures is analogous to science in modern, literate Western society, legend is analogous to history. Both legend and modern historical writing attempt to answer the question, "What happened in the human past?" Because the past explains and justifies the present, the telling of legends was an important activity in the cultural life of many peoples.

In legends, the central characters are human beings, not gods and goddesses. Although supernatural beings often play a part, their roles are subordinate to those of the human characters. The principal actors of legend are heroes and heroines. Drawn from the ranks of the nobility, they are kings and queens, princes and princesses, and other members of an aristocratic elite. They have extraordinary physical and personal qualities and are stronger, more beautiful, or more courageous than ordinary people.

Most peoples have no doubt that such legendary figures really lived, and members of important families regard themselves as descended from them. Whereas divine myth is set in a different or previous world-order, legendary events belong to our own order, although they took place in the distant past, at the very beginning of human time when mighty heroes and heroines lived on earth, cities founded, difficult quests undertaken, fearful monsters slain, and momentous wars waged. But early peoples had no way to compare their traditions with historical reality. Today, armed with the insights of archaeology and techniques of historical investigation, modern scholars recognize that the oral transmitters of traditional tales have little respect for historical truth, or even any concept of it. Myth tells us more about the circumstances and concerns of its transmitters than it does about life in the distant past.

Still, legends can contain an element of historical truth. Many or most of the figures of legend probably did live at some time. Modern scholars have long thought that legend does reflect, however dimly, major events and power relations of earlier periods. For example, there probably really was a Trojan War of some kind (Figure 1.1).

**FIGURE 1.1** The walls of Troy. The earliest settlement at Troy can be dated to about 3000 BC, but the citadel walls shown here belong to the sixth level of occupation (Troy VI), built around 1400 BC and destroyed around 1230 BC. Constructed of neatly cut blocks of limestone that slope inward, the citadel wall had at least four gateways, two of them protected by towers. Either Troy VI or its much poorer successor Troy VIIa, destroyed about 1180 BC, could have inspired Greek legends of the Trojan War. (Photo by Author)

# Folktale

Folktale is more difficult to define than is divine myth or legend because of the variety of traditional stories grouped together under this heading. Some scholars describe folktales as any traditional story that is not a divine myth or legend. This category would encompass such familiar fairy tales as "Cinderella" and "Snow White," among the many German stories written down from oral sources in the early 19th century by the brothers Jacob and Wilhelm Grimm. Likewise, we might also consider the beast fables attributed to the Greek writer Aesop (6th century BC), such as "The Tortoise and the Hare," as folktales, as we could a story such as "Sinbad the Sailor" from the *Arabian Nights* (c. AD 12th century) and most oral tales recorded in Oceania, North America, and Africa during the last two hundred years. In the "myths" of many cultures there is scarcely any divine myth or legend: All is folktale.

Within this diversity, we can still discern common traits. As in legend, the central characters in folktales are human beings, even though gods and spirits appear and play important roles. In folktales the main characters usually are ordinary men, women, and children rather than kings and queens and others of exalted personal qualities or social status, hence the term *folktale*, a story about common people. Even in fables, a kind of folktale in which the characters are animals, the animals speak and act as though they were ordinary humans.

Unlike legends, folktales do not pretend to tell us what happened in the human past. No one believes that Snow White, Cinderella, Hansel and Gretel, or the American Indian trickster Crow really existed, as the Greeks believed that Achilles, Helen, and Orestes did. Often, the main characters in folktales have low social status, at least at the beginning of the story, and are persecuted or victimized in some way by other characters. The folktale hero may be an outcast whose intelligence and virtue are not recognized by those in power. The hero often is the youngest child of three brothers or sisters, abused by siblings or by a wicked stepmother. Very often, the end of the story brings a reversal of fortune, the happy ending for which folktales are well known. Initially taken to be stupid or ineffectual, the folktale hero triumphs over all obstacles and receives an appropriate reward. The trickster, who gets what he wants by unexpected means, is common in folktale.

Whereas divine myths explain why the world is the way it is and legends tell what happened in the human past, the primary function of folktales is to entertain, although they may also play an important role in teaching and justifying customary patterns of behavior. Folktales draw on such universal human experiences as the child's place in the hierarchy of the family. They appeal to such universal human instincts as the belief that good is eventually rewarded and evil punished. In modern literate culture the novel and the feature film have functions analogous to those of the folktale in oral society. For this reason feature films almost without exception "end happily."

A distinctive aspect of the folktale is the regular appearance of identifiable **folktale types**, even in stories from cultures widely separated in space or time. Scholars recognize more than seven hundred folktale types in traditions around the globe. Sometimes a folktale type is named after a famous example. The "Cinderella type," for example, is any story in which an abused younger sister, assisted by a spirit, appears in fancy dress at a ball, disappears from the prince's admiring glance, and then is recognized and marries the prince.

Folktale types are made up of smaller elements called **folktale motifs**, which can be recombined in endless variety. A type may occasionally consist of a single motif, but folktales usually have several motifs, and we might think of folktale motifs as the cells that make up the body of a tale.

A folktale type is thus a constellation of motifs that constitutes an independent story, that is, a story that makes sense in itself and does not depend on its relation to some larger story. Some motifs making up the Cinderella type would be "the abused younger sister," "the spirit helper," "the glass slipper as a token," and "marriage to the prince." Different types may share the same motifs. For example, in any number of folktales the hero grows up and goes off into the world to seek his fortune. This motif by itself could hardly define a type. What defines a type is a recurring constellation of motifs.

Folktale motifs are not commonplace events, people, or incidents, and are always distinctive or unusual in some way. A "sister" is not a motif, but "an abused youngest sister of three" is. "The woman went to town" has no motifs, but "a hero put on his cap of invisibility, mounted his magic carpet, and flew to the Land Beyond the Sun" has four motifs: "the cap of invisibility," "the magic carpet," "the magic flight through the air," and "the wondrous land." Other common motifs are "the dragon that guards a spring" or "a magic object that protects against attack." Modern scholars have exhaustively described and organized the bewildering variety of folktale motifs, which number in the thousands, so you can look up a given motif and find where else it occurs throughout world folklore.

A common folktale type is the quest. In the quest, the folktale hero, compelled to seek some special object, journeys to a strange, terrifying, or wonderful land. There he must face a powerful antagonist: a dragon, a monster, an ogre, or a thoroughly wicked man. To overcome his antagonist, the hero needs the assistance of animals, ghosts, divine beings, or magical weapons or devices. The hero is often bold and chivalrous, a clever trickster, whereas his adversary is brutish, malicious, and stupid. His adversary succeeds in imprisoning, enchanting, or even killing the hero, but at last, often through a trick, the hero escapes, overcomes the enemy, and dispatches him in some cruel or gruesome way. Taking the object he sought, the hero returns to his native land, where his reward is marriage to a princess, or a part of the kingdom, or a great treasure.

Many of these motifs appear in the Greek story of Perseus, who was sent on a dangerous journey by an evil king who wanted to marry Perseus' mother. Assisted by nymphs, the goddess Athena, and an array of magical objects, Perseus goes to the ends of the earth and kills the deadly Gorgon. On his return journey, carrying the Gorgon's death-dealing head in a pouch, he kills a sea monster that threatens a young woman chained to a rock. He takes the woman back to Greece, marries her, and kills the wicked king.

This story illustrates the way Greek myth can use folktale motifs to elaborate on what would otherwise be considered a legend. About Perseus, for example, we are also told that he was born in the town of Argos and brought up by a poor fisherman on the island of Seriphus, that he accidentally killed his grandfather Acrisius in the town of Larissa, and that he moved to Tiryns and founded Mycenae, where his children later ruled. These are details appropriate to a widespread legend. The myth of Perseus, then, is neither pure legend nor pure folktale, but a mixture of the two.

| FORM | MYTH | LEGEND | FOLKTALE |
|---|---|---|---|
| conventional opening | none | none | usually |
| told after dark | no restrictions | no restrictions | usually |
| belief of audience | fact | fact | fiction |
| setting | some time and place | some time and place | timeless, placeless |
| time | remote past | recent past | any time |
| place | earlier or other world | world as it is today | any place |
| attitude of audience | sacred | sacred or secular | secular |
| principal character | nonhuman | human | human or nonhuman |

**CHART 1**   Comparison of features in myth, legend, and folktale.

(after A. Dundes, ed., *Sacred Narrative, Readings in the Theory of Myth* [Berkeley, 1984] Table 2)

The distinctions we have drawn between types of myth are of great value in organizing our thinking about myth, but we should remember that our distinctions are the results of intellectual analysis and are not recognized by mythtellers themselves (Chart 1)

## THE STUDY OF MYTH

The word *mythology* should mean "the study of myth" (by analogy with *biology*, *anthropology*), but in common usage *mythology* typically refers more loosely to the myths themselves, or to a particular group of myths, not to the study of myth. Such statements as "I like mythology" are therefore taken to mean "I like myths as such." To be clear, however, we avoid the ambiguous term *mythology* altogether, using instead *myth* or *myths*, on the one hand, and the *study of myth* on the other.

The study of myth is multifaceted. There are many different ways in which modern scholars approach the study of myth, but they can be grouped into four general categories:

- The recording and compiling of a given culture's myths
- The analysis of the role that specific myths play or played within the culture
- The study of how one culture's myths are related to those of other cultures
- Assessment of the lasting human significance of specific myths or groups of myths

Let us first discuss the recording and compiling of a given culture's myths. The spread of alphabetic literacy in the modern world, and now communication by the Internet, has greatly reduced the degree to which myths serve as a guide to everyday life, but many cultures still maintain an oral tradition vital to them (especially in India). One task undertaken by anthropologists and others who study such cultures is to record, in writing or by other means, the oral tales that are still passed on from generation to generation.

For ancient cultures like those of Mesopotamia, Egypt, Greece, and Rome, a direct recording of oral tales is, of course, no longer possible. We can study only the myths of these cultures that have, somehow, been recorded already. Typically the ancient myths were recorded not by scholars studying the myths for their own sakes, but by men (almost never women) who had other goals. In addition, oral tales exist in many different variants; the variant recorded on one occasion could be very different from that recorded on another. As a result, the records that have come down to us are contradictory, confusing, and incomplete. Careful study and considerable experience are needed to move from existing records to a coherent picture of any one myth.

The principal source for the study of myths is works of literature. A literary work can take the form of a narrative and thus have the same structure as an oral tale (beginning, middle, end; plot, character, setting). Literary works, encoded in writing, take their concepts of structure directly from oral tales. Therefore, the study of myth has much in common with the study of literature.

However, the structural similarities between the original oral tale and the written work of literature in which it is recorded can be deceptive. The literary work typically is the creation of a single person whose name we often know, whereas myths are anonymous. While creating one's own version of a given myth, the author of the literary work introduces variations not present in the different oral retellings of the tale. Moreover, the author may not have taken the myth directly from the oral tradition at all, but may have worked from versions recorded in previous literary works, so that often we are not sure whether we are dealing with the study of myths or with the study of literature.

Other valuable sources of information about myths are painting, sculpture, and other nonliterary artifacts, but a picture is not by itself a story. At most a picture can represent a character or scene from a myth. Still, much can be learned about a culture's mythic traditions by correlating artistic depictions with tales known from other sources. For this reason, the illustrations in this book, as much as is possible, come from the same time as when the myths were recorded, enabling us to see how contemporaries envisaged events and persons in myth. But in some cultures there are no such representations: In that case we have chosen as illustrations representations of the people themselves, the storytellers and those who listened to the stories.

A second way in which scholars approach the study of myth is to examine the functions of specific myths in the context of a given society. In a society with a living oral tradition, myths are told by someone to someone on some occasion. Both the tellers of tales and their audience have a certain identity and status within the culture. They are male or female, wealthy or poor, powerful or not. To understand the myth fully, we need to know how it functioned for the people who took part in its retelling. We have already mentioned that myths can be etiological, offering an explanation for beliefs or existing practices. But a myth can function in other ways. Did it enhance the prestige of those who told the tale or heard it told? Did it justify the existing distribution of power and wealth or perhaps express a protest? Did it strike a chord in the universal desire to know the meaning of action and of human life? Just what was so interesting to the people who listened to this tale?

A third way in which scholars study myth is to trace relationships between the myths of one culture and those of others. We have already mentioned that many folktale motifs are found in the same or similar form in many different cultures around the world. We can also look at the way that specific myths have migrated from one culture to another but were transformed to suit the adopting culture's needs and traditions. For example, the migration of myths from the ancient Near East to Greece is an event of extraordinary importance in the history of civilization.

Finally, some scholars involved in the study of myth are concerned above all with the assessment of myths. What is the deeper human significance of these tales? Why have they fascinated so many for so long, even after the culture that produced them ceased to exist? Is there some sense in which deep truths reside in these often fantastic tales?

Questions of the deeper meaning and truth of myth have played an important role dating back to antiquity. Some have sought to find philosophical or psychological truth in myth by moving beyond the obvious surface meaning to a hidden, less apparent meaning. But to say that this or that is the genuine meaning of a myth is always a matter for dispute. Although some interpretations can be more successful than others, it is never possible to offer conclusive proof.

Still, good interpretations require sensitivity and insight, knowledge of the society that produced the myth, and knowledge of one's own mind, which likes to see what it wants, unaware of its own prejudgments. In studying the history of the interpretation of myth, we truly study more how peoples' prejudgments have changed than we study myth itself. For some scholars, nonetheless, the assessment of a myth's meaning is the most important aspect of their study. Chapter 16 is devoted solely to an examination of the interpretation of myth and the many different theoretical frameworks.

## Key Terms

divine myths 5        folktales 5          folktale types 8
legends 5             etiological tale 6    folktale motifs 9

## Further Reading

Aarne, A., and S. Thompson, *The Types of the Folktale: A Classification and Bibliography*, 2nd rev. ed., trans. and enlarged by S. Thompson (Helsinki, 1961).

*Grimms' Fairy Tales.* Collection of 18th-century German folktales by Jacob and Wilhelm Grimm. There are many editions, most on the web at http://worldoftales.com/fairy_tales/Grimm_fairy_tales.html.

Hansen, W. F., *Ariadne's Thread: A Guide to International Tales Found in Classical Literature* (Ithaca, NY, 2002).

Thompson, S., *The Folktale* (New York, 1946; reprinted Berkeley, CA, 1977).

____, *Motif-index of Folk-literature*, 6 vols. (Bloomington, IN, 1993).

For bibliographic items dealing explicitly with the interpretation of myth, see the list at the end of Chapter 16.

# Mesopotamian Myth

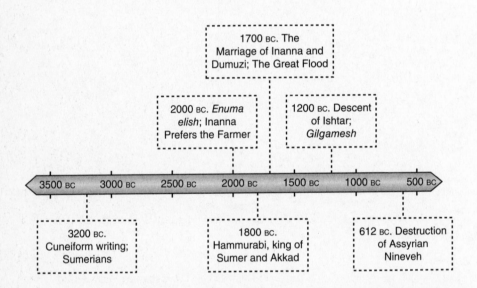

1700 BC. The Marriage of Inanna and Dumuzi; The Great Flood

2000 BC. *Enuma elish*; Inanna Prefers the Farmer

1200 BC. Descent of Ishtar; *Gilgamesh*

3500 BC   3000 BC   2500 BC   2000 BC   1500 BC   1000 BC   500 BC

3200 BC. Cuneiform writing; Sumerians

1800 BC. Hammurabi, king of Sumer and Akkad

612 BC. Destruction of Assyrian Nineveh

*Mesopotamia* in Greek means "the land between the two rivers," the TIGRIS and EUPHRATES, which flow down from the Taurus mountains in what is today the highlands of eastern Turkey. The headwaters of the Euphrates is about 20 miles from the headwaters of the Tigris. The rivers then flow through the plains of the north and come close together where Baghdad stands today (on the Tigris), a few miles from ancient BABYLON (on the Euphrates). Then the rivers diverge again, before coming together at the edge of the PERSIAN GULF (according to ancient writers, the rivers then had separate mouths) (Map 2).

Near the mouths of the rivers, and in the protected area where the rivers come close together, after one million years of little progress, homo sapiens laid the foundations of "civilization," about five or six thousand years ago. By *civilization*, we

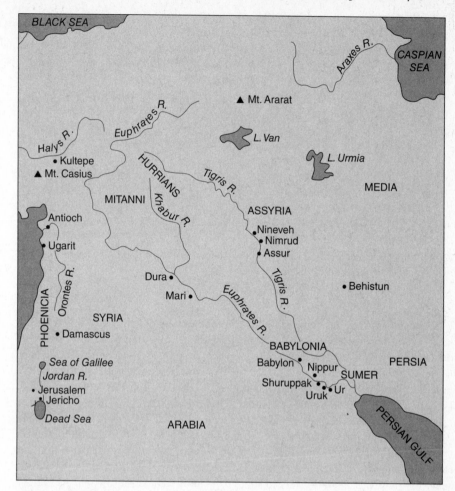

**MAP 2**   Mesopotamia.

ordinarily mean life lived in cities accompanied by the technology of writing. These developments had much earlier antecedents, about which we are poorly informed; here in Mesopotamia is said have been the Garden of Eden. From sometime in the 4th millennium BC—4000 to 3000 BC—we find the earliest known written records on earth in what is today southern and central Iraq. All modern civilizations are a direct outgrowth of what happened there, including the much later civilization of China. Only Mesoamerican civilization escaped the spell of Mesopotamia.

## SUMERIANS AND CUNEIFORM WRITING

The writing system of the Mesopotamians is called **cuneiform**, "wedge-shaped," after the practice of creating the signs by impressing the end of a wedge-shaped stylus into wet clay. The earliest myths in the world are in this script (Figure 2.1).

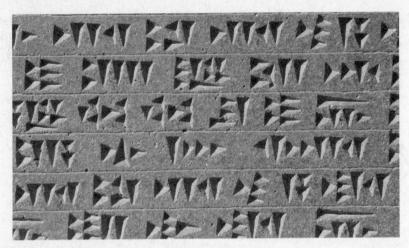

**FIGURE 2.1**   Cuneiform writing at a temple entrance, Çavustepe Kalesi, Urartu fortress (built 764-735 BC), near Van, Turkey (Gezmen / Alamy)

Cuneiform writing was invented by the **Sumerians** of southern Mesopotamia, a people of unknown ethnicity who spoke a language unrelated to any other known language. Probably the name of the Sumerians is the same as the biblical son of Noah, *Shem* (said to have been the ancestor of the Semites, who were not Sumerian!). The Sumerians lived in independent city-states near the Persian Gulf, dependent on irrigation agriculture. Geography was unfriendly to political unification, and except for brief periods the Mesopotamians were never politically unified. The city-states, and coalitions of city-states, warred against one another without cease over thousands of years.

We can understand the language of the Sumerians because of tablets that list equivalent words in Semitic languages, which are well understood and still spoken today. In linguistics, *Semitic* refers to a language family, including ancient Akkadian, Aramaic, Hebrew, Canaanite/Phoenician, and modern Arabic and Hebrew. It also refers to the culture of the speakers of these languages. In every respect the Sumerians are a conundrum of history, appearing in the 4th century millennium with a fully developed economy, with highly organized social classes, domesticated animals, irrigation agriculture, brick-making, pottery-making, metallurgy, and writing. The Sumerians seem to come from someplace else, and they speak of a mysterious Dilmun, perhaps today under the waters of the Persian Gulf. This early phase of Mesopotamian culture is called the *Sumerian phase*.

To some extent we can trace the evolution of cuneiform writing, the most important invention in the history of culture since the discovery of fire, from a very much earlier accounting system used all over the Near East (except Egypt). Somehow this accounting system made use of *tokens*, physical objects of different geometrical shapes carried in a pouch or on a string, apparently used to verify an economic transaction. The objects are found on many Near Eastern archaeological sites from as early as 8000 BC. At least some of the signs later traced into clay by means of a stylus have a similar shape to the independent tokens. How exactly sound became attached to the graphic signs, independent of the meaning of the signs, is unknown, but it was probably in response to the need to record names of people, places, and commodities in order to govern an urban economy based on irrigation agriculture.

Certainly phonetic elements are encoded in the graphic signs by c. 3200 BC, but it took many hundreds of years before the Sumerians wrote full texts, a kind of narrative. In its fully developed form, cuneiform writing has about six hundred signs, some of them with syllabic value, others that stand for whole words, and others that place the words in some or other category. It is a tremendously difficult script—very few people in the world can read it—and the meaning of most texts is unclear. Furthermore, documents survive principally on clay tablets, usually broken. When we read in English a text translated from cuneiform, for example Mesopotamian myths, really we read an interpretation based on highly complex and fragmentary evidence whose meaning is disputed. This is easy to forget.

In the 3rd millennium (3000–2000 BC) Semitic invaders, of different ethnic and linguistic background, came down from the north. *Semitic* originally designates a language group, then the cultures and ethnicities associated with speakers of this language family. They eagerly took over the alien culture of the Sumerians living in the south. The Semitic language of these invaders is called **Akkadian** after their (undiscovered) capital of Akkad. Akkadian was an early form of Semitic speech, although the Akkadians often wrote in Sumerian, the language of prestige very much as was Latin in the European Middle Ages.

A later group of Semitic invaders into the south was called the Amorites, who occupied Babylon. These Babylonians wrote in Akkadian too and achieved a brief political ascendancy under the great leader Hammurabi (c. 1800 BC), whose title was the "king of SUMER and Akkad." This is the *Babylonian phase* of Mesopotamian culture.

Later still, Semitic peoples from ASSYRIA, the area surrounding the northern Tigris River, occupied the southland, the ferocious and efficient **Assyrians**, introducing the *Assyrian phase* of Mesopotamian culture. The Assyrians wrote in a late form of Akkadian, usually called Assyrian. When their capital of NINEVEH on the upper Tigris River was destroyed in 612 BC, ending Assyrian hegemony forever, large libraries were preserved in the fire, including the standard text of *Gilgamesh*.

We have, then, three phases to Mesopotamian myth: Sumerian, Babylonian (writing in Akkadian), and Assyrian (writing in Akkadian/Assyrian). Babylonian and Assyrian versions are always similar, but the Sumerian versions of Mesopotamian myths may differ considerably.

## MYTH: THE AKKADIAN EPIC OF CREATION

We cannot be sure of the date of the composition of the Babylonian creation epic, but it may be as early as c. 2000 BC in the city of Babylon. The date of the poem depends on who was the original hero in the story. In our versions it is always Marduk, the great god of Babylon, but it could earlier have been **Enlil**, the Sumerian storm-god. Texts of our version come mostly from the 1st millennium BC (1000–0 BC), but probably it is the oldest creation story on earth. The story is a good place to begin our survey of world myth.

A tablet states explicitly that the epic was recited twice at the time of the New Year's Festival in Babylon. This myth is our clearest example from the ancient world of a story told in a ritual context (see Chapter 16). By telling of the creation of the world, the story had the power to magically rejuvenate the world.

## The Primordial Separation

The poem is known as *Enuma elish*, "When on high . . .," after its first two words in Akkadian:[1] Because the poem is highly abstract even in English versions and difficult to follow, we will intersperse it with commentary, making clear as we go the force and logic of the narrative:

> *When on high* the heavens had not been named,
> nor had the earth below received its name,
> Apsu, the first one, their begetter,
> and their maker Tiamat, who gave birth to them all,
> had intermingled their waters,
> but had not made pastureland
> nor a bed of reeds.

Before there was anything, everything was water—**Apsu** the sweet water and **Tiamat** the salt water. They were mixed together and there was nothing apart from them.

> When no gods were evident,
> nor names pronounced,
> nor destinies decreed,
> divinity took form within Apsu and Tiamat.

To name something is to bring it into existence. No gods have been named. Then gods are named:

> Lahmu and Lahamu came forth, their names spoken aloud.
> When they were fully formed, and had reached their maturity,
> Anshar and Kishar came into being, even greater than they.

*Lahmu* and *Lahamu* mean something like "Mr. Mud and Mrs. Mud," the primeval slime from which emerged the living things of the world. *Anshar* and *Kishar* mean "pivot of the sky" and "pivot of the earth," that is, the celestial poles, the principle of Up and Down, the space in which further creation is possible.

> They passed days, they added to the years.°
> Anu their first born son rivaled his forefathers.
> Anshar made Anu in his likeness,
> and Anu made Ea in his likeness.
> Ea was better than his forefathers.
> He had deep understanding, was very wise, had strong arms.
> Mightier by far than his forefather Anshar,
> he had no rival among the other gods.
>
> °*added to the years*: that is, grew old.

---

[1]Cf. S. Dalley, *Myths from Mesopotamia: Creation, the Flood, Gilgamesh, and Others* (Oxford, 1989); Samuel Noah Kramer, *Sumerian Mythology: A Study of Spiritual and Literary Achievement in the Third Millennium B.C.* (Philadelphia, 1944); James B. Pritchard, ed., *Ancient Near Eastern Texts Relating to the Old Testament*, 3rd edition (Princeton, 1996). See also, *Enuma elish*, http://www.sacred-texts.com/ane/enuma.htm; *Descent of Ishtar*, http://www.sacred-texts.com/ane/ishtar.htm; Andrew George, *The Babylonian Gilgamesh Epic* (Oxford, 1992); *Gilgamesh*, http://www.ancienttexts.org/library/mesopotamian/gilgamesh/.

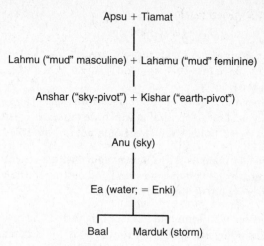

**CHART 2.1**  Akkadian gods of creation.

Anshar has begotten **Anu**, "sky"—that would be the sky when you look up. Anu (sky) has begotten **Ea** (Sumerian **Enki**), the god of water, who is strong and clever (see Chart 2.1).

## First Conflict between Older and Younger Gods

Then:

> The gods of that generation would gather
> and their hullabaloo disturbed Tiamat.
> They stirred up Tiamat's belly.
> They annoyed her as they played inside Anduruna.°
> Apsu could not quiet them down.
> Tiamat fell silent before them.
> However offensive their activity, however bad they were,
> she would endure.
>
> °*Anduruna*: name of the place of the gods' dwelling.

Tiamat and Apsu are disturbed by the clamor of the new gods taking place within Tiamat's body, but she is unwilling to harm her own progeny. Apsu the father is not so sure:

> Apsu, the begetter of the gods,
> cried to his vizier Mummu.
> "O vizier who pleases me, come, we will go to Tiamat!"
> They went and sat down before Tiamat.
> They discussed the doings of their children, the gods.
> Apsu spoke plainly,
> he spoke to Tiamat very loudly:
> "Their ways have become very burdensome to me!
> I can get no rest by day nor sleep by night.

I shall stop their ways! I shall scatter them!
May peace prevail. Let me get some sleep!"

When Tiamat heard this, she became very angry:

She shouted at her lover.
She shouted terribly. She was beside herself with rage.
"How could you allow to perish that which we ourselves created?
Even though they act offensively, we should put up with it."

The gods are organized as if in a human court, with a vizier to advise the king. The vizier **Mummu** advised that they go ahead and destroy the new gods, although it is not clear how they plan to do this:

Apsu was pleased with Mummu. His face brightened
when thinking of the evil he planned for the gods, his children.
Mummu hugged him. Mummu sat on Apsu's lap and
kissed him eagerly.

But the new gods learn of the plot to kill them. At first struck dumb (as often happens with Mesopotamian gods in a crisis), the clever water-god Ea soon takes over. He casts a spell on Apsu and his vizier Mummu:

But their plot was carried to the gods and to their sons.
The gods listened, they fell silent. They could not speak.
Superior in intelligence, very wise and crafty,
Ea who knows all learned of the plot.
He designed a counter-plot.
He laid out the plan. It was very clever.
His pure spell was effective.
He spoke the spell and the waters were stilled.
He poured sleep on Apsu so that he fell into a deep sleep.
He put Apsu to sleep. Vizier Mummu, the adviser,
he struck with a sleepless daze.
Ea undid Apsu's belt, he seized his crown.
He took away his radiant cloak and put it on himself.
He pinned Apsu down. He killed him.
He tied up Mummu. He laid him across Apsu.
He pitched his dwelling on top of Apsu.

By killing Apsu, Ea guarantees progress in the world. Ea will live on top of Apsu so that Apsu may never emerge. It appears that now the primordial waters have been overcome and will never be able to reabsorb its progeny. But danger lies ahead.

## The Birth of Marduk

The world of the gods as we know it has now come into being:

When he had overcome and killed his enemies,
Ea raised a triumphal cry over them.

Then he rested in peace within his house
which he named "Apsu." He set up chapels.
He made his residence there.

Ea and Damkina, his lover, lived in glory.
In the chamber of fates, the hall of designs,
Baal was born, wisest of the wise, wise man of the gods.
Inside Apsu, Marduk was created.
Inside pure Apsu, Marduk was born.

We do not know where Damkina comes from, any more than we know where
Mummu came from. She is just there, the consort of the god Ea. She gave birth to a wise
god named Baal (Semitic "lord," later a great Semitic storm-god). Then, inside the palace, built on Apsu, the storm-god **Marduk** is born, lord of Babylon, the hero of the poem.
Marduk was amazing in every way:

He had four eyes, he had four ears.
When he moved his lips, he sent forth fire.
His ears were huge,
likewise his eyes, which saw everything.
Highest among the gods,
he was very handsome.
His limbs were long, his height was amazing.

As a plaything for Marduk, the sky-god Anu made the four winds, which spun
and threw up dust devils, and once again disturbed the peace of Tiamat. The gods—
which gods we are never told—go to Tiamat to complain that they can never get any
rest. Something must be done. Tiamat is persuaded and Mother Hubur, mother of all
things, apparently an offspring of Tiamat,

contributed a weapon impossible to face.
She gave birth to monstrous snakes with hideous fangs.
Their bodies were filled with venom, not blood.
She dressed the serpents with rays.
She put on them shining cloaks,
like the gods.

"Whoever looks on them will collapse in terror.
Their bodies will be frozen, propped up continually,
they will never look away!"

Mother Hubur set up a serpent with horns,
a *mushusshu*-snake, and a *lahmu*-hero,
an *ugallu*-demon, a rabid dog, a scorpion man,
dangerous *umu*-demons, a fish man, and a bull man.
They all carried dreadful weapons,
without fear in battle.

In addition to these terrible monsters, Mother Hubur creates 11 more demons,
then appoints one **Kingu** as commander of the attack force, with absolute power to do

as he wishes. Mother Hubur gives Kingu the mysterious **Tablet of Destinies**, a power object with cuneiform writing on it that often appears in Mesopotamian myth.

The clever water-god Ea learns of Tiamat's preparations. He goes to Anshar (now said to be Ea's father) and explains the plight of the new gods. He notes that even his own children (who they are is unclear) have joined Tiamat. And Mother Hubur has put into the field a great assortment of monsters.

Anshar's reply is hard to make out because the tablet is broken. He seems at first to give the command to Ea, then to the sky-god Anu. In any event Anu is not equal to the task. He returns to the divine assembly in defeat. Is there not some other being who can take on the responsibility? Someone like Marduk, son of Ea?

## Marduk and Tiamat

The clever water-god Ea advises his son Marduk to submit his candidacy as heroic defender against Tiamat to Anshar. Anshar agrees but first sends his vizier (named Kakka) to Lahmu and Lahamu to report what is happening. The gods now test Marduk's power. They set up a constellation that Marduk, at their request, dissolves and then recreates.

Marduk prepares weapons by which to attack Tiamat (we hear no more of Mother Hubur)—a bow, a club, lightning, a net, and the four winds that Anu gave him as playthings. He fashions three other terrible winds:

> They advanced behind him to make awesome turmoil inside Tiamat.
> The lord raised his flood-weapon,° the great weapon,
> and ascended the terrible chariot of war that none can endure.
> He yoked a team of four. He harnessed as his team
> Killer, Pitiless, Racer, and Flyer.
> The horses sucked back their lips. In their teeth was poison.
> They never ever tire, they can only bring death.
> On his right he placed Dread Battle,
> on his left he placed Fight that Defeats All Comers.
> Marduk was cloaked in indestructible armor.
> A terrible radiance crowned his head.
>
> The lord set forth. He went up the road.
> He turned toward Tiamat, raging out of control.
> Between his lips he gripped a spell.
> In his hand he had an herb, an antidote to poison.

°*flood-weapon*: probably the lightning.

Marduk accosts Tiamat:

> The lord raised his flood-weapon, his great weapon.
> He sent a message to Tiamat, who pretended good will. He said:
> "Why are you friendly outside
> while inside you conspire to muster a battle force?

Just because the children were noisy and disrespectful to their fathers,
should you who bore them turn away pity?
You took on Kingu as your lover.
You gave him access to Anu-power that he did not deserve.
You devised evil for Anshar, king of the gods.
You have multiplied wickedness against the gods, my fathers.
Let your army get ready! Let them take up their weapons!
Or step aside, and you and I will fight in the hand to hand."

When Tiamat heard Marduk,
she went crazy, she lost her head.
Tiamat screamed in a loud passion.
Her lower parts shook, coming from the depths.
She recited her spell, she cast her spell.

Meanwhile the gods of battle sharpened their weapons.
They came face to face, Tiamat and Marduk, the wisest of the gods.
They entered combat, they closed for battle.
The lord spread his net and threw a circle around her.
He sent into her face the *imhullu*-wind, which he kept behind him.
Tiamat opened her mouth. She swallowed it.
He forced in the *imhullu*-wind so that she could not close her lips.
Violent winds expanded her belly.
Her insides were all jammed up.
She opened her mouth wide.
He shot an arrow that pierced her belly.
He split her right down the middle.
He cut her heart in half.
He conquered her. He snuffed out her life.
He cast down her lifeless body.

Marduk then rounded up the gods who had supported Tiamat and imprisoned them in the net. He put nose-ropes in the various monsters. He took possession of the Tablet of Destinies. As for the corpse of Tiamat:

He sliced her in half like a fish for drying.
Half he set above as the sky.
He drew a bolt across it, then set up a guard.
He arranged her waters so that none could escape.
He crossed the heavens and sought a shrine.
He leveled Apsu, the abode of Ea.°

°*abode of Ea*: apparently so that the primordial waters can never escape.

Marduk set up shrines to the great gods—Anu, Enlil, Ea—and puts up constellations in the heavens (Figure 2.2). He marked out the year. He set out the phases of the moon. All the gods hailed him as king. He put on a princely garment. He put on a crown and took up a scepter. He made for himself a brilliant palace in Babylon.

**FIGURE 2.2** Walking Dragon, symbolizing the god Marduk. Marduk is often shown in this guise. Part of the wall frieze of glazed tile from the Ishtar Gate in Babylon, erected under Nebuchadnezzar, c. 580 BC. (Vorderasiatisches Museum, Staatliche Museen, Berlin; Vova Pomortzeff; VPC Travel Photo / Alamy)

He proposed that the gods create man to be a slave of the gods. So the water-god Ea made man from the blood of the evil Kingu, Tiamat's lover, whom Marduk had killed. Babylon is built and a palace for Marduk.

In a great party Marduk is given his 50 honorific names, occupying about one fourth of the poem.

## OBSERVATIONS: SEPARATION AND SUCCESSION IN MESOPOTAMIAN CREATION STORIES

Creation is a process of separation. At first there was one thing, the primordial waters Tiamat and Apsu. Then the hero Marduk splits Tiamat in half, to make the heaven and the earth, the bubble in which progress is possible. Marduk is a **cosmocrator**, a "maker of the world." He does so by defeating a great monster, a dragon of chaos. From her dead body he fashions the cosmos. In Mesopotamian myth, dragon combat can be world-creation.

In the *Enuma elish*, first came a **theogony**, a "begetting of the gods," the generation of Apsu and Tiamat and their descendants. These new gods bring a principle of movement into the world (their activity and clamor), which contrasts sharply with the older forces of chaos, which stand for inactivity and inertia (symbolized by the older gods' desire to sleep). The primordial gods' resistance to change leads to a battle in which newer gods overthrow the older. This is the **succession motif**, whereby progress in creation takes place when a recent generation of gods replacing an earlier.

In the first round of the battle of the gods, the wise and clever Ea, god of fresh water, overcomes the wicked Apsu, god of the primordial waters. He does so by casting a spell. His magical power resides in the spoken word. Ea's wisdom and cleverness are contrasted with Apsu's brutish lust to destroy, a common folktale motif: The dragon-slayer is clever and tricky, his opponent is dull and stupid.

Tiamat manages to be both beneficent and malevolent, as so often with female divinities in Mesopotamian myth. She first opposes her husband's destructive designs, but when Apsu is killed, she herself becomes the destructive monster. Later, in a repetition of the succession motif, Marduk, the son of Ea, destroys his grandmother Tiamat and becomes ruler of the world. Marduk is a local Babylonian city-god, but in the myth he replaces Enlil, "lord of the wind," the ancient Mesopotamian wind and storm-god. There is little doubt that, before the reign of Hammurabi (18th century BC), Enlil was the hero of the tale.

## PERSPECTIVE 2
## The Biblical Creation Story

For many Westerners, the best-known story of creation is that reported in the biblical book of Genesis (1:1–8). The story is so familiar that many people find it hard to hear the words in their original meanings, but a close examination of the Hebrew text's opening lines reveals striking parallels with the creation myth of ancient Mesopotamia:

> In the beginning, when Yahweh created the heaven and the earth, the earth was a formless and unbounded mass, with darkness covering its fluid chaos and with a wind° from Yahweh sweeping over it. Yahweh said, "Let there be light!" and there was light.° Yahweh saw the goodness of the light and separated it from the darkness. The light he called° "day" and the darkness "night." Thus evening and morning came into being, a complete day. Then Yahweh said, "Let there be a partition° in the middle of the watery chaos, spreading out to separate the waters." So it came about, and the partition divided the waters below it from those above. Yahweh called the partition "sky." The evening came and the morning, making up the second day.

°*wind*: the word in Hebrew is *ruach*, which, like Greek *pneuma* and Latin *spiritus*, may mean "air in motion, breath, psychological power." °*light*: light is what makes it possible to distinguish things. °*called*: to name is to create. °*partition*: literally, "something solid."

The Hebrew text of Genesis, which did not reach its final form until perhaps 400 BC, is an edited account based on several earlier sources, some of which used different names for God. From these different sources Hebrew scholars created a text suitable to the doctrinal needs of a monotheistic religion. The Hebrew account differs from the Mesopotamian in its notion of a single transcendent God, with no rivals, who stands before and beyond the creation, but is similar to the Mesopotamian myth in its picture of a universe beginning in a watery mass that is split into an above and a below, Heaven and Earth (An and Ki).

In the Mesopotamian account, the great elements of nature are deified, whereas in the Hebrew account the powers that made the world are stripped of personal names and attributes. So An becomes simply "sky"; Enlil/Marduk, god of wind and storm, becomes the "wind" that moves across the water; Ki is the dry land; and Enki/ Ea is the waters from which the dry land is separated, the earthly waters as opposed to those that existed before the creation. For centuries Christian theologians have debated whether creation took place *ex nihilo,* "out of nothing," or out of something formless, but the Hebrew text, like its Mesopotamian forebears, envisions creation as a process of separation of something that was already there.

In *Enuma elish* the primordial waters are personified as the great dragon Tiamat, whom the creator of the cosmos must overcome. Although not a part of the biblical creation story, this myth of dragon combat as creation is dimly reflected in other biblical passages: "In that day Yahweh with his hard and great and strong sword will punish Leviathan ["twister," "coiler"], the fleeing serpent, Leviathan the twisting serpent, and he will slay the dragon that is in the sea" (Isaiah 27:1).

## MYTH: INANNA PREFERS THE FARMER

Marduk was a god of Babylon, whose inhabitants were Akkadian speakers; he does not exist in Sumerian myth. In the Sumerian genealogy, a son of Enki, "lord of earth" (= Akkadian Ea), was Enlil, "lord of the wind," instead of Marduk (sometimes Enlil's father was said to be Anu). Enlil's consort was Ninlil, "mother of the wind," and their child was Nanna (also called Sin), god of the moon. And Nanna's daughter was Inanna, greatest goddess in all the East, mistress of sexual love, of fertility, and of war (Chart 2.2).

Many stories were told about Inanna (= Akkadian Ishtar), whose name probably means "queen of heaven," especially about her relationship with the shepherd-god, Dumuzi (Figure 2.3).

In a badly broken text written in the Sumerian language is found a myth similar to the biblical story of Cain and Abel, sons of Adam and Eve, where in a quarrel over offerings the farmer Cain kills his brother, the shepherd Abel. Here too there is powerful enmity between the farmer and the shepherd. There are four characters in the Sumerian story: the fertility-goddess **Inanna;** her brother the sun-god **Utu;** the

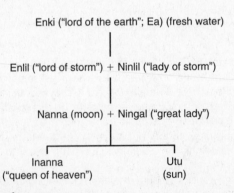

**CHART 2.2**    The descent of Inanna.

**FIGURE 2.3**  Inanna on the so-called Warka Vase, c. 3200–c. 3000 BC, made of carved alabaster, one of the oldest examples of narrative sculpture in the world. The goddess receives a basket of offerings made by a naked priest. Behind her are two of her symbols, a bundle of reeds with a pendant tied to the top. The carving may represent part of the "sacred marriage" (*hieros gamos*). From a cult vase from Uruk, Mesopotamia (Iraq). This vase was stolen during the American invasion of Baghdad in 2003 and returned, broken into 14 pieces, in the trunk of a car. (National Museum, Baghdad; University of Wisconsin Photo Archive)

shepherd-god **Dumuzi**, usually a child of Enki and a sheep-goddess (Ninsun); and the farmer-god **Enkimdu** (of uncertain descent).

In the story Inanna is ready to choose a spouse. Her brother Utu wants her to marry the shepherd-god Dumuzi, but she prefers the farmer-god Enkimdu. Dumuzi demands to know why she prefers the farmer because he, the shepherd, has everything that the farmer has, and more. Inanna does not answer, but Enkimdu, the farmer, tries to calm the aggressive and belligerent shepherd Dumuzi. Dumuzi will not be appeased, however, until the farmer promises to bring him all sorts of gifts, evidently including Inanna herself.

When we can next understand the broken text, the sun-god Utu speaks to his sister Inanna:

"O my sister, why don't you favor the
shepherd, who has everything?

O maiden Inanna, why do you not favor him?
His oil is good and his date-wine is good.
Everything he touches is bright, O Inanna,
Dumuzi who has everything . . .
full of jewels and precious stones.
Why do you not favor him?
He will eat his good oil with you.
He is protector of the king.
Why do you not favor him?"

But Inanna still refuses to be interested in Dumuzi, and says:

"I will not marry the shepherd who has so much,
I will not walk . . . in his new . . .,
I will not be praised . . . in his new . . .
I the maiden will marry the farmer,
who makes plants grow in abundance,
who makes the grain grow in abundance."

There is a break of around 12 lines. Inanna seems to continue to give reasons for preferring the farmer. Then the shepherd-god Dumuzi vigorously protests Inanna's choice:

"What does the farmer have more than I?
What does the farmer have more than I?
If he gives me his black garment,
I give the farmer, my black ewe.
If he gives me his white garment,
I give the farmer my white ewe.
If he pours me his first date-wine,
I pour him my yellow milk.
If he pours me his good date-wine,
I pour him my kid's milk.
If he pours me his heart-cheering date-wine,
I pour for the farmer my bubbling milk.
If he pours me his date-wine mixed with water,
I pour for the farmer my plant-milk (?).
If he gives me his good portions,
I give the farmer my *nitirda*-milk.
If he gives me his good bread,
I give the farmer my cheese.
If he gives me his small beans,
I give him my small cheeses,
more than he can eat, more than he can drink.
I pour out for him much oil,
I pour out for him much milk.
What has the farmer more than I?"

The next four lines are not clear. Then the farmer-god Enkimdu attempts to appease the shepherd Dumuzi:

"You, O shepherd, why do you begin a quarrel?
O shepherd Dumuzi, why do you begin a quarrel?
Why do you compare me with you, O shepherd?
May your sheep eat the grass of the earth.
In my meadows may your sheep pasture.
In the fields of Zabalam let them eat grain.
May all your folds drink the water of my river Unun."°

°*Zabalam . . . Unun*: these places are unknown.

But Dumuzi will not be satisfied:

"You shall not enter as a friend at my marriage.
You shall not enter as my friend, O farmer Enkimdu.
You shall not enter as my friend."

Thereupon the farmer Enkimdu offers to bring the shepherd Dumuzi all kinds of gifts:

"I will bring you wheat
I will bring you beans,
beans of . . . I will bring you.
I will bring you the maiden Inanna
and whatever pleases you.
The maid Inanna . . . I shall bring you."

There the poem breaks off, but evidently the shepherd Dumuzi was victorious over the farmer Enkimdu (unlike in the story of Cain/Abel) because other stories tell of Inanna's marriage to Dumuzi, as in the following myth.

## MYTH: THE WEDDING OF INANNA AND DUMUZI

Inanna is married to Dumuzi, whose death she later brings about. There is a considerable Mesopotamian literature about their marriage, which was the mythic basis for the *hieros gamos*, or "sacred marriage," which took place in Mesopotamian temples. During this ritual—we know this happened at the New Year's festival—a priestess or the queen would take on the role of Inanna and a high priest or the king would take on the role of Dumuzi. Their sexual union would bring fertility to the land, and the sexual union of Inanna and Dumuzi was the model for all lovemaking, as made clear in this Sumerian poem of uncertain date (perhaps c. 1700 BC).[2]

Inanna opened the door for him.
Inside the house she shone before him
like the light of the moon.

---

[2]Translation by D. Wolkstein and S. N. Kramer, altered, available at http://en.wikipedia.org/wiki/User:Arcehedron/sumerian_quotes.

Dumuzi looks at her joyously.

He pressed his neck close against hers. He kissed her.
Inanna spoke:
"What I tell you, let the singer weave into song.
What I tell you, let it flow from ear to mouth,

Let it pass from old to young.
My vagina, the horn,
the Boat of Heaven,
is full of eagerness like the young moon.
My untilled land lies fallow.
As for me, Inanna,
who will plow my vagina?
Who will plow my high field?
Who will plow my wet ground? . . ."

Dumuzi replies:

"Great Lady, the king will plow your vagina.
I, Dumuzi the King, will plow your vagina."
Inanna said:
"Then plow my vagina, man of my heart!
Plow my vagina!"

At the king's lap stood the rising cedar.
Plants grew high by their side.
Grains grew high by their side.
Gardens flourished luxuriantly . . .

"O Lady, your breast is your field.
Inanna, your breast is your field.
Your broad field pours out plants.
Your broad field pours out grain.
Water flows from on high for your servant.
Bread flows from on high for your servant.
Pour it out for me, Inanna.
I will drink all you offer."

Inanna sings:

"Make your milk sweet and thick, my bridegroom.
My shepherd, I will drink your fresh milk.
Wild bull, Dumuzi, make your milk sweet and thick.
I will drink your fresh milk . . ."

Dumuzi speaks:

"My sister,° I would go with you to my garden.
Inanna, I would go with you to my garden.
I would go with you to my orchard.
I would go with you to my apple tree.
There I would plant the sweet, honey-covered seed."

°*sister:* like "brother," a term of affection.

Inanna speaks:

"He brought me into his garden.
My brother, Dumuzi, brought me into his garden.
I strolled with him among the standing trees,
I stood with him among the fallen trees.
By an apple tree I knelt as is proper . . .
before my lord Dumuzi.
I poured out plants from my womb.
I placed plants before him,
I poured out plants before him.
I placed grain before him,
I poured out grain before him.
I poured out grain from my womb."

Inanna sings:

"Last night as I, the queen, was shining bright,
last night as I, the Queen of Heaven, was shining bright,°
as I was shining bright and dancing,
singing praises at the coming of the night—
He met me, he met me!
My lord Dumuzi met me.
He put his hand into my hand.
He pressed his neck close to mine.
My high priest is ready for the holy loins.
My lord Dumuzi is ready for the holy loins.
The plants and herbs in his field are ripe.
O Dumuzi! Your fullness is my delight!". . .

"Let the bed that rejoices the heart be prepared!
Let the bed that sweetens the loins be prepared! . . .
He put his hand in her hand.
He put his hand to her heart.
Sweet is the sleep when one hand is pressed to the other.
Sweeter still the sleep when one heart is pressed to the other."

°*shining bright:* Inanna was the morning star.

Inanna speaks:

"I bathed for the wild bull.
I bathed for the shepherd Dumuzi,
I perfumed my sides with ointment.
I coated my mouth with sweet-smelling amber,
I painted my eyes with kohl.°
He shaped my loins with his fair hands.
The shepherd Dumuzi filled my lap with cream and milk.
He stroked my pubic hair.
He watered my womb.
He laid his hands on my holy vagina.
He smoothed my black boat with cream.

He quickened my narrow boat with milk.
He caressed me on the bed.
Now I will caress my high priest on the bed,
I will caress the faithful shepherd Dumuzi.
I will caress his loins, the shepherd of the land,
I will decree a sweet fate for him."

The Queen of Heaven,
the heroic woman, greater than her mother,
who was presented to me by Enki,
Inanna, the First Daughter of the Moon,°
decreed the fate of Dumuzi:
"In battle, I am your leader,
In combat I am your armor-bearer,
In the assembly I am your advocate,
On the campaign I am your inspiration . . .
In all ways you are fit.
May your heart enjoy long days . . .
As the farmer, let him make the fields fertile.
As the shepherd, let him make the sheepfolds multiply,
Under his reign let there be vegetation,
Under his reign let there be rich grain."

The king went with lifted head to the holy loins.
He went with lifted head to the loins of Inanna.
He went to the queen with lifted head.
He opened wide his arms to the holy priestess of heaven . . .
"My blossom-bearer in the apple orchard,
my bearer of fruit in the apple orchard . . .
my fearless one, my holy statue . . .
How sweet was your allure . . ."

°*kohl*: a cosmetic made of lead and other ingredients, used as eye makeup.
°*the Moon*: Nanna.

# MYTH: THE DESCENT OF ISHTAR

The myth of the descent of **Ishtar** (Sumerian Inanna), goddess of fertility, sex and war, is known in an Akkadian version from the Late Bronze Age (c. 1200 BC), and later from the library at Nineveh (destroyed 612 BC). It is only 140 lines long. A considerably longer Sumerian version of 410 lines survives from the 3rd millennium BC, in which the goddess is Inanna. The Akkadian version seems to end with reference to a ritual in which a statue of Dumuzi, Ishtar's husband, is bathed, anointed, and laid out in state. Probably the myth of the Descent of Ishtar is attached to a ritual, as is the Akkadian myth of the creation. The story is an antecedent to the Greek myth of Persephone, taken by Hades to the underworld, and her mother Demeter, who sorrowed for her daughter so that nothing grew on earth.

According to the Akkadian version, for no clear reason Ishtar one day takes it into her head to descend to the underworld,

> to the house where those who enter can never leave,
> on the road where all travel is in one direction,
> to the house where for those who enter there is no light,
> where dust is food and clay is their bread.
> Dwellers there do not see light, they live in darkness.
> They are clothed like birds, they are clothed in feathers.

Ishtar comes to the gate of the underworld:

> "Here gatekeeper, open your gate,
> open your gate for me so that I may come in!
> If you do not open your gate for me to come in,
> I will smash the gate, I will force the bolt!
> I will smash the doorpost, I will overturn the doors!
> I will raise up the dead. They will eat the living!
> The dead will outnumber the living!"

> The gatekeeper made his voice heard.
> He said to great Ishtar,
> "Don't break down the door!
> Let me go and report your words to Queen Ereshkigal."

The death-goddess **Ereshkigal** cannot imagine why her sister Ishtar, goddess of fertility, wants to come into the underworld (Figure 2.4):

> "Surely not because I drink water with the Annunaki,°
> eat clay for bread, drink muddy water for beer?
> I must weep for the young man taken from his sweetheart,
> I must weep for the girl torn from her lover's lap.
> I must weep for the infant thrust out before its time.
> Go, gatekeeper, let her in."

°*Annunaki:* "those of royal blood": Even the gods have social class, and the Annunaki are the upper class.

**FIGURE 2.4**  Demonic figure, probably Ereshkigal, c. 1800 BC. We know that she is divine because of the headdress of horns and her wings. The owls are the ill-omened birds of the night, while the lions are a usual attribute of Inanna/Ishtar and Ereshkigal. She holds the rod and ring of justice. The plaque probably stood in a shrine. Baked straw-tempered clay, Babylonian. (British Museum, London; Photo by Author)

As Ishtar passes through each of the seven gates, she must remove an article of adornment or clothing. At the first gate she removes the *great crown on her head*; at the second gate, her *earrings*; at the third gate, her *bead necklace*; at the fourth gate, a *pectoral*, a kind of breast ornament; at the fifth gate, a *girdle of birth stones*; at the sixth gate, *bangles on her wrists and ankles*; at the seventh gate, *the proud garment of her body*. In other words, Ishtar has died.

To affirm Ishtar's death, Ereshkigal sends out 60 diseases to afflict her body. Then:

After Ishtar had gone down to the land of no return,
no bull mounted a cow, no male donkey covered a female donkey,

no young man impregnated a young girl in the street.
The young man slept in a private room,
the young girl slept with her friends.

The vizier of the gods, much concerned about Ishtar's fate, goes to Ea (Sumerian Enki), god of cleverness and fresh water. Ea creates a good-looking male to send down to Ereshkigal. The purpose of the male messenger is to get Ereshkigal to give him a water skin (evidently the corpse of Ishtar). Ereshkigal sees through the plot and curses the good-looking male—he will be an outcast eating garbage, drinking sewer water, with no place to crouch save beneath the city's walls!

As for Ishtar, the **Annunaki gods**—the upper-class gods—are called to witness the sprinkling of the water of life. Ishtar is given back her seven adornments. When she returns to the upper world, however, Ereshkigal requires that Ishtar's husband Dumuzi, "the lover of her youth," die as a substitute. Yet Belili, the sister of Dumuzi, affirms that one day Dumuzi will return.

## Observations: The Cycle of Life

This powerful story was to have great influence in Mesopotamia and elsewhere. Ishtar and Ereshkigal are the twin sides of the life force that makes nature grow and proliferate, then perish and die, then grow again. Ereshkigal is the sister of Ishtar, the other side of Ishtar. Death is the twin of Life. We are never told why Ishtar descends to see her sister.

Like a magnet Ereshkigal draws Ishtar in, who becomes ever less a person as she removes her clothes, then a nonperson, a piece of meat. No male force can reverse the process, as is clear from the failure of Ea's plot. But the female Ereshkigal of her own free will sprinkles the corpse of Ishtar with the water of life and restores her. Now a substitute must be found.

According to another version of the myth, on returning Ishtar finds that everywhere there is darkness and sorrow and grief because Ishtar is gone, except in the house of her husband Dumuzi, "who sat on a throne." A horde of demons carry him away. The male dies and the female lives. Yet the poem predicts that Dumuzi, too, will one day return to life.

## MYTH: THE GREAT FLOOD

There never was a universal flood that drowned everything and killed everybody, but there were periodic great inundations in Mesopotamia, especially of the Euphrates River. Vast tracts were threatened and certainly many died. There may well have been a man who foresaw the effects of such a flood and built a house that saved him. In the Babylonian myth of the Great Flood, this man was called **Atrahasis**, "exceeding wise." In Babylonian versions of the *Gilgamesh* epic he is also called **Utnapishtim**, which means "he found life," the Akkadian being an approximate translation of the earlier Sumerian **Ziusudra**. Possibly the Greek name of Prometheus, "forethought," is the same as Atrahasis: In the Greek tradition Prometheus is father to Deucalion, survivor of a universal flood in Greek tradition. "Noah" in the Hebrew version is evidently an abbreviation of Akkadian *(ut)napish(tim)*, as the name was pronounced in Palestine.

So powerful is the Mesopotamian myth of the universal flood that it has spread to virtually every culture, always adjusted to local conditions. For example, in the biblical account, it is the wickedness of humankind that drives God to destroy them, whereas in the Mesopotamian account the gods simply get tired of the endless commotion stirred up by humans. The gods prefer the way things were before the creation, when the waters of chaos were still.

## A Race of Slaves

From an Akkadian document c. 1700 BC, we learn of the origin of humans. It all began when the resentment of the **Igigi gods**, an order of gods beneath the Annunaki, boiled up against their masters, the Annunaki gods. The most important of the Annunaki gods are Anu as king, lord of the sky; Enlil as the wind- and storm-god, ruler of the earth; and Enki who dwells in the Apsu, or abyss, and controls the bolt releasing the fresh water onto the fields and crops. (In this Akkadian story, the Sumerian names of the gods are used: Sumerian Enki = Akkadian Ea. Apsu is also the name of the god of fresh water, as we have seen.)

The Igigi gods set fire to their tools and surround the palace. Enlil in a panic sends for Anu, king of the gods, and Enki, the clever god. Enlil, lord of wind and storm, says:

> "Is it against me that they rise up?
> Shall I go to battle? What did I see?
> A rabble gathering around my door!"

When Enlil learns that the lower-class Igigi gods are oppressed by labor, especially in keeping all the canals clear, he has an idea. He will fashion beings whose sole purpose is to bear the load: humans! Other Mesopotamian myths make the same point, that humans were created expressly to labor on behalf of the gods, to do all the dirty work required to keep the creation going. It is an etiological tale to explain the origin of human misery and the dogged, day-in, day-out work that life in Mesopotamian cities required.

At Enki's instructions, a god is killed (in Mesopotamian myth, gods are not necessarily immortal). Nintu, "lady of birth" a mother-goddess, mixes clay with the flesh and blood of the sacrificed god to make humans:

> Mami° made her voice loud
> and spoke to the mighty gods:
> "I have carried out to perfection
> your command.
> You have killed a god who has intelligence.
> I relieve you of your hard work.
> I have imposed your burden on humans."

°*Mami*: midwife to the gods.

## Lessening the Population

Thus humans came into being, but soon they grew so numerous and caused such an agitation that Enlil, lord of storm, decided to destroy them by means of disease:

> Six hundred years, less than six hundred years passed.
> The country grew too great.
> The people grew too populous.
> The country sounded like a bellowing bull.
> The gods couldn't stand the racket,
> Enlil had to listen to the noise.
> Enlil addressed the great gods:
>
> "The hullabaloo of humankind has become too much!
> I can't sleep from the noise!
> Give the command that the *shuruppu*-disease be let loose."

The tablet is broken here but evidently the disease does not work. The humans survive. Enlil then decides to send a famine:

> Adad° on high blocked the rain from falling.
> He stopped the flow of springs.
> Nissaba° turned her breasts aside.
> The dark fields grew white, the wide country
> covered with alkali.° Earth shut her womb.
> Nothing would grow, neither grain nor vegetation.
> Sickness fell on the people.
> The womb was too tight:
> The baby could not get out.

°*Adad*: another storm-god. °*Nissaba*: a vegetation-goddess. °*alkali*: that is, the fields were salinified.

Then:

> By the second year,
> the storehouse was empty.
> By the third year,
> starvation appeared in people's faces.
> By the fourth year,
> their shoulders were bowed in abject humility.
> By the fifth year,
> a daughter gave her mother the eye when she came,
> a mother would close the door to her daughter.°
> A daughter would eye the scales° when her mother was sold;
> a mother would eye the scales when her daughter was sold.
> By the sixth year,
> they served the daughter for food,
> they served the son as a meal.

°*her daughter*: because either might want to eat the other. °*eye the scales*: to make sure the balance is fair so that she gets the best price.

## The Universal Flood

Still, the famine does not succeed in eliminating the noisy offending humans. The storm-god Enlil at last decides on a huge flood that will drown everyone. Enki, who controls the bolt of the sea, tells his favorite mortal, a man named Atrahasis, "exceeding wise," what is coming. He must build a boat:

> "Tear down the house. Build a boat.
> Discard all that you own,
> save what still lives. Put a roof on your boat
> like on the Apsu, so that the sun cannot peer inside.
> Make two decks.
> Your ropes must be very strong.
> The bitumen caulking must be strong . . ."

> Enki released a sand clock. He showed
> how the flood would last for seven days and nights.

Atrahasis does as he is told and builds a huge boat. He puts within it flying things, cattle, and wild animals. Atrahasis throws a party. His family comes on board:

> They ate, they drank.
> He went in, he went out. He could not be still,
> could not rest crouched down.
> His heart was breaking. He was vomiting a black fluid.
> The weather changed. Adad roared from his clouds.
> When Atrahasis heard the thunder,
> he brought in bitumen and sealed up the door.
> As he closed the door,
> Adad roared from his clouds.
> The winds whistled. He went up.
> He loosed the mooring rope.
> He set the boat free.

The scribe relishes the details of the savage flood:

> You could see no one else.
> Everyone disappeared in the melee.
> The flood bellowed like a bull.
> The wind sounded like a wild ass screaming.
> There was total darkness.
> There was no sun.

However, not all the gods were pleased with the universal destruction. Nintu, the mother of humankind, wept with sorrow and complained:

> "What was Anu's intention as decision-maker?°
> The gods obeyed his command,

he who did not consider well,
but sent the flood,
who gathered the people for the catastrophe."

°*decision-maker*: Enlil sent the storm, but as god of the sky Anu was responsible for all that happens.

When the Annunaki gods discover that one man, Atrahasis, has in fact escaped the universal destruction, they become very angry. Enlil says:

"We the great Annunaki agreed on this.
We swore an oath, all of us.
No form of life should have escaped!
How did one man escape the disaster?"

Anu spoke aloud. He said to Enlil:
"No one but Enki would have done this!"

Enki spoke aloud,
he spoke to the great gods:

"I did this in defiance of you!
I saw to it that one escaped alive!"

The poem ends with a compromise, a deal struck between Enki, the sponsor of human life, and Nintu, the mother of humankind, and the other Annunaki gods. The whole human race will not be destroyed, but various women will henceforth be sterile or their young are killed by demons, so that the human population will never grow so dense again.

## OBSERVATIONS: DIVINE MYTH IN MESOPOTAMIA

These Mesopotamian stories are what we have called *divine myth*, concerned with gods and the creation of the world, the nature of death, the first humans, and the time that the world nearly came to an end. But as often with divine myth, the stories are close to folktale: Tiamat is the great dragon whom the hero, helped by special weapons, must slay.

The divine society of the Mesopotamians reflects the human. At the top is King Anu, lord of the heavens, and his ministers, especially Enlil, the wind- and storm-god, and Enki/Ea, the water-god. The great gods, the Annunaki, are an aristocracy who rule over a lesser order of gods, the Igigi. Humans are created in order to relieve the Igigi of their labor, but so great is the hullabaloo that the Annunaki gods, led by Enlil, decide to destroy all humankind. However, once the flood is over, the circumstances between humans and the Annunaki changes. A deal is struck, much as in the biblical account Yaweh agreed with Noah never again to destroy the earth by means of flood (Genesis 9:11): Henceforth, in the Akkadian account, humans will not be so numerous as before, thanks to infant mortality and restrictions on female fertility. Henceforth, there will be no more universal destructions. The flood was a return to the way it was before the creation, to universal chaos. But one man survived, to propagate a new race and a new beginning.

## MYTH: GILGAMESH

An entirely different kind of story survives in Akkadian manuscripts about five hundred years more recent than the tale of the Great Flood, from about 1200 BC, the story of **Gilgamesh**. It is a *legend*, the only one we find in ancient Mesopotamia. It is not a single story but a tradition of stories that often are contradictory. Apparently, there were many isolated legends about this Sumerian king, who seems really to have lived sometime between 2800 and 2600 BC, according to surviving king lists. Dumuzi, sometimes said to be Gilgamesh's brother, also appears in the king lists about this time. Although the real Gilgamesh must have cut a fine figure in his day, the stories about him, as with Mesopotamian divine myth, follow patterns common in folktale.

Around 1200 BC one Sin-leqe-unnini, an Akkadian scribe, assembled these disjointed written tales about Gilgamesh onto 12 tablets, thus creating the "Epic of Gilgamesh." It is by far the longest story from ancient Mesopotamia. We cannot tell how much Sin-leqe-unnini depended on any oral version he might have heard and how much he depended on his own ingenuity, or the ingenuity of earlier scribes.

So persistent are the stories about Gilgamesh that they were still influential during the composition of *The Arabian Nights* (8th through 13th centuries AD). There a certain Buluqiya—a name derived from "Gilgamesh"—sets out with his bosom friend to find immortality, in quest of the ring of Solomon; Gilgamesh too seeks immortality with his friend Enkidu. Just when success seems sure, the friend dies; so does Enkidu. Subsequently, Buluqiya goes through a subterranean passage and emerges in a land where the leaves are emeralds and the fruit are rubies; Gilgamesh does the same. Buluqiya meets a far distant king who has obtained immortality in a way no longer available to Buluqiya; so does Gilgamesh meet Utnapishtim, survivor of the flood. The king expounds to Buluqiya the early history of the world; Utnapishtim tells Gilgamesh about the great flood. Put to a different use—the Arabian story is used to foretell the coming of Mohammed—the tale of Buluqiya nonetheless preserves the basic story of *Gilgamesh* and even some of the details.

### Gilgamesh, Son of Lugalbanda

*Gilgamesh* opens with a preface surprisingly like the opening of Homer's much later *Odyssey* (c. 800 BC), which reads:

> Sing to me, Muse, of the man of many turns, who wandered
> far after sacking the holy city of Troy. He saw
> the cities of many men and learned their minds.

Gilgamesh opens:

> Of him who discovered all things, I shall tell the land.
> Of him who experienced all things, I shall teach the whole.
> He searched everywhere. He searched for the whole
> and was rewarded with complete wisdom.
> He found out what was secret, and he uncovered what was hidden.
> He brought back a tale of before the Flood.
> He had journeyed far and wide, weary and at last resigned.
> He wrote all his experiences up on a memorial stone.

He sought and he found (Figure 2.5). Strikingly, the opening lines of *Gilgamesh* declare the power of cuneiform writing, the technological basis for Mesopotamian civilization, to preserve the hero's quest (in the orally composed *Odyssey,* Homer never mentions writing). When Gilgamesh returned from his wanderings, he built the great temple complex called Eanna in Uruk in southern Sumer, west of the Euphrates (Map 2), dedicated to Ishtar. In this temple you will

> Look for the copper tablet box. Open its bronze lock,
> open the door to its secret. Remove the tablet of lapis lazuli.
> Read from it the story of the man Gilgamesh, who experienced so much.
> He was superior to other kings, a warrior of great stature,
> a hero from URUK, a goring wild bull.

Gilgamesh was the son of Lugalbanda, a mortal king of great renown, and of the goddess Ninsun, "lady wild cow." Somehow, he was two-thirds immortal and one-third

**FIGURE 2.5** Probably Gilgamesh, Assyrian relief from the palace of Sargon II (722–705 BC) in Khorsabad. The fully bearded figure holds a lion cub in one hand and a whip in the other: He is the lion-tamer. His long hair falls on his shoulders and his full beard is braided. (Musée du Louvre, Paris; Photo by Author)

mortal. Gilgamesh was a great leader but contemptuous of others, and he liked to have his way with young virgins. The citizens of Uruk called on the great mother-goddess Aruru ("arable land"?) to fashion a worthy rival to Gilgamesh (Aruru was a form of Ninhursag, "lady of the mountain," or Ninsun: all these mother-goddesses were in a way the same):

> When Aruru heard this, she pinched off
> a piece of clay and threw it into the open country.
> She made a primitive man, Enkidu the warrior.
> His whole body was shaggy with hair.
> He had the tresses of a woman.

## Enkidu

The primitive man **Enkidu** runs with the wild cattle and gazelle and drinks at the water hole. A hunter sees him, and complains to his father:

> Father, there was a young man who came from the mountain.
> He was strong, he was powerful.
> His strength was great, he came like a bolt of Anu.
> He walks about on the mountain.
> He eats vegetation with the cattle,
> with the cattle he places his feet in the watering place.

The wild man is pulling up all the hunter's traps so that the hunter can no longer hunt in the open country. The hunter is furious. The hunter's father advises his son to go into the city and request the services of a harlot. The hunter is led into the presence of Gilgamesh, who declares:

> Go, hunter, and take the harlot Shamhat.°
> When the wild man comes with the cattle to the watering hole,
> she must take off her clothes and bare her attractions.
> He will see her and go close to her.
> Then will the cattle, who grew up with him
> in the open country, avoid him as an alien being.
>
> °*Shamhat*: "voluptuous."

The hunter does as he is told. Soon Enkidu comes to the watering hole. The hunter says:

> "Here he is, Shamhat. Bare your breasts.
> Open wide your legs. Let him get a good look.
> Do not pull away. Take wind of him (?).
> When he sees you, he will approach you.
> Spread open your clothing. Let him lie upon you.
> Do for this primitive man what women do for men.
> Then his cattle, who grew up in the open country
> with him, will avoid him as an alien being."

Shamhat does as she is told:

His lovemaking he gave her.
For six days and seven nights he poured himself into her.
When he had had enough of her charms,
he set his sight on the wild cattle of the open country.
When the gazelles saw him, they ran away.
The wild cattle would not come close to his body.

Enkidu has changed, and his legs do not work so well any more. He has gained wisdom that sets him apart from the wild animals of his innocence. He sits down at the feet of Shamhat. She says to Enkidu:

"You have gained depth, you have become like a god.
Why roam the open country with the wild animals?
Let me take you to Uruk the Sheepfold,
to the pure house, where dwell Anu and Ishtar.
There Gilgamesh is perfect in strength,
a wild bull, superior to any of the people."

Enkidu agrees. He says that he will challenge Gilgamesh to a contest of strength, but Shamhat begs him not to:

"Look at him, see his face.
He is beautiful in manhood, dignified,
his body charged with seductive charm.
He is more powerful in strength of arms than you!
He doesn't sleep day or night.
Give up your plans for punishing Gilgamesh!
Shamash° loves Gilgamesh, and Anu, Enlil,
and Ea make him wise."

°*Shamash*: the sun-god (Sumerian Utu).

Shamhat then describes two dreams that she had heard from Gilgamesh's mother Ninsun, "lady wild cow." In one, a sky-bolt of Anu fell at Gilgamesh's feet, so heavy that he could not lift it. Gilgamesh loved the sky-bolt like a wife. This dream foretold the coming of a powerful companion. So did a second dream, in which an ax was thrown down to the street. People gathered around it. The ax, too, Gilgamesh loved like a wife.

The tablet is badly broken here, but it is clear that Enkidu challenges Gilgamesh as he is about to take the virginity of one more girl. They wrestle in the public square:

Enkidu blocks his access at the door of the father-in-law.
He won't allow Gilgamesh to enter.
They grapple outside the door of the father-in-law's house.
They wrestle in the street, in the public square.
They broke the door jamb, the walls quake.

The wrestling match is a draw, but each man admires the strength of the other. Gilgamesh and Enkidu fall into each other's arms, friends forever.

## Humbaba

When we can read the text again, the newfound friends have decided to go up against **Humbaba**, Lord of the Pine Forest. Humbaba'a shout is the flood-weapon, his utterance is fire, his breath is death. The storm-god Enlil has set up Humbaba as a protective spirit over the Pine Forest. He can hear 180 miles through the forest. The counselors of Uruk advise against the expedition, but the two friends decide to go anyway.

They set out. They come to the Lebanon (on the east coast of the Mediterranean) and dig a large pit to **Shamash**, the sun-god. Gilgamesh goes into the mountains and solicits three dreams. Enkidu interprets the first dream as foretelling victory over Humbaba. The second dream is in a broken part of the tablet. In the third dream:

> Heaven cried out, earth groaned.
> The day grew silent, darkness came out.
> Lightning flashed, fire broke out.
> Flames crackled, death rained down.
> Then sparks were dimmed. The fire was extinguished.

Somehow, Enkidu is paralyzed in both his hands; the text is very obscure here. Evidently, Gilgamesh cures Enkidu by rubbing Enkidu's hands with a healing plant. At last the two companions come to the Pine Forest:

> They stood before the forest,
> gazed and gazed at the height of the pines,
> gazed and gazed at the entrance to the pines
> where Humbaba made tracks as he went back and forth.
> The paths were well trodden and the roads were fine.
> They gazed at Pine Mountain, sacred to the gods, shrine of Irnini.°
> The pines were always luxuriant on the face of the mountain,
> the shade was excellent, filling one with happiness.
> Undergrowth grew everywhere and entangled the forest.
>
> °*Irnini*: a war-goddess assimilated with Ishtar.

Humbaba hears the adventurers at the entrance to the forest and comes out to meet them. Humbaba says:

> "The fool Gilgamesh and the brutish man ought to
> ask themselves why they have come to see me.
> Your friend Enkidu is a wretch who does not know his own father . . .
> I will bite through your windpipe, Gilgamesh,
> so that you will be a plaything of the birds of the forest,
> of roaring lions, and of birds of prey, and scavengers."

However, the sun-god Shamash intervenes on Gilgamesh's behalf. He summons 13 winds that blow against the Lord of the Pine Forest. Humbaba begs for his life. He

**FIGURE 2.6**  Gilgamesh and Enkidu kill Humbaba, guardian of the Pine Forest. On the right Enkidu, holding the monster by the hair, pins his shoulder with his foot and plunges a dagger into its breast. In the middle, Gilgamesh holds one of Humbaba's wrists while he brings down his mace. Perhaps the figure on the left, holding a staff, is Shamash. Babylonian, c. 1800 BC. Terracotta tablet. (Vorderasiatisches Museum, Staatliche Museen, Berlin; Editorial / Alamy)

promises to be the guardian of a special forest that will grow for Gilgamesh alone. Enkidu speaks against Humbaba, urging Gilgamesh to kill him:

> "My friend, finish him off! Kill him! Grind him up
> so that I may survive Humbaba, lord of the forest.
> Finish him off, kill him, grind him up
> so that I may survive Humbaba, lord of the forest!"

Gilgamesh does kill Humbaba (Figure 2.6). The friends make a raft of trees from the forest and float down the Euphrates.

## The Lust of Ishtar

When they have returned to Uruk, Gilgamesh washes out his filthy hair, lets his locks lie on his shoulders, throws away his dirty clothes, and puts on new clothes. He binds a sash around his waist. He is so handsome that when Ishtar sees him, she desires him:

> "Come to me, Gilgamesh, and be my lover!
> Give me the gift of your fruit.
> You can be my husband, and I will be your wife.
> Gilgamesh will have a golden chariot, and all his country will prosper."

In probably the most famous passage in Mesopotamian literature, Gilgamesh refuses her. He catalogues the sufferings of those whom Ishtar loved in the past:

"For Dumuzi, the lover of your youth,
you decreed that he should keep weeping year after year.
You loved the colorful *allalu*-bird—
you hit him and broke his wing.
Now he stays in the forest crying, 'My wing!'
You loved the lion, whose strength is great.
You dug seven and seven pits for him.
You loved the horse, trustworthy in battle—
for him you decreed the whip, the goad, and the lash.
You decreed that he should gallop twenty-one miles.
You decreed that he should be exhausted and thirsty.
You decreed endless weeping for his mother Sililu.°

"You loved the shepherd, the herdsmen, the keeper of flocks
who heaped up the piles of ash for you every day.°
He cooked young lambs for you every day.
Him you struck and turned into a wolf.
His own herdsmen hunt him down.
His own dogs nip at his haunches.°

"You loved Ishulannu, your father's gardener.
He gave you wild dates every day.
He adorned your table with them.
You lifted your eyes to him, you went to him.
'My own Ishulannu, let us enjoy your strength.
Reach out and touch my vagina.'

"But Ishulannu said to you,
'Me? What do you want of me?
Did not my mother bake for me and I did eat?
What is there to eat from you except loaves of shame and disgrace?
Rushes would be my only fence against the cold.'

"You listened to him.
You struck him and turned him into a frog,
left him to stay in the midst of his labors.
No more does the *shadduf* go up and down.°
And how about me? You will love me and then
treat me just like them."

°*Sililu*: otherwise unknown. °*every day*: the ashes of burned sacrificial animals. °*haunches*: as in the Greek myth of Actaeon, who saw Artemis while bathing and was turned into a stag and devoured by his own hounds. °shadduf *go up and down*: a *shadduf* is a primitive device for the transfer of water from one ditch to another consisting of a bucket on a counter-weighted pole supported in the center (still used in northeast Africa).

## The Bull of Heaven

Gilgamesh has deeply offended Ishtar by his reply. She goes up to heaven to the court of Anu. She begs Anu to send a monster, the Bull of Heaven, to destroy Gilgamesh. Anu at first refuses, but when Ishtar threatens to make the dead more numerous than the living (as Ereshkigal does in the Descent of Ishtar), he relents. The Bull appears in the streets of Uruk:

> At the snorting of the Bull of Heaven a chasm opened up
> and one hundred young men of Uruk fell in,
> two hundred young men, three hundred young men fell into it.
> At the second snorting of the Bull of Heaven another chasm opened,
> two hundred young men, three hundred young men fell into it.
> At the third snorting a chasm opened
> and Enkidu fell into it.

But Enkidu leapt out and seized the Bull of Heaven by its horns:

> The Bull of Heaven blew spittle into his face.
> He stirred up dung with its thick tail.

Gilgamesh then plunged his sword between the base of the horns and the tendons of the neck and killed the bull.

> When they had struck down the Bull of Heaven,
> they pulled out all its innards
> and set them before Shamash,
> backed away after setting them before Shamash.
> The two brothers sat down.
> Ishtar went up onto the wall of Uruk the Sheepfold.
> She was contorted with anger, she hurled down curses.
> "That man who reviled me, Gilgamesh, has killed the Bull of Heaven!"
> When Enkidu heard Ishtar saying this,
> he pulled out the shoulder of the Bull of Heaven
> and he slapped her across the face.
> "If I could get at you,
> I would do just the same.
> I would hang its guts on your arms!"

Gilgamesh makes a trophy of the horns of the Bull of Heaven and puts it beside his bed.

## The Death of Enkidu

Enkidu has a dream:

> Daylight came. Enkidu said to Gilgamesh,
> "O my brother, I had such a dream last night!

Anu, Enlil, Ea, and august Shamash were in the assembly.
Anu said to Enlil, "They have killed the Bull of Heaven,
and they killed Humbaba who guarded the Pine Forest."
Anu said, "One of them must die."
Enlil said, "Let Enkidu die, let Gilgamesh not die."
Then said august Shamash to valiant Enlil,
"Was it not in accordance with your own word
that they killed the Bull of Heaven and
Humbaba? Should now innocent Enkidu die?"
But Enlil turned in anger to august Shamash:
"In fact you accompanied them every day
as if you were their companion!"

Certainly Enkidu must die. In grief for the fate that will engulf him, Enkidu curses the hunter who saw him at the watering hole—he was better off in the wild. Then he curses Shamhat, the harlot who civilized him:

"Come, Shamhat, I will fix a fate for you.
Curses shall never cease.
I shall curse you with a great curse!
My curses shall rise up against you.
You shall never make your house voluptuous.
Your young bulls will never go into the girls.
Filth will sit in your beautiful lap.
The drunkard shall soak your party dress with vomit . . .
The crossroads will be the only place you sit down.
Waste ground will be your only lying place,
the shade of a city wall the only place you sit down.
Thorns and spines will sting your feet.
The drunkard and the thirsty shall slap your cheek."

The sun-god Shamash reproves Enkidu for his ingratitude, pointing out that, thanks to the harlot, he had fine food, abundant ale, a cloak, and a good friend in Gilgamesh, who would greatly honor Enkidu in death. Enkidu is then sorry for his curses against Shamhat, and he takes them back one by one.

Enkidu dreams of his impending death. He meets a young man with the face of an *anzu*-bird (a giant bird), the paws of a lion, and the talons of an eagle (cf. Figure 2.4). The demonic being seizes Enkidu and takes him

to the house where those who enter can never leave,
on the road where all travel is in one direction,
to the house of those without light,
where dust is their food and clay is their bread.
They are clothed like birds,
they are clothed in feathers.
They see no light and they live in darkness.

After the dream, Enkidu weakens and dies. Gilgamesh realizes that Enkidu's death is irrevocable when on the seventh day a maggot crawls from Enkidu's nose. Gilgamesh gives a long lament. Gilgamesh makes an image of Enkidu whose chest is lapis lazuli and whose skin is gold. Gilgamesh vows to make all the people bemoan Enkidu. He says that he will put on a lion-skin and wander the wilderness in sorrow.

## The Quest for Eternal Life

Gilgamesh says to himself:

"Will I die too? Am I not like Enkidu?
Grief pierces me, I am afraid of death.
I roam the open country. I shall take the road quickly
and go to see Utnapishtim, son of Ubara-Tutu."

Utnapishtim is a man who never died, a man who survived the Flood. Gilgamesh travels to the mountains of Mashu, someplace near the rising of the sun:

He reached the mountains of Mashu,
which daily guards the coming out of Shamash.
Their upper parts touch the foundation of the sky,
their breasts reach Allalu.°
Scorpion-men guard its gate.
Their aura is frightful, their glance is death.
They drape the mountains with terrifying radiant mantles.
They guard the sun at dawn and at dusk.
Gilgamesh beheld them, then fear and terror swept over him.

He took the initiative and greeted them.
A Scorpion-man shouted to his woman,
"Somebody has come. His body is like a god's!"
The Scorpion-man's woman answered him,
"He is two-thirds divine and one-third mortal!"

°*Allalu*: the underworld.

Gilgamesh declares his intention to travel to Utnapishtim, but to do so he must travel through a subterranean passage 36 miles long. There is no light anywhere:

The Scorpion-man spoke out loud and said:
"It is impossible, Gilgamesh, to travel
through the mountains' inaccessible tract."

Nonetheless, Gilgamesh walks down the dark tunnel. Eventually he emerges into a garden whose fruits are gems:

He came out in front of the sun.
Brightness was everywhere.
All sorts of thorny, spiky, prickly bushes

were everywhere, sparkling with gemstones.
Carnelian bore fruit, hanging in clusters,
lovely to look at. Lapis lazuli bore foliage,
bore fruit, delightful to behold.

In the jeweled garden lived Siduri, the ale-wife—an ale-wife in ancient Mesopotamia lived outside the protection of her male relatives and sold beer to travelers. At first frightened by his appearance because he wore only a lion-skin, Siduri locked herself inside the ale-house. Gilgamesh persuades her of his harmless intentions, and she opens the door. She asks why Gilgamesh is so distraught, why he wanders the open country? Gilgamesh explains that he grieves for a dead friend, Enkidu, whom he bemoaned for six days and seven nights until a worm dropped from his nose. Is he, too, doomed to such a fate? Does Siduri know the way to Utnapishtim, the man who never died? Gilgamesh wishes to learn the secret of immortality.

Siduri tells Gilgamesh to enjoy life and forget all about immortality. He should forego his quest, because it is pointless:

"Gilgamesh, where are you going?
The life that you pursue you shall never find.
When the gods made humankind,
death they set aside for humankind,
keeping life for themselves.
As for you Gilgamesh, keep your belly full,
make merry day and night.
Of every day make a feast.
Dance and play every day.
May your garments be fresh,
your head washed that you have bathed in water.
Pay attention to the little child who holds your hand.
Take your wife to your heart.
This is the task for humankind."

## The Man Who Never Died

Still, Gilgamesh will go. Unfortunately there is no ferry across the waters of death to where Utnapishtim resides. Only Shamash can cross these waters. Well, there is Urshanabi too, a boatman who *could* take him across. Urshanabi says that Gilgamesh must cut three-hundred poles each 90 feet long. Somehow these poles, which have special knobs, enable Gilgamesh to punt across the waters of death.

He reaches the land of Utnapishtim:

Utnapishtim spoke to Gilgamesh:
"Why are your cheeks so pale, your face cast down,
your heart so unhappy, your appearance worn out
and grief within? Your face is like that of a long-distance traveler.
Your face is weathered by cold and heat.
Wearing only a lion-skin you wander through the open country."

And Gilgamesh spoke to him, spoke to Utnapishtim:
"How would my cheeks not be sallow, my face cast down,
nor my heart unhappy, nor my appearance worn out,
nor grief within? . . .
My friend was the hunted mule, the wild ass of the mountain,
the leopard of the plain.
Enkidu was the hunted mule, the wild ass of the mountain,
the leopard of the plain.
We who came together and climbed the mountain,
we who seized the Bull of Heaven and killed it,
destroyed Humbaba, Lord of the Pine Forest,
killed lions in the passes of the mountains.°
My friend whom I loved so much, who endured hardships with me,
Enkidu whom I loved so much, who endured hardships with me,
the fate of mortals overcame.
For six days and seven nights I wept over him.
I would not allow him to be buried
until a worm came from his nose . . .
Am I not like him? Must I lie down too,
never to rise again?"

°*lions in the passes of the mountains*: this episode is lost in the earlier tablets.

Utnapishtim replies that

"because the gods made you from the flesh of gods and humankind,
because the gods made you like your father and mother,
death must come sometime, both for Gilgamesh and a fool . . .
Nobody sees death.
Nobody sees the face of death.
Nobody hears the voice of death.
Savage death just cuts you down.
Sometimes we build a house,
sometimes we make a nest.
Then brothers argue over the inheritance.
Sometimes there is hostility in the land,
but then the river rises and there is a flood.°
Dragonflies drift on the river.
Their faces turn toward the sun.
Then suddenly there is nothing."

°*flood*: that is, the flood wipes out every division of the land.

Utnapishtim explains that his immortality came about as a special case at the time of the flood. Ea warned him to build a great boat and to put all manner of things in it. The doors were slammed shut. The storm approached:

No man could see another.
People blended into the rain.

Even the gods feared the flood-weapon.
They withdrew, up to heaven.
They cowered like dogs down wind of the city.
Ishtar screamed like a woman giving birth.
The Mistress of the Gods,° sweet of voice,
was wailing.

°*Mistress of the Gods*: Ishtar.

The storm blows for six days and seven nights. Utnapishtim looks out:

The flood plain was flat like a roof.
I opened a porthole. Light fell on my cheeks.
I bent down, I sat down, I wept.
Tears ran down my cheeks.
I tried to see the banks, the limits of the sea.
Everywhere the land emerged.
The boat had come to rest on Mount Nimush.°
Mount Nimush held the boat fast, would not let her go.
On the first and second day Mount Nimush
held the boat fast, would not let her go.
On the third and fourth day Mount Nimush
held the boat fast, would not let her go.
On the fifth and sixth day Mount Nimush
held the boat fast, would not let her go.
On the seventh day I sent out a dove.

It went and returned. For no place
where it could perch appeared and it turned around.
I sent forth a swallow.
It went and returned. For no place
where it could perch appeared and it turned around.
I sent forth a raven.
The raven went and saw the waters recede.
It ate, it preened, it lifted his tail and did not return.
Then I put everything out to the four winds.
I prepared a sacrifice,
set out an offering on the mountain.
In fourteen jars
I poured the essence of reeds, pine, and evergreen.
The gods smelled the fragrance.
The gods smelled the lovely fragrance.
Like flies the gods gathered around the sacrifice.

°*Mount Nimush*: northeast of Kirkuk, Iraq.

When the storm-god Enlil arrives to the sacrifice, and learns that Utnapishtim
has survived the flood, he is furious. It could only be the doing of the clever water-god
Ea! Of course he did it, Ea admits, because Enlil had gone ahead with his plan to drown

every human being without consulting the other gods. There are plenty of other ways to reduce the numbers of humans without drowning them all—for example, famine and disease (although Enlil had already tried this). Enlil concedes Ea's point.

Utnapishtim goes on:

> "Enlil came up onto the boat.
> He took my hand and led me up.
> He led up my woman. He made her kneel down beside me.
> He touched our foreheads. He stood between us. He blessed us:
> 'Until now Utnapishtim was one of the mortals,
> but henceforth Utnapishtim and his woman will be as we are.
> Utnapishtim shall dwell far off at the mouths of the rivers.'
> They took me and made me dwell at the mouth of the rivers.
> Who can gather the gods on your behalf, Gilgamesh,
> and satisfy you with the eternal life you seek?"

## The Seven Loaves

It is impossible for Gilgamesh to conquer death. To prove his point, Utnapishtim challenges Gilgamesh to stay awake for six days and seven nights, for sleep is the brother of death. Gilgamesh sits down and immediately falls asleep. Utnapishtim mocks him to his wife, saying, "Look at this man who wishes to conquer death! He can't even conquer sleep!" He has her put a newly baked loaf of bread beside Gilgamesh on each day. On the seventh day Gilgamesh awakes. He says:

> "No sooner had sleep come upon me
> than you touched me and right away aroused me."

> Utnapishtim spoke to him, to Gilgamesh,
> "Look Gilgamesh, count your daily portions
> that the number of days you slept may be proved to you."

Gilgamesh sees the baked goods in progressive states of decay. He realizes that he is doomed to die and that nothing can be done about it. Utnapishtim commands that his guest nonetheless have his filthy hair washed and his wild skins thrown away:

> "Put a headband around his head,
> have him wear a robe as a proud garment
> until he comes to his city,
> until he comes to journey's end.
> The garment will not be discolored,
> but stay altogether new."

## The Plant of Rejuvenation

When Gilgamesh is already in the boat that will return him to Uruk, Utnapishtim's wife wonders what so weary a traveler has to take home with him. Utnapishtim calls out to Gilgamesh as he moves away, and Gilgamesh punts the boat near enough to

**FIGURE 2.7**   The walls of Uruk in modern times. (Nico Tondini / Robert Harding Picture Library Ltd. / Alamy)

hear. There is a certain plant of rejuvenation that Gilgamesh can acquire, Utnapishtim says, that Gilgamesh can get hold of. This will be compensation for his failure to discover the secret of eternal life. Gilgamesh must let himself down into the water by tying stone weights to his legs, then cutting the ropes once he has the thorny plant. Gilgamesh does this and so acquires the plant of rejuvenation.

Gilgamesh and Urshanabi, the man who ferried Gilgamesh across the waters of death and who for some reason now accompanies him, continue the journey to Uruk:

> At thirty leagues they stopped for the night.
> Gilgamesh saw a pool of cool water.
> He went down to the water and washed in it.
> A snake smelled the scent of the plant.
> Silently it approached and it ate the plant.
> As it took the plant away, the snake shed its skin.

And so Gilgamesh was deprived even of the ability to rejuvenate himself. The story is a typical etiology for why snakes can seemingly rejuvenate themselves by shedding their skins. The two travellers reach Uruk. Gilgamesh has Urshanabi go up onto the walls and walk around the great city, all made of baked brick (Figure 2.7).

## Observations: Gilgamesh, Archetypal Hero

The story of Gilgamesh follows patterns familiar from folktale. Enkidu is the wild man, made human by sex. He and Gilgamesh are buddies, devoted as only buddies can be. They reappear in Greek myth as Achilles and his friend Patroclus. The men endure

hardships and kill the spirit of the Pine Forest, who lives far f
there are no forests. So attractive is Gilgamesh when he re
that Ishtar, whose strong feelings are useful in sex and war, d
does not trust the sexual power of the female. The Bull of H
even this monster falls to the indomitable duo.

One can only go so far in defying the gods, and in i
go too far. Enkidu dies. Suddenly, the folktale of two men against the world bec
an anguished quest for eternal life, a theme inherited by the Greek Heracles, who
also wears a lion-skin: Heracles must be based to some extent on Gilgamesh. Surely
Utnapishtim, who never died and who lives at the mouth of the rivers, will know the
secret of eternal life.

In this version of the quest Gilgamesh must pass the Scorpion Men near the
Mountains of Mashu and penetrate a lightless tunnel through the mountain. At the
other end of the tunnel Siduri advises him to eat, drink, and be merry. Only Shamash
has crossed the water to the land of Utnapishtim. Gilgamesh nonetheless crosses.
Utnapishtim tells him the myth of the flood, to explain how he achieved his own immortality. But his was a special case, not repeatable. The most that Gilgamesh can hope
for is rejuvenation, but the snake eats the plant that would provide it. All that remains
are the splendid walls of Uruk, a human achievement in a human world.

## Conclusion: The Myths of Mesopotamia

The rich myths of Mesopotamia are generous in narrative detail. Prominent themes
are the cyclicity of vegetable life and the quest for immortality. In these stories the female is thoroughly deplorable, as Tiamat, who breeds monsters and holds up progress,
even the creation of the world, or Ishtar, with her treacherous sexuality. In human
relationships, the male friend is preferable. But when death wrecks such sympathy—
thanks to the female, who is death!—only human achievement is possible. Death is a
woman, Ereshkigal, but the sister of death is Ishtar, life itself. Although that life must
periodically disappear, its reappearance is just as certain.

The gods are ever bickering, like children in their petty wants, desires, and en-
mities. There is a dark, brooding quality to Mesopotamian myth. In part this owes to
the nature of the writing system, which allows only repetitive and simple expression:
Anything complex will not be understood in this writing that only vaguely supports
a spoken version. But the deep pessimism, and creative impulse, was to pass to the
Greeks through the traditions of the western Semites (see Chapter 4). Hence we in
the West are direct heirs of many of the mythic paradigms held in Mesopotamian
myth.

## Key Terms

cuneiform *15*      Enlil *17*       Ea *19*
Sumerians *16*      Apsu *18*        Enki *19*
Akkadian *17*       Tiamat *18*      Mummu *20*
Assyrians *17*      Anu *19*         Marduk *21*

## Further Reading

Frankfort, H., H. A. Frankfort, John A. Wilson, and Thorkild Jacobsen, *The Intellectual Adventure of Ancient Man* (Chicago, 1946). See also *Before Philosophy* (New York, 1949), a shortened edition of the same book.

Jacobsen, T., *The Treasures of Darkness: A History of Mesopotamian Religion* (New Haven, CT, and London, 1976).

McCall, H., *Mesopotamian Myths* (Austin, TX, 1990).

Sandars, N. K., *The Epic of Gilgamesh* (Baltimore, MD, 1972).

Schmandt-Besserat, D., *How Writing Came About* (Austin, TX, 1996).

Wolkstein, D., and S. N. Kramer, *Inanna: Queen of Heaven and Earth* (New York, 1983).

# Egyptian Myth

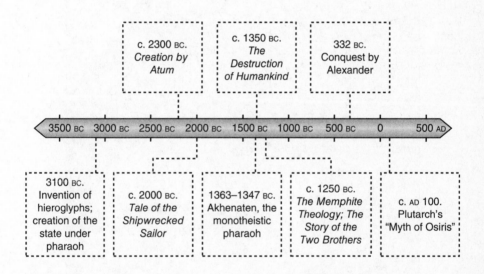

As the Greek historian Herodotus (5th century BC) noticed, Egypt is a gift of the Nile (Map 3). Rising south of the equator in streams that feed into Lake Victoria, the White Nile travels 3,000 miles north, joined by a single large tributary, the Blue Nile, at Khartoum in the Sudan. Most of the water and the silt come from the Blue Nile, which rises in Ethiopia. The Nile is the longest river in the world (the Missouri/Mississippi system is about as long).

North of Khartoum a series of six cataracts, outcroppings of granite in the river, form barriers to travel, the northernmost one at ASWAN, 400 miles south of modern Cairo and ancient MEMPHIS, the original capital of ancient Egypt, where the river meets the delta. Aswan was in history the logical border of southern Egypt. In the *Old Kingdom* (c. 2700–c. 2200 BC), Memphis was known as "the white walls," but at the

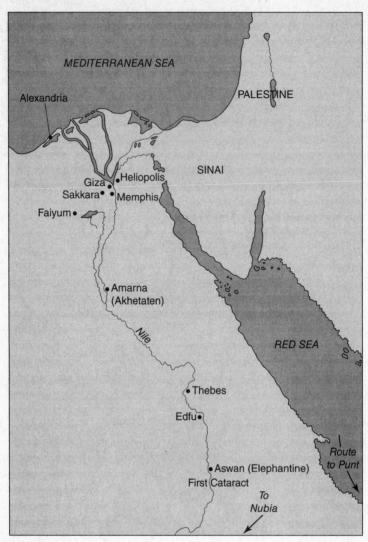

**MAP 3**   Ancient Egypt.

beginning of a period called the *New Kingdom* (c. 1570–c. 1070 BC), the city became known as *men nefer*, "the good place," which was corrupted in Greek to Memphis. In origin *men nefer* was the name of the pyramid of Pepi I (c. 2300 BC) of Dynasty 6, west of the city of Memphis.

After Aswan, the river, travelling north, forms a kind of tube through the desert (Figure 3.1). Along the shores of this tube arose one of the earliest and most interesting of all ancient civilizations. Its influence on art and morals has been profound, but it had a highly idiosyncratic, priestly intellectual life that left a deep impression on Egyptian myth.

**FIGURE 3.1**   The Nile near Aswan. (Photo by Author)

## THE BLACK LAND

It is literally possible to place one foot on the rich, black soil along the river and the other in the red, lifeless desert. The Egyptians called their own land *Kemet*, "the black land," after this rich soil. The sometimes high cliffs consist of limestone, because Egypt was in primordial times the bottom of a sea, but many other kinds of stone are available which made possible Egypt's extraordinary achievements in building with stone and in carving stone. Mesopotamia, by contrast, had no stone, and there buildings were made of dried mud (see Figure 2.7).

Each year the river flooded in late summer because of the spring rains in the highlands of Ethiopia. The flooding deposited rich soils along the banks. By catching the receding water in ponds, and then irrigating the dark, fertile soil from the ponds, it was possible to produce as many as three crops a year. Hence from an early time Egypt supported a huge population when compared with the rest of the ancient world, perhaps three million people during the heyday of the Pharaohs.

The valley of Egypt, between Aswan in the south and Memphis in the north, is known as *Upper Egypt*, because it is upriver (but it is lower on a map!). *Lower Egypt* is the delta, really a gigantic estuary in the shape of an inverted Greek letter delta Δ Lower Egypt is altogether different from Upper Egypt in its breadth and openness and flatness. We have very little information about the Egyptian delta from modern excavations because of the high water table. In any event, Egyptian civilization appears to have begun in the south along the river in Upper Egypt, around 3100 BC, with the invention of hieroglyphic writing and the establishment of the planet's first nation-state, centered on the divine kingship of Pharaoh.

## EGYPTIAN HISTORY

Archaic Period (c. 3100–c. 2700 BC): Dynasties 1–2

Old Kingdom (c. 2700–c. 2200 BC): Dynasties 3–6

Middle Kingdom (c. 2000–c. 1670 BC): Dynasties 10–12

New Kingdom (c. 1570–c. 1070 BC): Dynasties 18–20

   Akhenaten (reigned c. 1363–c. 1347 BC)

Post Imperial Egypt (c. 1070–c. 332 BC): Dynasties 21–31

*Pharaonic* Egypt begins with the first Pharaoh, sometime around 3100 BC, somewhat later than developments in Mesopotamia. Mesopotamia, however, never achieved political unity, except for the brief reign of Sargon the Great of Akkad, c. 2200 BC, and Hammurabi of Babylon, c. 1800 BC.

In prepharaonic Egypt, Egyptians lived in small villages along the Nile. Each village seems to have had its own god. Around 3100 BC a war leader from the south, near EDFU, who called himself a follower of the hawk- and sky-god Horus, overwhelmed the entire valley and the delta and became the first Pharaoh. The Egyptians always called him Menes, "he who upholds," but he seems also to have been called **Narmer**, "Fighting Catfish" (Figure 3.2). Narmer/Menes seems to have been preceded by several warlords, men who held power antecedent to Pharaoh. One was called King Scorpion.

Menes established his capital at Memphis where the valley joins the delta, at the "balance of the Two Lands." The "Two Lands" were Upper and Lower Egypt. The unification of power in a central authority was followed by an explosion of wealth. The next four hundred years are called the *Archaic Period*, Dynasties 1 and 2, when Pharaoh and his courtiers built huge tombs, sometimes with tens of thousands of grave objects and abundant human sacrifice.

A dynasty theoretically is ruled by a single family, and there were 31 of them in the about 3,000 years of pharaonic Egypt, which lasted to the conquest of Egypt by the Macedonian king Alexander the Great in 332 BC. The division of Egyptian history into 31 dynasties depends on a document written in the 3rd century BC in Greek by an Egyptian priest, one Manetho; one would never arrive at such a division by examining the monuments alone.

Around 2700 BC, in Dynasty 3, the *Old Kingdom* opened with the architectural genius Imhotep's design of the planet's first stone building, the so-called step pyramid complex in the Memphite necropolis. In Dynasty 4 were built the famous Giza pyramids, and many other enormous and spectacular pyramids were constructed to house the body of the Pharaoh, until the end of Dynasty 6 around 2200 BC.

What happened then is not clear, but for roughly two hundred years competing Pharaohs ruled the country. Then around 2000 BC, in Dynasties 10 and 11, central authority was reestablished, the so-called *Middle Kingdom*, which lasted until about 1670 BC. The

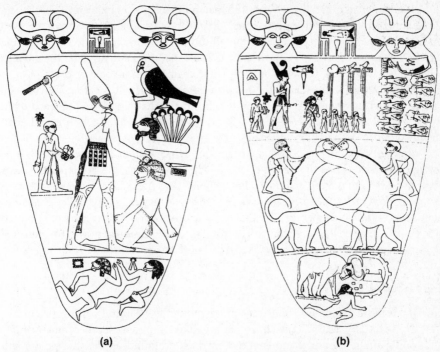

(a)                                                                    (b)

**FIGURE 3.2**   The Narmer pallet, c. 3100 BC, in the shape of a cosmetic palette, often taken as commemorating the victory of Narmer/Menes over the north. On the left (Figure 3.2a), the king, wearing the "white crown" of the south, is about to execute a prisoner. A symbolic representation in the upper right shows Pharaoh as Horus the hawk, holding by a nose-rope a dweller in the delta. In the register below, dead men lie outside their destroyed cities. The name of Narmer is written above in the center, *nrmr*, between two cow-goddesses, and various figures are labeled with some of the very earliest hieroglyphic signs. On the right (Figure 3.2b), the king, whose name *nrmr* is written before him in hieroglyphs, wears the "red crown" of the north, preceded by a confederation of allies, each with its fetish upon a standard. They review the dead in a recent battle. In the center fantastic animals (a Mesopotamian design) interlock their necks to leave a cavity suitable for grinding kohl, a kind of eye makeup (but this commemorative plaque was never actually used to grind kohl). In the bottom register the Pharaoh as a bull destroys a city and its inhabitants. (After J. E. Quibell, *El Kab*, London, 1898, pls. 12, 13; The University of Chicago Press)

biblical patriarch Abraham seems to have lived at this time. Then once again centralized authority collapsed and foreign invaders, called the Hyksos ("rulers of foreign lands"), evidently a Semitic people from PALESTINE, occupied the throne, at least in Lower Egypt.

The expulsion of the Hyksos around 1570 BC inaugurated the *New Kingdom*, Dynasties 18–20. With its capital now at Thebes, 400 miles south of Memphis, Egypt became an international power, exercising authority over PALESTINE and even parts of Syria, and in the south as far as the second cataract far south in arid Nubia. It was a period of immense sophistication and achievement in art and architecture, scarcely surpassed at any time.

At the end of Dynasty 18, Amenhotep IV ("Amon is content") came to power, who changed his name to *Akhenaten* ("servant of the Aten disk"), the first monotheist in history (reigned c. 1363–1347 BC). Akhenaten moved his capital from Thebes to an uninhabited cove in middle Egypt, which he called AKHETATEN, "horizon of the Aten disk." He closed the temples and attempted to impose worship of the Aten, the one God. He introduced an artistic revolution, the so-called AMARNA art, after the modern village near Akhetaten. The famous King Tutankhamen was his son-in-law.

After Akhenaten's death, the religion quickly reverted to earlier polytheism, and its ancient mythologies, but monotheism remained an underground teaching in Egypt. Probably, it influenced the later Moses, Egyptian for "child," a Hebrew raised in the Egyptian court, perhaps c. 1250 BC.

In the Post Imperial Period, after the 20th dynasty about 1000 BC, Egypt lost its foreign possessions and the wealth of empire. Still, it continued as an important Near Eastern power and is often mentioned in the Bible. After Alexander's conquest, the family of the Ptolemies, one of Alexander's generals, held power in Egypt. The Ptolemies continued until 30 BC when the last Ptolemy, the celebrated Cleopatra VII, committed suicide and Egypt fell under Roman control. For a long time Egypt was the personal possession of the Roman emperor: Once it had posed a grave threat to Roman power.

## EGYPTIAN WRITING

Nothing is more distinctive about ancient Egypt than its beautiful writing, product of the "House of Life," as the scribal offices attached to temples were called, and its influence on Egyptian literature, and Egyptian myth, is profound. Even as Egyptian myth is learned and rarefied, a plaything of scribes, so was the writing the joy and pride of the scribal class. Mesopotamian writing, by contrast, lacked the realism of Egyptian writing, but achieved high levels of narrative sophistication. In its writing lies the key to understanding Egypt of the Pharaohs.

The rules of Egyptian writing are complex and similar to the rules for cuneiform writing. For the Egyptians, writing was something very different than what it is for us. The language of ancient Egypt, which is now extinct, belonged to the so-called *Afro-Asiatic family* of languages. This large family includes such African languages as Berber (spoken in North African countries west of Egypt) and Cushitic (languages spoken in Ethiopia, Somalia, and Kenya). Afro-Asiatic also includes languages often called *Semitic* after Ham's brother, Shem: Akkadian, Babylonian, Arabic, and Hebrew.

First attested in writing somewhat around 3100 BC, the Egyptian language was spoken until the 11th century AD, when it died out except for use in ritual in the Coptic church, the ancient Christian church of Egypt. The Egyptian language spoken by the Pharaohs has an attested use of over four thousand years, more than any language on earth. After Islamic invaders from Arabia conquered the Nile valley in 641 AD, Arabic gradually replaced the native language. Arabic is the language of Egypt today, written in the syllabic Arabic script, a modification of the script of the ancient western Semites, first attested as early as 1400 BC in the writing of the Canaanites (see next chapter).

The Egyptian language coordinates in a rather complex way with forms of Egyptian writing. We need to remember that writing of whatever kind, including alphabetic writing, never represents speech directly, but is a system of thought with its own internal rules that makes use of the resources of speech. Egyptian writing is therefore not Egyptian language. Our perception of the speech that underlies the writing, and is attached to it in subtle and complex ways, is always highly imperfect. We simply cannot understand ancient myth without understanding the technologies that made it possible.

## The Forms of Egyptian Writing

We call the whole system of Egyptian writing *hieroglyphic* (not "hieroglyphics"), but distinguish three principal types: **hieroglyphic** proper ("sacred carving"); **hieratic** (Greek for "priestly"), and **demotic** (Greek "of the people"). In fact the hieroglyphic, hieratic, and demotic scripts are graphic variants of a single system, but such knowledge did not come easily.

*Hieroglyphic*, which consists mostly of stylized pictures, appears at the beginning of the pharaonic period, c. 3100 BC (Figure 3.3). Hieroglyphic signs, made up mostly of

**FIGURE 3.3**   Stele of King Djet, "King Serpent," 1st Dynasty (c. 2990–c. 2770 BC). His name consists of a single hieroglyph, the rearing cobra, within the stylized palace design, or *serekh*, surmounted by a hawk. The king proclaims himself as a manifestation of Horus. The serpent stands for the Egyptian word *dj[et]*, "serpent," and does not represent a serpent directly. The stele marked Djet's tomb in the Early Dynastic cemetery at Abydos in Upper Egypt. (Limestone. Louvre, Paris; Photo by Author)

**FIGURE 3.4**   The Egyptian word *ka* in detailed hieroglyphs, painted fresco from a tomb in the pyramid complex at Meidum, 4th Dynasty, c. 2575–c. 2450 BC. The upper basket stands for the consonant *k*, the vulture stands for the consonant *glottal stop* (the sound between the two syllables of "Uh-O," often written by scholars as *3*). We say "ka" but the pronunciation is conventional. (Egyptian Museum, Cairo; Alfredo Dagli Orti; The Art Archive)

recognizable objects but representing sounds of speech, not the object pictured, were still inscribed at the end of Egyptian civilization. The hieroglyphs were often treated with careful, even exaggerated attention, as miniature works of art (see Figure 3.4).The last known hieroglyphic inscription is on a temple near Aswan dated to AD 450.

*Hieratic* script is related to hieroglyphic script as our longhand is related to a printed text. It is nearly as old or as old as hieroglyphic script. Scribes seem to have learned by beginning with hieratic script, not hieroglyphic script, using brush and ink on papyrus. Hieratic was the "fast" hand used when keeping accounts or recording other kinds of information on perishable papyrus, rather as we use longhand when writing a letter (or once did) (see Figure 3.5).

Most surviving narrative accounts of Egyptian myths are in hieratic script. Although right to left was the usual direction, it was easy to shift to left-to-right writing to suit a larger artistic context. You can always tell in which direction Egyptian is being written because the figures in the hieroglyphs face toward the beginning of the text, against the flow of the reading. Hieroglyphic and hieratic were written side by side, by the same scribes, at the same time: hieroglyphic for things meant to last, like

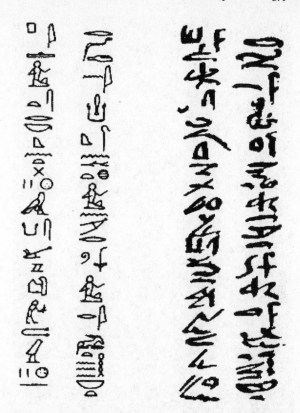

**FIGURE 3.5** Section from a private letter in the original hieratic script (right-hand columns), with a transcription into hieroglyphic (left-hand columns). The text is written from right to left and top to bottom, as always when Egyptian is written in columns, 11th Dynasty, c. 2040– c. 1991 BC. (after W. V. Davies, *Reading the Past: Egyptian Hieroglyphs*, Berkeley, 1990, Fig. 25)

expensive stone monuments, and hieratic for things of ephemeral or literary value. The last hieratic document comes from the 1st century AD.

Much later, around 650 BC, appeared the *demotic script*, a development of hieratic, but containing many ligatures (two or more signs written as one) and cursive forms. The last demotic document comes from the 4th century AD. Demotic is a very difficult script that few scholars can read. The hieroglyphic original underlying the demotic sign is lost.

The famous **Rosetta Stone**, from 196 BC during the reign of Ptolemy V—the most visited object in the entire British Museum—was carved in the upper register in *hieroglyphs* (the script of the priests), in *demotic* in the middle register (the script and language of everyday use at this time), and in *Greek* in the lower register (the script and language of the Macedonian rulers) (Figure 3.6).

The *Coptic script*, a slightly modified form of the Greek alphabet, accompanied a late stage of the language and served the Egyptian Christians, who in the 1st century AD wanted native-language versions of Christian documents. They wished to distinguish themselves from their pagan forebears, whose heritage they rejected, so they turned to the Greek alphabetic script of most Christian writings. Confusingly, like

**FIGURE 3.6**    The Rosetta Stone, carved in the hieroglyphic, demotic, and Greek scripts, the most visited object in the British Museum and one of the most famous objects in the world. (British Museum, London; Paul Briden / Alamy)

## PERSPECTIVE 3

### The Decipherment of Jean-François Champollion

Before Napoleon, in his rivalry with England, invaded Egypt in 1798, there was only a tiny amount of Egyptian hieroglyphic writing in Europe, some of it Roman fakes. In July 1799, one of Napoleon's officers was working on the defenses at a fort near the small port of ancient Rosetta, in the western delta. He found reused in a modern wall a basalt block inscribed in three scripts: hieroglyphic, an unfamiliar script (it is demotic), and Greek, the celebrated Rosetta Stone (see Figure 3.6). The stone was surrendered to the British in 1801 after the British fleet under Admiral Lord Nelson drove out the French invaders.

The importance of the Rosetta Stone was recognized at once as a possible key to decipherment, and copies made from direct impressions quickly circulated in Europe. Yet the decipherment was to take more than 20 years.

The Greek, easily understood, is a decree of 196 BC establishing a royal cult of Ptolemy V in return for the king's favors to the priests. Because the hieroglyphic portion, of which only 14 lines survive, was taken to be symbolic in nature, scholars focused their attention on the middle passage, the unfamiliar demotic script. It was assumed to represent the Egyptian language in some way, whose late form in Coptic script—a modified Greek alphabet—is well known. Presumably, the demotic script was not a system of symbolic representation, but in some way a phonetic writing, even an "alphabet" in which single signs represent single sounds, investigators thought.

One should be able to unravel the principles of the phonetic structure of the demotic text by finding *names* in the demotic text that correspond to *names* in the Greek text, which could be read. Having achieved some phonetic values in this way, it should be possible to unravel other vocabulary, known from Coptic.

While some of the values of the demotic signs were accurately determined, these values could not be made to yield results by applying them to the rest of the text. It became clear that there were far more characters in the demotic than you would expect to find in an "alphabet," where the average number of letters is less than 30.

From early childhood Jean-François Champollion (1790–1832) felt destined to decipher the hieroglyphs, and in preparation for the great day he mastered the Coptic language. Since the 17th century Coptic had been thought to be a late form of pharaonic Egyptian, as in fact it was, still used today in some Coptic churches. The Copts, or "Egyptians" (the word is a perversion of the Greek for "Egyptians"), preserved Egyptian prelslamic Christianity and, in fact, the ancient Egyptian language itself.

Champollion grew up during the French Revolution. He learned Greek and Latin at an early age, and at age 16, in 1806, five years after copies of the Rosetta Stone were available for study, he presented a paper on the Coptic etymology of Egyptian place names in the works of Greek and Latin authors. In Paris Champollion studied Persian and Arabic and at age 19 he won a chair at the University of Grenoble, an extraordinary achievement.

Already in the 18th century a scholar had suggested that the cartouches—enclosing circles resembling a bullet cartridge (French *cartouche*)—that surrounded some hieroglyphs contained divine and royal names. Unfortunately, only a single cartouche survived on the hieroglyphic portion of the Rosetta Stone, no doubt the name of Ptolemy. You would need at least a pair of names, however, that contain the same sounds if you want through cross-checking to establish the phonetic value of any one sign.

In 1822, Champollion received the transcript of the hieroglyphic writing on an obelisk transported recently to England, whose base, inscribed in Greek, contained the names of Ptolemy AND Cleopatra. One of the cartouches on the obelisk was the same as that on the Rosetta Stone—therefore, Ptolemy—and the other ended in two signs suspected of designating a female. That cartouche would belong to Cleopatra.

`We can follow Champollion's reasoning (Perspective Figures 3.1 and 3.2). The P appears as the first sign of PTOLEMIS (that is, Ptolemy), and as the fifth sign of Cleopatra,

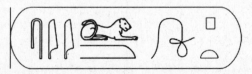

**PERSPECTIVE FIGURE 3.1**  PTOLMIS (Ptolemy), reading from right to left, from the Rosetta Stone (© The Art Archive / Alamy).

**PERSPECTIVE FIGURE 3.2**    KLEOPATRA (Cleopatra), reading left to right, top down, from an obelisk.

so that ☐ "stool" must have the value /p/. The "lasso" , third sign in one cartouche and fourth in the other, should have value /o/ (third sound in PTOLMIS and fourth in KLEOPATRA). The "reed" (for some reason doubled in PTOLMIS), third position in KLEOPATRA, should be /e/ or something like that. The "lion," fourth position in PTOLMIS and second in KLEOPATRA, should be /l/, allowing us to guess that "folded cloth" is /s/ (final sound of PTOLEMIS). The mouth must therefore be /r/ and the "vulture" is /a/ (last two sounds of KLEOPATRA (it is not really /a/ in this vowelless script but is used for /a/ to represent a foreign name, as is used for /e/). The sound for /t/ appears to be represented by both "bread loaf" and "hand" , but such duplications are common in writing systems.

Having already a group of signs, then, whose phonetic values seemed probable, Champollion turned to other cartouches. He deciphered the names of various Roman emperors, yielding sounds for around 40 hieroglyphic signs. By 1824, Champollion demonstrated that by applying the phonetic values already established in this way to words in continuous hieroglyphic text whose meaning could be guessed from context (son, father, mother), and to what appeared to be articles and personal pronouns, plausible Coptic equivalents could be found. He identified the names of numerous Egyptian gods known from Greek and Roman sources and explained how the name was always followed by what he called a nonphonetic marker, the picture of a god (now called a *determinative*).

When Champollion died suddenly at age 41 from a series of strokes, he was already reading Egyptian texts with remarkable skill and accuracy. His brilliant decipherment opened to humanity the thoughts and intellectual achievements of one of the world's great civilizations, including their myths, whose voice fell silent nearly 2,000 years ago, one of the greatest accomplishment of the 19th century.

*demotic*, *Coptic* refers both to a script and to one stage, the last, of Egyptian spoken language.

As Christianity took hold in Egypt, the older scripts were relegated more and more to the temples until by the end of the 5th century AD they ceased to be understood. Coptic script continued in everyday use until the 11th century AD when Arabic script, allied with the written Quran, prevailed along with the Arabic language, the script and language of Egypt today.

## MYTH: THE CREATION BY ATUM

Some very old myths—or rather, references to them—survive in the oldest religious literature on earth, from the 6th-Dynasty pyramids at Giza (c. 2300 BC), carved in hieroglyphs in the inner chambers. We can trace Mesopotamian myth back to c. 2000 BC, but the earlier Egyptian examples are more allusions to myth than they are myths themselves. The pyramid itself, in which these mythic references are carved, is like the primeval hill that first arose from **Nun**, the waters of chaos. On this primeval hill the first god **Atum** took his stand to create the other gods, according the *Creation by Atum* (cf. Chart 3). By referring to this myth (unknown in a narrative version), the

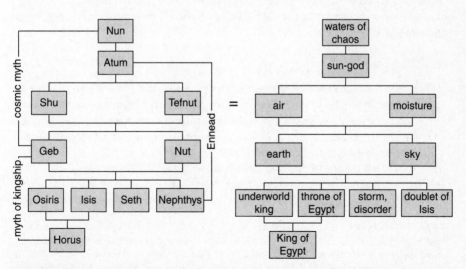

**CHART 3**  The creation by Atum; the descent of the Ennead, "group of nine gods," from Atum, and what these gods stood for.

texts guarantee the resurrection of the king buried in the pyramid, a clear example of myth used for magical ends. The *Enuma elish* served an analogous function in the Near Eastern New Year's Festival, to renew the world. In this case, the spirit of Pharaoh is renewed. The Egyptian Pyramid Text reads like this:[1]

> O Atum-Kheper, you who were on high on the primeval hill! You did arise as the *ben*-bird of the *ben*-stone in the *ben*-house in Heliopolis. You did spit out what was Shu, you did sputter out what was Tefnut. You did put your arms around them as the arms of a *ka*, for your *ka* was in them.

Atum, whose name means "the complete one," is the sun-god, always the great god in Egypt, the principle of unified creative power. **Kheper** is the scarab beetle, which has a name that looks like it means "the becoming one." Hence, the scarab beetle is the principle of generation, the force for progressive change (Figure 3.7). Atum-Kheper is therefore "the one god whose nature is to become."

The *ben*-bird, origin of our word *phoenix* (through the Greek), is another manifestation of the one creative principle, whose creative power bursts as a bird rising in the marshes. An image of this initial creative act is the alighting of the bird on the *ben*-stone, that is, on the pyramidal apex of an obelisk. The *ben*-house was in *Heliopolis* (Greek "city of the sun," of Atum), today a northeastern suburb of Cairo. In the Old Kingdom in Heliopolis, we know, was an open-air temple to Atum in whose central court stood a rather squat obelisk (unlike the slender New Kingdom obelisk of Figure 3.8).

The text puns on the names of **Shu** ("air") and **Tefnut** ("moisture"), which seem to mean "sputter" and "spit." The *ka* is a difficult concept, somehow the spiritual essence of a being that makes it alive, that leaves it at death, and receives nourishment

after death through offerings. The hieroglyphic sign of *ka* is ⊔, so Atum-Kheper "put his arms around Shu and Tefnut" when he imparted to them their *ka*. Such puns are not meant to be funny: In the resemblance of words to one another lie the deepest secrets of the universe.

The text continues:

> O Atum, put your arms around King Nefer-ka-Re ["beautiful is the *ka* of Re"], around this construction, around this pyramid, as the arms of a *ka*. For the *ka* of King Nefer-ka-Re is in it, enduring for all eternity. O Atum, may you protect King Nefer-ka-Re, his pyramid, and this construction of King Nefer-ka-Re. May you protect against anything evil happening to him through all eternity, as you set your protection over Shu and Tefnut.
>
> O great Ennead that is in Heliopolis—Atum, Shu, Tefnut, Geb, Nut, Osiris, Isis, Seth, and Nephthys—whom Atum begot, spreading wide his heart at his begetting you in your name of the Nine Bows. May there be none of you who will

---

[1]For the Egyptian texts, cf. J. B. Pritchard, ed., *Ancient Near Eastern Texts Relating to the Old Testament*, 3rd ed. (Princeton, 1969); M. Lichtheim, *Ancient Egyptian Literature*, vols. 1, 2 (Berkeley, CA, 1973, 1976); *New Revised Standard Version of the Bible* (Oxford, 1991). See also A. H. Gardiner, *Late Egyptian Stories*, Bibliotheca Aegyptiaca I (Brussels, 1932); R. O. Faulkner, trans., *Pyramid Texts* (Oxford, UK, 1969); R. B. Parkinson, *Voices from Ancient Egypt: Anthology of Middle Kingdom Writings* (London, 2006).

**FIGURE 3.7**    The scarab-headed god of creation Kheper seated on a chair holding a *was* ("power") scepter in his right hand and an *ankh* ("life") in his left hand. The columns above him mean, from left to right:
   *words to be spoken [by the god]: I have given you to eternity, like Re.*
   *words to be spoken: I have caused Re to appear in glory in the sky.*
   *words to be spoken: I have given you a seat in the holy land [the necropolis].*
   Over the god: *The great god Kheper loves you.*
Fresco in the tomb of Nefertari, chief royal wife of Ramesses II from her tomb in the Valley of the Queens in western Thebes, c. 1200 BC, 19th Dynasty. (The Art Gallery Collection / Alamy)

separate himself from Atum as he protects this King Nefer-ka-Re, as he protects this pyramid of King Nefer-ka-re, as he protects this his construction work—from all gods and from all dead, and as he guards against any evil happening to him through the course of eternity.

**Geb** is the earth, **Nut** is the sky, the children of Shu and Tefnut. They are up and down, the bubble within which everything takes place. This is a kind of divine myth, which in Chart 3 we call "cosmic myth," having to do with the creation of

**FIGURE 3.8**   Obelisk of Hatshepsut in the temple of Amun at Karnak. The obelisk is the *ben*-stone. (Thebes, Egypt; Photo by Author)

first principles, to distinguish it from the "myths of kingship," another kind of divine myth but having to do with origins of kingship, not of the world.

The most important Egyptian myth was evidently the myth of **Osiris** and **Isis** ("throne"), but the Egyptians never tell it; we have no Egyptian version of this myth. The myth must have seemed too special to give a narrative account, although there are countless references to details of the story. We learn, however, the following from the Greek Plutarch (c. AD 40–c. 120), writing at the beginning of the Christian era and knowing something about Egyptian traditions.

Osiris was an early king of Egypt. Osiris' evil brother **Seth**, represented by a strange unknown animal (see Figure 3.10), had secretly measured Osiris' height, built a beautiful sarcophagus, then at a banquet offered it to anyone who could fit inside. Osiris lay in it—a perfect fit!—and Seth's henchmen quickly nailed it shut and threw it into the Nile. Osiris' sister/wife set out in search of the corpse. She learned that the coffin had floated down the Nile and up the coast to Byblos in modern-day Lebanon, where it became embedded in the trunk of a cedar tree. The tree had been cut to make a pillar for the king's palace. She got hold of the coffin and put it on a boat back to Egypt, then left it in a marsh. While hunting, Seth found the coffin and cut the corpse into fourteen parts, which he scattered throughout Egypt. That's why there are so many temples to Osiris in Egypt!

Isis and her sister **Nephthys** ("lady of the house"), the wife of Seth, looked everywhere for the pieces and found 13; the 14th part, his penis, had been eaten by the Oxyrhyncus ("sharp-nosed") fish. In place of the missing penis she made a phallus out of gold, enlivened it by an enchantment, hovered over it like a bird, and so begot **Horus** ("above"), the hawk-god, whose incarnation every Pharaoh was. Osiris himself, resurrected, became Lord of the Dead.

According to Egyptian political myth, Horus was the reigning Pharaoh and Osiris was his dead father, whom Seth had drowned. Every Pharaoh was Horus and the father of every Pharaoh was Osiris, a principle so rigorously applied that we possess almost no personal details about the Pharaohs. They are never living, breathing men (except for the heretic Pharaoh, Akhenaten, of Dynasty 18), but were always absorbed into the myth.

According to the scattered Egyptian references to the myth, a great contest took place between the evil brother Seth and the good brother Horus, a struggle for the kingship that Horus won: He is the true king. Horus is not part of the **Ennead**, or group of nine gods beginning with Atum and ending with Nephthys (see Chart 3). They are often spoken of as a group, and sometimes in the plural form, as the *Enneads*, meaning "all the gods." The *Nine Bows* were the traditional enemies of Egypt, but the writer of the spell identifies them with the Nine Gods of the Ennead: The magic of the spell protects the dead Pharaoh against the potential enmity of the nine gods themselves—for the gods are forms of power and can be very dangerous!

## MYTH: CREATION IN MEMPHIS

There were rival versions to how the world came into being, though it is not clear that the Egyptians felt there was any contradiction.

Egyptian myth supported the reality of the Pharaoh's divinity and his right to rule as king. He was Horus, the legitimate son of Osiris, though posthumously begotten. In the 8th century BC, about the time of Homer, the nonEgyptian Kushites from south of Egypt held control of the country, the so-called 25th Dynasty (760–656 BC). Around 700 BC, the reigning Pharaoh, called Shabaka, claims to have found an old worm-eaten papyrus, whose contents he caused to be carved on a stone. Called the **Shabaka Stone**, it has been in the British Museum since 1805 (provenance unknown).

Scholars ignored the stone for a hundred years. It seems to have been used as a millstone, and the hieroglyphic text on it is hard to read and altogether lost in the center, where there is a large square hole. At first scholars thought that this text of c. 700 BC must go back to the Old Kingdom, the earliest days of Egyptian civilization when Memphis was the capital, because it is a celebration of the power of **Ptah**, the great god of Memphis, who represents the fecundating power of the earth (Figure 3.9). However, the text on the stone is now thought to be much younger than that, probably from Dynasties 19–20 (c. 1300–c. 1075 BC), four or five hundred years before Shabaka.

**FIGURE 3.9** Ptah, from the temple to Seti I (c. 1290-1270) BC. Ptah is mummified and holds the Egyptian symbols for "stability," "life," and "strength." He is often colored green. Ptah is always in human shape, wears a skullcap, a square beard, and an elaborate necklace with a counterweight. (Abydos, Egypt; Photo by Author)

Scholars call the text of the Shabaka Stone the **Memphite Theology**. We might call this a myth, because it is about how a god made the world, but it is also a symbolic way of thinking about ultimate realities. The text begins with a standard listing of the five official names of Pharaoh, then a note explains how the actual text came into being:

> This writing was copied afresh by his majesty in the house of his father Ptah-South-of-His-Wall,° for his majesty found it to be a work of the ancestors that was worm-eaten. It was unknown from the beginning to end. His majesty copied it afresh so that it became better than it was before, that his name might endure and his monument last in the house of his father Ptah-South-of-His-Wall in the course of eternity, as a work done by the son of Re,° Shabaka, for his father Ptah-Tenen,° so that he might be given life forever.

> °*Ptah-South-of-His-Wall*: the name of the temple to Ptah in Memphis; the "wall" is the wall of the palace. °*son of Re*: the living Pharaoh was Horus, son of Re; the dead Pharaoh was Osiris. °*Ptah-Tenen*: "Ptah who has emerged," a title for Ptah as identified with the first hillock, the arisen land.

The text goes on to discuss the conflict between Horus and Seth, the essence of the myth of Egyptian kingship. Horus was the rightful ruler, as the son of the dead king

Osiris, now king of the dead, but Seth, the brother and murderer of Osiris, claimed the kingship for himself. For a while they ruled jointly, or rather Seth ruled Upper Egypt and Horus ruled Lower Egypt, as the Shabaka stone reports:

> Geb [Earth], lord of the gods, ordered that the Ennead gather to him. He judged between Horus and Seth. He ended their quarrel. He made Seth king of Upper Egypt in the land of Upper Egypt, up to the place in which he was born, which is Su.°
>
> And Geb made Horus king of Lower Egypt in the land of Lower Egypt, up to the place in which his father Osiris was drowned, which is "Division-of-the-Two-Lands."°
>
> Thus Horus stood over one region and Seth stood over one region. They made peace over the Two Lands. That was the division of the Two Lands.

°*Su*: it is not clear where this is. °"*Division-of-the-Two-Lands*": Memphis.

This strange text seems now to refer to a ritual actually performed in which the participants, representing Horus and Seth, would move to certain places (in a temple?) standing for Upper and Lower Egypt and other locations important in the myth of kingship—or so some scholars have interpreted it:

> WORDS SPOKEN BY GEB TO SETH:
>
> "Go to the place in which you were born."
>
> SETH: *Upper Egypt.*
>
> WORDS SPOKEN BY GEB TO HORUS:
>
> "Go to the place in which your father was drowned."
>
> HORUS: *Lower Egypt.*
>
> WORDS SPOKEN BY GEB TO HORUS AND SETH:
>
> "I have separated you."
>
> *Lower and Upper Egypt.*

In any event, Geb, god of earth, regretted his division. He now decided to give the whole of the land to Horus:

> Then Geb thought that it was wrong that the portion of Horus was like the portion of Seth. So Geb gave to Horus his inheritance, for he is the son of his first-born son Osiris . . .
>
> Thus Horus stood over the entire land. He is the uniter of this land, proclaimed in the great name Ta-Tenen, South-of-His-Wall, Lord of Eternity. Then the two Great Magicians grew on his head. He is Horus who arose as king of Upper and Lower Egypt, who united the Two Lands in the Nome of the Wall,° where the Two Lands are united.

°*nome of the wall*: the district around Memphis. Apparently a "white wall" surrounded the palace of the king, which then came to symbolize the whole area.

Pharaoh, who is Horus incarnate, unites the Two Lands by right of inheritance. He unites the Two Lands, Upper and Lower Egypt, through his power as *Ta-Tenen*, which means "the land that has arisen," that is, the primordial mound that first emerged from the waters of the Nun, Chaos. The pyramid symbolized this primordial mound. He is also named after the temple to Ptah near the residence of Pharaoh, called "South-of-His-Wall, Lord of Eternity." The two *Great Magicians* are the crowns of Upper and Lower Egypt (see Figure 3.10). The *nome of the wall* is the district in which the palace ("the wall") of Pharaoh is built, that is, at the apex of the delta "where the Two Lands are united," in the fortress-city of Memphis.

> Reed and papyrus were placed on the great double door of the House of Ptah. That means Horus and Seth, reconciled and united, so that they fraternized and stopped their quarreling in whatever place they might reach, united in the House of Ptah, the "Balance of the Two Lands" in which Upper and Lower Egypt have been weighed.

The *reed* and the *papyrus* were emblematic of Upper and Lower Egypt; their union symbolized the union of the two lands, represented by Horus and Seth (Figure 3.10;

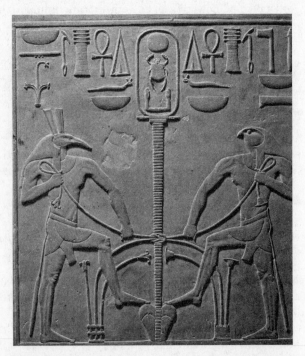

**FIGURE 3.10**   The symbolic union of Upper and Lower Egypt (called *sma-tawy*, "uniting of the Two Lands"): on the left the god Seth, holding the lotus (replacing the reed), and on the right the god Horus, holding the papyrus (symbolizing Upper and Lower Egypt respectively), tied around the hieroglyphic sign for "unity" (*sma*). The hieroglyphs above Seth on the left mean, from left to right: "May he be given all life, stability, power, lord of the South." Above Horus, from right to left: "May he be given all life, stability power, the great god, lord of the sky." One of the names of Senwosret I is in the cartouche: *Kheper-ka-re* or "the soul of Ra comes into being." Relief decoration on a limestone statue of Senwosret I, 12th Dynasty, c. 1918–c. 1875 BC. (Egyptian Museum, Cairo; Gianni Dagli Orti; The Art Archive / Alamy)

see also the design on the lower right side of the throne in Figure 3.7). The temple of Ptah in Memphis is like the point of a balance, exactly between Upper and Lower Egypt, and in it the Two Lands are one.

Now the text of the Shabaka Stone celebrates the power of Ptah, of whom all the other gods, even Atum, are but emanations:

> These are the gods who came into being in Ptah:
> Ptah-on-the-great-throne,
> Ptah-Nun, the father who made Atum,
> Ptah-Nunet, the mother who bore Atum.
> Ptah-the-Great is heart and tongue of the Ennead.
> Ptah who bore the gods,
> Ptah who bore the gods.
> Ptah Nefertem at the nose of Re every day.

Both Nun, and now Nun's female counterpart Nunet, are the primordial creative waters who begot Atum, the creator-god of the Heliopolitan cosmogony. But they are themselves only an aspect of Ptah, according to the Shabaka stone. "Ptah is the heart and tongue of the Ennead" because he is the desire (the "heart") for creation, and the source of the words by which the creation takes place ("the tongue"). The "Ennead" simply means "all the gods." "Nefertem," perhaps "the beautiful one who closes," is the cosmic lotus that appeared on the primal sea of Nun, whose delicious scent the sun-god Re partakes of each day.

> There came into being as the heart, there came into being as the tongue the form of Atum. For the very great one is Ptah, who gave life to all the gods and their *ka*s through this heart and through this tongue in which Horus had taken shape as Ptah, in which Thoth had taken shape as Ptah.
>     Thus heart and tongue gained control over all the limbs in accordance with the teaching that he, Ptah, is in every body and he, Ptah, is in every mouth of all gods, all men, all cattle, all creeping things, everything that lives, thinking whatever he wishes and commanding everything he wishes.

The creator-god Atum came into being through the thought of Ptah and through the speech of Ptah. In this way the divine power of Ptah was transmitted to all the other gods. **Thoth** (pronounced *thoth*) is the god of writing and magic, represented as an ibis or a baboon (see Figure 3.11), and often associated with Horus. Here Horus and Thoth are "thought" and "speech":

> Ptah's Ennead is before him as teeth and lips. That is the same as the semen and the hands of Atum. For the Ennead of Atum came into being through his semen and his fingers. But the Ennead is the teeth and lips in this mouth that pronounced the name of every thing, from which Shu and Tefnut came forth, and which gave birth to the Ennead.

The difficult text refers to a Heliopolitan myth whereby Atum, the first created being, gave birth to the second order of beings, Shu ("air") and Tefnut ("moisture"), through masturbation—he was after all completely alone. Evidently, he took the semen into his mouth, then "sputtered" out Shu and "spit" out Tefnut. But the Memphite Theology denies this: No, instead, Ptah held the creative thought in his *heart* and then he *spoke* ("teeth and lips") the world into existence:

> The sight of the eyes, the hearing of the ears, the breathing of the nose—they report to the heart and it makes every concept come forth. The tongue, it announces what the heart has devised. In this way all the gods were born and his Ennead was completed. For every word of the god came about through what the heart devised and the tongue commanded.

The senses report to the heart. Making use of this material, the heart devises thought. The tongue passes it into effective utterance:

> Thus all the faculties were made and all the qualities determined, they that make all provisions and all nourishment, by this speech. Thus justice is done to him who does what is liked and punishment to him who does what is hated. Thus life is given to the peaceful, death is given to the criminal. Thus all work, all crafts are made, the action of the hands, the motion of the legs, the activity of every member according to this command that is devised by the heart and comes forth on the tongue, and fashions the value of everything.
>
> So it is said of Ptah: "He who made everything and brought the gods into being."
>
> He is Ta-Tenen, who gave birth to the gods, and from whom all things came forth, foods, provisions, offerings to the gods, all good things. Thus it is recognized and understood that there is no god as strong as he.
>
> Thus Ptah was satisfied after he had made all things and all divine words. He gave birth to the gods, he made the towns, he established the districts, he placed the gods in their shrines, he settled their offerings, he established their shrines, he made their bodies according to his wishes.
>
> Thus the gods entered into their bodies of every wood, every stone, every clay, of everything that grows upon him in which they came to be. Thus he gathered to himself all the gods and their *ka*s, content and united with the Lord of the Two Lands.

All things were spoken into existence by the speech of Ptah, including the moral order that requires that wrong-doing be punished and right-doing rewarded. Not only is everything in the world of Ptah, but the meaning of the world comes from Ptah. The phrase *"everything that grows upon him"* refers to Ptah as **Ta-Tenen**, the risen land. The gods are not the statues made of wood or clay; they come from outside and enter the statues, as a *ka* enters a body. All these gods are of Ptah, as is Pharaoh, the "Lord of the Two Lands."

> The Great Throne, which causes joy in the heart of the gods in the House of Ptah, is the granary of Ta-Tenen, the mistress of all life, through which the sustenance of the Two Lands is provided, owing to the fact that Osiris was drowned in his water while Isis and Nephthys watched.
>
> They beheld him, they attended to him. Horus quickly commanded Isis and Nephthys to grasp Osiris and prevent his submerging. They heeded in time

and brought him to land. He entered the hidden portals in the glory of the lords of eternity, in the steps of him who rises in the horizon, on the ways of Re at the Great Throne. He entered the palace and joined the gods of Ptah Ta-Tenen, lord of years.

The temple of Ptah at Memphis is the "Great Throne," the granary that keeps Egypt alive. After all, Osiris was drowned here, where the valley meets the delta. Osiris is the grain-god, who through his death brings new life, as the grain dies, then sprouts from the ground in new life. The text is highly obscure, but evidently Isis and Nephthys only saved their brother Osiris from eternal death "when they heeded in time." They saw Osiris enter "the hidden portals in the glory of the lords of eternity," that is, he became god of the dead. Osiris went into the other world at the very site of the temple of Ptah in Memphis, "in the steps of him who rises in the horizon." He exercises his resurrective powers just as Re, the sun-god, is raised every morning from the darkness. In this way the powers of Osiris and the powers of Re are the same, but both are aspects of Ptah Ta-Tenen, the source of all that is.

Thus Osiris came into the earth at the Royal Fortress, to the north of the land to which he had come. His son Horus appeared as king of Upper Egypt, appeared as king of Lower Egypt, in the embrace of his father Osiris and of the gods in front of him and behind him.

Pharaoh is Horus and Horus is the son of Osiris. Pharaoh's residence, the "Royal Fortress," is at Memphis, the Balance of the Two Lands, where Osiris entered the earth and became lord of the dead.

As lord of the dead, Osiris was also judge of the dead. Judgment after death, according to the quality of one's deeds in life, which has famously entered popular Christianity, is an Egyptian invention (Figure 3.11).

**FIGURE 3.11** The judgment of the dead from the *Book of the Dead of Ani*, from Thebes, Egypt, 19th Dynasty, c. 1275 BC. (British Museum, London; The Trustees of The British Museum / North Wind Picture Archives / Alamy)

Figure 3.11 represents the Judgment. In the top register are seated the gods who will judge the dead man, a scribe named Ani; each god is named. In the lower scene, from left to right, the dead man and his wife enter the Hall of Judgment. In the central scene is the weighing of the heart on a scales (in the left-hand pan) against the feather of Truth (*maat*, in the right-hand pan). The heart is the essence of the man. Anubis reads out the favorable result, of which Thoth, scribe of the gods, makes a record. Were the result to prove unfavorable, the heart would be thrown to the Devourer, the monster with a crocodile's head, foreparts of a lion, and hind parts of a hippopotamus. Then the dead man would cease to exist.

## MYTH: THE TALE OF THE SHIPWRECKED SAILOR

In the Middle Kingdom appear the earliest narrative tales, recorded in hieratic script on papyrus. One Egyptian tale, c. 2000 BC, is the oldest known example of the story of a castaway on a fabulous island, who returns home laden with riches. The stories of Odysseus, sung 1200 years later around 800 BC, and of Sinbad the Sailor, from *One Thousand and One Nights*, c. AD 1100, belong to the same tradition.

The learned story is set artificially in a frame. A high official has returned from a failed expedition. Anxiously he awaits his reception at Pharaoh's court. One of his attendants attempts to cheer him up with some fatherly advice about how to behave in Pharaoh's presence, and by relating an incident that he himself experienced years before, at first disastrous, then it turned out successfully. At the end, however, the official remains despondent.

The story looks like a folktale, but in fact it is a highly sophisticated scribal composition, alluding through symbolic means to the power of the sun-god. The story survives on a single papyrus, now in Moscow. Where it comes from, no one knows:

> The wise attendant said, "Take heart my lord! We have come back home. We have seized the hammer and driven in the mooring post. The prow rope is tied. Praise is given, God° is thanked, and all embrace. We have come back in good health. We've lost not a man. We have left Wawat° behind, we have passed Senmut,° we have reached our land.
>
> "Now listen to me, my lord—I do not speak too strongly. Wash yourself, pour water over your fingers. You must answer when questioned. You must keep your wits when speaking with the king. Don't stammer when you answer! A man's words may save him. His speech leads to forgiveness. Or do as you wish! I am tired of arguing with you.
>
> "But I shall tell you of something similar that happened to me. I was going to the mines of Pharaoh. I went to sea in a ship one hundred and twenty cubits long and forty cubits° wide, with one hundred and twenty of the best Egyptian

---

°*God*: Egyptian texts often speak of a singular "God" almost as do later monotheistic texts; probably something like "the divine order, the intelligence that pervades the world" is meant, though it is a matter of debate among Egyptologists. °*Wawat*: probably Nubia on the Red Sea. °*Senmut*: location unknown. °*cubit*: the distance between the elbow and tip of the hand, about one and one half feet. The ship is about 180 feet long and 60 feet wide—huge by ancient standards.

sailors. Whether they looked at the sky, or at the land, their hearts were stronger than lions. They could foretell a storm, or a tempest.

"But as we approached the land, a storm came up, and cast up a wave eight cubits high. As for me, I seized a piece of wood but all the others perished, not one surviving. A wave threw me on an island. I spent three days alone, my heart my only companion. I lay in a thicket. I sought the shade.

"Then I stretched my legs to find something to eat. I found there figs and grapes, fine vegetables, sycamore figs both notched and unnotched,° and cucumbers that seemed to be tended. There were fish and fowl, nothing was lacking. I stuffed myself, then left on the ground what was left over, because I had more than I could carry. I cut a fire drill and made a fire. I made a burnt offering to the gods.

"Suddenly I heard a thundering noise, which I took to be a wave of the sea. The trees shook, the earth moved. I uncovered my face, and I saw a snake come near. He was thirty cubits long and his beard longer than two cubits! His body was overlaid with gold. His eyebrows were of true lapis lazuli.°

"He coiled himself before me. Then he opened his mouth while I lay on my face before him, and he said to me, 'Who brought you, who brought you, little one, who brought you? If you do not answer speedily and tell me who has brought you to this island, I will make you find yourself reduced to ashes, as a thing unseen.'

"I said, 'Although you are speaking to me, I do not hear you. I am before you, without knowing myself.'°

"Then he took me in his mouth and carried me to his resting-place and laid me down without hurting me. I was whole and sound, and nothing was taken from me. Then he opened his mouth while I lay on my face, and he said, 'Who has brought you, who has brought you, little one, who has brought you to this island that is in the sea, whose shores are in the midst of the waves?'

"Then I answered, holding my arms low before him, saying, 'I was going to the mines of Pharaoh. I went to sea in a ship one hundred and twenty cubits long and forty cubits wide, with one hundred and twenty of the best Egyptian sailors. Whether they looked at the sky, or at the land, their hearts were stronger than lions. They could foretell a storm, or a tempest.

" 'But as we approached the land, a storm came up, and cast up a wave eight cubits high. As for me, I seized a piece of wood but all the others perished, not one surviving except myself. I am here with you now. A wave threw me up on this island.'

"Then he said to me, 'Fear not, fear not, little one, and make not so sad a face, now that you have come to me. It is a god who has saved your life and brought you here to this island of the *ka*, where nothing is lacking, which is filled with all good things. See now, you shall pass one month after another until you will complete four months on this island. Then a ship will come from your

---

°*unnotched*: for sycamore figs to ripen they must be infested by a certain fly or be notched by hand with a knife. °*lapis lazuli*: a deep blue stone from Afghanistan common in Egyptian jewelry, from which this image is taken. °*without knowing myself*: he seems to be dazed.

land with sailors that you know, and you shall leave with them and go to your own country. You shall die in your town.

" 'How happy he is to tell of what he has experienced, when the pain in gone. So I will tell you that something similar happened on this island. I was here with my brothers and their children all around me. There were seventy-five serpents all told, children, and relatives, without mentioning a little daughter whom I obtained through prayer. Then a star fell and they went up in flames. It so happens that I was not with them when this happened. I could have died from grief when I found the heap of corpses.'

" 'As for you, if you are strong, and if your heart waits patiently, you shall press your children to your breast. You shall embrace your wife. You shall return to your house full of good things. You shall see your land where you will dwell in the midst of your brothers.'

"Stretched out on my belly, I touched the ground before him. I said, 'I shall tell Pharaoh of your power. I shall make him know of your greatness. I will send you sacred oils and perfumes and the incense of the temples by which all gods are honored. I shall tell what happened to me, what I saw of your power. Praises will be rendered to you before all the councilors of the land. I shall slaughter oxen for you as a burned offering. I shall sacrifice geese for you. I shall send you ships full of all kinds of the treasures of Egypt, as is done for a god, a friend of men in a far country of which no one knows.'

"He smiled at what I had said, which seemed foolish to him. He said, 'You are not rich in myrrh and all sorts of incense. I am lord of the land of Punt,° and I have myrrh. The oil and perfumes that you say you would bring are common on this island. Moreover, when you shall depart from this place, you shall never more see this island. It shall become water.'

"Then the ship came, just as he foretold. I got up into a high tree. I recognized those who were within it. I came and told him, but he already knew. He said to me, 'Farewell, farewell, go to your house, little one, see your children again, and let your name be good in your town. These are my wishes for you.'

"Then I bowed myself before him and held my arms low before him, and he gave me gifts of precious myrrh, of precious oils, cinnamon, perfume, eye paint, giraffe's tails, great lumps of incense, ivory tusks, greyhounds, long-tailed monkeys, baboons, and all kinds of precious things.

"I loaded all in the ship that had come. Then, throwing myself down on my belly to thank him, he said, 'You will reach home in two months. You shall press to your breast your children. You shall rest in your tomb.'

"After this I went down to the shore to the ship. I called to the sailors who were there. On the shore I gave praise to the master of this island and those in the ship did the same.

"We sailed north to the residence of the king. We reached the residence in two months, just as the serpent had said. I went into the king and presented him with the gifts I had brought from the island. He praised God for me in the presence of the councilors of the land. I was made an attendant and given slaves.

°*Punt*: probably southeast of Egypt in northern Somalia.

"Cast your eye on me after I reached land! After I told what I had experienced! Listen to me! It is good for people to listen."

"He said to me,° 'Don't even try, my friend. Who would give water at dawn to a goose that will be slaughtered in the morning?' "

°*he said to me*: that is, the man in need of cheering spoke to the man who had been stranded on the island.

This strange story reflects the Egyptian's deep attachment to his land. No wanderer like the Greek, the Egyptian wanted a wife, children, a home, and a nice tomb when he died, all of which the storyteller received. The island is a never-never land, the land of the *ka*. Everything there is luxuriant and abundant, like the garden of jewels to which Gilgamesh comes after passing through the dark tunnel. It is only in this world temporarily and will soon sink beneath the waves, never to appear again, as if the world beyond, the watery world of the chaos, of the Nun, came for a moment into this world.

The serpent is a common symbol in Egyptian art, often embracing the disk of the sun, or biting its tail as a symbol of eternity. The story of the death of the 75 relatives of the serpent from an apparent meteor proves that there is always hope, no matter how grave the disaster. And in fact there is plenty of hope, because the sailor escapes the island with great wealth.

Still, such fantastic tales of things gone badly, then coming out well, makes little impression on the man whom the narrator is trying to cheer. Thus the final remark about the goose watered at dawn and killed in the morning—it is useless to try to cheer one who is certainly doomed! the man insists.

## MYTH: THE DESTRUCTION OF HUMANKIND

The story of the first part of a longer work called the *Book of the Cow in Heaven* is first found in hieroglyphic writing on the outermost of the four shrines that enclosed the sarcophagus of the New Kingdom Pharaoh Tutankhamen of Dynasty 18 (c. 1341–c. 1323 BC), son-in-law of the radical monotheistic reformer Akhenaten. Later the *Book of the Cow in Heaven* appears in other royal tombs of the New Kingdom.

The myth tells how Re sets out to destroy the human race because they plot rebellion. He sends out his Eye to destroy them, but after initial success he reconsiders. By then the Eye can only be stopped by a trick. Re is the same as Atum, the sun, the creator of the world:

This happened in the time of the majesty of Re, the self-begotten and self-created, after he had assumed sovereignty over men and women, and gods, and things, the one god. Men and women plotted against him, while his majesty—life, strength, and health to him!°—had grown old, and his bones became like silver, and his flesh had turned into gold and his hair was like true lapis lazuli.

His majesty heard the complaints that men and women were uttering, and his majesty said to his followers, "Summon to me my Eye, and Shu, and

°*life, strength, and health to him*: added every time after the name or title of Pharaoh, hereafter omitted in the translations.

Tefnut, and Geb, and Nut, and the fathers and mothers who were with me when I was in Nun, and also the god Nun. Let there be brought along with my Eye his ministers, and let them be led to me secretly, so that men and women may not perceive their coming and may not therefore lose heart. Come with them to the Great House, and let them fully declare their plans. I may return to Nun, the place wherein I brought about my own existence."

Re, creator of the world, has grown old, as shown by his bones turning to silver and his flesh to gold. He hears reports of humankind rising in rebellion, and so summons a council of all the gods, including Nun, to which he threatens to return. The power of Re is symbolized by his Eye, whom he also summons, which is separable from him.

Probably the Eye was in origin a device for turning away the maleficent power of the evil eye, exalted into a cosmic principle. It is also called the *Eye of Horus*, but Horus is a sun-god when he wants to be. The "Great House" (*pr-aa*) where the secret council is held is on earth Pharaoh's palace, in heaven the palace of Re, the origin of the biblical word *Pharaoh* (a title never used of the Egyptian king in Egyptian sources).

The text continues:

> The gods were drawn up on each side of Re and they bowed down before his majesty until their heads touched the ground. He spoke in the presence of the maker of men and women, the king of people, the eldest father.° The gods said to his majesty, "Speak to us, for we are listening to your words."
>
> Then Re spoke to Nun, "O first-born god from whom I came into being, O gods of ancient time, my ancestors, take heed to what men and women are doing. Those who issued from my Eye are uttering words of complaint against me. Tell me what you would do in the matter, and consider this thing for me, and seek out a plan for me. I will not kill them until I have heard what you say to me concerning it."
>
> Then the majesty of Nun spoke to his son Re, "You are the god who are greater than he who made you, you are the sovereign of those who were created with you. Your throne is set, and the fear of you is great. Let your Eye go against those who have schemed against you."

°*the eldest father*: Nun.

Men and women originated as a tear from the Eye according to a pun whereby the word for "eye" is *remetch* and the word for "tear" is *remyt*—another unfunny pun revealing the secret reality of the universe. A story told of the Eye is that once when it returned from a mission it found that a second Eye had grown in its place. Re placated the first Eye by setting it on his forehead as the uraeus serpent, the cobra that symbolized deadly pharaonic power (cf. Figures 3.12, 3.13). Here he makes use of that destructive power:

> And the majesty of Re said, "Look, they have fled into the desert, for their hearts are afraid because of the words I may speak to them."
>
> Then the gods said to his majesty, "Let your Eye go forth and let it destroy those who revile you! No Eye is more able to destroy them for you. May it journey forth in the form of Hathor!"
>
> Thereupon this goddess went forth and slew the men and the women who were in the desert. And the majesty of this god said, "Come, come in peace, O Hathor, for the work is accomplished."

Then this goddess said, "You have made me to live, for when I gained the mastery over men and women, it was sweet to my heart." And the majesty of Re said, "I myself will be master over them as their king, and I will destroy them." And so the Powerful One, Sakhmet, came into being.

The Eye does what it is told and destroys large swathes of humankind in the guise of Hathor, whose name means "house of Horus," a major Egyptian goddess of love and drunkenness (Figure 3.12). Then Hathor changes into **Sakhmet**, whose name means "the powerful female one," a lioness goddess who brings victory in war.

**FIGURE 3.12** The goddess Hathor/Isis leads Queen Nefertari by the hand, 19th Dynasty, c. 1290–c. 1220 BC. Nefertari wears a vulture crown surmounted by a sun-disk and two feathers. On Hathor's back dangles a *menat*, a female sexual symbol and necklace counterweight. Hathor is crowned by a cow's horns (her power to nourish is like that of a cow) embracing a solar disk (her power is like that of sun), from which is suspended a uraeus serpent. She carries a *was* scepter (*was* = "power"). Her iconography is that of Hathor, but the inscription in front of her face identifies her as Isis: The two goddesses can embody the same feminine power. (Tomb of Nefertari, Valley of the Queens, Thebes, Egypt; The Print Collector / Alamy)

Re regrets his decision to destroy all humankind, yet is unable to call off the ferocious and destructive Sakhmet:

> The beer-mash of the night for her who would wade in their blood, beginning at Hnes:° The majesty of Re spoke, "Cry out, and let there come to me swift speedy messengers who may run like the body's shadow."
>
> Straightway messengers of this sort were brought to him. The majesty of this god spoke, "Let these messengers go to Yebu° and bring to me red ochre in great quantity." And when this red ochre was brought to him the majesty of this god gave them to the Sidelock-Wearer-in-Heliopolis,° the high priest, to grind.
>
> And when the maidservants were crushing barley for making beer, this ochre was placed in the beer mash and it became like human blood. They made seven thousand vessels of beer. The majesty of Re, the King of the Upper and Lower Egypt, came with the gods to look at the vessels of beer.
>
> When dawn appeared of the day on which the goddess would destroy all humankind in their time of traveling south (?), the majesty of Re said, "If the beer is good, it is good. I will save humankind with it." And Re said, "Let them take up the vases and carry them to the place where she plans on slaughtering the men and women."
>
> Then the majesty of the king rose up before dawn to have this sleeping draft poured out. The fields were flooded three palms high by the beer that the majesty of this god had poured out. When the goddess came in the morning, she found them flooded, and she was very pleased. She drank of the beer and her heart rejoiced, and she became drunk and paid no further attention to men and women.

°*Hnes*: a city near the Faiyum, the large oasis southwest of Memphis. °*Yebu*: Elephantine, an island in the Nile near Aswan. °*Sidelock-Wearer-in-Heliopolis*: Horus as a young god wore his head shaved except for a sidelock, but here it seems to be the title of the priest.

The rest of the story has to do with the creation of certain names and customs, including the custom of drinking vast quantities of beer at festivals to Hathor, for which this detail is etiological. The story of the destruction of humankind has a clear parallel in the biblical story of the flood, when Yahweh attempts to destroy humankind because of their wickedness; even the flood itself is paralleled by the ocean of beer that the drunken goddess consumes. But there is no myth of the Great Flood as such in Egypt.

The easy way in which divine power slips in and out of different forms—now Re, now the Eye, now Hathor, now Sakhmet—is typical of Egyptian religion and myth. These gods have little personality because they are forces with many manifestations.

## MYTH: THE STORY OF THE TWO BROTHERS

Surviving on a papyrus written in hieratic script, c. 1250 BC, is a story whose two main characters are gods, **Anubis** (see Figure 3.11) and **Bata**, a minor god, but who act in the story as humans. It is the oldest example in world literature of the so-called Potiphar's wife motif, whereby a married woman attempts to seduce a young man, is rejected, and then lies to her husband that she has been raped. The story-type is named after the biblical account of Joseph, recorded around 550 BC. The biblical tale

(Genesis 39) reads like an historical account, moralizing how with Yaweh's help the Hebrew Joseph survived the foreign devil:

> Joseph was taken down to Egypt, and Potiphar, an officer of Pharaoh, the captain of the guard, an Egyptian, bought him from the Ishmaelite° who had brought him there. Yaweh° was with Joseph, and he became a successful man in the house of his master the Egyptian, and his master saw that Yaweh was with him ... and left all that he had in Joseph's charge ...
>
> Now Joseph was good-looking and attractive. After a time his master's wife cast her eyes upon Joseph, and said, "Lie with me." But he refused and said to his master's wife, "Look, by having me as his servant my master has no concern about anything in the house, and he has put everything that he has in my hand ... How then could I do this great wickedness, and sin against Elohim?"°
>
> And although she spoke to Joseph day after day, he would not listen to her and have sex with her or be with her. But one day, when he went to the house to do his work, and none of the men of the house was present, she caught him by his garment and begged him, saying "Lie with me!"
>
> But he left his garment in her hand and fled and got out of the house. And when she saw that he had left his garment in her hand ... she called to the men of her household and said to them, "See, he [Potiphar] has brought among us a Hebrew to insult us. He [Joseph] came in to me to lie with me and I cried out with a loud voice, and when he heard that I lifted up my voice and cried, he left his garment with me and fled and got out of the house ..." Then she laid up his garment by her until his master came home, and she told him the same story ... And Joseph's master seized him and put him into the prison.

°*Ishmaelite*: that is, an Arab. °*Yaweh*: the tribal god of the Hebrews, probably the volcanic spirit that lives in the Sinai, usually translated as *Lord*. °*Elohim*: a plural form in Hebrew meaning "gods," but here meaning simply "God." *El* is an ancient Semitic word for God.

Joseph is finally freed when he interprets Pharaoh's dreams. The folktale is a religious myth, glorifying God's protection of his people.

The Egyptian story is much older and set to serve a political, not a moral, interpretation:

> Once upon a time there were two brothers, as the story goes, who had the same mother and father. Anubis was the name of the older brother and Bata was the name of the younger brother. As for Anubis, he had a house and a wife, and he viewed his younger brother as if he were a son. The older brother made clothes for the younger while the younger brother followed behind his cattle to the fields. It was the younger brother who had to plow and who reaped for the older brother. The younger brother did for him every chore in the fields. In fact his younger brother was an excellent man. There was none like him in the whole land, for a god's strength was in him.
>
> After many days had passed, the younger brother was tending his cattle according to his daily habit. He returned to his house every evening, laden with every vegetable of the field, with milk, wood, and with all good produce of the

field. He would place them before his older brother while he sat with his wife. He drank and ate, then left to spend the night in his stable among his cattle.

When the next dawn came, the younger brother took foods that were cooked and placed them before his older brother. He took bread for himself for the fields, and he drove his cattle to let them graze in the fields. He walked behind his cattle and they would tell him, "The grass of such and such a place is good." He listened to all that they said and took them to the place with the good grass that they desired. Thus the cattle in his charge became handsome and fine and they multiplied exceedingly.

At plowing time the older brother said, "Have a team of oxen made ready for plowing. The soil has emerged and is just right for tilling. Also, come to the field with seed because we will begin to cultivate tomorrow."

So he said to him. Then the younger brother made all the preparations that his older brother had told him to make. After dawn the next day, they went to the field carrying their seed. They began to plow. Their hearts were exceedingly pleased with this work that they had undertaken.

Many days later, while they were in the field, they needed seed. The older brother sent his younger brother, saying, "Go and fetch us seed from town."

The younger brother found the wife of his older brother seated, braiding her hair. He said to her, "Get up and give me seed so that I may hurry off to the field. My older brother is waiting for me. Don't delay!"

She said to him, "Go, open the storeroom and take what you want. Don't make me leave my hairdressing unfinished."

The youth entered his stable and took down a large vessel, for he wished to take out a lot of seed. He loaded himself with barley and wheat and came out carrying it. Then she said to him, "How much is it on your shoulder?" And he told her, "Three sacks of wheat and two sacks of barley, totaling five, that are on my shoulder." Thus he spoke.

Then she said to him, "There is great strength in you, for I have been watching your daily exertions." She desired to have sex with him. She got up, seized hold of him, and said, "Come, let us spend an hour together in bed. You will like it. I will make you nice clothes."

Then the youth became like a leopard in his rage over the wicked proposition that she made, and she became very frightened. He rebuked her, saying, "You are like a mother to me and your husband is like a father. My older brother has brought me up. What can you mean? Don't repeat it! But I will tell no one. I will not let it escape my mouth."

He picked up his load and went off to the field. He reached his older brother and they began work on their undertaking. Afterward, when the day was done, his older brother left work for his house while his younger brother was still tending his cattle. He loaded himself with produce of the field and drove his cattle before him to let them spend the night in their stable in the village.

But the wife of the older brother was afraid because of what she had said. She took grease and fat and made herself look like she had been assaulted, in order that she might tell her husband, "Your younger brother has assaulted me."

Her husband returned in the evening according to his daily habit. He reached his house and found his wife lying down, pretending to be sick. She did not pour water on his hands as she usually did, nor had she lit a fire. The house was in darkness as she lay vomiting.

Her husband said to her, "Who has quarreled with you?" She said, "No one, except your younger brother. When he came back to get some seed, he found me sitting alone and said, 'Come, let's spend an hour in bed. Loosen your braids.' That's what he said, but I would not. I said, 'Aren't I like a mother to you and your brother is like a father?' And he became afraid and beat me so I wouldn't tell you. Now if you let him live, I'll kill myself! As soon as he returns, you must kill him. I am ill from this evil plan that he was going to carry out this morning."

Then the older brother became like a leopard. He sharpened his spear and held it in his hand. The older brother stood behind the door of his stable in order to kill his younger brother when he returned in the evening to let his cattle enter the stable.

When the sun set, the younger brother loaded himself with all sorts of vegetables of the fields, as was usual, and came back to the stable. The lead cow entered and said to its herdsman, "Look, your older brother is standing in wait for you to kill you with his spear! Run away from him!"

The younger brother understood what his lead cow had said. When the next one entered, she said the same. He looked under the door of his stable and saw his older brother's feet as he was standing behind the door with his spear in his hand. He put down his load and took off at a run, and his older brother went after him with his spear.

Then his younger brother prayed to Re-Harakhti,° saying, "My good lord, it is you who distinguishes wrong from right."

Thereupon Re heard all his petitions, and Re caused a great gulf of water to come between him and his older brother, infested with crocodiles, so that one of them came to be on one side and the other on the other side.

His older brother struck twice on the back of his hand because he had failed to kill his younger brother. Then his younger brother called to him from the other side, "Wait there until dawn. As soon as the sun rises, I shall contend with you in presence of this god, and he shall hand over the wicked to the just. I will never again be present in your company, nor will I be present in a place where you are. I shall go to the Valley of the Pine."

After dawn and the next day had come, Re-Harakhti arose, and the brothers looked at each other. The youth rebuked his older brother, saying, "Why do you pursue me, wishing to kill me unjustly before you have heard my side of the story? I am still your younger brother. You are like a father to me and your wife is like a mother, is that not so? When you sent me to fetch seed, your wife said to me, 'Come, let's spend an hour sleeping together.' Look, it has been twisted around backwards."

---

°*Re-Harakhti*: "Re-Horus of the Two Horizons," a form of the sun-god identified with Horus who rises like a hawk at each sunrise (see Figure 3.13).

**FIGURE 3.13** Wooden stele of the Lady Taperet as she prays to the god Re-Harakhti. The god, holding a flail and an *ankh* ("life") and the scepters of power, sends his rays in the form of flowers beneath a shrine supported by the lotus and papyrus representing Lower Egypt and Upper Egypt, growing from a hieroglyph meaning "earth." They support a curved sign, the hieroglyph for "sky." Taperet stands by a heaped offering table, wearing a transparent robe and raising her hands in adoration. Offerings are listed in hieroglyphs behind her: "thousands of loaves of breads, beer, meat, and poultry." At the top, the solar disk flanked by magical eyes; beneath, the name Re-Horakhte is written. The hieroglyphs written in the box above the lady's head exhort the gods to provide her with all she needs in the beyond. 10th-9th centuries BC, 22nd Dynasty. (Musée du Louvre, Paris, France; The Art Gallery Collection / Alamy)

Then he told him all that happened between him and his wife. He swore by Re-Harakhti, saying, "As for your coming to kill me unjustly, you carried your spear on the testimony of a worthless slut!"

Then he took out a reed knife, cut off his penis, and threw it into the water. The catfish swallowed it, and the younger brother grew weak and became feeble. His older brother became sick at heart and stood weeping for him aloud. He could not cross over to where his younger brother was because of the crocodiles.

Then his younger brother called to him, saying, "If you have recalled a grievance, can't you recall a kindness or something that I have done for you? Go back to your home and take care of your cattle, for I shall not stay in a place where you are. I shall go off to the Valley of the Pine. What you shall do for me is this: Come and care for me if you learn that something has happened to me. I will take out my heart and place it on top of the flower of the pine tree. If the pine tree is cut down and falls to the ground, you must come to search for it. If you spend seven years searching for it, don't let your heart become discouraged. When you find it, place it in a bowl of cool water, then I will become alive that I may avenge the wrong done to me. You will know that something has happened to me when a beaker of beer is delivered to your hand and it ferments. Do not delay when you see that this happens to you."

Then he went off to the Valley of the Pine, and his older brother went off to his home with his hands placed upon his head and his body smeared with dirt.° Presently he reached his home. He killed his wife, cast her to the dogs, and sat down in mourning over his younger brother.

Many days later, his younger brother was in the Valley of the Pine with no one with him. He spent all day hunting desert game. He returned in the evening to spend the night under the pine tree on top of whose flower his heart was. After many days, he built for himself a country villa with his own hands in the Valley of the Pine, filled with all sorts of good things. He hoped to establish a home for himself.

Presently he went out from his country villa and encountered the Ennead as they were walking along governing the entire land. The Ennead spoke in unison, saying to him, "O, Bata, Bull of the Ennead, are you alone here, having abandoned your town because of the wife of Anubis, your older brother? See, he has killed his wife, and thus you have been avenged for every wrong done to you."

Because the Ennead were very sorry for him, Re-Harakhti told Khnum,° "Please fashion a marriageable woman for Bata so that he does not have to live alone."

So Khnum made a companion for him who was more beautiful than any woman in the entire land, for every god was in her. Then the seven Hathors° came to see her and said all together, "She shall die by the knife."

He desired her very much. She sat in his house while he spent all day hunting desert game, bringing it back and putting it before her. He told her, "Don't go outside or the sea may carry you away. I will be unable to rescue you from it, because I am a female like you° and my heart lies on top of the flower of the pine tree. But if another finds it, I will fight with him." Then he revealed to her all his inmost thoughts.

Many days later, while Bata went hunting according to his daily habit, the maiden went out to stroll under the pine tree next to her house. Then she saw the sea surging up behind her, and she hastened to flee from it and entered her house. The sea called to the pine tree, saying, "Seize hold of her for me." And the pine tree removed a curl from her hair.

The sea brought it to Egypt and deposited it in the place of the launderers of Pharaoh so that the scent of the curl of hair got in the clothes of Pharaoh. The king quarreled with the launderers, saying, "A scent of ointment is in the clothes of Pharaoh!" The king came to quarrel with them daily, but they didn't know what to do.

The chief launderer of Pharaoh went to the bank highly vexed because of the daily quarreling. Then he realized that he was standing on the shore opposite

°*smeared with dirt*: signs of mourning. °*Khnum*: a ram-headed creator-god, who fashioned humans on a potter's wheel. °*seven Hathors*: birth spirits who determine an individual's fate.
°… *female like you*: because he has cut off his penis.

the curl of hair that was in the water. He had someone go down and get it. The scent was found exceedingly fragrant, and he took it away to Pharaoh.

The learned scribes of Pharaoh were summoned and they said, "As for this braid of hair, it belongs to a daughter of Re-Harakhti in whom there is the seed of every god. It is a greeting to you from another country. Send forth envoys to every foreign country to search for her. As for the envoy who will go to the Valley of the Pine, have many men go with him in order to fetch her." Then his majesty said, "What you have said is good." And off they went.

Many days later, the men who had gone abroad returned to report to his majesty, except those who had gone to the Valley of the Pine, for Bata had killed them, leaving only one alive to report to his majesty. Then his majesty again sent forth many soldiers as well as charioteers in order to get her, and with them was a woman who had all kinds of beautiful feminine adornment.

The woman returned to Egypt with Bata's wife,° and there was jubilation in the entire land. His majesty loved her very much and appointed her chief lady. The king spoke with her and asked about her husband, what he was like, and she said to his majesty, "Have the pine tree cut down and cut up." The king sent soldiers bearing copper tools to cut down the pine tree. They reached the pine tree. They cut off the flower on which lay Bata's heart, and he fell dead at the very same moment.

After dawn on next day, after the pine tree had been cut down, Anubis, the older brother of Bata, entered his house and sat down and washed his hands. He was handed a cup of beer, and it fermented. A cup of wine was handed him, and it turned bad. He took his staff and sandals as well as his clothes and his weapons, and he journeyed in haste to the Valley of the Pine.

He entered the country villa of his younger brother and found his younger brother lying dead on his bed. He wept when he saw his younger brother lying there dead, and he went to search for his younger brother's heart beneath the pine tree under which his younger brother slept in the evening.°

He spent three years searching for it without finding it. When he had begun the fourth year, his heart desired to return to Egypt, and he said, "I will leave tomorrow." So he said in his heart.

After dawn on the next day, Anubis again walked under the pine tree and spent all day searching for the heart. In the evening he gave up. Again he spent time to search for it, and he found a pine cone. He left for home with it.

The pine cone was really his younger brother's heart! Anubis fetched a bowl of cool water, dropped the heart into it, and sat down according to his daily routine. When night had come, the heart absorbed the water. Bata shuddered over all his body and looked at his older brother while his heart was still in the bowl. Anubis, his older brother, took the bowl of cool water in which was his younger brother's heart and let him drink it. His heart assumed its proper position so that he became as he used to be.

Then each embraced the other, and they conversed with one another. Then Bata said to his older brother, "Look, I shall become a large bull that has

---

°*Bata's wife*: that is, the woman whom Khnum had made   °... *evening*: the narrator has forgotten that the pine is now cut down.

every beautiful color, whose kind is unknown, and you shall sit on his back. By the time the sun has arisen, we shall be where my wife is, so that I may avenge myself. You shall take me to where the king is, for every sort of good thing will be done for you. You will be rewarded with silver and gold for taking me to Pharaoh. I shall become a great marvel and there shall be jubilation for me in the entire land. Then you shall depart to your hometown."

After dawn on the next day, Bata changed into the form that he had described. Then Anubis, his older brother, sat down on his back until dawn. He reached where the king was, and his majesty was informed about him. His majesty saw the bull and became joyful over him. He made for him a grand offering, saying, "It is a great marvel that has come to pass." And there was jubilation for him in the entire land. His weight was made up in silver and gold for his older brother, who again took up residence in his hometown. The king gave him many servants and many goods, for Pharaoh preferred him over anybody else in the entire land.

Now many days later, the bull entered the kitchen and stood in the place where the chief lady was. He began speaking with her, saying, "See, I'm still alive!" She said to him, "Who are you, I ask?" And he told her, "I am Bata. I realize that when you caused the pine tree to be cut up for Pharaoh it was on account of me, to keep me from staying alive. See, I'm still alive, but as a bull!"

The lady became very frightened because of the speech that her husband made to her. Then he left the kitchen, and his majesty sat down and made a feast with her. She poured drinks for his majesty so that the king was exceedingly happy in her company. She said to his majesty, "Swear to me by God as follows, 'Whatever she will say, I will listen to it.'" And he heard all that she said. "Let me eat the liver of this bull, for he never will amount to anything." So she said. The king became very annoyed over what she said, and the Pharaoh was very sorry for the bull.

After the next day had dawned, the king proclaimed a grand offering, the sacrifice of the bull. The king sent a chief royal slaughterer to sacrifice the bull. When he had been sacrificed and while he was being carried on the shoulders of the men, he trembled in his neck and caused two drops of blood to fall beside the two doorposts of his majesty, one landing on one side of the great portal of Pharaoh and the other on the other side. They grew into two large Persea trees,° each superb (Figure 3.14). Someone went to tell his majesty, "Two large Persea trees have grown this night as a great marvel for his majesty beside the great portal of his majesty." There was jubilation for them in the entire land, and the king presented an offering to them.

Many days later, his majesty appeared at the audience window of lapis lazuli with a wreath of every sort of flower on neck. He mounted a golden chariot and came out from the palace to inspect the Persea trees. The chief lady came out in a chariot following Pharaoh. His majesty sat down under one Persea tree and the chief lady sat under the other. Bata spoke to his wife, "Ha, you liar! I am Bata. I'm alive in spite of you. I realize that when you had the pine cut down for Pharaoh it was on account of me. And I became a bull, and you had me killed."

°*Persea tree*: an Egyptian tree associated with the rising sun (see Figure 3.14)

**FIGURE 3.14**   The sun-god Ra, in his cat form, kills the snake god Apophis, a chaos demon, under a Persea tree. The tree represents the resurrective power of the sun-god, triumphant over death. Detail of a wall painting, 19th Dynasty, c. 1295–c. 1186 BC. (Tomb of Sennedjem (a workman's tomb), Deir el-Medina, Thebes, Egypt; Stock Connection Blue / Alamy)

Many days later, the chief lady stood pouring drinks for his majesty and the king was happy in her company. She told his majesty, "Swear to me by God as follows, 'Whatever she will say, I will listen to it.' So you shall say." And he heard all that she said. She said, "Have these two Persea trees cut down and made into fine furniture."

The king heard all that she said, and after a moment his majesty sent skilled craftsmen. The Persea trees were cut down for Pharaoh. The queen, the chief lady, observed it being done. A splinter flew up and entered the chief lady's mouth. She swallowed it and became pregnant in the space of a split second. The king had the Persea trees made into whatever she desired.

Many days later, she bore a son, and someone went to tell his majesty. "A son has been born to you." The child was brought in, and nurse and maids assigned to him. There was rejoicing in the whole land, and the king sat down and feasted and held the infant on his lap. From that instant his majesty loved him very much, and the king appointed him Viceroy of Kush.°

Many days later, his majesty made him crown prince of the entire land. Many days after this, when he had completed many years as crown prince in the entire land, his majesty flew up to the sky.° Then the new king said, "Have my great royal officials brought to me that I may inform them regarding all that has happened to me."

°*Kush*: southern Egypt and northern Sudan. °*flew up to the sky*: he died.

The wife was brought to him. He judged her in their presence. A consensus was reached among them. His older brother was brought to him, and he appointed him crown prince in the entire land. He spent thirty years as king of Egypt. He departed from life, and his older brother acceded to his throne on the day of death.

The story begins in a realistic mode with the wife's attempt to seduce the young, virtuous boy. When he prays to Re-Harakhti, the story suddenly, drops its realistic guise, and becomes an exploration in symbolic form of ever-renewed vitality, in this case the vitality of Pharaoh, who embodied Egypt: Repeatedly Bata dies and is reborn. Death is repeatedly brought by a woman's treachery, but always overturned through pharaonic vitality. The *folktale* is a political myth.

The gulf of water that separates the two brothers is the waters of death. The brothers can never be together again. The younger brother will go the Valley of the Pine, a tree associated with fecundity through its phallic straightness and its pine cones, filled with seed. The Valley of the Pine is also like the land of the dead.

The younger brother cuts off his penis and throws it into the water, where a catfish swallows it. Similarly, the Oxyrhyncus fish swallowed the penis of Osiris, whose myth governs much of the imagery in this story. Bata grows weak and feeble, that is, he dies once again. His heart is his essence, represented by the heart scarab—a stone carved in the form of a dung beetle—placed in the chest of the mummy and by the heart weighed against the feather of Truth (see Figure 3.11). The heart is made to live by being placed on the bloom of the flower.

The older brother covers himself in mud in mourning for his brother, and then kills the wife. In the meanwhile Bata hunts daily in the desert, a scene represented in many tombs as an idealized otherworld. The theme of the treachery of woman is repeated when the gods make for Bata a lovely female companion, whom Bata desires very much. Instead she crosses the uncrossable waters and goes to the court of Pharaoh. She treacherously orders that the pine be cut down and the flower toppled, killing Bata once again.

But every death implies a resurrection, so that the beer in the older brothers' hands now ferments, telling him that he must find his younger brother's heart and resurrect him by placing the heart in a bowl of water. Anubis cannot find the heart, but a pine cone instead (filled with seeds), which turns out to be the heart after all. Returning to human form, Bata then takes on the shape of a bull, and animal associated with a powerful vitality. The bull comes to Pharaoh's court. A title of Pharaoh was Bull of his Mother—that is, he is self-begotten. The bull is repeatedly identified with Pharaoh on, for example, the Narmer Palette (Figure 3.2).

But the woman is responsible for the bull's death, asking for its liver. The blood of the bull, which holds the life, is resurrected now as two Persea trees, an Egyptian tree associated with nourishment and the rising sun. When the Persea trees are cut down, Bata dies again, but because a splinter flies into the woman's mouth he is again reborn, this time from the woman herself. Becoming the king's favorite, the child is awarded the kingship, as in any good folktale. Bata judges the dead Pharaoh's wife with the consent of the royal ministers—that is, he condemns her to death. He makes his brother Anubis chief minister and, when Bata dies, king himself.

And so all came out right in the end.

The story type appeals to the same male fear of woman's power that underlies tales about the Mesopotamian Aphrodite, the vindictive Inanna/Ishtar who attempted to seduce Gilgamesh, then sent the Bull of Heaven. The same folktale appears in Homer's *Iliad*, told about the Corinthian hero Bellerophon (bel-**ler**-o-fon). After Bellerophon rebuffed the wife of King Proetus (**prē**-tus) while residing at Corinth, the king sent him to his father-in-law in Lycia, carrying sealed tablets with instructions, "kill the bearer" (the only reference to writing in Homer).

The king of Lycia sent Bellerophon on impossible tasks. First, he must kill the dread Chimera (kī-**mē**-ra), but Bellerophon mounted the winged horse Pegasus and killed the monster. He then had to fight the Amazons and perform other tasks, but he was always successful and in the end married the princess and received a portion of the kingdom. The folktale is a heroic myth, with the familiar ingredients of dangerous woman, treacherous king, conquest of a monster, victory, marriage, and kingship.

The Greeks told a similar story memorably in the myth of Hippolytus, whose stepmother Phaedra fell in love with him and, one day, propositioned him. When he brusquely refused her, she killed herself and accused Hippolytus of rape in a note pinned to her dress. It is a family drama, worthy of modern TV. Hippolytus' father Theseus, reading the note, cursed his own son, who died tangled in the reins of his chariot, its horses panicked by a bull from the sea. In one of the oldest stories in the world, when a respectable woman charges rape, nothing will save the man, guilty or innocent.

## Conclusion: Egyptian Myth

Egyptian myth is striking for its lack of legends. There are none that we can identify. Instead, all myth is *divine myth*, concerned with the doings of gods, strongly colored by *folktale*, whereby the downtrodden and oppressed wins through in the end. Egyptian myth was a plaything of the scribes who served the Pharaoh closely and had little attachment to popular traditions, even if such traditions existed. Divine myth blends in with the myths of kingship, whereby it was the purpose of the story to prove that the king ruled by divine right as the incarnation of Horus, the son of Osiris. This made the king a kind of god, only slightly removed in power and influence from the sun itself, whose representative on earth he certainly was. The world's first nation-state rested upon this theory of the divine kingship. As the sun shines on the earth, making it fruitful, so does Pharaoh shine in life on Egypt, as he continues to do in death.

# Key Terms

Narmer 60
hieroglyphic 63
hieratic 63
demotic 63
Rosetta Stone 65
Nun 69
Atum 69
Kheper 70
Shu 70

Tefnut 70
Geb 71
Nut 71
Osiris 72
Isis 72
Seth 72
Nephthys 73
Horus 73
Ennead 73

Shabaka Stone 73
Ptah 73
Memphite Theology 74
Thoth 77
Ta-Tenen 78
Sakhmet 85
Anubis 86
Bata 86

# Further Reading

Allen, J. P., *Middle Egyptian: An Introduction to the Language and Culture of Hieroglyphs*, 2nd ed. (Cambridge, UK, 2010).
Assmann, J., *The Search for God in Ancient Egypt*, translated by D. Lorton (Ithaca, NY, 2001).
Collier, M., B. Manley, and R. Parkinson, *How to Read Egyptian Hieroglyphs: A Step-By-Step Guide to Teach Yourself* (Berkeley, CA, 1998).
Pope, M., *The Story of Decipherment: From Egyptian Hieroglyphs to Maya Script*, rev. ed. (New York, 1999).
Quirke, S., and J. Spencer, *The British Museum Book of Ancient Egypt* (London, 1992).
Shaw, I., ed., *The Oxford History of Ancient Egypt* (Oxford, 2000).
Wilkinson, R. H., *The Complete Gods and Goddesses of Ancient Egypt* (London, 2003).

# The Myths of Canaan

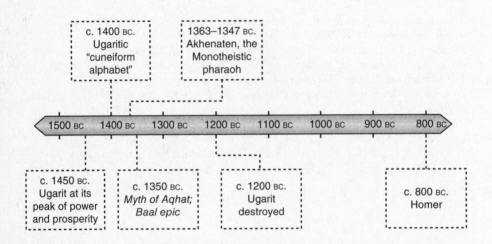

c. 1400 BC.
Ugaritic
"cuneiform
alphabet"

1363–1347 BC.
Akhenaten, the
Monotheistic
pharaoh

| 1500 BC | 1400 BC | 1300 BC | 1200 BC | 1100 BC | 1000 BC | 900 BC | 800 BC |

c. 1450 BC.
Ugarit at its
peak of power
and prosperity

c. 1350 BC.
*Myth of Aqhat;
Baal epic*

c. 1200 BC.
Ugarit
destroyed

c. 800 BC.
Homer

Ancient **UGARIT**, modern Ras Shamra near Latakia in northern Syria, was a cosmopolitan port city on the Mediterranean coast. Although its prehistory reaches at least back into the Neolithic period, c. 6000 BC, the site reached its greatest influence in power from c. 1450 BC until c. 1200 BC, when it was destroyed by unknown hands. It never rose again (Map 4).

Perhaps the city was destroyed by the mysterious Sea Peoples, who ravaged coastal cities at this time and even invaded Egypt: Murals on the walls of splendid Egyptian temples celebrate the Egyptian victory over them. A letter written in Akkadian cuneiform from the king of Ugarit to a king in CYPRUS, very near the time of the destruction of Ugarit, survives in the Hittite archives in central Anatolia—how it came to be there is unknown—and explains why help is needed:

> My father [the king in Cyprus], behold, the enemy's ships came here; my cities were burned, and they did evil things in my country. Does not my father know that all my troops and chariots are in the Land of Hatti [that is, in Anatolia, in

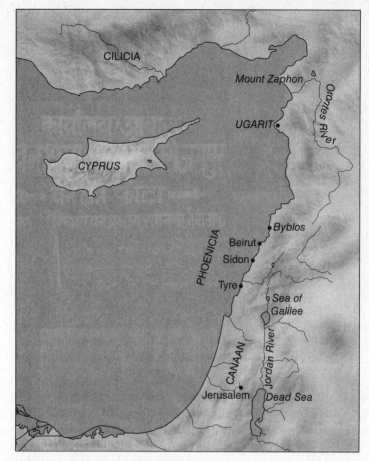

**MAP 4**   Ugarit on the north Syrian coast.

central Turkey], and all my ships are in the Land of Lukka [in Lycia, in southern Turkey]? . . . Thus, the country is abandoned to itself. May my father know it: The seven ships of the enemy that came here inflicted much damage upon us.[1]

The help never came.

Although the leaders of Ugarit spoke a Semitic language, the culture was deeply influenced by Egypt, which maintained trade and diplomatic connections with Ugarit. There were also Mycenaean Greeks living in the city.

## THE DISCOVERY OF UGARIT

Ugarit's location was forgotten until 1928 when a farmer accidentally opened an ancient tomb while plowing a field. Excavations have since revealed an important city from the end of the Bronze Age. It was the principal port and the entrance to the

---

[1]After J. Nougaryol et al., *Ugaritica* V (Paris, 1968), 87–90, no. 24.

**FIGURE 4.1**   Entrance to the royal palace at Ugarit. The stairs ascend steeply, and then turn sharply to the left before opening into a court. (dbimages / Alamy)

inland trade with the Euphrates and Tigris lands of Mesopotamia, shut off from the Mediterranean Sea by the high Lebanon mountains that run close to the coast all along the Eastern Mediterranean, except to the south in Palestine. A second range of mountains, the Anti-Lebanon mountains, runs inland parallel to the Lebanon mountains, making the barrier still more effective. A pass near Ugarit leads inland through the mountains.

Excavations have revealed a royal palace of 90 rooms laid out around eight enclosed courtyards and many ambitious private dwellings (Figure 4.1). Crowning the hill on which the city was built were three main temples: one to **Baal**, "lord," the great storm-god of the Canaanites; one to **El**, "God"—the same as Islamic *Allah* and the singular of the Hebrew plural form *Elohim*—who like Mesopotamian Anu stood above all and to some extent was eclipsed by his successors; and one to **Dagon** ("grain"), a god of fertility and growth of wheat and, in Ugaritic tradition, equated with El, the father of Baal.

Excavators discovered a palace library, a temple library, and—apparently unique in the world at the time—two private libraries, all dating from the last phase of Ugarit, around 1200 BC (Figure 4.2).

The tablets in the libraries contain diplomatic, literary, and economic texts, written in four languages: *Sumerian*, the classic language, in cuneiform script; *Hurrian*, a language of unknown affinities spoken by a kingdom on the middle Euphrates, in cuneiform script; *Semitic Akkadian*, the language of diplomacy at this time throughout the ancient Near East, in cuneiform script; and *Semitic Ugaritic*, a West Semitic dialect of which nothing had been known before, closely related to Hebrew, Aramaic,

**FIGURE 4.2**  Central court in Ugarit off which were found the two personal libraries. (Egmont Strigl / Alamy)

and Phoenician. West Semitic are simply those Semitic dialects spoken in the western portions of the Semitic language area. By East Semitic we mean those eastern dialects spoken in places like Babylon, whose writing system was cuneiform. The West Semitic dialects tended to be recorded in a syllabic system of writing for which the Ugaritic "cuneiform alphabet" is the earliest evidence, c. 1400 BC. The writing appears to be cuneiform, but the script is unrelated to Mesopotamian cuneiform. Three other scripts were found at Ugarit: Egyptian hieroglyphs; Luwian (or Hittite) hieroglyphs, used in central Anatolia (modern Turkey); and Cypro-Minoan, a syllabary derived from Cretan writing. Truly, Ugarit was the most cosmopolitan city in the world in the Late Bronze Age! The myths of Ugarit were to influence deeply the Greeks, who after all were living in Ugarit, and the Ugaritic writings are in the same tradition of written records that resulted in the Hebrew Bible.

## UGARITIC WRITING

The Ugaritic **"cuneiform alphabet,"** which records the Ugaritic language, discovered in the ruins of Ugarit is one of the most important archaeological discoveries of all time. It is the oldest evidence, from c. 1400 BC, for what was to become the Phoenician writing, then the Greek alphabet and all modern alphabets. It is, however, not an alphabet and is not cuneiform script. It is a syllabary consisting of around 30 characters in which the reader is expected to provide the appropriate vowel sounds according to the context; only the consonantal values of the syllable is expressed. Its around 30 signs are in roughly the same order as the Phoenician and Greek writing,

**FIGURE 4.3** The Ugaritic "cuneiform alphabet," which was not an alphabet and, although consisting of signs impressed into clay with a stylus, is unrelated to Akkadian cuneiform. The signary has around 30 signs that go from top to bottom, left to right on this tablet. Each sign represents the consonantal sound of a syllable (except for the last three, which represent full syllables). (National Museum, Damascus, Syria; Robert Harding Picture Library / SuperStock)

although their outer forms bear no resemblance to West Semitic characters (Figure 4.3).

Ugaritic literature found on tablets in the unique personal libraries include mythical texts, letters, legal documents such as land transfers, a few international treaties, and lists of administrative offices. Fragments of several poetic works have been identified, including those we will examine here: the "Myth of Aqhat" and the "Baal epic," a poem about the storm-god Baal that describes Baal's fight with the chaos-monsters Sea (*Yam*) and Death (*Mot*).

The discovery of the Ugaritic archives has enlightened study of the Bible because these archives for the first time provided a detailed description of the religion of CANAAN during the period directly preceding Israelite settlement. *Canaan*, perhaps meaning "lowlands," is an ancient term that appears in Egyptian and Akkadian texts. It refers broadly to all the area west of the JORDAN RIVER, but also up the coast to include the cities of TYRE, SIDON, BEIRUT, BYBLOS, and in the Bronze Age Ugarit, a territory that we call PHOENICIA in the scholarly literature, but was never known as such by the ancient inhabitants. The texts show significant parallels to biblical Hebrew literature, and to Greek epic, which is in some way related to Canaanite oral song.

The Baal cycle certainly influenced later Israelite cult and myth, where the volcano-god Yahweh takes on the role of Baal in Baal's struggle with the chaotic sea. While El is the chief of the Canaanite pantheon, he is barely mentioned in the mythical texts: The high god slips into the background while a new warrior deity moves to center stage, as Marduk replaced Enlil in Babylonian myth.

Goddesses in the stories are **Anat**, **Asherah**, and **Astartê**, although they play minor roles. Asherah is El's consort, and hence mother of the gods. She is sometimes identified with Astartê, said to be her sister but her name is probably a variation of Asherah; she is the least mentioned of the three. Anat, whose name means "Mistress Sky," stands out more than any. She is the sister and wife of Baal and allied with him in promoting fertility and repressing the forces of chaos (Chart 4).

The craftsman of the gods is **Kothar-wa-Hasis** ("skilful-and-wise") who lives either in Crete or Egypt, the source of Ugaritic artistic objects. He has little personality but, like the Greek Hephaestus, provides the gods with weapons and beautiful places to live. **Mot** is "Death," embodiment of the sterile western desert where nothing grows, as **Yam**, or "Sea," is the sterile and dangerous waters, like Tiamat.

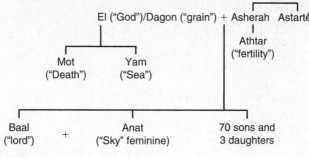

**CHART 4**   Some gods of Ugarit.

## MYTH: THE MYTH OF AQHAT

Three tablets, supposedly from c. 1350 BC, bear the story of **Danel**, which means "El is judge," in about four hundred lines, but break off before the story is finished. The story is called "The Myth of Aqhat."

King Danel has no son. He engages in an incubation rite, that is, he sleeps in the temple in hope of communicating with the gods in his sleep. On the seventh day of his incubation, Baal persuades the other deities to intercede with El, who takes pity on Danel, blesses him, and grants him a son, **Aqhat**.

The craftsman deity Kothar-wa-Hasis presents Danel with a bow to give to Aqhat. The goddess Anat, who presides over war as well as sex and fertility, desires the bow and tries several times to obtain it, even offering Aqhat immortality for the bow. In a scene reminiscent of Ishtar's attempt to seduce Gilgamesh, Aqhat roundly rejects her offer: "Old age and death are inevitable—it is useless to pretend otherwise," he says.

Anat, with the consent of El, sends her attendant in the form of a hawk to steal the bow, but it is broken and lost in the sea. Aqhat dies, bringing drought to the land. Aqhat's sister **Pagat** seeks revenge, but discovers that the killer she has contracted—one Yatpan—is in fact the murderer of her brother. Here the narrative breaks off, but most assume that Aqhat is somehow brought back to life. With his resurrection comes renewed fertility.

Such is the plot behind the text:[2]

Then may Danel, the man of healing,
the hero, the follower of Harnam,°

°*Harnam*: probably Danel's capital, perhaps on the Orontes River that flows north between the Lebanon and the Anti-Lebanon mountains. The "follower of Harnam" seems to mean "the follower of Baal," the god of Harnam.

---

[2]For the Ugaritic texts, cf. James B. Pritchard, ed., *Ancient Near Eastern Texts Relating to the Old Testament*, 3rd ed. (Princeton, 1969); Lilinah biti-Anat, *The Ugaritic Myth of Ba'al* (http://webspace.webring.com/people/nl/lilinah_haanat/mythobaal.htm, 1995–1997). See also A. Herdner, *Corpus des tablettes cunéiformes alphabétiques découvertes à Ras Shamra-Ugarit, en 1929 à 1939* (Paris, 1963) (CTA 17–19); J. C. Gibson, *Canaanite Myths and Legends*, 2nd ed. (London, 1978); M. D. Coogan, *Stories from Ancient Canaan* (Louisville, KY, 1978); Simon B. Parker et al., eds., *Ugaritic Narrative Poetry* (Atlanta, 1997); M. N. Wyatt, *Religious Texts from Ugarit*, 2nd ed. (London, 2002).

give food to the gods,
give drink to the gods.

May he go to his mat, may he lie down.
May he go to his pallet where he may pass the night.

One day passed. On the second day
Danel fed the gods,
gave the holy ones to drink.
Three days passed, and on the fourth day
Danel fed the gods,
gave the holy ones something to drink.
Five days passed, and on the sixth day
Danel fed the gods,
gave the holy ones something to drink.

Danel went to his mat and lay down
on his pallet, where he spent the night.
Then, on the seventh day,
Baal came to intercede for Danel:

"Danel, the man of healing, is miserable,
the hero, the follower of Harnam.
He has no son, like his brothers,
no heir, like his relatives.
Unlike his brothers, he has no son.
Unlike his kinsmen, he has no heir.
Yet he has given the gods to eat.
He has given the holy ones to drink.

"So father El, the bull, surely you must bless him.
Creator of all, will you not show him favor?
May he have a son in his house,
an heir in his palace.
May he set up a stone for his divine ancestor,
a family shrine in the sanctuary.
Sending his breath into the earth when he dies,
into the protective dust, he shall stop the breath
of those who speak against the son.°
He will drive away the son's enemies.
He will hold the son's hand when he is drunk.
He will hold him up when he is full of wine.
He will patch the son's roof when it leaks,
wash his clothes when dirty."

°*the son*: when the father dies, he will become a protective spirit, watching over
the son.

El took a cup in his hand,
a goblet in his right hand.
He blessed Danel, the man of healing.
He favored the hero, the follower of Harnam.

"May the vitality of Danel revive, the man of healing,
the passion of the hero, the follower of Harnam.
May he go to his bed.
When he kisses his wife, she will conceive.
When he embraces her, she will be with child.
May she become pregnant, may she give birth.
There will be a son in his house,
an heir in his palace
to set up a stone for his divine ancestor,
a family shrine in the sanctuary.
Sending his breath into the earth when he dies,
into the protective dust, he shall stop the breath
of those who speak against him.
He will drive away his enemies."

About 20 lines are missing here, probably telling of the conception and birth of Aqhat. Then:

Danel's face was joyful
and his brow shone above.
He smoothed his brow and laughed,
he put his feet on a stool,
he lifted his voice and cried:

"Now I can sit down and relax,
now my heart inside me can relax.
A son will be born to me, like to my brothers,
an heir, like to my relatives.
May he set up a stela for his divine ancestor,
a family shrine in the sanctuary.
Sending his breath into the earth when he dies,
into the protective dust, he shall stop the breath
of those who speak against his own son.
He will drive away his son's enemies.
He will hold his son's hand when he is drunk.
He will hold him up when he is full of wine.
He will serve up his son's portion in the house of Baal,
he will serve up his portion in the house of El.°
He shall patch his roof when it leaks,
wash his clothes when dirty [Figure 4.4]."

°*house of El*: that is, Aqhat when dead will establish by means of appropriate offerings communications between his own son and the god.

**FIGURE 4.4** Statuette probably of Baal, c. 1300 BC, in "striking god" posture, adapted from a posture common in Egyptian art. He wears the Egyptian white crown (associated with Upper Egypt). His crown and head are covered in gold leaf. Found in the harbor of Ugarit. (Musée du Louvre, Paris, France; Zev Radovan / BibleLandPictures.com / Alamy)

> Danel came home,
> Danel arrived at his palace.
> The skilful goddesses entered his house,
> the daughters of Enlil°,  the bright ones.
> Danel, the man of healing,
> the hero, the follower of Harnam,
> killed an ox for the skilful goddesses,
> he gave food to the skilful goddesses,
> drink to the daughters of Enlil, the bright ones.
>
> One day passed. On the second day
> he gave food to the skilful goddesses,
> drink to the daughters of Enlil, the bright ones.
> Three days passed, and on the fourth day

°*Enlil*: the Mesopotamian storm-god.

he gave food to the skilful goddesses,
drink to the daughters of Enlil, the bright ones.
Five days passed, and on the sixth day
he gave food to the skilful goddesses,
drink to the daughters of Enlil, the bright ones.
Then on the seventh day,
the skilful goddesses left his house,
the daughters of Enlil, the bright ones

The pairing of thought—"food to the skilful goddesses" and "drink to the daughters of Enlil"—and the repetitiveness of the style show that this text, unlike the Mesopotamian and Egyptian texts, are dictated oral texts. The style is similar to the poetic style of the Hebrew Scriptures (that is, the Old Testament of the Bible). Apparently, these Ugaritic poems were made by a poet dictating to a scribe. The scribe wrote down what he heard, not of course recoverable from the written document itself, but recoverable to a native speaker who used the written phonetic clues to remind him of words he knew from speech. Both Mesopotamian cuneiform and Egyptian hieroglyphs, by contrast, contain many nonphonetic signs that communicate information without the intercession of speech, but the Ugaritic "alphabet" contains no nonphonetic signs. There are no dictated oral texts in Mesopotamian cuneiform or Egyptian hieroglyphs. To be intelligible, the Ugaritic text had to be simple and predictable, governing this and biblical poetic style.

About 130 lines are missing; then Kothar-wa-Hasis speaks:

"I will bring a bow there,
I will provide the arrows."

And then, on the seventh day,
Danel, the man of healing,
the hero, the follower of Harnam,
got up and sat at the entrance to the gate
beneath the trees near the threshing floor.
He judged the cases of widows,
the cause of the orphans.°

Then he raised his eyes and looked
a thousand miles, ten thousand leagues away.
He saw Kothar coming,
he saw Hasis° approaching.
He was bringing a bow.
He had also provided arrows.
Then Danel, the man of healing,
the hero, the follower of Harnam,
called to his wife:

°*orphans*: that is, he behaved as a good Near Eastern king, protecting the powerless.
°*Kothar . . . Hasis*: "skilful" and "wise," the same god.

"Listen, Mistress Danataya,
prepare a lamb in flour
for the appetite of Kothar-wa-Hasis,
for the desire of the skilful craftsman.°
Give food and drink to the god.
Wait on him and honor him,
the lord of Egypt, the god of it all."

Mistress Danataya did as she was told.
She prepared a lamb in flour
for Kothar-wa-Hasis' appetite,
for the desire of the clever craftsman.

After Kothar-wa-Hasis arrived,
he placed the bow in Danel's hands,
he placed the arrows on his knees.
Then Lady Danataya gave food and drink to the god.
She waited on him and honored him,
the lord of Egypt, the god of it all.

Kothar departed for his tent,
the skilful one for his home.
Danel, the man of healing,
the hero, the follower of Harnam,
bent the bow and blessed it,
on Aqhat's account he bent it . . .

°*craftsman*: the gods behave very like men; there is scarcely any distinction, and Kothar-
wa-Hasis expects to be fed when he pays a visit.

There is a gap of about 60 lines, with only a few words remaining. Apparently,
Danel gives the bow to Aqhat. Then:

Anat poured her cup on the ground [Figure 4.5].
She raised her voice and cried,
"Listen, Aqhat the hero,
if you want silver, I will give it to you.
Or gold—I will make it yours.
But give your bow to Anat,
let the beloved of the Powerful One° have your arrows."

But Aqhat the hero replied,
"Give me wood from the Lebanon,
tendons from the wild ox,
horns from the mountain goats,°

°*Powerful One*: Baal. °*goats*: he is talking about the "composite bow," a powerful bow made of
wood and horn laminated together whose tips when unstrung bent forward. The composite bow
may have been invented around 2000 BC and was effective from horseback and chariots.

**FIGURE 4.5** The lid of a round ivory box showing a goddess of fertility feeding two wild goats and standing on a mountain top in the posture of "mistress of the animals." She holds a sheaf of wheat in either hand. The lid was found in a grave in the harbor of Ugarit, but the bare-breasted woman with conical cap, flounced skirt, and tresses falling down is Creto-Mycenaean in style. There were Greeks living in Ugarit at this time. We cannot be sure of the goddess's name, but to a large degree all Near Eastern goddess were the same: Anat along with Inanna/Ishtar/Asherah/Astartê. (Musée du Louvre, Paris, France; Zev Radovan / BibleLandPictures.com / Alamy)

> sinews from the ankles of a bull,
> reeds from the vast marshes:°
> Give them to Kothar-wa-Hasis.
> He will make a bow for Anat,
> arrows for the beloved of the Powerful One."
>
> But the virgin Anat answered,
> "If you want to live forever, Aqhat the hero,
> if you want never to die, I will give this to you,
> immortality—I will make it yours.
> You will match years with Baal,

°*marshes*: to make the arrows.

months with the sons of El.
Alive, Aqhat will make a feast,
alive he will be feasted and given drinks.
The singer will sing a song in Aqhat's honor,
a pleasant refrain for him."

But Aqhat the hero replied:
"Don't lie to me, virgin!
With a hero your lies are wasted.
A man—what does he get in the end?
What does a mortal finally get?
Plaster on his head,
lime on top of his skull.
As every man dies, I will die,
yes, I will surely die.
And I have something to tell you:
Bows are for men!
Do women hunt?"

Anat laughed, but not in her heart,
and she said: "Listen, Aqhat the hero,
listen while I speak. I will surely
meet you on the path of rebellion,
on the path of pride I will make you fall
under my feet, handsome fellow,
strongest of men."

She stamped her feet and left the earth.
She headed toward El
at the source of the two rivers,
in the double springs of the deep.
She opened El's tent and entered
the shrine of the king, the father of time.
At El's feet she bowed down and adored him,
she prostrated herself and worshiped him.
She spoke ill of Aqhat the hero.
She slandered the child of Danel, the man of healing.

The virgin Anat said:
"Do not rejoice in your well-built house,
in your well-built house, El,
do not rejoice in your high palace.
Do not rely on them!
I will smash your head,
I will make your gray hair run with blood,
your gray beard with gore.
Then you may call to Aqhat.

He can save you!
Call to the son of Danel—he can save you
from the hand of the virgin Anat!"

El the kind, the compassionate, replied:
"I know you, daughter, that you are without pity.
There is no contempt like yours among goddesses.
Leave, unscrupulous daughter!
You will store it up in your heart.
Take whatever is in your mind,
whatever you desire you will do.
Whoever opposes you will be crushed."

Virgin Anat left.
She headed toward Aqhat the hero,
a thousand miles, ten thousand leagues at each step.
Virgin Anat laughed.
She raised her voice and cried,
"Listen, Aqhat the hero,
you are my brother and I am your sister . . ."

There are 12 lines of which only a few words survive. Then:

The virgin Anat left.
She headed for Yatpan, the drunken soldier.
She raised her voice and shouted:
"Pay attention, Yatpan,
Aqhat is now in the city of Abilim,
Abilim, the city of the moon . . ."

Yatpan, the drunken soldier, replied:
"Listen virgin Anat,
will you really kill him for his bow,
kill him for his arrows, not let him live?
The handsome fellow, the hero, has fixed a meal.
He is all alone in the tent."

Virgin Anat replied:
"Pay attention, Yatpan, and I'll give the orders.
I will put you in my pouch like a falcon,
in my bag like a bird.
When Aqhat sits down to eat,
the son of Danel to his meal,
falcons will swoop over him,
a flock of birds will soar above.
I will be swooping among the falcons.

I will set you over Aqhat.
Strike him twice on the skull,
three times over the ear,
make his blood run like a murderer,
run to his knees like a butcher.
Let his breath run out like a wind,
like spittle his spirit,
like smoke from his nostrils.
His vitality will leave his nostrils.
I will not let him live!"

She took Yatpan, the drunken soldier,
she put him in her pouch like a falcon,
in her bag like a bird.
When Aqhat sat down to eat,
the son of Danel to his meal,
falcons swooped over him,
a flock of birds soared above.
Among the falcons swooped Anat.
She set Yatpan over Aqhat.
He struck him twice on the skull,
three times over the ear.
He made his blood run like a murderer,
run to his knees like a butcher.
His breath left him like wind,
like spittle his spirit,
like smoke from his nostrils . . .
and she wept.

About 10 lines are missing here.

Into the water it fell,
the bow shattered.
Virgin Anat returned.
She picked up his quiver.
She held Aqhat as a singer holds his lyre.
Her teeth were like a chisel.
She devoured his entrails.
She split him like a tree.
She cut the corpse in two,
she divided the cadaver,
she dismembered the body.

"I killed him only for his bow,
I killed him for his arrows.
I did not let him live,
but I have not got his bow.

Because of his death
the first fruits of summer have withered,
the ear in its husk . . ."

Danel, the man of healing,
the hero, the follower of Harnam,
got up and sat at the entrance to the gate,
beneath the trees near the threshing floor.
He judged the cases of widows,
the cause of the orphans.

Pagat° raised up her eyes and looked.
On the threshing floor the greenery had dried.
It drooped, it withered.
Over her father's house falcons swooped,
a flock of birds soared above.
Pagat wept in her heart,
she cried inwardly.

She tore the clothes of Danel, the man of healing,
the clothes of the hero, the follower of Harnam.
Then Danel, the man of healing
cursed the clouds in the devastating heat,
the rain from clouds that falls in summer,
the dew that drops on the grapes:
"For seven years Baal will fail,
for eight, the rider on the clouds.
No dew, no showers,
no surging of the two seas,
no benefit of Baal's voice.
The clothes of Danel, the man of healing,
have been torn,° the garments of the hero,
the follower of Harnam."

Danel called to his daughter:
"Listen, Pagat, who carry water on your shoulder,
who brush the dew from the fleece,
who know the course of the stars—
saddle an ass, harness a donkey,
attach my silver trappings, my golden bridle."

Pagat obeyed, who carried water on her shoulder,
who brushed the dew from the fleece,
who knew the course of the stars.
In tears she saddled the ass,

°*Pagat*: Aqhat's sister. °*torn*: as a sign of mourning.

in tears she harnessed the donkey,
in tears she lifted her father,
put him on the ass's back,
on the splendid back of the donkey.

Danel drove to inspect his fields.
He saw a shoot in the fields,
he saw a shoot in the plots.
He embraced the shoot and kissed it.

"If only the shoot could grow in the heat-cracked field,
in the heat-cracked field the shoot could grow,
in the wilted plots the plant,
the hand of Aqhat the hero would harvest you,
place you in the granary."°

He inspected his plots.
He saw an ear of wheat growing in the plots,
an ear growing in the heat-cracked fields.
He embraced the ear and kissed it.

"If only the ear could grow,
in the plots the ear grow,
in the heat-cracked fields the plant,
the hand of Aqhat the hero would harvest you,
place you in the granary."

He had just spoken his words,
this speech had just come from his lips,
when Pagat raised her eyes and looked.
Two young boys were coming . . .

About 10 fragmentary lines. Then Danel, whose curses because of Aqhat's death
have brought about drought, receives from an unidentified source an exact description
of how Aqhat was killed:

"He was struck twice on the skull,
three times over the ear . . ."
Tears poured like shekels . . .
"We have news for you, Danel.
Virgin Anat made his breath leave him like wind,
his spirit like a breeze,
like smoke from his nostrils."

They arrived, they raised their voices and cried:
"Listen, Danel, the man of healing,

°*granary:* Danel sees the first result of his curse against the rain and hopes that a counterblessing
will reverse it.

Aqhat the hero is dead.
The virgin Anat made his breath leave him like wind,
his spirit like a breeze."

Danel's feet shook,
his face broke out in a sweat,
his back was as though shattered,
his joints trembled,
his spine was weakened.
When he raised his eyes and looked
he saw falcons in the clouds.

He raised his voice and cried:
"May Baal shatter the falcons' wings,
may Baal shatter their pinions!
May they fall at my feet!
I will split their gizzards and look inside.
If there is fat, if there is bone,
I will weep and I will bury my son.
I will put him into the pit of the earth gods."

He had just spoken these words,
this speech had just come from his lips,
when Baal shattered the falcons' wings,
Baal shattered their pinions,
and they fell at his feet.
Danel split their gizzards and looked inside.
There was no fat, there was no bone.

Danel raised his voice and cried:
"May Baal rebuild the falcons' wings,
may Baal rebuild their pinions.
Falcons, up and fly away!"

When he raised his eyes and looked upward,
he saw Hirgab, the father of falcons.

He raised his voice and cried:
"May Baal shatter Hirgab's wings,
may Baal shatter his pinions!
Let him fall at my feet!
I will split his gizzard and look inside.
If there is fat, if there is bone,
I will weep and I will bury my son,
I will put him into the pit of the earth gods."

He had just spoken these words,
this speech had just come forth from his mouth,

when Baal shattered Hirgab's wings,
Baal shattered his pinions,
and Hirgab fell at Danel's feet.
Dane' split Hirgab's gizzard and looked inside.
There was no fat, there was no bone.

He raised his voice and shouted:
"May Baal rebuild Hirgab's wings,
may Baal rebuild his pinions!
Hirgab, up and fly away!"

When he raised his eyes and looked upward,
he saw Samal, the mother of falcons.

He raised his voice and cried:
"May Baal shatter Samal's wings,
may Baal shatter her pinions!
Let her fall at my feet!
I will split her gizzard and look inside.
If there is fat, if there is bone,
I will weep and I will bury Aqhat.
I will put Aqhat into the pit of the earth gods."

He had just spoken these words,
this speech had just come from his lips,
when Baal shattered Samal's wings,
Baal shattered her pinions.
She fell at his feet.
He split her gizzard and looked inside.
There was fat, there was bone.

From them he took Aqhat.
He wept and he buried him.
He buried him in a tomb, in an urn.

Then he raised his voice and cried:
"May Baal shatter the falcons' wings,
may Baal shatter their pinions,
if they fly over my son's grave
and wake him from his sleep!"

King Danel cursed the spring of water:
"Woe to you, spring of water,
for near you Aqhat the hero was killed,
the young lion of El's house met his end.
Now flee forever,

from now on and forever."
He destroyed his royal scepter.

Danel arrived at the city of Abilim,
Abilim, the city of Prince Moon.

Danel raised his voice and shouted:
"Woe to you, city of Abilim,
for near to you Aqhat the hero was killed.
May Baal dry up your wells, now and forever,
from now on and for all generations."
Danel destroyed his royal scepter.

Danel came to his house.
Danel reached his palace.
The mourning women entered his palace,
the mourning women entered his court.
Those who gash their skin wept,
they shed tears for Aqhat the hero,
the child of Danel, the man of healing.
Days grew to months,
months grew to years.
For seven years they wept for Aqhat the hero,
they shed tears for the child of Danel, the man of healing.

In the seventh year Danel spoke, the man of healing,
the hero, the follower of Harnam,
raised his voice and declared,
"Leave my house, keeners!
Leave my palace, mourners!
Leave my court, you who lacerate your flesh!"

He sacrificed to the gods,
he offered up incense to heaven,
an offering for the god of Harnam to the stars . . .

Pagat, who carries water on her shoulder, said,
"My father, you have sacrificed to the gods.
You have sent an offering up to heaven,
incense for the god of Harnam, to the stars.
Now bless me so that I may go with your blessing.
Show me favor so that I may go with your favor.
I will kill my brother's killer,
I will destroy whoever destroyed my mother's son."

Danel, the man of healing, replied:
"Pagat, may your spirit flourish,

you who carry water on your shoulder,
who brush the dew from the fleece,
who know the course of the stars.
Truly I will live again
when you have killed your brother's killer,
when you have destroyed whoever
destroyed your mother's son."

She washed in the sea.
She put on rouge from a shellfish.
She applied cosmetics from the sea.
She put on a warrior's clothes,
She placed a knife in her sheath.
She placed a sword in her scabbard,
and over all this she put on women's clothes.

When Shapash,° torch of the gods, went down,
Pagat went down to the fields.
When Shapash, torch of the gods, went down,
Pagat arrived at the camp.

Yatpan was told:
"Our mistress has come to your tent,
Pagat has come to the camp."

Yatpan, the lady's man, replied:
"Let her in. She will give me wine.
She will take the cup from my hand,
the beaker from my right hand."

Pagat was received. She gave him drink.
She took the cup from his hand,
the beaker from his right hand.

Then Yatpan, the lady's man, said:
"The hand that killed Aqhat the hero
can kill a thousand enemies."
Twice she gave him wine to drink,
she gave him wine to drink.

Then Danel, the man of healing,
the hero, the devotee of the god of Harnam,
made an offering for the gods to eat,
made an offering for the holy ones to drink . . .

°*Shapash*: the sun, Mesopotamian Shamash (except Shapash is female).

Here the text breaks off, but we can assume that Pagat kills Yatpan, the murderer of her brother; Aqhat is resurrected; and fruitfulness returns to the land.

## OBSERVATIONS: THE LEGEND OF DANEL

The Danel of the Canaanite legend is not the Daniel of the Book of Daniel, probably written in the 2nd century BC, but he may be the same as the righteous and wise Danel of the Book of Ezekiel (14:14), written in the 6th century BC, nine hundred years after the Ugaritic text: "The word of Yahweh came to me: 'Son of man, if a country sins against me by being unfaithful and I stretch out my hand against it to cut off its food supply and send famine upon it and kill its men and their animals, even if these three men—Noah, Danel, and Job—were in it, they could save only themselves by their righteousness.'" Then in Ezekiel (28:3), Danel is noted for his wisdom in the prophecy addressed to the king of Tyre: "You are indeed wiser than Danel, no secret is hidden from you." Danel is also given as the father-in-law of Enoch in Jubilees (4:20). In likelihood Danel was a real man. The story is a *legend*, a type of story that we never find in Egyptian myth, and in Mesopotamian myth only in the story of Gilgamesh. But the story has been drawn into the Near Eastern preoccupations with the cyclicity of nature. As Aqhat dies, so does the land: It becomes infertile and dry, as in the story of Ishtar's descent to the underworld. Only, we presume, when Aqhat is resurrected does fruitfulness return to the land.

Just like Dumuzi, the young man dies, then is brought back to life. His death is caused by the aggression of Anat, who covets his bow. She is merely Ishtar in West Semitic guise. The bow as a weapon whose arrows penetrate is a symbol for masculine potency, and Anat's longing for the bow is a kind of sexual desire. The result of Anat's desire is Aqhat's death. Even so the sexually aggressive Ishtar threatened Gilgamesh.

Gods and humans interact in a seamless way so that we can never be sure whether we are looking at divine myth with a legendary flavor, or a legend with features of divine myth. The story of a mortal man who wants a son has been submerged in a story about the cyclicity of the natural world explained by a god's death and (presumed) resurrection.

## MYTH: THE MYTH OF BAAL

The Canaanite god Baal, also known as **Hadad**, god of storm and fertility, was the central figure in a whole cycle of tales from Ugarit. Many of them are fragmentarily preserved on clay tablets, but we can reconstruct most of the story of Baal and his struggle with Sea, or Yam, and Death, or Mot. Here we will use the English equivalents for the Ugaritic names.

In the story Sea wants to rule over the other gods and be the most powerful god of all, but Baal opposes Sea and kills him. With the support of Anat (Baal's wife) and Asherah (or Astartê, El's wife), Baal persuades El to allow him to build a palace. Baal commissions Kothar-wa-Hasis to do the work. Then as king of the gods and ruler of the world, Baal attacks Death, but instead Death overwhelms Baal. In revenge Anat brutally kills Death, grinds him up, and scatters his ashes.

Baal, resurrected, returns to MOUNT ZAPHON to the north of Ugarit (see Map 4). Death, having recovered from being ground up and scattered, again challenges Baal, but Baal refuses to fight with him. Death gives in and Baal rules again. Baal is king of the gods. Such is the outline of the myth.

## El Surrenders Baal

The beginning of the story of the battle between Baal and Sea is highly obscure, preserved on tablets badly broken. When the story becomes clear, the messengers of Sea have come to the assembly of the gods and demanded that Baal be given over to them. El complies:

> Sea sends two messengers, saying to them:
> "Go, turn not away, go to the Assembly in council
> meeting at the center of the mountain of night.
> Do not fall down at the feet of El,
> do not prostrate yourselves before the Assembly in council.
> Stand up and say what you have to say,
> repeat what you know, and say to the bull, my father,
> 'The message of Sea, your master, of your lord Judge River:°
> Give up him whom you are hiding, O gods,
> the one the multitudes are hiding!
> Hand over Baal, the son of Dagon, and his henchmen
> that I may humble him, that I may assume his inheritance!'"
>
> The messengers sped away, they did not delay.
> They made straight for the mountain of night,
> the Assembly in council. There the gods sat down to eat,
> the holy ones, to eat a meal. Baal stands beside El.
> As soon as the gods catch sight of the messengers of Sea,
> the envoys of Judge River, they lower their heads
> to their knees and onto their princely thrones.
>
> Baal rebuked them, "Why do you lower your heads
> onto your knees and onto your princely thrones?
> I see that you are cowed by the messengers of Sea,
> the envoys of Judge River. Lift up, O gods,
> your heads from the top of your knees,
> from your princely thrones. I will answer the messengers
> of Sea, the envoys of Judge River."
>
> Standing up and saying what they had to say,
> the messengers repeated what they knew.
> They seemed like one fire, like two fires,
> their tongues were like sharpened swords.
>
> They spoke to the bull, his father El:
> "The message of Sea your master, of your lord Judge River:
> Give up him whom you are hiding, O gods,
> the one the multitudes are hiding!
> Hand over Baal, the son of Dagon, and his henchmen
> that I may humble him, that I may assume his inheritance!"

°*Judge River*: another name for Yam.

And the bull, the father El, answered,
"Baal is your slave, O Sea, your slave forever.
O River, the son of Dagon is your prisoner!
He must bring tribute to you, like the gods.
He must bring tribute like the holy ones . . ."

## Baal Defeats Sea

There is a break in the text. When the story resumes, Baal has already started to battle Sea, to whom he has been surrendered, but is in despair at Sea's power. Kothar-wa-Hasis encourages Baal and brings two divine clubs for Baal's use. He gives them magic names and strikes Sea the first two times himself. Baal then drags out Sea and finishes him off. Baal cries out that Sea is dead, and that now he shall be king:

"And the Sea will be the sieve of destruction.
The Sea will be the lungs of death.
In Judge River will be the gnawers.
There maggots move about . . .
The mighty will fall to the earth."

Scarce had come these words from her [Anat's?] mouth,
this speech from her lips,
when Kothar-wa-Hasis groaned from beneath
the throne of Prince Sea. Thereupon answered Kothar-wa-Hasis:

"Truly, I keep telling you, O Baal, rider of the clouds!
You must slay your enemy, you must silence your foes.
Then will you take your kingship for all time,
your dominion forever."

Therewith Kothar brought down
two weapons and proclaimed their name:

"Your name is, Chaser.
Chaser, chase Sea,
chase Sea from his throne,
Judge River from his dominion.
Swoop down from the hand of Baal,
like a hawk from between his fingers.
Strike the back of Prince Sea,
between the shoulders of Judge River."

The weapon swooped down from the hand of Baal,
like a hawk from between his fingers.
It struck the back of Prince Sea, between the shoulders
of Judge River. But strong is Sea, he does not sink down,
his joints do not quiver, his form does not collapse.

Kothar brings down the two weapons
and he proclaimed their name:
"Your name is Driver.
Driver, drive Sea,
drive Sea from his throne,
Judge River from his dominion.
Swoop down from the hand of Baal,
like a hawk from between his fingers.
Strike the skull of Prince Sea,
between the eyes of Judge River."
And the weapon swooped down from the hand of Baal,
like a hawk from between his fingers.
It struck the skull of Prince Sea, between the eyes
of Judge River. Sea collapsed, he fell to the earth.
His joints quivered and his spine shook.

Then Baal dragged out Sea and wished to hack him into pieces.
He would make an end of Judge River.
Astartê° shouted Baal's name:
"Hail mighty Baal! Hail rider on the clouds!
Our captive is Prince Sea, our captive is Judge River."

°*Astartê*: here she seems to be a separate goddess from Asherah.

About 16 broken and fragmentary lines follow.

## A Banquet for Baal

Next comes a description of the Palace of Baal. A banquet is thrown in honor of Baal
on Mount Zaphon, with a bard in attendance:

Then Radamin° served the mighty Baal.
He waited on the prince, lord of the Earth.
He arose, he prepared food and gave it to him to eat.
He divides a breast before him with a sharp blade,
he cuts up a fatling. He gets up, makes ready a feast
and gives him drink. He places a cup in his hands,
a goblet in his two hands, a large beaker, a jar
that would amaze a mortal, a goblet
that Asherah must never set her eyes on [Figure 4.6].
He takes a thousand pitchers of harvest wine,
he mixes in ten thousand portions.
While mixing it, he rose up, he chanted, he sang.
There were cymbals in the hands of the poet.
With his sweet voice he sang of Baal
on the heights of Zaphon.

°*Radamin*: the court singer, an oral poet, as Homer was.

**FIGURE 4.6** Asherah, Canaanite goddess of fertility, the consort of El, sister of Astartê, clay figurine, c. 10th–7th century BC. Nude, with an Egyptian style hairdo, she wears a necklace and holds flowers in both hands and has an exaggerated pubic triangle. (National Museum, Damascus, Syria; Zev Radovan / BibleLandPictures.com / Alamy)

He caught sight of the daughters of Baal,
he sets his eye on Pidray, daughter of light,
also on Talay, daughter of rain.

About 23 lines are missing.

## The Anger of Anat

When the text resumes, Anat closes the door of her mansion and meets her servants in a valley where there are two cities, perhaps Ugarit and its port. For reasons unclear, she kills the guards and warriors and drives away the townspeople. She slaughters the guards and warriors in her own palace, turns the furniture into warriors and kills them too, then makes a peace-offering. Surely, great is the destructive power of Anat!

She comes, bathed in the scent of henna,
enough for seven maidens, in a scent of saffron
and perfume. Anat closes the gates of her house.
She meets the messengers° at the base of the mountain.
Anat gives battle in the valley. With power she cuts in pieces
the people of the two cities. She slaughters the people
of the western shore, she destroys the men
of the eastern sunrise. Beneath her heads roll like balls,
hands fly above her like locusts. Like avenging grasshoppers
are the hands of the quick warriors. She hangs
heads on her back, she binds hands to her belt.
She wades up to her knees in the soldiers' blood,
she wades to her thighs in the warriors' gore.
With her staff she drives out the enemies,
with her bow-string the foes.

Then Anat came to her house,
the goddess goes to her palace.
But she is not satisfied with the fighting in the valley,
her cutting down the sons of the two cities.
She made the chairs into soldiers,
she set up the tables as troops,
footstools for heroes. Greatly she battled
and looked. Anat hewed and smashed.
She looked. Her insides swelled with laughter,
her heart was filled with joy,
the liver of Anat with thrilled to triumph.
She waded in blood up to her knees,
to her thighs in the gore of quick warriors.
She fought in the house until satisfied.
She smashed and hacked in the midst of the tables.

Wiped from the house was the blood of swift soldiers.
Poured out was the oil of peace from a bowl.
She washed her hands, the virgin Anat,
the Maid of the People washed her fingers.
She washed from her hands the blood of soldiers,
she washed from her fingers the gore of the warriors.
She made the chairs again into chairs,
the tables into tables, the footstools into footstools.
She scooped up water and washed
in dew of the Heavens, oil of the Earth,
rain from rider on the clouds,
dew that the heavens pour out,

°*messengers*: it is not clear who these are.

rain that the stars pour out, spray the stars shed.
She adorns herself with perfume,
one thousand miles from its source in the sea.

About seven missing and fragmentary lines follow. When the text resumes, Baal
addresses his messengers, telling them to call off Anat's attack and to have her come
to Mount Zaphon. There in his stronghold he will show her the secret of the lightning,
which he controls. Anat joins Baal on Zaphon:

Baal spoke to his messengers:
"For the love of Baal,
for the love of Pidray, daughter of Light,
for the desire of Talay, daughter of Rain,
for the love of Arsay,° daughter of the floods,
go forth, lads, enter, fall down at Anat's feet.
Do homage to her, and say to the virgin Anat, the Maiden,
repeat to the Mistress of the Peoples, 'Message of Baal
the conqueror, word of the mightiest of warriors:
Withdraw war from the earth, set in the land the flowers
of love, pour forth peace in the midst of the earth,
rain a libation of love like honey from a pot
in the heart of the fields. Hurry! Hasten! Rush!
Run to me with your feet, hasten to me with your legs.
I have a tale to tell, a story to recount, a tale
of trees and a whisper of stones, the sighing of the heavens
to the earth, of the seas to the stars. I understand lightning
not known to the heavens, a tale not known to humankind,
not yet understood by the multitudes of the earth.
Come and I myself will reveal it in the midst
of my mountain, the divine Zaphon, the holy place,
the mountain of my inheritance, the pleasant place,
the hill of my triumph.'"

Anat saw the two gods Gapen and Ugar.°
Her feet started to tap, her back seemed as if to shatter,
her face broke into a sweat, her joints convulsed,
the spine quivered.°

She raised her voice and cried,
"Why have Gapen and Ugar come?
Does some enemy rise against Baal,
foe of the rider on the clouds?

°*Arsay*: the third of Baal's daughters. °*Gapen and Ugar*: Baal's assistants, whose names
mean "vineyard" and "grain field," stressing Baal's control of the fertile life-giving earth.
°*quivered*: a typical response to an unexpected visit.

Did I not demolish the darling of El, the Sea?
Did I not make an end of the divine river, whose name is Rabim?
Did I not snare the dragon, envelope him?
I demolished the twisting serpent,
the tyrant with seven heads.
I demolished the darling of the gods, Desire,
I silenced the divine calf, the Rebel,
I destroyed the bitch of the gods, Fire,
I made an end of El's daughter, Zabib, the Flame.
I battled for the silver, I took possession of the gold.
Has Baal been driven from the heights of Zaphon?
Has Baal been driven from the throne of his kingdom,
from the cushion of his platform, from the seat of his power?
What foe rises against Baal? What enemy against the rider on the clouds?"

And the gods answered Anat: "No foe rises
against Baal, an enemy of the rider on the clouds.
This is the message of Baal,
the word of the mightiest of warriors:
'Withdraw war from the earth.
Put on the earth an offering of loaves.
Set in the land the flowers of love.
Pour forth peace in the midst of the earth.
Rain a libation of love like honey from a pot
in the heart of the fields. Hurry! Hasten! Rush!
Run to me with your feet, hasten to me with your legs.
I have a tale to tell, a story to recount, a tale
of trees and a whisper of stones,
the sighing of the heavens
to the earth, of the seas to the stars.
I understand lightning
not known to the heavens,
a tale not known to humankind,
not yet understood by the multitudes of the earth.
Come and I myself will reveal it in the midst of my mountain,
the divine Zaphon of the north, the holy place,
the mountain of my inheritance,
the pleasant place, the hill of my triumph.'"

The virgin Anat replied, the Mistress of the Peoples:
"I will withdraw war from the earth,
will set in the land the flowers of love,
will pour forth peace in the midst of the earth,
will rain a libation of love like honey from a pot
in the heart of the fields. I have something else to say:
Go, go, divine powers! You are slow but I am swift.

Is not my mountain far from El, my cave far from the gods?
Two measures beneath the wells of the earth,
three measures under the caves."

Then she headed toward Baal in the heights of Zaphon,
across a thousand fields, ten thousand tracts at every step.
Baal saw his sister coming, his father's daughter coming quick.
He sent away his wives° from his presence.
He set an ox before her, a fatling too.
She scooped up water and washed in dew
of the heavens, oil of the earth,
rain from rider on the clouds,
dew that the heavens pour out,
rain that the stars pour out, spray the stars shed.

°*wives*: like any Eastern king, El has many wives.

Mount Zaphon, known as Mount Casius to the Greeks, is near the mouth of the Orontes River on what is today the Syrian-Turkish border about six miles north of Ugarit (Map 4). On its bare limestone peak the site of Baal's sanctuary is represented archaeologically by a huge mound of ashes and debris, 180 feet wide and 26 feet deep. Only the first six feet have been excavated. According to Isaiah (14:13), the gods assembled on this mountain, the Mount Olympus of the Near East.

The text continues:

For you [Anat] said to yourself,
"I will ascend to heaven and set my throne above God's stars.
I will preside on the mountain of the gods
on the heights of Zaphon.
I will climb to the highest heavens
and be like the Most High."

Several lines are missing here from the Ugaritic text.

## Baal and Anat Bribe Asherah to Support the Building of a Palace

When the text resumes Baal complains to Anat that he does not have a house, nor a court like other gods, meaning that he must live in the house of his father El. Having a palace was a way to show that you were a king:

"But Baal does not have a house like the other gods,
no court like the sons of Asherah,°
the house of El, the shelter of his sons,
the home of Asherah of the sea,
the dwelling of Pidray, daughter of light,
the shelter of Talay, daughter of rain,
the dwelling of Arsay, daughter of the floods
the home of the beautiful brides."

°*sons of Asherah*: Asherah was said to have 70 sons.

Virgin Anat replied: "My father El, the bull,
will attend to me and I will tell him what I will do.
I shall drag him like a lamb to the ground,
I shall make his gray hairs run with blood,
the gray hairs of his beard with gore,
if he will not give Baal a house like the gods
and a court like the sons of Asherah!"

She stamped her feet and left the earth.
Then she set her face toward El
at the source of the two rivers,
in the midst of the springs of the two oceans.°
She came to the tent of El and entered
the shrine of the king, father of time.

°. . . *two oceans*: the two rivers would be the Tigris and the Euphrates, whose headwaters are
near in the mountains of eastern Turkey. The oceans could be the Mediterranean and the
Persian Gulf.

About 10 missing or fragmentary lines follow. Anat threatens El. She will make
his gray hair run with blood unless he allows Baal to have a palace:

The virgin Anat spoke: "Don't rejoice in your mansion,
O El, do not rejoice in your well-built mansion,
do not rejoice in the height of your palace,
I shall drag you like a lamb to the ground,
I shall make your gray hairs run with blood,
the gray hairs of your beard with gore."

El replied from the seven chambers,
through the eight entrances of the closed rooms:
"I know, daughter, that you can be gentle,
but there is no restraint among goddesses.
What do you want, O virgin Anat?"

And the virgin Anat said, "Your decree, El, is wise,
your wisdom is everlasting, eternal.
A life of good fortune is your decree.
But our king is Baal the conqueror, our judge.
There is none higher. All of us must bear his goblet,
all of us must bear his cup."

El the bull cried out loudly, her father,
the king who created her.

Asherah and her sons shouted,
the goddess and her company of offspring:
"But there is not a house for Baal like the gods,
no court like the sons of Asherah, the dwelling of El,

the shelter of his son, the home of Asherah of the sea,
the dwelling of Pidray, daughter of light,
the shelter of Talay, daughter of rain,
the dwelling of Arsay, daughter of the floods
the home of the beautiful brides."

There are about 38 missing or fragmentary lines. Baal dispatches attendants of Asherah to deliver a message to Kothar-wa-Hasis, whose home is in Egypt. The attendants deliver Baal's message: Kothar-wa-Hasis should fashion gifts for Asherah, presumably so she will support Baal's bid for a palace. He enters his forge and produces magnificent pieces of furniture, a pair of sandals, and a decorated table and bowl:

In the hands of Kothar-wa-Hasis are the tongs.
He smelts silver, he hammers out gold,
he casts silver into a thousand bars,
by the thousandfold he hammers out ten thousand pieces.
He casts a canopy and a couch,
a divine platform fit for a god of twice ten thousand pieces,
a divine platform coated with silver,
overlaid with a film of gold,
a divine seat with a cushion, fit for a god,
a divine footstool fit for a god . . .
And divine sandals with straps of gold,
a divine table filled with all things given
by the earth's foundations, a divine bowl
fit for a god whose handle is shaped
like a lamb, whose base is like the land
of Yaman° where ten thousand wild oxen graze.

°*Yaman*: an unknown location.

About 16 lines are missing. When the text continues, Asherah is performing her woman's work by the seashore when she sees Baal and Anat approach. She wonders whether Baal has come to kill all her sons and relatives. However, her anger subsides when she sees the elegant gifts that Kothar-wa-Hasis has made, and so supports Baal in his bid.

Asherah, who is entertaining Baal and Anat, calls on her attendants to cast a net into the sea so she may have provisions with which to entertain the guests:

On a stone she grasps her spindle in her hand,
the spindle she holds high in her right hand.
She tears off the covering of the flesh, she flings
her robe into the sea, her two garments into the rivers.
She places a pot on the fire, a vessel on the coals.
She implores El, the bull, the compassionate.
She entreats the creator of all.
When she raises her eyes, she beholds the approach of Baal.

Asherah sees the approach of the virgin Anat,
the speedy approach of the Mistress of the Peoples.

Then her feet stamp, it seems her back will crack.
Her face bursts into a sweat, she bends to shake
the joints of her hips. Her muscles quake, and her spine too.
She lifts her voice and cries, "Why does Baal the conqueror
come here? Why has the virgin come here?
Have my enemies come to kill my sons?"

But as soon as Asherah saw the gleam of silver,
the handiwork of silver and the shine of gold,
she rejoiced, Lady Asherah of the sea.

She cried aloud to a lad, "Look at the marvelous gifts!
Now pay attention, O fisherman of Lady Asherah of the sea.
Take a net in your hand . . .

A large chunk of text survives only in fragments. It is clear that Asherah makes a feast for her visitors, and presumably they urge her to intercede for Baal with El. In the surviving text, Asherah goes to El's house and makes her case.

Reluctantly, El agrees to a house for Baal. Baal is instructed to collect cedar-wood, bricks, and precious metals to build his house. Kothar-wa-Hasis builds the palace, but Baal insists that it be left without windows in case his daughters may escape, or in case Sea may come again. In a kind of reverse alchemy, the palace, built of precious materials, is set afire and the precious materials are turned into ordinary brick and stone (evidently to explain the actual temple of Baal on Mount Zaphon). The work is finished and Baal throws a big party:

Lady Asherah of the sea replied:
"Listen, holy and most blessed one, fisherman
of Lady Asherah of the sea!° Saddle a donkey,
harness an ass, put on it trappings of silver,
a bridle of gold. Fasten the trappings of my she-asses."

The holy and most blessed one obeyed.
He saddled a donkey, harnessed a jackass,
put on it trappings of silver, trappings of gold.
He got ready the trappings on the she-asses.
The holy and most blessed one put his arms around her,
then set Asherah on the back of the donkey,
on the splendid back of the donkey.
The holy and most blessed one took a torch and blazed the trail.
The holy and most blessed one was like a guiding star.
And while Baal left for the heights of Zaphon,
Anat followed. But Asherah right away turned her face

---

°fisherman of lady Asherah of the sea: it is not clear who this is.

toward El at the source of the two rivers,
in the midst of the headwaters of the two oceans.

She went to the tent of El and opened it,
the shrine of the king, father of time.
She bowed at the feet of El and did him homage.
She prostrated herself and adored him.
When El saw her, he opened his mouth and laughed.
His placed his feet on the footstool, and he snapped
his fingers with excitement.

He lifted his voice and cried:
"Why has Lady Asherah of the sea come here?
What moves the mother of the gods to come here?
Are you hungry or faint, having journeyed so far?
Or are you very thirsty, having traveled all night?
Well eat then, yes, come and drink, eat bread
from the tables. Drink wine from the goblets,
drink the blood of vines from cups of gold.
Or does love for El the king excite you?
Desire for the bull arouse you?"

Lady Asherah of the sea replied:
"Your decree, O El, is wisdom, your wisdom
is everlasting. A life of good luck is your decree.
Our king is Baal the conqueror, our judge, none higher.
We must bear his chalice. We must bear his cup."

But El cried out, El the king who begot her.
Asherah and her sons cried out, the goddess
and her pride of lions: "But Baal does not have a house
like the other gods, no court like the sons of Asherah:
the dwelling of El, the shelter of his son;
the dwelling of Lady Asherah of the sea;
the dwelling of the beautiful brides;
the dwelling of Pidray, the daughter of Light;
the shelter of Talay, daughter of rain;
the dwelling of Arsay, daughter of the wide floods."

Then answered El the compassionate:
"So am I a slave of Asherah?
So am I a slave to hold a trowel,
a slave to mould the bricks?
Let a house be built for Baal as for the gods,
and a court like the sons of Asherah."

Lady Asherah of the sea answered:
"You are great, O El, you are truly wise.

The gray hairs of your beard instruct you . . .
Baal will appoint a season for his rain,
the season for wadis in flood. He will peal his thunder
from the clouds, flash his lightning to the earth!
Let him complete his house of cedar,
let him build his house of bricks.
Let Baal the conqueror be commanded:
'Call a caravan into your house, a wagon train
in your palace. The mountains will bring you
abundant silver, the hills the choicest gold.
They will yield the noblest gems, the camels
will bring jewels to build a house of silver and gold,
a house of purest lapis lazuli.'"

The virgin Anat rejoiced. She stamped her foot
and left the earth. Straightaway she headed
toward Baal in the heights of Zaphon,
a thousand fields, ten thousand tracts at each step.

The virgin Anat laughed, she raised her voice
and cried: "Be of good cheer O Baal!
I bring glad tidings. A house will be built for you
like for your brothers, and a court like for your cousins.
Call a caravan into your house, a wagon train
in your palace. The mountains will bring you
abundant silver, the hills the choicest gold.
They will yield the noblest gems, the camels
will bring jewels to build a house of silver and gold,
a house of purest lapis lazuli."

Baal the conqueror was glad. He called a caravan
into his house, a wagon train into his palace.
The mountains brought him abundant silver,
the hills the choicest gold. The camels brought him
jewels. He sent messengers to Kothar-wa-Hasis.

## Kothar-wa-Hasis Builds a Palace for Baal

Kothar-wa-Hasis, being summoned, arrives:

After Kothar-wa-Hasis had arrived,
they set an ox before him, a fatling at his disposal.
They made ready a chair and he was seated
at the right hand of Baal the conqueror.
When the god Kothar-wa-Hasis had eaten and drunk,
then exclaimed Baal the conqueror, the rider on the clouds:
"Kothar-wa-Hasis, hurry, build a mansion.

Hurry, raise a palace. Hurry, build a mansion.
Hurry, build a palace on the heights of Zaphon.
May the house cover a thousand fields,
ten thousand tracts."

And Kothar-wa-Hasis answered:
"Listen, Baal the conqueror, pay attention,
O rider on the clouds:
Should I not put a casement in the house,
a window in the middle of the palace?"
But mighty Baal answered, "Do not put a casement
in the house, a window in the midst of the palace . . ."

And Kothar-wa-Hasis said, "You will recall my words."
Kothar-wa-Hasis repeated his speech:
"Should I not put a casement in the house,
a window in the middle of the palace?"
But Baal the conqueror answered,
"Do not put a casement in the house,
a window in the middle of the palace . . ."

Quickly they built his house, quickly they raised
the palace. Men brought from Lebanon trees for timber,
From Sirion° they brought its precious cedars.
They went to Lebanon for its timbers,
to Sirion for its finest cedars.

Fire was set to the house, so that the palace
went up in flames. A day and a second day,
the fire consumed the mansion.
The flames consumed the palace.
A third, a fourth day, the fire fed on the house,
the flames consumed the palace.
A fifth, a sixth day, the fire ate the house, the flames
consumed the palace.
On the seventh day, the fire died down,
the flames died down in the palace.
The silver had turned into blocks, the gold into bricks.
Baal the conqueror rejoiced:
"I have built my mansion
of silver, my palace of gold."

Baal prepared the house, he made the preparations.
He slew oxen and sheep,
he slaughtered bulls and fatted rams, yearling calves.

---

°*Sirion*: Mount Hermon, north of the Sea of Galilee in southern Syria.

He strangled lambs and kids.
He called his brothers into his mansion,
his relatives into the midst of his palace.
He called the seventy children of Asherah.
He entertained the gods with lamb and wine.
He entertained the goddesses with ewes and wine.
He entertained the gods with oxen and wine.
He entertained the goddesses with cows and wine.
He entertained the gods with thrones and wine.
He entertained the goddesses with thrones and wine.
He entertained the gods with jars of wine.
He entertained the goddesses with jugs of wine.
The gods ate and drank endlessly.
They were supplied with a suckling pig.
With a sharp knife they carved a tender breast of fatling.
They drank flagons of wine,
the blood of vines from cups of gold.

Here the text is broken. When the text resumes, Baal recalls his triumph over Sea, then marches out, conquering many cities. For some reason he consents to having windows in his palace after all and Kothar-wa-Hasis installs them, reminding Baal that "I told you so" (the meaning of the incident with the windows is obscure). As Kothar builds the windows, Baal (the storm-god) opens a slit in the clouds and thunders through it, terrifying his enemies. Baal takes his place on his throne in his palace, king of the world. He doesn't even need to send messengers announcing his power—for example, to Baal's great enemy Death—for it is obvious to all:

Baal marches from city to city, from town to town.
He captures 66 towns, 77 towns,
Baal sacks 80 towns, then 90.

Baal returns to his house. Baal the conqueror speaks:
"I will put it in, Kothar-wa-Hasis, this very day,
this very hour. Let a window be opened in the mansion,
a casement in the middle of the palace.
Then I'll open a slit in the clouds,
according to the word of Kothar-wa-Hasis!"

Kothar-wa-Hasis laughed.
He raised up his voice and cried: "Did I not say to you,
O Baal the conqueror, you would come back
to my word?" He opened a window in the mansion,
a casement in the middle of the palace, and Baal
opened a slit in the clouds. Baal gave forth his holy voice.
Baal repeatedly thundered from his lips.

His holy voice shook the earth, at the thunder of his lips . . .
The earth's high places shook. The enemies of Baal
fled to the forest, the enemies of Hadad° to the hollows
of the mountains.

Baal the conqueror spoke:
"Enemies of Hadad, why are you quaking?
Why do you quake?" Baal's eye guided his hand,
as he swung a cedar° in his right hand.
Straightaway Baal sat and dwelled in his house.
"Neither king nor commoner on earth shall install
himself on this throne! I will not send a message to divine Death,
a herald to the beloved of El, the youth, the hero.°
May Death cry to himself!
Let the beloved one grumble in his heart!
For I alone am king over the gods,
give fatness to gods and men,
satisfy the multitudes of the earth."

°*Hadad*: that is, Baal. °*cedar*: perhaps his scepter of authority. °*beloved of El, the youth, the hero*: that is, Death.

## Death Kills Baal

About 10 lines are missing. Baal has changed his mind about not sending a message to Death, "the darling of El," El's son. He sends two messengers, apparently Gapen and Ugar, giving them careful instructions about how to get to the watery and dangerous underworld and how they should behave toward mighty Death when they get there. Gapen and Ugar are to deliver the message that Baal has built his palace and is now king of the world:

"Now set your faces toward Mount Targuziza,
toward Mount Tharumagi,° toward the two hills
that bound the earth and block the way to the underworld.
Lift the mountain with your hands,
raise the hill up with your palms,
then descend to the depths of the earth
to be counted among those who go down into the earth.
Then turn your faces toward divine Death
in the midst of his city, to Slime, his royal house,
to the filth of the earth, which is his province.
Yet be on your guard, divine messengers of the gods:
Approach not close to El's son, Death, unless
he make you like a lamb in his mouth,
like a kid in his gullet! You will both be crushed.

°*Targuziza . . . Tharumagi*: locations unknown.

Shapash the sun, the torch of the gods, is glowing hot.
The heavens shimmer under the hand of the beloved of El,
Death. At each step a thousand tracts, ten thousand fields.
At the feet of Death do homage and adore him,
prostrate yourselves and do him honor.
And say to El's son, Death, repeat to the darling of El,
that hero, 'This is the message of Baal, the powerful,
the word of Baal the conqueror: I have built
my house of silver, my palace of gold . . .'

"When I killed Lotan, the fleeing serpent,
finished off the twisting serpent,
the seven-headed monster, the heavens drooped helpless,
like the folds of your robe . . .

[something missing]

Now you will descend into the throat of El's son,
divine Death, into the watery depths, the gorge
of the beloved of El, the youth, the hero!"

Lotan is the same as the biblical Leviathan (mentioned six times in the Hebrew Bible), a seven-headed sea serpent or dragon, either a pet of Sea or an aspect of Sea himself. He represents the destruction of floods, oceans, and winter and lives in a palace in the sea. When Baal killed Sea, he killed Lotan (as the biblical Yahweh killed Leviathan).

There is a break in which presumably the message is delivered. Gapen and Ugar return to Baal. But Death, like a lion in the desert, hungers constantly for flesh and blood:

The gods left, they did not tarry. They turned toward
Baal on the heights of Zaphon. Then Gapen and Ugar spoke:
"Message of El's son, divine Death, word of the beloved of El,
the youth, the hero: 'My appetite is like that of lions.
The appetites of lions naturally crave sheep,
as the desire of a dolphin is for the sea, or a pool
attracts wild oxen, a spring does the same to deer . . .'"

There are about 18 obscure or badly broken lines. When the text continues, Death threatens Baal and Baal admits his fear of Death, then instructs his messengers Gupen and Ugar to tell Death that, after all, he will be Death's slave, news to which Death rejoices:

One lip down to the earth, one lip to the heavens,
Death stretches his tongue to the stars.
Baal must enter his mouth and must descend into his throat,
like bread stuffed with olives, like the produce of earth,
the fruit of the trees.

Baal the conqueror was afraid,
terrified was the rider on the clouds.
He spoke to his messengers:
"Be gone! Speak to El's son Death,
repeat to the beloved of El, the youth, the hero:
'Message of Baal the conqueror, the word
of the mightiest of warriors: Hail, divine Death, El's son Death!
I am your slave, I am your bondsman forever.'"

The messengers left, they did not tarry. They turned
toward divine Death in the midst of his city,
the Swamp, Slime, his royal house,
down into the pit of Death they descend,
to the filth of the earth, which is his province,
Phlegm, the land of his inheritance.
They raised their voices and cried,
"The message of Baal the conqueror,
the word of the mightiest of warriors:
'Hail, El's son, divine Death! I am your slave,
I am your bondman forever.'"

Divine Death rejoiced, El's son, Death.
He raised his voice and cried, "How Baal comes
to make merry along with my companions,
how Hadad tarries awhile with my comrades!"

There are about 75 missing or badly preserved lines. Apparently, **Shapash** the sun-goddess addresses Baal. She promises to bury Baal's body, and advises him to go to the two mountains at the entrance of the underworld and to move them aside. He is to go down into the earth where he will be as if dead. Baal finds a heifer in the fields and on it begets a child, whom he dresses in his robes and presumably offers as a gift to Death. Shapash speaks:

" . . . I will put him in a hole of the gods of the earth.
And as for you, take your clouds,
your winds, your thunderbolts, your rains.
Take with you your seven men,
your eight noble serving maids.
Take with you Pidray, daughter of light,
and Talay, daughter of rain. Turn toward
Mount Kankaniya.° Lift the mountain with your hands.
Raise the hill upon your palms and go down
to the house of freedom in the earth's depth.
Be counted among those who go down
into the earth. You will know nothingness,
you will become as one who has died!"

°*Kankaniya*: location unknown.

> Baal the conqueror obeyed. He had sex with a heifer
> in the desert pastures, a cow by the shore
> of the realm of Death. He had sex with her 77 times,
> she allowed him to mount 88 times,
> and she conceived and gave birth to a boy.
> Baal the conqueror clothed him with his robe . . .

When the text continues, two deities arrive at El's house. They announce that they have searched for Baal, but found him dead by the bank of the river. El comes down from his throne. He sits on the ground and mourns, strewing dust on his head, mourning for the dead Baal. He puts on sackcloth, shaves off his beard, and beats his chest. Anat too wears sackcloth when she finds the dead body of her brother/husband Baal. The sun-goddess Shapash aids Anat in burying Baal on Mount Zaphon. Anat slaughters large numbers of oxen, sheep, goats, and asses as a memorial:

> The two messengers departed, they did not tarry.
> They turned to El at the sources of the two rivers,
> amid the headwaters of the two deep oceans.
> They came to the tent of El, father of years.
> They raised up their voices and cried:
> "We two did go around to the edges of the earth,
> to the limits of the watery region.
> We came to the pleasant place, the desert pasture,
> the lovely fields on the shore by the realm of Death.
> We came upon Baal. He had fallen to the ground.
> Dead is Baal the conqueror! Perished is the prince,
> master of the earth!"

> Right away kindly El, the compassionate,
> came down from his throne. He sat on his footstool.
> He came down from his footstool, he sat on the ground.
> He poured the ashes of mourning on his head,
> on his skull the dust in which he wallowed.
> He covered his loins with sackcloth.
> He cut his skin with a knife, with flint for a razor
> made incisions. Cheeks and chin he scraped.
> He raked his arm with a reed. He plowed his chest
> like a garden. He furrowed his back like a valley.
> He raised his voice and cried, "Baal is dead!
> What will become of the people? Dagon's son gone!
> What of the multitudes? I will go down into the earth
> in Baal's place."

> Anat too wandered on every mountain
> in the heart of the earth, over every hill
> in the heart of the fields. She came to the pleasant place,
> the desert pasture, the lovely fields of the shore of Death.

She came upon Baal: He had fallen to the earth.
She covered her loins with sackcloth.
She cut her skin with a stone knife,
she made incisions with a razor, cheeks and chin
she gashed. She plowed her chest like a garden,
she raked her back like a valley. She cried,
"Baal is dead! What will happen to the people?
Dagon's son gone! What of the multitude?
We will go down into the earth in Baal's place."

Torch of the gods, Lady Shapash the sun,
went down with her. When she had her fill
of weeping, had drunk her tears like wine,
then loudly she called to the torch
of the gods, Lady Shapash the sun,
"Lift Baal the conqueror, I pray you, onto me."

The torch, Lady Shapash the sun, obeyed.
She raised up Baal the conqueror, she set him
on the shoulders of Anat. And she brought him
to the heights of Zaphon. She wept for him,
she buried him. She laid him in the hollows of the gods
of the earth. She slaughtered 70 wild oxen
as a funeral offering to Baal the conqueror.
She slaughtered 70 plow oxen
as a funeral offering to Baal the conqueror.
She slaughtered 70 sheep, small cattle,
as a funeral offering to Baal the conqueror.
She slaughtered 70 deer
as a funeral offering to Baal the conqueror.
She slaughtered 70 mountain goats
as a funeral offering to Baal the conqueror.
She slaughtered 70 asses
as a funeral offering to Baal the conqueror.

## Athtar, Son of Asherah, Is Made King

Anat returns to El and tells Asherah and her family (many of whom were on the side of Death) that they can rejoice: Baal is in fact dead. El asks Asherah whom he should appoint in Baal's place. She suggests **Athtar** ("fertility"), a male counterpart to Astartê, a son of Asherah. Athtar sits down on Baal's throne, but he is not tall enough, confirming El's suspicion that he is not equal to the position. Athtar is struck dead and becomes king of the underworld (it is not clear how this fits in with Death's role in the underworld):

Then right away Anat headed for El at the sources
of the two rivers, in the midst of the springs
of the two oceans. Anat entered the tent of El,

entered the shrine of the king, father of years.
At the feet of El she did homage and fell down
and adored him. Anat prostrated herself and did
him honor. She raised up her voice and cried:
"Now may Asherah and her sons rejoice,
she and her pride of lions. For Baal the conqueror
is dead! Perished is the prince, the master of the earth!"

El cried aloud to Lady Asherah of the sea,
"Listen, O Lady Asherah of the sea,
give me one of your sons that I may make him king."
And answers Lady Asherah of the sea,
"Yes, let us make king him who has knowledge
and intelligence." But kindly El the compassionate answered,
"One feeble in strength cannot run like Baal,
nor release the spear like Dagon's son
when the time is right."
Lady Asherah of the sea answered,
"No! Let us make Athtar king,
let the awesome Athtar be king!"
Thereupon right away the awesome Athtar
went up into the heights of Zaphon.
He sat in the throne of Baal the conqueror.
His feet did not reach the footstool.
His head did not reach the headrest.
And spoke Athtar the awesome,
"I cannot be king in the heights of Zaphon!"
And down came the awesome Athtar.
He descended from the seat of Baal the conqueror.
and he became king of the underworld, the whole of it.

## Anat Kills Death

About 34 lines are missing. When the text continues, Anat looks for her brother/husband Baal. She comes to Death and demands that Death restore her brother/husband Baal. However, Death answers that he had searched for him everywhere and finally found him at the entrance of his domain. Then he simply ate him. Anat continues her search until she loses patience, attacks Death with a sword, shakes him, burns him, crushes him, then throws his remains to the birds:

One day passed, then two passed.
Virgin Anat was drawn to Baal.
Like the heart of a cow for her calf,
like the heart of a ewe for her lamb,
was the heart of Anat for Baal.
She seized Death by the edge
of his garment, she seized him by the hem of his robe.
She raised up her voice and cried, "Come, Death!
Give up my brother!"

But Death answered, El's son Death,
"What do you desire, O virgin Anat?
I wandered every mountain to the heart of the earth,
every hill to the heart of the fields. I felt a desire
for human beings, a desire for the people
of the earth. I came to the pleasant place,
the desert pasture, the lovely fields
on Death's shore.
I approached Baal the conqueror. I put
him in my mouth like a lamb, and like a kid
he was carried away in my gullet."

Lady Shapash the Sun, the torch,
luminary of the gods, burned hot.
The heavens shimmered under the hand
of El's son, of Death. A day, days passed.
From days to months.
Virgin Anat felt drawn to him, like the heart of a cow for her calf,
like the heart of a ewe for her lamb
was the heart of Anat for Baal. She seized
the son of El, Death, and with a blade she split him,
with a fan she winnowed him,
with fire she burned him,
with a mill-stone she ground him.
In the field she scattered him.
His pieces were devoured by birds.
His limbs were consumed by fowl.

## The Resurrection of Baal and Death

About 40 lines are lost. When the text resumes, Anat returns to El and announces that Baal is dead, but El dreams that Baal lives. Soon after, Baal comes back to life, and with his return life and vitality is restored to the land.
    Probably Anat speaks:

"For surely Baal has perished.
If Baal the conqueror is alive, if the prince,
the master of the earth, has revived,
then in a dream of kindly El, the compassionate,
let the heavens rain oil, the valleys run with honey.
Then I will know that Baal the conqueror is alive,
that the prince, master of the earth, has revived."

In a dream of kindly El, the compassionate,
in a vision of the creator of all,
the heavens rained down oil,

the valleys flowed with honey.
Kindly El rejoiced, the compassionate.
He placed his feet on the footstool.
He opened his mouth and laughed.
He raised up his voice and cried,
"Now I can be at ease, my heart within me may relax.
For alive is Baal the conqueror!
Revived is the prince, master of earth."

El called to the virgin Anat, "Listen, O virgin Anat!
Say to the torch of the gods, to Lady Shapash the sun,
'Dried are the furrows of the fields, O Shapash.
Dried are the furrows of El's fields.
Baal has neglected the furrows of his plowland.
Where is Baal the conqueror? Where is the prince,
the master of the earth?'"

The virgin Anat departed.
She turned toward the torch of the gods,
to lady Shapash the sun.
She raised up her voice and cried,
"Message of the bull, El your father,
the word of the kindly one, your begetter:
'Dried are the furrows of the fields, O Shapash.
Dried are the furrows of El's fields.
Baal has neglected the furrows of his plowland.
Where is the prince, the master of the earth?'"

And replied the torch of the gods,
Lady Shapash the sun, answered,
"Pour sparkling wine from its container,
bring a garland for your brother,
and I will look for Baal the conqueror."

And the virgin Anat replied,
"Wherever you go, O sun, O Shapash,
may El protect you . . ."

About 40 lines are missing. The resurrected Baal affirms his kingship, his power,
but Death comes back to life too and complains to Baal of all he has suffered. He demands that Baal surrender one of his brothers as a substitute sacrifice, a compensation
for all he has been through.

Instead the two gods, Death and Baal, fight on Mount Zaphon. Shapash arrives
and warns Death that fighting Baal is useless because El is now on Baal's side and will
overturn Death's throne. Death is afraid and declares that, after all, Baal is king:

Together, Anat and Lady Shapash the sun
searched for Baal and returned him to his palace.

Now Baal will make fertile the harrowed land
with his rain, with his water. He will put his voice
in the clouds and he will flash lightning to the earth.
Baal seized the sons of Asherah,° he struck
great ones on the shoulder, he struck the waves
with his club. He pushed Death to the ground.
Baal sat on the throne of his kingship,
on the cushion on the seat of his dominion.

A day, days passed, from days to months,
from months to years. Then in the seventh year
spoke the son of El, Death, to Baal the conqueror,
he raised his voice and cried:
"Because of you, Baal, I suffered shame.
Because of you I experienced splitting with the sword.
Because of you I experienced burning with fire.
Because of you I experienced grinding with a hand mill.
Because of you I experienced winnowing with the sieve.
Because of you I experienced scattering in the fields.
Because of you I experienced sowing in the sea.
Give one of your brothers so that I may eat
and the anger that I feel will turn back . . .
Let Baal give me his own brothers to eat,
the sons of his mother to consume!"
He returned to Baal in the heights of Zaphon.
He raised up his voice and cried,
"Let Baal give me his own brothers to eat,
the sons of his mother to consume!"

They butted each other like camels.
Death was strong, Baal was strong.
They gored like wild oxen. Death was strong,
Baal was strong. They bit like serpents.
Death was strong, Baal was strong.
They kicked each other like stallions.
Death fell down, Baal fell down.
Lady Shapash the sun cried out from above:
"Listen, I beseech you, El's son Death.
How can you battle with Baal the conqueror?
If El, the bull, your father hears you,
surely he will undermine the foundations of your throne,
will break the scepter of your rule."

Divine Death was afraid. Terrified was the beloved of El,
the youth, the hero. Death was afraid at Shapash's call.

---

°*sons of Asherah*: he means Death and his followers; Death's mother is Asherah.

About 10 lines are missing. Apparently, Shapash speaks to Baal:

"You will eat the fresh meat.
Yes, you will surely eat the sacrificial meal.
Yes, you will drink the wine of offering."
Lady Shapash judged the healers,
Lady Shapash, the sun, judged the divine ones:
"O gods, Death is yours, and Kothar is yours,
and your acquaintance Hasis is yours.
In the sea are Desire and the Dragon.
Let Kothar-wa-Hasis banish them,
let Kothar-wa-Hasis drive them away!"

There the myth ends, with an extraordinary and unique note indicating that the poem was dictated by a priest to a scribe, at the instruction of the king:

*The scribe was Ilimilku from Shubbani. The reciter was Attanu-Purlianni, the head priest, the head herdsman. The sponsor was Niqmaddu, king of Ugarit, master of Yargub, lord of Tharumani.*

## PERSPECTIVE 4

### The Hittite Myth of Kingship in Heaven

Other important Eastern myths come from the mighty Indo-European Hittites, who ruled the central Anatolian plain (modern central Turkey) in the Late Bronze Age. Their powerful capital was near modern Ankara, and offshoots of their art and culture were strong well into the 8th century BC in what is today southeastern Turkey and northern Syria. Only small portions of a Hittite poem called "Kingship in Heaven" survive (in Mesopotamian cuneiform script but Hittite language), but the story of the victory of the storm-god (Teshub) over a predecessor bears clear parallels to Canaanite and Mesopotamian myth.

The poem goes like this:

In earlier years, Alalush was king in heaven.

Alalush sits there on his throne.

And strong Anush [= Anu, Sky], first of the gods, is his servant.

He bows to him at his feet.

He always gives him great cups

to drink into his hand.

For nine years of rule, Alalush was king in heaven.

After nine years, Anush made war against Alalush.

He defeated Alalush

who fled under the dark earth,
but Anush sat on the throne.

Anush is there on his throne
and strong Kumarbi always gives him food to eat
and he always bows at his feet
and always gives him great cups into his hand.

For nine years Anush ruled as king in heaven.
In the ninth year, Anush made war with Kumarbi.
The eyes of Kumarbi he could not defeat.
He slipped from Kumarbi's hand and fled.
Anush the eagle flew in the sky
and Kumarbi closed in behind him,
grabbed his feet
and pulled him down from the sky.
Kumarbi bit off Anush's genitals.
Anush's sperm went into Kumarbi's stomach.
He swallowed Anush's sperm
and Kumarbi was happy and he laughed.

And Anush turned back to him
and began to speak to Kumarbi:
"You are really pleased about your stomach.
It swallowed my sperm.
You should not rejoice!
I have placed a load in your middle.
First, I have made you pregnant with the storm-god;
second, with the river Aranzakh;
third, with the heavy Tasmishu.
And I placed the burden, the terrible gods into your middle!
You will perish, hitting your head on the mountain Tashshu°!"

When Anush finished speaking, he disappeared.
Then Kumarbi went high into the heavens.
He spit from his mouth.
The stricken king spit from his mouth upward.
That which had been ingested, Kumarbi spit out . . .

°. . . *Tashshu*: the storm-god is Teshub; Aranzakh is the Tigris River; Tasmishu is an attendant of the storm-god; Tashshu is an unknown location.

There the tablet breaks off. When it resumes, we learn that Anush argued with the storm-god (Teshub), still within the body of Kumarbi, over how the storm-god should escape from Kumarbi's body. Kumarbi felt dizzy and asked Aya (= Ea/Enki) for something to eat. He ate something that hurt his mouth. At last the storm-god, warned not to come forth through various openings, especially not through Kumarbi's anus, came out of the "good place," apparently Kumarbi's penis. The rest is lost, but somehow the storm-god Teshub escaped from Kumarbi's body, overthrew him, and became king of heaven.

Like *Enuma elish*, the Hittite "Kingship in Heaven" is based on the succession motif: First Alalush was king, then Anush (Sky), then Kumarbi, then Teshub (storm-god). The motif of a primordial god (Kumarbi) castrating his father Sky (Anush) is exactly paralleled in the Greek story that the primordial Cronus castrated Uranus, "sky" (see Chapter 5).

So this is an oral, dictated poem—like Homer. But we knew that anyway from the stylized formulas and repetitions.

## OBSERVATIONS: THE TRIUMPH OF BAAL

The theme of this very ancient myth is the triumph of Baal the conqueror. It is a way of explaining how Baal came to be the chief god of the Canaanites. Baal became king by defeating the forces of chaos, embodied in Sea and in Death. Sea is the water from which all things come, and may always return, just as in *Enuma elish* Tiamat and Apsu, the mixed waters, are parents of the gods. Death is of course the ultimate dissolution undergone by all things.

The first surviving episode begins with Sea's divine ministers demanding the surrender of Baal. The council of the gods is terrified. El, "God," gives in and delivers Baal to Sea. Unlike Anu, "sky," in the Mesopotamian myth, El seems to be in alliance with Sea. But Baal rebukes the gods: He would himself be king of all the gods and he will not give in.

Instead, assisted by two clubs that Kothar-wa-Hasis, the craftsman-god, prepares, he overcomes Sea. Baal is the power of storm and the fertilizing rain brought by storm. Baal's title "rider on the clouds" underlines his similarity to the Mesopotamian Marduk, "son of the storm," as it anticipates the role of Zeus, the "cloud-gatherer" in Greek myth.

In Hebrew myth Baal as storm-god is remembered in the description of Yahweh, tribal god of Israel (Psalm 104:3–4):[3]

Yahweh makes the clouds his chariot
and rides on the wings of the wind.

He makes winds his messengers,
flames of fire his servants.

As Baal defeated Sea, so did Yahweh defeat Rahab, demon of the sea (Job 26:12–13):

By his power Yahweh churned up the sea,
by his wisdom he cut Rahab to pieces.

---

[3]Biblical quotations based on *New Revised Standard Version of the Bible* (Oxford, 1991).

By his breath the skies became fair,
his hand pierced the gliding serpent.

Now comes an interlude in which Anat, sister and wife, shows her own powers in war, but because the tablet is broken above and below we cannot tell how this episode fits in. In any event, Baal sends messengers to Anat calling her back from fighting and ordering her to his side.

The second and longest episode concerns the construction of a house, or palace, for Baal. Without this structure he cannot be considered a king. El gives his permission, perhaps persuaded by Anat, sister and wife of Baal, but he also must have the permission of Asherah, El's wife. Asherah is reluctant, then won over by the bribe of precious objects manufactured by Kothar-wa-Hasis.

Asherah prophesizes the beginning of the rainy season, once the house is complete. The house is built of the most precious materials, but in a curious reverse alchemy turned to ordinary brick and lumber after seven days of firing.

Baal throws a lavish party: Likewise, Marduk's victory is celebrated by a great party. In the Hebrew tradition, David designs and Solomon builds around 1000 BC the great temple to Yahweh in JERUSALEM, although the prophets had railed against building a "house of cedar" for God (II Samuel 7:5–7). Solomon's architects and craftsmen were Phoenicians, Levantine Semites, who used cedar from Lebanon. The Hebrew temple was dedicated with words appropriate to Baal (I Kings 8:36):

> Teach them the right way to live, and send rain on the land you gave your people for an inheritance.

The transfer of power from a primordial god to a storm-god is a myth spread over all the ancient Near East and Greece. Thus in Mesopotamia Marduk replaces Tiamat; among the Hittites Teshub replaces Kumarbi; and in Greece Zeus replaces his father Cronus, just as in Cannanite Myth Baal replaces El as king of the gods.

The detail of the disagreement over the window in the palace is puzzling. At first Baal refuses, then after a brief military campaign agrees to the window. Perhaps this can be explained by a passage in Jeremiah (9:21), one of the few times that Death personified is named in the Bible:

> Death has come up through our windows.
> It has entered our palaces
> to cut off the children in the streets,
> the young men in the town squares.

In fact Death attacks Baal soon after Kothar-wa-Hasis makes the window.

But Baal's defeat of Sea, personified as the serpent Lotan, had caused a cosmic collapse. As punishment Baal must go into the maw of death, whose all-consuming appetite Attanu-Purlianni vividly describes. The sequence of the narrative is, however, impossible to follow very well, because only 40 percent of it survives. In what we can make out, Baal is frightened by Death's messengers and surrenders to Death. After sex with a heifer (perhaps his wife Anat in bovine form), he descends to the underworld with his sons and daughters and all the accouterments of storm—wind, lightning, rain. When El learns of Baal's death, he mourns, as does Anat. Anat buries him, with Shapash the sun as helper, and offers a sacrifice. The void left by Baal must be filled, but Asherah's son Athtar proves unequal to the task.

In the meanwhile all fertility is gone from the land, just as when the human king is ailing or dies the crops will fail. Anat finds the answer: She kills Death, cutting him to pieces. She treats him as if he were the seed of agriculture: She splits him, winnows him, burns him, grinds him, sows him. The death of Death leads to Baal's revival and fertility returns. Still, after seven years, Death returns too. Defeat of the forces of sterility is not permanent; it is part of an unending cycle that goes round and round, bringing now benefice, now darkness and sorrow.

## Key Terms

| | | |
|---|---|---|
| Ugarit 98 | Anat 102 | Danel 103 |
| Baal 100 | Asherah 102 | Aqhat 103 |
| El 100 | Astartê 102 | Pagat 103 |
| Dagon 100 | Kothar-wa-Hasis 102 | Hadad 119 |
| "cuneiform alphabet" 101 | Mot 102 | Shapash 137 |
| Canaan 102 | Yam 102 | Athtar 139 |

## Further Reading

Cross, F. M., *Canaanite Myth and Hebrew Epic: Essays in the History of the Religion of Israel* (Cambridge, MA, 1997).

Drews, R., *The End of the Bronze Age: Changes in Warfare and the Catastrophe ca. 1200 BC* (Princeton, 1995).

Schniedewind, W. M., *A Primer on Ugaritic: Language, Culture, and Literature* (Cambridge, UK, 2007).

Smith, M. S., *The Origins of Biblical Monotheism: Israel's Polytheistic Background and the Ugaritic Texts* (Oxford, UK, 2001).

____, *Untold Stories: The Bible and Ugaritic Studies in the Twentieth Century* (New York, 2001).

West, M. L., *The East Face of Helicon: West Asiatic Elements in Greek Poetry and Myth* (Oxford, UK, 1997).

# 5

# Greek Myth

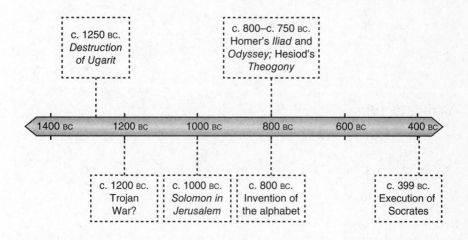

Greece was a poor country, barren and dry, in ancient times as today. Unlike the rich river valleys of Egypt and Mesopotamia, the rugged Balkan peninsula, the south-eastern-most extension of Europe, does not seem to be a likely setting for the ancient civilization it produced. The Greek achievement must depend on the nature of the Greek people themselves, who seem to have moved into the Balkans sometime around 2100 BC, on very scant information. The body of myth that they generated is equaled only by myths of the Indian subcontinent, and naturally we can say only a little in a single chapter.

## GREEK LANDSCAPE

In Greece the rivers are too small to be navigable, and they dry up in the blazing heat of the mostly rainless summers. High mountains dominate the Greek landscape and occupy about three-quarters of the land. The towering PINDUS range runs down the

**MAP 5**    Ancient Greece.

center of the Balkan peninsula, then continues into the sea, where peaks appear as dry, rocky islands (Map 5).

The Pindus is intersected by other ranges that cut across the peninsula. Between these ranges lie a series of small, isolated plains, the only places in Greece suitable for agriculture. Here, in these pockets nestled between the mountains and the sea, Greek civilization developed.

To the northeast on the Balkan peninsula lie the plains of THESSALY and MACEDONIA. To their south lies the plain of **BOEOTIA** (bē-ō-sha, "cow-land"), in which the principal settlement in ancient times was the city of THEBES. Hesiod (8th century BC), whose poem the *Theogony* we will examine in a moment, lived in a small town in Boeotia.

On these small plains the ancient Greeks grew wheat and barley and manufactured olive oil for cooking, cleansing and anointing the body, and burning in lamps.

Wine grapes grew on vines planted on the slopes that surrounded the plains. Goats, sheep, and pigs were kept for wool, milk, cheese, leather, and meat, but cattle were few because of the lack of forage. Horses were also scarce and highly valued. They were a source of great prestige, the pride of the ruling class.

As cultivable land was limited in Greece, so were other resources. There was some gold in THRACE, but none in Greece proper. Egypt, by contrast, was awash in gold from the earliest times. There were a few deposits of silver, such as at Laurium in ATTICA, which contributed to Athenian economic and military power. Most iron was imported. Greece imported copper from CYPRUS (see Map 4 ). The source of tin, alloyed with copper to produce bronze, remains unknown.

The Greeks did have access to excellent deposits of limestone and clay. The best limestone was found on the island of EUBOEA (yū-bē-a), just east of the mainland not far from ATHENS, on several smaller islands, and in Thessaly. Under high pressure, lime-stone crystallizes into marble, a lovely, workable stone used by the Greeks for sculpture and for their finest temples, such as the Parthenon in Athens that celebrated the goddess Athena. Important deposits of marble also occur on Mount Pentelicus near Athens and on the islands of NAXOS and PAROS.

The finest clay, especially that found near Athens and CORINTH, provided material for pottery, which the Greeks produced in great abundance and variety. Once fired, ceramic material is breakable, but its fragments are virtually indestructible. Exquisitely decorated Greek pots have been found all over the Mediterranean world and especially in Italy. Such pots were often made expressly for use in burials, where they have been found in modern times. The pictures painted on these pots provide us with vivid illustrations of Greek myths and wonderfully illuminate many details of Greek social life.

But perhaps Greece's greatest natural resource was the sea. The AEGEAN (ē-jē-an) SEA between the Balkan peninsula and ASIA MINOR (modern western Turkey) played a central role in the life of the ancient Greeks, more so than in Ugarit. Most Greeks lived near the sea and took from it the fish that were a staple of their diet, although Homeric heroes preferred to eat only flesh. The sea was an avenue of communication with the world beyond the mountains that enclosed the isolated Greek communities.

Because of the islands scattered across the Aegean Sea, a sailor is almost never out of sight of land, and the Greeks learned early to travel long distances in small open boats. Several large islands dominate the others. CRETE, the southern-most Aegean island, had an especially important role in the early history of Greece (see Figure 5.1).

The paucity of cultivable land and natural resources led the Greeks to trade with other peoples. A mastery of the sea allowed them to transport goods to and from foreign lands. They exported wine, olive oil, and pottery and brought back the metals and other goods they needed, especially grain and prestige items of exquisite quality. Myths reflect the fact that the Greeks were the greatest seafaring people of the ancient world (together with the Semitic Phoenicians), as exemplified by the story of Odysseus, whose perilous sea journey home from the Trojan War lasted 10 years.

**FIGURE 5.1**   Fleet fresco from the town of Akrotiri, 16th century BC, Santorini (Thera), Greece. A boat in the lower left, manned by rowers and a steersman, pull into the harbor. Along the harbor are multistoried houses, from the tops and windows of which people watch the spectacle. In the Nilotic landscape at the top, a river embraces the town along which bound desert animals and along which grow desert plants. The Cretans had intimate contact with Egypt and Cretan frescoes from about the same time as this picture have been found in the delta there. (University of Wisconsin Photo Archive)

## INDO-EUROPEAN ORIGINS

The people later called the "Greeks" belonged to the cultural and linguistic group called the **Indo-Europeans**, whose original homeland seems to be in central Asia, east of the Caspian Sea. They are unrelated to the Sumerians, the Semites, and the Egyptians. Beginning in the 4th millennium BC, the Indo-Europeans apparently migrated in all directions into Europe and Asia, bringing with them their linguistic and cultural traditions. They could not get into the well-fortified urban settlements along the Tigris/Euphrates and the Nile, so they veered off into Greece, northwest India, and Europe. The exact date of their arrival in Greece cannot be established definitively, but the destruction of existing settlements around 2100 BC suggests the arrival of a new people. From about the same time we find the first evidence in Greece of the domestic horse, an animal elsewhere associated with the Indo-Europeans.

Much of what little we know about the Indo-Europeans today is inferred by scholars from a reconstruction of the language they spoke, called protoIndo-European. Although we have no written record or other direct evidence of this long-extinct hypothetical language, some of its vocabulary, and even some of its grammatical structure, can be deduced from the many ancient and modern languages descended from it. Every language spoken today in Europe (except

Basque, Finnish, Hungarian, and Estonian) belongs to this family. Today mo₁ than 1.6 billion people, on every continent, speak or at least understand Indo-European languages. The spread of the Indo-European language family, now further assisted by the Internet, is one of the most remarkable events in the history of the human race.

The Greek language of later eras was not the tongue of the early Indo-European immigrants but developed over the centuries after their arrival. The basic vocabulary of Greek is derived from the hypothetical protoIndo-European parent language, but many words—particularly those for places, plants, animals, and gods—were taken from the language of the earlier inhabitants, just as in America the names Manhattan, Chicago, and Wisconsin were taken from languages of preEuropean inhabitants. There were also many Semitic words in Greek, reflecting the Greeks' enormous debt to earlier Semitic culture.

## THE ALPHABETIC REVOLUTION

About 800 BC, someone familiar with Phoenician syllabic writing, probably a Semite, perhaps from north Syria near Ugarit, invented the Greek alphabet by requiring that a rough indication of the vowel accompany each consonantal sign. Phoenician syllabic writing, of which the Ugaritic "cuneiform alphabet" is the oldest attested ancestor, had signs only for consonants and could not be pronounced except by a native. Phoenician writing was an odd but purely phonetic syllabary with around only 22 signs.

The Greek alphabet was the first writing that encoded an approximation of the actual sound of the human voice, hence a script potentially applicable to any human language. It is the most important invention in the history of culture after the invention of writing itself. It is the basis for Western civilization and today, to a remarkable extent, for world civilization. Except for minor changes, the Greek system was the same system of writing that appears on these pages. In its Roman and related forms, the Greek alphabet is today found everywhere.

Within a generation, the revolutionary alphabetic technology had spread throughout the Greek people. At the same time the Greeks sent out colonies to the west, to southern Italy and Sicily, where they built cities and prospered. The period of political and cultural revival that began with the invention of the alphabet around 800 BC marks the beginning of a new era in Greek and human history.

Greece was never socially stratified in the fashion of the heavily populated and extravagantly wealthy river monarchies along the Nile and in Mesopotamia. The Greeks' dependence on the sea further reduced class distinctions. The sudden dangerous storms of the Aegean threatened captain and crew alike. Claims to good birth and upbringing had no survival value. Seafaring encouraged extreme individualism and offered rich rewards to the skilled adventurer willing to take risks. Seafaring was practiced almost entirely by free citizens, and in the *Odyssey* (8th century BC) the Greeks invented a world of danger and wonder on the high seas, a journey that came to symbolize the quest for knowledge itself.

Although the proud and politically independent city-states struggled constantly and murderously against one another, very much as had the city-states of Mesopotamia, the Greeks nonetheless maintained the sense of being a single people.

ommon language, used a common technology of writing, and called
llenes (**hel**-ēnz), implying a common descent from the legendary
) (a male, not to be confused with Helen of Troy!). The term *Graioi*,
Greeks," comes from the Romans, who took it from a northwestern Greek tribe living
in EPIRUS, the backward territory across the IONIAN SEA from Italy. Greeks worshiped
the same pantheon of gods and participated in panHellenic religious and athletic festivals, especially at the Olympic games held in the northeast PELOPONNESUS, "the island
of Pelops," really the peninsula of southern Greece separated from the mainland by a
narrow isthmus at the city of Corinth.

## GREEK POLYTHEISM

The Greeks had many gods. Their polytheism was similar to the Mesopotamian or
Canaanite, to whom the Greeks certainly owed a debt. Zeus was the leader, but Void
(Chaos), Earth (Gaea), Night (Nyx), and other gods existed before him and his brothers, sisters, and children—the Olympians. These early gods continued to exist even
after Zeus, like Baal, achieved ascendancy by force. No Greek god was all-powerful,
but each controlled a sphere of interest that sometimes overlapped with that of other
gods, just as the Mesopotamian and Egyptian and Canaanite gods, with whom the
Greek gods had so much in common.

Like the Mesopotamian and Canaanite gods, the Greek gods had personalities
and struggled with one another for position and power. They did not love humans
(although some had favorites) and did not ask to be loved by them. They did not impose codes of behavior. They expected respect and honor but could act contrary to
human needs and desires. They did not reveal their will in writing. Their priests, having no writings to interpret, were required only to perform appropriate rituals.

The appropriate religious ritual was in Greece always a form of sacrifice: the
killing of an animal or many animals or the offering of foodstuffs. Although human
sacrifice is often mentioned in Greek myths, it appears to have been highly uncom-
mon during the historical period, and archaeology has produced only one clear example from the Bronze Age (from Crete). The underlying logic of sacrifice was always
the same: In order to gain the god's goodwill, destroy what you value most. That will
place the god firmly in your debt. We find similar modes of thinking in the ancient
Near East.

Sacrifice was performed outside the god's house on an altar, usually to the east
of the temple. The temple was not itself a place of worship. There was no official
priestly organization with social or political missions in ancient Greece, unlike in the
Near East. Priests and priestesses came from local families or were sometimes chosen
by lot. They did not serve the state, as in Mesopotamia and Egypt: There was no state
to serve.

When one wanted to know the god's will, one went to a seer or to an oracle.
Religious activity—appropriate sacrifice—could help in this life, but had no effect
on one's lot in the next world (the mysteries at ELEUSIS were a notable exception).
Notions of guilt or sin, which arise from disobeying God's rules of universal application, were unknown. There were no such rules to obey.

The Greek gods were capricious and terrifying, not to be taken lightly. Yet the Athenian comedians made fun of them, and Greek intellectuals criticized them for the immoral behavior reported in Greek myths. A small minority of Greeks even questioned the existence of the gods and sought other than divine causes behind the phenomena of the world. The thinking of these radical intellectuals led to the proposition that gods do not fashion human misery or happiness, success in war or love, or anything else. Humans make their own world, a fundamental principle of what we think of as Western civilization. We owe this to the Greeks. No such notions ever appeared in the ancient Near East.

## HOMER AND HESIOD

Although many Greek myths may have taken shape during primordial times, it was not until around 800 BC, the same time as the introduction of the alphabet, that myths were committed to writing. According to the best explanation, the Greek alphabet was devised expressly in order to record oral verse, that is, myths, very much as Ilimilku of Shubbani recorded the dictation of Attanu-Purlianni in Ugarit. Consequently, we derive most of our knowledge of Greek myth from writings of this and later periods.

Additional information comes from the 50,000 pictured Greek vase paintings that survive and occasionally from sculpture. They date from about 650–350 BC, so later than the old Greek poets. Scholars estimate surviving pictured vases to represent about one percent of the original production, giving us some idea of the explosion of images that flooded ancient Greece and Italy in this period, for which there is no parallel in the ancient world. Whereas mythic images are rare in Near Eastern Art, although we have here attempted to illustrate several, in Greek art mythic images are astoundingly prevalent. The Greeks invented the narrative style in art, where art tells a story and does not just illustrate a power. Many images on Greek pots represented myths inspired by literary accounts that have been lost.

The earliest Greek literature is the oral poems the *Iliad* and the *Odyssey*, of **Homer**, who seems to have composed his poems some time in the 8th century BC, or the late 9th, although there is not very much evidence. We know nothing for certain about Homer's life. Later tradition has him born somewhere in Asia Minor, perhaps in the city of Smyrna or on the island of Chios, but his poems show wide knowledge of the Aegean and Greece. One of the reasons we think that he lived just at the moment that the alphabet was introduced into Greece is that, with one exception, Homer's stories never refer to writing; in the one instance he does refer to writing, he does not understand it.

The *Iliad*, a long poem of about 16,000 lines, is set in a period of several weeks during the 10th year of the Trojan War. It would have been impossible to record Homer in the earlier Phoenician syllabic script because the complex rhythms of his poetic line depend on the alternation of long and short vowels, which that script could not notate. Its principal theme is the wrath of Achilles, his anger over being mistreated by the leader of the expedition, Agamemnon. Within this frame Homer includes a wealth of subordinate myths. The *Odyssey* is about 12,000 lines long and narrates the return of Odysseus to his home after an absence of 20 years. Unlike the Indian *Mahabharata* and other epics in world literature, which exist in many versions, the *Iliad* and the *Odyssey* exist in a single version by a single author.

Under what conditions Homer may have sung songs as long as the *Iliad* or *Odyssey* remains unclear. These poems probably were never presented in the form in which we have them. The poems we have are the result of artificial conditions created by the writing down of the poems, when the poet was no longer forced to sing rapidly and had no audience to entertain. He was free to greatly expand his narrative. But the Homeric poems are mysterious. In spite of hundreds of years of analytical and historical scholarship no one has explained what they are for, what was their purpose. There was certainly no reading public in the days of Homer.

Views differ widely about the reality of the world Homer portrays. On balance it seems plausible that Homer incorporated various features from earlier periods preserved through the oral tradition, but that his poems, and especially the social and religious values that move the actors, reflect Homer's own age, the late 9th, early 8th century BC.

Although we do not know the purpose of Homer's poems, their influence on Greek and later culture is inestimable. He was the textbook by which alphabetic writing was learned. Less influential but perhaps more important to the study of myth is his near or virtual contemporary **Hesiod** (800–750? BC). Unlike the anonymous Homer, who conceals his personality, Hesiod tells us a little about himself in his two surviving poems, the *Theogony* ("origin of the gods") and *Works and Days*, a sort of combination moral treatise and almanac. His father had lived in Asia Minor, Hesiod tells us, then moved to mainland Greece to a small forlorn village at the foot of Mount Helicon near Thebes, where Hesiod lived. The alphabet, which preserved the songs of Hesiod, was invented on the island of Euboea, just miles away.

Like Homer, Hesiod was a singer, an oral poet. According to the opening lines of the *Theogony*, the **Muses**, inspirers of poetry, came to him in a vision while he was tending his flocks on Helicon. They gave him the power of song (thus, *Helicon* is synonymous with poetic inspiration in the Western literary tradition).

Hesiod's remarkable description of the Muses and his meeting with them contains many unfamiliar names, but is worth quoting here because the description identifies Hesiod as the first European author (Homer never identifies himself), gives the first definition of a *poet* ("maker"), and explains why a poet can speak with authority about past, present, and future: because he is inspired by the Muses with a mission divinely ordained.[1]

Let us begin our song with the Muses of Helicon,
who dwell upon the great and rugged mount of Helicon
and dance with gentle feet around the indigo spring
and around the altar of Cronus' mighty son.°
When they have washed their tender bodies
in Permessus, or in the Horse's Spring, or holy Olmeius,
they make lovely, longing dances on the top of Helicon

°*mighty son*: Zeus.

---

[1] For the Greek texts, cf. B. B. Powell, *Classical Myth*, 7th ed. (New York, 2011). See also, A. N. Athanassakis, *Hesiod: Theogony, Works and Days, Shield* (Baltimore, 1983); G. Most, *Hesiod*, 2 vols. (Cambridge, MA, 2006–2007); A. T. Murray, *Homer: Odyssey*, 2 vols., revised by G. E. Dimock (Cambridge, MA, 1995); R. Fagles, *The Odyssey* (New York, 1999); B. B. Powell, *A New Translation of the Odyssey* (New York, 2014).

and move with thumping feet. From there they rise, go forth by night,
veiled in dark mist to utter their song in darling voice,
singing of Zeus who holds the aegis° and mistress Hera
of Argos, who walks on golden sandals,
and of the blue-eyed Athena, daughter of Zeus the aegis-holder,
and of Phoebus Apollo, and Artemis who thrills to the arrow,
and Poseidon, who holds the earth and shakes it,
and honorable Themis ["Law"] and glancing-eyed Aphrodite
and Hebê ["Youth"] with crown of gold and beautiful Dionê,
Leto, Iapetus,° and Cronus of crafty counsels,
Eos [Dawn] and great Helius [Sun] and bright Selenê [Moon],
Earth too, and great Oceanus [the river around the world] and dark Night
and the sacred race of all the other ones who never die.
One day they taught Hesiod glorious song
while he was shepherding his lambs under holy Helicon.

°*aegis*: a magic shield. °*Dionê, Leto, Iapetus*: Dionê according to some accounts is the consort of
Zeus; Leto is the mother of Apollo and Artemis; Iapetus is a Titan from the preOlympian race of
gods, probably the same as the biblical Japheth.

And how much truth do myths contain?

Here is the first word [*muthos*, hence our "myth"] the goddesses said to me—
the Muses of Olympus, daughters of Zeus who holds the aegis:
"You stupid rustic shepherds, bellies and nothing more,
we are the ones who can tell you lies that look like truth.
We can also, if we please, proclaim what indeed is true."
So spoke the trustworthy daughters of mighty Zeus,
and gave me a leafy branch of laurel to pluck for a staff.
Then into me they breathed the inspired art of the poet,
to sing of things of the past and those that are yet to be.
They told me to sing of the blessed immortal race of the gods,
always beginning and ending my song with the Muses themselves.

Hesiod, *Theogony,* 1–33

Poetry, and its burden of myth, can be true or not true, and it can be hard to tell
the difference. This sobering reality is always before us when we use myth to reconstruct the truth about the past.

## MYTH: THE CREATION OF THE WORLD

Hesiod's thousand-line poem, the *Theogony*, composed in the 8th century BC, is in
external form an elaborate hymn to Zeus, the Greek version of the Indo-European
storm-god. The story owes a great deal to Mesopotamian myth, telling how Zeus overcame an earlier generation of gods and monsters in battle and established his own
power. In Hesiod's other surviving poem, *Works and Days*, Hesiod tells us that he sang
at funeral games in honor of a dead prince on the nearby island of Euboea, a detail that

may explain how poems by this oral poet came to be written down: The Euboeans were the earliest possessors of the Greek alphabet.

In contrast to the familiar story told in the biblical book of Genesis, where God stands outside of the creation and exists before it, Hesiod, like his Mesopotamian forebears, tells of the origin of the universe through succeeding generations of gods. **Cosmogony**, a story that explains the "origin of the world" (*kosmos* = "world," *gony* = "origin"), is for Hesiod the same as **theogony** (*theos* = "god"), a story that explains the "origin of the gods" and their rise to power. To explain Zeus's supremacy in the world Hesiod must go back to the beginning of all things, to the generations of **Chaos** (kā-os), "chasm"; **Gaea** (jē-a), "earth"; and **Uranus** (**yur**-a-nus), "sky."

## The Children of Chaos

Hesiod begins his account:

> Chaos was first to appear, then Gaea, Earth, the broad-bosomed,
> unshakable base of things, then Tartarus, windswept and dark,
> deep in the caverns of broad-wayed earth. And Eros, the fairest
> of all the immortals, arose, who frees us all from our sorrows,
> but ruins our hearts' good sense, breaking the wisest intentions
> of gods and mortals alike. From Chaos came Erebus, darkness,
> and Nyx, night, mother of Aether, radiance, and Hemera, day;
> these Nyx conceived by uniting with Erebus, gloomy and somber.

Hesiod, Theogony, 116–125

Hesiod's cosmogony is hard to understand, and its meaning is still debated. Certainly first came Chaos, a being of some kind that was not always there (Chart 5.1).

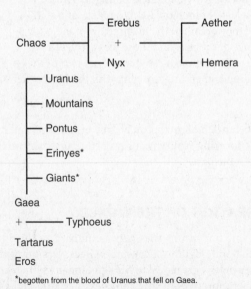

**CHART 5.1**   The primordial beings of the Greek cosmogony.

Where Chaos comes from, Hesiod does not say, and we are not sure what Hesiod meant by it. Chaos is related etymologically to our words *gap* and *yawn*; we might translate it as "chasm," and some understand it as the opening from which the other primordial beings arose. Implicit in the word is the separation of two things to make a gap in the middle, in the Mesopotamian tradition.

After Chaos came Gaea, Mother Earth, the personification of the earth beneath us, the solid, sure foundation of the world. Tartarus, a name of unknown meaning, is some place below Earth and often confused in Greek myth with the abode of Hades, but Hesiod personifies Tartarus as one of the primordial creatures by which Gaea later has offspring. Hesiod struggles to delineate space in mythical terms, working toward the scheme Olympus/topmost, Gaea/middle, and Tartarus/bottommost.

After Chaos also appeared **Eros**, "sexual love" or "attraction," the first motion, which brings sexual beings together to produce still more offspring. Eros is a being as well as the force that drives Hesiod's complex genealogies. Hesiod does not say that Gaea, Tartarus, and Eros sprang from Chaos, and some think that he meant the four to represent independent aspects of the primeval stuff from which the world emerged: a gaping (Chaos), the foundation of all that is (Gaea), the underside of that foundation (Tartarus), and the principle of sexual attraction, which ensures future generation and change (Eros). We follow this interpretation in Chart 5.1. However, Hesiod's statement that Erebus (**er**-e-bus), "darkness," and Nyx (nux), "night," came from Chaos may imply that the other primeval beings did too; certainly the Near Eastern myths on which Hesiod bases his account had sought for a *single* origin to the multiplicities of the world.

## The Children of Gaea: The Titans

From Earth, the foundation of all that is, sprang a host of beings, bewildering in their complexity and in the obscurity of their origins and nature. Most important were the **Titans** (**tī**-tans), but the monstrous **Cyclopes** (sī-**klō**-pēz) and the even stranger **Hecatonchires** (he-ka-ton-**kī**-rēz) had important roles to play in the world's early days.

According to Hesiod, Gaea first bore, asexually, Uranus ("sky"), and the Mountains on her upper side that rise into the sky. Then she bore her watery doublet, Pontus ("sea") (Chart 5.1). In sexual union with her son Uranus/Sky, Gaea/Earth produced the six male and six female Titans, a word of unknown meaning (Chart 5.2).

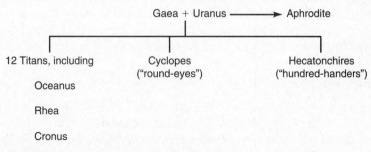

**CHART 5.2**  The children of Gaea and Uranus.

**Cronus** (krō-nus), who will contend with Uranus ("sky") for power, is named as the last born. The Titans rarely are represented in art and do not often play a role in later stories or in religious cult. However, their unions were to produce a whole cycle of divinities:

> The first of the children of Gaea, equal in size to herself,
> hiding her body completely, was Uranus, star-studded heaven.
> The blessed gods needed solider ground to support their feet.
> She bore long ranges of mountains, pleasant haunts of immortals.
> Pontus she bore, the unharvested sea with its raging swell,
> without the pleasure of love. Thereafter Gaea was bedded
> with Uranus, lord of heaven, and bore deep-swirling Oceanus,
> Coeus, Crius, Hyperion, Iapetus, Theia, and Rhea, Themis,
> Mnemosynê, gold Phoebê, and fair-featured Tethys.
> Last of all she gave birth to Cronus, that scheming intriguer,
> cleverest child of her brood, who hated his lecherous father.

Hesiod, Theogony, 126–138

Uranus evidently was the same size as Gaea and covered her completely, as if locked in perpetual sexual embrace. The birth of Pontus, "sea," reminds us of the watery nature of the primordial element in the Mesopotamian, Egyptian, and Canaanite myths. Although the oppositions of up/down, Sky/Earth have now appeared, the separation of the primal opposites is yet to be fixed and made permanent.

Two notable Titans are the watery male **Oceanus** (ō-sē-a-nus) and the female **Tethys** (tē-this). Tethys is probably a corruption of "Tiamat." According to a passing reference in Homer, Oceanus and Tethys themselves gave birth to all the gods: a good example of a different cosmogony parallel to Hesiod's. Oceanus is a river that encircles the world, where the dome of the sky touches the flat surface of the earth. All the waters that emerge from wells, springs, fountains, and rivers are also fed by the flow of Oceanus. Oceanus and Tethys united to give birth to the six thousand Oceanids (ō-sē-a-nids), spirits of the sea, rivers, and springs.

Coeus, Crius, and Theia, "divine," are scarcely more than names. Phoebê, "brilliant," must have something to do with the light of the sky, as Themis, "law," refers to the earth, that which is fixed and settled, like the oracles delivered in her name. The oracular shrine of Delphi belonged to Themis before Apollo took it over. Themis will bear children to Zeus, as will Mnemosynê (nē-**mos**-i-nē), "memory." The name of Iapetus seems related to that of the biblical Japheth, the son of Noah, who survived the great flood, and, in the biblical account, the ancestor of Europeans. Cronus and **Rhea** (rē-a), doublets for Uranus and Gaea, are parents or grandparents of the 12 Olympians, including Zeus, the king of the gods and the central subject of praise in Hesiod's poem.

## Cyclopes, Hecatonchires

In addition to the Titans, Gaea bore, after union with Uranus, three Cyclopes, "round-eyes," and the mighty Hecatonchires, the "hundred-handers" (Chart 5.2). Sometimes, we can understand the meaning of their names, usually allegories, but not always, and they have little role to play as individuals in Greek myth:

Then Gaea gave birth to Cyclopes, strong and abrupt of emotion,
Brontes, Steropes, Arges, stubborn, determined of spirit,
forgers of thunder for Zeus and makers of bolts of his lightning.
For the most part, they resembled in features the other immortals,
but each had only one eye, in the middle part of his forehead.
Violence, power, and shrewdness attended each of their actions.
Still other children were born to Uranus, bedded with Gaea:
three huge powerful beings, whose names can scarcely be spoken,
Cottus, Briareus, Gyes, offspring of terrible power.
A hundred terrible arms hung down from their muscular shoulders,
and fifty heads surmounted their mighty necks and their limbs.
Invincible terrible power glared out from each of the monsters.
Of all the children descended from Uranus, husband of Gaea,
these their father most hated, from the very day of their birth.

Hesiod, *Theogony,* 139–155

Unlike the famous shepherd Cyclops Polyphemus, son of Poseidon, who imprisoned Odysseus in his cave, Hesiod's Cyclopes combined the wisdom of the metallurgist with great strength. They were the clever smiths of the gods. Taking raw iron from the depths of earth, their mother, they made the irresistible weapon of victory: lightning. Their names Brontes, "thunderer"; Steropes, "flasher"; and Arges, "brightener" reflect the noise and brilliance of their marvelous weapon.

Finally, Uranus and Gaea bore the three Hecatonchires, who each had one-hundred arms that shot from his shoulders, as well as 50 heads, beings who can easily crush any opponent in their mighty hands.

## MYTH: CRONUS AGAINST URANUS

Although Uranus and Gaea bore many children, none could come forth into the light, for Uranus/Sky hated his own offspring:

As soon as each child was conceived, Uranus kept it well hidden,
refusing it access to light, deep in the womb of the earth,
and gloated over his action, while Gaea groaned in her travail.
But she planned a treacherous scheme. First inventing gray steel°
(till that day unknown), she fashioned a terrible sickle.

She told her children the plan, hoping to stiffen their courage,
though sorely disturbed herself: "O children, you whom I bore
to a wicked and terrible father, if you will only support me,
we can avenge the shame and disgrace he has loaded upon you.
For he it was who first devised such hideous actions."

At that fear silenced them all. Nobody dared give an answer,
till the wily Cronus bravely replied to the lady his mother.

°*steel:* the sickle is said to be *adamantine,* "invincible," a mythical hard substance often translated "steel," which it probably was not. The word is the source of our *diamond.*

"Mother, I am quite ready to carry through with this matter,
for I scorn our accursed father, who plotted such terrible things."

So he spoke, and the heart of Gaea leaped up in delight.
She hid him, couched in an ambush, and into his hands she delivered
the sickle, toothed like a saw. Her plot worked out as she planned it.
When Uranus came to her presence, bringing with him the darkness,
and, panting with lust, embraced the mighty body of Gaea,
from ambush Cronus' left hand seized the genital parts of his father.
He reached out his right with the sickle, saw-toothed, deadly, and sharp.
Like a reaper, he sliced away the genitals of his own father,
flinging them over his shoulder, to roll wherever chance sent them.
But they did not fly from his hand down to the earth, ineffective,
for Gaea absorbed the gory drops that rained down upon her,
and after a year had passed she bore the frightful Erinyes,
the Giants gleaming in armor, holding long spears in their hands,
and the Melian Nymphs, whom mortals reverence all the world over.

Hesiod, *Theogony*, 156–187

Although Hesiod speaks of Uranus "bringing with him the darkness and panting with lust," the meaning of the story depends on an image of Uranus/Sky and Gaea/Earth locked as a unity in perpetual intercourse. Uranus/Sky lay constantly across Gaea/Earth, fecundating her but never allowing his children to emerge from the mother's body. There is no space where the activity of the world can take place. By slicing away his genitals, Cronus broke away Sky, allowing him to rise to the place where he belongs.

A provisional separation of the two primal elements is now made permanent. The world has reached its proper configuration, Sky above and Earth beneath, with Tartarus attached somewhere below. All around flows Oceanus, the primordial water.

But the permanent separation of the first elements is bought at the high cost of deceit and violence of son against father. Uranus/Sky mightily cursed his treacherous son Cronus. Fecundated by the drops of blood that fell from the ghastly wound of Uranus/Sky, Earth gave birth to the Erinyes (e-**rin**-i-ēz), the Furies, ferocious female spirits who haunt anyone who violates oaths or sheds kindred blood, driving them into madness (Chart 5.1). The Erinyes are especially malignant because kindred blood is, in a sense, one's own. From other drops of the bloody gore sprang up the **Giants**, "earthborn ones," beings of enormous strength and unbridled violence, who one day will bring their power to bear against Zeus and his Olympian brothers and sisters.

## The Birth of Aphrodite, Monsters, and Sea Deities

Hesiod goes on to describe the birth of Aphrodite, Greek equivalent to the Mesopotamian Inanna/Ishtar/Astartê (the name *Aphrodite* seems somehow to derive from that of the Eastern goddess):

As for the genitals, slashed away by the sickle of steel,
their impetus carried them out from shore to the tide of the sea.
For years the waters swirled them about, as white foam kept oozing

from out the immortal flesh. Within it there grew up a maiden
who drifted first to holy Cythera,° then on to Cyprus.
There she emerged from the sea as a modest and beautiful goddess
around whose slim-ankled feet arose all the flowers of springtime.
Gods and mortals alike call her *Aphro*dite, the *Foam*born,
or else Cytherea, to honor the island where first she was seen.
Eros walked by her side, and fair Desire came after
as she joined the race of the gods. These are the honors she holds:
the giggling whispers of girls, the smiling deceptions they practice,
as well as the honeyed delights and all the allurements of passion.

Hesiod, *Theogony,* 188–206

°*Cythera*: an island off the southeastern coast of the Peloponnesus where there was an early temple to Aphrodite.

The blood fell on the earth, but the genitals themselves fell into the sea. The sea foam, mixed with semen, sloshed around them until from the "foam" (Greek *aphros*) appeared a being of dreadful power, Aphrodite, goddess of sexual love (Figure 5.2).

Born from the bloody genitals of a cosmic deity, Aphrodite represents the universal force of irresistible sexual desire, a fruit of mutilation and violence. The destructive power of sexual attraction is a central theme in Greek myth, as in the story of the Trojan War where the passion of Helen and Paris caused the deaths of thousands.

**FIGURE 5.2**  Birth of Aphrodite, from the Ludovisi Throne, a Greek relief probably from southern Italy, c. 460 BC. The women raising up Aphrodite are probably the Seasons (Horae). (Museo Nazionale Romano. (Photo by Author))

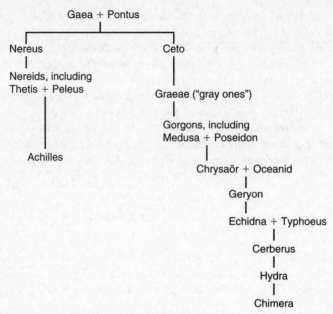

**CHART 5.3**  Offspring of Gaea and Pontus.

The Titans, the Cyclopes, and the Hecatonchires were born of Gaea's union with her son Uranus, but she also had sexual relations with Pontus ("sea"), another of her sons. From this union came a host of other offspring, most of whom have little importance in later myth or make only a brief appearance in heroic legend (Chart 5.3).

Some are notable for their monstrous shape or, like the sea that begot them, are changeable in appearance. The Greeks invented their own ways to portray monsters in their art, although they preserved the Near Eastern practice of combining parts from different creatures or simply reduplicating normal parts. The Gorgons had a woman's body to which wings were attached, snakes instead of hair, and boar's tusks for teeth. Geryon (**jer**-i-on), an enemy of Heracles, had three bodies joined at the waist; his dog Orthus had two heads. **Cerberus** was a 50-headed (or 3-headed) hound who guarded the gates of Hades' realm (Figure 5.3).

The water-serpent Hydra, "watery," sometimes had seven heads. Echidna was an ordinary woman from the buttocks up, but a serpent below, "a glimmering flesh-eater in the inky caverns of hallowed earth," as Hesiod puts it. Most bizarre was the Chimera (ki-**mē**-ra), "she-goat," a lion with a snake's tail and a goat's head growing from its back (Figure 5.4).

The shapes of the descendants of Gaea and Pontus could also be drawn from nature, although they possessed extraordinary powers. Ceto (**sē**-to), "sea monster," was a whale or enormous fish. The Graeae (**grē**-ē), "gray ones," were "fair-cheeked hags, gray from birth," as Hesiod describes them. Nereus (**nē**-rūs) was the wise Old Man of the Sea, a prophetic deity, as are many sea-gods. Ordinarily he had a human shape, but he could also change his shape at will into fire, a leopard, a serpent, or a tree. He

**FIGURE 5.3** Heracles captures a two-headed Cerberus. Heracles wears his lion-skin cap and carries a sword and quiver. He has leaned his club against a tree and holds a chain in his left hand with which to bind the beast. The column indicates that this is the entrance to the House of Hades. Behind Heracles stands Athena wearing a helmet and the snake-fringed aegis and carrying a spear. Snakes protrude from Cerberus' head and his tail is a snake. Athenian water jug, c. 480 BC. (Musée du Louvre; The Art Gallery Collection / Alamy)

sired the 52 Nereids (nē-re-idz), a group of sea-spirits hard to distinguish from their cousins the Oceanids but far fewer in number (the suffix -*id* means "daughter" or "descendant"). The Nereids live at the bottom of the sea seated on golden thrones and embody the lovely, gentle aspect of the sea. The best-known Nereid was Thetis (**thē**-tis), mother of Achilles. Like her father, Thetis could change her shape at will.

**FIGURE 5.4** The Chimera of Arezzo, 400–350 BC, of Etruscan manufacture. (Museo Archeologico, Florence. (Photo by Author))

# MYTH: THE WAR AGAINST THE TITANS

Hesiod tells how Uranus tyrannized Gaea with his sexual demands, smothering her and keeping her and all else down. With the overthrow of Uranus/Sky, Cronus became the first king of the world. He ruled over a complex realm filled with many new beings. He had to be underhanded, violent, and suspicious to maintain his power. Told by his parents that he would fall victim to one of his children, Cronus feared his children and swallowed them as fast as they issued forth from his wife and sister, Rhea. These children were Hestia, Demeter, Hera, Hades, Poseidon, and Zeus, six gods who would one day divide the power of the world among themselves:

> Rhea, submitting to Cronus, bore to him wonderful children:
> Hestia, gold-sandaled Hera, Demeter, and Hades the mighty, implacable,
> him whose dwelling is under the earth in the darkness;
> Poseidon, thundering shaker of earth, and Zeus the wiliest schemer,
> father of gods and men, whose thunder shatters the cosmos.
> Each of them Cronus devoured as they came from the holy womb
> to the knees of Rhea. All this, lest she bear him a lordly successor,
> to hold high honor and rule in heaven among the immortals.
> For his fate, as starry Uranus told him, and Gaea, his mother,
> was one day to fall from his throne, displaced by one of his children,
> in spite of the power he held, through the plottings of great Zeus.
> He therefore kept vigilant watch, and lay in wait to devour
> each of his children at birth. Rhea mourned, but she never forgot.

> Hesiod, *Theogony*, 453–467

Rhea went to her parents, Gaea and Uranus, for advice. They instructed her to journey to Crete and there to bear her youngest child, Zeus. This she did, then hid him in a mountain cave, where he was brought up by nymphs on milk from the goat Amalthea (am-al-**thē**-a) and honey from Melissa, the "bee." His infant cries were drowned by the clashing cymbals of the Corybantes (kor-i-**ban**-tēz), perhaps "whirlers." When Cronus asked for the latest child, she gave him a stone wrapped in swaddling clothes. Stupid Cronus gulped it down. In this way Zeus was saved and grew into manhood.

## PERSPECTIVE 5

### Goya's Saturn Devouring his Children

Francisco de Goya (1746–1828), a Spanish artist of eccentric vision, stood apart from his contemporaries in his perception of demonic forces and the terrors of the human experience. Late in life, suffering from deafness, witness to many horrors, he retired to his house and covered the walls with nightmarish devil-worshipers, subhuman monsters, and other haunting images, including a representation of Saturn devouring his children (Perspective Figure 5).

**PERSPECTIVE FIGURE 5**  Francisco de Goya (1746–1828), Saturn Devouring His Children (detail), 1819–1823; oil on plaster transferred to canvas. (Museo del Prado, Madrid; Masterpics / Alamy)

Saturn ("the sower"), an Italian spirit of the harvest, appears in Latin authors as the ruler of Italy in the Golden Age, but also as a cynical old man (giving us the English word *saturnine*, "gloomy"). He was the Latin equivalent of "crooked-counseling Cronus," whom Greek intellectuals equated with Chronos ("time"). In this way, the myth of Cronus eating his children could be explained as an allegory for "time devours all things." The scythe of our Father Time, hence of a popular representation of Death, is the sickle whereby Cronus (= Chronos) severed his father's genitals.

Hesiod tells us that Cronus swallowed his children whole, as if in one gulp, but Goya heightens the horror through an exaggerated fantasy of Saturn as a ghastly cannibal giant, chomping up one child—male or female, we cannot tell—bit by bit. Even so does ravenous, unforgiving Time destroy all in its bloody, grinding jaws: Even so do the demonic forces in human nature, reflecting savage nature itself, destroy all that is childlike and innocent.

Hesiod is strangely silent about what happened next, noting only that Zeus eventually forced Cronus to vomit up the children, Zeus's brothers and sisters. Later sources say that the Oceanid Metis, "cleverness," gave Cronus an emetic potion and that Cronus vomited out the children in reverse order to his swallowing them. The stone came out too and was later displayed for all to see in Apollo's shrine at Delphi (see Map 5). Conical and decorated, this stone was called the *omphalos*, "navel." Oil was poured on it every day, and unspun wool decked it during festivals.

Now Zeus became king of the gods, and he and his brothers and sisters took up their abode on Mount Olympus (except for Hades, who ruled the underworld). But the Titans resented their rule. They banded together and attacked the Olympians in the stupendous **Titanomachy**(tī-tan-o-ma-kē), "battle of the Titans" (*machê* in Greek means "battle"). Only the Titan Themis and her son Prometheus (prō-mē-thūs) dared side with Zeus in the gruesome conflict:

> For a long time the Titans and the other gods sprung of Cronus
> savagely battled each other. The lordly Titans came charging
> down from the heights of Othrys;° the gods, bestowers of blessings,
> whom fair-haired Rhea had borne, bedding in union with Cronus,
> counterattacked from Olympus.° For ten full years did they battle,
> no rest, no truce in the strife, no victory crowning their efforts.

Hesiod, Theogony, 629–638

°*Othrys*: a mountain south of the plain of Thessaly, in northern Greece. °*Olympus*: north of the Thessalian plain.

Zeus learned from Gaea that he could win the battle only with the help of the three Hecatonchires, the Hundred-handers. He released them and the Cyclopes from Tartarus where Uranus, fearing their power, had imprisoned them. Weakened from long confinement, the Hecatonchires partook of a mythical drink called *nectar* (perhaps meaning "that which overcomes death") and an equally mythical food known as *ambrosia* ("deathless stuff") and soon regained strength. In gratitude, the Cyclopes, wonderful smiths, made for Zeus the thunderbolt, his special weapon:

> On that very day the immortals began their terrible contest,
> male and female, the Titans and those descended from Cronus,
> and those whom Zeus had freed from Erebus,° deep in the darkness,
> back to the light of day. A hundred hands, strong and brawny,
> grew from the shoulders of each, with fifty heads in the middle.
>
> Forward they marched to war with the Titans, giving no quarter,
> each one brandishing broken-off fragments of cliff as his missiles.
> Against them advanced the Titans, each one urging his fellows,
> each side eagerly vaunting the strength and skill of its ranks.
> The mighty sea howled around, and the earth resounded beneath them.

°*Erebus*: "darkness," used here for Tartarus.

Broad heaven trembled above, and the roots of Olympus were shaken
by the clash of immortals, resounding louder than echoing thunder,
as far as windy Tartarus—rushing of feet as they hurried,
screaming darts in their flight, shouting cries as they rallied.
All this rang to the stars as the two sides clashed with each other.

Now Zeus no longer held back his might. From now on his spirit
seethed in his rage as he showed the full extent of his power.
Down from the heaven he rushed, from the highest peak of Olympus,
hurling in endless showers the flashing bolts of his lightning.
Forth from his mighty hand flashed glare commingled with thunder,
ceasing for never a moment. Earth, giver of life, could but cower,
tormented and scorched by her burns. Great forests choked in the fire,
as the water of earth boiled off, and the surging tides of the ocean,
even the harvestless sea. The fiery blast soared on upward
to the quiet expanse of the heaven, and down to the arrogant Titans,
shriveling sight from their eyes.

Hesiod, *Theogony,* 666–698

The tide of battle turned. Helped by the three Hecatonchires (Hesiod names
them), Zeus cast the Titans into black distant Tartarus:

Leading the bitter struggle were Cottus, Briareus, Gyes,
lusting for battle, each hurling a good three-hundred terrible boulders
in fire so rapid the stones quite overshadowed the Titans.
Some they hurled to their ruin, down under the wide-wayed earth
as far underground as earth itself is lower than heaven,
where they bound them in biting chains, curbing their arrogant spirit.
Drop an anvil from heaven; it falls nine days and nine nights,
reaching the earth on the tenth. Just so a great brazen anvil,
if dropped from the earth, for an equal time would go hurtling downward,
and would land at last on the tenth day, deep in Tartarus' depths.

Round Tartarus runs a wall of brass, at whose narrowest portion
threefold night gushes out. Below are the roots of the earth,
and those of unharvested sea. Within it the Titans are buried
by design of Zeus who assembles the clouds. No way of escape
lies open, for mighty Poseidon set gates of bronze, and around them
the wall hems them in on both sides. There Cottus, Briareus, Gyes,
mighty of heart, all dwell,° strong henchmen of Zeus of the aegis.

Hesiod, *Theogony,* 713–729

°*all dwell*: as jailers.

Atlas, either a Titan (a son of Uranus) or a Giant (son of an Oceanid), was
condemned by Zeus to live at the edge of the world, where he held up the heavens,
ensuring the continued separation of Sky and Earth (Figure 5.5).

**FIGURE 5.5**   Atlas supporting the world, with Prometheus tied to a stake, his liver devoured by Zeus's eagle because he gave fire to man. Black-figure drinking cup from Sparta, c. 550 BC. (Museo Gregoriano Etrusco, Vatican Museums; INTERFOTO / Alamy)

Later, Atlas was equated with a mountain range in Morocco near the Atlantic Ocean (the origin of its name) and gave his name to the fanciful continent Atlantis, said by Plato to lie in the far west beyond the Pillars of Heracles—the hills of Gibraltar on one side and of Ceuta in Morocco on the other.

## MYTH: THE WAR AGAINST TYPHOEUS

But Zeus's struggles were not ended. Gaea, who had advised Zeus to summon the Hecatonchires in his struggle against her own children the Titans, for some reason now resented Zeus's victory. She became his greatest enemy. Coupling with Tartarus, she gave birth to the monstrous **Typhoeus** (tī-fḗ-ūs), also called Typhon (**tī**-fon) (Chart 5.1):

> When Zeus had driven the Titans out of the sky into exile,
> mighty Gaea gave birth to the last of her children, Typhoeus,
> born of Tartarus' lust and the wiles of gold-haired Aphrodite.
>
> Typhoeus had muscular arms, fit for laborious action,
> and the tireless feet of a god of might. Surmounting his shoulders
> sprouted the hundred heads of a terrible serpentine dragon,
> flicking their dark livid tongues. The eyes of each sinister forehead

spat out a jet of flame from under its shadowing eyebrows,
and each indescribable mouth had a voice of ineffable volume,
uttering words only gods can know: now the arrogant cry of a bull,
a lordly bellow of strength, now the terrible roar of a lion,
shameless and angry. Again, the eager bark of the mastiff,
or the hunter's echoing whistle that makes the mountains resound.

No defense could be found, from the day of birth of the monster,
and Typhoeus would soon have been despot alike of gods and of humans,
had not the wit of the father of mortal men and immortals
seen through the threat and sounded his irresistible thunder.
All earth quaked at the sound, and the wide-flung arches of heaven,
the springs of Ocean, the seas, and the gloomy depths of the earth.
Under the thundering tread of its monarch marching to battle,
huge Olympus was shaken, and all earth trembled and whimpered.
The purple face of the sea was seared by the flames of both rulers,
by Zeus's thunder and lightning, by fire that flashed from Typhoeus:
the lightning bolts of the one, the scorching winds of the other.

All earth boiled, and all heaven. The sea surged over its headlands,
its crashing waves driven up and around by the blast of the powers.
Uncontrollable shaking seized all the earth and the heavens,
and even Hades, the lord of the lifeless shades, shook in terror,
and the Titans, buried in Tartarus, huddled together with Cronus.

Now Zeus kindled his rage and eagerly snatched up his missiles,
thunder and lightning and fire from heaven, crashing and blazing.
He bounded forward and shot from the lofty top of Olympus.
The fiery blast ignited the marvelous heads of the monster.
Typhoeus, scourged and shattered by Zeus's terrible weapons,
hamstrung, sank to his knees as the mighty earth groaned in despair.
From the fall of the stricken ruler, blasted by heavenly lightning,
flames leaped out like those in the woods of rugged Mount Etna,°
when it too is struck. For miles the whole great earth was enkindled
by the blast of heavenly wind. It melted like wax in a ladle
worked by a brawny-armed smith, or iron, toughest of metals,
smelted in mountain forests and worked in the heat of a forge.
Just so the earth was melted in the white-hot gleam of the fire.

Hesiod, *Theogony*, 820–867

°*Etna*: in Sicily.

The three male gods, Zeus, Hades, and Poseidon, now cast lots to divide the world between them. Zeus took the heaven, Poseidon the gray sea, and Hades the dark mist at the world's end. But the earth and the heights of Olympus were common to all.

## OBSERVATIONS: PROMINENT THEMES IN HESIOD'S STORIES OF THE EARLY DAYS

The Greek story of the creation of the world and of the gods as told by Hesiod is a good example of *divine myth*. Its subject is the actions of gods and the description of grand events and their consequences. Yet the narrative patterns underlying the story owe much to *folktale*, as does the myth of Marduk and Tiamat. Here gods act as ogres (Uranus, Cronus) and tricksters (Cronus, Zeus); goddesses behave as sexual victims (Gaea, Rhea), as dangerous enemies (Gaea), and as beneficent protectors (Gaea, Rhea). Typhoeus is a dragon; Zeus is his enemy. Vicious family conflict drives the action: Wife plots against husband (Gaea against Uranus), son against father (Cronus against Uranus, Zeus against Cronus), and father against children (Uranus against the Titans, Cronus against the Olympians). Ancient traditional material of Eastern origin has been remodeled to make an exciting tale that answers the question, "How did Zeus come to rule the world?"

The universe portrayed by Hesiod is no static creation, spoken into existence by God once and for all, but comes from successive growth and change, from progressive proliferation and differentiation away from original unity. First was Chaos/Chasm, from which emerged Night and Darkness, primal entities that generate their opposites, Day and Radiance. Then came Gaea/Earth, the first really animate being, female in nature, who nonetheless gave birth without sexual intercourse to Pontus/Sea and Uranus/Sky. But Eros/Love propelled the expanding creation, and later Gaea/Earth had intercourse with her own children. Henceforth, with few exceptions, reproduction is by sexual means.

The Greek cosmogony/theogony is a tale of the gradual ascent to power of male over female. In the beginning was the female Gaea/Earth, mother of all; in the end the male Zeus rules the universe. At the beginning of the evolutionary development, Gaea produced children asexually; at the end, Zeus does the same according to a story that Athena sprang fully armed from Zeus's head. For the Greeks it seemed natural to suppose that an orderly universe, like an orderly household or city, would be ruled by a clever and powerful male. This was the social ideal. But the power of Gaea/Earth can never be removed completely. She is the ultimate base on which depends the whole world. In the cycle of Greek creation myths, the motifs of separation, succession, and dragon-combat familiar to us from the ancient East are ingeniously melded to tell the story of the fashioning of the ordered and diverse world from the disordered and homogeneous one that preceded it.

In both the *Enuma elish* and Hesiod's *Theogony*, the first generation of gods is made up of primal pairs: Apsu, the male fresh waters, and Tiamat, the female salt waters, and Uranus and Gaea. The fathers Apsu and Uranus hate the first children, who are begotten within the mother. In an initial round of conflict the clever sons Ea and Cronus overthrow their fathers. In a second round of conflict, gods of the third generation—Marduk and the storm-god Zeus—revolt against an earlier divine generation. Terrible monsters are overcome: Tiamat and her army in *Enuma elish*; the Titans, Typhoeus, and the Giants (which we have not discussed), all children of Gaea, in the Greek story. The storm-god is then made king. Mesopotamian and Greek myths alike report a cosmic history that begins with mighty powers of nature and ends in the organization of the universe as a monarchic, patriarchal state.

Similarities between the Hittite (Perspective 4) and Greek myths are equally striking. According to the Hittite "Kingship in Heaven," first a primordial god (Alalush) was ruler; then the sky-god (Anush) ruled; then another god (Kumarbi); and then, probably, the storm-god (Teshub). The same sequence of generations appears in Hesiod: First came Chaos (= Alalush?), then Uranus/Sky (= Anush), then Cronus (= Kumarbi), then the storm-god Zeus (= Teshub). Both Anu ("sky") and Uranus ("sky") were castrated by their sons, and gods were born from the severed organs.

As long as heaven and earth are locked in sexual embrace, forming a solid whole, there is no space within which the created world can appear. Castration was a real practice imposed on enemies taken in war, but in the logic of the myth castration is separation, and separation is creation. Both Kumarbi and Cronus have children within themselves. The children of each, Teshub and Zeus, both storm-gods, overcome their fathers to win victory in heaven.

There are differences in detail and profound differences in tone between the Near Eastern and the Greek stories. The writing systems of the Mesopotamians and Hittites, unlike the Greek alphabet, were unable to record the suppleness and color of spoken language. Nonetheless, striking similarities prove that the myth is Eastern in origin. The Canaanite tradition, too, reports the conflict between younger and older gods and the ultimate triumph of the storm-god, Baal (but we should note that the Egyptian myth of Osiris avoids this pattern: There the conflict is between brothers). The Greek cosmogonic traditions are old and have been passed across linguistic, cultural, and racial lines. Greek cosmogonic myth partly reflects the Greeks' own attitudes, but its basic structure, and many of its cultural assumptions, come from nonGreek peoples.

## MYTH: ODYSSEUS IN THE CAVE OF POLYPHEMUS

Hesiod's story is *divine myth*, but by far the most famous event in the body of Greek *legend* is the Trojan War, about which many stories were told. The war was waged by a mainland coalition of warriors against the city of TROY at the entrance to the DARDANELLES, a strait that leads first to the SEA OF MARMORA, then through the Bosporus into the BLACK SEA. Troy was a mighty city defended by powerful walls.

The war began when Helen, married to a mainland prince named Menelaus, ran off with Paris, a prince of Troy. Helen was the most beautiful woman in the world, begotten by Zeus in the form of a swan on Helen's mother Leda (Figure 5.6). Menelaus launched a military campaign, together with his brother Agamemnon, to recover Helen from Troy.

Homer's very long *Iliad* (about 16,000 lines) recounts events in several weeks of the 10th year of the war. The protagonist is Achilles, the greatest fighter on the Greek side, who quarrels with Agamemnon about a girl taken as booty. At the end of the *Iliad* Achilles is still alive (but soon to be killed), while Hector, the greatest Trojan fighter, is dead.

After the city fell, the heroes returned home. One of the greatest Trojan fighters, Odysseus, ran into a lot of trouble in his journey home. Only after 20 years did he return to his home on Ithaca, as reported in Homer's long *Odyssey* (about 12,000 lines). There he found his son's life threatened, his father living like a pauper, and his wife besieged in their house by lascivious, greedy, and politically ambitious men.

**FIGURE 5.6**  Leda and the Swan, fresco from a house in Herculaneum, c. AD 50. She is naked except for a cloak and holds the swan by the neck. The swan claws at her genitals while kissing her on the chin. (Museo Archeologico Nazionale, Naples; Sites & Photos / Alamy

Without allies, except experience and high intelligence, Odysseus appeared in disguise among his wife's suitors and, on a feast day of Apollo, killed them all in cold blood. Of this wonderfully gory story of revenge Homer made a parable of the human journey from life into death and return again to life. The Canaanite Myth of Baal told of such a resurrection too, but the *Odyssey* tells its tale of rebirth completely through symbolic means.

Odysseus recounts the story of his adventures while dining on the island of Scheria, somewhere in the west (the classical Greeks thought it was Corfu). The inhabitants of Scheria live in a storybook world somewhere at the fringes of the real world. In the course of his narrative, he tells of his imprisonment by the dangerous monster **Polyphemus**, a Cyclops (but unlike Hesiod's Cyclopes, this one is no smith). This story, one of the most famous stories in the world, may have had an independent

The judgment of the dead from the *Book of the Dead of Ani,* from Thebes, Egypt, 19th Dynasty, c. 1275 BC. (British Museum, London; The Trustees of The British Museum / University of Wisconsin Photo Archive)

The goddess Hathor/Isis leads Queen Nefertari by the hand, 19th Dynasty, c. 1290–c. 1220 BC. Nefertari wears a vulture crown surmounted by a sun-disk and two feathers. On Hathor's back dangles a *menat,* a female sexual symbol and necklace counterweight. Hathor is crowned by a cow's horns (her power to nourish is like that of a cow) embracing a solar disk (her power is like that of sun), from which is suspended a uraeus serpent. She carries a *was* scepter (*was* = "power"). Her iconography is that of Hathor, but the inscription in front of her face identifies her as Isis: The two goddesses can embody the same feminine power. (Tomb of Nefertari, Valley of the Queens, Thebes, Egypt; Photo by author)

A blue four-armed Vishnu asleep on Ananta, the serpent of eternity/chaos, c. 1870. (Victoria and Albert Museum, London; V&A Images, London / Art Resource, NY)

Goddess Devi (or Durga) the buffalo-demon. From the clouds celestial beings watch the event. In her eight arms she holds: a sword, a shield, a noose, a goad, a bow, a bell, a mace, and a spear. Her head is crowned with lotuses. She rides on her tiger that attacks the demon. The head of the demon, emerging from the neck of the buffalo, has been pierced by two arrows. The demon carries a sword a shield. The decapitated head of the buffalo lies at his feet. Watercolor, c. 1730. (http://upload.wikimedia.org/wikipedia/commons/f/f5/Durga_Mahisasuramardini.JPG)

Rostam battles his son Sohrab in a page from an illustrated 15th century manuscript of the *Shahnameh*. Rostam and the Iranians are on the right, Sohrab and his Turanians on the left. The men carry long swords, wear helmets, and are armed with bow and arrows. Sohrab carries a small shield. The horses are caparisoned. A man lies dead at the bottom of the hill. (British Museum, London; Photos 12 / Alamy)

Many of the symbols on this stone from Gotland from the 8th century AD seem to refer to the cult of Odin. The three interlocking triangles are known as a *valknut*, the "knot of the slain." They are adjacent to an eagle, Odin's bird, in front of a tree from which a man is hanging. Above the tree flies a figure (hard to make out, her head is to the left), probably a Valkyrie. Below the *valknut* are two men, one with a spear, who seem to place a corpse inside a burial mound, or to be sacrificing a prisoner on an altar. Behind, to the right, stand four warriors, three with shields and upraised swords led by a fourth man who holds a large bird of some kind. (Larbro, Gotland (Statens Historiska Museet, Stockholm; sacrificial_scene_on_Hammars_(I).jpg: Berig http://en.wikipedia.org/wiki/File:Sacrificial_scene_on_Hammars_(II).png));

Page from the Dresden codex, a Maya book of the 11th or 12th century of the Yucatecan Maya in CHICHEN ITZA. The Maya codex is believed to be a copy of an original text of some three- or four-hundred years earlier. It is the earliest known book written in the Americas. It is an astronomical text showing a section of a season of 260 days. Each picture is a day, its name and number given in the Maya glyphs written above the figure. From the top left: a human-headed serpent; a jaguar; an armed warrior; a god; Quetzalcoatl ferrying a woman; an eagle biting a serpent; Quetzalcoatl again, holding a war-ax; a god; a god sitting in a shrine. It is eight inches high and eleven feet long. (Royal Library at Dresden, Germany; The Print Collector / Alamy Images)

Ranginui raua ko Papatuanuku / The legend of Rangi and Papa

40ᶜ

N E W   Z E A L A N D

Carving from the front of a storehouse depicting the Maori gods, Rangi or Father Sky and Papa or Mother Earth, as a couple copulating on top of Po, or chaos. In Maori myth they were finally separated from their embrace only by the intervention of Tane, god of the forests. The children of Rangi and Papa are shown as three heads in the carving. New Zealand, Maori, 18th century, wood. Otago Museum, Dunedin, New Zealand. (Sergey Komarov-Kohl / Alamy)

Reliquary mask from Gambia made of copper inlaid with silver strips. Such masks are worn in rituals to arouse the attention of the ancestors. (The Art Archive / Alamy)

The birth of Venus, by Sandro Botticelli (1445–1510), c. 1485. (Classic Image / Alamy)

existence before Homer adapted it to the story of Odysseus, but Homer has given it an elegant narrative twist. Like the myth of Marduk and Tiamat, or Zeus and Typhon, it pits hero against ruthless monster, though now the hero is a Trojan fighter, not the creator of the world:

Forward we sailed, regretful of all we were leaving behind.
In time we came to the land of the arrogant lawless Cyclopes,
who sow no crops with their hands, nor harvest the ripened grain,
but entrust all that to heaven; so all their needs are supplied—
wheat and barley and vines which bear them wine in abundance,
fostered by Zeus's rain, without labor of seedtime or harvest.
They never unite in assembly for common decisions or laws,
but live in echoing caves on the highest peaks of the mountains,
alone, each ruling his wife and children, ignoring all others.

A little outside a harbor along the Cyclopean coastline
stretches a wooded island, a breeding place for wild goats,
untroubled by wandering humans or hunters in search of game.
No danger ever concerns them as they wander over the hillsides,
no goat pens cumber the island, no plowland limits their range.
No humans inhabit the region, unplowed and fallow forever,
unharvested through the ages, a pasture for bleating goats.
For Cyclopes know nothing of ships with red-painted gunwales.
They have no shipwrights to build vessels of well-fitted benches,
to sail to the cities of men and return with whatever they lack—
crossing the sea in their vessels in search of something to trade.

Traders, in fact, might make of the island a prosperous city,
a source of all that is good, with nothing to threaten its safety.
By the coast of the foaming sea lie rich and well-watered meadows
which, planted with grapes, would yield almost perpetual vintage.
Plowmen could easily harvest abundant crops in their season
from the island's soil, so easy to harrow, so deep and so fertile.
The harbor, moreover, is perfect; a ship has no need of an anchor
or hawsers at either end, to hold her fast in her place.
Just beach her and leave her alone, for as long a time as you want,
till the men are ready to sail and following breezes are rising.
Abundant fresh water runs from springs at the head of the harbor,
rising deep in a cave whose mouth is surrounded by poplars.

Some god was surely the pilot who guided us into the harbor,
through the dark of night, for the dawn had not begun to appear.
Deep fog enveloped the ships, no moon was shining in heaven;
clouds had covered her face. No one saw the loom of the island,
nor did we see the long crests of the breakers rolling ashore,
till our vessels had already grounded and run on the sandy beach.

We jumped out into the water, removed the gear from the vessels,
then pulled our ships to safety and clambered up on the seashore,
where we sank into deepest slumber to wait for the breaking of dawn.

Rose-fingered dawn at last revealed the coming of morning.
Gaping about in surprise, we wandered all over the island,
whose nymphs, the daughters of Zeus, the god adorned with the aegis,
roused up herds of wild goats, as breakfast for all my comrades.
From the ships we took curved bows and deeply socketed lances,
split ourselves into three groups, and then set off to the hunt.
The gods gave us wonderful luck: Nine goats were allotted to each
of the dozen ships of my fleet, and ten to me as commander.

So we spent the whole day, till the sun was setting at evening,
feasting on endless fresh meat washed down with mellow old wine.
For the wine in our ships as yet was not completely exhausted,
wine that was part of our loot from the holy Ciconian city.°
This we had poured in great jars and distributed plenty to each.
All that day we watched the land of the nearby Cyclopes,
seeing their smoke and hearing the sound of men and their flocks.
But after the sun had set and darkness come over the heavens,
we finally laid ourselves down to sleep by the edge of the water.

Rose-fingered dawn at last revealed the coming of morning.
I rose to my feet, called the men, and issued them these as orders:

"My comrades, stay here a bit, while I and the crew of my vessel
go out to spy on the natives, what sort of people they are.
Uncivilized, maybe, and savage, having no vestige of honor,
or possibly kindly to strangers, with minds inspired by heaven."
At this I climbed in my ship and ordered my comrades to follow,
to cast off the hawsers, board, and seat themselves at the oars.
Quickly they hurried aboard and took their place on the benches.
Swinging together they caught at the foaming sea with their oars.

When we got to the nearby mainland we could see the mouth of a cavern,
down by the edge of the sea, high-vaulted, shaded by laurels,
where sheep and goats liked to sleep. Its front was a sort of corral,
fashioned of rough quarried stones piled up as high as the roof,
braced by long slender firs and trunks of high-foliaged oak trees.
Inside, there slept by himself a man of incredible stature,
a hermit, watching his sheep, avoiding the rest of his fellows,
in solitude making up fantasy, dreaming his god-accursed dreams.

---

°*Ciconian city*: Odysseus and his men had earlier sacked a town in Thrace.

His frame was enormous, atrocious, unlike that of bread-eating humans;
rather, he looked like a craggy spur of a desolate mountain,
standing alone and apart, its trees all gnarled and contorted.

The rest of my loyal crew I told to remain with the vessel,
and to pull it up on the beach, while I myself with a dozen,
the best of the men, set out. With me I carried a goatskin
of wine, black, potent, and sweet, which Maron, son of Euanthes,
priest of Ismarean Apollo, gave me when we protected
him with his wife and son, out of reverence for Apollo.°
For Maron lived in a tree-studded meadow, the property of the god.
He had given magnificent gifts—seven talents of workable gold
and a bowl of the purest silver. As crown to this he included
fully a dozen double-eared jars, into which he decanted
a sweet and powerful wine, a drink to delight the immortals.
Nobody knew it existed, not even the slaves of the household;
Maron alone, his wife, and his stewardess knew of the secret.
Whenever he drank of the crimson wine with a heart sweet as honey,
he filled one cup and then added full twenty measures of water;°
at once the bowl breathed out a bouquet of heavenly fragrance,
a scent which I knew full well no man would dream of resisting.
With this I filled up a wineskin and hid it all in a knapsack,
for deep in my heart I suspected I soon would encounter a being
armed with invincible strength, but savage, barbaric, and lawless.

We quickly got to the cave, but did not find its owner within it,
for he was herding fat sheep and moving from pasture to pasture.
Into the cave we wandered and looked around in amazement:
baskets loaded with cheeses, pens crowded with kids and with lambs,
milling about, group by group, the oldest, middling, and weanlings;
containers—pans, bowls, and buckets—carefully fashioned for milking.
Uneasily then my companions began to urge me, suggesting
that we borrow a few of the cheeses, and maybe a kid or a lamb,
driving them out from the sheepfolds. Then, hurrying back to the ship,
we should depart at once and set off on the briny dark waters.
But I refused their advice (later on, how I wished I had listened!),
for I wanted to see the owner, and see what gifts he might offer.°
(In fact, when he did appear, he was not at all nice to my comrades.)

So we sat inside by a fire and nibbled bits of the cheeses,
offering some to the gods, while we waited for him to come back.
At last he returned from the pasture, with a heavy load of dry wood,

---

°*... reverence for Apollo*: when they sacked the Ciconian city in Thrace. °*water*: ordinarily
one mixed one part wine to two parts water; wine was never drunk straight. °*offer*: Odysseus
hopes to receive the gifts appropriately given as an expression of "guest-friendship" (*xenia*).

to give him light for his supper. He threw this down on the floor
inside the cave with a crash that frightened us off to a corner,
while he himself went out, to return with the ewes and the nannies,
leaving the rams and the billies corralled outside in the forecourt.
He then picked up a great rock and set it to serve as a barrier.
Twenty-two four-wheeled wagons could not shift it up from its threshold,
yet he easily moved this towering rock to block up the doorway.
Then down he sat to milk the ewes and the bleating nannies,
setting their young under each, with everything neat and in order.
Half the white milk he collected to curdle in wickerwork baskets;
the rest he poured into bowls, to take and drink for his supper.
He busied himself at his task, but when at last he was finished,
he blew up his fire, looked around, saw us, and thus he addressed us:

"Gentlemen, who might you be? From where did you cross the waters?
Are you come hither to trade, or are you wandering at random,
like pirates over the sea, cruising now this way, now that,
forever risking your lives and bringing destruction to others?"
So he inquired, and we felt our poor hearts shatter within us,
hearing his thundering voice and seeing the mass of his body.

Yet I managed to answer his question in these diplomatic words:
"We are Achaeans, returning home from our warfare at Troy.
Winds of all sorts have scattered and driven us over the surges,
some in the way they would go, but us by a far different journey.
No doubt the inscrutable mind of Zeus has determined our fortune.
Know you that we are the people of Atreus' son, Agamemnon,
whose fame is the greatest of all men living under the heaven,
for the mighty city he sacked, the many peoples he conquered.
For our part, now we have met you, we beg you for only one thing:
Grant us a kindly reception with a trifle to bid us good-bye,
the usual gift to a stranger, or show due respect to the gods.
Suppliants we kneel before you, whom Zeus, defender of strangers,
defends as fully as those to whom honor is owed to as guests."

From deep in his evil heart the Cyclops gave me his answer,
"Stranger, you really are stupid, or else live a long way off,
if you warn me to dread the gods or fear that they may be offended.
We Cyclopes pay no attention to Zeus or the other immortals,
because we are stronger by far. And if a whim should possess me,
my fear of the anger of Zeus would not save you or your friends.
But tell me, where did you moor your stout and well-founded ship,
close by, or off at a distance? I really would like to know."

His clumsy attempt to trap me did not deceive my astuteness.
I innocently gave him an answer in lying treacherous words:
"Poseidon, Shaker of Earth, has smashed my ship on a reef

as a rising wind drove her close to a point we wanted to weather.
Only these men and I survived her utter destruction."

Even this tale did not soften the flinty heart of the Cyclops.
Springing erect, he grabbed with his hands, caught two of my sailors,
and smashed them down on the rock, as you kill a superfluous puppy.
Their brains burst out from their skulls and ran all over the floor.
He twisted one limb from another (his way of preparing his supper),
and, crunching them down like a wildcat, left never a morsel uneaten,
not entrails or muscle, not even the bones and their succulent marrow.
What could we do but rage as we lifted our hands to the heavens,
while watching this horrible crime? Despair crushed all other emotion.

When the Cyclops finally ended stuffing his monstrous great belly
with swallows of human flesh, washed down with milk by the bucket,
he stretched himself out in his cave, in the very midst of the sheep.
For a moment I planned to approach, to draw the sword by my side,
to feel for the lethal spot where the diaphragm covers the liver,
and stab him under the chest. But second thought gave me pause:
We too would die in the cave and suffer a horrible ending,
for I saw no way human hands could budge his rock from the doorway.
So all night long we lay groaning and waiting for dawn to appear.

Rose-fingered dawn at last revealed the coming of morning.
The Cyclops rekindled the fire and milked his magnificent sheep,
in smooth and efficient fashion, then set each lamb to its mother.
Next, this duty completed, he grabbed two more of my comrades
to gobble them up for his breakfast. Then he easily lifted the stone,
drove his fat sheep outdoors, and put back the boulder behind them,
just as one does when replacing the lid on a quiver of arrows,
and with many a merry whistle drove off his flock to the mountains.
There I was, left to brood and to fashion a terrible vengeance,
hoping Athena would grant my prayers and an opportune moment.

This plan suggested itself to my heart as by far most effective:
the Cyclops had cut a bludgeon of olive, still pliant and green,
and left it to dry by the pens. To us it looked fully as heavy
as the mast of a twenty-oared ship, black-sided, broad in the beam,
plodding its way through the surge, heavily loaded with cargo;
such was its length to our eyes, such was its cumbersome thickness.
From this I chopped off a piece, a length fully six feet long,
and handed it on to my comrades to smooth it and taper it down.
They made the shaft of the weapon all smooth and easy to handle,
while I first pointed the tip, then hardened it well in the fire.
This done, I carefully hid it by burying it under a dungheap,
plenty of which, of course, was everywhere piled in the cavern.

Lastly, I told the men to draw lots to decide who should join me
in the perilous job of lifting and twisting the ponderous timber
around in the Cyclops' eyeball, when he drifted off to sweet dreams.
Four volunteers they chose, and I added myself to the number.

At evening he reappeared, his wooly sheep going before him.
He drove the fat creatures onward, into the depths of the cavern,
this time not leaving a one outside in the spacious forecourt;
perhaps some deity moved him, or perhaps he suspected the truth.
Once more he lifted the boulder and set it over the doorway,
then sat him down to his milking of bleating nannies and ewes
in smooth and efficient fashion, then set each lamb to its mother.
Next, this duty completed, he seized two more of my comrades
and devoured them for his supper. At last I spoke to the Cyclops,
standing beside him and holding a large bowl of strong black wine.

"Cyclops, drink up," said I, "now your cannibal orgy is over,
so you may learn what sort of drink we carried as cargo.
See, I have brought you a drop. I hope you will show me your mercy
and send me back to my home, giving up your boorish behavior,
which I really can stand no more. How can you dream for a minute
that anyone ever will come, from any nation of mortals,
if they hear the way you have acted, and the nasty way you behave?"

At that he reached for the bowl and drained it all at a gulp.
The sweet wine delighted his heart, and thus he addressed me again:
"Give me another big drink. But tell me, what is your name?
I shall certainly give you a present, one you will surely enjoy.
O yes, our land, rich in grapes, yields us Cyclopes a vintage
good in its way, and fostered by showers sent us by Zeus.
But that with which you have plied me is truly a fountain of nectar!"
So he exclaimed, and I poured him a sparkling bumper of wine.
Three times I offered him more; three times he drank in his folly.

At last, when the fumes had addled the brain and wits of the Cyclops,
I spoke to him once again with words deceitful of purpose:
"Cyclops, a moment ago you asked me to tell you my name.
I shall tell you, if you in return give me the present you promised.
'Nobody' is my name, for my dear mother and father
gave me this name at my birth, and since then all my companions."

These were my words, and this the reply of his arrogant heart:
" 'Nobody,' then, will be last, after all his friends, to be eaten.
Before him, the rest will go down. That will be my farewell gift!"°

°*farewell gift*: the gift of Cyclops parodies, by inversion, the custom of *xenia*—Odysseus's gift
will be to be eaten last!

Collapsing, he sprawled on his back, his head drooping off to one side,
and slumber, who conquers all mortals, received him into its charge.

The wine and the half-chewed flesh of humans spewed from his gullet,
vomited up by the drunkard. Then I thrust the stake in the embers,
and, while it heated, inspired the hearts of all my companions,
hoping that no one would fail me or flinch in a spasm of terror.
Green though it was, the olive-wood stake was about to catch fire
and shone with a red-hot glare. Approaching, I lifted it out.
The others stood by me to help, and some god fired their courage.

They picked up the olive-wood log, red-hot and sharp at the tip,
and swung it into his eye. Against it I threw my whole weight
and spun it around, like a shipwright drilling a hole in a timber:
He guides the drill, while his helpers, standing on either side,
saw the thong back and forth as the drill° sinks deeper and deeper.
So I and my men rotated the stake in the eye of the Cyclops.

Hissing, his blood spurted out, and the heat-singed eyelid and brow.
The eyeball, scorched to its roots, crackled and boiled in the fire.
As when a blacksmith is quenching a big bronze° adze or an ax-head,
he plunges it into cold water, which makes it sizzle and scream,
but gives the temper required, the strength and toughness of iron;
just so his eyeball squealed as the stake of olive-wood entered. [Figure 5.7]

He let out a horrible cry, which the rocky cavern reechoed,
scaring us back in terror. He plucked at the blood-smeared stake,
wrenched it out from his eye, and in torment hurled it away.
He shouted to other Cyclopes, who lived in the nearby caves
dotted about the wind-blown hillsides, to come to his rescue.

Hearing his call, they came at a run from every direction,
and standing before his cave, they asked him what was the matter:
"What troubles you so, Polyphemus, making you call us to help,
and rousing us from our slumber, so late in the god-given night?
Perhaps some rascally mortal is trying to rustle your sheep,
or is somebody bent on your murder by treachery or brute force?"

---

°*drill*: the auger described here is like a bow drill, whose forward thrust comes from the
weight of the user as he leans against it. The twist of the drill came from a long thong
wrapped in a single turn around it. Men at each end pushed and pulled so it turned, now
clockwise, now counterclockwise, like the drill of someone starting a fire by friction. But the
simile is somewhat mixed: How could Odysseus both guide the stake and twist it, especially
if its weight was carried by four other men? °*bronze*: when Homer was composing, iron was
replacing bronze, so the smith is said to quench a bronze ax that gives "the strength and
toughness of iron."

**FIGURE 5.7** The blinding of Polyphemus, fragment of an early Argive wine-mixing bowl, c. 650 BC. In art he is often shown with three eyes, one in the middle of his forehead, which may be the case here. (Archaeological Museum, Argos, Greece; INTERFOTO / Alamy)

The mighty Polyphemus replied from the mouth of his cave:
"*Nobody* wants to kill me by treachery, not by brute force."
To this the others replied in words aimed right at the mark:
"If nobody's using force on a man alone and defenseless,
you must have an inescapable sickness, sent by great Zeus.
The best thing for you to do is to pray to your father Poseidon."
With this retort they departed. I laughed in my inmost heart,
gloating over my shrewdness, and seeing them tricked by my name.

The Cyclops groaned in his pain and suffered spasms of torture.
Groping about with his hands, he lifted the rock from the doorway,
meanwhile feeling around, as he sat him there at the entrance,
expecting to catch whoever might try to get out with the sheep,
and even hoping that I might be foolish enough to attempt it.
But I was pondering deeply, to make things turn out for the best,
and to find some way to avoid disaster for me and my comrades.
In this matter of life and death, in the face of imminent peril,
this was the method that seemed the best of all possible courses:
The cave held plenty of well-fed rams with thick shaggy fleeces
(big ones, handsome, all covered with heavy dark-colored wool),
which I quietly tied in threes with pliant shoots of the willow
where the monster Cyclops slept, planning his criminal horrors.
The rams in the middle each carried a man; the two on the outside
trotted along beside them, and thus protected my comrades.
So three rams carried each man, but I myself was left over,

as also the noblest ram of the flock enclosed in the sheepfold.
Approaching the beast from behind and stretching under its belly,
I lay there, my hands holding tight to the animal's glorious wool.
So we lay in discomfort and awaited the light of the dawning.

Rose-fingered dawn at last revealed the coming of morning.
The Cyclops drove all the males of the flock away to the pasture,
but the unmilked females remained, with udders swollen to bursting,
bleating in pain, in the cave. Tormented by horrible anguish,
their owner felt the back of each ram as it went out to pasture—
dumbo! He never suspected my men were lashed under their bellies.
Last of all the bellwether approached and was nearing the doorway,
slowed by the weight of his wool and of me, a man of resources.

Gently caressing its back, the mighty Polyphemus addressed it:
"My good old ram, how is it that you are last of my flock
to hurry out of the cavern? The others have never outstripped you,
as you proudly galloped along, the first to taste of the grasses,
to get to the stream, and to hurry home to the fold in the evening.
But today you are last of all. Is it grief for your master's eye,
which Nobody blinded, the scoundrel, he and his evil companions,
after getting me drunk? But I tell you, he hasn't yet gotten away
from the death he deserves. How I wish that you could stand here beside me
and tell me in human speech how he managed to duck from my power!
I'd smash him down on the floor, his brains would spatter all over
in every part of the cave! And that would lighten the burden
of all the sorrow I feel, which that no-good Nobody caused me."

With this he dismissed the ram to go free from the door and away.
As soon as the ram and I were far enough from the doorway,
I freed my hands from the wool, and undid the bonds of my comrades.
Turning the fat and shambling sheep away from their pasture,
we drove them back to the ship and were greeted with great relief—
those of us who survived. For the rest they began to lament,
but sorrow I could not allow and shook my head at each mourner.
Instead, I told them to hurry and load the heavy-wooled sheep
down in the bilge of the ship's timbers, and set sail on the billowy ocean.
At once they hurried aboard and took their place on the benches;
swinging together they caught at the foaming sea with their oars.

When we had gone as far as the sound of a man's voice will carry,
I shouted back at the Cyclops in words of taunt and abuse:
"Cyclops, your luck was bad. No coward was he, whose companions
you seized with violent hands in the hollow cave and devoured.
Your sin has found you out, your insolent treatment of strangers.

Unscrupulously you killed and ate them, right in your dwelling!
Revenge has fallen upon you from Zeus and the other immortals."

So I jeered at the Cyclops, who raged even more in his heart.
He broke off the topmost peak of a mighty mountain nearby
and flung it out at the ship. Flying over, it landed beyond us.
The cresting sea swelled up where the rock fell into its waters,
in a surge which hurtled our vessel headlong back to the shore,
a huge wave out of the deep, driving us in to destruction.
Hastily grabbing a spar, I reached it down to the bottom,
fended her off, and in silence signaled the oarsmen to heave,
to strain at the oars, if they hoped to break away from the peril.
They fell to their oars and rowed, until, by churning the sea,
we had opened a gap twice as wide as that we had earlier trusted.

Again I taunted the Cyclops, while my sailors tried to restrain me,
assailing me from all sides with clever attempts at persuasion:
"Why do you have to keep on infuriating this savage?
Just now he hurled that great rock beyond us out into the ocean,
washing us back to the shore, where we fully expected destruction.
If you had made the least sound, or if he had heard what you uttered,
he would have smashed our bodies and ships into one bloody mess
with the toss of one jagged rock at that incredible distance."
So they attempted in vain to persuade my imperious spirit.

Once more I called in an angry voice and showed my defiance:
"Cyclops, if ever a human asks how you came by your blindness,
or who it was that disfigured your eye, just give him the answer:
'Odysseus put out my eye, Odysseus, sacker of cities,
the son of Laërtes, who dwells in Ithaca, lord of its palace.'"

Hearing, he gave a great moan and sadly made this reply:
"Alas, the words of a prophet have now returned to my mind.
There once was a seer among us, a prophet wise and sagacious,
Telemus, son of Eurymus, a man who excelled at divining,
grown old among the Cyclopes, for whom he practiced his science.
Long ago he assured me I was doomed to loss of my eyesight
at the hands of a certain Odysseus. This man, I assumed, would appear
big and impressive to look at, wearing the trappings of power.
But the man who put out my eye is little, feeble, and sluggish,
who could only do what he wanted by getting me drunk on his wine.
Come back to me then, Odysseus, so I can give you a present
fitting for your departure, by persuading the Shaker of Earth
to escort you off on your way and grant you a prosperous voyage.
For I am his son, and Poseidon is proud that he is my father;
he himself, if he pleases, will escort you off on the journey,
not leaving the task to another, be it human or blessed immortal."

He tried to wheedle me so, but I quickly gave him my answer:
"I wish I were able to rob you of life and send you to Hades!
Still, even the Shaker of Earth can never restore you your vision."

So I replied. The Cyclops then prayed to lordly Poseidon,
lifting his suppliant hands to the star-studded heaven above:
"Hear my prayer, Poseidon, thou dark-haired Shaker of Earth:
if I am truly your son, if you boast of being my father,
grant that the sacker of cities, Odysseus, son of Laërtes,
whose house is in Ithaca, never again may return to his home.
But if Fate ordains that he must revisit the land of his father,
that he look on his friends again and enter his well-built palace,
grant this: May he come as a beggar, a vagrant for long weary years,
bereft of his comrades' lives, with no one left to support him;
may he come in a ship not his own, and find his household a chaos."

Such was his prayer, and the dark-haired god approved his petition.
But the Cyclops seized on a rock, far bigger in size than before,
which he whirled up over his head, and exerting incredible force,
he threw it a little behind the stern of the dark-sided vessel,
barely failing to carry to the blade of the oar of the helmsman.
The cresting sea surged up where the rock fell into its waters,
making our dark ship yaw and plunge headlong right to the island.
We made our way to the shore, where our other well-fitted ships
lay drawn up all in a group, with their worried crews sitting alongside,
always keeping a lookout and waiting till we should appear.
Arriving, we beached the vessel, and pulled her up on the sand.
We ourselves disembarked there by the side of the water,
brought the sheep of the Cyclops from out of the smooth-gliding vessel,
and divided them up so no one should leave without a fair share.
But to me as a special portion my well-armed comrades awarded
the noble ram who had brought me out of the cave of the Cyclops.
Of him I made an offering there on the shore of the ocean,
to dark-clouded Zeus, son of Cronus, ruler of all that has being,
the animal's succulent thighs.° But Zeus ignored my offering,
and schemed to destroy my well-fitted ships and trusty companions.

Homer, Odyssey, 9, 105–555

°thighs: he burned the thigh bones in the fire, as was customary in Greek sacrifice.

## OBSERVATIONS: THE MAN WHO CAME HOME

Homer's *Odyssey*, viewed as a whole, is the story of a man who came home after a long absence and many dangers, found his household in the hands of usurpers, and killed them to reestablish his ascendancy. The poem ends with sex between Odysseus and Penelope and a mock wedding celebration. The older generation—tough, smart, and wise in the need for just behavior—is triumphant over the younger generation—brash, indolent, and self-indulgent, taking what they want. But they are stupid, like the Cyclops. Because the youthful usurpers threaten traditional property rights, wishing to possess Penelope and wasting the wealth of the household, the poem appears to be a simple tale of revenge, of human justice triumphant over wrong. Not the gods' enmity but the suitors' own thoughtless behavior brings about the their destruction.

Zeus sets this powerful moral theme in the beginning of the poem when he complains that humans blame gods for their troubles, when in fact their own recklessness brings them to grief. Justice is based on restraint, on the ability to hold back and not give in to one's animal appetite. But sometimes such simple morals, typical of folktales, are contradicted by the story itself. Although Zeus explains that humans are responsible for their own troubles, Poseidon, a god, harasses Odysseus in revenge for the blinding of the Cyclops Polyphemus, where the fault seems to lie heavily on the monster's side.

But the underlying structure of the story is much older than the moral posture Homer gives it. Earlier, we noticed how the epic of Gilgamesh and Homer's *Odyssey* begin with nearly the same words. In these stories the hero goes on a journey where deadly dangers threaten, but eventually he returns. The hero must slay his dragon and resist the temptations of such females as Circe and Calypso, who promise even eternal life. Even the 108 suitors who besiege Odysseus' home are, in a realistic mode, a kind of dragon, described as voracious ("devouring his substance") and sexually threatening—they want to have intercourse with Odysseus' wife! He overcomes the beast with 108 mouths by a trick: He enters the palace in disguise, surprises the suitors in the dining hall, then even as they drink kills them with a special bow that no one else can string. As the dragon-slayer in later European folklore receives a princess as reward, Odysseus too "marries" the woman, Penelope.

In Mesopotamian cosmogonic myth and in Hesiod, such stories describe the triumph of the ordered world over the disordered, of life and progress over death and stagnation, even as a prominent theme in Homer's *Odyssey* is the hero's victory over death—so closely interwoven are myths of creation, the epic hero, and the folktale hero. Declared by all to be dead, Odysseus travels across water, the element of chaos. Water is death and its god, Poseidon, is Odysseus' relentless enemy. Even so the enemies of Baal are first Sea, then Death.

Like the Cyclops Polyphemus, death is a cannibal, devouring the living in the tomb's dark and hungry maw. Within the dark cave of the Cyclops, Odysseus is "Nobody"—nameless, without identity, nonexistent. As dragons of death are stupid, so Polyphemus is made drunk by wine, fooled by the trick of the name, then wounded by the special weapon of the pointed stake. When Odysseus escapes from the cave, passing from darkness into light, from death into life, he takes his name back and shouts to Polyphemus, "I am Odysseus!" He is victorious, and the world begins anew.

## Key Terms

Boeotia *150*
Indo-Europeans *152*
Homer *155*
Hesiod *156*
Muses *156*
cosmogony *158*
theogony *158*
Chaos *158*

Gaea *158*
Uranus *158*
Eros *159*
Titans *159*
Cyclopes *159*
Hecatonchires *159*
Cronus *160*
Oceanus *160*

Tethys *160*
Rhea *160*
Giants *162*
Cerberus *164*
Titanomachy *168*
Typhoeus *170*
Polyphemus *174*

## Further Reading

Bloom, H., ed., *Homer's The Odyssey* (New York, 1988).
Clay, J. S., *The Wrath of Athena* (Princeton, NJ, 1983).
Finley, M. I., *The World of Odysseus*, 2nd ed. (New York, 1978).
Louden, B., *The Odyssey: Structure, Narration and Meaning* (Baltimore, MD, 1999).
Malkin, I., *The Returns of Odysseus* (Berkeley, CA, 1998).
Powell, B. B., *Homer*, 2nd ed. (Oxford, UK, 2007).
Stanford, W. B., *The Ulysses Theme* (Ann Arbor, MI, 1968).
____, and J. V. Luce, *The Quest for Ulysses* (New York, 1974).

# Roman Myth

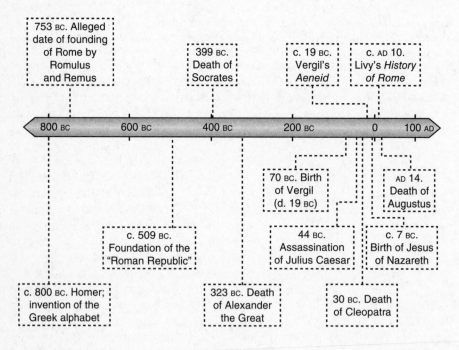

399 BC. Death of Socrates

c. 19 BC. Vergil's *Aeneid*

c. AD 10. Livy's *History of Rome*

800 BC    600 BC    400 BC    200 BC    0    100 AD

70 BC. Birth of Vergil (d. 19 BC)

AD 14. Death of Augustus

c. 509 BC. Foundation of the "Roman Republic"

44 BC. Assassination of Julius Caesar

c. 7 BC. Birth of Jesus of Nazareth

c. 800 BC. Homer; invention of the Greek alphabet

323 BC. Death of Alexander the Great

30 BC. Death of Cleopatra

Roman religious and social patterns of thought were quite different from those of the Greeks, as were their economic and political institutions, but they early on adopted the Greek alphabet and became steeped in Greece's literary culture. They had few myths of their own, and those mostly of a political flavor; therefore, they made Greek myth into Roman myth. For this reason we rightly speak of Greco-Roman culture, the direct antecedent to modern Western alphabetic culture.

In the native Roman tradition, there is no creation story and almost no divine myth. Roman myth is Roman *legend*, intimately bound up with Roman history and equated with it by the Romans themselves. Nonetheless, there is little that is truly historical in these legends. Mostly they are myths in our modern sense, propaganda designed to elicit support for social patterns, and they did prove remarkably effective in maintaining Roman power.

The Romans knew that their legends worked as propaganda but nonetheless accepted their validity, just as American educators once taught children (or still do!) that George Washington cut down a cherry tree and, because he could not tell a lie, confessed the crime to his father. Even if George Washington never did this, he *might* have done so. The moral of the story is more important than its historical truth. Roman "myth," then, looks like traditional storytelling and is modeled after Greek myth, but moral and political purposes have become paramount.

The stories of early Rome have exercised a profound influence on Western civilization and continue to do so today. Whenever one is asked to suppress one's personal interests for the common good, the wonderful deeds of early Rome take on fresh meaning. Such has always been an important function of myth: to define a culture to itself, to inform a people what is real in their world and important in their personal and social lives, and to offer bases for the difficult decisions everyone must face.

## ROMAN GEOGRAPHY AND CULTURE

When Alexander "conquered the world" in 336–323 BC, he did not conquer Italy or any other region west of the Adriatic Sea (Map 6.1). The western lands were still remote, although Greek cities had flourished in Italy and Sicily since the 8th century BC. But even in Alexander's day a small tribe of Indo-European speakers south of the TIBER RIVER, living in and near the city of Rome and possessing a superior political and military organization, had begun a course of relentless expansion without parallel in human history (Map 6.2). Controlling perhaps a few hundred square miles in the 6th century BC, by the time of Christ the Romans governed virtually the entire Mediterranean world and large territories to the north, east, and south of the Mediterranean. Greece itself became a Roman province in 146 BC, as did Asia Minor in 133 BC and Syria in 63 BC, but the Roman Period in ancient history may conveniently be dated from 30 BC, when Egypt, and the center of Hellenic culture in Alexandria, fell into Roman hands. The Western Roman Empire crumbled in the 5th century AD, but its Greek-speaking eastern part lasted until AD 1453, preserving virtually all the records we have of ancient Greece.

As Rome was in early times surrounded by hostile peoples speaking different languages, so it was isolated by geography. Greece is made up of innumerable islands, large and small, and, on the mainland, coastal pockets suited to seaborne commerce and international exchange with the extraordinary riverine cultures of the East. Italy, by contrast, is a long boot-shaped peninsula, split down the middle by the rugged APENNINE RANGE that cuts off Italy from the East.

Seas to the east and west of the Italian peninsula are noted for their sudden storms, and the whole peninsula had few good harbors, only one (at BRINDISI) on the coast facing Greece. To cross Italy from east to west, the traveler had to go over high, bandit-ridden mountains. Traffic from north to south by land was slow and dangerous until the construction of the famous Roman military roads. The first, the Appian Way, connecting Rome with the eastern port of Brindisi, was not built until 312 BC. We need not be surprised, then, that Italy remained so long on the periphery of ancient Mediterranean culture.

**MAP 6.1**    Ancient Italy.

Italy was a melting pot of diverse peoples who spoke many languages. The Romans spoke Latin, an Indo-European language, but there were many other Indo-European dialects in Italy whose speakers could scarcely understand each other. North of Rome lived the powerful and influential **Etruscans** who, like the Greeks, resided in independent city-states. The modern name of Tuscany is derived from the ancient name ETRURIA.

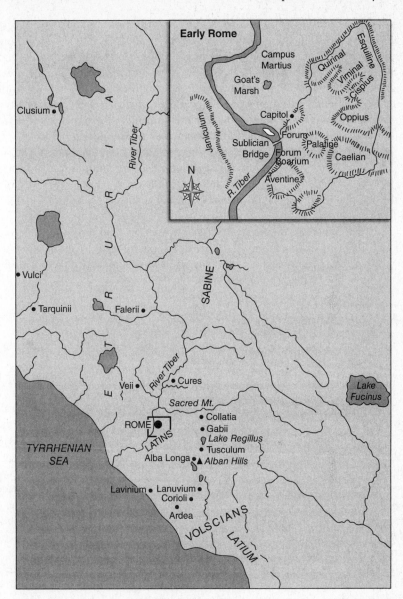

**Early Rome**

Campus Martius

Goat's Marsh

Quirinal

Esquiline

Viminal

Cispius

Janiculum

Capitol

Oppius

Forum

Palatine

Sublician Bridge

Forum Boarium

Caelian

R. Tiber

Aventine

N

River Tiber

Clusium •

E T R U R I A

Vulci •

SABINE

Tarquinii •

Falerii •

River Tiber

Veii •

• Cures

Lake Fucinus

Sacred Mt.

ROME •

• Collatia

• Gabii

Lake Regillus

LATINS

• Tusculum

TYRRHENIAN SEA

Alba Longa •

▲ Alban Hills

Lavinium •

Lanuvium •

Corioli •

Ardea •

VOLSCIANS

LATIUM

**MAP 6.2**    Rome and her neighbors.

Their origin is unknown, but some think the Etruscans emigrated from Asia Minor sometime in the 12th century BC. Although the culturally powerful Etruscans spoke a non-Indo-European tongue of unknown affiliation, they took over the Greek alphabet within decades of the alphabet's invention around 800 BC, from Greeks living near the Bay of Naples. The Etruscans gave this writing to the Romans, who gave it to us, the writing on this page. With the alphabet came the riches of Greek culture and, above all, Greek myth.

The Etruscans ruled the city of Rome during the 6th century BC, bequeathing a rich legacy to Roman society, government, and religion (although the name *Roma* appears to be Greek, meaning "strength"). The Roman gladiatorial games developed from Etruscan funeral games in which prisoners were killed in honor of the dead as a form of human sacrifice. The unique genius of the Roman people was to absorb cultural achievements from foreign peoples, especially Greek and Etruscan, and yet remain Roman. Rome's insatiable appetite for territory and resources suited its voracious appetite for cultural forms. In the 4th century AD they even took over the Christian church, of Jewish origin. Whereas other peoples made things of beauty, the Roman destiny was to rule efficiently and justly, as the Romans often explained to themselves their own historical role.

The direct ancestors of the Romans were the tribe of the *Latini* (la-tē-nē) who may have entered the Italian peninsula as early as 1500 BC and occupied the site of Rome by 1200 BC. They gave their name to LATIUM (lā-shum), the territory west of the central Apennine range and south of the Tiber as far as the fertile plain of CAMPANIA, behind the Bay of NAPLES.

Dominating Latium on the south and east rose the ALBAN HILLS, where many important Latin towns rose up in the 6th and 5th centuries BC. Among these were **ALBA LONGA**, at the western edge of the hills, and **LAVINIUM** toward the coast, which figure in stories about the early Roman state.

## ROMAN GOVERNMENT AND HISTORY

How did a small village on the Tiber become the center of one of the largest empires the world has ever known, and certainly the most successful? Many have speculated on this extraordinary and unparalleled development in human history, starting with the Romans themselves.

In its earliest days, Rome was ruled by kings. About 500 BC an alliance of wealthy land-owning Latin families, the *patricians*, "fathers," destroyed the foreign Etruscan monarchy. Thereafter the patricians met together in the Senate, "body of old men," to pass laws and decide on peace and war. Those excluded from this privileged class, the majority, were called *plebeians*, "commoners," who, especially in the 4th century BC, struggled to gain their own representation and voice in the affairs of the state, with real but limited success.

Under the *republic*, as modern historians call the period of Roman rule after the expulsion of the kings (from the Latin *res publica*, "business of the people"), elections, usually rigged, were held among the members of the ruling patrician oligarchy. There were never more than 30 or so ruling families at any time. Under the republic the legislative branch, we might say, normally held the power, whereas the weaker executive branch consisted of two *consuls*, elected annually. The power of the consuls was checked by their short term of office and the power of veto each held over the other.

A consul possessed *imperium*, the "power" to command the army and enforce the law, including imposition of the death penalty, a vestige of royal power inherited by the new ruling patrician oligarchy. The symbol of *imperium* was the *fasces*, an ax surrounded by a bundle of rods carried by bearers called lictors, who preceded the consul wherever he went. The rods were for whipping and the ax for beheading. From this word comes the modern term *fascism*, because the 20th-century Italian political leader Benito Mussolini claimed to be reconstructing the ancient Roman state (see Perspective 6).

Having set up a government controlled by small cliques belonging to a restricted social class, the patrician families fabricated legendary traditions about their ancestors to justify their monopoly of power. So successful was their form of government, wherein a self-sacrificing, idealistic oligarchy was pitched against much less efficient foreign constitutions, usually monarchical, that the rule—and the wealth—of Rome expanded enormously. The system was tested to the utmost in the 3rd and 2nd centuries BC, when Rome waged three long and bitter wars against Semitic Carthage. In the early 2nd century BC the great Carthaginian commander Hannibal led his war elephants over the Alps, destroyed army after Roman army, and camped within sight of the walls of the city. But he lost in the end. Roman victory over Hannibal became archetypal for the steadfastness and devotion to duty that leads to success, as rule by the senatorial oligarchy seemed superior to that of foreign governments.

Still the strain of expansion was too great. **Julius Caesar** (100–44 BC), a key figure in the disintegration of the republic, was in his enemies' eyes a man who placed personal ambition before the interests of the state, that is, the interests of the privileged patrician class. With brilliance and ruthless efficiency he destroyed the senatorial armies that opposed him. In defiance of Roman tradition he became sole ruler, but conspirators cut him down as he stood before the senate to speak. As he fell—Shakespeare tells the story in his play *Julius Caesar*—Caesar cried out to the assassin Marcus Brutus, his good friend, *Et tu, Brute,* "You too, Brutus?" Not so coincidentally, this same Marcus Brutus claimed descent from a legendary earlier tyrant-slayer also named Brutus, alleged founder of the patrician oligarchic republic some five hundred years before, around 500 BC.

Caesar's patrician enemies thought that his death would restore the power of the senatorial oligarchy, but Caesar's party rallied under **Marc Antony** (83–30 BC), Caesar's general, and under Caesar's grandnephew and heir, **Octavian** (63 BC–AD 14), who after 27 BC was called **Augustus**, "greater than human." Octavian and Marc Antony conquered the senatorial armies and divided the world between them, Octavian taking the West and Antony the East. Antony's infamous affair with the Macedonian queen Cleopatra of Egypt, descended from a general of Alexander the Great, and other quarrels led in 31 BC to a war between the onetime partners. Octavian was victorious in 30 BC.

The old patrician oligarchic republic now gave way to a new quasimonarchy under Augustus. Pretending that the Republic still existed, Augustus modestly called himself *princeps*, "first citizen" (the source of our *prince*) and *imperator*, "commander" (or "emperor"). Modern historians call this new monarchy the Roman empire, when *imperium* resided permanently in the hands of a single man and not with the representatives of a privileged social class. Henceforth Rome was in reality a monarchy, ruled by one man. The monarchy instituted by Octavian/Augustus was to last (in the East) until the fall of Constantinople to the Turks in AD 1453.

## ROMAN GODS EQUATED WITH GREEK

Mostly native Roman gods were bloodless abstractions, without personalities like those associated with the Eastern and Greek gods. They were called *numina*, singular **numen**, "nodders," because they possessed the power to nod in agreement or disagreement with what was proposed. It was hard to tell stories about them (Figure 6.1). When the Roman poets fell under the influence of the Greeks living in southern Italy, they began to think of these *numina* as being like the anthropomorphic gods of the Greeks. The Roman equivalents to Greek gods as named in Vergil and other poets were largely

**FIGURE 6.1** A river *numen*, marble sculpture, c. 2nd century AD. Almost everything had its indwelling spirit. This one was labeled "Marforio" evidently sometime in the medieval period, for reasons unclear. Most medieval and Renaissance paintings of the baptism of Christ have a figure representing the *numen* of the River Jordan. (Musei Capitolini, Rome, Italy; Photo by Author)

a poetic invention with little basis in native Roman religion, although there were also important political motivations, especially during the reign of Augustus (27 BC–AD 14) for establishing such identifications.

The first syllable of the name of **Jupiter** (also called **Jove**, spelled "Juppiter" in Latin), originally the *numen* of the bright sky, is etymologically identical to Zeus (see Chart 6.1).

Jupiter must descend from the common cultural, linguistic, and racial heritage shared by all speakers of Indo-European languages. Jupiter became the incarnation

| Roman | Greek |
| --- | --- |
| Jupiter | Zeus |
| Juno | Hera |
| Ceres | Demeter |
| Diana | Artemis |
| Mercury | Hermes |
| Neptune | Poseidon |
| Apollo | Apollo |
| Mars | Ares |
| Minerva | Athena |
| Faunus | Pan |
| Venus | Aphrodite |
| Vesta | Hestia |

**CHART 6.1** Roman *numina* equated with Greek gods.

**FIGURE 6.2**   The Hellenized Roman gods, marble relief from the Arch of Trajan at Beneventum (in southern Italy), AD 114–117. In the Greek anthropomorphic style, Jupiter stands in forefront with his staff and thunderbolt, which he hands to Trajan in the next panel; to his right, Minerva with her helmet; to his left, Juno dressed as a priestess with cloak pulled over her head. Jupiter, Minerva, and Juno are called the Capitoline Triad. The great temple on Capitol Hill (to Jupiter Optimus Maximus) celebrated their cult. Behind the triad, left to right: Hercules (with his club), Bacchus (with vines in his hair), Ceres (with the torch), and Mercury (with winged helmet). The sculptural style goes back to the Athenian Parthenon. (Arch of Trajan, Benevento, Italy; Photo by Author)

of the striking power of the Roman state, and his emblem, the eagle, appeared on the standards of the Roman legions. His magnificent temple sat on top of the Capitoline Hill, hence our word *capitol* (Figure 6.2).

**Juno** was the *numen* who presided over women as members of the family and was easily equated with Hera; she had close ties with the moon. Ceres, *numen* of wheat, was from an early time equated with Demeter. Diana, the Roman Artemis, shares the same Indo-European root *di-*, "shining," with Zeus, Jupiter, the Indian sky-god Dyaus, and the Norse war-god Tiu. Perhaps in origin a spirit of the wood, Diana, like Juno, was associated with women and childbirth.

**Mercury** has no ancient Italian heritage but is simply Hermes introduced to the Latins under a title suggestive of his commercial activities (*merx* is Latin for "merchandise"). **Neptune** was the *numen* of water, although not specifically the sea until identified with Poseidon. Apollo was never successfully identified with a Latin *numen*, but kept his ancient name as he came early to Latium through Etruria and the Greek colonies of southern Italy.

The origins of **Mars**, assimilated to the Greek Ares, are obscure. Closely associated with the wolf, he may once have protected flocks or been a primordial god of war (a spear kept in the Forum Romanum had the name *Mars*). He gave his name to the month of March, a good time for beginning military operations. Minerva, an Etruscan import, was *numen* of handicrafts, hence associated with the Greek Athena. Faunus (**faw**-nus), "kindly one," is named euphemistically: He was *numen* of the unreasoning terror of the lonely forest and so identified with Pan.

**Venus** seems once to have been a *numen* of fresh water, especially springs. Water is, of course, essential for the cultivation of plants, especially in gardens, and the name of the *numen* may derive from the Latin word for "pleasant," *venustus*. From being a *numen* of vegetable fertility, Venus, under Greek influence, also took animal and human fertility under her protection. Vergil's *Aeneid* (c. 19 BC) presents Venus functioning as would any Greek god in the poems of Homer, protecting her son Aeneas in his trials.

## GODS OF THE FAMILY AND STATE

The divinities associated with the Roman family always retained their own identities, despite Greek influence, either because the Greeks had no deities to correspond with these particular gods or because they were so embedded in Roman life that nothing could replace them. One such deity was the protective spirit called a **Lar** (plural Lares, **lar**-ēz), the name apparently derived from the Etruscan word for a spirit of the dead. The Lares probably began as protective ghosts of the fertile field, then came to protect all kinds of places: the household, streets, even whole cities (Figure 6.3). They were worshiped in small shrines at crossroads where the boundaries of four farms came together.

Similar to the Lares were the **Penates** (pe-**na**-tēz), who protected a household's things and especially its food. Penates and Lares were often confused, but Penates are portable and Lares were always fixed to a specific location. In origin the Penates were the *numina* of the storehouse—*penus* means "cupboard," the origin of our *pantry*. Later the Penates became identified with the welfare of the Roman state. The Trojan gods whom Hector's ghost entrusted to Aeneas as he fled the burning city of Troy were identified with the state Penates.

The religious activity of the family revolved around the *gens* (gānz, plural *gentes*), roughly "clan," and the *familia*, "household," including slaves. Citizenship meant membership in a *gens* and was confined to males. The head of the *familia*, at least in theory, had absolute power over all members of the *familia*, including the right to kill even his own sons (some instances are recorded). The *patria potestas*, "power of the father," invested in the *paterfamilias*, "father of the family," rarely was exercised to the full, but was always a real threat, especially for slaves.

One term from the Roman religion of the family, *genius* (**gān**-i-us), has passed into our own speech, although its meaning has changed. A man's *genius*, "begetter," was a sort of double, the part of himself that he inherited from his father and would

**FIGURE 6.3**  Shrine of the household gods in an atrium of the House of Vetii, c. AD 60. In the center stands the *genius*, or generative spirit of the house, head veiled for offering a sacrifice, surrounded by two Lares, each holding a horn of plenty. At the bottom is a good-luck snake, the *agathos daimon*, about to eat a honey cake set out for it. (Casa dei Vettii, Pompeii, Italy; Photo by Author)

pass on to his sons (see Figure 6.3). Citizens throughout the Roman world worshiped the *genius* of Augustus, and later emperors. Not the man, but his *genius* was the object of adoration, the Romans insisted, but the distinction was lost on subject peoples, who came to view the Roman emperors as gods themselves.

The Romans felt that the state was a family writ large, a notion clear in the cult of the *numen* **Vesta**, whose name corresponds etymologically to the Greek Hestia. Like her, Vesta is protectress of hearth and home. Six Vestal Virgins served her, each chosen at the age of seven from the great families. The Vestals served for 30 years, after which they could marry, although few did. In their round temple in the Roman Forum they served the state as unmarried girls served in a private home: baking, cleaning, tending the hearth, whose sacred flame, never allowed to go out, Aeneas had brought from Troy (Figure 6.4).

If a Vestal was caught having sexual relations, she was buried alive in a tomb containing a loaf of bread, a jug of water, and a lighted lamp (some did meet their end in this way). Although Vesta was among the most sacred and revered deities of Roman

**FIGURE 6.4**  Reconstruction of three columns of the temple of Vesta in the Roman forum. The original was destroyed in a fire in AD 191, then rebuilt, then destroyed again. Present reconstruction was the work of Benito Mussolini in the 1930s (see Perspective 6). (Fabrizio Ruggeri / Alamy)

religion, she had few myths (like the Greek Hestia), but remained an abstract *numen* throughout Roman history.

Perhaps the Romans' vision of the state as an enlarged family is most clear from the exaltation in myth and other propaganda of a set of duties called *pietas* (pē-e-tas). The term has little in common with its English derivatives *piety* and *pity* but refers to the extraordinary devotion that one shows first to the *paterfamilias*, then by extension to the abstraction of the state itself and its gods. The Roman exaltation of *pietas* as the highest virtue was prominent from an early time and was claimed in titles used by Roman emperors and the poets who wrote for them, especially Vergil, who calls his legendary hero *pius Aeneas*. No doubt it was the native Roman predisposition to regard abstractions as divine that enabled them to transfer pious devotion from the head of a family to an invisible entity of great power, the Roman state. Mesopotamian, Canaanite, and Greek religious anthropomorphism, by contrast, stood in the way of granting obedience to a divine abstraction, and neither Canaan, nor Mesopotamia, nor Greece ever evolved a nation-state.

# MYTH: THE LEGEND OF AENEAS

Augustus calmed the remains of the old senatorial party, who under the empire remained an advisory elite, by retaining the outward trappings of republican government. The religious, artistic, and literary program he sponsored, from which come most surviving accounts of Roman myth, was heavily propagandistic, with the aim of making the new regime appear to be a continuation of the old republic. In reality the old republic had ceased to exist. Two writers particularly important in Augustus' cultural program were **Vergil** (70–19 BC) and the historian **Livy** (59 BC–AD 17), but many other writers prominent under Augustus, especially Ovid, allude often to the tales of early Rome, linking the present political situation with a mythical past.

Vergil, in his immensely complicated and influential poem the *Aeneid*, used the legend of Aeneas, the founder of the Roman race, to create a literary document that might rival those of the Greeks, even Homer. Vergil was born in 70 BC near MANTUA, in northern Italy. In 41 BC, according to his own verses, he lost his farm in the political turmoil. Helped by Maecenas, a friend and minister of Augustus, he became a trusted member of Augustus' art council. He wrote the *Eclogues*, graceful pastoral poetry celebrating the uncorrupted emotions and clever wit of imaginary shepherds, and the *Georgics*, a long poem ostensibly on farming, praising the physical beauty of Italy and the old-fashioned virtues of its peoples. During the last 10 years of his life Vergil worked on the *Aeneid*, which he left not quite finished when he died in 19 BC. Although the poet ordered his poem to be burned, Augustus himself intervened to save it.

In Homer's *Iliad*, Aeneas was the son of Anchises and Aphrodite and a cousin of Hector, prince of Troy. He hoped to succeed Priam as king of Troy, although they were on bad terms. It is unusual for a hero to have a mortal father and a divine mother, yet the same was true of Achilles.

Aeneas was destined to survive the Trojan War. One day his descendants would rule over the Trojans, as Poseidon explains to Artemis and Hera in the *Iliad* just as Achilles is about to kill Aeneas:

> "Come, let us bring Aeneas away from the clutches of death,
> averting the fury of Cronus' son,° if he learns that Achilles
> has killed the man whom destiny calls to escape from this fate—
> all this so that Dardanus' line° may not perish in total oblivion,
> Dardanus, dearer to Zeus than all the rest of the children
> born as the fruit of Zeus's loving embrace with the daughters of men.°
> You know how the son of Cronus now hates the household of Priam;
> know too that mighty Aeneas is to hold the rule of the Trojans,
> he and his children's children, for generations to come."

Homer, Iliad, 20.300–308

°*Cronus' son*: Zeus. °*Dardanus' line*: the Trojans. °. . . *daughters of men*: Dardanus was an early king of Troy.

And so Poseidon saves Aeneas from death. Because the Romans had no native explanation for their origins, but were from the 8th century BC steeped in Greek

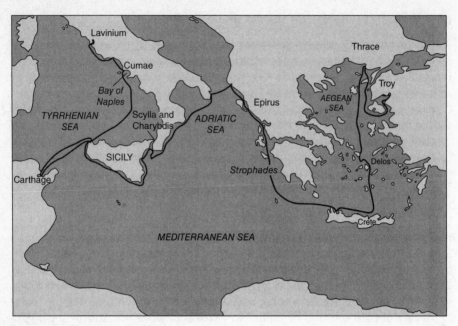

**MAP 6.3    The travels of Aeneas.**

literature, this passage from the *Iliad* suggested a possible illustrious ancestor, complete with divine parent, Venus/Aphrodite.

Long before Augustus, the Romans elaborated a myth about Aeneas based on the passage in the *Iliad*: Aeneas had fought valiantly for Troy, yes, but when the city burned around 1200 BC (in modern dating) he escaped to the far West where his Trojan descendants, the Romans, were destined to rule all the lands around them (Map 6.3). On his journey **Dido** (dī-dō, perhaps = "virgin" in Phoenician), queen of Carthage, attempted to hold Aeneas back from his goal, but driven by destiny he abandoned her and sailed to Italy. There he founded Lavinium in Latium. His son **Iulus** (ī-ūl-us), claimed as ancestor by the Julian clan to which Julius Caesar and Augustus belonged, left Lavinium and founded the town of Alba Longa. Hundreds of years later the descendants of Aeneas, Romulus (**rom**-u-lus) and Remus (**rē**-mus), born in Alba Longa, founded the city of Rome around 750 BC. Aeneas was *paterfamilias* of the whole race of victorious Romans and the direct ancestor of Augustus.

The *Aeneid* is a modern poem, composed in writing and not orally, that makes self-conscious use of mythical traditions to justify present conditions in the world. It is never just a story, but always an explanation of the problems that Romans faced and the moral and political solutions that gave Rome ascendancy over the world.

## Arrival at Carthage

The *Aeneid* opens with an explanation, in mythical terms, of the ferocious and bitter rivalry that would one day exist between CARTHAGE, a Phoenician colony in North Africa close to modern Tunis, and Rome. The name of Carthage is from Semitic *qart hadasht,* "newtown" (Naples too is Greek *Neapolis,* "newtown"). Although Vergil places the founding of Carthage at the same time as the burning of Troy, perhaps about 1200 BC, in fact Phoenicians settled the site about 800 BC, the same time as the Greek western expansion reflected in the *Odyssey.*

Juno is the protector of Carthage, as Venus, mother of Aeneas and sponsor of the Julian clan, favors Rome:[1]

> I sing of ancient wars and an exile, by the order of Fate,
> who sailed from the seashore of Troy, pursued over land and sea
> by the might of the gods who heeded great Juno's implacable anger.
> To Italy's mainland he came, to the coast of the land of Lavinia.
> Once more he fought to the death, as he tried to establish a city
> and settle his gods in Latium, whence rose the race of the Latins,
> the noble rulers of Alba, and the towering ramparts of Rome.
>
> O Muse, recall to my mind the insulted godhead of Juno:
> What did the queen so resent that she forced so pious° a hero
> to suffer such trials and labor? Can divinity harbor such passion? [Figure 6.5]
> There once was an ancient city, founded by Tyrian settlers,°
> far to Italy's south, but facing the mouths of the Tiber,
> Carthage, dowered with wealth, skilled and resourceful in warfare.
> Juno is said to have cherished this city more than all others,
> Samos alone excepted°; here she kept her weapons and chariot.
> Even as early as this the goddess was planning and helping
> to make—if fate should permit—of her city the ruler of nations.
> She heard that a race was arising from the conquered rulers of Troy,
> which some day would dash to the ground the new-built Tyrian city.
> From this race was destined to come a warlike imperial people,
> Libya's° bane and destruction. And the fated time was approaching.
>
> Saturnian° Juno trembled at this, but remembered the struggle
> which once she had waged at Troy at the head of the Argives° she loved.
> The cause of that war and the bitter resentment it roused in her spirit
> had never vanished away: Deep down in her heart she remembered

°*pious*: the first reference to the *pietas* of Aeneas—his respect for family, country, and gods. °*Tyrian settlers*: that is, Semitic Phoenicians, from Tyre. °*Samos alone excepted*: on the island of Samos, just off the coast of Asia Minor, was an early cult to Hera (Juno) and one of the earliest temples in Greece (8th century BC). °*Libya's*: that is, North Africa's; after a hundred years of war Rome destroyed Carthage in 146 BC. °*Saturnian*: Roman Saturn (a *numen* of the harvest) = Greek Cronus, father of Juno/Hera; hence Juno is "Saturnian." °*Argives*: the Greeks.

---

[1]For the Latin texts, cf. B. B. Powell, *Classical Myth,* 7th ed. (New York, 2011). See also R. A. B. Mynors, ed., *P. Vergili Maronis Opera* (Oxford, 1969); H. R. Fairclough and G. P. Goold, eds., *Eclogues, Georgics, Aeneid 1–6; Aeneid Books 7–12, Appendix Vergiliana* (Cambridge, Mass., 2001); S. Lombardo (trans.), *The Aeneid* (New York, 2005); F. Ahl (trans.), *The Aeneid* (Oxford, 2007); Robert Fagles (trans.), Bernard Knox (intro.), *The Aeneid* (New York, 2008); B. O. Foster (trans.), *Livy: History of Rome,* Vol. I, Books 1–2 (Cambridge, Mass., 1919); Aubrey De Selincourt and Stephen Oakley (trans.) *Livy: The Early History of Rome,* Books I–V (New York, 2002).

**FIGURE 6.5** Vergil, dressed in a tunic and Roman toga, between the Muses Clio and Melpomenê, muses of history and tragedy, reading from lines 8 and 9 of his *Aeneid*, where he invokes the Muses. The Latin reads: *Musa, mihi causas memora, quo numine laeso quidve*, "O Muse, tell to me the causes, her divinity [Juno's] being offended by what, or [suffering] what . . ." Clio holds a papyrus with some history text on it; Melpomenê holds a tragic mask. Sousse, Tunisia, c. AD 3rd century. (Musée National du Bardo, Tunis, Tunisia; Photo by Author)

the judgment of Paris, the wounding shame that her beauty was slighted,
her rival's° hated descendants, and abducted Ganymede's honors.°
Already embittered by this, she had blocked the way for the Trojans
(survivors of war with the Greeks and the wrath of savage Achilles),
and driven them over the seas, far from the promise of Latium.
Truly a mighty task was the founding of Rome and its people!

Vergil, *Aeneid*, 1.1–33

°*rival's*: the nymph Electra, on whom Zeus/Jupiter fathered Dardanus, ancestor of the Trojans.
°*Ganymede's honors*: Ganymede, a Trojan prince brought to the Olympian court, was also rival to Juno's affections.

Aeneas and 12 shiploads of refugees have for seven years wandered across the Mediterranean, drifting ever westward. They have just left the south coast of Sicily when Juno persuades Aeolus, king of the winds, to raise a terrible storm. The storm destroys some of Aeneas' ships, but others reach North Africa. Aeneas' mother, Venus, sends Cupid, "desire," to breathe passion into Dido, queen of nearby Carthage and herself a refugee who left Phoenician Tyre after the treacherous murder of her husband Sychaeus (si-kē-us). She swore to Sychaeus' beloved ghost a vow of perpetual chastity.

At a banquet in honor of the newcomers, Aeneas tells Dido and her court the story of the fall of Troy: the wooden horse, the death of Priam, his own escape through darkened streets, the disappearance into the shadows of his wife Creüsa. Carrying on his shoulders his lame father, Anchises, and his household gods, the Penates, he led his son Ascanius (as-kān-i-us, another name for Iulus) through the fire and carnage to safety, a striking image of the Roman patriarchal family. He and other refugees managed to build ships and sail away.

In a voyage deliberately reminiscent of Odysseus' travels, Aeneas describes how he and his companions stopped in THRACE, but a ghost warned them away. From Thrace they sailed to the sacred island of DELOS, where Apollo's oracle told them to seek "the land of the founder of their race, Dardanus." This they supposed to be CRETE, but on Crete a plague beset them. Dardanus, Aeneas now learned, was not born in Crete, but in Italy. Sailing north, the Trojans put in at one of the STROPHADES, the island of the Harpies, winged "snatchers," demons of Greek myth who make an unsettling prediction: They will travel until "hunger makes them eat their tables."

Disheartened, the Trojan refugees make their way up the coast of what today is Albania. Putting to land in EPIRUS in northwestern Greece, they meet the Trojan prophet Helenus, himself a refugee and the last surviving son of Priam and Hecabê. Helenus describes the route to Italy and warns Aeneas to land on its western coast. He must found his city in a secluded valley by a stream, where he will find a white sow with 30 piglets.

They head west across the Adriatic, edge around the boot of Italy, and land in SICILY. An enraged and recently blinded Polyphemus attacks them—Odysseus had just been there! They continue west along the coast of Sicily. Aeneas' father Anchises dies and is buried. As they set out again, the great storm catches them that brings them to Dido's palace.

Dido, inspired with hopeless love for Aeneas (thanks to Cupid's arrows), listens to the story that Aeneas tells at a banquet with fascination. A few days later, Aeneas and Dido are out hunting. Dido is sworn to chastity after her brother murdered her husband Sychaeus and forced her to flee from Tyre on the Phoenician coast. A thunderstorm bursts and the two royals take refuge in a cave. They fall into each other's arms. The rumor of their hot affair soon reaches the ears of a neighboring king whom Dido had refused to marry because of her vow to her dead husband. In anger the local king prays to Jupiter, who sends Mercury: Aeneas must abandon Dido and leave Africa. His destiny is to found the Roman race, not to idle away his life in the arms of a foreign queen.

## Suicide of Dido

When Dido hears of Aeneas' preparations to leave, she accuses him:

> "Traitor, did you expect to conceal the crime you were planning,
> and quietly sneak away from my land? Was our love unable to hold you,
> or the mutual vows that we gave, or the thought of Dido abandoned,
> doomed to a piteous death? Pray, why pick the middle of winter
> for hurriedly readying ships to sail into a furious tempest?
> Have you no heart?"

So Dido poured out her pain, but Aeneas, by Jupiter's order,
displayed no trace of emotion and repressed his anguish of heart.
At last he muttered an answer: "If the choice were entirely mine,
not a single word of the many which you so justly can utter,
O queen who deserved so much better of me, would I try to deny.
As long as self-consciousness lasts, or body hearkens to spirit,
never will I be ashamed to acknowledge my debt to Elissa.°

"Still, the plain truth demands a few words of exculpation.
I never tried to conceal my hurried departure—no, never!
I never held the bridegroom's torch, nor acknowledged a marriage.
If destiny so had allowed, I would live my life as I pleased,
easing the cares that attack, in whatever way seemed to me best.
I would cherish the city of Troy and whatever remained of my people.
Priam's great hall would survive, and the Pergama° shake off its ashes,
raised up by my own hand, restored to a once beaten people.

"But now such a prospect is gone. The voice of Grynean° Apollo
and the Lycian tablets of fate° have expounded Destiny's order:
To Italy now must I voyage, to great Italy turn my endeavors.
That is the land that I love, and that is the land of my fathers.
Mighty Carthage detains you, and the sight of your Libyan city,
Phoenician though you were born. By what right, then, do you murmur
if the Trojans at last find their promised home in Ausonia's land?°
Surely we too are entitled to a kingdom in lands not our own.
Night never covers the earth with misty shadows and darkness,
the stars never rise in the east to march on their fiery courses,
but the troubled ghost of my father brings panic into my slumber,
urging me on to my task. My son, too, appears in my dreams,
reproaching me for my damage to the hopes of one so beloved,
in cheating him of a kingdom, his destined Hesperian° acres.
And last, great Jove himself—I swear by your head and my own—
has sent his herald to bring my orders down through the tempest.
By the clearest light of the day I saw him enter the city,
and when he addressed me I listened with all my closest attention.
So please, give over inflaming both yourself and me with your protests.
Though not by my own free will, to Italy I make my venture!"

Vergil, *Aeneid*, 4.305–361

°*Elissa*: Dido's real name. Dido ("virgin") is an epithet of the Phoenician goddess Astartê in
her role as moon-goddess. °*Pergama*: "citadel," "stronghold," a word Homer uses to describe
the walls of Troy.  °*Grynean*: the epithet derives from Apollo's shrine in Mysia, south of Troy.
°*Lycian tablets of fate*: that is, the oracles of Apollo that Aeneas received on Delos: Lycian is
a common epithet of Apollo. °*Ausonia*: the borderland between Latium and Campania; here
simply Italy. °*Hesperian*: that is, "western."

Dido loses her self-control and threatens suicide. Aeneas sails anyway, just before sunrise. As he goes, he turns to see distant smoke rising from Dido's funeral pyre,

spiraling into the sky. Dido has died by her own hand. With her last breath she curses Aeneas and all those begotten of him, a mythical explanation of the terrible wars one day to come between Rome and Carthage.

The Trojan fleet stops again in Sicily, now to hold funeral games for Anchises. The Trojan women rebel against their long wandering and attempt to burn the ships. Aeneas leaves them behind with the older, weaker men to found their own colony. The Trojans travel north toward what is today the Bay of Naples, where the helmsman Palinurus falls overboard and is drowned, for Neptune had demanded a death before he would allow a safe landing.

## Descent to the Underworld

At Cumae on the northern lip of the Bay of Naples, Aeneas prepares for a descent into the underworld. Many popular conceptions about the other world still current today lead back directly to Vergil's description, which incorporates Greek and Roman myth, religion, and philosophy.

He must descend to the underworld through an opening near sulphurous Lake Avernus, north of the Bay of Naples, to speak with his dead father, Anchises. The Romans thought the etymology of Avernus to be "birdless" because the foul vapors kill even birds that fly over it. First he needed to find Apollo's onetime love, the **Sibyl of Cumae**, Cumae being an early Greek colony near Avernus. The goddess Hecatê had revealed to the Sibyl how to enter the nether realms. Now an old woman, the Sibyl will be his guide. Aeneas plucks a magical golden bough from a sacred wood, a sign that he is chosen by fate, then in the Sibyl's company he descends into the realm of Dis, the Roman god of the underworld (from *Dives*, "wealth").

After sacrificing to the gods beneath the earth, Aeneas and the Sibyl set forth at the earliest rays of the rising sun. At the entrance to the underworld hovers a crowd of personified abstractions, a tree filled with deceptive dreams, and beyond it a crowd of monsters. Their journey soon brings them to the river **Acheron** (ak-er-on, "sorrowful"), the boundary proper of Dis's realm. If the dead have the fare, they are soon taken aboard the boat of the grim ferryman **Charon** (kār-on); if not, they must wait a hundred years to cross:

> From there the downward way led them to Acheron's waters,
> whose black and sluggish current eddied in whirlpools of mud.
> A filthy old guardian boatman kept watch on the banks and the river,
> Charon, whose red flaming eyes peered over a greasy gray beard,
> dressed in a dirty old scarf looped around and over his shoulder.
>
> Scorning the help of a crew, he alone handles punt pole and sail,
> and loads the dead to the gunwales of his rusty, leaky old hull—
> an old man now, but old age in a god is green and resilient.
>
> Great crowds of the dead swarmed out and rushed on down,
> to the slimy banks of the water in an endless torrent of humans—
> mothers of children, their husbands, great-hearted heroes,
> schoolboys, unmarried maidens, young men scarcely mature,
> but laid on the funeral pyre before the eyes of their parents.

A crowd like swirling leaves that fall from the branches in autumn,
when nipped by the first cold blast, or like the flocking of seabirds,
when icy winter drives them in flight from the open sea
in search of a warmer climate. Just so the dead, passing number,
came stretching their hands in longing to cross to the opposite shore.

Vergil, Aeneid, 6.295–314

Among those who hold out their hands in longing for the further bank is Palinurus, the helmsman of a ship of Aeneas. Palinurus, overcome by sleep, had fallen overboard and drowned and begs for a proper burial. Charon allows Aeneas and Sibyl to enter his boat and ferries them over the gloomy water. Having human bodies, they very nearly swamp the boat (Dante will imitate this scene in his *Inferno*, c. AD 1300). On the other bank, the Sibyl drugs the ferocious Cerberus with a honey cake (cf. Figure 5.3):

Having completed this part of the journey, Aeneas and Sibyl
drew near the bank of the stream. The pilot, from out in the river,
noticed them making their way through the silent gloom of the forest
and hurrying down to the shore. He raised a threatening clamor:

"Whoever you are, approaching in arms the bank of my river,
stop right there where you are! Speak up! Say why you have ventured
to a place belonging alone to dreams, to night, and to shadows.
I may not carry the living across in my Stygian ferry° …"

… To this the Sibyl replied,
"Although you remain unimpressed by this man's feelings of duty"°
(drawing the golden bough from her cloak, she showed it to Charon),
"even so you will recognize this."

Anger died in his swelling heart as he looked down in silence
at the awesome gift of the Sibyl. At last he slowly directed
his gloomy prow to the shore, drove out the rows of the spirits,
and cleared a way for the pair. When mighty Aeneas was boarding,
the rickety vessel creaked and groaned at the weight of the hero
and was nearly swamped by the water that lapped in over its gunwales.
But Charon finally landed the prophet and hero in safety,
to splash their way through the mud and drifted weeds of the river.

From his triple throat the snarls of Cerberus rang to the sky
as he crouched, immense, by his cave, straddled across their pathway.
The Sibyl glanced at his neck, already bristling with vipers,
and threw him a morsel of honey and dough made narcotic with drugs.
Stretching three ravenous jaws, he snapped at the bait in the air.

°*Stygian ferry*: belonging to the underworld river Styx. °*duty*: the Latin word is *pietas*, duty to family, country, and gods: At the command of Jupiter he has come down to the underworld to ask his father about the destiny of Rome.

At once his taut-muscled back went slack on the ground where he lay,
filling with his huge bulk the entire width of the cavern.
As the beast lay snoring, Aeneas hastily ran for the portal
and hurriedly ran on beyond the stream no mortal recrosses.

Vergil, Aeneid, 6.384–425

The Sibyl and Aeneas next come to the region of the great mass of the dead, who are divided into various groups. The first is those who died too soon: infants, those wrongly convicted of crime, suicides, and those who have died for love. Aeneas espies the ghost of Dido:

Among them Phoenician Dido was wandering deep in the forest,
still showing her wound. As Aeneas came, he peered through the shadow,
like a man who sees or imagines the rise of the dim new moon,
gleaming faint through the clouds. Unable to hold back from weeping,
and touched by still tender affection, Aeneas spoke through his tears:

"So the word, poor Dido, was true, that reported that your life had ended,
and that you had met your fate from a weapon in your own hands!
Was I the cause of your death? I swear by the stars in the heaven,
by the gods above, by whatever has force in the depths of earth,
that I sailed away from your country, O queen, against my desire.
The orders of heaven forced me, and the gods' irresistible power,
which forces me now to explore this region of darkness and mildew.
How could I have foreseen what anguish my leaving would bring you?
No, no! Wait for a while. Turn not away from my presence.
This is the last time ever that fate will allow me to plead."

With words like this, with a flood of tears, Aeneas attempted
to mollify angry Dido's scowling implacable specter.
She fixed her eyes on the ground, and, silently turning her back,
seemed no more moved by his pleading than would be a block of flint
or a statue of Parian marble.° At last she regained control,
and, still unforgiving, ran off to the shadowy depths of the forest,
where at once her husband Sychaeus consoled her with mutual affection.
Aeneas still watched as she went, deeply shaken by Dido's misfortune,
shedding his tears of pity as long as she still could be seen.

Vergil, Aeneid, 6.450–476

°*Parian marble*: a high-quality stone from the Aegean island of Paros.

Nearby are soldiers who fell in battle, especially the dead of the Trojan War.
Now they come to a fork in the road. The way to the left leads to Tartarus, in Vergil's poem a place of eternal torment. There reside the great sinners, including Tantalus, who fed his son to the gods, and Sisyphus, whose punishment was to roll a rock to the top of a hill, only to see it tumble down again. The Titans are there too, sent

to Tartarus by the thunderbolts of Zeus according to Hesiod's *Theogony*. The crime of Vergil's great sinners is impiety against the gods, but Vergil universalizes the moral vision of crime punished and virtue rewarded to include the fates of ordinary humans. We do not actually behold the torment of Vergil's sinners, however. Even the Sibyl is not allowed to see, but has learned about them from Hecatê, goddess of witchcraft and the crossroads:

> Here are those who in life detested and envied their brothers;
> those who attacked their fathers, who cheated and swindled dependents,
> who refused to offer to others a part of their chance-given riches,°
> but in avarice hoarded it all; of the greedy the number is legion.
>
> Here were the men who were slain in the very act of adultery.
> And faithless breakers of oaths° who fought for a criminal cause—
> all these, loaded with chains, lie dreading the penalty waiting . . .
> Sadly they cry a warning in a voice that rings through the shadow:
>
> "Be warned by my words. Learn justice. Do not belittle the gods."
> Here is the traitor who peddled his country and set up a tyrant,
> who for a bribe would establish bad laws and abolish the good;
> here the incestuous man who corrupted the bed of his daughter—
> darers of horrible crimes, who enjoyed the fruit of their daring.
> If I had a hundred mouths, I could not exhaust their offenses,
> nor could I even begin to expound the torments they suffer.
>
> Vergil, *Aeneid*, 6.608–627

°*chance-given riches*: magnanimity ranked high as a virtue in the ancient world and miserly greed as a great vice. °*breakers of oaths*: that is, the opponents of Augustus in the civil wars with Marc Antony.

Aeneas leaves the golden bough as an offering to Proserpina (Persephonê), queen of the dead, in front of the gate to Pluto's palace, king of the dead, and he and the Sibyl hurry on to **Elysium**. There dwell the ghosts of heroes who died in battle and of many other sages and poets. They await reincarnation:

> They passed to the happy region of green and flowering glades,
> the groves where the favored dwell, the blessed haunt of the heroes.
> A purer air enfolds them and clothes them in larger soft light.
> A sun of their own shines above, their own stars call them to slumber.
> Some find delight in wrestling in rings made soft by the grass;
> some exercise well-trained muscles in arenas of golden sand.
> Others delight in the steps of the dance or the singing of verses.
>
> Orpheus,° dressed as a bard, fits musical notes to the epic,
> sweeping the lyre with his fingers, or plucking with ivory plectrum.

°*Orpheus*: the legendary singer who could entrance even the trees and stones.

Here dwell the noble descendants of Teucer,° a glorious lineage,
great-hearted heroes, the men of an earlier, happier age—
Ilus, Assaracus, back to Dardanus, founder of Ilium.
Aeneas gazed at their ghostly weapons, their hurrying chariots,
no longer loaded with fighters; at spears, just stuck in the ground;
at their horses, now grazing in peace. Yet the joy of their owners
in chariots, horses, and weapons, which once they enjoyed while alive,
remained with these fortunate spirits, whose bodies lay in the earth.

And others Aeneas observed, relaxing at ease in the meadows,
picnicking, singing, or dancing, or raising a paean in chorus,
all through the perfumed thickets of laurel, watered by brooklets
bickering down through the woods, from great Eridanus on earth.°

Here were those who alive had shed their blood for their country
and those who all through their days were pure and reverend prophets,
wise men, uttering oracles worthy of Phoebus Apollo himself.
Here were those whose talents have rendered life more attractive,
and all who deserve our remembrance as generations roll onward.

Vergil, Aeneid, 6.638–663

°*Teucer*: the first king of Troy. Ilus, Assaracus, and Dardanus were among his successors.
Aeneas himself belonged to this house, and from his son Iulus sprang the Roman Julii (by a bad
etymology), including by adoption Augustus, Vergil's patron. °*Eridanus on earth*: the PO.
Because the lower world is a sort of copy of that above, its rivers presumably have the same source.

Aeneas sees the spirit of his father, Anchises, and vainly attempts to embrace
it. Nearby, ghosts drink from the River Lethê, "forgetfulness," and Anchises explains
that these spirits will soon reincarnate, purified of crimes committed in earlier lives.
Anchises points out to Aeneas the souls of Romulus, the other early kings of Rome, the
great generals of Rome, and the spirit of Augustus himself.

Anchises' words about Rome's destiny are central to this highly political poem:

Others° will chisel the bronze so subtly it seems to be breathing;
others, no doubt, will extract a lifelike face from the marble.
Tongues more fluent than ours will plead the rights of their clients;
sages will measure the heavens and tell of the rise of the stars.
But you, Roman, never forget your duty to govern the nations.
Your god-given skill will be this: to impose good conduct on peace,
to thrust the proud from the throne, to forgive the beaten and humble.

Vergil, Aeneid, 6.847–853

°*Others*: the Greeks.

## Latium

After returning to the upper world, Aeneas and his followers board their ships and sail
north to the mouth of the Tiber, in Latium. In Latium they encounter the local king,

Latinus. His daughter, Lavinia, was betrothed to **Turnus**, king of a nearby people, but a prophecy directed Latinus to give Lavinia to a foreigner instead. When Aeneas accepts her, war erupts between the indigenous Italians and the Trojan invaders. The angry, jilted Turnus organizes a coalition of local warriors, including Camilla, a warrior-maiden from a neighboring tribe.

The river-god Tiber persuades Aeneas to form an alliance with King Evander, a Greek settled on the Palatine Hill, the future site of Rome. On the way to Evander, Aeneas sees a white sow with a litter of 30 piglets: Here he will found Lavinium, according to the prophecy of Helenus. Evander shows Aeneas sites near the Palatine later to be famous in Rome, and he agrees to support Aeneas in the war. He suggests that they also strike an alliance with a faction of the Etruscans led by the mighty Tarchon.

Meanwhile, Turnus has surrounded the Trojan camp. In a skirmish Ascanius/ Iulus, Aeneas' son, kills his first man. In a glorious scene of battle, Turnus is trapped alone inside the walls of the camp (as once in fact was Alexander the Great). Single-handedly, he kills many Trojans, then dives into the river and escapes. In the company of Pallas, the son of Evander, Aeneas returns to the Trojan camp, but Turnus lies in wait and kills the young Pallas.

At last Aeneas and Turnus agree to settle the quarrel by single combat. The winner will marry Lavinia and rule over Latium. Aeneas wounds Turnus, who falls to the ground and begs for his life. Aeneas nearly shows mercy, but when he sees Pallas' sword-belt tied to Turnus' chest as a trophy, he angrily plunges his sword into the breast of the Italian warrior.

So ends the *Aeneid*.

## OBSERVATIONS: THE *AENEID*, A MYTH OF REBIRTH

Vergil was highly literate, steeped in written Greek poetry and philosophy and in personal contact with the most powerful men in the world. Vergil's poem was painstakingly learned, self-conscious, and created in writing with deliberate compression and elegant expression. Greek oral epic, usually complete in a single sitting, differed with every performance: Our Homeric and Hesiodic poems are snapshots of a single artificially extended performance. The *Aeneid*, composed in writing, was not finished even after 10 years.

Vergil's myths are purposeful propaganda, to prove that Augustus deserved his place in the world and that Rome's destiny in history was willed by divine intelligence. Characters and events in Vergil's myths have various levels of meaning; they stand for more than meets the eye. All events and characters are subordinated to his patriotic purpose of satisfying Rome's need for a tradition of national origin, a tale telling in the language of legend how this great empire was made. Its story of far away and long ago, when cows munched grass on the Palatine hill, satisfied contemporary literary taste for an escapist setting while making it possible for Vergil to proclaim, in symbolic form, the divine necessity of Rome's conquest of the world and of Augustus' ascendancy in it.

Vergil's complex myth places empire in the context of a divine plan for human history while glorifying the moral qualities necessary for the foundation of empire. The quality of *pietas*, devotion to duty, is the most important positive quality in a ruler. Vergil also shows what features a ruler should not have. Aeneas during his seven years of wandering has purged himself of material and sexual excess, which the exotic eastern city of Troy symbolized in ancient literature. He spurns the glorious new city that Dido is building and rejects his passion for her, so like that between Paris and Helen, who in placing personal desire above communal good gave rise to the catastrophic Trojan War.

## PERSPECTIVE 6
### Aeneas, Augustus, and Mussolini

In the 1930s, Benito Mussolini (1883–1945), the ruler of Italy's fascist regime, joined forces with Nazi Germany in a failed bid to retake the Mediterranean by storm, just as imperial Rome had done 2,000 years earlier. Roman legend and archaeology inspired the madcap scheme. Mussolini was called *il Duce*, "the leader," in Latin *dux* (*der Führer* in German had the same meaning). He sponsored excavations to recover evidence of Rome's heroic past, which he displayed prominently, and he built new monuments to promote continuity between Rome's imperial past and the fascist present.

When the famous Altar of Augustan Peace was discovered in the late 1930s, it was hastily excavated and restored (with fragments known since the 1500s), then exhibited inside a specially built glass enclosure near the mausoleum of Augustus on the Campus Martius (see Map 6.2). The altar consists of a central stone for animal sacrifice surrounded by a marble rectangular screen wall, decorated in high relief in a style reminiscent of the sculptures on the Parthenon in Athens. In 1939, Mussolini rededicated the restored altar on Augustus' birthday (September 23) in a grand gesture designed to inaugurate a new empire.

Apparently, Augustus himself directed the design and erection of the ancient altar. Ovid tells us in his calendrical poem the *Fasti* (1.709–722) that Augustus dedicated it on the 30th of January 9 BC, the birthday of Augustus' powerful wife, Livia. The altar was the site of annual sacrifices to celebrate the peace that followed Augustus' ascension to absolute power, called the *pax Augusta*, "the Augustan peace."

Some figures carved in the marble are unidentified, but numerous scenes are mythical. The general theme is to celebrate Augustus' military success, divine roots, extended family, heirs, and promise of a renewed "golden age," the *aetas aurea*. The *numen* Roma appears at rest atop a heap of captured weapons in a gesture of triumph and the peace that follows war. Mars, father of the Roman people, entrusts his sons Romulus and Remus to a shepherd. In one scene (Perspective Figure 6.1) a bearded Aeneas stands before a shrine to the Penates and prepares to sacrifice a sow, whose presence, according to prophecy, marked the site of Lavinium (but here there are no 30 piglets).

He wears a cloak over his head, as always with officiants at Roman sacrifice. A damaged figure behind him could be Iulus. Two attendants stand beside the sow. Thus does Augustus renew Rome with a fresh founding of the state. As Augustus cultivated continuity with the heroic age of Aeneas, Mussolini, in his patronage of the altar's recovery and display, sought legitimacy in his own bid for empire.

Augustus himself appears on the altar among members of the imperial family, with his head veiled in the same manner as Aeneas: Augustus is the new Aeneas, as is Mussolini, whose Italian fascist state in 1930 published postage stamps with scenes

**PERSPECTIVE FIGURE 6.1**    Aeneas about to sacrifice a sow before the sanctuary of the Penates, marble relief from the Altar of Augustan Peace (ara pacis Augustae), Rome, 13–9 BC. (Photo by Author)

**PERSPECTIVE FIGURE 6.2**    Italian postage stamp, 1930, with the scene of Tellus Mater (or some other fertility goddess) holding Romulus and Remus, from the Altar of Augustan Peace. (Biblioteca Treccani Istituto della Enciclopedia Italiana)

from the altar to commemorate the two thousandth anniversary of Vergil's birth. One stamp (Perspective Figure 6.2) shows Tellus Mater, "Mother Earth," with two suckling babes, probably Romulus and Remus, from the front panel of the Altar of Peace.

Engraved beneath is a quotation from Vergil's pastoral poem (*Georgics* 2.173): *salve magna parens frugum, Saturnia tellus*, "Greetings, great mother of abundance, the land of Saturn [that is, Italy]." In the left-hand panel, *secondo millenario Virgiliano*, means "on the two thousandth birthday of Virgil." The panel on the right is also a quotation from Vergil, *antiquam exquirite matrem*, the advice that Vergil received from an oracle on Delos that the Trojans should "seek your ancient mother."

Mussolini's other monuments in and around Rome included the Foro Italico, decorated with murals of Greek and Roman myth, and the Stadio dei Marmi (Stadium of Statues) for the 1944 Olympic Games (these were cancelled, but the stadium was used for the games in 1960). A towering Egyptian obelisk dedicated in 1932 was inscribed "Mussolini Dux." Mussolini planned a gigantic new forum in the center of Rome with a colossal bronze statue of himself as Heracles, but in 1945 antifascist partisans placed him before a firing squad, then hung his corpse, and that of his mistress, upside down in a gas station, for all to see, to spit on, and despise.

In Dido, Vergil embodies many mythical and historical associations: Dido is not only like Helen of Troy, who gave in to her passion, but also like Circê and Calypso, enchantresses in the *Odyssey* who would sway the hero from his purpose. In her the contemporary Roman reader would recognize Cleopatra too, who seduced Marc Antony and turned him against Augustus and Rome. Dido represents the moral failings of broken faith and Eastern passion. Although she swore to Sychaeus that she would have no other, she slept with Aeneas. Instead of transcending her heartbreak and pain (as a true Roman woman would), she took her life in an act of vindictive self-destruction. Dido also is an incarnation of Carthage, Rome's greatest enemy, who under the extraordinary general Hannibal (247–183 BC) nearly destroyed the Roman state. Such was the working out of Dido's curse on Aeneas and his descendants.

The Romans were an amalgam of many clans and tribes whose primitive tribal identity was submerged in the greater being of the state. In Vergil's poem, Latinus the Latin, Tarchon the Etruscan, and Evander the Greek stand for the peoples who were fused into Rome. All work together toward the common enterprise. Brazen and hot-headed, Turnus is too like Achilles or Marc Antony or Alexander the Great to survive. Morally, he is not wrong; he may be right. After all, he was engaged to Lavinia before Aeneas appeared and carried off the bride already promised to Turnus. Still, Turnus must lose because he opposes the pattern of destiny. The personal and local pride that Turnus represents must succumb if empire will bestow its many benefits on humankind.

## MYTH: ROMULUS AND REMUS

Roman intellectuals had to fill in the embarrassing gap of 450 years between the burning of Troy, traditionally placed at about 1200 BC, and the conventional date of the founding of Rome in 753 BC (according to the modern calendar). The usual story is that Aeneas founded the town of Lavinium, named after his wife Lavinia, then after three years died in battle. His son Ascanius/Iulus founded the nearby town of Alba Longa in the southeast of Latium, about 12 miles from the later site of Rome (archaeologists are not sure of the site of Alba Longa). There he was succeeded by a sequence of kings.

In the 12th generation after Aeneas—that is, about 450 years later—**Romulus** and **Remus** were born, the sons of Mars, as Aeneas was the child of Venus. Romulus and Remus founded Rome on seven low hills on the banks of the Tiber River. In this way Roman mythographers brought together the legends of Aeneas and Romulus and Remus, in origin no doubt separate traditions of how the city began.

Titus Livius or Livy (59 BC–AD 17) wrote an enormous history of the Roman people in 142 papyrus rolls, of which 35 survive, called *Ab urbe condita*, "From the founding of the city," after its first three words. Livy celebrated the political settlement of Augustus, who had personally encouraged him to write his history. Livy's prose version of the story of Romulus and Remus is a good specimen of how the Roman understood his early past. Livy has been describing the early kings of Alba Longa who succeeded Ascanius: (Chart 6.2):

> The next king [of Alba Longa] was Proca. He had two sons, Numitor and Amulius. To Numitor, the older, he bequeathed the ancient throne of the Silvian dynasty.° But neither a father's intention nor respect for the claims of an elder son proved to be any match for violence when Amulius drove his brother out into exile. Then, piling crime on crime, Amulius killed all Numitor's sons, and stripped away all hope of male issue from his brother's daughter Rhea Silvia by giving her the empty honor of being a Vestal, and thus condemned to lifelong virginity.
>
> But surely the origin of so great a city, and an empire second only to the domain of the gods, must be ascribed to Fate itself. The Vestal presently gave birth to twins, the result, she claimed, of violent rape. She named Mars as their father, either because she really believed it, or because she felt that putting the responsibility on a god would lessen her own dishonor. Be that as it may, neither gods nor man defended the Vestal or her sons from the savagery of the king. She was chained and flung into a dungeon, and an order was given for the boys to be thrown into a running stream.

°*Silvian dynasty*: so called from Aeneas Silvius, grandson of Aeneas.

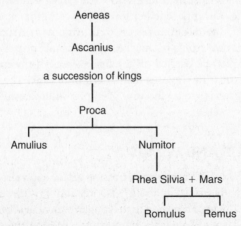

**CHART 6.2**  Descent of Romulus and Remus.

By some piece of divine providence it happened that the Tiber had over-flowed its banks and spread out into sluggish ponds, so that its normal bed could nowhere be approached. This led the men who were carrying out the babies to hope that they could toss them into any water that was moving, how-ever slowly, and could thus feel that they were carrying out the royal command. So they abandoned the boys on the nearest mud bank, by the site of the present *Ficus Ruminalis* ["fig tree of the sucklings"], which, it is said, was then called the Romular ["of Romulus"].

Now in those days there were wild areas all through the region. The story goes on that when the slow-moving water ebbed away, it left the basket that car-ried the boys stranded on the dry bank. Presently a thirsty she-wolf from the nearby hills came down to drink. Hearing a childish wail, she turned aside to the boys and offered them her teats so gently that, when a shepherd of the king's block found her a little later, she was licking them with her tongue. The shep-herd's name is said to have been Faustulus ["lucky"].

He brought the boys back to his hut and gave them to his wife Larentia to bring up. True, some people maintain that Larentia was the local whore to whom the shepherds gave the nickname of Lupa ["she-wolf"], and that this was the source of the story—be it legend or miracle.

Livy, *History of Rome*, 1.3.10–1.4.7

The origin of the legend of Romulus and Remus, perhaps the best-known foun-dation story from all classical myth, is not clear. Some think it a genuine Roman tra-dition, but other scholars find in it a compendium of elements drawn consciously from Greek models. Native elements would include Romulus' name, the origin of Roma, probably from the Greek word for "strength." No one has been able, however, to explain the name of Remus.

The detail about the Ruminal Fig seems to be an etiological tag to explain a real tree venerated as the site of a *numen* called Rumina, "breast nourisher" (be-cause the milk of the fig looks like milk from the human breast). Faustulus is per-haps related to the Roman woodland-spirit Faunus, identified with the Greek Pan. A *numen* with underworld associations, said to be mother to the Lares, was also called Larentia.

But the narrative details of the story recall Greek examples. The exposure of the children reminds us of the Greek myth of Oedipus, a foundling, and other figures like Paris, exposed and suckled by a bear, and Zeus, suckled by a goat (Figure 6.6). Sargon of Akkad (c. 2500 BC), greatest ruler of Mesopotamia in the 3rd millennium; the Hebrew Moses (c. 1200 BC); and Cyrus the Great, founder of the Persian empire in the 6th century BC, were all, like Romulus and Remus, abandoned in baskets on a river: So difficult is it to disentangle history from myth.

Royal brothers also appear in Greek myth (notably in the story of the twins who founded Thebes). Danaë, a virgin like **Rhea Silvia**, was imprisoned in an underground cavern, but Zeus seduced her anyway and she and her child were set afloat on the sea. The rivalry between the colorless Numitor and Amulius may be consciously modeled on that between the sons of Oedipus, who fought the war of the Seven Against Thebes; the ancient motif occurs earlier in the biblical stories of Cain and Abel and Jacob and

**FIGURE 6.6**   The great she-wolf, an Etruscan bronze c. 500 BC. The two babies—Romulus and Remus—are Renaissance additions, probably by Antonio Pollaiuolo in the 15th century. In the 1930s Benito Mussolini sent copies of this sculpture to three American cities. A copy of the one he sent to Cincinnati still stands in a city park there. (Musei Capitolini, Rome; Photo by Author)

Esau and in the Egyptian story of Osiris and Seth. We cannot determine whether such elements were borrowed deliberately from Greek or even Eastern stories to concoct a Roman foundation myth or whether the story arose from a parallel native tradition.

In any event, when Romulus and Remus grew up, they became great hunters (like many traditional heroes), first of animals, then of bandits, whose loot they honorably divided with other shepherds. But one day bandits captured Remus and handed him over to King Amulius, who for some reason gave him to his hated brother, the disenfranchised Numitor, for punishment. Numitor recognized his grandson, Romulus was brought into a conspiracy, and the father and brothers united to kill the wicked Amulius. Livy continues:

> Thus the throne of Alba was restored to Numitor. But Romulus and Remus were eager to build a city in the place where they had been exposed and brought up. There were already too many people in Alba, both Albans and Latins, and beside them there were the shepherds—so many, all told, that it was quite reasonable to believe that Alba and Lavinium would look like little hamlets compared to the town now being founded. But into these rosy dreams intruded the ancestral blight of ambition to be king, and a shameful quarrel arose from a trifling argument.
>
> Since Romulus and Remus were twins, respect for seniority could not determine whose name should be given to the new city and which of them should rule once it was founded. Romulus therefore occupied the Palatine and Remus

the Aventine° to observe the signs by which the local gods might show them the answers. Remus, so goes the story, was the first to receive a portent, six vultures. But this sign had just been announced when twice that number appeared to Romulus. Both men were promptly hailed as king by their own henchmen, Remus on grounds of priority, Romulus on grounds of number.

They began to argue, but their quarrel soon turned to violence, and in the fighting Remus was killed. There is a better-known story that Remus contemptuously jumped over his brother's half-built wall [the *pomerium*]. Romulus, furious at the slight, killed him, adding the bitter jest: "This is what will happen to anyone else who tries the same!" Thus Romulus became sole ruler, and his name was given to the city he had founded.

Livy, *History of Rome*, 1.6.3–1.7.3

°*Aventine*: another of the seven hills of Rome.

In later speculation the founding of Rome in fratricide was sometimes interpreted as foretelling the civil wars of the 1st century BC, but in origin the story of the two brothers may have advocated the sanctity of the consuls' dual rule in the state as the best refuge against kingship and tyranny. A recent theory suggests that the original story told of the foundation by Romulus alone, who gave his name to Rome, and that Remus was added to the story much later, in the 4th century BC, to represent the plebeians, who in a prolonged struggle resisted the power of the patricians, represented by Romulus. That Rome claimed the murder of Remus by Romulus as the story of its founding is a tantalizing puzzle.

## MYTH: THE RAPE OF THE SABINE WOMEN AND THE DEATH OF ROMULUS

Rome was founded and named, but there was no one to live in it except runaway slaves, bandits, and murderers who assembled from the hills. If the Romans were to grow in number, they needed wives. Romulus approached local communities and requested women for wives, but no one wanted to marry his daughter to a Roman bandit. Romulus therefore conceived a plan. During a festival large crowds flocked to Rome from neighboring Latin townships, including the **Sabines** (sā-bīnz). As soon as the festival began, the Romans rushed into the crowd and seized the young Sabine women. The festival broke up in a panic, but the girls' parents, shouting curses, were forced to abandon their daughters.

The abducted women were angry and fearful, but Romulus assured them that everything would turn out well. They would enjoy the privileges of married women. Their children, when they came, would bind them closely to their new husbands, whom they would learn to love. The men spoke honeyed words and swore that passionate love had prompted their offense, a tactic, as Livy observes, that "touches a woman's heart." In fact the women soon forgot their resentment.

No doubt the Sabines did contribute significantly to the early Roman bloodline, but behind the story must also lie an early custom of the communal exchange of women, forced or voluntary. Such practices occur in many societies. Even in classical

Roman marriage the maid was pulled away from her mother in a mock show of force and her hair parted with a spear.

Romulus died mysteriously. He was holding an assembly at the Campus Martius when the day went black, and when it came light again, he was nowhere to be found. One tradition reports that senators jealous of his power murdered him, dismembered his body, and hid it under their togas. Another holds that he was raised into heaven. In any case, he became a god and was ever after worshiped as the ancient *numen* Quirinus, who embodied the military and economic strength of the Roman people.

After its foundation by Romulus and Remus, supposedly in 753 BC, Rome was ruled by seven kings, the first four Romano-Sabine, the last three Etruscan. In an artificial schema, the odd-numbered kings were valiant and warlike, the even-numbered devoted to the arts of peace.

## MYTH: THE ETRUSCAN DYNASTY AND THE WICKED TULLIA

The jealous sons of the fourth king killed Tarquin the Elder, the fifth king of Rome, who had come to Rome from Etruria to establish his ascendancy (Chart 6.3).

However, the sons did not succeed in regaining the throne, which fell next to one Servius Tullius, "Tullius the slave's son." His mother had been a slave in the royal house when the household Lar, taking the form of a phallus of ash on the hearth, leapt out upon the girl. When Servius Tullius was a child, flames danced around his head, convincing Tarquin the Elder's wife, Tanaquil, a prophetess, that he was a man of destiny. After her husband's murder, Tanaquil conspired to place Servius Tullius on the throne.

Servius Tullius ruled long and well, and his daughters, both named Tullia, married sons of Tarquin the Elder, the murdered fifth king of Rome. (Roman women had no first names: They bore the name of their *gens* with a feminine ending.) When Servius Tullius grew old, one of the Tullias began a passionate love affair with her brother-in-law, soon to be the seventh and last king of Rome, **Tarquin the Proud**. Tullia I urged Tarquin to murder his wife Tullia II (her sister) and his brother (her husband) and to get rid of her father, King Servius Tullius, so that together they could rule Rome. Soon Tullia II was dead, Tarquin's brother was dead, and Tullia I and Tarquin were married to one another.

One day Tarquin, soon to be "the Proud," sat down in the king's seat in the Senate house. When the old king came to see what was happening, Tarquin picked

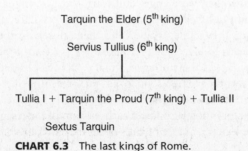

**CHART 6.3**  The last kings of Rome.

him up and hurled him down the steps into the street. At that very moment the wicked Tullia I arrived in the Forum in her carriage. Livy tells the story:

> Everybody agrees that Tullia, driving her carriage into the forum, paid no attention to the assembled crowd of men, but shouted to her husband to come out from the senate house, and was the first to hail him as king. He told her to go away, because the crowd might become dangerous. But on her way home she had just reached the top of Cyprian Street (where the temple of Diana stood until a little while ago) and was turning right onto the Urbian Hill to get to the Esquiline Hill, when her coachman halted in terror, reined in the horses, and showed her the mutilated body of Servius Tullius as it lay in the road.
>
> The savage and brutal act Tullia then committed is commemorated by the place it occurred, which they now call Crime Alley (vicus sceleratus). For it was there that Tullia, crazed by the vengeful spirits of her murdered sister and husband, is said to have driven her carriage right over her father's corpse. She herself was spattered with his blood, and on the gory vehicle she brought back bits of his flesh to the household of herself and her husband. The gods of the home were so enraged by this terrible start of Tarquin's reign that an equally terrible end presently caught up with the pair.

Livy, *History of Rome*, 1.48.5–7

Surely in the days of Tarquin the Proud the patrician hatred of excessive power in one man's hands was fully justified! The king laid terrible burdens on his people and was feared by all.

## MYTH: LUCRETIA AND THE END OF MONARCHY

Several young army officers, including Tarquin the Proud's son **Sextus Tarquin** ("Tarquin the Sixth") were on military service near Rome. They were comparing the beauty and virtue of their wives, each boasting that his own wife was most virtuous. To settle the argument they visited Rome unannounced to see what the women were doing. They found most of the women indecorously drinking and gossiping, but **Lucretia** (lu-krē-sha), wife of a certain Tarquin Collatinus, was virtuously spinning wool with her women servants. Sextus Tarquin, astonished by her beauty no less than by her virtue and modesty, formed a vile plan.

Returning alone a few nights later, he was politely received, but as soon as the house was quiet he drew his sword and demanded that she yield to him. When she indignantly refused, he threatened to kill her and one of her slaves, then tell her husband that he had found the pair together in bed, thus joining shame to her death. Lucretia sadly gave in, but the next day summoned her family and a few friends, including Lucius Brutus, associate of her husband and a cousin of the Tarquins. His real name was Lucius Junius, but to ensure his safety he had carefully cultivated the appearance of a fool, and so received the nickname Brutus, "stupid":

> Shattered by such a horror, Lucretia sent the same message to her father in Rome and her husband in Ardea, to come to her, each with one trustworthy

friend. Both speed and action were imperative; something dreadful had happened. Spurius Lucretius came with Publius Valerius, the son of Volesus, and Tarquin Collatinus with Lucius Junius Brutus, with whom he happened to be returning to Rome when he met the messenger.

They found Lucretia sitting dejectedly in her bedroom. Tears sprang to her eyes when her husband asked her, "Are you all right?" "Certainly not," she answered, "How can a woman be all right when her shame and modesty have been torn away? In your bed, Collatinus, are the marks of another man. But only my body has been violated. My soul is still guiltless—and this I shall prove by my death. But this you must promise: The adulterer shall not go untouched. He is Sextus Tarquin, who came last night in the guise of a friend, but in fact a bitter enemy, and made a plunder of this delight, a plunder deadly to me—and, if you are men, to himself."

One after the other the men promised what she asked, meanwhile trying to console her sorrow by shifting the blame from the victim to the guilty man: Crime, they assured her, was a matter of the mind, not the body, and where there was no intent there could be no offense.

But Lucretia only answered, "You must determine his punishment. As for me, even though I acquit myself of guilt, I must still pay the penalty. From now on no adulteress can live with Lucretia as her model." She had hidden a dagger in her clothing. At this she plunged it into her heart and fell dying upon her wound.

Livy, *History of Rome,* 1.58.5–12

Brutus drew the gory dagger from her breast, and on its hilt swore to drive out the Tarquins. He summoned the people, repeated the tale, and led them in the expulsion of the tyrant and his brood. A new order was established. Henceforth, the state would be ruled by the Senate, presided over by two consuls, and there would be no more kings. The state was to be a *res publica,* a "public affair," not a plaything of kings. The first two consuls were Brutus himself and Tarquin Collatinus, the husband of Lucretia. According to a traditional, but entirely artificial chronology, the expulsion of Tarquin the Proud took place in 510 BC, about the time of the foundation of the democracy in Athens.

## OBSERVATIONS: AN IMAGINARY PAST PRESERVES THE PRESENT

There was little change in Rome's system of government for five hundred years. The external world, by contrast, changed enormously, swiftly, and radically between the founding of the Republic in the 6th century BC, when Rome controlled perhaps one hundred square miles, and the murder of Julius Caesar, when Rome controlled most of Europe, the Near East, and the Mediterranean world. Rarely in human history has a small power grown so large so fast, and never has a political power lasted so long. The Roman political achievement is unparalleled in history and is likely never to be equaled.

Roman violence was terrifying, but Rome was not a tyrant state, gobbling up everything in its path, taking what it wanted and offering nothing in return. Control by Rome was in most cases preferable to the dangers of freedom. Rome offered military protection in a cutthroat world, safe communication, free trade across the wonderful Roman roads, equal treatment (in theory) under written law, and relative freedom from religious and social persecution. Military superiority may grant any state an initial advantage over its neighbors, but only moral advantage can bestow permanence to conquest and rule. Moral advantage, according to the Romans' own understanding of their history, was in fact responsible for Roman victory where others failed. The ideal of selfless devotion appears again and again in Roman myth.

The Romans also wanted to know where they came from and how they got to where they were, but surviving traditions about the early days were unreliable. Greek historians of Sicily first suggested the Trojan ancestry of the Romans, which Romans readily agreed to after entering into close relations with Greeks living in the West. Perhaps building on a local story, the Romans claimed that the Trojan Aeneas' descendants, Romulus and Remus, had founded the city of Rome 450 years after Aeneas.

But the monarchy of Romulus concentrated power in the hands of one man, hateful to the ideals of the expanding Roman state and the powerful oligarchy within it. The Republic, by contrast, spread power among this small class, which directed Rome's expansion and benefited from it. Thus did Roman myths support ideals of the Roman Republic through examples of men who at first helped the city, then came to a bad end for "aiming at the kingship." The enemies of Julius Caesar accused him of just this ambition.

During the one-man rule of Augustus and his successors the challenge was to pretend that nothing had changed from the days of the *res publica*. For this reason Augustus called himself *princeps*, "first citizen," never *rex*, "king." Few were fooled. Roman legend was an important force in stabilizing and conserving the Roman state, but in the end Time, the great devourer, swallowed that too.

## Key Terms

| | | |
|---|---|---|
| Etruscans *190* | Neptune *195* | Acheron *205* |
| Alba Longa *192* | Mars *196* | Charon *205* |
| Lavinium *192* | Venus *196* | Elysium *208* |
| Julius Caesar *193* | Lar *196* | Turnus *210* |
| Marc Antony *193* | Penates *196* | Romulus *214* |
| Octavian *193* | Vesta *197* | Remus *214* |
| Augustus *193* | Vergil *199* | Rhea Silvia *215* |
| numen *193* | Livy *199* | Sabines *217* |
| Jupiter/Jove *194* | Dido *200* | Tarquin the Proud *218* |
| Juno *195* | Iulus *200* | Sextus Tarquin *219* |
| Mercury *195* | Sibyl of Cumae *205* | Lucretia *219* |

# Further Reading

Bloom, H., *Virgil: Modern Critical Views* (New York, 1986).
Bremmer, J. N., and N. M. Horsfall, *Roman Myth and Mythography* (London, 1987).
Conte, G. B., *The Poetry of Pathos: Studies in Vergilian Epic* (Oxford, UK, 2007).
Feeney, D. C., *The Gods in Epic: Poets and Critics of the Classical Tradition* (Oxford, UK, 1991).
Galinsky, G. K., *Aeneas, Sicily, and Rome* (Princeton, NJ, 1969).
Grant, M., *Roman Myths* (New York, 1986).
Johnson, W. R., *Darkness Visible: A Study of Vergil's* Aeneid (Berkeley, CA, 1976).
Livy, *The Early History of Rome*, trans. Aubrey de Sélincourt (Baltimore, MD, 1960).
Wiseman, T. P., *Remus: A Roman Myth* (Cambridge, UK, 1996).
_____, *Roman Drama and Roman History* (Exeter, UK, 1998).
_____, *The Myths of Rome* (Exeter, UK, 2005).

# Myth in India

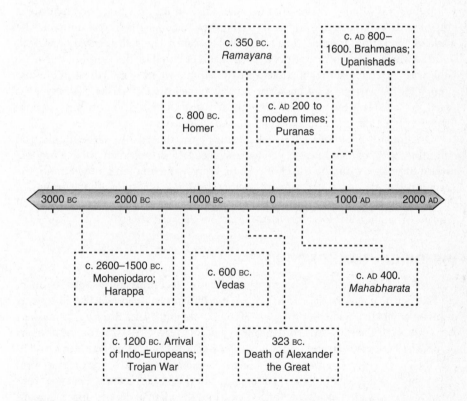

So great is the wealth of myths of the Indian subcontinent that one could spend a lifetime in study without exhausting it. Only the body of Greek myth approaches it in extent. Unlike Greek myth, however, the myths of India continue to be a part of the everyday life of the peoples who live in India, to inspire them directly with models for behavior and explanations for the way the world is. In 2010 there was a presentation on the radio of the *Ramayana*, an Indian epic, which lasted for 120 episodes!

There are more than a billion followers of the religion of Hinduism with which Indian myth is inextricably involved, if we may characterize Hinduism as a single religion. There are many gods in Hinduism, related to each other in a most haphazard way. Unlike Christianity and Islam, Hinduism had no founder, but is derived from many diverse traditions. Like the religions of Mesopotamia, Canaan, and Egypt, it is a religion of evolution, not a religion of revelation. The vast majority of Hindus— that is, practitioners of indigenous Indian religions—live in India, but there are other countries with large Hindu populations: Nepal, Bangladesh, Mauritius (an island east of Madagascar), and the island of Bali (in Indonesia).

Here we will examine several typical myths. Indian myth, unlike Mesopotamian, Egyptian, Canaanite, Greek, and Roman myth, is deeply rooted in a sometimes very abstract philosophy that veers off constantly into religion to form a basis for belief, hence action. *Philosophy* is a Greek word that means "love of wisdom" and is concerned with general and fundamental problems: the nature of existence, values, knowledge, mind, and language, addressed through rational argument.

Indian philosophy teaches that the world is infinitely diverse, and anything is possible within it, but the world is always **maya**, illusion—it is simply not real. The world of oppositions is unified in a true invisible reality. The path to salvation is open to those whose ascetic practice purifies the soul, polluted by the world of dualities. Otherwise the soul will remain attached to an eternal wheel of rebirth, each lifetime atoning for the wrongs of a previous according to the justice of **karma**. *Karma* means "deed" or "act." It is the universal principle of cause and effect, action and reaction, that governs all life: If I harm another, I must be harmed.

One must follow *dharma*, which means "law," that is, discharge the natural obligations that come from caste, gender, and occupation. Only then can one proceed toward liberation from the wheel of rebirth. Only by meditation on the **atman**, the deepest personal essence, does one realize that the *atman* is at one with the **brahman**, the creative principle of the universe, from which everything comes and to which all returns: "That thou art" (*Tat tvam asi*)—a famous Sanskrit saying.

## HISTORICAL BACKGROUND

The stories as we have them have a curious distance, a curious abstract quality in accord with their philosophical underpinning. But Indian myth depends, like all systems of myth, on history. Sometime around 1500–1200 BC in the Late Bronze Age invaders from east of the CASPIAN SEA, from the mountains of the KOPET DAGH (on the frontiers of modern Turkmenistan and Iran), came over BALUCHISTAN (in modern Afghanistan) into the PUNJAB, the "five waters" (in modern Pakistan), where five rivers join to form the mighty INDUS RIVER that flows (through modern Pakistan) into the PERSIAN GULF (Map 7). The invaders also went further east into the plain along the upper GANGES RIVER (in modern India). These were the so-called **Indo-Aryans** or **Indo-Europeans**.

In what is today Pakistan, the Indo-Europeans found the very advanced urban civilization that has left impressive remains at MOHENJODARO, HARAPPA, and a thousand smaller sites. Deeply influenced by the Sumerians in southern Mesopotamia, the civilization seems to have flourished from 2600 to 1500 BC. Presumably the population was Dravidian, that is, they were related to modern speakers of Dravidian languages

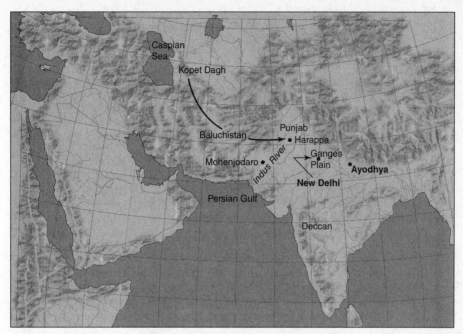

**MAP 7**   Indo-European migration into the Punjab, c. 1500–c. 1200 BC.

(Telugu, Tamil, Kannada) who live mostly in the DECCAN ("south") in southern India. We can presume that the Indo-European invaders pushed them there, yet the Dravidians left an impression on the religion of the invaders, to whom they may have been distantly related. Sometimes we can see such influence in the myths.

For example, a seal from Mohenjodaro shows an ascetic in yogic posture, but we usually associate the ascetic yogi with the Hindu religion, that is, the religion of the invading Aryans (Figure 7.1). The square seal depicts a nude male deity with three faces, as Hindu art shows many multi-faced figures. Five symbols of the undeciphered Indus script appear on either side of the headdress. The headdress is made of two outward projecting buffalo-style curved horns, with two upward projecting points: Similarly this special headdress designates the gods in Hindu art.

Nonetheless the Indo-European invaders later had their own sacred texts and an elaborate ritual life supported by these texts. Indian myth consists of the stories that these peoples told. The descendants of these early Indo-European invaders are the Brahmans of today, who in a not very successful attempt to prevent racial admixture with the indigenous population created the infamous Indian caste system that rigorously governs whom one can marry.

## THE SOURCES FOR INDIAN MYTH

How do we know of Indian myth? The oldest sources are the **Vedas**, "knowledge," a large collection of hymns, formulas, and spells that every handbook, and pious fiction, dates to around 1200 BC. Such cannot be the case, however, because writing was not introduced into India until perhaps c. 600 BC. Studies in oral verse-making have

**FIGURE 7.1**    Seal showing yogi, c. 2600 BC. A single branch with three leaves rises from the middle of the headdress of buffalo horns. Seven bangles adorn the right arm and eight adorn the left arm. Hands rest on the knees, and the heels are pressed together under the groin. The feet project beyond the edge of the throne, which has legs carved as bovine hoofs. A grooved and perforated boss is on the back of the seal. Five signs in the undeciphered Mohenjodaro script are engraved above the figure. (National Museum of Pakistan, Karachi, Pakistan; Borromeo / Art Resource, NY)

shown that verbatim repetition is impossible without the stabilizing effect of writing, so we cannot be sure of any original form. We cannot say how old the Vedas are, but they are the earliest Indian writings and some of them go back to 600 BC.

The Vedas are in the Indo-European Sanskrit language and in various scripts. In modern times Sanskrit is usually written in Devanagari script ("divine town" script), which a modern scholar will learn who wishes to read the ancient Sanskrit. Devanagari, easily recognizable for having what appears to be a horizontal line from which the characters are suspended, seems to have originated around AD 1200 and is used for several Indian languages today, including Hindi (Figure 7.2). Like all Indian scripts, Devanagari is derived from syllabic West Semitic writing. It is unclear in what script the Vedas first appeared, but perhaps it was in the so-called Brahmi script, the earliest attested Indian writing, surviving only on monuments from the reign of the powerful king Asoka (304–232 BC), who ruled the entire Indian subcontinent and Pakistan. In his promulgations, carved into stone, the great Asoka advocated the teachings of the Buddha, our earliest evidence for the existence of this religious philosophy.

The Sanskrit Vedas do not tell myths as such, but refer to them, often very obliquely. The **Brahmanas** ("teachings of the Brahmans," the priestly caste) describe the Vedic rites. Like the Vedas they are in the classical Sanskrit language and usually Devanagari script. They comment on the meaning of the Vedic rites and explicate

**FIGURE 7.2**   Information signboard in front of a building in Devanagari script. (Jim Corbett National Park, Ramnagar, Nainital, Uttarakhand, India; PhotosIndia.com LLC / Alamy)

various features according to etymologies and by telling myths. We cannot date the Brahmanas, but they were written between AD 800 and 1600. The earliest **Upanishads** ("sitting down near" a teacher), too, are very early, but they were still being composed in the medieval and early modern period. The Upanishads are the basis for the widespread religion or philosophy of **Vedanta**, which holds that one can attain cosmic consciousness through realization of the true nature of the self, the *atman*, as *brahman*. Vedanta is from "Veda-end," apparently the goal and purpose of the Vedas.

Finally the **Puranas** ("of ancient times"), at last offer what we think of as myths: stories of the history of the universe, its creation and ultimate destruction and recreation, genealogies of gods and heroes, all mixed up with Hindu philosophy. The oldest Puranas are in the Sanskrit language and come from the 3rd to 5th centuries AD, but they were still being added to in the 16th century AD and perhaps even today. It is hard to date the Puranas accurately. Usually they are written as a story told by someone speaking to another. The Puranas usually give precedence to one or another deity and were used by Brahmans who advocated the power of their own special deity.

In addition there are two very long epics, the Sanskrit **Mahabharata**, "the great story of the Bharata dynasty," the longest epic poem in the world with over ninety thousand verses, long passages in prose, and 1.8 million words. According to tradition it was composed by one Vyasa, who supposedly also composed the Upanishads, the Puranas, and who wrote down the Vedas. We cannot really date Vyasa, although he may belong to the time when writing was introduced into India about 600 BC. He was presumably a man who had something to do with fixing the Hindu sacred texts in writing, but the

*Mahabharata*, as well as the Upanishads and Puranas, contains much later material. The poem did not settle down into something like its modern form until AD 400.

In the *Mahabharata* a king is in conversation with a trusted adviser concerning the war between the Pandavas and their cousins the Kauravas. The Pandavas are victorious in the war. The poem is a chaos of myth and historical and geographical description. It contains the *Bhagavad Gita* ("song of god"), a song of about seven hundred lines in which **Krishna**, an incarnation of **Vishnu**, a creator-god, explains to the Pandava bowman Arjuna the need to do his duty, to follow *dharma*, to uphold the moral order, even if it means killing his cousins.

Similar obscurities attend the date and origin of the shorter **Ramayana**, "the journey of Rama," with twenty-four thousand verses, about one fourth as long as the *Mahabharata*, or nearly as long as the *Iliad* and *Odyssey* combined. It is attributed to a single poet, Valmiki, who plays a minor role in the epic, but it contains much later material. Valmiki may have lived in the 4th century BC, so at least a core of the story may go back to this time. There are many much later accretions. The *Ramayana* tells the story of Rama, like Krishna an incarnation of the creator-god Vishnu, and his wife Sita, "furrow," an incarnation of **Lakshmi**, "good fortune," consort of Lord Vishnu. In the heart of the story a 10-headed demon-king steals Sita, whom Rama then rescues with the assistance of Hanuman, the monkey-king.

We cannot form a neat genealogy of the Hindu gods and goddesses, as is the case with the Greek gods, but here is a list of those divine beings with whom we will be most concerned in this chapter (Chart 7):

| | |
|---|---|
| *Brahma* | Creator of the world (*brahman* is the principle of the oneness of existence) |
| *Vishnu* | The creator of Brahma, who grows like a lotus flower from Vishnu's navel |
| *Lakshmi* | Vishnu's consort |
| *Krishna* | An *avatar* (manifestation) of Vishnu |
| *Shiva* | The destroyer and creator of the world, identified with Brahma or Vishnu |
| *Kali* | The feminine principle as destroyer |
| *Ganesha* | Son of Shiva, the elephant-headed god who removes all obstacles |
| *Indra* | A storm-god important in the Vedas, where he is "king of the gods," later replaced by Vishnu and Brahma |
| *Rama* | A hero, and also an avatar of Vishnu |
| *Sita* | An avatar of Lakshmi |
| *Ravana* | A demon king |

**CHART 7**  Some Hindu gods.

Let us first consider divine myth in India.

# MYTH: BRAHMA CREATES THE WORLD

In one of the most famous of the *Puranas*—the so-called *Vishnu Purana*—perhaps from around AD 500, deeply imbued with Indian philosophy, is told the story of the creation:[1]

> Created beings, although they are destroyed at the periods of dissolution, are still affected by good or evil *karma*. They are never exempt from its consequences. When Brahma creates the world anew, the created beings are the progeny of his will in the fourfold condition of gods, men, animals, and inanimate things.

The god who actually makes the world is **Brahma** (whereas the oneness of existence as a principle is *brahman*; the superior priestly caste of the Brahmans are named after *brahman*). The world is a cycle of birth and destruction: One day the world will end as it has many times before. But when Brahma remakes the world, he does so in accordance with justice, with *karma*. As an individual consciousness, an *atman*, you must pay for your offenses and will be rewarded for your virtues, even though at the end of an age you cease to exist as an individual. Each time that Brahma recreates the world, he does so through his will. There are four kinds of things in the world: gods, men, animals, inanimate objects.

The *Vishnu Purana* continues:

> Brahma, desiring to create the four types of "waters"—gods, demons, ancestors, and men—gathered his mind into itself. While he was thus concentrated, darkness pervaded his body. Thence the demons were first born, coming from his thigh. Brahma then abandoned that form made up of the root of darkness. When deserted by him, the form became night.
>
> Continuing to create, but taking on a different shape, Brahma experienced pleasure. From his mouth came the gods, endowed with goodness. The form abandoned by him became day, in which the goodness is dominant. For this reason the gods are most powerful by day and the demons are powerful by night.
>
> He next adopted another form in which the root of goodness also was dominant. Seeing himself as the father of the world, the ancestors [*pitaras*, "fathers"] were born from his side. When he abandoned the body, it became the evening twilight, the space between day and night.
>
> Brahma then assumed another form, pervaded by passion, and from this humans, in whom passion is dominant, were made. Quickly abandoning that body, the form became the morning half-light, or dawn. At the appearance of this light of day, humans feel most vigor while the ancestors are most powerful during the evening.

---

[1]For the Indian texts, cf. D. A. Mackenzie, *Indian Myth and Legend* (London, 1913); H. H. Wilson, *The Vishnu Purana* (orig. 1840); J. Eggeling (trans.), *The Satapatha Brahmana*, Part I, Sacred Books of the East, Vol. 12 (London, 1882); Anand Aadhar Prabhu (trans.), *Bhagavatam: The Story of the Divine Play of the Supreme Lord* (http://bhagavata.org/, no date); Kâshinâth Trimbak *Telang* (trans.), *The Bhagavadgîtâ*, Volume 8, The Sacred Books of the East (1882); Kisari Mohan Ganguli (trans.), *The Mahabharata* (London, 1883–1896); F.E. Pargiter (trans.), *The Markandeya Purana* (Calcutta, 1904); M. N. Dutt, *The Ramayana* (Calcutta, 1891). See also, E. F. Bryant (trans.), *Krishna: The Beautiful Legend of God (Srimad Bhagavata Purana Book X)* (New York, 2004); R. Menon (trans.), *The Bhagavata Purana* (New Delhi, 2006); J. D. Smith (trans.), *Mahabharata* (New York, 2008); William Buck and B.A. van Nooten (trans.), *Ramayana* (Berkeley, 2000).

It is not clear what the Purana means by "waters," but in any event from Brahma come all qualities—darkness and light. They are equals, two halves of a single harmony. The dark and the demons are from Brahma's thigh, in the human body the location of sexual passion. The light and the gods are from his mouth, the higher articulate functions. The battle between the gods and the demons is a central theme in Indian myth, the war between light and dark that are really two sides of the same coin. The ancestors—the ghosts of dead men whom you must honor—are from one side, the twilight; humans, presumably from the other side of Brahma, are of the passionate body because that is their nature. Ancestors are good and humans are bad, but you need both in the balance of the cosmos.

Next Brahma took another body in which passion was predominant, and from Brahma hunger was born, anger was born. And the god put forth in darkness beings emaciated by hunger, of hideous aspect, with long beards. Those beings hurried to the god. Those who exclaimed, "O preserve us! [*raksyatam*]" were called Rakshasas [a class of demons]. Others, who cried, "Let us eat! [*yaksanat*]", were called from that expression Yakshas [a class of semidivine beings, mostly benevolent].

Seeing how disgusting they were, the hairs of Brahma shriveled up. First falling from his head, they were then renewed upon it. They became snakes, called serpents [*sarpa*] from their creeping [*sarpana*] and snakes [*ahi*] because they had departed [*hina*] from his head.

Then the Creator of the Universe became angry, and he created beings who had anger as their essence. Because of their tawny [*kapisa*] color, these fiends are eaters of flesh [*pisitasanas*]. The Gandharvas [celestial musicians] were next born as he sang. They were born drinking of the goddess of speech, and from this came their name [*gam dhayantas*, "drinking of the goddess of speech," a false etymology].

All things come from Brahma—qualities, feelings, desires, demons, snakes, other beings. We may think of puns as amusing, but the Indian mythographer, like the Egyptian, sees a similarity of sound as reflecting a similarity of essence.

Of his own will the divine Brahma made other beings. He made the birds [*vayamsi*] from his own youthful vigor [*vayas*]. He made sheep from his breast, goats from his mouth, cattle from his belly and sides. From his feet he made horses, elephants, donkeys, oxen, deer, camels, mules, antelopes, and other animals. From the hairs of his body sprang grasses, fruits, and roots.

*Vishnu Purana*, 1.5.26–48, 59–65

All things are from Brahma. He is the creator of all things that exist. But he is not prime in the creation. That is Vishnu. Brahma springs from the navel of Vishnu, and Vishnu himself lies asleep on the great serpent Sesha, called **Ananta**, "endless" (Figure 7.3). In Figure 7.3, four-armed Vishnu, blue in color and sound asleep, reclines on Ananta, the serpent of endlessness, whose many heads hang over him in a kind of canopy. Ananta floats on the waters of chaos. Vishnu is lord of creation and wears a crown of pearls. His emblems the scepter, lotus bloom, and conch are at his side. Vishnu's wife Lakshmi, representing the feminine principal, massages his foot as a good wife will. From Vishnu's navel grows a lotus, and from the lotus comes the four-headed Brahma, creator of the world.

**FIGURE 7.3**   A blue four-armed Vishnu asleep on Ananta, the serpent of eternity/chaos, c. 1870. (Victoria and Albert Museum, London; V&A Images, London / Art Resource, NY)

In Indian philosophy/myth there are four great ages, called *yugas*, which means "yoke" in the sense of an "era" or "age." The ages see a gradual decline of *dharma*, wisdom, knowledge, intelligence, and life span and an increase in immoral behavior and violence. Four *yugas* make up a *mahayuga*, or "great age," when the cycle of *yugas* begins again. The four *yugas* are called the *Satya Yuga* (or *Krita Yuga*), the *Treta Yuga*, the *Dvapara Yuga*, and the *Kali Yuga*. Different theories exist about their lengths, but in the following we give a standard interpretation:

- *Satya Yuga*: *Satya* means "truth," a golden age that lasts for 1,728,000 years, when humankind is ruled by gods and all humans pursue *dharma*. Its other name, *Krita Yuga*, means "best" throw of the dice. Humans are 30 feet tall. Goodness reigns supreme and life spans reach 100,000 years.
- *Treta Yuga*: *Treta* means "triple," because during this age three parts of truth prevail. Humans are 21 feet tall and live 10,000 years. The age lasts 1,296,000 years.
- *Dvapara Yuga*: *Dvapara*, "past two," is named from the third best throw of the dice. There is half virtue and half sin. People are around 10 feet tall and live 1,000 years. The Dvapara Yuga lasts 864,000 years.
- *Kali Yuga*: *Kali* means "dark," and this is an age of darkness, our own. There is only one quarter virtue and three quarters sin. Normal human stature is five or six feet and human life less than a hundred years. Toward the end of the Yuga, life span will sink to 20 years. This age lasts 432,000 years (for some reason the present Kali Yuga began in 3102 BC).

The cycles repeat like seasons, which they resemble. One thousand *mahayugas* make up a day in the life of Brahma; two thousand *mahayugas* make up a day and a night of Brahma. Brahma lives for one hundred years, or 311.04 trillion human years, when the universe is completely destroyed, then recreated anew.

So great are the spans of time in Hinduism, reducing a human life to a speck of dust in the wind!

## MYTH: VISHNU'S INCARNATION AS A DWARF

On many occasions Vishnu entered the creation of which he (or the serpent of endlessness) is the ultimate source. These are the *avatars* of Vishnu (in Sanskrit *avatar* means "descent," that is, from heaven), which became popular after the 6th century AD. Other Hindu deities also had *avatars*, but Vishnu's avatars are the best known. Different numbers are given, but 10 is usual, or they were without count. Krishna (see below) and Rama (see below) are the best known avatars of Vishnu, widely worshiped, whose stories are told in the *Mahabharata* and the *Ramayana*. Well known too is the myth of the avatar of Vishnu as a dwarf, told in one of the Brahmanas set in the context of the epic battle between demons and the gods:

> The gods and the demons, both sprung from Prajapati,° were contending for su-periority. The gods were worsted, and the demons thought, "To us alone belongs this world." Thereupon they said, "Well then, let us divide this world between us. Having divided it, let us live upon it." Accordingly they set about dividing it with strips of ox-hide from west to east.
>
> The gods heard of this and said, "The demons are dividing up the earth. Come, let us go to where the demons are dividing it. For what will become of us if we get no share in it?"
>
> Placing Vishnu, the sacrifice,° at their head, they went there and said, "Let us share in this earth along with yourselves. Let a part of it be ours!" The demons replied rather grudgingly, "As much as this Vishnu lies upon, and no more, we give you."
>
> Now Vishnu was a dwarf. The gods, however, took no offense, but answered, "They have given much to us. They have given what is equal in size to the sacrifice."
>
> They laid Vishnu down with his head pointed toward the east. Then they enclosed him on all sides with the meters of the Veda, saying on the south side, "With the Jayatri meter I enclose you!" On the west side, "With the Trishtubh meter I enclose you!" On the north side, "With the Jagati meter I enclose you!"
>
> Having enclosed him in this way on all three sides, and having placed Agni° on the east side, they continued to worship and toil with him.° Therefore from him they obtained the entire earth.° And because they obtained [*samavindanta*, from *vid*] by it the entire earth, therefore the sacrificial ground is called the *altar* [*vedi*]. For this reason they say, "As great as the altar is, so great is the earth," for by the altar they obtained the entire earth. And, truly, he who understands this, likewise takes the entire earth from his rivals and excludes his rivals from all share in it.

*Satapatha Brahmana*, 1.2.5.1–9a

°*prajapati*: "lord of creatures," an epithet of Brahma or any number of other creator-gods. °*the sacrifice*: that which is to be killed to make creation possible, in this case the god Vishnu himself. °*Agni*: the fire-god, but here the sun. °*with him*: that is, Vishnu, the sacrifice. °*the entire earth*: because through the agency of the Vedic poetic meters Vishnu expanded to a gigantic size.

The myth of the avatar of Vishnu as dwarf explains many things. It explains why the gods rule the world and not the demons. It explains the name of the altar, which in Vedic ritual is said to encompass the whole earth: It is through the magic of the Vedas that the dwarf is made to take in the whole world. It is a myth of the very great contained in the very small, a common theme in Indian myth, as we see from the myth of what was in Krishna's mouth.

## MYTH: THE MYTH OF WHAT WAS IN KRISHNA'S MOUTH

Another of Vishnu's avatars was as Krishna, "the dark one," one of the most renowned figures in Indian myth. Hari ("khaki-colored") is an epithet of Vishnu, so *Hari Krishna* is the incarnation of Vishnu as Krishna. The motif of the great contained in the small, implicit in the myth of Vishnu's incarnation as a dwarf, is foremost in the myth of what was in Krishna's mouth, but the depiction of Lord Krishna as a prankish child is very striking. The story is in the *Bhagavata Purana* from c. 9th to 10th centuries AD:

> After a short time passed, both of the young boys, Rama° and Krishna, began to crawl on the ground of the village with the strength of their hands and knees. They crawled in the muddy places in the village made up of cow dung and cow urine. They slithered through the slime like serpents, and the sound of their ankle bells was very charming. They followed people, then, suddenly bewildered, they went back to their mothers.
>
> Covered in filth, the babies still looked very beautiful. When they went to their mothers the women picked them up with great affection, embraced them, and allowed them to suck the milk from their breasts. While sucking a breast, the babies smiled and their small teeth were visible, causing their mothers to feel a transcendental happiness.
>
> The cowherd ladies enjoyed seeing the pastimes of the babies Rama and Krishna. They caught the tails of calves, and the calves dragged them about. When the ladies saw these pastimes, they stopped their household activities and laughed and enjoyed watching the babies.
>
> But the mothers were always anxious in trying to protect the babies from horned cows, fire, animals with claws and teeth (such as monkeys, dogs, and cats), and from knives, water, birds, and thorns. In fact they were unable to do their housework.
>
> After a short time both Rama and Krishna stopped crawling and began to walk easily on their legs by their own strength. Then the lord Krishna played with Rama and the other children of the village, giving great pleasure to the village women.
>
> When the wives of the cowherds saw Krishna's very charming boyish pranks, they would approach his mother and say, "Our dear friend, your son sometimes comes to our houses and releases the calves before the milking of the cows! When the master of the house shouts at him, your son just smiles. Sometimes he steals curd, butter, and milk, which he then eats and drinks. When the monkeys get together, he divides it with them. If he doesn't eat the

°*Rama*: not the Rama of the *Ramayana*.

food, he breaks the pots! Sometimes, if he cannot steal butter or milk from a house, he becomes angry at the householders and makes the children cry, then he runs away.

"Then when the milk and curd are kept high on a swing hanging from the ceiling and Krishna cannot reach it, he reaches it by piling up pillows and whatever else he can find. If he knows that the curd and milk is placed in pots suspended high in a net, he pokes holes in the net. While the wives of the cowherds do their household chores, Krishna sometimes goes into a dark room and makes his body with its valuable jewels and ornaments into a lamp so that he can steal.

"Such are his activities, which are sometimes very naughty. Sometimes, in his anger, Krishna pees and shits in a neat clean place in our houses! But now, this expert thief is sitting before you like such a good boy."

When the mother heard this tale from the wives of the cowherds, who sat there looking at his fearful eyes and beautiful face, his mother laughed and could not punish him.

One day while Krishna was playing with his small playmates, including Rama and the other sons of the cowherds, all his friends got together and lodged a complaint to Krishna's mother, saying, "Mama, Krishna has eaten dirt!"

When his mother heard this from Krishna's playmates, she became anxious about Krishna's well-being, and she picked Krishna up to look into his mouth and reprimand him. With fearful eyes she said, "Dear Krishna, why have you secretly eaten dirt? All your playmates have made this complaint against you, including your older brother Rama. How can this be?"

Krishna answered, "My dear mother, I have never eaten dirt. All my friends complaining about me are liars! If you think they are telling the truth, you can look straight into my mouth to see what you can see."

"If you have not eaten dirt, then open your mouth wide," his mother challenged, and Krishna opened his mouth—Hari, the god of unchallenged sovereignty who had in sport taken the form of a human child.

When Krishna opened his mouth wide at his mother's command, she saw within all the moving and nonmoving entities, outer space, all directions, mountains, islands, oceans, the surface of the earth, the blowing wind, fire, the moon, and the stars. She saw the planets, water, light, air, sky, and space itself. She also saw the senses, the mind, the elements, and the qualities of goodness, passion, and ignorance. She saw the time given to living creatures. She saw instinct and the reactions of *karma*, and she saw desires and different kinds of bodies, moving and nonmoving.

Seeing all these forms of life and time and nature, and her own village, and herself, she became afraid and confused about her son's nature, and asked herself, "Is this a dream, or is it an illusion made by a god? Is it a delusion of my own perception? Is it a foretelling of the natural powers of my own child? I bow down to the god whose nature is beyond human speculation, the mind, behavior, words, arguments, who is the original cause of this universe, by whom the entire cosmos is maintained, by whom we can conceive of its existence. The god is my refuge, and through his maya alone do I think that there is an 'I,' that 'this is my husband' and 'this is my son' and that 'I am the wife of the village mayor and all the wealth of cows and calves are my possessions and all the cowherds and their wives are my subjects.'"

When the cowherd's wife understood in this way the truth about reality, again the supreme master spread his maya in the form of a mother's love. Immediately the cowherd's wife forgot what she had seen. She took her son on her lap. She was like before, but with an increased affection in her heart for her transcendental child.

*Bhagavata Purana*, 10.8.21–45

A similar motif appears in the *Mahabharata*. It is told of a sage that he floated in the cosmic ocean after the dissolution of the cosmos. He saw a boy sleeping under a banyan tree. He entered the mouth of the boy—who was Vishnu—and there he saw the entirety of the universe. Then he came back out of the mouth.

## THE BHAGAVAD GITA

Normally Vishnu's avatars descend with a certain mission. A passage in the *Bhagavad Gita*, "the song of God," describes the role of an avatar of Vishnu: to return *dharma* to the social order:

When right-doing disappears and wrong-doing grows, I sent myself forth.
To protect that which is good, to destroy the evil,
and to establish righteousness,
I come into being time and again.

*Bhagavgad Gita*, 4.7–8

### PERSPECTIVE 7
### Mughal Miniatures

A form of art common in India is called *Mughal art* or *Mughal miniatures*. They are bright-colored watercolors from 6 × 8 inches to the size of a coffee-table book. Originally they were painted as illustrations for the Mughal court, designed to be held in the hand or placed in albums but never hung on walls. The Mughals were Muslims of Mongol origin who ruled much of India from the 16th to the 19th century. The first Mughal emperor of northern India, Akbar (1556–1605), employed more than a hundred painters in his new capital near Delhi. Although they followed Islam, they were interested in the native myths and often illustrated them.

A typical Mughal miniature, "The Transfer of Babes," illustrates the well-known Hindu myth of the saving of Krishna (Perspective Figure 7). It is a frame-by-frame continuous narration. The story starts in the upper-left corner. Krishna's parents, imprisoned by a wicked king, make plans to save their unborn child. In the next scene, to the right, the baby-size Krishna appears, worshiped by his parents with gods in

**PERSPECTIVE FIGURE 7**   Indian The Transfer of Babes early 19th century Watercolor, opaque watercolor, and gold on paper, Chazen Museum of Art, University of Wisconsin-Madison, Gift of Mr. and Mrs. Earnest C. Watson, 69.28.16

the clouds above. In the top center frame, the parents plot to release Krishna by exchanging him with another baby. Directly below this scene, the prison door opens while the guards sleep. Below the prison doors, the father takes the baby Krishna and prepares to cross the river and take the child-god to safety, protected by the serpent-god Vasuki.

In the bottom right the father places the baby Krishna (identified by a bluish complexion in the original) on the bed of a certain Yashoda; Yashoda's newborn daughter sleeps in a nearby chamber. Back to the upper right, Krishna's father takes Yashoda's newborn daughter (white complexion) and gives her to Krishna's mother. In the meanwhile (in the lower left) the guards and the wicked king walk toward the prison, unaware of the exchange. Thus is Lord Krishna saved.

Because the Mughal emperors wanted visual records of their deeds as hunters and conquerors, their artists accompanied them on military expeditions or missions of state, or recorded their prowess as animal slayers, or depicted them in great dynastic marriage ceremonies. Painters focused mostly on court scenes, royal portraits, natural scenes, and landscapes, but some miniature paintings illustrated manuscripts of Jains and Buddhists and such Indian epics as the *Ramayana*, *Mahabharata*, *Bhagavata Purana*, and *Kama Sutra*, "sayings on sexual lore."

Indian miniature paintings are renowned worldwide for their bright, beautiful colors and impeccable details. As an educational and historical resource, they have great value. Bygone tastes and beliefs, vanished modes of life, and forgotten nuances of behavior can all be found in Mughal paintings.

Such is Krishna's mission in the long philosophical, not mythical conversation that Krishna carries on with Arjuna, prince of the Pandavas, as he is about to go into battle against his one hundred cousins near modern Delhi. The *Bhagavad Gita* is one of the most important texts in Indian literature. Here Krishna reveals himself as the Supreme Being himself, the Divine One.

He addresses Arjuna's confusion over having to fight his cousins, explaining that he must do his duty as a prince and a warrior. On the way he elaborates various philosophies. The *Gita* is a concise guide to Hindu theology and to how one should lead one's life. The *Gita* has earned the status of an Upanishad, a revealed document.

## SHIVA, LORD OF THE DANCE

**Shiva**, "auspicious," came late into Hindu religion, anticipated in Vedic times by a god named Rudra, "roarer." Shiva may be an epithet of Rudra that evolved into an independent god. By the first centuries AD he was well established. Shiva brought the nonVedic worship of the *linga* ("sign") or phallus, his usual form in cult, the erect penis ready to fertilize the *yoni*, the "female genitalia."

He also introduced the practice of asceticism: Shiva is the god of yogis. He is the moon-god of the mountains, who wears the moon tangled in his hair, heavily matted because of his ascetic practice. Through the matted hair of Shiva flows the Ganges River, breaking up into many streams instead of a single inundating flow. To the mountain the yogis go to practice their yoga, "the art of union" with *brahman*. Shiva is the father of the Brahmans who can read the Vedas.

To some sects Shiva is the destroyer or transformer, while to others he is the Supreme God, or one of the five primary forms of God. Followers of Shiva are called Shaivites, today one of Hinduism's most influential sects. When not represented as a *linga*, Shiva is shown as a comely youth either lost in meditation or dancing on the "demon of ignorance" as Lord of the Dance (Figure 7.4). Shiva is the father of **Ganesha**, the very popular elephant-headed god who removes all obstacles (Figure 7.5). Once Ganesha's wife Uma held her hands over Shiva's eyes: At once all lights in the cosmos were extinguished, and so he grew a third eye. The glance of Shiva's third eye is death: He is the god of Death, the ultimate dissolution that awaits all created things, as he is also the creator-god, identified with Brahma and Vishnu.

In Figure 7.4, which shows Shiva as king of the dance, he holds in his upper right hand a small drum in the shape of an hourglass, for beating the rhythm. The upper left hand holds a tongue of flame, the agency of destruction at the end of the world. These are the opposites—the rhythm of life (the drum) and consuming death (the flame)—that meet in the central figure, who dances away all contradiction.

The other right hand is posed in the "fear not" position (*mudra*). The other left hand is pointed down to the upraised left foot, the foot of release, the position of the hand imitating the trunk of the elephant-headed Ganesha. The god dances on the prostrate body of the dwarfish demon of ignorance. To conquer the demon is to attain truth and freedom.

Shiva dances in a ring of fire, signifying the vital processes of the universe, nature's dance as moved by the dancing-god within. The hair of this god of the

**FIGURE 7.4**   Shiva as Lord of Dance, from Tamil Nadu, India. Chola Dynasty, copper alloy, c. 1000. Los Angeles County Museum of Art, M.75.1 (http://en.wikipedia.org/wiki/File: Shiva_as_the_Lord_of_Dance_LACMA_edit.jpg)

yogis is partly long and matted, streaming free, and partly stacked into a pyramid. Supernormal life energy flows in his hair. The whole scene takes place atop the lotus of creation that comes from Vishnu's navel (see Figure 7.3).

Dancing is an ancient form of magic, a means of self-transformation and of the discovery of spiritual truth. No wonder that the god of the ascetic is also the god of the dance. The dance is creation. By it the dancer summons the hidden energies through which the world is brought into being, and then dissolved. Life is the cosmic dance of Shiva.

By the same token Shiva is the center of the cult of Tantra ("loom," hence "doctrine"), wherein the universe is viewed as a divine play between Shiva and **Shakti** (from Sanskrit "to be able"), one personification of the divine female creative power. Sometimes Shakti is called "The Great Divine Mother." A feature of the famous Tantric ritual is sexual intercourse through which one enters into the powers that bring the universe into being, often illustrated in books of the 18th and 19th centuries. The male takes on the role of Shiva and the female the role of Shakti, thus releasing, through intercourse, knowledge of the divine.

**FIGURE 7.5** Ganesha, the Indian god who removes obstacles. In one left hand he hold an ax and in the other a lotus; in a right hand he holds a necklace and a bowl of fruit, one of which he reaches to his mouth with his trunk. He emerges from a lotus and wears lotuses on his crown. Miniature painting from Kashmir in northwestern India, c. 1730. National Museum, New Delhi, India. (http://upload.wikimedia.org/wikipedia/commons/6/64/Ganesha_Basohli_miniature_circa_1730_Dubost_p73.jpg)

## MYTH: GODS AND DEMONS CHURN THE OCEAN TO OBTAIN AMBROSIA

The oddness of much Indian myth is prominent in the famous story of how the gods found **ambrosia** by churning the ocean, told in the immensely long *Mahabharata*, "the great story of the Bharata dynasty" (c. AD 400?). Ambrosia is the substance that makes gods "gods." When they eat it, they become immortal. They were not immortal before (and in many cases, after):

> There is a shining mountain named Meru,° looking like a heap of glory. Its golden peaks outshine even the rays of the sun. The gods and Gandharvas° dwell on its golden beautiful slopes, unapproachable by men of *adharma*.° Dreadful beasts of prey wander over it, and many divine life-giving herbs illuminate it. The mountain kisses the heavens with its height. It is the first of mountains. An

---

°*Meru*: the golden mountain, the center of the world. °*Gandhaarvas*: celestial musicians.
°*adharma*: the opposite of *dharma*; the pursuit of making things the way they should not be.

ordinary person would not even think of ascending it, graced with trees and streams and resounding with the charming sounds of birds.

Once the gods, who dwell in heaven and are of great vigor, rich in ascetic power, all came together on its slopes covered in gems. They sat and took counsel how they might obtain ambrosia.°

While the gods were conferring, Narayana° said to Brahma, "You should churn the ocean with the gods and the demons. By doing so, you will obtain ambrosia and all the herbs and gems. Churn the Ocean and you will discover ambrosia."

There is a mountain called Mandara adorned with cloudlike peaks. It is the best of mountains and is covered all over with intertwining herbs. Countless birds pour forth their melodies. Beasts of prey roam at will. Celestial spirits and gods and Kinnaras° visit the place. It rises upwards eleven thousand leagues and descends down as much.

The gods wanted to uproot it and use it as a churning rod, but being unable to do so they came to Vishnu and Brahma, who were sitting together. The gods said, "Devise some effective scheme for how Mount Mandara may be dislodged to our advantage."

Vishnu and Brahma assented, and the lotus-eyed one° laid the hard task on the mighty Ananta,° the prince of snakes. The powerful Ananta, under the direction of Brahma and Narayana, tore up the mountain along with the woods and the creatures who lived in those woods.

The gods came to the shore of the ocean with Ananta and addressed the ocean, saying, "O Ocean, we have come to churn your waters for obtaining ambrosia." And Ocean replied, "But let me have a share of it. Then I can bear the prodigious agitation of my waters caused by Mount Mandara."

The gods then went to the king of tortoises and said, "O tortoise king, you will have to hold the mountain on your back!" The tortoise king agreed, and Indra contrived to place the mountain on the back of the tortoise. The gods and the demons made of Mount Mandara a churning staff and of the serpent Vasuki° a cord, and they set about churning the deep for ambrosia.

The demons held Vasuki by the hood, and the gods held him by the tail. Ananta, who was on the side of the gods, and the blessed Narayana at intervals raised the snake's hood and suddenly lowered it. Because of the stretching that Vasuki received from the demons and the gods, black vapors with flames came from Vasuki's mouth, turned into clouds charged with lightning, and poured forth showers to refresh the tired gods. They were refreshed too by the flowers that fell on the gods from the trees on whirling Mount Mandara.

Then out of the deep came a tremendous roar like the roar of the clouds at the cosmic dissolution. A variety of aquatic animals, crushed by the great mountain, perished in the salt waters, and many denizens of the lower regions of hell were killed. As Mount Mandara spun, huge trees filled with birds were torn up by the roots and fell into the water. The friction of those trees produced fires that

---

°*ambrosia*: a drink that makes one immortal. °*Narayana*: "son of man" or "son of the waters," a name for Vishnu. °*Kinnaras*: "what-men," demigods with heads of horses and bodies of men, or the other way around. °*lotus-eyed one*: Vishnu. °*Ananta*: "infinite," the serpent on which Vishnu sleeps. °*Vasuki*: one of the great serpent kings.

blazed up over the mountain, which looked like a mass of dark clouds charged with lightning. The fire consumed the lions, elephants, and other creatures on the mountain until Indra extinguished the fire by pouring down heavy showers.

After the churning had gone on for a good while, gummy exudations of various trees and herbs that contained the properties of ambrosia mingled with the waters of Ocean. From these juices, and from drinking water mixed with those gums and with a liquid extract of gold, the gods achieved immortality. By degrees, the water of the agitated deep turned into milk, then clarified butter, because of those gums and juices.

But ambrosia still did not appear. The gods came before Brahma, grantor of boons, and said, "Lord, we are worn out. We have no strength left to churn further. Ambrosia has not come from our efforts. We have no resource save Narayana."

On hearing them, Brahma said to Narayana, "Vishnu, grant the gods strength to churn the deep anew."

Narayana, acceding to their prayers, said, "You wise ones, I grant you sufficient strength. Go, put the mountain in position again and churn the water."

Thus reinvigorated, the gods began to churn again. After a while arose Soma,° the mild moon with its cool rays, then the sun of a hundred thousand rays emerged from the ocean. Then sprang forth Lakshmi, dressed in white, from the clarified butter; then the goddess of wine; then the White Horse of the Sun; then the celestial gem Kaustubha° that adorns the breast of Narayana, born of the ambrosia. And at length rose the great elephant Airavata,° of huge body and with two pairs of white tusks. Indra took him, the wielder of the thunderbolt.

But while the churning was still going on, the poison Kalakuta appeared at last and engulfed the earth, blazing like a smoky fire. The poison paralyzed the triple world. Then Shiva, at Brahma's request, held the poison in his throat, and that why he is called "blue-throat."°

When Lakshmi, wine, moon, and the horse swift as thought had come forth, they went upon the path of the sun that leads to immortality. Then were born the magic tree and the magic cow from which come the fulfillment of all that one desires. At last the god Dhanvantari° came forth holding the ambrosia in a white pot. When the demons saw this, they cried out, "It is mine!"

But the lord Narayana called his bewitching maya to his aid and took on the form of an enticing female. She went to the demons. They were charmed by her exquisite beauty and grace. They lost their reason and placed the ambrosia in her hands. The goddess made of illusion gave the ambrosia to the gods to drink, but did not give it to the demons who were all seated in a row.

The demons equipped themselves with wonderful armor and all kinds of weapons. They attacked the gods. Then the valiant Vishnu, in the form of the enticing female accompanied by Nara,° deceived the mighty demons and took away the ambrosia from their hands. And all the gods drank the ambrosia with delight, receiving it from Vishnu.

°*Soma*: originally an intoxicating drink, the water of life; the god of the moon. °*Kaustubha*: a fabulous jewel. °*Airavata*: "born of the milky ocean," the white elephant, Indra's mount. °*blue throat*: Shiva is usually represented as blue. °*Dhanvantari*: "moving in a curve," the physician of the gods. °*Nara*: "the man," the primeval man associated with Narayana.

While the gods were eating that which they had so much desired, a demon named Rahu took on the guise of a god and drank it too. And when the ambrosia had reached Rahu's throat, the moon and the sun reported it, and Narayana with his discus cut off the head of the demon drinking the ambrosia without permission.

The great head of the demon, cut off by the discus and resembling a mountain peak, at first fell to the ground, then rose up to the sky and uttered terrible cries. The demon's headless trunk, falling on the ground and rolling, made the earth tremble with her mountains, forests, and islands. And from that time there is a long-standing quarrel between Rahu's head and the moon and the sun. To this day it swallows the moon and the sun.°

Then Narayana left his enchanting female form and routed the demons. He hurled many awesome weapons. The most dreadful battle between gods and demons began on the shores of the salt sea. Sharp-pointed javelins and spears and other weapons fell by the thousands. Mangled by the discus and wounded with swords, arrows, and maces, the demons in large numbers vomited blood and lay prostrate on the earth. Sharp double-edged swords cut off heads adorned with bright gold from the trunk. Demons fell continually on the field of battle.

Their bodies drenched in gore, the great demons lay dead everywhere as mountain peaks crimson with mineral ore. The sun grew red with the blood of the thousands of warriors as they struck one another. Cries of distress filled the sky. They fought hand-to-hand, with clubs of iron or gold, and those fighting at close quarters killed one another with their fists, filling the air with shrieks of "Cut!" "Break!" "At 'em!" "Knock him down!" "Advance!"

When the battle was fiercely raging, Nara and Narayana entered the field. Seeing the celestial bow in the hand of Nara, Narayana remembered his own weapon, the demon-destroying discus. Suddenly the discus, called Sudarsana,° came out of the sky like Agni° in brilliance, dreadful in battle.

Ferociously energetic Narayana, having arms like the trunk of an elephant, hurled with great power that weapon of astounding brilliance, shining like a blazing fire, terrible, capable of ruining the enemy's towns. That discus, blazing like the fire that consumes all things at the end of an age, hurled with force by Narayana, cut down the demons by the thousands. Sometimes it consumed them, struck them down as it coursed through the sky. Sometimes, falling on the earth, it drank their blood like an evil spirit.

But the demons, white as the clouds from which rain drops, with great strength and bold heart ascended the sky. They hurtled down thousands of mountains, harassing the gods. Those terrible mountains, like masses of clouds, with their trees and tops broken off, collided with one another as they fell from the sky. They produced a tremendous roar. The warriors on the battlefield roared incessantly at one another as the mountains with the woods still on them fell all around. The forested earth trembled.

°*moon and sun*: in an eclipse. ° *Sudarsana*: "beautiful." °*Agni*: god of fire.

The divine Nara came into the dreadful conflict. With his gold-headed arrows he shattered the mountain peaks amidst the bands of terrible demons. Great demons, overwhelmed by the gods, seeing the furious discus scouring the fields of heaven like a blazing flame, entered the bowels of the earth or plunged into the salt sea.

Having gained the victory, the gods offered due respect to Mount Mandara and placed him again in his proper place. Like water-bearing clouds, the gods made the heavens resound with thunderous shouting as they rejoiced. Indra, who shatters armies, and the other deities gave to Narayana the vessel of ambrosia for careful keeping.

*Mahabharata*, 1.15.5–13; 1.16.1–40; 1.171–30

The story of the war in heaven, with gods fighting demons, is critical in Indian myth. In a way all of existence is seen in these terms, of light fighting darkness, but light winning in the end, until it is apparent that the light and darkness are the same thing: just part of the dream of Vishnu. This story is notable for its cosmic compass, with mountains ripped from their roots and used as a stirring implement by beings of immense power. Vishnu kills a great demon and from his head a mountain is made, which continues its evil ways in regularly swallowing the sun and the moon. In the meanwhile the gods dine on a magical food that makes them immortal, and only they possess it.

## MYTH: DEVI KILLS THE BUFFALO DEMON

**Devi** just means "goddess." She is sometimes said to be Shiva's consort. She is the feminine side of things, the Eternal Feminine. She takes on many forms, including Shiva's consort Shakti; the terrible Kali ("black goddess": see Figure 7.7); Parvati ("daughter of the mountain" Himalaya), another consort of Shiva; Uma ("O! Don't," uttered by her mother when she practiced asceticism), also the daughter of Himalaya, sometimes a wife of Ganesha; and many others. Really, these are all different aspects of the same goddess.

The best-known myth about Devi (often called Durga) tells how she killed the buffalo demon. One of the Puranas (*Markandeya Purana*) has the oldest version, from c. AD 1000, which focuses on the undoing of the savage monster:

When his own army was destroyed, the buffalo demon assumed his own form as a buffalo. He terrified the goddess's troops. He abused some with his muzzle, others he trampled under his hoofs. He lashed some with his tail and others he pricked with his two horns. Others he rushed at, roared at, whirled around. Others he coughed to the ground with his hurricane breath.

When he had overwhelmed the vanguard of Devi's army in this way, the great demon attacked her lion in order to kill him.° Now she was very angry. The great hero° was angry too. He pounded the earth with his hooves and tossed mountains high with his horns. He roared. The earth was ruined

---

°*kill him*: Devi is usually accompanied by a lion. °*great hero*: the buffalo demon.

by his poundings. He lashed the ocean with his tail so that it overflowed on both sides. The clouds were pierced by his swinging horns and were broken into fragments. Hundreds of mountains fell from the sky, cast down by the blast of his breathing (Figure 7.6).

**FIGURE 7.6**  Goddess Devi (or Durga) the buffalo-demon. From the clouds celestial beings watch the event. In her eight arms she holds: a sword, a shield, a noose, a goad, a bow, a bell, a mace, and a spear. Her head is crowned with lotuses. She rides on her tiger that attacks the demon. The head of the demon, emerging from the neck of the buffalo, has been pierced by two arrows. The demon carries a sword a shield. The decapitated head of the buffalo lies at his feet. Watercolor, c. 1730. (http://upload.wikimedia.org/wikipedia/commons/f/f5/Durga_Mahisasuramardini.JPG)

Seeing the great buffalo demon swollen with rage and advancing towards her, fat with anger, the goddess was determined to kill him. She flung her noose over him and bound the great demon. Thus bound in the great battle, he left his buffalo form and suddenly became a lion. When Devi cut off the head of his lion form, he took the appearance of a man with a sword in his hand and a hide shield. Immediately Devi pierced him with her arrows. Then he became a big elephant. The elephant tugged at her great lion with his trunk and roared loudly, but as he was dragging the lion Devi cut off his trunk with her sword. The great demon then resumed his buffalo shape and shook the three worlds° with their movable and immovable objects.

Deeply angered, the furious mother of the universe drank the supreme wine over and over. Her eyes reddened and she laughed. The demon roared, puffed up by his own power and strength. He ripped up mountains with his horns and hurled them at the goddess. She pulverized them with a shower of arrows.

Then she spoke to him, her passionate syllables all mixed up from the intoxication of the divine wine. Devi said, "Roar, roar all you want while I drink this wine. Soon the gods will roar here too when I have killed you."

Having so spoken, she jumped and landed on the great demon, kicked him on the neck and struck him with her trident. The demon came halfway from his own buffalo mouth, completely overcome by the valor of Devi. As the great demon named Buffalo came halfway out, fighting, Devi struck off his head with her great sword and he fell. Then, crying in consternation, the whole demon army perished and his band of friends, when he had bewitched the triple world.

When the buffalo demon fell, all the crowds of gods, demons, and men in the triple world shouted out, "Victory!" A cry of consternation went out as the demon army was destroyed and all the bands of gods rejoiced. The heavenly gods and the great sages all sang Devi's praise, the Gandharva° leaders sang, the bands of celestial spirits danced.

*Markandeya Purana*, 80.21–44

°*three worlds*: the earth, the sky, and heaven above. °*Gandharva*: celestial musicians.

The demon had terrorized the triple world—the earth, sky, and heaven. He can assume any form, for he is the principle of chaos itself, peering out from every angle. To defeat a chaos demon you must become a chaos demon, and the mother of all things shows her savage destroying side in her drunken wildness and rage.

More particularly Devi as the destroyer is **Kali**, "the black goddess," bedizened with necklaces of skulls, with toothed and bloody maw (Figure 7.7). Paradoxically, Kali is said to be Brahma, the creator of all. Kali too killed a demon, according to a myth about her. The battle between the gods and demons is never complete. Even though Devi killed the buffalo demon, the demons go on, they live, and they are a fact in life on which you can depend.

**FIGURE 7.7**   Kali, the "black goddess," lord of time and annihilation. She tramples on her consort Shiva. In one hand she holds a trident, in another a scimtar, in another a severed head, and in the fourth a pan into which drips the gore of the severed head. Her tongue is lolling and she wears a necklace of severed skullls and a girdle of severed arms. Contemporary illustration. (Vidura Luis Barrios / Alamy)

## MYTH: THE ABDUCTION OF SITA

The hero **Rama** too came to be viewed as an avatar of Vishnu, although he was earlier simply a great hero. He is the subject of the very long *Ramayana*, the Sanskrit epic of very obscure date that tells how the 10-headed demon **Ravana** stole Rama's beloved wife, **Sita**. Sita was born in Nepal, where her father was king. An avatar of Lakshmi, consort of Vishnu, she sets the standard for womanly and wifely behavior among the Hindus. The epic is well known in modern times and often used to clarify events, a kind of template for behavior.

There was a Maharajah named **Dasaratha**, king of a place called AYODHYA in northern Indian near Nepal (Map 7). He was the father of Rama. Dasaratha had three wives: Kaushalya, Sumitra, and Kaikeyi. Rama was the son of Kaushalya; **Lakshmana** and Shatrughna were the sons of Sumitra; and Bharata was the son of Kaikeyi.

When the boys were grown, Dasaratha decided to retire and make Rama king, his eldest son. But before the coronation, the ambitious Kaikeyi reclaimed a promise Dasaratha once had made to her, to give her any two things she asked. She asked that her own son Bharata be made king and that Rama be forced to leave Ayodhya for 14 years. Dasaratha could not disobey, because he had promised, but died of grief not long after Rama had gone into exile.

In the following excerpt is told what happened then, and how the demon Ravana first saw Sita, whom Rama has married, and how Ravana snatched her away. Rama and his wife Sita and his half-brother Lakshmana are traveling south:

Rama and Sita and Lakshmana headed south into the deep jungle. They visited various holy sages. They crossed the Vindhya mountains to the Deccan, where they wandered for a long time. At Pachavati, near the source of the Godavari River, the royal couple built a hut with four rooms. There they lived peacefully, piously, for thirteen and a half years.

One day there came to the hut a Rakshasa woman, a demon, sister to Ravana, king of Lanka,° named Surpanakha. She was badly misshapen and quite hideous, and her voice grated and antagonized. When she saw Rama, handsome as a lotus and tall, she fell deeply in love. Emboldened by her love, she resolved to change her appearance and induce Rama to abandon his faithful Sita.

She came again to the king, this time as a striking young beauty, and she said, "Who are you, who have come here to live alone in a place swarming with Rakshasas?"°

Rama replied, "I am Rama, the oldest son of Maharajah Dasaratha. I live here because of the decree of my father Dasaratha with my wife, Sita, and my half-brother Lakshmana. But why do you wander about all alone, you who are as beautiful as the bride of Vishnu?"

Surpanakha replied, "I am a Rakshasa woman, the sister of Ravana. I have come here because I love you. I have chosen you as my husband. You shall rule over my mighty empire. Your Sita is pale, she's deformed, she's not worthy of you. I by contrast am of surpassing beauty. I can assume any form I wish. I must consume your Sita and your brother. We may wander the jungle together, and the hills behind."

Then Rama said, "Sita is my bride. I love her. I would never leave her. But Lakshmana has no one. He can be your husband."

Surpanakha left Rama. She went to Lakshmana, who jested with her.

Then, enraged, the Rakshasa woman leapt toward Sita in a jealous rage, but Rama pushed her back. Like a lightning bolt Lakshmana leapt to the rescue and cut off Surpanakha's ears and nose. She shrieked aloud and fled, wailing like a storm. The rocks echoed her anguished cries.

Surpanakha hurried to her brother Khara, disfigured and bleeding. "Only a god could have done this!" he said. "Today I will drink the blood of Indra as a crane drinks water!"

Surpanakha told what had happened. "Rama and Lakshmana attacked me because they were protecting the woman named Sita. I wanted to drink her blood. Bring her here now, I beg of you!"

°*Lanka*: Ceylon, off the southwest coast of India. °*Rakshasas*: a race of demons.

Khara summoned fourteen Rakshasas and ordered them to capture the three royal hermits who lived in the jungle. They hurried off and Surpanakha went with them, but soon returned, wailing: Rama had killed all the Rakshasas with his divine arrows!

Khara at once called his brother Dushana. He said, "Gather an army of fourteen thousand Rakshasas. Bring my weapons and my chariot drawn by a white horse. Today I will kill the hated Rama!"

There were bad omens as the army marched off: Jackals howled, birds screamed at dawn, the sky was as red as blood, the demon Rahu° swallowed the sun, and a headless apparition appeared in the sky. Smoke arose from Rama's arrows.

Rama said to Lakshmana, "Take Sita and hurry to a secret cave in the mountains. Keep her safe. I will battle the demons alone."

Lakshmana did as he was told. Rama put on his glowing armor. Taking up his divine bow and his many arrows, he waited the coming of his enemies. At first the Rakshasas held back, terrified by Rama's appearance, like Yama° at the end of a Yuga. Then up came Khara in his chariot. He urged his followers on and they came like a storm, like great black clouds rushing to the rising sun.

A thousand weapons fell on Rama. He fired his flaming arrows, which fell on the Rakshasas like fire in a sun-parched forest. Many were mangled and killed. But Khara and his brother pressed forward when Rama seized his divine weapon and killed Dushana and scattered the demon army. Khara tried to avenge his brother's death, but Rama drew back his bow and shot him with a blazing arrow. So the battle was won. Sita came out of the cave. She embraced her husband. She kissed him.

Of all the demon host only Surpanakha escaped. She hurried to the ten-headed King Ravana in Lanka and told him of the death of his brothers. She said, "You can never beat Rama in battle. But you may overcome him by deception. He has a beautiful wife. Her name is Sita and he loves her more than life. If you capture her, Rama can be taken. He cannot live without her."

Ravana said, "I will bring Sita here in my chariot."

On the next day Ravana and his brother Maricha, whom Rama had earlier driven across the ocean with his divine weapon, traveled to the hut in the forest. They rode in a chariot that soared through the air like a mighty bird, drawn by asses that had the heads of Rakshasas.

Maricha took on the form of a golden deer with silver spots. Its horns were tipped with sapphire and its eyes were like lotus blossoms. This beautiful animal, seeming so gentle, grazed beneath the trees when Sita came out to pick wild flowers. She called to Rama, "A wondrously beautiful deer is wandering through the trees. I would love to take my ease on its golden skin."

"O Lakshmana," Rama said, "I can only hope to fulfill every one of Sita's desires. Watch her while I capture this animal."

He took up his bow and hurried through the trees. Lakshmana spoke to Sita: "I am worried. The wise men have reported that Rakshasas like to take on the shape of deer. Many a time have kings been waylaid in the forest by skillful demons come to lure them away."

°*Rahu:* the demon who devours the sun and moon in an eclipse. °*Yama:* "bridle," god of the dead, king of hell and the south.

Rama chased the deer for a long time through the forest. At last he shot an arrow that pierced its heart. In agony Maricha leapt out of the deer's body and cried out, imitating Rama's voice, "Sita, Sita, save me! Save me, Lakshmana!"

Then he died. Rama realized that he had killed the Rakshasa Maricha, brother of Ravana.

Sita was alarmed when she heard the Rakshasa speaking in Rama's voice. "Hurry and help my Rama," she said to Lakshmana, "he is calling for help!"

Lakshmana replied, "Don't be afraid, O fair one. No Rakshasa can harm Rama. I must obey his command—to stay at your side. The call you heard is an illusion made by demons."

Sita was angry. Her eyes flashed and her voice trembled as she spoke: "Have you grown callous? Are you your brother's enemy? Rama is in danger and yet you do not hurry to save him. Have you come to this forest wishing that he die so you could possess his widow by force? You are deluded if that's what you think—I will live not one second after he dies! Therefore it is useless for you to remain here."

Lakshmana replied, his eyes filled with tears, "I am not afraid for Rama. O Sita, your words burn me! You are as a mother to me. I cannot answer. There is no base desire in my heart. Alas that erratic women with poisonous tongues should try to set brother against brother."

Sita wept. Lakshmana, sorry that he had spoken so strongly, said, "I will obey you and go after Rama. May the spirits of the forest protect you! I am troubled—I have seen bad omens. When I come back, I hope to see Rama at your side."

Sita said, "If Rama has been killed, I will drown myself, or take poison, or hang myself. I cannot live without Rama."

All the while Ravana was watching. When he saw Lakshmana leave the hut, he took on the form of a wise man of the forest. He went to the sad and lonely Sita. The jungle fell silent. Ravana saw that Sita was very beautiful, like the moon at midnight when it shines in the gloom of the forest.

He said to her, "O woman of golden beauty, O shy one in full blossom, dressed in silk and adorned with flowers, are you Gauri,° or the goddess of love, or a nymph of the forest? Your lips are red like coral, your teeth shine, love lives in your soft and lustrous eyes. You are slender and tall, and have shapely limbs, and your bosom is like ripe fruit. Why, fair one with long and shining hair, do you linger here in the lonely jungle? You belong in a handsome palace. Choose a royal suitor, be a king's bride. What god is your father, O lovely one?"

Sita respected the old man, whom she thought was a Brahman. She told him how the Maharajah Dasaratha had exiled Rama. She said, "Wait here and rest until the brothers return from the jungle to greet you."

But Ravana said, "I am no Brahman but the king of the vengeful Rakshasas! I am Ravana, King of Lanka, whom even the gods fear. Your beauty, dressed in yellow silk, has taken my heart. I want you to be my chief queen, O Sita. Five thousand handmaids will wait on you. Share my empire and my fame."

Sita's eyes flashed with anger and she said, "Do you know Rama, the divine hero who wins every battle? I am his wife. Do you know Rama, who is without sin, like a saint, who is well-armed and courageous and bold? I am his wife. Are

°*Gauri*: a name of Shakti.

you mad, to woo the wife of so mighty a warrior? I follow Rama as a lioness follows her lion. How can you, a wandering jackal, hope to obtain a lioness? Go snatch from the jaws of a lion the calf it devours, or touch a cobra's fang when it attacks its victim, or tear up a mountain by its roots, or seize the sun in heaven—before you try to win the wife of avenging Rama!"

Ravana then boasted of his power. "Why, I can even slay Yama! I can torture the sun! I can shoot arrows through the earth! How little you know of my glory."

Then he changed his shape. He stood up as a gigantic demon with huge body and ten heads and twenty arms.

Seizing Sita, he soared through the air with her even as Garuda° carries off the queen of the serpents. He put her in his chariot. He went swifter than the wind.

The invisible spirits of the forest looked on. They heard Sita's cries as she called to Rama and Lakshmana—in vain. The king of the vultures, Jatayus, heard her. He fell on Ravana like the thunderbolt of Indra. A ferocious battle took place in mid air. Jatayus destroyed the chariot and he killed the asses, but Ravana took Sita in his arm and, soaring above the vulture king, he killed him with his sword.

Ravana continued his journey to Lanka. As they passed over the Mountain of Apes, Sita took off her ornaments. They dropped to the earth like falling stars. The five apes found them and said, "Ravana is carrying off some beautiful woman who calls on Rama and Lakshmana."

When Ravana reached his palace he turned Sita over to the Rakshasa women. He commanded that they guard her day and night.

Long and loud did Rama lament when he returned to the hut and found it empty. He knew that Sita had been abducted, but where he did not know.

°*Garuda*: a huge bird, the mount of Vishnu.

## MYTH: HOW RAMA REJECTED SITA

After many adventures and a savage war, at last Rama recovered Sita from Ravana, only to suspect her virtue. In the following excerpt Sita is summoned to the court:

When he saw Sita standing near him and bowing low, Rama spoke with anger deep in his heart.

"You have been won back by me after I conquered the enemy in battle, my dear lady! I accomplished that which I did through my manliness. I have satisfied my jealousy and wiped out the insult. I have obliterated the enemy along with the offense. Today all have seen my manly strength. Today my efforts have borne fruit. Now I have fulfilled my promise. Today I am the master of myself. The wrong done to you, when an outrageous demon took you because fate decreed it, I have corrected as a human being.

"What is the use of the prowess, however great, of a weak-minded man who does not wipe out insult through his own energy? The great deeds of Hanuman° in leaping across the water and destroying Lanka has today borne

°*Hanuman*: "having large jaws," name of the monkey-king who assisted Rama to win back Sita.

fruit. The efforts of Sugriva,° who showed himself able in the battle and always gave good advice, have today come to fulfillment. Furthermore, the efforts of Vibhishana,° who deserted his evil brother and sought me out, has today borne fruit."

When she heard Rama's words, Sita was bathed in tears, her eyes wide opened like a doe's. King Rama's heart, as he saw Sita (whom he loved) near him, again blazed with anger, as when you throw butter into a fire.

In the midst of the monkeys and Rakshasas, Rama spoke as follows to Sita, whose eyes resembled a lotus flower, whose hair was dark and curly, whose hips were fine:

"I have done what honor demands in killing Ravana and wiping out the insult. I have won you, Sita, just as the sage Agastya° won the southern quarter for the world of the living, purified by asceticism. But be sure that this effort of war, which my friends waged successfully, was not for your sake. I did it to wipe out the evil words from every side, and the insults to my dynasty, illustrious as it is. But you, whose character is suspect, stand before me as one very unpleasant, like a light shone to one suffering from a disease of the eye.

"Go wherever you like, in any direction, my dear lady! I can have nothing to do with you. What man of nobility, born into an illustrious race, will take back a woman who has lived in another's house, no matter how eager he is to do so? I can't stand to look at you, who were ravaged by Ravana's groin—how can I take you back when I come from so high a lineage?

"I won you with that end in view, to retrieve my lost honor, which is now restored. I feel no attachment to you. Go wherever you want, my lady! I have decided. Go to Lakshmana or Bharata,° as you wish, O Sita! Or set your mind on Sugriva, or on Vibhishana the demon—whatever you want! Seeing your beautiful and attractive form, Ravana would not have held back long when you were living in the same house!"

Hearing such unpleasant speech from her beloved husband after such a long time, Sita, who was used to hearing only pleasing words, burst into tears, like a creeping vine attacked by the trunk of an elephant. As Rama spoke to her in such anger, her hair stood on end. Sita was deeply disturbed. Hearing the harsh words of her husband, never heard before and now in a large gathering of people, Sita bent low with shame. As though the words had pierced her limbs, like arrows with pointed tip, Sita wept profusely.

Then, wiping her tear-streaked face, she said, slowly, in a stammering voice:

"O brave Rama! Why do you speak such harsh words, violent to hear, like a common man speaking to a common woman? I am not such as you believe. Have faith in me. I swear that I have behaved properly. Because of the conduct

°*Sugriva*: "having a fine neck," a monkey-king who with his agent Hanuman assisted Rama in recovering Sita. °*Vibhishana*: a brother of the demon Ravana who threw in his lot with Rama and was rewarded with kingship over Lanka. °*Agastya*: "mountain-thrower," a great sage. °*Bharata*: a half-brother of Rama.

of vulgar women, you distrust the entire race of women. Give up your doubt, because you have tested me, O lord. It was not my fault that Ravana took me. I was helpless. Do not blame me. My heart, that I control, is always attached to you. What could I do, helpless as I was, with regard to my body that had fallen into another's power? If you, who have honored me, still do not know me, although we have lived together, I am ruined!

"O king! You sent the great hero Hanuman to find me in Lanka. My hero! I would have gladly given up my life if the monkey king told me you deserted me . . . Then you would not have wasted all this effort crossing to Lanka and fighting the mighty Ravana, nor would your friends have suffered so, and for nothing.

"Tiger among men! You, like a feeble man, gave into your anger! I prefer women. You who know so much about virtuous conduct! Although I derive my name from Janaka,° I actually am borne from the earth.° You have not honored my conduct. You have not acknowledged my chaste hand, taken in our childhood.° You have ignored my devotion and my nature!"

So Sita spoke, weeping and stammering with tears. She then said to Lakshmana, sad and pensive, "O Lakshmana, make a pyre for me, a remedy for this disaster. I no longer wish to live abused by false blame. I will enter the fire to find the only course appropriate for me. My husband has abandoned me in an assembly of men. He is no longer satisfied with my virtue."

Hearing the words of Sita, Lakshmana, the destroyer of enemy warriors, gave way to anger and looked toward Rama. But he understood what was in Rama's heart by the expression in his face. The valiant Lakshmana prepared the pyre.

Sita walked around Rama, who stood with his head bent low, and she proceeded toward the blazing fire. Having offered salutation to the gods and the Brahmans and joining her palms near the fire, Sita spoke:

"As I never wavered from Rama, so may this fire, witness of the world, protect me from all sides."

So speaking, Sita walked up to the blazing fire and entered it without hesitation. A large gathering of children and old people saw the shining Sita enter the fire. As she did so a horrified cry of terror arose from the Rakshasas and the monkeys alike. The virtuous Rama was pensive, afflicted by melancholy, and his eyes filled with tears.

Thereupon wide-famed Kubera,° Yama who wears away those who are hostile, the thousand-eyed great Indra, Varuna° who roasts his enemies, illustrious Shiva the great deity who bears the device of a bull on his banner and has three eyes, Brahma the creator of all the worlds and the best among those who know the Vedas—all these came together in their celestial chariots shining like the sun. They journeyed to the city of Lanka. Lifting their long arms, hands decked with ornaments, they spoke to Rama who stood there with his palms joined:

"How do you, the maker of the whole cosmos, foremost among those endowed with knowledge, ignore Sita who is falling into the fire?° How do you not

°*Janaka:* "begetting," father of Sita. °*from the earth:* because Sita means "furrow." °*taken in our childhood:* when they married. °*Kubera:* lord of wealth, guardian of the north. °*Varuna:* god of the waters and lord of the west. °*into the fire:* because Rama is an avatar of Vishnu.

recognize yourself to be the foremost of the troop of gods? Formerly you were the progenitor of all the Vasus.° You are the self-created, the first creator of the three worlds, the eighth Rudra° of the Rudras,° the fifth among the Sadhyas.° The twin Asvins° are your ears. The sun and the moon are your eyes. The destroyer of the adversaries, you are seen at the beginning and at the end of creation. Yet, you disregard Sita as if you were a common man."

Hearing the words of the guardians of the world, Rama, the lord of creation, foremost among protectors of *dharma*, said to those chiefs of the gods:

"I think of myself as a human being, by name Rama, the son of Dasaratha. O lord, tell me who I am, whose son, where do I come from?"

Then said Brahma, the foremost among those who know the Vedas:

"Listen to my true word, O truly brave lord! You are the Lord Narayana° himself, the glorious god, who carries four weapons.° You are the divine boar° with a single tusk, the conqueror of your past and future enemies . . . Sita is no other than the goddess Lakshmi while you are Vishnu, Krishna, Prajapati.° You have a shining dark-blue hue. For the destruction of Ravana, you entered a human body, here on this earth, and you have completed this task for us, O foremost among the supporters of *dharma*! Ravana has been killed. Rejoice, return to your divine abode ..."

When the shining fire heard the words of Brahma, the fire rose up with Sita in his arms and he placed the daughter of Janaka in Rama's arms. She shone brightly as the rising sun, decked in ornaments of refined gold, attired in a red robe with dark curly hair and adorned with garlands that did not wither.

Then the purifying fire, the witness of the whole world, spoke to Rama:

"Here is your Sita. There is no sin in her. This lady's character has been good. She has never been unfaithful to you either in speech or in mind or by her glances. When you left her alone in the forest, miserable and helpless, she was carried away by the Rakshasa Ravana, proud of his virility. Although hidden away in the women's quarter, this Sita fixed her mind and intent on you alone. Frightful deformed female demons guarded her, tempted her, threatened her, but she never turned her mind away from you and she ignored that Rakshasa. Take back Sita, who is sinless, with a pure character. She should not be struck. I hereby command you!"

Rama, of great energy and forbearance, whose mind was set on *dharma*, said to the best of the 33 gods, "It was necessary that Sita enter the purifying fire in the presence of the people of the triple world because she resided long within

---

°*Vasus*: a group of eight gods once headed by Indra, then Vishnu. °*Rudra*: "roarer," the Vedic equivalent of the malevolent Shiva, associated with wildness and danger. °*Rudras*: the armies of Rudra. °*Sadhyas*: "to be attained," a group of 12 celestial beings who inhabit the region between the sun and the earth. °*Asvins*: "horsemen," horse-gods, twin sons of the sun and a mare. °*Narayana*: "son of man" or "son of the waters," an epithet of Vishnu. °*four weapons*: conch shell, discus, mace, and lotus, held in the god's four hands; see Figure 7.3. °*divine boar*: one of Vishnu's avatars is the boar, which became his emblem. °*Prajapati*: "lord of creators," an epithet of Brahma or any of a class of creator-gods.

the woman's quarters of the demon Ravana. Had I not purified her, the world would chatter against me, saying that Rama, the son of Dasaratha, was lustful and childish.

"I also know that Sita, the daughter of Janaka, is undivided in her affection to me. Ravana could not violate this woman, protected by her own splendor, any more than an ocean could transgress its bounds. But in order to convince the three worlds, I allowed Sita to enter the fire. The evil-minded Ravana could not rape this woman, even in thought, for Sita blazes like a flaming tongue of fire. This lovely woman could not have ruled over the women's quarters of Ravana for she belongs to no one but me, even as sunlight belongs to the sun. Sita, the daughter of Janaka, has been purified in all the three worlds and I can no longer renounce her, as a good name cannot be cast aside by a prudent man. Certainly I will carry out your good advice, you who are the affectionate guardians of the world, who say what is conducive to our welfare."

When he had said this and was praised by the mighty because of the deeds he had accomplished, the mighty Rama, a scion of Raghu dynasty, was united with his beloved and enjoyed the happiness that he deserved.

*Ramayana*, 6.103.1–25; 6.104.1–27; 6.105.1–12, 25–26; 6.106.1–20

## OBSERVATIONS: QUEEN MAYA, LORD OF ALL

The dramatic tale of husband and wife, of deep love, suspicion, rejection, then acceptance turns out to be a mask for the cosmic union of male and female principles, Vishnu and Lakshmi, for whom there can never be any but an illusory separation. The story emphasizes the cruelty of Rama because on this earth events must play out in a certain way; the wife must remain above suspicion or die. Yet in a grand scheme all is right in the world and the eternal feminine unites with the eternal masculine, the *yoni* (the vulva, widely respected in cult) with the *linga* (the phallus as religious emblem, often united with the *yoni* in cult). Such myths are the basis of much erotic art in early Indian and South Asian sculpture.

The battle between gods and demons may contrast good with evil, but from the myth of the body of Brahma we learn that demons come from the thighs of the god, the gods from the mouth. The gods took the ambrosia, and now they will live forever, and they destroyed the demons, one of whom ravished Sita. But one day gods and demons alike will be submerged in the universal return to the still waters before the creation, when creation begins anew.

Indian myth is as strange for its hundreds of figures, some very important in Hindu ritual and cult, as it is for its philosophizing. The stories are told in a flat, non-dramatic style, though sometimes reaching for literary effect. Indian myth constantly philosophizes about the nature of reality, showing that Queen Maya, princess of illusion, rules all.

## Key Terms

Maya 224
karma 224
atman 224
brahman 224
Indo-Aryans 224
Indo-Europeans 224
Vedas 225
Brahmanas 226
Upanishads 227
Vedanta 227

Puranas 227
Mahabharata 227
Krishna 228
Vishnu 228
Ramayana 228
Lakshmi 228
Brahma 229
Ananta 230
Shiva 237
Ganesha 237

Shakti 238
ambrosia 239
Devi 243
Kali 245
Rama 246
Ravana 246
Sita 246
Dasaratha 246
Lakshmana 246

## Further Reading

Buitenen, J. A. B. van, *Tales of Ancient India* (Chicago, 1969).
Campbell, J., *Myths of Light: Eastern Metaphors of the Eternal* (Novato, CA, 2003).
Dallapiccola, A. L., *Dictionary of Hindu Lore and Legend* (London, 2004).
____, *Hindu Myths* (Austin, TX, 2003).
Doniger, W., *Hindu Myths: A Sourcebook Translated from the Sanskrit* (New York, 2004).
Macdonell, A. A., *Vedic Mythology* (1897; reprinted New Delhi, 1995).
Walker, B., *Hindu World* (New Delhi, 2005).
Williams, G., *Handbook of Hindu Theology* (Oxford, UK, 2008).
Zimmer, H. R., and J. Campbell, *Myths and Symbols in Indian Art and Civilization* (Princeton, NJ, 1972).

# Persian Myth

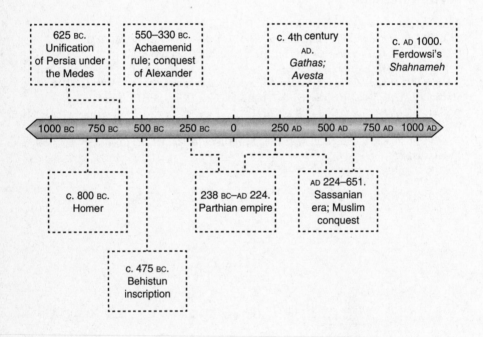

Today Persia, or Iran, is a country in central Asia with a population of about 75 million. The name *Iran*, first attested in the *Avesta*, has been in native use since the Sassanian era, AD 224–651, but came into the West only in 1935; before, the country was known as Persia. The Sassanian era was the last preIslamic Persian empire, encompassing many neighboring countries, ruled by the Sassanian family, one of the two main powers in the Western world in competition with the Roman empire and its successor, the Byzantine empire. The name *Iran* is a cognate of *Aryan* and means

"Land of the Aryans." Both terms are common, but *Iran* is used mostly in the modern political context and *Persia* in a cultural and historical context.

Iran is a country of special strategic significance because of its location midway between West and East, bordered on the north by ARMENIA and TURKMENISTAN and, beyond the inland CASPIAN SEA, by Kazakhstan and Russia; bordered on the east by AFGHANISTAN and PAKISTAN; on the south by the PERSIAN GULF; and on the west by IRAQ (Map 8).

Iran is home to one of the world's oldest continuous major civilizations. Iran was never colonized, unlike neighboring states in the region, so it retains native traditions relatively unaffected by European traditions.

Iran is one of the world's most mountainous countries, its rugged ranges separating various basins from one another. The populous western part is the most mountainous, with the CAUCASUS in northwest Iran, and the ZAGROS MOUNTAINS separating the Iranian plateau from Mesopotamia. The highest peak on the Persian plateau rises to eighteen thousand feet, the highest mountain on the Eurasian landmass west of the Hindu Kush mountains in modern Pakistan and Afghanistan.

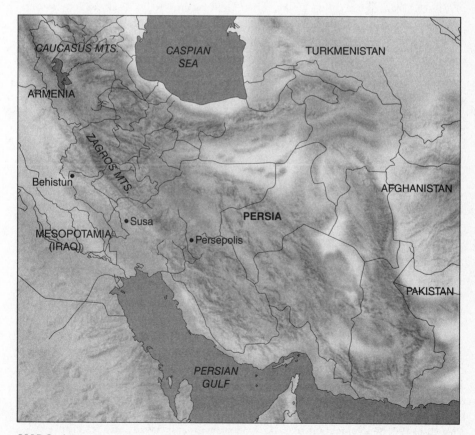

**MAP 8**   Iran.

The northern part of Iran is covered by dense rain forests. The eastern part consists mostly of desert basins. The only large plains lie along the coast of the Caspian Sea and at the northern end of the Persian Gulf. Iran's climate ranges from arid to subtropical along the Caspian coast, where temperatures rarely fall below freezing and the area remains humid for most of the year.

## HISTORY OF IRAN

The primordial Iranians seem to have moved down onto the Persian plateau sometime in the 3rd and 2nd millennia BC, close cousins to the Indo-Europeans who moved into northwest India at this time and founded Indian civilization (see Chapter 7, MYTH IN INDIA). The original homeland of these peoples may have been east of the Caspian Sea and they spoke closely related dialects of Indo-European.

We do not know much about the Iranians, however, before the tribe called the Medes, who lived in the Zagros range between Mesopotamia and Iran, unified Iran into an empire in 625 BC. In the 6th century BC the Medes were succeeded by the Achaemenid dynasties (530–330 BC), who came from the mountains of Pars in southwest Iran, hence called the *Persians*. Their ceremonial capital was PERSEPOLIS (Greek "city of the Parsoi"), from which important ruins remain (Figure 8.1).

We cannot exaggerate the power and importance of Persia in the ancient world. Under Cyrus the Great (c. 600–c. 530 BC) and Darius the Great (ruled 522–486 BC) the

**FIGURE 8.1** A palace at Persepolis started under Darius I in 510 BC and completed by Xerxes in 486 BC. Images of tribute-bearing dignitaries are carved on either side of the podium of the terrace. This palace, called Tachara ("winter palace'), was one of the few structures at Persepolis not burned by Alexander the Great in a wild party in 330 BC. Persepolis was the ceremonial capital of the Achaemenid empire (c. 550–c. 330 BC), situated 50 miles northeast of the modern city of Shiraz in modern Iran. (Photo by Author)

Persian empire became the largest and most powerful empire ever seen on this planet. Encompassing one million square miles, and united by a system of roads, the borders of the Persian empire stretched from the Indus River in the east, in modern Pakistan, to the Mediterranean Sea in the west and included Anatolia—modern day Turkey— and Egypt. It also included Thrace and Macedonia in Greece.

Persian rule brought peace, security, and prosperity where commerce prospered and the standard of living for all people of the region improved. The Achaemenids (550–330 BC) strictly followed the rules and ethics of the teachings of **Zoroaster**. They adopted policies based on human rights, equality, and the banning of slavery. Zoroastrianism spread unopposed during the time of the Achaemenids and, through contacts with the exiled Jewish people in Babylon, Zoroastrianism deeply influenced the Abrahamic religions—Judaism, Christianity, and Islam.

In 499 BC Athens lent support to a revolt in the Greek city of Miletus on the coast of Asia Minor. The Persian local capital of Sardis, 75 miles inland from the coast, was burned and sacked. This act led to an Achaemenid campaign against Greece known as the Greco-Persian Wars, the principal subject of the Greek Herodotus' (c. 484– c. 425 BC) celebrated history, the first historical study ever. After defeating a Greek coalition led by Sparta at the battle of Thermopylae (ther-**mo**-pi-lē) in 480 BC, one of the most famous battles ever fought (thanks to Herodotus' thrilling description), Persia went on to raze Athens to the ground, then withdrew after a string of Greek victories (Perspective 8).

Alexander the Great invaded the Persian empire in 334 BC, allegedly to take revenge for the Persian attack one hundred fifty years earlier. In 330 BC Alexander burned the Persian ceremonial capital, Persepolis, after a drunken party. He killed the Achaemenid king Darius III after three great battles and installed his officers

## PERSPECTIVE 8
### Frank Miller's *300*

The 2007 American action film *300* about the battle at Thermopylae grossed about $500 million. The film's opening was the twenty-fourth largest in box office history and the third biggest opening ever for an R-rated film. It is adapted from a graphic novel by Frank Miller, who also produced the film. King Leonidas (lē-o-**nì**-das, Gerard Butler) leads 300 Spartans into battle against the Persian king Xerxes (**kserk**-sēz, Rodrigo Santoro) and his army of more than one million soldiers! The film is a shot-for-shot adaptation of the comic book using the "bluescreen" technique, whereby the actors stand before a blue screen later replaced with background footage. More than 1,500 special effects shots were incorporated into the film in this way.

Dilios, a Spartan soldier, narrates the story of Leonidas from childhood to his being crowned king of Sparta. A Persian messenger arrives at Sparta demanding submission to the Persian king Xerxes. Leonidas and his guards throw the messenger into a pit. Knowing a Persian attack will come soon, Leonidas visits the Ephors, ancient priests stricken with leprosy, whose blessing he needs before the Spartan council will authorize war. He proposes that they meet the immense army of Persians up north at Thermopylae ("hot gates"). The Ephors consult an oracle, who decrees that Sparta must not go to war during their religious festival. Two agents of Xerxes appear who bribe the corrupt Ephors with whores and gold.

Leonidas follows his plan anyway, setting out with only 300 soldiers. He knows that he is on a suicide mission, but hopes his sacrifice will spur the council to action. On the way, other Greeks join the Spartans. At Thermopylae, they build a wall across the pass. Leonidas meets Ephialtes (ef-i-**al**-tēz), a hunchbacked Spartan in exile whose parents fled Sparta to spare him from infanticide. He asks to join the fight and warns Leonidas of a secret path by which the Persians could outflank them. Leonidas turns him down. Ephialtes cannot hold a shield properly, and he would compromise the Spartan phalanx.

The Persians arrive and demand surrender. Leonidas refuses. Advancing in a tightly knit phalanx, the Spartans use the narrow terrain to knock back the Persian army. Xerxes parleys with Leonidas, offering him wealth and power in exchange for surrender. Still Leonidas declines. Xerxes sends the feared Immortals, his elite troops, to attack the Spartans, but the Spartans finish them off. Xerxes then sends black-powder bombs and giant war beasts at Spartans, but all attacks fail.

Angered by Leonidas' rejection, Ephialtes tells the Persians about the secret path. When they realize that Ephialtes has betrayed them, the Greek allies retreat. Leonidas orders Dilios to return to Sparta to tell the council what is about to happen.

In Sparta, the treacherous Spartan Theron demands that Gorgo, Queen of Sparta (Leonidas' wife), have sex with him in exchange for persuading the Spartan council to send reinforcements. She complies, but Theron then argues just the opposite. Gorgo kills him, repeating his own words as he raped her, "This will not be over quickly!" Her dagger pierces his purse. Persian coins spill from his robe revealing he is a traitor. At last the council agrees to unite against Persia.

In the meanwhile at Thermopylae, the Persians use the goat path to outflank the Spartans. Leonidas hurls his spear at Xerxes, cutting the king on the cheek. Disturbed by his own mortality, Xerxes watches the Persians slaughter all the Spartans by a massive barrage of arrows. Moments before his death, Leonidas pledges his love to Gorgo.

Concluding his tale before an audience of Spartans on the edge of the battlefield a year after Thermopylae, Dilios relates how the Persian army was long baffled by the bravery of a mere 300 Spartans. Word of their valiant resistance spreads across Greece, inspiring the city-states to unite against the Persians. Now the Persians face ten thousand Spartans leading thirty thousand free Greeks. Dilios then leads the Greeks in a successful charge against the Persian army in the battle of Plataea.

The film has been praised for portrayal of the Spartans' heroic code, but decried for the portrayal of the Persians as a monstrous, barbaric, and demonic horde. Officials of the Iranian government, including President Mahmoud Ahmadinejad, denounced the film: The film was banned in Iran. There is no doubt that *300* was meant to reflect on current political issues. Just prior to its release, the creator of *300*, Frank Miller, said: "For some reason, nobody seems to be talking about who we're up against and the sixth-century barbarism that they actually represent. These people saw off people's heads. They enslave women. They genitally mutilate their daughters. They do not behave by any cultural norms that are sensible to us. I'm speaking into a microphone that never could have been a product of their culture and I'm living in a city where three thousand of my neighbors were killed by thieves of airplanes they never could have built."

as caretakers of the empire. After Alexander's death the empire was split up. The Hellenic Seleucids ("sons of Seleucus," a general of Alexander) then ruled Iran until the Parthians, Iranians from northeast Iran and Afghanistan, regained control of the plateau.

The Parthian empire (238 BC–AD 224) was the third Iranian kingdom to dominate the plateau, after that of the Medes and the Achaemenids. They intermittently controlled Mesopotamia and were Rome's constant and implacable enemy, limiting Rome's expansion beyond central Anatolia (modern Turkey). Rome's acclaimed general Marc Antony (83–30 BC) led a disastrous campaign against them in 36 BC in which he lost 32,000 men.

In AD 224 one of the Parthian kingdom's vassals defeated the Parthian king to establish the fourth Iranian empire under the Sassanids. The Romans suffered repeated losses in wars against the Sassanids. During the Parthian, and later Sassanid era, trade on the Silk Road, which passed through Persia, was vigorous and significant in the development of civilization in China, Egypt, Mesopotamia, Persia, the Indian subcontinent, and Rome. In AD 632, raiders from the Arab peninsula overthrew the last of Sassanids and prepared for the Islamic conquest of Persia, which was slow and complex. By the 9th century, however, Islam was dominant in Persia, although in some parts of the country Zoroastrianism remained strong.

## WRITING DOWN THE PERSIAN LANGUAGE

The oldest attested *written* form of Persian is called Old Persian and seems to have been invented about 520 BC in the court of Darius the Great (Darius I), that is, about three hundred years after Homer. The signs are made by impressing a stylus into clay (or by imitating such signs), but are unrelated to the Mesopotamian cuneiform. Old Persian writing is a syllabary based on the Aramaic syllabary (that is, Phoenician writing, the ancestor of the Greek alphabet). Three signs make explicit the vowel sound implicit in an accompanying sign—it is not alphabetic writing.

By far the longest text in Old Cuneiform is carved high on a cliff face at a place called BEHISTUN in the Zagros mountains between Mesopotamia and the Iranian plateau. The inscription functioned much as the Rosetta Stone in enabling a decipherment of cuneiform writing, in the mid-19th century, but unfortunately the decipherers never explained how they had reached their conclusions. The Old Persian text, in a special cuneiform script, is repeated in two other languages—Semitic Akkadian in the complex Mesopotamian cuneiform script and Elamite, a language without known relatives, in a somewhat simplified cuneiform script. The Elamite language, spoken in southwestern Iran with an important capital at SUSA, has not been deciphered. The Behistun inscription beneath the carved relief tells how Darius came to power and gained victory over many rebels under "the grace of Ahura Mazda," the earliest reference to this Zoroastrian god.

But Persian administration was conducted mostly in the *Aramaic language* written in the Aramaic syllabary (of which the modern Hebrew and Arabic writing

**FIGURE 8.2**  Ahura Mazda, Lord of Wisdom, supreme god of the Zoroastrian religion of Persia, from the Royal Audience Hall of King Darius I (548–486 BC) at Persepolis, built c. 500 BC. He wears a king's cap and holds in his left hand the ring of eternity, repeated in the central ring. The iconography is based on that of the Egyptian sun-god. (Ann Ronan Picture Library, Persepolis, Iran; © World History Archive / Alamy)

are direct descendants). Sometimes the *Persian language* itself was written in the Aramaic syllabary, which during the Parthian and Sassanian periods developed into a script called *Pahlavi* or Middle Persian. Probably in the 3rd century AD Pahlavi gave rise to *Avestan*, an alphabetic script used only to record the sacred scriptures of Zoroastrianism, used side by side with Pahlavi.

After the Arab conquest in the 7th century AD, Arabic script gradually replaced Pahlavi and today is predominant (although the Persian language has also been recorded in Russian Cyrillic and in the Latin alphabet). The 9th and 10th centuries were the last in which Zoroastrians had the means to engage in creative work on a grand scale, and most of what we know about Zoroastrianism, apart from the *Avesta* (probably = Persian "praise"), comes from texts composed in this period. At first there was a severe struggle between Zoroastrianism and Islam, but the struggle declined in the 10th and 11th centuries as most of the country became Islamicized.

## THE RELIGION OF ZOROASTER

Zoroaster, a Latinized form of the Persian Zarathustra (perhaps "he of the golden light"), seems to have lived sometime around 600 BC. Therefore he lived at the same time as Confucius and Lao Tse in China, Siddhartha the Buddha in India, the Second Isaiah in Palestine, and Thales in Asia Minor, one of the most extraordinary periods in the evolution of religious thought on this planet.

In some form, Zoroastrianism was the state religion of a significant portion of the Iranian people for many centuries. The political power of the preIslamic Iranian dynasties lent Zoroastrianism immense prestige in ancient times, and some of its leading doctrines were adopted by other religious systems, including Judaism and Christianity. The Magi of the New Testament were Zoroastrian priests.

It is hard to be sure what Zoroaster taught, but hymns attributed to him, called the **Gathas** ("hymns") lie at core of Zoroastrianism, a religion still observed by 145,000 adherents, mostly in India where they are known as Parsees. The 17 *Gathas* are written in alphabetic Avestan and are close in language to the Sanskrit of the Vedas but the language is otherwise unknown. It is impossible to date the *Gathas*, but also impossible that they were passed on orally unchanged since the days of Zoroaster. The difficult language of the *Gathas* can be understood, if at all, by analogy with later forms of Persian or with the language of the Vedas. In any event the *Gathas* form the oldest part of the **Avesta** (meaning unknown), the primary collection of sacred texts of Zoroastrianism, composed in the **Avestan** language and script, which includes hymns from a much later date.

Because the Avestan alphabet was invented probably in the 4th century AD, fully a thousand years after Zoroaster, the relationship between the *Gathas* and anything Zoroaster might actually have said remains a difficult problem. There may have been a written form of the earliest portions of the *Avesta* before the 4th century AD, but we have no evidence. In fact the oldest existing copy of an Avestan language text dates to AD 1288.

The *Avesta* does not mention the Achaemenids or any Iranian tribes such as the Medes, Persians, or Parthians. Information about Zoroaster's life comes mostly from the *Avesta*, complemented by legends from Zoroastrian texts of the 9th to 12th centuries AD, which describe such family events as the marriage of Zoroaster's daughter. Other 9th to 12th-century stories of Zoroaster, as in the *Shahnameh*, "book of kings" (see following section), are assumed to be based on earlier texts, but again there is no evidence.

In the *Gathas*, Zoroaster presents the human condition as the mental struggle between Truth and the Lie: We imagine that this teaching reached back to the 6th century BC and to Zoroaster himself. The cardinal concept of Truth is at the foundation of all Zoroastrian doctrine. **Ahura Mazda** is the Truth, opposed by **Angra Mainyu** (or **Ahriman**), the Lie or Destructive Principle. Ahura Mazda is the beginning and the end, the creator of everything that can and cannot be seen, the Eternal, the Pure, and the only Truth (Figure 8.2).

The purpose of humankind, like all the creation, is to sustain the Truth through active participation in life and the exercise of good thoughts, good words, and good deeds. This active participation is central to the Zoroastrian concept of free will, and Zoroastrianism rejects all forms of monasticism and asceticism so popular in India. Such behavior, admired by many religious traditions, would be to flee from the experience of life, the very purpose of human existence.

There is no dualism of *matter* and *spirit*, only of *good* and *evil*. The spiritual world is similar to the material. Humans bear responsibility for situations they find themselves in and in the way they behave toward one another. Reward, punishment, happiness, and grief all depend on how you live. The creator Ahura Mazda is all good and no evil originates from him. Good and evil have distinct sources, then, with the Lie trying to destroy the creation of Ahura Mazda and the good trying to sustain it.

Ahura Mazda is the one universal and transcendental God, the one uncreated creator to whom all worship is directed. Ahura Mazda will ultimately prevail over

Angra Mainyu/Ahriman, when the universe will undergo a cosmic renovation and time will end. All of creation will be reunited at last in Ahura Mazda.

In Zoroastrianism, *water* and *fire* are agents of ritual purity, and associated purification ceremonies are the basis of ritual life. Zoroaster did not teach the worship of fire but sought to use the flame as a symbol of the pure and wise spirit of universal and supreme dominance. Zoroastrians usually pray in the presence of some form of fire. Both water and fire are represented within the precinct of a fire temple. Fire is considered a medium through which spiritual insight and wisdom is gained, and water is considered the source of that wisdom.

During life, the *fravashi*, a sort of guardian spirit, looks over and protects the individual. On the fourth day after death, the soul is reunited with its protective spirit and the experiences of life in the material world are collected for the continuing battle in the spiritual world. There is no reincarnation. The corpse is a host for decay, a residence of the Lie, so that traditionally the dead were exposed to vultures in the "towers of silence" (a problem in modern times because in India, where most Zoroastrians live, all the vultures have been killed).

Zoroaster was born into a polytheistic religion, which included animal sacrifice and the ritual use of intoxicants similar to the early forms of Hinduism of India. All this Zoroaster rejected. According to tradition, his religion spread when he converted a powerful prince. By the time of the Achaemenid empire in the 6th–4th centuries BC, Zoroastrianism was well established.

## THE CULT OF MITHRAS

In Hellenistic times (323 BC onward, the year of the death of Alexander the Great), the greatest of all mystery cults was the worship of the Persian **Mithras**. The Mithraic cult was restricted to males and spread over the Roman empire through the propagandizing of Roman legions recruited in the Near East. The cult arose in Iran and long persisted in its homeland despite the militant opposition of the followers of Zoroaster. By the time Mithraism reached Rome, however, it had absorbed many of Zoroaster's teachings. It was chiefly through Mithraic cult that Zoroaster's religion exerted an influence on Christianity.

The Mithraic cult portrayed a militant god born from a great stone. He engaged in valiant exploits, causing water to gush forth from a rock struck by his arrows, and he survived the flood in a specially built boat. Mithras celebrated a last supper with the sun-god before ascending into heaven. This sun-god, called in Latin *Sol Invictus* ("unconquered sun"), was a degeneration of Ahura Mazda. Mithras was conceived as the greatest champion of the sun-god in his struggle with the god of darkness (that is, Angra Mainyu). In recognition of his slaying a sacred bull, Mithras was made immortal and exalted to the status of intercessor for the human race among the gods on high (Figure 8.3).

The adherents of the Mithraic cult worshiped in caves and other secret places, chanting hymns, mumbling magic, eating the flesh of the sacrificial animals, and drinking the blood. Three times a day they worshiped, with special weekly ceremonials on the day of the sun-god. The most elaborate observance of all was the annual festival of Mithras at the winter solstice on December 25: Christmas was in origin a Mithraic celebration (nothing is known of the date of the birth of Jesus of Nazareth).

**FIGURE 8.3**   Mithras slaying the bull. In the upper right and left corners are the sun and the moon. The bull's tail is a stalk of wheat, indicating the rebirth of new life. A serpent at the bottom, and a dog at the right, both attack the bull in this formulaic composition, but their significance is not understood. The act takes place within a cave, as indicated by the rough rock above and at the sides. From a sanctuary to Mithras in Rome, where the cult of Mithras was strong, 2nd–3rd century AD. (Musée du Louvre, Paris; Photo by Author)

It was believed that the partaking of the Mithraic sacrament ensured eternal life, the immediate passing, after death, to the bosom of Mithras, there to tarry in bliss until the Judgment Day. On the Judgment Day the Mithraic keys of heaven would unlock the gates of Paradise for the reception of the faithful. When a man died, he went before Mithras for judgment. At the end of the world Mithras would return to earth to summon the dead from their graves to face the last judgment. The wicked would be destroyed by fire, and the righteous would reign with Mithras forever. Much of this teaching entered popular Christianity.

There were seven levels of initiation through which a male could pass. Later, the wives and daughters of the all-male believers were admitted to temples of the Great Mother that adjoined the Mithraic temples. The women's cult was a mixture of Mithraic ritual and ceremonies from the Anatolian cult of the Great Mother goddess Cybelê.

## FERDOWSI'S *SHAHNAMEH*

There was little room for myth—narrative about gods and heroes—in the religion of Zoroaster, concerned as it was with moral behavior and salvation through union with the *fravashi* after death. Little myth attached to Mithras either, apart from his having fired arrows into a mountain to produce water, his killing of a bull, and his last supper with the sun-god. In the 9th century AD, when Islam was overwhelming the ancient religion of the Zoroastrians, enough Zoroastrian literature survived, however, to enable the remarkable Persian poet **Ferdowsi** (AD 940–1020) to embody much of it in his *Shahnameh* ("book of kings"), still today the national epic of the Persian-speaking world. The *Shahnameh* tells the mythical and historical past of Iran from the creation of the world up until the Islamic conquest in the 7th century AD.

The *Shahnameh* is written in the Arabic syllabic script in a pure Persian unmixed with foreign loan words. It was pivotal in the revival of the Persian language after the Islamic conquest. The work is huge: 62 tales and over 50,000 rhyming couplets, more than three times the length of Homer's *Iliad*. This enormous work, regarded by Persian speakers as a literary masterpiece, also reflects Persia's history, cultural values, and the ancient religion of Zoroastrianism. Illustrated copies of the work are among the most sumptuous examples of Persian miniature painting.

Ferdowsi's epic is probably based mainly on an earlier prose version that was itself a compilation of Old Persian stories and historical facts and fables. However, many of Ferdowsi's sources may be oral. The work is not precisely chronological, but there is a general movement through time. Some of the characters live for hundreds of years, though most have normal life spans. Many kings come and go, as well as heroes and villains. The tone of the poem on the whole is dark, reflecting the Arab conquest and the last days of Persian Zoroastrianism. The best characters have serious flaws, and the worst have glimpses of humanity.

## MYTH: ROSTAM AND SOHRAB

Here we have chosen one of the *Shahnameh*'s 62 stories, the story of **Rostam** ("brave in development") and **Sohrab** ("right-visaged") as exemplary of the character of Persian myth. After an opening in praise of God, the *Shahnameh* gives an account of the creation of the world and of humans. This introduction is followed by the story of the first man, who also became the first king after living for a long time in the mountains. His grandson accidentally discovered fire and established a feast in its honor.

Eventually Rostam was born, by Caesarean section, one of the greatest of the early heroes. Rostam was the champion of champions and is the subject of many tales. As a child he killed the mad white elephant of the king with one blow of a mace owned by his grandfather. He then tamed the famous horse **Rakush**. His tragic contest with his son Sohrab is one of the best-known Persian myths (Chart 8).

Rostam was one of the favorites of Kaykaus, king of Iran. Following his lost horse Rakush, he entered the kingdom of Samangan in Turan, a territory

```
        Zal + Rudabeh                King of Samangan
            |                              |
        Rostam (prince of Iran)  +  Tahmina (princess of Turan)
                            |
                         Sohrab
```

**CHART 8**   Descent of Rostam and Sohrab.

neighboring Iran. There he became the guest of the king and married his daughter, Tahmina. However, he soon left the kingdom, never to return.

Tahmina gave birth to a son and named him Sohrab. Rostam and Sohrab never met until a new war between Iran and Turan started many years later. By then Sohrab had become known as the best fighter of the Turan army.

Sohrab knew that his father was named Rostam, but he did not know the name of the hero of the Iranian army. The two warriors met on the battlefield, and Sohrab even told his rival that he would never fight against Rostam. For some reason Rostam does not reveal his name. After a long battle between the two men, Rostam killed his son, who while dying reveals his identity. The father Rostam, torn by grief, gives Sohrab an elaborate burial:[1]

> Listen to the combat between Sohrab
> and Rostam, a tale filled with many tears.
>
> One day Rostam rose from his couch,
> his mind filled with foreboding.
> He thought he'd go out to hunt,
> so he saddled his horse Rakush
> and filled his quiver with arrows.
> He went into the wild country near **Turan,**°
> toward the city Samangan.
> When he came near, he came on a herd
> of wild asses, and he killed many
> until he tired. He caught one and roasted it
> and broke the bones for the marrow,
> then he lay down to sleep while
> Rakush grazed on the nearby pasture.
>
> While he slept, seven horsemen came by
> from Turan. They saw Rakush and they
> desired him. They tried to ensnare him
> with their ropes, but Rakush pawed the ground
> in anger and he attacked as if falling on
> a lion. He bit off the head of one horseman,
> and another he trampled down underfoot.
> He would have killed them all, but

---

°*Turan:* The ancient Iranian name for central Asia, literally meaning "the land of the Tur"; the original Turanians were an Iranian tribe of the Sassanian period. Although identified in the *Shahnameh* with the Turks, there is no relationship between Turanians of the *Shahnameh* (who spoke an Indo-European language) and the ancient Turks (who spoke Turkic languages).

---

[1]For the Persian texts, cf. H. Zimmern, *The Epic of Kings: Stories Retold From Firdusi* (New York, 1883). See also J. K. Motlagh, ed., *The Shahnameh*, 12 vols., Bibliotheca Persica (New York, 1988–2009); J. W. Clinton (trans.), *The Tragedy of Sohrab and Rostam: From the Persian National Epic, the Shahname of Abdol-Qasem Ferdowsi,* 2nd ed. (Seattle, WA, 1996); R. Levy (trans.), *The Shahnameh: The Persian Book of Kings* (New York, 1996). Abolqasem Ferdowsi, D. Davis (trans.), *Shahnameh: The Persian Book of Kings,* (New York, 2006).

there were too many. They ensnared him
and dragged him to the city, thinking,
"Surely we've made a catch!"

When Rostam awoke, he was sad and
perplexed that his horse was gone. He said,
"Now how will I cross the desert?"
His heart was full of trouble, and he
searched for the trail. He followed the tracks.

Now when the people within the city saw Rostam,
that he had no horse, the king and the nobles
came out to greet him. They asked him how
this had come about. Rostam told them
how Rakush had disappeared in the night.
When he followed his tracks, he came
to this gate. Then he swore a great oath.
He said that if his horse was not given back
right away, many a head would fall
from its trunk! When the King of Samangan
saw how angry Rostam had become,
he spoke soothing words. He said that no one
would harm him and begged that he
enter his house and stay with him until
the horse was found. "Surely Rakush cannot
be concealed!" he said.

Rostam liked his words
and put aside his suspicion and entered the house
of the king. There he feasted and passed the hours
and the time in drinking wine. The king
was happy that Rostam was his guest. He brought
out fine singers and honored him. When night
came he personally led Rostam to a couch
scented with perfume and roses. He wished him
a sweet sleep and said again that all would be well
with him and his horse.

When part of the night was passed, and the morning star
was high in the heaven, the door to Rostam's chamber
opened and a murmur came from the threshold.
A slave entered with a scented lamp. A woman
came behind, veiled, in her musky robes.
They came to hero's bed, who was heavy with wine.
He was amazed when he saw them and, rising up,
said, "Who are you? What is your name?
What are you looking for in this dark night?"

The woman answered, "I am **Tahmina**, daughter
of the king of Samangan, of the race of the leopard
and the lion. No prince on earth
is worthy to marry me. Nor has any seen me
without my veil. But now my heart is filled with pain,
and my heart is torn by desire. I have heard
of your famous deeds, how you fear neither
demon, nor lion, leopard, nor crocodile, how your
hand is quick to strike, and how you have eaten
wild asses, and the earth groans beneath your feet,
and men die from your blows, how even
the eagle dares not to attack its prey when
he sees your sword. All this and more they have
told me, and my eyes long to look on your face.
God now has brought you within my father's palace.
I have come to say that I am yours if you
want me. If not, I will marry no other. Consider
only how love has wrecked my reason
and leads me beyond discretion. Yet maybe
God will give me a son like you in strength
and bravery, who will inherit the empire of the world.
If you will hear me, I will bring out before you
your steed Rakush, and I will place beneath
your feet the land of Samangan."

While this moon of beauty spoke, Rostam looked
on her. He saw her beauty, and that she was wise.
When he heard of Rakush, his mind was made up.
The adventure would come out well. And so in secret
they passed the night together.

On the next day Rostam sent to the king and asked
for the hand of Tahmina. The king
rejoiced. They concluded the alliance according
to custom, observing all the rites. All the men,
both young and old, in the palace and in the city
were glad and called down blessings on Rostam.

When Rostam was alone with his wife, he took
from his arm a bracelet known to all the world.
He gave it to her, saying, "Cherish this jewel,
and if heaven gives you a daughter, fasten it
in her hair, a protection from evil. But if
you give birth to a son, fasten it on his arm
so that he may wear it like his father." When
Tahmina heard his words, she was glad.

When the day had passed, the king came to them. He said
he had learned of Rakush and that the horse would soon be
inside the palace gates. When Rostam heard, he was filled
with desire for his horse and he hurried out
to caress him. He fastened the saddle with his own hands
and thanked Ahura Mazda, who had brought
him joy. The time to depart had come. Rostam opened
his arms and held Tahmina close, bathing
her cheek with his tears. He covered her hair with kisses.
Then he mounted Rakush and the swift horse bore him
quickly from sight, and Tahmina too was filled with sorrow.
-months ran their course. Tahmina bore a son
in the likeness of his father, his mouth filled
with smiles. So they named him Sohrab ["bright-faced"].
When he was one-month old, he was like a child
of twelve. When he was five, he was skilled in arms
and the arts of war. When he was ten, there was none
in the land who was better in games of strength.

He came before his mother and spoke words of daring.
He said, "Because I am taller and stronger than my peers,
teach me my race and background. What shall I say
when men ask for my father's name? If you
won't answer, I will not allow you to live a moment longer!"

When Tahmina saw her son's passion, she smiled
within, thinking how like he was to his father.
She opened her mouth and said, "Listen to me,
my son, and be glad, and do not give in to anger.
You are Rostam's son and since God
made the world there has never been one like him."

She showed him a letter that Rostam had written
and three rubies set in gold, that Rostam sent.
She said, "Cherish these gifts and be thankful.
Your father sent them. But remember—
speak not of these things! The land of Turan
groans under the hand of **Afrasiyab**,°
Rostam's enemy. If Rostam learns of your strength,
he may call you to his side, and so break
my heart."

Sohrab replied, "Nothing can be hidden
forever. All men know of Rostam's deeds.
Why have you kept this from me, that I am of such
high birth? I will gather a force of gallant Turks

°*Afrasiyab*: an evil Turanian sorcerer and king.

and lead them into Iran. I will drive **Kaykaus°**
from his throne. I will give Rostam the crown.
Then together we will conquer the land of Turan.
Afrasiyab will fall by my hand. I will
mount the throne in his place, and you shall
be the queen of Iran. Because Rostam is my father
and I am his son, no other king will rule
in this world. We alone shall wear the great crown.
I lust for battle and the glory it brings. But first
I need a horse, strong and powerful. I must not
go on foot among my enemies."

When Tahmina heard these words,
she was happy. She asked the herdsmen
to lead out the horses before Sohrab, her son,
and so they did. Sohrab looked them over.
He tested their strength as his father had of old,
but was not satisfied. So for many days
he looked for a worthy steed until he learned
of a foal sprung from swift Rakush. The foal
came before him. Sohrab smiled, he tested it,
and the horse was strong. He saddled the horse
and leaped on its back, saying, "Now that
I own a horse like you, the world will be made
black for many!"

He prepared for war.
The nobles and fighting men gathered around him.
When everything was prepared, he came before the king
of Samangan and asked his advice for the war
and for his quest to find his father. The king
opened the doors of his treasury and gave
richly from his wealth. He was filled with pleasure
at the boy.

In the meanwhile Afrasiyab heard of Sohrab's
preparations, and he learned of Sohrab's bravery
and his intention to drive Kaykaus from his kingdom.
Afrasiyab was thrilled. He called
before him his captains Human and Barman the mighty
and he ordered them to gather an army
to join the ranks of Sohrab. He told them
his secret purpose, which they were to tell
no one. He said, "Fallen into our hands
is the power to settle the course of the world.
Sohrab is sprung from Rostam, but we must hide

°*Kaykaus*: the king of Iran, which neighbors Turan.

that it is Rostam who opposes him. Perhaps
Rostam will die at the hands of this young lion
and Iran, without Rostam, will fall into my hands.
Then we will subdue Sohrab too, and the world
will be ours. But if Sohrab falls to Rostam,
then grief from having killed his own son
will bring him to his grave."

So spoke Afrasiyab
in his deceit, and he ordered the warriors to go
to Samangan. They carried with them valuable gifts
and a letter filled with deceptive words. The letter
praised Sohrab for his decision, and said
that once Iran was subdued the world would know
peace, and on Sohrab's own head would rest the crown,
and Turan and Iran would be as one.

When Sohrab read the letter, and saw the gifts,
he was glad. Now none could stand against his power.
The cymbals of departure were clashed
and the army got ready to march forth.
Sohrab led them into the land of Iran.
They left in their path a desolation, utter destruction,
sparing nothing as they passed. Everywhere
fires burned. They marched on without opposition
until they came to the White Castle, the fortress
in which Iran laid all its trust.

The guardian of the castle was **Hujir**
and Gustahem lived there too, but now grown old
and helpless except to give advice. There
Gustahem's daughter **Gurdafrid** lived, ferocious in war,
a fine rider, skilled in the fight. When Hujir
saw from a long way off the dark cloud of armed
men, he came out to meet them. Sohrab drew
his sword and asked his name.

"Prepare to meet your end,"
Hujir said, and taunted the man who had
come alone to stand against a lion. Hujir
answered Sohrab with other taunts, and said
he would cut off his head and send it
as a trophy to King Kayvaus. Sohrab only smiled
when he heard him speak.

"Come near," Sohrab said,
and they clashed in combat. Fiercely
they struggled with one another, and strong

and mighty were their blows. But Sohrab
overwhelmed Hujir as if he were a child,
and he bound him and sent him a captive
to Human, captain of the wicked Afrasiyab,.

When those inside the White Castle
learned that their chief was a prisoner, they cried
out loud. They were afraid. Gurdafrid too,
when she heard, was sorrowful and ashamed
for Hujir's fate. She took out her gleaming mail
and wrapped it around her. She hid her hair
under a Roman helmet. She climbed on a battle
horse. She came forth before the walls like
a warrior. She uttered a thunderous cry.
She insulted the men of Turan.
She challenged their champions to come forth
in single combat. But no one came, seeing
how strong she was. They did not know it was a woman
and were afraid.

But Sohrab stepped forth and said,
"I accept your challenge. A second prize will fall
to my hands." He made ready for battle.
The woman showered arrows upon him.
They fell like hail. They whizzed past his head.
Sohrab, angry and ashamed, could not
defend himself. He covered his head with
a shield and attacked the woman. When she
saw him come near, she dropped her bow,
took up her spear, and stabbed at Sohrab
with all her might, nearly knocking him
from the saddle. Staggered, Sohrab ran
in a fury, seized the reins of her horse,
caught her by the waist, and threw her
to the ground. Before he could raise his
hand to strike, she drew her sword and
splintered his spear, then leaped on her
horse. Weary of fighting, she hurried
back to the fortress.

But Sohrab remounted
and followed her, very angry. He grabbed her,
he took hold of her, he wrenched the helmet from her head.
He wished to see who was this man who could withstand
the son of Rostam. Then rolled forth the dark
locks and he saw it was a woman. Astounded,
he managed to say, "If the daughters of Iran are
all like you, none can stand against this land!"

Then he took his rope and bound her in its
snare, saying, "Don't try to escape, O moon
of beauty. I have never before taken such prey."

Gurdafrid, full of deceit, turned her face to him,
unveiled—for she saw no other escape—
and she said, "Flawless hero, do you wish to
make me captive, and parade me before your men?
They have seen us fight, they've seen
how I overcame you. Surely they will laugh
when they learn that a woman stood up against your
power. Best to conceal this adventure, or
your cheeks will grow red with shame. Let us
make a pact. The White Castle is yours, and all it holds.
Follow me and take possession of what is now yours."

Sohrab, listening, was tricked by her words
and enchanted by her beauty. He said, "You do well
to make this peace with me. Truly these walls
could never resist my power."

He followed her up to the castle.
He stood with her before its gates.
Gustahem opened the gate and Gurdafrid stepped
inside. When Sohrab made to follow, she
slammed the door upon him! Sohrab saw that
she had fooled him. He was overcome with anger.
She came out on the battlements and scoffed
and counseled him to return from where he came,
he who could not stand against a woman.
Surely he would fall easy pray to Rostam
once Rostam learned that robbers from Turan
had broken into the land!

Angered even more,
Sohrab departed from the walls. He spread
terror where he went, and he vowed he would
bring the woman to submission.

Meanwhile, the aged Gustahem called a scribe and told
him to write to tell Kaykaus all that had
happened, how an army came from Turan,
how a child led it, yet like a lion
in his form; how Hujir was bound and how
the fortress would soon fall to the enemy's
hands. There were none to defend it

except himself and his daughter, and
he hoped the king would come to their aid.

On the next day Sohrab prepared his attack.
But when he came near, he found that the White Castle
was empty. The doors stood wide open, no warriors
appeared on its walls. He was surprised.
Little did he knows that the inhabitants had fled
by an underground passage. He searched
everywhere for Gurdafrid, for his heart
yearned for her in love. He cried aloud,
"Alas, that this moon is vanished behind the clouds!"

When Kaykaus received Gustahem's message,
he was sorrowful and afraid. He called to
his nobles and asked advice. He said,
"Who will oppose this Turk? Gustahem
says he is like in power to Rostam." The warriors
cried with one voice, "We must appeal to Rostam!"

Kaykaus heard their voice. He called for a scribe.
He dictated a letter. He wrote to Rostam and
blessed him and told him what had happened
and how fresh dangers threatened Iran, and how
Rostam alone could save them. He recalled
all that he Rostam done for him in the past.
He begged Rostam to save them, saying, "When you
get this letter, don't say a word, and if you
hold roses in your hand, don't stop to
smell them, but hurry to help us in our need."

Then Kaykaus sent forth his messenger to Zabulistan.°
He ordered him to neither to rest nor linger until
he stood before Rostam. He said, "When you
have accomplished your mission, return immediately
to me. Do not dawdle there or on the road."

The messenger did as ordered. He neither ate
nor rested until he set foot inside Rostam's gates.
Rostam greeted him kindly and asked why
he had come. When he read the message, he said,
"I would hardly be surprised if a great hero arose
in Iran, but that a warrior of such fame
should come from the Turks—I cannot believe it!
But you say that no one knows from where he comes from.
I myself have a son in Samangan, but he is

°*Zabulistan*: a region in the border area of today's Iran and Afghanistan, the realm
of Rostam.

yet little. His mother writes to say that he rejoices
in the sports of his age. Although he may one day
be a great man among men, his time is not come.
What you say he has accomplished, surely this is
no work of a babe! But come into my house
and we will talk about what should be done."

Rostam's cooks made ready a wonderful banquet.
He feasted the messenger, giving him a lot of wine
so that he forgot his cares and how much time had passed.
In the morning the messenger remembered the king's
command that he not linger but return with speed.
He spoke again to Rostam and asked for his
decision. Rostam said, "Don't worry. Death will
come to these men of Turan. But stay still another
day and rest. Make wet your dry lips. Although
Sohrab is a hero, yet he shall fall by my hands."

And he prepared another banquet. For three
days they made merry. But on the fourth day
the messenger rose resolutely and came before
Rostam, dressed to travel. He said, "I must
go back. Kaykaus is a hard man, and fear of Sohrab
weighs upon his heart. He is impatient,
he cannot sleep, he hungers and thirsts because
of this. He will be angry if we delay
still longer." Rostam said, "Don't be afraid. No one
on earth dare be angry with me!"

He prepared his army. He mounted Rakush and set forth
from Zabulistan, and a great army followed him. When they
came near to the king's court, Kaykaus' nobles
came out to meet them to do homage. Rostam
dismounted from Rakush and hurried to his lord.

But Kaykaus was angry and would not speak.°
His brows were furrowed with fury. When Rostam
had done obeisance before him, he unlocked
the doors of his mouth and words of folly
came from his lips. He said, "Who is this Rostam
that he deifies my power and disregards my command?
If I had a sword in my hand, I would split his head
like an orange! Seize him! Hang him on the nearest
gallows! Let no one ever speak his name!"

°*would not speak*: Kaykaus is angry because of the Rostam's delay in coming.

When the messenger heard these words, he trembled
and said, "Do you put forth your hand against Rostam?"
When the king heard these words, he was beside himself.
He cried in a loud voice that the messenger be hanged
along with Rostam. He commanded that the men be seized,
and so they were. But Rostam broke away from his
captors and stood before Kaykaus, and the nobles
were filled with fear when they saw his anger.

He reproached King Kaykaus, recalling to him his folly,
and how except for Rostam he would not now be seated
on the throne of light. He should threaten Sohrab
the Turk with his gallows! Rostam said, "I am a free
man, no slave. I am a servant to God alone. Without
Rostam, Kaykaus is nothing. The world is subject to me.
Rakush is my throne. My sword is my seal. My helmet
is my crown. But for me, your eyes would never have looked
on this throne. If I desired it, I could have sat
in its seat. I am weary of your foolishness. I will turn
away from Iran, and when this Turk shall have put
you under his yoke, I shall nave nothing to do with it."

Then he turned and strode from the chamber. He leaped
on Rakush, who waited outside, and he vanished
before the nobles had recovered from their astonishment.
They were downhearted, oppressed with care. They held
counsel about what to do, for Rostam was their foundation.
Without his help, they could never stand against
this Turk. They blamed Kaykaus. They counted the deeds
that Rostam had done for him. They spoke for a long time.
At last they resolved to send a messenger to Kaykaus.
Their aged representative spoke long and without fear.
He reviewed all that Rostam had done. He reproached
Kaykaus for his ingratitude. He said that Rostam was
the shepherd, that the flock needed their leader.
Kaykaus heard him to the end. He knew that he
spoke the truth. He was ashamed of what he had done.
He humbled himself and said, "What you say, it is right."

He asked the nobleman to go and find Rostam.
May he forget the evil words of his king.
May he save Iran. And the nobleman hastened
forth to do as King Kaykaus desired. He told the nobles
and they joined him in seeking Rostam. When they
found him, they threw themselves in the dirt.
They told him why they had come. They said

that Kaykaus was without understanding, his thoughts
overflowed like an inflaming wind. The nobles said,
"Although Rostam is angry at the king,
yet the land of Iran has done no wrong that it should
perish at Rostam's hands. Yet, if Rostam does not save it
Iran surely will fall to this Turk."

But Rostam said,
"Well, there are limits to my patience, and I fear none
but God. Why should this Kaykaus anger me?
I have not deserved the rotten words he spoke,
but I will think of them no more. I will cast
aside all thought of Iran."

When the nobles
heard these words they grew pale, and fear
took hold of their spirits. But the wise Gudarz, a noble,
opened his mouth and said, "O Rostam! When Iran
learns of this, they will think that Rostam has fled
before this Turk. When men believe that Rostam
is afraid, they will lose heart. Iran will be beaten
down at the hands of the Turk. So do not turn away
from your loyalty to the king. Do not
tarnish our glory by retreat. Do not allow
the downfall of Iran to rest on your head.
Put from you the words that Kaykaus spoke
in his empty anger. Lead us forth to battle
against this Turk. Let it not be said that Rostam
was afraid to fight a beardless boy!"

Rostam listened.
He pondered these words in his heart.
He knew they were good, but said, "I have
never known fear. Nor has Rostam avoided
the clash of arms. I depart not because of Sohrab,
but because contempt and insults have been my reward."

Yet when Rostam thought further
about the matter, he saw that he must return
to the king. And so he did what he knew
was right. He rode until he came to the gates
of Kaykaus. He strode proudly into his presence.
When the king saw Rostam from a distance,
he stepped down from his throne and stood before
him. He asked his pardon for what had happened.
He said that he had been angered because Rostam
delayed in his coming, that he was born to haste,

and that he had forgotten himself with his words.
But now he was repentant. And Rostam said,
"The world belongs to the king. It is right that you act
as you think right toward your servants. I shall be faithful
to you until old age. May your power and
majesty be yours forever."

And King Kaykaus answered,
"O Rostam, may your days be blessed to the end!"
He invited him then to a feast. They drank wine
until far in the night. They considered how they should act.
The slaves brought rich gifts to Rostam
and the nobles rejoiced. All was well once
more in the gates of the king.

When the sun came up
and clothed the world in its rays of love, the clarion call
of war sounded throughout the city. Men prepared
to go forth against the Turks. The legions of Persia
came at the king's command. Their countless thousands
covered the earth, the air was dark with their spears.

When they came to the plains where stood Hujir's fortress,
they set up their tents in the usual manner.
The watchmen saw them from the battlements
and set up a great cry. Sohrab heard the cry. He asked
the reason for it, and when he learned that the enemy had
come, he was glad. He demanded wine, and drank,
to their destruction. He called forth the captain Human and showed
him the army. Sohrab told Human to be of good cheer. He saw
in its ranks no hero, mighty of mace, who might
stand against himself. He called his warriors to the feast
and a banquet of wine. He said they would dine until
it was time to meet the enemy in battle. And so they did.

When night came, throwing her mantle of darkness over
the earth, Rostam came before the king. He asked
for permission to go beyond the camp to see what sort
of man was this youth from Turan. Kaykaus agreed,
and said it was worthy of him. So Rostam went forth disguised
as a Turk. He entered the White Castle in secret. He came into
the chamber where Sohrab held his feast. When he looked
on the boy, he saw that he was like a cypress of good sap.
His arms were sinewy and powerful, like the sides
of a camel. His stature was tall. He saw around him
many gallant warriors. Slaves poured wine from golden
cups. They all were glad. No one dreamed of sorrow.

Now while Rostam was watching, Zindeh changed
his seat and came near to where Rostam
watched. Zindeh was brother to Tahmina. She had
sent him forth with her son Sohrab that he might
point out to Sohrab his father Rostam, whom he alone of all
the army recognized. She did so to avoid any harm if the
heroes should meet in battle. Now Zindeh, when he
changed his seat, thought that he espied someone watching.
He walked over to where Rostam was hiding. He came
before him and said, "Who are you? Come into
the light so I may see your face." But before he
said another word, Rostam raised his hand
and struck him and Zindeh fell to the ground dead.

When Sohrab saw that Zindeh had gone out, he was
disturbed. He asked his slave why Zindeh had not returned
to the banquet. They went to find him, and found Zindeh
lying in his own blood. They reported to Sohrab what
had happened. Sohrab could not believe it. He ran
to the place, he called for torches, and all the warriors
and singers followed him. When Sohrab saw it was
true, he was much saddened, but insisted that the banquet
go on. He did not wish that his men's spirits be subdued
with pity. So they all went back to the feast.

Meanwhile Rostam returned to the camp. As he was
about to enter the lines, he came on a sentry who,
seeing a tall man dressed as a Turk, drew a sword and
made ready for combat. But Rostam smiled and spoke,
and the sentry knew his voice. The sentry asked
him what he was doing in the darkness. Rostam told him.
Then Rostam went before King Kaykaus and described what he had
seen. No man, he said, like this Sohrab had appeared
before among the Turks.

When morning, came, Sohrab put
on his armor. He went to a high place from where he
could look down over the Iranian camp. He took
Hujir with him. Sohrab spoke, saying, "Do not deceive me.
Do not depart from the path of truth. If you answer
my question truthfully, I will loosen your bonds and give
you treasure. If you deceive me, you shall languish until
you die in your chains."

And Hujir said, "I will answer you
according to what I know." Then Sohrab said, "I want to
question you about the nobles down there. You will name those

whom I point out. You see that tent of gold weave,
adorned with leopard skins. Before it stand a hundred
war elephants. In its gates is a turquoise throne. Over the tent
floats a violet flag with a moon and sun at its center.
Tell me, whose pavilion is this that stands in the midst
of the camp?"

Hujir replied, "It belongs to the king of Iran,
King Kaykaus." Sohrab said, "On its right hand is another tent
draped in the colors of mourning. Above it floats a flag on which
is portrayed an elephant."

And Hujir said, "It is the tent of Tus,
son of Nuder, who carries an elephant as his sign."
Then Sohrab said, "And whose camp is that where many warriors
stand rich in armor? A golden flag, with a lion, waves above it."
And Hujir said, "That camp belongs to the brave Gudarz.
Those who stand about him are his sons. He has fathered
eighty men of might."

Then Sohrab said, "Whose tent is that
covered in green? There is a nobleman on its throne.
His head strikes the stars. And beside him stands a horse
as tall as he is. His standard shows a lion and a twisting dragon."

When Hujir heard this question, he thought to himself,
"If I reveal the signs by which he might recognize Rostam,
surely he will fall on him and seek to destroy him.
It seems to me best that I keep silent and leave out
his name from the list of heroes."

So he said to Sohrab,
"This is some ally who has come to King Kaykaus from far
China. I don't know his name."

When Sohrab heard this, he was downcast, and his heart
was sad that he could nowhere see Rostam. Still he
asked again the name of the unknown warrior, and yet again
Hujir denied it to him, for it was written that that
should happen that had been decreed.

Sohrab asked, "Well, who is that beneath the standard
with the head of a wolf?" Hujir said, "It is Gew,
son of Gudarz, and men call him Gew the brave."

Then Sohrab said, "Whose is the seat over which
are awnings and weaving of Rome, that glisten

in the sunlight?" And Hujir said, "It is the throne of
Fraburz, son of King Kaykaus. "It is right that the king
surround himself with such splendor." And he pointed
to a tent with trappings of yellow encircled
by flags of many colors. Whose was that?

Hujir answered, "Guraz the lion-hearted is its lord."
Then Sohrab questioned Hujir about Rostam, his
father, and he asked still a third time about the green
tent. But Hujir replied that he did not know who
stayed there. When Sohrab pressed him about Rostam,
he said that Rostam lingered still in Zabulistan. For it was
the feast of roses. But Sohrab refused to accept
that Kaykaus would go to battle without the help
of Rostam, whose might was like no other's. So he said,
"If you do not show me the tent of Rostam, I will
cut your head from your shoulders! The world will
fade before your eyes. Choose—the truth or your life!"

Hujir thought to himself, "Though one hundred men
cannot withstand Rostam when he is roused, I fear that he
may find the equal in this boy. Because he is younger,
he may even subdue Rostam. What is value of my life
against the well-being of Iran? I will
abandon myself into his hand rather than show him
where he can find Rostam."

So he said, "Why do you seek
to find Rostam? Surely you will know him in battle,
and he will strike you dumb, and crush the
pride of your youth. I will not show him to you."

When Sohrab heard these words he raised his sword
and struck Hujir, making an end of him with
a great blow. Then he made ready for the fight.
He leaped on his battle steed. He rode until he came
to the Iranian camp. He broke the barricades with his spear.
Fear seized everyone when they saw his powerful form
and the majesty of his bearing. Then Sohrab opened
his mouth, and his voice of thunder was heard to the
far ends of the camp. He spoke words of pride and
summoned the king to battle. He swore with a loud
voice that the death of Zindeh would be avenged.
When Sohrab's voice rang through the camp, confusion
spread, and none who stood around the throne would
accept his challenge. With one accord they cried
that Rostam was their sole support. His sword alone
could cause the sun to weep.

And Tus sped to the court
of Rostam, and Rostam said, "Kaykaus always gives
me the hardest jobs." But the nobles would
not permit him to linger, nor to waste time in words.
They buckled his armor on him. They threw a leopard
skin around his shoulders. They saddled
Rakush. They made the hero ready for battle.
They sent him forth and called after him, "Hurry up!
This is no common combat. Ahriman stands
before us!"

Now when Rostam came before Sohrab,
and saw the youth, so brave and strong, Rostam said,
"Let us go apart. Let us step far from the lines."
For there was an area between the two camps
that none could cross. Sohrab agreed and they
stepped out into the no-man's land and prepared for single
combat. When Sohrab was about to fall on him,
Rostam was filled with compassion. He did
not wish to kill a boy so fair and brave. He said,
"Young man, the air is warm and soft, the earth
is cold. I take pity on you. I would not rob you
of the gift of life. Yet if we meet in the contendings,
you will fall by my hands. No one has withstood
my power, not demons, not dragons.° Lay off,
quit the ranks of Turan. Iran needs fighters like
you."

While Rostam spoke in this fashion, Sohrab's heart
went out to him. He said, "I will ask you a question,
and please tell the truth. Tell me your name.
May my heart rejoice, for I think that you are
Rostam, the son of Zal, the son of Saum, the son
of Neriman."

But Rostam replied, "You are mistaken.
I am not Rostam. Nor do I spring from the line
of Neriman. I am a slave without crown
or a throne."

Rostam said this so Sohrab might take
fear when he realized that a greater power was
still hidden in the enemy's camp. But Sohrab was
saddened by these words. His high hopes were
shattered. A day once bright had turned black.

°*dragons*: in other adventures Rostam slays demons and a dragon.

He prepared for combat. They fought until their
spears were shattered and their swords were hacked
like saws. When their weapons were bent,
they took up clubs and fought until they too
were broken. They fought until their mail
was torn and their horses worn out. Even then
they did not give up the fight, but tore at one
another with bare hands until sweat mingled
with blood covered their bodies. They contended
until their throats were dry and their bodies
weary, but neither could win the victory.
Then they rested. Rostam thought how in all
his days he had not fought such a hero. He thought
that his fight with the White Demon had been
nothing compared to this.

When they had rested, they fell to fighting again.
They fought with bow and arrow, but neither could
surpass the other. Rostam tried to hurl Sohrab
from his horse, but he could no more shake
him from the saddle than a mountain can be
moved from its seat. They set to once again with
clubs. Sohrab took aim and struck Rostam.
Rostam reeled, he bit his lips. Sohrab boasted
his advantage. Maybe Rostam should try to find
a fair match—clearly he was not up to the
strength of a youth!

Thus they parted. Rostam attacked
the men of Turan, spreading confusion far and wide.
Sohrab raged against the lines of Iran, and men
and horses fell to his attack. But Rostam was sad in
his heart. He turned with sorrow to his camp.
When he saw the destruction Sohrab had done,
he grew angry. He challenged the youth once again
to single combat. But because the day was over,
they put off the fight until the next day.

Rostam went before
King Kaykaus. He told him of this boy of valor. He prayed
to Ahura Mazda that he would give him the strength
to overcome this enemy. Yet he made preparations
to die, sending kind words to his mother Rudabeh
and to his father Zal. Sohrab too praised the power
of Rostam. He said the fight had been severe,
its outcome uncertain. He said to Human,
"I wonder about this old man, my adversary.
He is about my size. He is as my mother described Rostam.

My heart goes out to him. I wonder if it is my father
Rostam. I really should not fight him. How has this
come to pass?"

Human said, the captain of Afrasiyab, "Often enough I've
seen Rostam fight. I've witnessed his bravery.
This man is not like him at all. He uses the
club in a completely different fashion." So spoke Human
in his vileness. For Afrasiyab had encouraged
him to lead Sohrab to destruction. Sohrab
said no more, but he was still not so sure.

When dawn broke and the shadows were swept away,
Rostam and Sohrab advanced midway between
the two armies. Sohrab carried a great club,
and the dress of battle was about him. His mouth
was full of smiles. He asked Rostam if he had
slept well, and Rostam said, "Why be stirred up for
battle? Cast away this mace and sword of revenge.
Let's take off our armor. Let us sit together
in friendship. Let us drink wine and forget our
deeds of anger. This fight is not right. If you will hear
my desire, I will speak to you of love. I will cause
tears of shame to swell in your eyes."

And Sohrab said, "For this reason I ask you
once again. Tell me your name! Do not
hide it any more. I see that you are of a noble
race. I think you are Rostam, the chosen one,
the lord of Zabulistan, the son of Zal, the son of Saum."

But Rostam answered, "You are of a young age,
and we are not here to parley but to fight.
I am not tempted by your words. I am old,
you are young, but we are geared up for battle.
The ruler of the world will decide."

Sohrab said,
"Old man, why will you not hear the words
of a youth? I wish that you had died in bed,
but you have chosen to die in combat.
Well, that which must be, must be. Let us prepare
to fight."

They prepared. They harnessed their horses.
They fell upon one another. The crash of their
meeting was like thunder. They fought from
morning to when the sun went down [Figure 8.4].

**FIGURE 8.4**  Rostam battles his son Sohrab in a page from an illustrated 15th century manuscript of the *Shahnameh*. Rostam and the Iranians are on the right, Sohrab and his Turanians on the left. The men carry long swords, wear helmets, and are armed with bow and arrows. Sohrab carries a small shield. The horses are caparisoned. A man lies dead at the bottom of the hill. (British Museum, London; Photos 12 / Alamy)

When the day was nearly
gone, Sohrab seized Rostam by the belt around
his waist and threw him to the ground. He drew
his sword. He made ready to sever head from trunk.

Rostam realized that only a trick could save
him. "Young man," he said, "you know not
the ways of combat. It is written in the
laws of honor that he who defeats a brave
man for the first time should not kill him,
but preserve him for a second time, when
it is fine to kill the man."

Sohrab heard Rostam's
crafty words. He stayed his hand. He let
the warrior go. Because the day was ended,
Sohrab wished to fight no more.

Sohrab turned aside
and hunted deer until the night was spent.
Human came to him and asked about the
day's adventures. Sohrab told him how he
had vanquished the tall man, how he then

granted him freedom. Human reproached him
with the folly and said, "Young man, you
have walked into a trap. This not at all the
custom among the brave! And now, perhaps,
you will fall victim to this warrior."

Sohrab was
taken aback by Human's words, but said,
"Be not aggrieved. In an hour we meet again
in battle. He will never stand for a third time
against the strength of my youth."

In the meanwhile
Rostam had gone to a running creek, where he
washed his limbs. He prayed to God. He entreated
Ahura Mazda to grant him the strength
to win the victory. Ahura Mazda heard him, and
gave such strength to Rostam that the rock
where he was standing could not bear him. Rostam saw
that the power was too great and prayed that
a part of it be taken from him. And Ahura Mazda
heard his voice.

When the time for combat had
come, Rostam set out for the meeting place.
His heart was filled with care, his face with tears.
Sohrab came forth like a refreshed giant,
and he ran at Rostam like a crazed elephant,
and he cried with a thunderous voice, "You
who fled from battle—why have you come
once more against me? I say to you, this time
your guileful words will do you no good."
Rostam heard him and looked on him
and was seized with misgiving. He was afraid.
He prayed to Ahura Mazda that he restore
to him the power he had taken back. But
he did not reveal his fears to Sohrab. They
made ready to fight. Rostam closed on
Sohrab with his new-found power. He shook
Sohrab to the foundation. Though Sohrab met
his attack with vigor, the hour of his destruction
had come.

Rostam took him by the belt around
his waist and hurled him to the earth. He broke
his back like a reed. He drew out his sword
to cut his body in half. Sohrab knew it was
the end. He gave a huge sigh and writhed

in agony. He said, "That which has happened
is my fault. Hereafter will they laugh at my
youth. But I never sought glory—I went to
seek my father. My mother told me how I
would know him. I perish, longing for him.
All is useless. I have not looked on his face.
Yet I say to you—if you became a fish in
the sea, or a star in the farthest sky, my father
would find you and avenge my death upon you,
once he has learned how I lie in my grave.
For my father is Rostam the son of Zal, and he
shall learn how Sohrab, his son, perished
when trying to find him."

When Rostam heard these
words, he dropped his sword, shaken with
alarm. He groaned from deep in his heart.
The earth grew dark before his eyes. He sank
down lifeless beside his son. But when he
opened his eyes once more, he cried to Sohrab
in the agony of his spirits. He said,
"Do you wear a token of Rostam, so that I may
know that what you say is true? For I am Rostam the
miserable. May my name be struck from the lists
of men!"

Sohrab heard these words in bottomless
sadness. He cried, "If you are in fact my father,
then have you stained your sword with the life
blood of your son. And you did if from stubbornness.
For I sought to befriend you, I asked you for your
name. I thought I recognized the tokens.
I appealed to your heart, in vain. But open
up my armor, and you will see the jewel on
my arm. It is a gemstone that my father gave me,
as a token whereby he could know me."

Rostam did as Sohrab asked. He opened his mail.
He saw the gemstone. He tore his clothes in anguish.
He covered his head with ashes. The tears of
repentance poured from his eyes. He roared aloud
in his sorrow.

But Sohrab said, "In vain. There is
no remedy. Do not weep. Doubtless it is written
that this should be."

When the sun had set
and Rostam had not returned to camp, the nobles

of Iran grew afraid. They went forth to find him.
When they were gone but a little way, they came
on Rakush. When they saw he was alone,
they raised a great wailing. They thought that
for sure Rostam had been killed. They went to tell
Kaykaus. He said, "Let Tus go out and find if
this is in fact the case, that Rostam is fallen.
Let the drums of battle roll, so we may avenge
Rostam on this Turk."

When Sohrab saw from afar
the men who came to find Rostam, he said, "I ask
that you do me an act of love. Let not
the king fall on the men of Turan. They came
not through enmity to the king, but to do
my desire. I alone am responsible for this
campaign. I do not wish that all the men of Turan die
when I no longer can defend them. As for me,
I came like the thunder, I vanish like the wind.
Perhaps we will meet again in the great beyond" [Figure 8.5].

Rostam promised to do what Sohrab wanted.
He went before the men of Iran. When they saw
that he was still alive, they raised a great shout. But
when they saw that his clothes were torn,
and that he bore the mask of sorrow, they asked
what had happened.

He told them how he
had caused a noble son to perish. And they
grieved for him and joined in the wailing.
He asked one of them to go to the camp of Turan
and give a message to Human. Rostam sent him
word, saying, "The sword of vengeance must
sleep in its scabbard. Now you are leader of
the host. Go back to where you came from. Depart
across the river before many days have passed.
As for me, I will fight no more. Nor will I
speak to you again. For you did hide from my son
the tokens of his father. Through your wickedness you
have led Sohrab into this pit."

When he had so spoken
Rostam turned again to his son. The nobles
went with him. They beheld Sohrab. They heard
his groans of pain. When he saw the boy's agony,
Rostam was beside himself. He would have
made an end to his own life, but the nobles

**FIGURE 8.5** Sohrab, wounded by a bowshot, lies dying before his boastful father Rostam, who wears his leopard skin as a helmet. Sohrab's dead horse lies at the lower left. The Iranians are mounted on horses and a war elephant. The Turanians are mounted on horses and a camel. At the top a Turanian blows a war trumpet. 19th century, Mughal miniature. (National Museum, Delhi; dbimages / Alamy)

would not let him. They stayed his hand.
Then Rostam remembered that Kaykaus had an
unguent that could heal anything. He asked Gudarz
to go to the king, bearing a message from
Rostam, his devoted servant. He said, "O king,
if ever I have done something good for you,
if ever I have raised my hand in your defense,
remember now in my hour of need. Send me
now, I pray, the unguent in your treasures so that
my son may be healed."

And Gudarz ran like the
wind, bearing the message to the king. But the
heart of Kaykaus was hardened. He could
not remember the benefits he had received from

Rostam, but only the proud words Rostam had spoken.
And he feared that the power of Sohrab might
be joined to that of his father, that together
they might become more powerful than he
and turn against him. Therefore he shut his ear
to Rostam's plea.

Gudarz carried back the answer
and said, "The heart of Kaykaus is like flint,
his evil nature like a bitter gourd.
I suggest that you go before him yourself,
if perhaps you might soften this rock."

And Rostam did as Gudarz advised. He turned
to go to the king when a messenger came up
and said that Sohrab was dead. Rostam set up
a howling like which the earth has never heard.
He reproached himself. He did not cease
complaining that he had killed his own son.
He cried continually, "I who am old have killed
my son. I who am strong have uprooted this
mighty boy. I have torn my child's heart,
I have killed the fruit of my own begetting."

He made a great fire and flung into it
his tent with many colors, and the trappings
of Rome, his saddle, his skin of leopard, his
armor proven in battle, and his throne. He
stood beside it and looked to see his pride
utterly humbled. He tore his flesh. He cried
aloud, "My heart is sick unto death." He
commanded that Sohrab be covered in rich
golden weavings, worthy of his body.

When they
had wrapped him, Rostam learned that the
Turanians had left the camp. He prepared his
own army to return to Zabulistan. The nobles
marched in front of the bier, their heads
covered with ashes, their garments torn.
The drums were shattered, the cymbals broken,
the tails of the horses cropped to the root,
all the signs of mourning abroad.

Now Zal, when
he saw the host returning in sorrow, was amazed
at what had happened. He saw Rostam at the
army's head, so he knew they were not wailing

for his own son. Then Rostam led him to the bier
and showed him the young man so like in feature
to Saum the son of Neriman.° Rostam told Zal
what had happened, how this was his son, in
years a child, in battle a hero.

Rudabeh, Rostam's mother, too came
out to behold the child. She joined her lamentation
with theirs. They built for Sohrab a tomb in the
shape of a horse's hoof. Rostam laid him within
a chamber of gold, scented with perfume. He
covered him in weavings of gold.

When the tomb was finished
the house of Rostam became like a grave,
its courts filled with the whisperings of
sorrow. Rostam took pleasure in nothing, and
it was a long time before he raised his head.

Meanwhile the news spread to Turan. There too
did men weep for the brave child, cut down in
his bloom. The king of Samangan tore his vestments
and his daughter, learning what had happened, was beside herself
with sorrow. Tahmina cried for her son. She
bewailed the fate that took him. She piled black
earth in her hair. She tore her hair. She wrung her
hands. She rolled on the ground in agony.
Constantly she gave a sad cry. She had
Sohrab's garments brought to her, and his throne and
steed. She regarded the objects. She stroked the
horse. She poured tears upon it. She cherished
the robes as if they still clothed her child. She
pressed his horse's head into her breasts. She kissed
the helmet he had worn. Then with a sword she
cut off the tail of the horse and set fire to
the house of Sohrab. She gave the gold and the
jewels to the poor. When in this way a year had
rolled over her bitterness, her breath departed from
her body. Her spirit went forth to Sohrab, her son.

°*Saum the son of Neriman:* Saum is Rostam's grandfather and Neriman his
great-grandfather.

The great hero Rostam met his death when his jealous half-brother Shaghhad
plotted with the king of Kabul to kill him. They had dug a deep pit, lined it with spears,
and disguised it with ferns. They invited Rostam on a hunting trip and led him to the
trap. Rostam's horse Rakush was impaled on the spears and killed, and Rostam was

fatally injured. Realizing his half-brother's treachery, the wounded Rostam begged Shaghhad to string his bow for him so that he could protect himself from wild animals while he lay dying. Shaghhad obliged and Rostam shot him dead, pinning him to a tree with his well-aimed arrow.

## OBSERVATIONS: FERDOWSI'S *SHAHNAMEH*

Modern Persian has existed as a living language for around 1,100 years. Persian speakers today read the *Shahnameh* in its original form, although it is more than 1,000 years old. In fact the *Shahnameh* created the modern Persian language, which still looks to this book for canons of expression and style. *Beowulf*, by contrast, or the Norse *Eddas*, cannot be understood by the modern speakers of English or Icelandic. Because the *Shahnameh* is written in a living language, and because it has sustained Persian poetry through the centuries, the *Shahnameh* has shaped the modern identity of its Iranian readers.

According to Persian tradition, Rostam is based on a historical character named "Retzehem," supposedly an Achaemenid general of the 6th century BC. Retzehem was said to have helped the Persians conquer the city of Sardis in 546 BC by climbing up its walls, throwing down a rope, and pulling up his fellow soldiers. Like the Irish hero Cuchulain (see Chapter 9), he killed a ferocious beast as a young man, slew his son in combat, is virtually invincible in combat, and, in the end, was murdered by treachery while killing his murderer with his last breath. Many of these themes are also echoed in Homer's *Iliad* and *Odyssey*: Rostam's dispute with Kaykaus is like Achilles' dispute with his superior Agamemnon; Rostam's penetration of the enemy camp in disguise is like Odysseus' penetration of Troy in disguise; Hujir's explanation of the enemy's camp is like Helen's identification of the Greek forces while standing on the walls of Troy. In the postHomeric tradition, the Amazon queen Penthesilea, killed by Achilles, is very like the warrior-queen Gurdafrid. Such may be standard narrative devices evolved independently in parallel traditions, or more likely the Greek tradition has influenced the Persian.

The *Shahnameh* is an exciting tale of heroic behavior in a world where violence decides all. Love is passionate and part of a rigorous code of conduct. But it all ends badly. What can you do?

At the end of the *Shahnameh* Ferdowsi wrote:

> I've reached the end of this great history
> and all the land will talk of me. I shall
> not die. These seeds I've sown will save
> my name and reputation from the grave.
> Men of sense and wisdom will proclaim,
> when I have gone, my praises and my fame.

And so they have.

## Key Terms

| | | |
|---|---|---|
| Zoroaster *259* | Mithras *264* | Tahmina *269* |
| *Gathas 263* | Ferdowsi *266* | Afrasiyab *270* |
| *Avesta 263* | *Shahnameh 266* | Kaykaus *271* |
| Avestan *263* | Rostam *266* | Hujir *272* |
| Ahura Mazda *263* | Sohrab *266* | Gurdafrid *272* |
| Angra Mainyu *263* | Rakush *266* | |
| Ahriman *263* | Turan *267* | |

## Further Reading

Allan, T., C. Phillips, and M. Kerrigan, *Wise Lord of the Sky: Persian Myth* (New York, 2000).

Curtis, V. S., *Persian Myths* (Austin, TX, 1993).

Hinnelis, J., *Persian Mythology* (New York, 1997).

Mackey, S., and W. Scott Harrop, *The Iranians: Persia, Islam and the Soul of a Nation* (Ann Arbor, MI, 2008).

Shahbazi, A. S., *Ferdowsi: A Critical Biography* (Cambridge, MA, 1991).

Wiesehöfer, J., *Ancient Persia* (New York, 2001).

# Japanese Myth

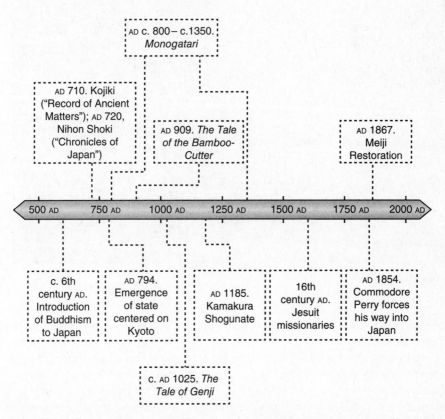

AD c. 800– c.1350.
*Monogatari*

AD 710. Kojiki
("Record of Ancient
Matters"); AD 720,
Nihon Shoki
("Chronicles of
Japan")

AD 909. *The Tale
of the Bamboo-
Cutter*

AD 1867.
Meiji
Restoration

| 500 AD | 750 AD | 1000 AD | 1250 AD | 1500 AD | 1750 AD | 2000 AD |

c. 6th
century AD.
Introduction
of Buddhism
to Japan

AD 794.
Emergence
of state
centered on
Kyoto

AD 1185.
Kamakura
Shogunate

16th
century AD.
Jesuit
missionaries

AD 1854.
Commodore
Perry forces
his way into
Japan

c. AD 1025. *The
Tale of Genji*

Japan lies in the Pacific Ocean near the coast of China, Korea, and Russia (Map 9). The name *Japan* comes from a Dutch and Portuguese version of a Malay version of a Chinese rendering of the characters that make up Japan's name. In Japanese these nonphonetic characters are pronounced *Nippon* or *Nihon*. The two characters can in Japanese also mean "sun origin," supposedly referring to the myth whereby the

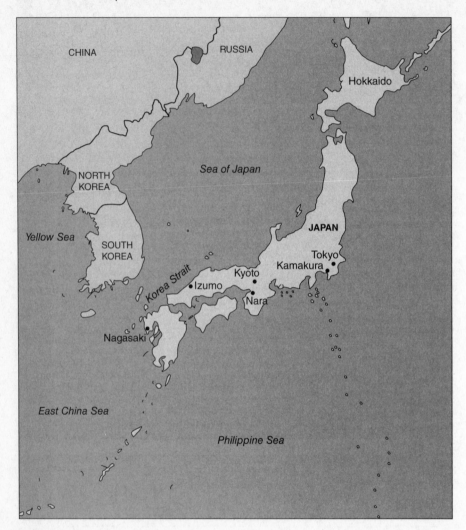

**MAP 9**   Japan.

emperor of Japan is a direct descendant of the sun-goddess. Japan is therefore the "Land of the Rising Sun," taken in reference to China—Japan lies to the east of China.

Although there are 6,852 islands in the Japanese archipelago, the four largest islands make up most of the land, which is mountainous and volcanic. The immense volcano of Mount Fuji, near Tokyo, is the highest peak (see Figure 9.1). Most land is unsuitable for agricultural, industrial, or residential use, because of the steep elevation and risk of landslides caused by earthquakes, soft ground, and heavy rain. Therefore the inhabitable coastal areas are densely populated in Japan.

The Greater Tokyo Area is today the largest metropolitan area in the world, with over 35 million residents. About 130,000 million people today speak Japanese, almost entirely ethnic Japanese. Because of the extreme complexity of the writing system, there are very few nonJapanese readers, writers, and speakers of Japanese.

**FIGURE 9.1**  *The Great Wave at Kanagawa,* from the series *Thirty-six Views of Mount Fuji* by Katsushika Hokusai (1760–1840). Massive waves curling with white foam smash down on a small boat while Fuji looms in the background. The prow of a second boat is shown on the right. The artist's name and the title of the print appear in the upper left. Polychrome woodblock print, 1831–1833. (Newark Museum, Newark, New Jersey; INTERFOTO / Alamy)

## BACKGROUND: CHINESE MYTH

Japanese culture was a spin-off of Chinese culture so that in discussing Japanese culture one must always say something about its roots in China, although the Chinese were a wholly foreign people and spoke languages completely unrelated to Japanese. In primordial times the Chinese racial group moved into the Yellow River basin in eastern Asia. They were remarkable for their ability to get along with one another, but warred successfully against another racial group in eastern Asia that eventually escaped the Old World, long ago, to enter the New World across a land bridge over the Bering Strait—the ancestors of the native peoples of North and South America. The dwellers in the Yellow River Valley built one of the oldest cultures in the world, later than developments in Mesopotamia, but still existing today. The great challenge of Chinese culture today is to adapt an ancient culture, with its bizarre system of writing, to modern conditions.

Naturally there were periods of internal breakdown when one Chinese group contested with another for power, but pacific tendencies, a close family life, and an elaborate bureaucracy so favored the Chinese people that today one out of every four or five humans is Chinese, about 1.2 billion people. The earliest historical period is called the Shang Dynasty, conventionally dated c. 1800 BC–1120 BC, around the time of the Egyptian Middle Kingdom, the days of Abraham. From the late Shang Dynasty, c. 1200 BC, come the earliest examples of Chinese writing in caches of oracular bones numbering in the tens of thousands. The bones are the scapula of sheep, part of the shoulder, or the belly of the tortoise. The bones are inscribed with what appear to be questions that usually can be answered by Yes or No, such as Will the child be a boy? Will the weather be good? Will the battle be won? The operating shaman, who may have been the emperor himself, carved a small pit into the bone. Then a hot tip probably of metal was placed in the indentation. In the pattern of cracks that developed lay the answer to the question. More than 150,000 of these oracle bones, the earliest Chinese writing, have been found!

Not all of the signs on the oracle bones can be read, but still there is continuity between writing in the late Shang and modern Chinese writing, a tradition of at least 3,200 years, nearly as long as the West Semitic tradition of writing represented by modern Arabic script. Perhaps the West Semitic tradition goes back to about 1800 BC. But there are no myths of any kind in the Shang writing. There must have been a period of development antecedent to the oracular bones of the Shang, but we have no evidence. Evidently, writing was used otherwise exclusively on perishable material, such as the bamboo strips known from later times.

From, c. 600–c. 221 BC (the late Chou Dynasty) come some texts that we may classify as literary, beginning about two hundred years after Homer, but the period of greatest literary production comes during the Han Dynasty, 202 BC–AD 220. We might think of the Han Dynasty as the classical period of Chinese culture, the golden age in which many texts took on the appearance that they have today. Of course we would like to know something of Chinese myths, but the nature of their system of writing makes this task exceedingly difficult.

Chinese writing does not work like any writing with which we are familiar. There are 50,000 signs in the full range of Chinese writing, but no one knows them all. You need to know about 4,000 signs to read a newspaper, and college educated students may know as many as 7,000 signs. An alphabet-user need know only 25–35 signs! Chinese writing is what historians of writing call a *logography*, that is, there is in general a separate sign for every word. It is true that Chinese signs consist (mostly) of two elements, one phonetic and the other not phonetic, but in practice these different elements of a sign are not recognized. The phonetic element of a sign is in any case more a phonetic hint than the representation of an exact sound.

This fact is very hard for an alphabet-user to understand—that there is no sound attached to Chinese signs, although the Chinese Communist revolution has attempted to make the Mandarin pronunciation of the Beijing dialect of Chinese the official pronunciation, and there is today a system of Roman alphabetic characters (called *pinyin*) that children learn in order to become familiar with Mandarin pronunciation. The power of the Chinese writing is that communication is possible independently of the dialect that one speaks (many Chinese dialects are mutually unintelligible), a perfect tool of empire, but it places the written version of any text separate from any spoken version of it.

Impossible to appreciate in translation is that a Chinese written text gains its aesthetic power and its meaning from the beauty of the signs. For this reason, as one scholar has remarked, it is almost impossible to make Chinese literature in translation interesting to a Western reader. A translation into English is a reconstruction in a completely different medium. The Chinese reader is facing a symbol whose meaning is encoded in no single spoken symbol, with beautiful flourishes and elegant and sometimes very personal touches, a work of art. The Japanese were to inherit this tradition and this taste in their own writing.

Laboring under such obstacles to understanding, we may nonetheless say that the Chinese saw the earth as four-square in shape, topped by the globe of the sky, supported by four pillars. Chinese myth has little to say of the underworld, the realm of the Greek Hades or the Mesopotamian Ereshkigal or the Egyptian Osiris. Whereas Mesopotamian and Indian myth saw the primeval substance from which world was made as being watery, in Chinese thought it is a kind of vapor. At the moment of creation, this vapor became solidified into male and female, Yin and Yang, hard and soft, and other binary qualities. There is no creator, nor any being that exerts will, as does Vishnu. The creation just happens. One Chinese cosmology, however, claims a Fu Hsi ("prostrate breath"?) as a primordial god and says that he invented the system of the Eight Trigrams, all the different possible combinations of Yin and Yang in a group of three lines. There are also stories about the founders of Chinese culture, but it is impossible to disentangle legend, folklore, and history, which are further colored by religion and philosophy.

In ancient China arose the philosophical school of the **Tao**, or the "Way." The Taoists were followers of Lao Tze ("old master"), c. 6th century BC, author of the Tao Te Ching, "The Classics of the Way and of Virtue." The Tao is the path on which all opposites are perfectly blended so as to form a seamless whole. Taoism has both a philosophical and a religious aspect. Philosophical Taoism emphasizes inner contemplation and mystical union with nature. One should let things take their natural course and not interfere by purposive action based on wisdom or knowledge. Simplicity and nonaction are the rule. The religious aspect of Taoism developed later, c. 3rd century AD, and incorporated features from Buddhism (see later) and established a monastic system for followers.

The Yin/Yang duality is the basis of Taoist thought. Though opposites, they are in perfect harmony and each contains the seed of the other. Taoism is important to the study of Chinese myth because our most important sources for Chinese myths are Taoist documents, especially *The Classics of Mountains and Seas*, by many hands from about 300 BC to 100 AD. This book is a compilation, an account, mostly fabulous, of the geography and culture of early China. Along the way we are told many Chinese myths, such as they are, but the book is never a narrative. Early scholars categorized the book as a bestiary. The myths are rarely longer than a paragraph, as is usual in Chinese documents.

For example, there are many stories of the Yellow Emperor. The Yellow Emperor had power over Responding Dragon (Ying Lung) and his daughter, Drought Fury. He overcame and killed Ch'ih Yu, a god of war and rain who invented metal weapons (in transliterating Chinese names into Roman characters, the apostrophe ['] indicates a *glottal stop*, when the throat constricts as between the syllables of "Uh-O"):

> In the wilderness there is a great mountain called Pu-chü. Rivers and the sea flow into it. Bowmen did not dare to go north of the mountain. There was someone dressed in green clothes, the emperor's daughter Drought Fury. Ch'ih Yu put on his armor and attacked the Yellow Emperor. The Yellow Emperor ordered Responding Dragon to counterattack in the wilderness of Chi province. Responding Dragon stored up all the water. Ch'ih Yu asked the Wind God and the Rain Master to let down a cloudburst. The Yellow Emperor sent his daughter Drought Fury and dried up all the rain. Then he killed Ch'ih Yu.
>
> *Shan hai ching* ("The Classic of Mountains and Seas"), *Ta huang tung ching*, Ssu-pu pei-yao edition 17.4b-5.b[1]

---

[1]This version based on the translation given in A. Birrell, *Chinese Mythology: An Introduction* (Baltimore, MD, 1993).

Chinese myth, then, survives only in fragments, written in a lapidary and often highly obscure style. Translations make specific what in the original Chinese is only implicit and ambiguous, so we might say there are as many versions of a Chinese myth as there are translations of it. However, such fragments formed part of the literature assiduously studied between the 4th century BC to the later Han Dynasty in the 3rd century AD, so they became familiar to many, and of course such texts survive to the present day. But China had no Homer, Hesiod, Vergil, or Ferdowsi to give shape and color to their mythic traditions, or in fact a tradition of writing that was capable of supporting such a poet. Their myths exist only as isolated references in other texts, making difficult a study and appreciation of Chinese myth.

## JAPAN IN HISTORY

Japan is first mentioned in Chinese history texts from the 1st century AD, that is, about 1,700 years after the beginning of the Shang Dynasty. Around 500 BC wet-rice farming, a new style of pottery, and metallurgy came to Japan, brought by migrants from China and Korea. Somewhat later, Buddhism influenced the ruling class and gradually became predominant, alongside the native religion of Shinto (see section "Japanese Religions"). In the 8th century AD first emerged a strong central Japanese state, centered on an imperial court. At this time were written in Chinese characters and Chinese language the massive chronicles that contain the earliest of all Japanese myths.

The emperor moved the capital from Nara, where the emperor had originated, 30 miles north to **Kyoto** in AD 794, where it remained for more than a millennium. For long Kyoto was the only city in the land. Perhaps a hundred thousand people lived there. Kyoto is a kind of bowl, surrounded on three sides by high mountains that trap the heat in the summer. Rivers flow on either side of the city. Kyoto was laid out in a gridlike pattern, in imitation of Chinese cities. At its center stood the emperor's palace, occupying 300 acres. The emperor was served by a small aristocratic elite. Otherwise there were bureaucrats, peddlers, servants, and monks, but no middle class. At this time, in Kyoto, a distinctly indigenous Japanese culture emerged, noted for its art, poetry, and literature.

In Japan one had a personal name and a clan name. The clan name is written first, so that *Fujiwara no Tadzane* means "Tadzane of the Fujiwara clan." The *no* is like German *von*, except it precedes the personal name.

The central fiction of Japanese politics is that the emperor holds absolute power, but in reality power was held by an official who ruled in the emperor's name. It is amazing that the emperor was not simply removed, but he never was, and he remains the ultimate political authority in Japan today.

The few born to power cut an extraordinary figure and often are important in Japanese stories. A ruling class of warriors emerged, the samurai, whose code of honor was inviolable and deeply affected Japanese society. Since the late 19th century this code has been known as *bushido*. American troops in the South Pacific, after December 7, 1941, learned to their sorrow the power of this code of self-sacrifice.

In AD 1185, following the defeat of the rival Taira clan, Minamoto no Yoritomo was appointed shogun and established a base of power in the city of Kamakura on the coast near modern Tokyo. *Shogun* simply means "commander of a force." The shogun was generalissimo under the nominal authority of the emperor, but wealthier than the emperor and more influential.

The Kamakura shogunate repelled invasions in 1274 and 1281 by Islamic Mongols, aided by a storm that the Japanese interpreted as *kamikaze*, "divine wind." After a long period of political instability, during the 16th century, traders and Jesuit missionaries from Portugal reached Japan for the first time, introducing commercial and cultural exchange between Japan and the West. Although in 1639 the shogunate introduced the isolationist policy that lasted two and a half centuries, some contacts continued through a Dutch enclave in Nagasaki. On March 31, 1854, the American Commodore Matthew Perry of the United States Navy forced the opening of Japan to the outside world.

Adopting Western political, judicial, and military institutions, the shogunate resigned in 1867, and a cabinet introduced a constitution and assembled an imperial diet. This so-called Meiji Restoration—because the power of the emperor was in theory restored—transformed Japan into the industrialized world power that it is today.

## JAPANESE WRITING

Chinese writing is first found in Japan in the 1st century AD, but only on metal and stone, serving an amuletic function. Then in the 8th century appeared the oldest Japanese literature, the **Kojiki** ("Record of Ancient Matters," AD 712) and *Nihon Shoki* ("Chronicles of Japan," AD 720), written entirely in Chinese characters. They contain the oldest Japanese myths. Because such characters do not have sound attached to them, but stand for words, it is difficult to say whether these chronicles are in the Chinese language, or in the unrelated Japanese, or a mixture. Some signs in the *Kojiki* are used with syllabic value, however, suggesting that the text was read in Japanese, no doubt the aristocratic Japanese of the court in the city of Nara where the capital then was. Not long after, when the capital was moved to Kyoto, a system of syllabic signs, evolved from the Chinese signs that *do* have sound attached to them. At first such signs were used to give the sound in the Mandarin dialect of Chinese (that spoken around Beijing), but were soon applied to notate the Japanese language.

Although there have been several reforms since the 8th century, the highly complex system of writing that appeared at this time is still used in Japan. There are three main scripts. (1) **kanji** ("Han writing," that is, Chinese writing), consisting of word-signs from Chinese characters without a sound attached (as in the numbers 1, 2, 3, the sound being different in every language); there are about 2,000–3,000 kanji in common usage, but complete inventories run as high as 100,000! There are two systems of syllabic signs, called **kana** ("script"): (2) *hiragana* ("ordinary script"), with 46 signs for native Japanese words, and (3) *katakana* ("fragmentary script," that is, the signs are graphically a part of kanji signs) for foreign loan words and sometimes to replace kanji or hiragana for emphasis; there are 51 basic signs in katakana. Although the language could be written phonetically by means of kana alone, the Japanese prefer to write with a mixture of kanji and kana.

Writing is done in columns from top to bottom and right to left (Figure 9.2). Some say that Japanese is the most difficult writing system in the world, but there are other highly difficult systems, especially the Chinese from which Japanese writing is derived. In any event the complexities of the system effectively shut out nonJapanese from direct apprehension of Japanese culture. Our English versions of Japanese tales are a good distance from the original expression, filled with an elaborate system of honorifics that reflects the hierarchical nature of Japanese society. Verb forms and vocabulary also indicate constantly the relative status of speaker and listener. A literal

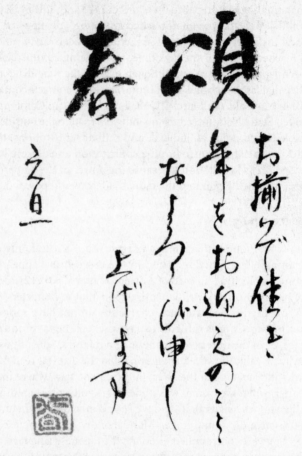

**FIGURE 9.2**  Japanese calligraphic kanji, 18th century. (J Marshall – Tribaleye Images / Alamy)

translation of Japanese texts is quite bewildering to a Western ear. Like Chinese writing, Japanese writing cannot separate beauty of form from significance of meaning. Hence calligraphy is of cardinal importance, as in the Figure 9.2, where the beauty of the characters is independent of their signification.

The Japanese language is not related to any other language. The language works, however, somewhat like Turkish in being *agglutinative*: that is, words are formed by adding morphemes (meaningful units) to a stem. Sometimes English is agglutinative, as in the formation of *shame-less-ness*, where the first word establishes the realm of meaning; the second *-less-* tells you that there is a lack of this quality; the third *-ness-* tells you that it is an abstract noun. (But English, like Chinese, is in general an *isolating language* in which units of meaning are separate words.) About half the words in Japanese are taken directly from Chinese.

## JAPANESE RELIGIONS

**Shinto** (Chinese for the "way of the gods") is a 19th-century word used to describe the body of Japanese religious practices that came before, and after, the introduction of Buddhism, and that justified the power of the emperor as dependent on his descent from **Amaterasu**, the sun-goddess. In Shinto there is a large body of gods that exist side by side with the gods of Buddhism, sometimes in opposition to them, but generally in harmony.

The gods of Shinto are known through mediums, dreams, and shamanistic possession, usually by monks. Shinto practices were first recorded in the *Kojiki* and *Nihon Shoki* in the 8th century, although these writings do not refer to a unified "Shinto religion," but to a disorganized folklore, history, and myth. Shinto today is a term that applies to public shrines suited to such purposes as war memorials, harvest festivals, and historical monuments. Practitioners express their beliefs through a standard language and behavior, adopting an ancient style in dress and ritual. The vast majority of Japanese people who take part in Shinto rituals also practice ancestor worship.

Taoism, Confucianism, and Buddhism from China had for long influenced Japanese beliefs and customs. **Confucianism** is a Chinese ethical and philosophical system developed from the teachings of the Chinese philosopher Confucius (K'ung-fu-tzu, "Master Kong," 551–478 BC). It is a complex system of moral, social, political, philosophical, and religious thought according to which human beings are improvable and perfectible through personal and communal effort. A dominant theme in Confucianism is the cultivation of virtue and the development of moral perfection.

**Buddhism** began probably in Nepal around 550 BC with the teachings of a man named **Siddhartha Gautama**, commonly known as the *Buddha* (= Sanskrit "the awakened one"), a religion and philosophy encompassing a variety of traditions, beliefs, and practices. He is also known as *Sakyamuni*, "Sage of the Sakyas"; the Sakyas are an ethnic group of which Siddhartha Gautama was a member. Nothing real is known of his life or teachings, but Buddhists believe that accounts of his discourses and monastic rules were memorized and first written down about 400 years after his death.

The Buddha is recognized by his followers as an enlightened teacher who shared his insights to help sentient beings end their suffering, achieve nirvana—a state free of suffering and individual existence—and escape the cycle of rebirth. From India, Buddhism spread to Southeast Asia, central Asia, China, and Korea, but by AD 600 had faded in its native India and largely in China. Buddhism came to Japan around AD 600, more than a thousand years after its inception, and flourishes there today. Zen Buddhism, developed in China in the 7th century AD, was introduced to Japan in the Kamakura period (AD 1185–1333) and became popular among the samurai class. Zen de-emphasizes theoretical knowledge in favor of direct realization of reality through meditation.

Buddhism is a religion of monks, all male, and in Japanese stories there are very many monks of a great variety. The religious or quasireligious members of Japanese society were large in number. Often the son of a great lord would become a monk. Monks had acolytes and students. They were usually attached to a temple or shrine, which could be elaborate and densely populated, with even thousands of adherents.

The Buddhist scriptures are called *sutras*, a Sanskrit word referring to texts taken as having been spoken by the Buddha himself. Japanese stories often refer to the Lotus Sutra. The monk would recite the sutra in the Chinese language, which he probably did not understand.

Sakyamuni, an honorific name of the historical Buddha, was known in Japan as *Shaka*. He was just a man, not a god, who taught the unreality of the world, including the round of birth and death, reincarnation. Always this teaching remained basic to Buddhism. Although the cosmos became filled with many Buddhist gods, their ultimate unreality, as against the truth of perfect being, was never doubted. For this reason enlightenment is not necessarily separate from living a life in this world, which in its unreality is in essence the true nature of being—a Buddhist paradox.

Buddhism came to explain that Shaka was just one in a line of Buddhas that extended indefinitely into the past and indefinitely into the future. The next Buddha after Shaka is Miroku, who at present is only a **bodhisattva**. A bodhisattva is a being who has renounced Nirvana until everyone can join him, and in the meanwhile works to save those caught in the web of birth and death. Miroku will descend to this world after many eons. He awaits his descent from what is called the Tosotsu Heaven, one of several Buddhist heavens. The Tosotsu Heaven is associated with salvation reached through the Lotus Sutra.

The **Amida** ("infinite light," "infinite life") **Buddha**, depicted as a simple Buddha in meditation, presided over a splendid Paradise in the far West to which one might aspire through calling out the name *Amida*. At the moment of death, Amida would come in a blaze of glory preceded by the bodhisattvas **Kannon** and Seishi. Those present at the death could not see the vision, but only smell the sweet incense of salvation.

The Amida Buddha does not work actively in the world, unlike Kannon and Seishi who serve him. Kannon is an especially important bodhisattva, sometimes having 11 faces to represent his accessibility to all, and one thousand arms to represent the many ways in which he helps humankind. For some reason he is called the Goddess of Mercy, though he is always represented as a male, and of course females cannot be bodhisattvas. He presides over an earthly heaven, somewhere unreachable in the far West; the Dalai Lama of Tibet is thought to be an incarnation of Kannon (Figure 9.3).

## MYTH: JAPANESE CREATION OF THE WORLD

Following a bloody and long-drawn out internal competition for power, the victorious emperor Tenmu (AD 631–686) ordered the writing down of the oral tales that would justify his victory by celebrating his descent from the sun-goddess Amaterasu. In AD 710 his command was completed in the *Kojiki*, or "records of ancient matters," which we mentioned earlier. The *Kojiki* is divided into three parts. The first part deals with divine myth, with gods and goddesses and the divine origin of clans. In the second and third parts Japanese divine myth slides into Japanese legend, telling stories of the exploits of the powerful descendants of the sun-goddess leading up to the early 7th century. The purpose of the *Kojiki* is explicitly to glorify the reigning emperor through tracking his origin back to the gods. Japanese myth and history are always tangled up like this, although the more sober *Nihon Shoki*, written in classical Chinese and completed in AD 720, is a more dependable reporting of history.

The account of the creation of the world in the first part of the *Kojiki*, in its emphasis on separation of an initial unity, is like accounts in the ancient Near East:[2]

> The names of the gods born in the Plain of High Heaven, when the heaven and earth began, were *Lord Midst-of-Heaven God*; next born was *High Creative Force*

---

[2]For the Japanese texts, cf. B. H. Chamberlain, *Transactions of the Asiatic Society of Japan*, vol. x (London, 1882); T. P. Williston, *Japanese Fairy Tales*, Second Series (New York, 1911). See also, René Sieffert, *Bulletin de la Maison Franco-Japonaise*, Nouvelle Série 2 (1952); D. Keene, *Monumenta Nipponica*, Vol. 11, No. 4 (Tokyo, 1956); D. Keene (trans.), *The Tale of the Bamboo Cutter (Taketori Monogatari)*, illustrated by Miyata Masayuki (Tokyo, 1998); Haruo Shirane, ed., *Traditional Japanese Literature* (New York, 2007).

**FIGURE 9.3**  Seated bodhisattva Kannon. Usually Kannon has six arms (sometimes he has one thousand!). He sits in a lotus posture wrapped in a cloak. Kyoto, 20th century. (Jeremy Hoare / Alamy)

*God*, then *Divine Creative Force God*. These three gods were born alone. Their forms were invisible.

At first, before the separation of heaven and earth, all was one thing. When they separated, when the world came into being, there were three divine principles, a division into three of the basis of reality. The three divine principles worked from the invisible world.

Next, when the land was young and like floating oil, drifting around like a jellyfish, a thing sprouted forth like reed shoots, *Glorious Root Shoot God*, then *Standing Forever Heaven God*. These two deities were also born alone, and their forms were invisible.

These five deities are the *Separate Heavenly Deities*.

The names of the gods that were born next are *Standing Forever Land God* and *Abundant Clouds Field God*. These two gods were likewise born alone, and their forms were invisible.

The names of the gods born next were the deity *Clay Male God*, then his spouse *Mud Female God*.

Next, the *Emerging Form God* came into being, along with his spouse the *Living Form God*.

Next, *Great Male Organ* God and his spouse *Great Female Organ God*.

Next, the god Izanagi or *He Who Invited God*, and his spouse Izanami, or *She Who Invites God*.

These gods, from *Standing Forever Land God* to Izanami, are termed the *Seven Generations of the Age of Gods*.

*Kojiki*, part I

After the creation of the world, governed by a trinity of powers, came into being two powers embodying the principles of growth (*Glorious Root Shoot God* and *Standing Forever Heaven God*, a place for the roots to grow). The next two gods are the earth and the sky above (*Standing Forever Land God* and *Abundant Clouds Field God*), All things come from the earth (hence *Clay Male God* and *Mud Female God*), from which they take form (the *Emerging Form God* and the *Living Form God*). Now sexual reproduction is possible (*Great Male Organ God* and his spouse *Great Female Organ God*), leading to the first beings with real personality, **Izanagi** and **Izanami**.

## MYTH: ORIGIN OF THE JAPANESE ISLANDS

Hereupon all the heavenly deities commanded the two gods Izanagi and Izanami to "make, consolidate, and give birth to this drifting land." Giving them a jeweled spear, the gods entrusted them with this mission. Standing on the Floating Bridge of Heaven, Izanagi and Izanami pushed down the jeweled spear and stirred with it. When they had stirred the brine till it made a sound, they drew the spear up. The brine that dripped down from the end of the spear was piled up and became the Island of Onogoro, probably "self-curdling island," a mythical land:

Descending from heaven to this island, they erected a heavenly pillar and built a huge palace.

Then Izanagi, the Male-Who-Invites, said to Izanami, the Female-Who-Invites, "How is your body made? And she said, "My body is made in one place insufficiently." Then Izanagi said, "My body is in one place made in excess. I would like to place that part of my body made in excess inside that part of your body that is insufficient. Thus we can give birth to the land. What do you say?"

And she said, "That would be fine."

He said, "Let us go around the heavenly pillar, and when we meet on the other side, let us unite. You go around from the left, and I will go around from the right."

When they met, Izanami spoke first, saying, "Ah, what a handsome and lovely young man!"

Then Izanagi said, "Ah, what a handsome and lovely young woman!" But afterward he said, "It is not right that the woman speak first!"

The child that was born to them was a leech. When it was three years old it could still not stand up straight. So they placed the leech child in a boat of reeds and let it float away. Next they gave birth to an island of foam. This likewise is not considered to be one of their children.

The two gods took counsel and said, "The children to whom we have given birth are not good. It will be best if we announce this to the heavenly gods."

They went up to heaven and inquired of the heavenly gods. Then the heavenly gods performed a divination and said, "They were not good children because the woman spoke first. Go back again and correct your words."

They went back and again went around the heavenly pillar. Now Izanagi spoke first, saying, "Ah! what a handsome and lovely maiden!" Afterward his wife Izanami spoke, saying, "Ah! what a handsome and lovely youth!"

Then they united and Izanagi bore a child, Awaji Island. Then they bore the double island of Iyo. This island has one body and four faces, and each face has its own name. So the land of Iyo is called *Lovely Princess*; the land of Sanuki is called *Grain Spirit Possessed Man*; the land of Awa is called the *Great Food Woman*; and the land of Tosa is called *Fierce Spirit Possessed Man*.

Next they gave birth to the triple island of Oki, another name for which is *Heavenly Great Heart Youth*. This island likewise has one body and four faces, and each face has its own name.

*Kojiki*, part I

Here the *Kojiki* gives a long list of the islands of the Japanese archipelago. So long as there was an incorrect order of things, with the woman speaking first, there could be no proper offspring. Once the male takes his correct precedence over the female, all is in order. And so the Japanese islands came into being through sexual reproduction of the primordial pair.

## MYTH: THE TRIUMPH OF AMATERASU

When they had finished giving birth to countries, they began afresh giving birth to gods … [many gods are named]. Then they gave birth to the *Swift Burning Fire Deity*. Through giving birth to this child Izanami's genitals were burned, and she became sick and lay down. The name of the god born from her vomit was the *Metal Mountain God*. The names of the gods born from her feces were the *Clay Earth God* and the *Clay Earth Goddess*. The names of the gods born from her urine were the *Goddess of Irrigation* and, next, the *God of Agricultural Creation*. The child of this god was the *Goddess of Food*. And so Izanami, through giving birth to the god of fire, at length passed away.

*Kojiki*, part I

In revenge for the death of Izanami, Izanagi kills the fire-god, then journeys to the other world, called Yomi, to visit with Izanami. But Izanami, like Persephone in the Greek story, has eaten of the food of the underworld. She sends demons after her husband (as did the Mesopotamian Ereshkigal), but according to the common folktale motif, Izanagi casts objects behind him that delay his pursuers:

Izanagi, wishing to meet and see his spouse Izanami, followed after her to the land of Yomi. When she raised the door and came out from the palace to meet him, Izanagi said, "O my beloved spouse, the lands that you and I were making are not yet complete. Come back!"

Then Izanami said, "You should have come sooner! For I have eaten at the hearth of Yomi. O my husband, I am honored that you have come. I will discuss my desire to return with the gods of the land of Yomi. Do not look at me!" Having said this, she went back inside the palace.

Because she was away a long time, he could not wait. He broke off one of the teeth of the comb that he stuck in the left side of his hair, lit a fire, and went in and looked.

Maggots swarmed everywhere. She was rotten … Izanagi was astonished. He fled back, whereupon his wife Izanami said, "You have put me to shame," and at once she sent the hags of Yomi to pursue him. Izanagi loosened the black vine that tied his hair and threw it down. Instantly it bore grapes. While the hags picked them up and ate them, he fled on, but because they still pursued him he broke away the teeth of the thick comb he kept in the right bunch of his hair and threw them down. Instantly they turned into bamboo shoots. While they pulled them up and ate them, he fled on.

Finally Izanagi reaches the upper world, but realizes the need to purify himself:

Then the great god Izanagi said, "I have come from a hideous and polluted land—I have! So I will perform a purification."

He went out to the plain of Awaki at the mouth of a river near Tachibana in Himuka on the island of Tsukushi. He purified and cleaned himself. As Izanagi took off his clothes, various gods sprang up from the items of clothing. When he went to wash his left eye, up sprang the goddess Amaterasu, the Great Heaven Shining Goddess. When he washed his right eye, Tsukuyomi was born, the *Moon Counting God*. The name of the god that was next born, as he washed his nose, was Susanoo, *Ferocious Virulent Male God* …

At this time Izanagi greatly rejoiced, saying, "Begetting child after child, I have at my final begetting begotten three illustrious children." With these words, taking off his necklace and shaking it so that it jingled, he gave it to Amaterasu. He said, "You will rule the heaven."

Next he said to Tsukuyomi, "You rule the night." Thus he charged him.

Next he said to Susanoo, "You rule the sea."

*Kojiki*, part I

In some versions of the myth, Susanoo, a storm-god, rules not only the seas but also all elements of a storm, including snow and hail.

Later, after many adventures, Amaterasu unites with a god called *High Creative Force Deity* and they produce a child, *Heavenly Grain*, who in turn, uniting with a daughter of High Creative Force Deity, produces Ninigi, Amaterasu's grandson. Amaterasu sent Ninigi out of heaven down to earth to introduce rice cultivation. Ninigi was the great-grandfather of Jimmu, the first emperor of Japan, from whom all subsequent emperors claim descent.

## MYTH: AMATERASU AND SUSANOO

One story tells of Susanoo's bad behavior toward Izanagi. Because of Susanoo's constant complaining, Izanagi banished him to Yomi, the underworld. Susanoo agreed, but first went to heaven to bid farewell to his sister the sun-goddess, Amaterasu.

Amaterasu suspected his intentions and readied herself for battle. "Why do you come here?" she asked. "To say farewell," said Susanoo.

Amaterasu demanded a contest to decide on Susanoo's good faith. Whoever could give birth to more divine children would win. Amaterasu made three women out of Susanoo's sword. Susanoo made five men from a decorative chain that Amaterasu wore. Amaterasu claimed victory on the grounds that because the five men were made from her belongings, they belonged to her and that the three women belonged to Susanoo.

Amaterasu's claim drove Susanoo to violence. He flayed a pony—sacred to Amaterasu—and flung it into Amaterasu's weaving hall, killing an attendant. Amaterasu fled and hid in the cave and darkness covered the world. All the celestial beings tried to coax Amaterasu out of the cave, but she refused. At last the goddess of merriment, Uzume, placed a large bronze mirror on a tree opposite Amaterasu's cave. Uzume dressed in flowers and leaves, turned over a washtub, and danced on it, booming out the rhythm. Uzume shed the leaves and flowers and danced naked, causing the male gods to roar with laughter.

Amaterasu grew curious. She peeked outside and a ray of light escaped. Amaterasu was dazzled by the beauty of the goddess she saw, not realizing it was her own reflection in the bronze mirror. A quick-thinking god pulled her out of the cave and sealed it up. Amaterasu now agreed to return her light to the world (Figure 9.4).

**FIGURE 9.4**  The sun-goddess Amaterasu emerging from the earth with the blaze of the sun behind her. During her retirement in a cave there was no light on earth until she reemerged, looking into a magical mirror, to illuminate the emperor and his court. On her brow is the sun disk. She looks at the emperor, and his wife, in the lower left. The mirror is suspended above the empress. Uzume, the goddess of merriment, is beneath the goddess against the rock of the cave. On the right is the decorated washtub that a courtier beats. An inscribed pennant hangs over it. Various courtiers, in fancy dress, witness Amaterasu's reappearance. The rays of the sun are like wall linings from which tassels hang. Utagawa Kunisada (Toyokuni III) (1786–1865), Japanese woodblock print. (PD-US http://en.wikipedia.org/wiki/File:Amaterasu_cave_edit2.jpg)

## MYTH: THE *TALE OF THE BAMBOO-CUTTER*

Roughly between AD 822 and 1350 appeared a large "tale literature," the **Monogatari**, in 45 collections. This form of literature was made possible by the invention of *kana*, syllabic signs that gave hints to the reader about how the word is sounded, unlike the Chinese signs (*kanji*) that have no sound attached to them. Because words in the Japanese language are open-syllables, and each *kana* stands for a syllable, the *kana* made possible an intimacy with spoken Japanese that Chinese signs could never have. Hence arose stories that explored the psychology of its characters. Eventually this development led to *The Tale of Genji*, perhaps the world's first psychological novel, of the early 11th century AD (but unreadable by a modern Japanese without special study). The *Monogatari* were never considered serious literature, but of interest only to aristocratic women and children. Serious literature was chronicles and poetry, written mostly in *kanji* by learned males.

It is only possible to give here a taste of this vast literature, which consists of stories of great range. Mostly they treat of Buddhist topics, invoking, for example, the miraculous origin of some temple or image, or telling the lives of famous monks. Other tales treat of life at court, its many affairs and courtesies and entertainments. The smallest category of tales is what might be called folktales, but they are of great interest. Of course by no means are these tales of the folk, though in some cases they may depend on folk traditions. They were composed by and for the highly educated aristocratic elite.

Oldest of all the *Monogatari* is *The Tale of the Bamboo-Cutter* (*Taketori Monogatari*), from around AD 909:

> Once upon a time there was an old bamboo-cutter. Every day he would go out into the fields and the forest to gather bamboo, from which he made all sorts of things. The man's name was Sanuki no Miyakko. One day he saw a light burning at the base of a bamboo stalk. Thinking how strange this was, he went over to examine it. He was surprised to see that the light was within the stalk of bamboo, and that a pretty girl was sitting there, about three inches high.
>
> "I have found you here in the bamboo where I look every day. You must be meant to be my daughter."
>
> He took her up into his hands and took her home to his aged wife. She was a darling, and they kept her in a special cradle so that they might care for her.
>
> Ever after that the bamboo-cutter would find bamboo stalks filled with gold, and soon he became very rich.
>
> They took excellent care of the child, who grew rapidly. In three months she was a fully grown woman,° whom they thought should be suitably dressed. They did her hair up in a bun and put on her a long robe.° They took the greatest pains with her education. She was not allowed even to leave the curtained chamber. The child was so beautiful that the house was filled with her light. When the old man was in low spirits, just to look at her would fill him with joy. Soon his anger was gone.

°*woman*: she grew as fast a bamboo. °*robe*: part of the maturity rites for girls was to put up the hair and don a long gown.

So for many years the bamboo-cutter continued with his work, and he became very rich. When the girl had reached her maturity, they called in the diviner to give her a woman's name. He called her Nayotake no **Kayuga-hime**, the Shining Princess of the Young Bamboo. On the day of her name-giving they held a great feast with every manner of entertainment, and the feast went on for three days. Men and women alike were there, and it was a splendid entertainment.

## The Suitors

Every man in the realm, both of high and low estate, hoped to win Nayotake no Kayuga-hime, or at least to behold her beauty. Just the report of her drove men mad with love. But it was no easy thing for those who staked out the fence and gate to catch a glimpse of her. At night, unable to sleep, they would poke holes in the fence, hoping to see something—the fools! When they addressed members of the household, nobody paid attention. Many a young noble spent his days and nights by the compound, refusing to go away. At last those faint hearts went home, having decided they were wasting their time.

But five famous lovers would not give up. They spent every night and day outside the house. They were Prince Ishizukuri; Prince Kuramochi; the Minister of the Right° Abe no Nimuraji; the Grand Counselor° Otomo no Miyuki; and the Middle Counselor Isonokami no Marotari. Whenever they heard of someone who was just sort-of good looking, they burned to see her, although there were plenty of such women around.° It was hardly surprising that they gave up all nourishment in their anxiety to see Kayuga-hime, and languished for her. They went to her house and wandered around aimlessly, although there was little chance that anything would come of it.

They wrote her letters, which she did not answer. They composed odes of lamentation, but she did not notice. All the same they kept up their suit, both in the cold of December and in the heat and lightning of July.

Once they called in the old bamboo-cutter, and on bended knee they begged, each one of them, that he be given the girl. The old man only answered, "I am not her father and she does not have to do what I say."

Thus did the days, weeks, and months pass. At last all returned to their own houses, where they sank into meditation, praying to the gods for assistance. However much they wished to forget Kayuga-hime, they could not. In spite of what the old man had said, they thought that the girl must one day marry, and this gave them hope. They went about with looks of consecrated devotion.

Seeing them, the old bamboo-cutter said, "My darling, I realize that you are a divinity in human form, but I have tried my best to raise you in a suitable manner. Will you not listen to an old man?"

°*Minister of the Right*: the Minister of the Left served immediately below the chancellor, the highest administrative post, but his duties were often performed by the Minister of the Right; an extremely exalted post. °*Grand Counselor*: a high post, but beneath the Minister of the Right. °*women around*: Japanese men rarely saw Japanese women, even their wives, because there were always veils between them, or darkness.

Kayuga-hime answered, "What could you possibly ask that I would deny you? I do not know for certain if I am immortal, and I view you as the only father I have."

"How happy your words make me," said the old bamboo-cutter. "I am now over seventy years old, and who knows if today I breathe my last. In this world it is customary that men and women marry, and so the family flourishes. Why then will you not marry?"

Kayuga-hime answered, "Why should I do such a thing?"

The old bamboo-cutter said, "Even though you are a transformed deity, still you have a woman's body. So long as I am in this world you can remain unmarried, but when I am gone, you will be all alone. These suitors have come here faithfully for weeks and even years. Why not hear them out, and marry the one you choose?"

"All I can say," said Kayuga-hime, "is that I would bitterly regret it if I were to marry someone, in spite of my unattractiveness, whose heart was shallow, who in the end proved fickle. It hardly matters how grand the suitor is—if he is not sincere."

"I do agree with you, my darling. Let me only ask: What qualities exactly do you expect in a husband? All these men have shown remarkable devotion."

"I am not seeking any great depth of emotion … It is only a little thing that I ask. All five of them seem to have the same feelings. How can I tell them apart? If one of them will show me something I desire, that will prove his affections the most noble, and I will belong to him. Talk to the men when they come again and tell them this."

"An excellent idea," said the old bamboo-cutter.

Around sunset the men gathered as usual. One of them played a flute, another recited a poem, another sang a song, or they whistled and beat time with their fans.

The old man came up to them. "You are to be commended—for months and even years you have come to see my daughter. I am very grateful. Now as it is I do not know if today will be my last. I have suggested to Kayuga-hime that she choose one of you as her husband. She would, however, like to know how genuine are your affections, as is natural. She says that she will serve the one who shows her something she desires. It is a good plan, for then no one of you will resent her choice."

The five men agreed that it was a good plan, and the old bamboo-cutter went back into the house.

Kayuga-hime said, "I should like Prince Ishizukuri to bring me the stone begging bowl of the Buddha. Prince Kuramochi should go to the mountain in the eastern sea called Horai° and fetch me a branch of a tree that grows there whose roots are silver, its trunk gold, and its fruits precious jewels. The next man should bring me a robe made of the fur of Chinese fire-rats.° The Grand Counselor Otomo must bring me the jewel of five colors from a dragon's head. Isonokami should bring me the swallow's charm for an easy birth."°

°*Horai*: the mountain of Paradise. °*fire-rats*: a mythical rat. °*birth*: the swallow is imagined as giving live birth; the charm is a cowry shell, whose name in Japanese means "easy-delivery shell."

The old bamboo-cutter said, "These are very difficult tasks. None of these objects are within Japan. How shall I break the news to them?"

"I don't see why these tasks are so hard," said Kayuga-hime.

"Anyway, I'll tell them," said the old man and went outside.

When he had related all that she said, they replied, "Why doesn't she just tell us not to come around any more?" And they went away in disgust.

## The Stone Begging Bowl of the Buddha

All the same the five men felt that they could not live without seeing the girl, and they said, "Is there any thing we would not bring to the girl, even if from India?"

Prince Ishizukuri was a clever man, and he realized how unlikely it was to find the one begging bowl of the Buddha, not even if he traveled a hundred, a thousand, a million miles, and even went to India. Leaving a message, however, that he was on that very day departing for India, he was gone for three years.

At a mountain temple in the province of Yamato he found a bowl that was blackened with soot from having hung before an image of Binzuru.° He put it in a brocade bag to which he attached a spray of artificial flowers and carried it to Kayuga-hime's house. When he showed her the bowl, she looked at it with suspicion. She opened the note enclosed. It said, "I have worn myself out journeying over the sea and the mountains. In quest of the stone bowl of the Buddha my tears have flowed."

Kayuga-hime looked to see if the bowl gave off a light,° but there was not so much as the light given off by a firefly. She gave back the bowl with the note, "I should have thought the bowl of Buddha would give off the sparkle of the fallen dew. Why did you bring the bowl from the Mountain of Darkness?"

The prince threw away the bowl at the gate and answered with a note, "When it met the Mountain of Brightness perhaps it lost its glow. Now I discard the bowl, but I maintain my hopes."

He sent this note into the house, but Kayuga-hime did not lower herself to answer him. As she would not listen to his pleas, he went away in sorrow, muttering to himself.

°*Binzuru*: a kitchen-god. °*light*: as sacred objects were thought to do.

## PERSPECTIVE 9
## Japanese Woodblock Prints

*Ukiyo-e* ("pictures of the floating world") is the main genre of Japanese woodblock prints (or woodcuts), produced between the 17th and the 20th centuries. Widely admired in America at the end of the 19th century, Japanese woodblock prints were a major source of information about Japanese art and culture.

The roots of *ukiyo-e* can be traced to the urbanization of the late 16th century and the development of a middle class of merchants and artisans who wrote stories and painted pictures and picture books, such as the 1608 edition of *Tales of Ise* by Hon'ami Koetsu. The art form gained great popularity in the urban culture of Edo (Tokyo) during the second half of the 17th century. *Ukiyo-e*, affordable because they were mass produced, were mainly meant for urbanites who could not afford an original painting but wanted to display their knowledge of culture.

Woodblock printing featured landscapes, such as Hiroshige's "Views of Mount Fuji"; myths and tales from history, such as *The Tale of Genji*; the theater, including portraits of famous actors; and the pleasure quarters, such as the many portraits of courtesans engaged in appealing activities. The woodblock prints directly inspired such artists as Edouard Manet, Vincent van Gogh, James Abbott McNeill Whistler, Claude Monet, Edgar Degas, Henri de Toulouse-Lautrec, and Paul Gauguin, and artists living in America. This influence is known as *Japonisme*, characterized by an interest in asymmetry, two-dimensionality, flat bright color, shallow perspective, and an interest in fragmentary everyday scenes almost unknown to the neoclassicism dominant in European painting at this time.

A good example of a woodblock print showing a dramatic performance is Perspective Figure 9 from the *Chushingura*, the name for fictionalized accounts of the revenge by forty-seven *Ronin* (leaderless samurai) of the death of their master, Asano Naganori. Supposedly the incident was historical (Perspective Figure 9).

**PERSPECTIVE FIGURE 9**    Kabuki actor Eisaburō Onoe I in the play *Chushingura* ("The 47 Ronin"). He carries two swords, one long and one short, and is elaborately costumed. Inscriptions appear in the upper left and lower right. Color woodblock print by Utagawa Toyokuni I, c. 1800. ( PD-US http://en.wikipedia.org/wiki/File:ToyokuniActor.jpg)

The story has been told in *kabuki* (a highly stylized stage play), puppet-plays, films, novels, television shows, and other media. With 10 different television productions in the years 1997–2007 alone, the *Chushingura* ranks among the most familiar of all stories in Japan.

*Chushingura* recounts a famous case involving the samurai code of honor, *bushido*, and vividly expresses a significant part of the traditional Japanese worldview. The story tells of a group of samurai who were left leaderless after their master Asano Naganori was forced to commit *seppuku* (ritual suicide) for assaulting a court official, Kira Yoshinaka, who had insulted him. The Ronin avenged their master by killing the court official after patiently waiting and planning for over a year. In turn, they were themselves forced to commit *seppuku* for committing the crime of murder, an outcome they well knew in advance. The tale is about the honorable fulfillment of duty, especially to an honorable leader.

## The Jeweled Branch from Paradise

Prince Kuramochi, wily in his ways, announced to the court that he would be taking the waters at Kyushu. He left word with Kayuga-hime that he was off to find the jeweled branch of Paradise. He was accompanied from the capital° as far as Naniwa° by his retainers. Announcing his intention to travel incognito, he released his large band of followers and retained only his personal servants, and set out from Naniwa. The retainers all returned to the capital. Three days later, when he had pretended to leave, he had his ship rowed back empty to the port.

In the meanwhile, Prince Kuramochi had summoned six of the finest jewelers of the day and sequestered them in an out-of-the-way location, and built a triple wall around their workshop. Now in secret Prince Kuramochi traveled to the enclosure. He had summoned all the resources of his 16 domains to recreate a jeweled branch such as Kayuga-hime described. Having thus cleverly managed everything, the prince now returned to Naniwa with the branch. He sent word ahead to his family how he was returning to Naniwa by ship, acting as if he were in great anguish.

A large number of people flocked to Naniwa to welcome the ship. The prince placed the jeweled branch in a long wooden box, which he carefully wrapped and brought ashore. Word soon got out—it was rumored that he had brought back an *udonge* flower° to the capital. When Kayuga-hime heard this, she feared in her heart that somehow Prince Kuramochi had defeated her.

Just then there was a knocking at the gate. Prince Kuramochi had arrived. Hearing that the prince had come in his traveling clothes, the old bamboo-cutter went out to greet him.

"At the risk of my life, I have brought the jeweled branch," the prince announced. "Please show it to Kayuga-hime." The old man took it inside. Attached to the branch was a note, "Even at the cost of my life, I would have broken away the jeweled branch."

While the lady was reading with some sorrow the verse, the bamboo-cutter rushed in. "The prince has brought back from Paradise the jeweled branch, just

°*capital*: Kyoto. °*Naniwa*: an outlying village. °udonge *flower*: a mythical plant said to bloom once every three thousand years.

as you requested. What more can you ask? He has even come here straight off the road, in his traveling clothes, without first going home."

The lady was very unhappy and she made no secret of it, resting her head on her arm.

"There need be no further discussion at this time," said the prince, and stepped up on the veranda.° The old man saw that this was true. He said, "I do not see how you can deny him. He has brought you the jeweled branch from Paradise. Also, he is a very handsome fellow."

"It was because I did not wish to refuse you outright that I made up such preposterous tasks. It is altogether annoying that he should surprise me by actually bringing back the branch."

Paying no attention to her words, the father prepared the nuptial chamber.

The old man asked, "The branch is so beautiful. What was it like where you found it?"

The prince replied, "About three years ago, in the second week of the second moon, I set out from Naniwa by boat. I had no idea what direction to go, but knew that I must have the branch at any cost, even my life. I let the ship go wherever the winds blew. I thought to myself that if I died, that would be an end to it, but so long as I was alive I would keep sailing on and, who knows, maybe come to Horai mountain. I rowed out into the waves and gradually left Japan behind. Sometimes the seas became so high that I feared we would be capsized. Sometimes the winds carried us to strange lands where demon-faced beings attacked us. Sometimes we drifted aimlessly and knew not where we were. Sometimes we ran out of food and had to eat the roots of plants, or the shellfish of the sea, just to survive. Sometimes great monsters rose up from the deep and attacked us.

"None could help us on this journey. We allowed the ship to wander where it pleased. At around 9:00 of day 500 of our journey we perceived on the horizon the faint shape of a mountain. We gazed at it intently. The mountain was tall and graceful. This, I thought, must be the mountain that I seek. Nonetheless I was afraid. For two or three days we sailed around the mountain, when a celestial women emerged from the side of the mountain. She was dipping the water with a silver cup. I went ashore and asked her the name of the mountain.

" 'This is the mountain of Horai,' she said, filling me with joy.

" 'Who are you?' I asked.

" 'I am Ukanruri,' she said, and disappeared into the mountain.

"There seemed no way to climb the mountain. I walked around it and saw trees of a kind I've never seen before. Streams gold, silver, and emerald poured down the mountain, crossed by bridges made of precious stones. Beside them stood glittering trees. I took the branch from one of these, not the most splendid either. However, because it corresponded closely with the lady's description, I took that one.

"The mountain was delightful, but after securing the branch, its pleasures held no attraction for me. I boarded ship and, favored by the wind, I returned

---

°*veranda*: the lady appears to be within the house, concealed by screens; the suitor overhears the father's words and steps up from the court onto the veranda that ran around Japanese houses, but he cannot see the lady.

after a voyage of four hundred days. Perhaps my prayers speeded our voyage. Only yesterday did I leave Naniwa for the capital, and without changing my brine-soaked clothes, I have come here."

When he had finished, the old man recited a verse, "In all the years that I have cut bamboo in the forest, I have never undergone such suffering."

The prince said, "For many days I have been anxious, but now I am at peace." Then he answered the old man's verse with a verse of his own, "My sleeve has dried today,° I shall forget my many hardships."

Just then six men suddenly burst into the garden. One held a letter on a split stick. He said, "I am Ayabe no Uchimaro, an artisan with the Office of Handicrafts. For 1,000 days I devoted all my energies on making a jeweled branch for you, and during all that time I abstained from the five cereals.° This is not a small matter, and I must be paid at once so that I may pay my assistants."

He proffered the note. The old man did not know what to do, having no idea what the artisan was talking about. The prince was dumbfounded and quite lost his composure.

"Bring me the letter!" commanded Kayuga-hime. This is what it said: "For 1,000 days the prince remained in hiding with us lowly workmen and had us make a wonderful jeweled branch. He promised to grant us in return posts as officials. Recently we thought this over and decided that the branch must have been the one requested by Kayuga-hime, about to become the prince's wife. We have therefore come to ask compensation from this household."

Kayuga-hime on hearing the cry "we must be paid!" felt all her gloom and darkness instantly dissipate, replaced by a feeling of freedom and joy. She called to her father. "Really I thought it was a branch from a tree in Paradise. But it is evidently a shameful counterfeit. Please give it back at once."

The old man nodded. "Now that we know it is a fake, it is a simple matter to return it."

Kayuga-hime was content. She wrote in reply to the verse that accompanied the branch, "I examined the branch and found it to be counterfeit. The branch is as false as your words."

So she returned the branch. The old bamboo-cutter was dismayed that he had tried so hard to persuade her to marry. The prince was uncomfortable whether he sat or stood, and when night fell, he slunk away.

Kayuga-hime summoned the workmen who had so bitterly complained. "Happy men!" she exclaimed and she compensated them richly for their labors.

They departed happily, saying "This is why we came." But on the road home they met with Prince Kuramochi, who had them beaten so that the blood flowed. He took every bit of treasure from them, and they fled for their lives.

"Life can hold no humiliation more bitter," said the prince. "I have not won the girl and I am ashamed to think of what the world thinks of me."

He went off by himself. Although the court official and all his attendants searched, they could not find him anywhere, and so concluded that he must be dead.

°*dried today*: because the Japanese wept copiously at misfortune (in one story the character hides a bottle of water in his sleeve to mimic tears). °*five cereals*: the success of a project was guaranteed if the practitioner did not eat the "five cereals" (which they are, is not clear).

## The Robe of Fire-Rat Skins

The Minister of the Right Abe no Mimuraji was a wealthy man with a large house. He wrote a letter to a man named Wang Ching, from China, asking him if he could purchase a robe made of the skins of the fire-rat. He sent his letter to the port of Hakata with Ono no Fusamori, one of his servants noted for his ability. The servant took the letter to Hakata and presented it to Wang Ching with a sum of gold.

After Wang Ching read the letter he said, "Robes made of fire-rats do not exist in my country. I have heard of such things, but I have never seen one. If they really do exist, it is odd that no one has ever turned up in China. In short, it is a difficult purchase to negotiate ... Nonetheless, I will make inquiries among the rich of India, to see if they have one there. If I can not find one, I will return your money with your servant."

Wang Ching departed from China, then returned to Japan. The Minister of the Right, Abe no Mimuraji, learning that Ono no Fusamori, his servant, had returned and was on his way to the capital, sent him a swift horse, and in seven days he galloped to the capital.

He brought a letter from Wang Ching: "I have managed at last, by sending messengers everywhere, to obtain a robe of fire-rat skins, which I am sending. This has been no easy task. I learned that a great Indian priest had deposited such a robe in a temple in the mountains in the west. At last, with the help of the authorities, I obtained it. The officials told my agent that the money you had sent was not enough, and so I added some funds of my own. I would appreciate it if you forwarded fifty ounces of gold by the return voyage of the ship. If you prefer not to send the money, please return the robe."

When the minister read these words, he exclaimed, "Well, whatever can he be thinking? Of course I'll part with the paltry sum he requests! This is wonderful—he's found the robe!"

He bowed deeply in the direction of China.

The box holding the robe was exquisitely made, inlaid with precious stones. The robe itself was a dark blue color. A golden glow came off the tips of the hairs, a treasure of great beauty. Its loveliness surpassed even its unique invulnerability to flame. "This must be the robe that Kayuga-hime desires. It is wonderful!"

He attached the box with the robe to a branch and, assuming that he would be spending the night in Kayuga-hime's arms, made himself very handsome. He composed a poem:

I have wept for endless love.
Today my sleeves are dry,
wearing a robe impervious to fire.

The minister Abe no Mimuraji took the box at once to Kayuga-hime's gate, and there he waited. The old bamboo-cutter came out, accepted the gift, and showed it to Kayuga-hime.

"Truly a lovely robe," Kayuga-hime said, "but how can I be sure it is genuine?"

"Whether it is or it isn't," said the bamboo-cutter, "nonetheless I'll invite him in. There is not such another fur robe in all the realm. You would do right to think it genuine. You shouldn't make people suffer in this way!" He invited the minister inside.

When the old woman saw how the minister was ushered in, she thought that surely this time Kayuga-hime would marry. The old man was aggrieved that his daughter was so reluctant to marry, although he constantly sought a suitable husband for her. It was of course not right that he force her into something she didn't want to do.

Kayuga-hime said, "If I put this fur robe in the fire, and it does not burn, then I will believe it is what the minister claims."

"That is reasonable," said the old man and he told the minister.

The Minister of the Right said, "I had great difficulty in coming by this robe, which was not available even in China. What doubt could there be? All the same, by all means do test it in the fire."

They put it in the flames, where it burned brightly.

"Just as I thought," said Kayuga-hime. "It was not the correct fur."

The minister turned the color of leaves of grass. Kayuga-hime was very happy. She wrote a poem in answer to the minister's poem, which she put in the jeweled box:

> Had I but known
> that it world burn,
> leaving no trace,
> I would have kept it
> from the flames.

The minister departed.

## The Jewel in the Dragon's Head

Otomo no Miyuki, the Grand Counselor, summoned together all the members of his household and said, "There is a shining jewel of five colors in a dragon's head. Whoever can get this for me, will have whatever he desires".

His men, receiving the commission, said, "Jewels are hard to come by, especially those fixed in a dragon's head."

The Grand Counselor said, "Servants should not question their lord's desires, but do their best to fulfill them, even at the risk of their lives. I am not asking for something from India or China, but what I desire is found in Japan. Dragons are constantly rising from the sea, or the mountains, or descending from the heavens. Why do you think it is so difficult?"

They replied, "In that case we will do as you say, O master, and bring back the jewel, no matter how hard it may be."

The Grand Counselor Otomo no Miyuki said, "You have the reputation for doing what your master asks. How could you disobey me?" With these words, he sent them out to find the jewel, providing them with silk and copper coin for their journey.

"Until you return, I will eat only vegetables. But don't come back without the jewel."

The servants departed with their instructions. "He told us to bring back the jewel, so we might as well let our feet lead the way. This is craziness!" they said.

They divided up the valuables they had been given. Some went home and shut themselves up, others went to this or that place they wished to visit.

"Although he is our parent and lord," they complained, "he should not send us on such ridiculous assignments."

One day the Grand Counselor said, "I cannot expect Kayuga-hime to live in so run-down a place." He had a beautiful house built for her. It was entirely varnished with lacquer with inlaid gold leaf. The roof was thatched with silken threads made of many colors. In every alcove hung lovely paintings on damask. The Grand Counselor's concubines hastened to prepare for the arrival of Kayuga-hime. But the Grand Counselor's first wife spent her days and nights alone.

The Counselor anxiously awaited his men's return, but by New Year's he had heard nothing. Greatly impatient, he disguised himself and went in secret to Naniwa, accompanied by only two retainers. He asked around town, "Have you heard anything about Otomo's men, who were off to find a dragon and remove the jewel from its head?"

"What a strange story!" a boatman would reply. "We have no boats here for that sort of thing. The Grand Counselor said, "Just the sort of stupid answer you'd expect from a boatman. He simply doesn't know." Then he thought to himself, "Why I am a good bowman, no doubt strong enough to kill a dragon myself and take the jewel. No need to wait for those rascals!"

He boarded a ship and rounded one arm of the sea after another, until he came to the distant ocean off Kyushu. What then? A ferocious gale came up, the sky turned black, and the storm engulfed them. The wind blew the ship here and there. It seemed certain to sink to the bottom of the sea. The waves lashed all around the ship, sucking it down, and lightning danced on the mast.

The Grand Counselor was bewildered. He said, "I have never been in such a predicament. What will happen to me?"

The steersman replied, "In all the many years that I have sailed the seas, never have I seen such a storm. If we don't capsize, we shall be struck by lightning. If by the gods' good blessing we are somehow spared, still we will be driven to the southern seas. This is all because I have a cruel master!" And he burst into tears.

When the Grand Counselor heard these words, in between bouts of violent vomiting, he said, "When aboard a boat, I always trust in what the steersman says. Why do you speak like this?"

The steersman answered, "I am not a god, and I don't know what to do. It is because you intended to kill a dragon that the wind is howling and the waves are raging. Thunderbolts rain down on our head. This storm is whipped by the dragon's breath! You should pray at once to the gods."

"Very well," said the Grand Counselor. "O god of steersmen, hear my words! I hoped in my folly to kill a dragon and take the jewel from its forehead. I promise henceforth to do no harm to dragons!" He stood up and sat down and stood up again as he uttered this prayer. He shouted, he wept. He repeated these words a thousand times.

At last the thunder stopped. The steersman said, "This is a dragon's doing. Now the wind is blowing fair, just where we want."

For three or four days they drove before the wind and came at last to land. The sailors recognized the place as Akashi in Harima. However, the Grand Counselor, thinking that they had been driven to somewhere in the southern seas, fell on his face in despair and lay in the bottom of the ship. The sailors informed the local officials, and they all came out to greet the Grand Counselor. He could not get up. He continued to lie in the bottom of the ship. They spread a mat for him under some pines and carried him to it.

Realizing at last that he was not in the southern seas, the Grand Counselor managed to stand up. He looked like a man who was horribly sick, his belly all distended and his eyes like plums. The local officials could not help but smile. The Counselor gave order that a sedan be prepared and in it, groaning and moaning, he was carried home. When he arrived, the men he had sent out, who had heard he returned, appeared at his gate and explained that they had been unable to find the jewel in the dragon's head and that is why they did not return to his service. "Now that you know how hard it is to find this jewel, we have decided to come back, hoping that you won't be too hard on us."

The Grand Counselor sat up. "You did well not to bring it back. Dragons and Thunders are just alike, and if you had tried to get that jewel, many of you would have died. If you had caught a dragon, that would have been the death of me. I'm glad you didn't catch one! That thief Kayuga-hime was trying to kill us. I'll never go to her house again. And don't you go anywhere near!"

He bestowed on the men who had failed to get the jewel what little of his wealth remained. When his—now former—first wife learned of this, she laughed until her sides ached. The roof thatched with silken threads was carried off by hawks and crows to make their nests.

## The Easy-Delivery Charm of the Swallows

When the Middle Counselor Isonokami no Marotari ordered all those in his employ to tell him if any swallows made a nest, naturally they wondered why he wished to know. He answered, "I want to get the easy-delivery charm that they carry."

One man said, "I have killed many swallows in my day, but I've never seen anything in their belly. How could they pull out a charm just when they were about to give birth?"

Another man said, "The swallows are building nests in the holes all along the palace kitchen. If you set up so that someone can watch them, you will see many swallows born and have a chance to grab the easy-delivery charm."

The Middle Counselor was quite pleased. "Why that is extraordinary. I had never heard anything about it. This is an interesting idea."

He ordered some twenty dependable men to climb up on perches and watch the swallows. From his mansion he sent an incessant march of messengers to find out if they had succeeded in acquiring the easy-delivery charm.

The swallows, terrified by all the men who climbed up on perches, did not return to their nests. When the Middle Counselor heard of this, he did not know what to do. Just then an old man named Kuratsumaro, who worked the palace kitchen, said, "I have a plan to acquire the easy-delivery charm."

Kuratsumaro was brought before the Middle Counselor. "You are trying through clumsy means to obtain the easy-delivery charm. You will never get it by these means. Your men have made such a stir climbing up to their perches that the swallows are frightened away. You should remove the perches and withdraw the men. Put one good man in an openwork basket with a rope attached. When the swallow is about to give birth, hoist up the basket and quickly grab the charm. This is the best plan."

The Middle Counselor said, "Surely this is an excellent plan." So the men were dismissed and the perches taken down.

The Counselor asked Kuratsumaro, "How will we know when is the moment to haul up the basket?" Kuratsumaro answered, "When the swallow is about to give birth it raises up its tail and flies in a circle seven times. As soon as it has circled seven times, haul up the man in the basket."

The Counselor was overjoyed at the man's plan. "How the gods have heard my prayers! Even if this man is not in my direct employ." He offered the old man his cloak and said, "Come tonight to the palace kitchen."

When it grew dark, the Middle Counselor went to the kitchen and discovered that in fact the swallows were building nests there. He did just as Kuratsumaro said. A man was put in a basket that they hoisted at just the right moment, but he called down that he could not feel anything in the nest. The Counselor retorted in anger, "You just aren't doing it in the right way! Nobody here can search as well as I can. I shall go up myself."

He got into the basket and was hauled up. He peered into the nest. A swallow had lifted its tail and was circling madly. At once he stretched out his arm and felt in the nest. He touched something flat. "I have it!" he exclaimed. "Lower me down now—I have it!"

His men all gathered around, but in their haste to lower the basket quickly, they pulled too hard and the rope snapped. Down plunged the Middle Counselor, coming to rest on top of a large cauldron. His men rushed up and lifted him in their arms. He was motionless. The whites of his eyes showed. The men gave him some water, and he drank a little. At last he came to. They carried him by the hands and feet and lifted him down from the cauldron. When they asked him how he felt, he answered beneath his breath that though he had some idea of where he was, he could not seem to move his back. "But I am glad that I got the charm. Here, bring a torch, and let's have a look."

He lifted his head and opened his hand. He was holding some bird-dung!

"Alas, it was all for nothing," he cried.

The Counselor tried to keep people from finding out what had happened, a constant worry that was more debilitating than his injuries. He was more depressed by the thought that people might find out about the escapade and laugh at him than by the fact that he had not gotten the charm. Every day his anxiety increased. He decided that it was better that he die of his injuries than that people find out what had happened. Kayuga-hime, hearing of his distress, sent him a poem of inquiry:

> The years pass by without the waves returning
> to the pines of Suminoe where I waited.
> You have not found the charm
> I have heard. Is it true?

The Counselor asked that the poem be read to him. He feebly lifted his head. He was barely able to write, and then only painfully while someone held up the paper. "I failed to get the charm and was about to die in desperation, but have you not saved me?"

Then he died. Kayuga-hime was touched.

## The Imperial Hunt

When the emperor heard of Kayuga-hime's great beauty, unrivalled in his realm, he said to a maid of honor, "Please find out what sort of woman this Kayuga-hime is, who has ruined so many men and will not marry."

The lady accepted his charge and departed. When she arrived at the house of the old bamboo-cutter, the old woman reverently let her in. The maid of honor said, "I have been commissioned by the emperor to find out if Kayuga-hime is as beautiful as they say. I come for this reason."

"I will tell her," said the old woman and went inside. She said to Kayuga-hime, "Please go out to meet the messenger of the emperor."

Kayuga-hime said, "How can I go when I am so unattractive?"

"Don't be absurd. How could you possibly show such disrespect to the emperor's messenger?" said the old woman.

"Even if it is a command of the emperor, I am not overawed," said Kayuga-hime, showing no sign of willingness to meet the emperor's representative. Although Kayuga-hime was as if a child of the old woman's own body, nonetheless the old woman felt reserved around her and unable to scold the girl as she liked, even when she was so disrespectful.

The old lady returned to the emperor's messenger and said, "I must apologize. The girl is highly disrespectful and will not see you."

The maid of honor said, "I was told to have a look at her without fail. If I do not, how shall I return? Can it be that someone living in the realm would deny a royal request? Please do not allow her to act in so unreasonable a fashion." She spoke these words in an attempt to shame Kayuga-hime into responding, but instead, when Kayuga-hime heard these words, she refused all the more vehemently. "If I am violating a royal command, let me suffer immediate execution," she said.

The maid of honor returned to the palace and told what had happened. When the emperor heard, he said, "I can see that she is a person capable of causing the deaths of many."

However, he still had his heart set on her and would not accept defeat. He summoned the old bamboo-cutter and his wife and declared, "Please send Kayuga-hime to me, whom you have in your keeping. I heard reports of her beauty and sent a messenger to you, but she was unable even to get a glimpse of her. Are we going to allow such disrespect?"

The old man replied, "The girl does not intend to serve at court, and frankly we are at a loss what to do about her. Nevertheless, I shall return home and report your commands."

The emperor said, "Why should a child whom you have raised as your own not obey you? If you present the girl for service in the court, how can I do otherwise than appoint you a court rank?"

The old man was overjoyed and went home. He reported his conversation to Kayuga-hime. "These are the emperor's commands. Do you dare to disobey?"

Kayuga-hime answered, "I utterly refuse to serve at court. If I am forced, I shall vanish. Your court rank will mean my death."

"Never do such a thing!" the old man answered. "What use is it to hold a place in court and be unable to look upon my child? But how can you avoid service at court? Would it really cause your death?"

"If you do not believe me, then force me to serve the court and you will see. Many men have shown me great affection, but all for nothing. If I obey the emperor's commands, I will be ashamed of what people think of my earlier callousness."

The old man replied, "My rank at court is as nothing when compared to the danger to your life. I shall go to court and report that you still refuse to serve."

He reported to the emperor, "When, overawed by the presence of your commands, I attempted to persuade the child to enter your service, she said that service in the court would result in her death. She is not a child of my body, but one I found long ago in the mountains. Her ways are not like those of common people."

The emperor said, "I understand that your house is near the mountains. What if, under pretext of a royal hunt, I were to glimpse the maid?"

"This is a good plan," said the old man. "If the imperial procession comes by at just the right moment, when she least expects it, there might be a chance of seeing her."

The emperor at once set up a day for the hunt. During the course of the hunt, the emperor ended up in Kayuga-hime's house. Looking around it, he saw a person sitting there of such beauty that she filled the room with light. The emperor thought, "This must be she," and approached her. Kayuga-hime attempted to hide, to flee within, but the emperor caught her by the sleeve. She covered her face, but just by the glimpse he knew this was a woman of exceptional beauty.

"I shall not let you go!" he announced. But when he attempted to lead her away, she said, "If my body were born on earth, then I could have served you. But as it is you cannot take me with you."

The emperor replied, "How can that be? Surely I will take you with me."

He summoned his palanquin. At that very instant Kayuga-hime vanished. Realizing that she was in fact no mortal, the emperor was amazed.

"I won't insist that you come with me, then, only please return to your former shape," the emperor said. "Just one look at you, and I shall be off."

Kayuga-hime resumed her former appearance [Figure 9.5].

But the emperor could not dam the tide of his love. He showed his pleasure with the bamboo-cutter who had made the meeting possible, and the old man in turn offered a splendid banquet to all the emperor's officers. The emperor

**FIGURE 9.5** Aristocratic lady and her servant. She wears an elaborate hairdo with decorations and is dressed in a silk gown embroidered with a dragon. There is an inscription in the upper left. Woodblock print. Japan, 19th century. (Victoria and Albert Museum, London; V&A Images, London / Art Resource, NY)

regretted bitterly that he was returning to the palace without Kayuga-hime. As he left the hut of the bamboo-cutter, he felt as though he left his soul behind.

When he had entered the palanquin, he penned this poem to Kayuga-hime:

On my journey back to the palace,
I will be sad. I turn back,
I return because of Kayuga-hime.

In reply Kayuga-hime wrote this poem:

How could one who lives in a house
overgrown with weeds
visit a jeweled palace?

The emperor was even more regretful to leave when he saw the poem, but as he could not stay the night, he went home. The palace ladies could not be compared with Kayuga-hime, and the emperor even wondered whether she belonged to the same race, although before he had always thought them lovely. In his heart there was room only for Kayuga-hime, and he kept to himself. Without giving a reason, he kept away from all his consorts. He wrote letters to Kayuga-hime, and her replies were friendly. Sometimes he would send her a poem attached to a flower, when he found one of especial beauty.

## The Celestial Robe of Feathers

So for three years they consoled one another by correspondence. Then in the spring of the new year Kayuga-hime looked out and saw the moon rising in all its splendor, and she fell into a pensive mood. Someone standing nearby admonished her: "You should never look directly at the moon." But when no one was near, Kayuga-hime would often stare at the moon, and weep.

During the full moon of the seventh month Kayuga-hime sat outside lost in thought. Her maidservants told the bamboo-cutter, "Kayuga-hime has always looked at the moon, but her mood of late has changed. There must be something deep inside that worries her. You should keep an eye on her."

The old man asked Kayuga-hime, "What troubles you that you gaze at the moon with such sadness? The world should be a place of happiness ..."

She answered, "When I look at the moon, the world seems a place of sadness. What could cause me worry?"

He went over to Kayuga-hime and looked at her. She seemed so melancholy. "My dear, what can be troubling you?"

"Nothing troubles me, except I find that the world is depressing."

"You shouldn't look at the moon. Whenever you do, you worry."

"How could I live without gazing at the moon?"

Whenever the moon rose, Kayuga-hime would sit outside, lost in thought. On dark moonless nights she would emerge from her reverie, but when the moon reappeared she would sigh and weep. Her maidservants whispered to one another, "There really is something wrong," but no one knew what it was.

On a moonlit night of the eighth month, Kayuga-hime, who was sitting outside, suddenly burst into tears. She wept without care for the opinion of others. When her parents saw, they were much alarmed, and asked what the matter was. Kayuga-hime, in tears, answered, "I have intended for a long time to tell you. But I was afraid I would upset you. I can be silent no more—I must tell you all. I am not of this world. I come from the Palace of the Moon. I visited this world because of an obligation I incurred in the past. Now the time has come that I must return, and on the next full moon my people will come for me. I must go. The thought of the unhappiness that this event must bring you has made me sad all this spring."

She wept bitter tears.

The old man cried, "What's that? I found you in a stalk of bamboo. You were no bigger than a seed. I have brought you up, my child, until now you are as tall as I. Who is going to take you away? Do you think I will let them?" He added, "If they do take you away, surely I will die." The old man wept inconsolably.

Kayuga-hime said, "I have a father and a mother in the Palace of the Moon. When I came here from my country, I said that it would be for just a little while. But I have spent many years in this land. I have stayed here for a long time, without thinking of my parents on the moon. I feel no joy now that I am about to return, but only sadness. Yet, though I do not choose it, I must return."

The old man and Kayuga-hime wept uncontrollably. Her maidservants, who had served her for many years, thought how they would regret separation, how they would miss her exquisite nature and her beauty, to which they had grown accustomed. Choked with emotion, they too gave into grief.

When the emperor learned what was happening, he sent a messenger. The old man, weeping inconsolably, came out to meet him. His beard had turned white from sorrow, his back was bent, and his eyes had swelled. He was only seventy years old, but his sorrows seemed suddenly to have aged him. The imperial messenger reported the emperor's words, "Is it true that you have suffered painful affliction?"

The bamboo-cutter answered in tears, "On the night of the full moon, people will come from the Palace of the Moon to take Kayuga-hime. I am deeply honored by your interest. I beg the emperor to dispatch troops to intercept who-ever comes on that night from the Palace of the Moon."

The messenger transmitted the old man's request. When the emperor thought, "If I who saw her only an instant am so smitten, how hard must it be for someone who has lived wither her for years."

On the 15th of the month the emperor issued commands to his officers and sent 2,000 troops. As soon as they arrived, 1,000 men took up position on the roof and 1,000 on the wall. Together with the numerous members of the household they made an impregnable defense. They all had bows and arrows. The womenfolk guarded the interior of the house.

Inside the strong room of the house the old lady held Kayuga-hime in her arms. The old man, having fastened the door tight, stood on guard. He announced, "Even people from heaven will not easily overcome this force." To the men on the roof he shouted, "If you see even a faint glimmer in the sky, shoot it." They shouted back, "Even if a mosquito goes by, we will shoot it down." Their words greatly reassured the old man.

Kayuga-hime said, "In spite of all these preparations, you cannot defeat the people from the moon. You will be powerless to shoot your arrows. No matter how strongly you fortify the house, when they come all will be useless. No matter how your resist them, when they come, even the bravest men will be able to do nothing."

The old man cried, "If they come, I will tear out their eyes with my long nails. I'll grab them by the hair and throw them to the ground. I will make them ashamed by exposing their behinds to all the officers to see," he shouted in his wrath.

"Don't speak so loudly," said Kayuga-hime. "The men on the roof must not hear you talk that way. It pains me deeply that I have been unable to show my gratitude toward you. It was against fate that we should remain together. Soon I must go. Thus I am very sad. It pains me that I was never able in any way to repay you for your kindness to me. When I went outside to sit by the moon, I begged that I might stay for one more year with you. It was useless. That is why I have been so unhappy. It breaks my heart that I must upset you so, and then leave. The people of the moon are very beautiful, and they do not grow old nor do they worry. However, I am not happy to be going there. I am torn with regret when I realize that I will not be able to care for you in your old age." She spoke in tears.

With anger the old man said, "Please do not say such painful things. No matter how beautiful these people are, they will not stand in my way."

By now the evening was past. Around midnight the area around the house was lit by a light brighter than the sun at noon, the brightness of ten full moons, so bright that the pores of the skin stood out. Down from the heaven came men riding on clouds. They ranged themselves about five feet above the ground. Those inside and outside the house were frozen with fear. None could resist. They tried to take up their bows and arrows, but their hands were without strength, which were as paralyzed.

Some especially valiant man tried to shoot their arrows, but they fell harmlessly to the side. They were unable to put up a fight. They could only watch stupefied.

The men standing before them were arrayed in raiment of matchless beauty. They brought with them a winged chariot with a canopy made all of silk. The one among them who appeared to be the king called out, "Miyakomarro, come here!" The old man, who earlier had spoken so boldly, now prostrated himself before the stranger. He felt like he was drunk.

The king said, "Old man, because of some trifling good deeds that you performed, we sent this young lady for a short while into this world to help you. Many years have gone by, and you have become quite wealthy. You have become a different man. Kayuga-hime was forced to remain with you humble people because of something she did, but the term of her punishment is now run out and we have come for her. It doesn't matter how much you lament—she cannot stay. Bring her forth at once."

The old man said, "Kayuga-hime has been in my care for over twenty years. When you say 'for a short while' I wonder if you aren't thinking of some other Kayuga-hime, in a different place. Beside, the Kayuga-hime who is here is suffering from a serious illness and can not come outside."

He did not answer but guided the winged chariot to the roof of the house. He called out, "Kayuga-hime, why have you remained so long in such a filthy abode?" The door of the room flew open, and the lattice-work windows opened by themselves. Kayuga-hime, whom the old woman had clasped in her arms, stepped forth. The old woman could not hold her back, but only look up and weep.

Kayuga-hime went to where the bamboo-cutter lay prostrate, weeping. She said, "Not by own will do I now depart. At least, please watch me as I ascend to the sky."

"How can I watch you go when it is so painful? Are you going to go to heaven, abandoning me to whatever fate has in store? Take me with you!"

Kayuga-hime was at a loss. "I shall write you a letter before I leave. Whenever you long for me, take the letter and read it."

Crying, she wrote, "Had I been born in this land, I would never have caused you such unhappiness. Our moment of parting is an agony to me. Take this cloak, which I now remove, as a memento of me. On nights when the moon shines, gaze at it, and I will feel as if I am returning from the sky to the parents I must now leave."

Some of the celestial beings carried boxes. In one was a robe of feathers, another the elixir of immortality. "Take some of the elixir in this jar," said one celestial being. "You must be in poor health after eating in so filthy a place."

Kayuga-hime tasted the elixir. Thinking the elixir might serve as a small remembrance, she wrapped it in the cloak she had just removed, but one of the celestial beings stopped her. They took out the robe of feathers and wished to put it on her, but Kayuga-hime said, "Just wait. When you don this robe, one's heart changes. I have still some things to say." She wrote another letter.

The celestial beings cried, "It is late!"

Kayuga-hime said, "Do not betray your lack of understanding for human feelings." Perfectly calm, she gave the letter to someone to carry to the emperor. She showed no signs of agitation.

The letter read: "Although you sent many people here, escorts have come who cannot be denied. Now they are taking me away, regretful as I am. I would not enter your service, and I have been so troublesome that no doubt you thought my behavior incomprehensible. It is a heavy weight on my heart that you must have thought my refusal to obey your commands a sign of disrespect."

To this she added a poem:

Now when I am about to don
the robe of feathers, I think
longingly on my lord.

Kayuga-hime attached to the letter some of the elixir of immortality and asked the commander of the guards to offer it the emperor. One of the celestial beings passed the gift to the commander. No sooner had he taken it than Kayuga-hime put on the robe of feathers, and at once lost all recollection of her sorrow and pity for the old man. Those who wear this robe know no grief. Kayuga-hime climbed into the winged chariot and, accompanied by one hundred celestial beings, rose into the air.

Although the old bamboo-cutter and his wife wept bitterly, it was to no avail. When they had her letter read to them, they cried out, "Why should we go on living? For whose sake? All is emptiness."

They would not take their medicine, and they never left their beds again.

The commander returned to the palace with his men. He reported in some detail what had happened, and why they were unable to stop Kayuga-hime's departure. He presented the letter with the elixir. The emperor was much distressed when he read Kayuga-hime's words. He would neither eat, nor permit entertainment. He summoned his ministers and counselors and asked them which mountain is closest to heaven. One man answered, "There is in Saruga a mountain both close to the capital and to heaven."

The emperor wrote the poem:

What is the use of this elixir
of immortality, I who float
in tears shed because
I will never see her again.

He gave the poem and the jar containing the elixir to a messenger. He ordered him to take these things to the summit of the mountain in Saruga. He instructed him to place the letter and the jar side by side and to set them afire. Let them be consumed in the flames. The man accepted the command and climbed the mountain with many other soldiers. They gave the name Fuji°
to the mountain. Even now the smoke is said to rise to the clouds.

°*Fuji*: it means "not die," as if named for the elixir.

## OBSERVATIONS: THE *TALE OF THE BAMBOO-CUTTER*

*The Tale of the Bamboo-Cutter* draws on several strands in oral tradition. It falls into four parts: (1) the story of the poor bamboo-cutter who becomes rich through a chance find, as often in folktales throughout the world; (2) the stories of the five suitors; (3) the story of the emperor's suit for the lady's hand; and (4) the ascension of the shining princess to the moon. Other tales told of a shining princess from heaven who wore a robe all of feathers, which she lost and so was unable to return to heaven. She recovers the robe and returns to heaven.

The story is also concerned with the origin of place-names, as in the case of Mount Fuji at the end. The courtship by the five aristocratic suitors appears as an addition. Here the author presents a satiric portrait of greed, deceit, lust, and attachment. The suitors are of the very highest rank—prince, Minister of the Right, Major Counselor, Middle Counselor—but none acts like a refined aristocrat. They are all buffoons.

In the suitor section, Kayuga-hime appears as heartless, cold, and cruel, but in the final section she is humanized when she thinks of her love for her earthly parents. There is a contrast between the beautiful, clean moon, and its happy denizens, and the dirty polluted earth, with all its misery. The moon suggests the western paradise of Buddhism. The connection is clear from the descent of the moon people, just as in one form of Buddhism the dead are greeted by heavenly beings who descend on clouds.

Even though the earth is a place of exile and punishment for Kayuga-hime, she comes to appreciate human beings and to value their emotions. The robe of feathers represents the divide between the two worlds, and she is reluctant to put it on. Likewise the emperor does not drink the elixir of immortality, because "what is the point of living forever if you cannot have that which you love?" The world of men, of sadness, death, and pathos, is juxtaposed with the divine world of the moon, a Buddhist paradise of no attachment and no suffering.

## Key Terms

| | | |
|---|---|---|
| Tao 299 | Amaterasu 303 | Kannon 304 |
| Kyoto 300 | Confucianism 303 | Izanagi 306 |
| Kojiki 301 | Buddhism 303 | Izanami 306 |
| kanji 301 | Siddhartha Gautama 303 | Monogatari 310 |
| kana 301 | bodhisattva 304 | Kayuga-hime 311 |
| Shinto 302 | Amida Buddha 304 | |

## Further Reading

Ashkenazi, M., *Handbook of Japanese Mythology* (Oxford, UK, 2008).
Birrell, A. M., *Chinese Mythology: An Introduction* (Baltimore, MD, 1999).
Davis, F. H., *Myths and Legends of Japan* (1913; reprint New York, 1992).
Tyler, R., trans., *Japanese Tales* (New York, 2002).
An Yang, L., D. J. A. Turner, *Handbook of Chinese Mythology* (New York, 2008).

# Celtic Myth

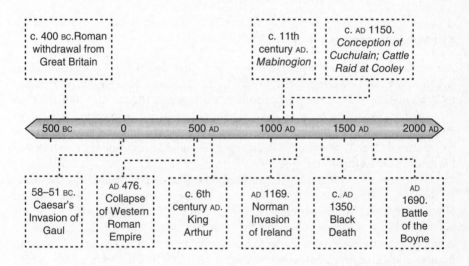

The term *Celtic* (keltik) was first used by the Romans to describe tribes in central
Gaul, today France and Belgium. In modern times, beginning in the 18th century,
the term has been used to describe speakers of an Indo-European language family
called "Celtic," who lived in England, Ireland, Spain, France, northern Italy, Austria,
southern Germany, the northern Balkans, and a patch in Anatolia/Turkey (Galatia),
where the Gauls invaded the highlands of modern Turkey in the 3rd century BC (thus
Paul's *Epistle to the Galatians*) (Map 10.1).

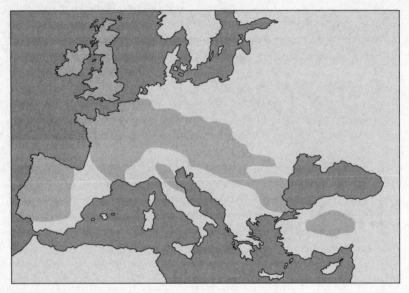

**MAP 10.1**    The Celtic world in the 3rd century BC.

## CELTIC RECORDS

Aggression in the first century BC, mostly under Julius Caesar (102–44 BC), Romanized large portions of Celtic territories so that Celtic languages were gradually replaced by descendants of Latin—French, Spanish, Portuguese, Italian, and Romansh (in Switzerland). Still today, however, several hundred thousand people speak Celtic languages, and millions of inhabitants of northern Europe are of Celtic stock. The Celts (pronounced "keltz") constitute a large linguistic and ethnic group of enormous importance in the history of Europe.

The Romans, writing in the 1st and 2nd centuries AD, commented in a few places on the Celts, noting the importance of a priestly caste among them called the **Druids**, but the early Celts had no writing of their own and so left no contemporary accounts of their myths. It is hard to coordinate the Roman evidence with what we know of the later Celts. We have a lunar calendar in Latin script from the 2nd century AD found in France, containing only names, and we have several hundred names in a native script called **Ogham**, from the 4th to 10th centuries AD (see Figure 10.1). From the 5th to 12th centuries there are alphabetic notations in a language called Old Irish in the margins of Latin texts, but we must await the Irish and Welsh documents of the 11th and 12th centuries AD for continuous narrative. These documents are written in the Latin alphabet in a language called Middle Irish, spoken throughout Ireland and in Scotland and on the ISLE OF MAN at this time. From the 12th century Middle Irish evolved into Modern Irish in Ireland, Scottish Gaelic in Scotland, and Manx on the Isle of Man.

Our whole notion of Celtic myth derives from these documents, but they are badly skewed toward a Christian point of view. Although Ireland and WALES (southwestern Britain) were peripheral to the great centers of Celtic power in France and further East, these documents are all that we have in testimony to Celtic myth. It is the earliest of all European literatures in a vernacular language.

**FIGURE 10.1**    Stone inscribed with Ogham writing. Ogham was a writing system developed in the 4th century AD and lasted until the 10th, used to record a primitive form of the Irish language. Approximately 400 inscriptions, mostly names, survive in Ireland, and also in Wales and Scotland. The alphabetic letters in the script are made by a single vertical stroke crossed by horizontal strokes (visible here) to the right, or to the left, or at an angle, to make the different letters. (On the Dingle Peninsula, County Kerry, Ireland; Holmes Garden Photos / Alamy)

## MYTH: CUCHULAIN OF IRELAND

Three collections of stories survive from Ireland:

- The *Mythical Cycle* from c. AD 1050, which includes the *Book of Invasions* and the *Book of Places*. The *Book of Invasions* is a kind of pseudo-history that traces the invasion of Ireland from before the flood, culminating in the coming of the Celts along with numerous gods and goddesses. The *Book of Places* is a collection of topographical lore.
- The *Ulster Cycle* preserved in manuscripts from c. 1150 AD and later, but containing earlier material. Its most important stories make up *The Cattle Raid at Cooley* (*Táin Bó Cuailnge*), which celebrated the deeds of the semidivine **Cuchulain** (ku-**khel**-in, "Culann's hound," known as **Setanta** when young).
- The *Fionn Cycle* (pronounced "fin"), from AD c. 1150, which chronicles the deeds of the mighty Finn and his band of supernatural followers.

Here we will concentrate on the Ulster Cycle and the famous deeds of the legendary Irish hero Cuchulain.

## The Birth of Cuchulain

There are a number of versions of Cuchulain's birth, but the best known is given in a prose narrative called the *Conception of Cuchulain* from the 12th century AD. ULSTER, Cuchulain's home, is in Northern Ireland, one of the four ancient Irish provinces (Map 10.2). His mother **Deichtine** (dĭkh-tē-ne) is the daughter of **Conchobar** (**konkh**-a-war) mac ("son of") Nessa, king of Ulster, himself son of the Druid Cathbad. She is also Conchobar's charioteer and accompanies Conchobar as he and the nobles of Ulster hunt a flock of magical birds.

As they hunt, snow falls and the Ulstermen seek shelter. They find a house where they are welcomed. The host's wife just then happens to go into labor. Deichtine assists at the birth of a baby boy. A mare gives birth to two colts at the same time. The next morning, the Ulstermen find themselves at the "Bend of the Boyne," in the BOYNE

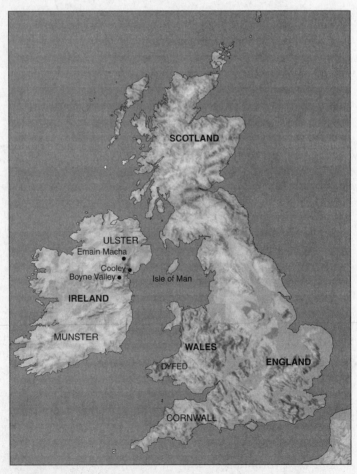

**MAP 10.2**   United Kingdom (England, Wales, and Scotland) and Ireland.

VALLEY (which contains ruins from the Neolithic period: Its graves, from c. 3500 BC, are older than the Egyptian pyramids). The house and its occupants have disappeared! But the child and the colts remain.

Deichtine takes the boy to her palace, but after a few years he falls sick and dies. The god Lugh appears to her. He tells her that *he* was their host on that night, and that now he has put his child in her womb, who is to be called Setanta.

Deichtine's pregnancy is a scandal because she is engaged to a local nobleman. The Ulstermen suspect her own father Conchobar of being the father. She aborts the child, marries the noble, and conceives another son whom she calls Setanta. All the nobles of Ulster work together to educate the boy in the arts of speaking and fighting.

## Youthful Deeds of Cuchulain

The stories of Setanta's childhood are told in a flashback in the 12th century *The Cattle Raid at Cooley*. As a small child, he sets off to a place called EMAIN MACHA (a-win makh-a), apparently a prehistoric center of power (where there is also a Neolithic site). He runs onto the playing field without first asking for the boys' protection, as was the custom. The boys view this as a challenge and attack him, but for the first time he enters a kind of berserker frenzy where he loses all sense of himself and becomes indestructible. Setanta beats the boys single-handedly. Conchobar, the king of Ulster, comes in to stop the fight and explains to Setanta the custom of offering submission before entering the playing field. Setanta therefore puts himself under the boys' protection, then chases after them demanding they put themselves under *his* protection!

Setanta received his much better known name Cuchulain in the following way. Culann, a smith, invited King Conchobar to a feast at his house. Before the appointment, Conchobar watched the boys play hurling, a team sport played with a stick called a hurley and a ball, a game still played. He was so impressed by the boy's performance that he suggested that he join the feast. Setanta said he would come as soon as the game was over. But Conchobar forgot to tell Culann this, and Culann let loose his ferocious hound to protect the house. When Setanta arrived, the giant dog attacked him. Setanta killed it by driving a *sliotar*—a hurling ball—down its throat with his hurley.

Culann was so devastated by the loss of his faithful hound that, until a replacement could be raised, Setanta promised to guard Culann's house himself! Henceforth, said the Druid Cathbad, he would be called Cuchulain, "the hound of Culann" (Irish *Cú Chulainn*).

## PERSPECTIVE 10

## The Druids

Most of what we know of the Celts comes from a literary tradition that begins around AD 1000 or somewhat later. But classical sources in Greek and Latin sometimes speak of a priestly and learned class in northern Europe called the Druids (perhaps, "men of the oak"), though there is no trace of them in the literary record after the 2nd century AD, and no Romano/Celtic inscription (that is, in Latin but with clear Celtic associations) has the word. From the little we know, they were famous for their wisdom; they were always male; they shared in some kind of oral tradition in which cultural knowledge was secretly transmitted. But not a trace of any Druidic literature survives. In religion, from what we can tell from Roman sources, they appear to have taught reincarnation and to have conducted religious rituals involving oak trees and the mistletoe that grew on them. Perhaps the use of mistletoe at Christmas to encourage fertility is Druidic in origin.

Julius Caesar (102–44 BC) wrote about the Druids in his *The War in Gaul* (6.13) of c. 50 BC:

> With regard to the Druids' actual course of studies, the main object of all education is to imbue their scholars with a firm belief in the indestructibility of the human soul, which, according to their belief, merely passes at death from one body to another. By such doctrine alone, they say, which robs death of all its terror, can the highest form of human courage be developed. Subsidiary to the teachings of this main principle, they hold various lectures and discussions on astronomy, on the extent and geographical distribution of places on the globe, on the different branches of natural philosophy, and on many problems connected with religion.

The Romans Julius Caesar, Cicero (106–43 BC), Lucan (AD 39–65), and Suetonius (c. AD 69/75–after 130) all refer to gruesome Druidic rites of human sacrifice, causing the emperor Tiberius (42 BC–37 AD) to outlaw the religion. A 10th-century marginal note in Latin to Lucan's report of Druidic human sacrifice claims that sacrifice to the Druidic gods Teutates (Mercury), Esus (Mars), and Taranis (Jupiter) took place by drowning, hanging, and burning, respectively. Diodorus Siculus (1st century BC) remarks on the role of Druids in sacrificial ritual (5.31.2):

> They predict the future by observing the flight and call of birds and the sacrifice of special animals. All orders of society are in their power ... When it is a matter of high importance, they prepare a human victim, then plunge a dagger into his chest. By observing how his limbs twitch as he falls and the gushing of blood they are able to predict the future.

Archaeological excavations in Picardy, France, have discovered bodies that have been interpreted as Druidic human sacrifices, but it is hard to tell why a man was executed. At a bog in Lindow in England professional peat-cutters discovered in 1984 a body now called "Lindow Man," who may have been the subject of Druidic sacrifice, unless he was executed as a criminal or was the victim of violent crime (Perspective Figure 10).

The man was bludgeoned, he was garroted, and then his throat was cut. He may have been stabbed in the chest. He had just eaten a meal of grains and charred bread. He was in his 20s and had never performed manual labor. The date of the body seems to be c. AD 100. The unique conditions of the bog make the preservation of such bodies possible, and about 1,860 bog bodies, or parts of them, have been found in the United Kingdom and, mostly, in Europe. They are dated to the 1st to 4th centuries AD, the period of Druidic prominence.

The Roman historian Tacitus (AD 56–117) described the Druids as ignorant savages who "thought it their duty to stain the altars with the blood of captives and to consult their gods by examining human entrails" (14.30). Wales seems to have been the last holdout of the Druids, but they were extinguished by the 7th century AD, when the Christianization of Wales was complete. Nonetheless, the role of bard or "seer" persisted in medieval Wales, and bards and seers are prominent in early Irish literature.

In the 18th century interest in the Druids revived in England and Wales. At this time Stonehenge was connected with them—its actual date is c. 2500 BC—and other

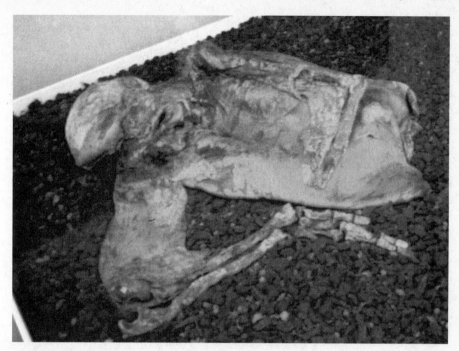

**PERSPECTIVE FIGURE 10**   Lindow Man, a bog man discovered in 1984, c. AD 100 (?). (Mike Peel (www.mikepeel.net) http://en.wikipedia.org/wiki/File:Lindow_Man_1.jpg)

megalithic monuments too. The Ancient Druid Order, who selected the British poet William Blake (1757–1827) as their "Chosen Chief," was founded in London in 1717 and remained intact until it split into two groups in 1964. Druids figured widely in popular culture with the advent of Romanticism in the second half of the 18th century. Many novels and operas featured Druids and Druidesses in important roles. Forged texts appeared, claimed to be written by Druids. Some strands of contemporary NeoDruidism, a religion that promotes harmony and the worship of nature and respect for the environment, is a continuation of this 18th century revival, built around writings produced in the 18th and 19th centuries. NeoDruidism has no connection whatsoever with the ancient religion.

One day at Emain Macha, Cuchulain overheard the Druid Cathbad while he taught his pupils. Here is a passage from *The Cattle Raid at Cooley* that tells of this incident and its consequences. An Ulster warrior named Fiachu son of Firaba is talking to Ailill, king of Connacht, about the youthful Cuchulain's deeds. They are about to be attacked by Cuchulain, and the king wants to learn all he can about his enemy:[1]

"The little boy [Cuchulain] performed a third deed in the following year," said Fiachu son of Firaba.

---

[1]For the Irish texts, cf. Lady Augusta Gregory, *Cuchulain of Muirthemne: The Story of the Men of the Red Branch of Ulster* (London,1902). See also *Táin Bó Cúalnge* from the *Book of Leinster* at http://www.ucc.ie/celt/published/T301035/index.html; J. Gantz (trans.), *Early Irish Myths and Sagas* (London, 1981).

"What deed was that?" asked King Ailill.

"Cathbad the Druid was with his son, Conchobar, teaching his pupils. He had eight eager pupils in his class of Druidic cunning, that's how many he had. One of them asked his teacher what fortune there might be for that day, whether good or ill. Cathbad said, 'The little boy that takes arms this day will be renowned for deeds of arms. Tales of his high deeds will be told forever. But he won't live long.'

"Cuchulain overheard what he said, although he was far off playing. He threw away all his toys and hurried to Conchobar's bedroom to ask for arms.

" 'May all that is good come to you!' cried the little lad.

" 'You seem to be looking for something. What is it?' said Conchobar.

" 'To take up arms,' the boy answered.

" 'Who has advised you, little boy?' asked Conchobar.

" 'Cathbad the Druid,' Cuchulain said.

" 'Well, he would never deceive you, little boy,' said Conchobar.

"Conchobar gave him two spears, a sword, and a shield. The little boy shook and brandished the arms in the middle of the house until they flew into tiny pieces! He gave him another spear and a shield. Cuchulain brandished them in the middle of the house so that soon nothing remained of the fifteen sets of armor in Conchobar's household!

" 'Truly these arms are no good, O Conchobar, my master,' the young man cried. 'They are not good enough for me!'

"So Conchobar gave him his own two spears and his own shield and his own sword. Cuchulain shook and brandished them. He bent them so that the tip of the spear touched its butt. And he could not break the armor, which bore up against his assault. He saluted the king whose arms they were. 'Truly, these arms are good,' said the little boy. 'They are suited to me. Hail to the king whose arms and equipment these are. Hail to the land from where he comes!'

"Just then Cathbad the Druid happened to come into the tent. He said, 'So, has he taken the arms?'

" 'So it must be,' Conchobar answered.

" 'By God I wish they were not taken today,' said Cathbad.

" 'Why do you say that? Did not you yourself advise him so?' Conchobar asked.

" 'Surely not I,' said Cathbad.

" 'What do you mean?' cried Conchobar to Cuchulain. 'Have you told us a lie?'

" 'Don't be angry, my master Conchobar,' said the little boy. 'I have told no lie. But he did advise me when he was teaching this morning. His pupil asked what luck might lie in the day, and he said that the youth who took arms on this day would be illustrious and famous, but would be short-lived.'

" 'That's right,' said Cathbad. 'The day is good, and he will be glorious and renowned, whoever takes up arms today, but short-lived!'

" 'A noble gift!' cried Cuchulain. 'What do I care if I should be only one day and one night in the world, if only the fame of me and of my deeds live after?'

"On another day one of the pupils asked the Druid what that day would be good for.

" 'Whoever mounts a chariot today,' Cathbad answered, 'will be famous over Erin° forever.'

"Cuchulain mounted the chariot. He laid his hands between the two poles of the chariot and mounted it, and it tossed until it was reduced to splinters. He mounted a second chariot, but he made small pieces of it in the same way. The same with a third chariot. And so he made small pieces out of the seventeen chariots that Conchobar kept for the troop of boys in Emain. They simply could not withstand his strength.

" 'These chariots are not any good, O my master Conchobar,' said the little boy. 'They are not good enough for me.'

" 'Where is my charioteer Ibar, the son of Riangabair?' asked Conchobar.

" 'I am here,' Ibar answered.

" 'Take my own two horses and yoke my chariot.'

"The charioteer took the horses and yoked the chariot. The little boy mounted the chariot. He shook the chariot, and it withstood the shaking. He could not break it.

" 'This chariot is good,' cried the boy. 'This chariot is suited to me.'

" 'Very well,' said Ibar, 'come out of the chariot now and let the horses go to pasture.'

" 'It is yet too soon, O Ibar,' the lad answered. 'Only let us go on a circuit of Emain today and you will have a reward, for this is my first day of taking up arms.'

°*Erin*: Ireland.

Three times they drove around Emain. Ibar took Cuchulain to a high promontory and showed him all of Ulster. Soon they come to the fort of the sons of Necht. Cuchulain asked:

" 'But are those not Necht's sons, who boast that there are not more Ulstermen alive than they have killed?'

" 'That's them,' answered Ibar.

" 'Then let us go down to the fort of the mac Nechta,' cried the little boy.

" 'Don't say it—It is dangerous!' said Ibar.

" 'Let's go,' answered Cuchulain.

" 'Let any man go who wishes, but count me out,' said Ibar.

" 'Dead or alive, you shall go there!' the little boy cried.

" 'Alive I shall go to the south,' answered Ibar, 'and dead I shall be left at the fort—this I know—at the fort of the mac Nechta.'

"So they pushed on to the fort. The little boy sprang out of the chariot onto the green. On the green was a pillar-stone and an iron band of prowess around it, and there was writing in ogham on the stone. The writing said, 'Whoever should come to the green, if he be a champion, it is forbidden that he depart from the green without undergoing single combat' [Figure 10.1].

"The boy deciphered the writing. Then he put his arms around the pillar-stone and flung it with a cast of his hand into the moat so that a wave passed over it.

" 'I'm afraid that won't do any good,' said Ibar. 'We're going to get what we came for—death, doom, and destruction!'

" 'Yes, of course. But Ibar, spread out the chariot-coverings and its skins so that I may snatch a little sleep.'

" 'Alas that you say this,' said Ibar. 'The land of the enemy is not a place for diversion!'

"Ibar arranged the chariot-coverings and its skins under Cuchulain, and the lad fell asleep on the green grass.

"Then came one of the mac Nechta onto the fair green, Foill son of Necht.

" 'Don't unyoke those horses, boy,' cried Foill.

" 'I have no desire to,' answered Ibar. 'You see that I still hold the reins in my hand.'

" 'Whose horses are those, then?' Foill asked.

" 'Two of Conchobar's horses,' answered Ibar. 'The two with the dappled heads.'

" 'I have heard of these horses. What has brought these steeds here to the borders?'

" 'Amongst us a tender youth has today taken up arms. He has come to the edge of the marshes for luck and good omen, to display his good looks.'

" 'May it not be for victory or triumph, this first taking of arms!' exclaimed Foill. 'If I thought he was fit for action, he should go back dead to Emain and not alive.'

" 'Truly, he is not fit for action,' Ibar answered. 'By no means. It is only seven years since he was taken from the crib.'

"Then the little lad raised his face from the ground and drew his hand over his face, and he became crimson from head to toe. 'Aye, but I am fit for action!' he cried.

" 'Fine,' said the champion. 'But it seems to me that you are not fit for action.'

" 'You will know that better if we go to the ford. But go, get your weapons, for I slay not charioteers nor attendants nor folk without arms.'

"And so the man went quickly after his arms.

" 'You should beware this man that comes to meet you, little boy,' said Ibar.

" 'And why so?' asked the lad.

" 'Foill son of Necht is the man. Neither points of spear nor edges of weapons can harm him.'

" 'Don't worry, Ibar,' said the lad. 'I will cast my iron-headed mace and it will light on the disc of his shield and then the flat of his forehead and it will carry away his brain out through the back of his head as though through a sieve-hole, till the light of the sky will be visible through his head.'

"Foill son of Necht came at him. Cuchulain took the mace in hand and threw it from him so that it lighted on the disc of his shield and then the flat of his forehead and carried his brain out through his head as through a sieve-hole, till the light of the sky could be seen through it. Cuchulain went to him and struck off the head from the trunk. He bore away his spoils and the head with him.

"Then came the second son out on the green, his name Tuachall ["cunning"] son of Necht.

" 'You would boast of this deed,' said Tuachall.

" 'No point of boasting for slaying one champion,' said Cuchulain, 'when I can soon boast of two. You'd better find your armor, for you are unarmed.'

"The man rushed to get his armor.

" 'You should be careful of this man, my boy,' said Ibar.

" 'How so?' the lad asked.

" 'Tuachall son of Necht is the man you behold. And he is not badly mis-named, for you can't take him by arms. Unless you get him with your first blow or with your first shot or with your first touch, you will never get him. He'll know your game and anticipate every blow.'

" 'Not to worry, O Ibar,' cried the lad. 'I will use Conchobar's well-tempered lance. It will land on the shield over his belly, it will crush through his ribs on the farther side after piercing his heart in his breast. That would be the throw of an enemy and not the friendliness of a countryman! Then I'll watch him die.'

"Tuachall son of Necht came forth on the green. The lad laid his hand on Conchobar's lance, and it struck the shield above his belly and broke through the ribs on the farther side after piercing his heart within his breast. He struck off his head before it reached the ground.

"Then came the youngest of the sons forth on the green, Fandall son of Necht.

" 'Those were fools who fought with you here,' cried Fandall.

" 'Really?' cried the lad. 'Come, let us meet at the pool, so deep that your foot cannot find the bottom.'

"Fandall rushed to the pool.

" 'You should be wary of him, little boy,' said Ibar.

" 'Why should I then?' asked the lad.

" 'Fandall son of Necht is the man before us. He bears the name Fandall ["swallow"] because like a swallow or weasel he skims over the sea. The swimmers of the world cannot reach him.'

" 'You should not say this, Ibar,' said the boy. 'You know the river in our land, in Emain, the Callann. When the boys play near it, I carry a boy over the river on either of my palms and a boy on either shoulder, and I do not myself wet my ankles under their weight.'

"They met on the water and seized hold of one another. The little boy closed his arms over Fandall so that his face was under water. Then he gave him a deft blow with Conchobar's sword, chopping off head from trunk. He let the body float downstream, and he carried off the head and the spoils with him.

"Cuchulain went into the fort and pillaged the place and burned it so that the buildings were no higher than walls around the fort. Then they turned towards Sliab Fuait, carrying the three heads of Necht's sons with them.

"When they came to Sliab Fuait, there was a herd of wild deer in front of them.

" 'What are those many animals, Ibar, those nimble ones up the road?' asked the boy. 'Are they tame or wild?'

" 'Truly those are wild,' Ibar answered. 'Herds of wild deer haunt the wastes of Sliab Fuait.'

" 'Urge on the horses—into the bog, to see if we can take some of them.'

"The charioteer drove a goad into the horses, but the king's fat steeds could not keep up with the deer. The boy jumped down from the chariot and took off at a run, charging through the bog, and he caught two of the swift, stout deer. He fastened them to the back poles of the chariot with thongs.

"They continued their way towards Emain, when they saw a flock of white swans flying near them.

" 'What are those birds there, O Ibar?' the boy asked. 'Are they tame or wild?'

" 'Truly they are wild birds,' Ibar answered. 'They come from the rocks and crags of the islands in the great sea to feed on the plains of Erin.'

" 'Which would be more wondrous to the Ulstermen, Ibar—for them to be fetched alive to Emain or dead?' asked the lad.

" 'Alive would be more wondrous,' Ibar answered. 'For few succeed in taking the birds alive, while there are many who take them dead.'

"Then did the little boy perform one of his lesser feats upon them. He put a small stone in his sling and brought down eight of the birds, but did not kill them. Then he performed a greater feat: He threw a large stone at them and brought down sixteen. He fastened them to the hind poles of the chariot with thongs.

" 'Take the birds along with you, O Ibar,' cried the lad to his charioteer.

" 'I have a problem,' answered Ibar. 'It is not easy to go.'

" 'Why is that?' asked the lad.

" 'The horses have become wild. If I stir from where I am, the chariot's iron wheels will cut me down because of their sharpness and because of the strong and mighty power of the horses. If I make a move, the horns of the deer will pierce and gore me.'

" 'Ha! Some champion you are, O Ibar,' said the lad. 'I will give the horses such a look that they will not depart from the straight way. And I shall give the deer such a look that they will bow their heads in fear and awe of me. They will dare not move. It will be safe for you even though you pass right before their horns.'

"So they went on till they reached the fair plain of Emain. Then Lebarcham, on the watch in Emain Macha, saw them, she who was the daughter of Aue ["ear"] and of Adarc ["horn"].

" 'A single chariot-fighter comes towards Emain Macha,' cried Lebarcham, 'and his coming is fearful. The heads of his enemies hang red in his chariot beside him. Beautiful, all-white birds hover around the chariot. With him are wild, untamed deer, bound and fettered, shackled and pinioned. For sure, if we do not take care of him tonight, blood will flow over Conchobar's province and the Ulster youth will fall by his hand.'

" 'We know him, that chariot-fighter,' said Conchobar. 'I'm sure that it is my sister's son, who went to the edge of the marches at the beginning of the day, who has reddened his hands and is still not sated with combat. Unless he be attended to, all the youths of Emain will fall by his hand.'

"And they agreed to follow this plan: to let out the womenfolk to meet him, one-hundred-fifty stark-naked women, at one and the same time. Their leader, named Scannlach ["wanton"], would go before them, revealing all their shame.

"So the young women got up and marched out, and they displayed their nakedness and all their shame to him. The lad hid his face and turned his gaze on the chariot so he might not see the nakedness or the shame of the women.

"Then the boy was lifted out of the chariot. They placed him in three vats of cold water to extinguish his wrath. The first vat into which he was put burst its staves and hoops like the cracking of nuts. The next vat into which he went boiled with bubbles as big as fists. The third vat into which he went—well, some men might endure it and others not. Then the boy's wrath cooled down. He came out, and his festive garments were put on him.

"His handsomeness stood forth. Seven toes he had to each of his two feet, and seven fingers to each of his two hands, and seven pupils to each of his two kingly eyes, which shone like gems. Four spots of down on each cheek: a blue spot, a purple spot, a green spot, and a yellow spot. Fifty strands of bright-yellow hair from one ear to the other, like a comb of birch twigs or like a brooch of pale gold in the face of the sun. A clear, white, shorn spot on the top of his head, as if a cow had licked it. A fair, laced green mantle about him, held by a silver pin over his white breast. He wore a hooded tunic made of golden threads.

"The boy was seated between the two feet of Conchobar, and the king began to stroke his close-shorn hair.

"A mere lad accomplished these deeds at the end of seven years after his birth," continued Fiachu son of Fiarba. "He overcame heroes and battle-champions at whose hands two thirds of the men of Ulster had fallen, and there was no opportunity for revenge, until that boy rose up for them."

## More Youthful Deeds of Cuchulain

Cuchulain was so handsome that the Ulstermen worried that, unless he soon got a wife of his own, he would seduce their wives and debauch their daughters. They searched all over Ireland for a suitable wife, but Cuchulain was in love with a certain **Emer**, daughter of Forgall Monach. Forgall was opposed to the match. He suggested that Cuchulain train in arms with the renowned warrior-woman **Scathach** (**skath**-akh) in Scotland, hoping that he would be killed. But Scathach befriended Cuchulain and taught him the arts of war, including how to throw a barbed spear with his foot, so terrible that it must be cut from its victim. His fellow trainees included one Ferdiad, who became Cuchulain's best friend.

During his time in Scotland, Scathach faced a battle against Aife (a-**if**-e), her rival and in some versions her twin sister. Scathach, knowing how powerful Aife was, feared for Cuchulain's life and gave him a powerful sleeping potion to keep him from the battle. However, because of Cuchulain's strength, the potion put him to sleep for only an hour, and he soon joined the fight. He took on Aife in single combat. They seemed evenly matched, but Cuchulain distracted and seized her. He spared Aife's life on condition that she settle her enmity with Scathach—and that she bear him a son!

Leaving Aife pregnant, Cuchulain returned from Scotland fully trained. Forgall still refused to let him marry his daughter Emer. Cuchulain stormed Forgall's fortress, killed 24 of Forgall's men, abducted Emer, and stole Forgall's treasure. Forgall fell from the ramparts to his death.

King Conchobar has *droit du seigneur*, the "right of the first night" with anyone who marries in his kingdom. However, he feared Cuchulain, if he exercised it in this case. On the other hand, he would appear to diminish his authority if he does not. The Druid Cathbad has a solution: Conchobar will sleep with Emer on the night of the wedding, but Cathbad will sleep between them!

Eight years later, Connla, Cuchulain's son by Aife, came to Ireland looking for his father, but in a typical pattern Cuchulain took him as an intruder and killed him when he refused to identify himself. Cuchulain was grief stricken at killing his own son.

While abroad in Scotland, Cuchulain rescued **Derbforgaill**, a Scandinavian princess, from being sacrificed to the Fomorians, a race of divine spirits older than the gods, like the Greek Titans. Derbforgaill fell in love with Cuchulain, and, in the form of a pair of swans, she and her handmaiden came to Ireland to find him.

Cuchulain was out hunting. He cast his sling at a flying swan—in fact Derbforgaill—bringing her down. He saved her life by sucking the stone from her side. She regained her human form, but for some reason once he tasted her blood he cannot marry her. He therefore gave her to a foster son to marry.

But the women of Ulster hated Derbforgaill because she was so sexually desirable, and they attacked and mutilated her. Derbforgaill died of her wounds, her husband the foster son died of grief, and Cuchulain took revenge by demolishing the house in which the women of Ulster sought refuge. He killed one-hundred fifty of them.

## The Cattle Raid at Cooley

At age 17, a single-handed Cuchulain defended Ulster from the army of the neighboring province of Connacht in *The Cattle Raid at Cooley*. **Medb** (mev), queen of Connacht, has mounted the invasion in order to steal a great stud bull kept in the town of Cooley in Ulster. Cuchulain is with a woman when the queen arrives at the border, and so Ulster is taken by surprise. A curse has disabled all the men of Ulster, so Cuchulain stops Medb's army by invoking the traditional right of single combat at fords: He defeats champion after champion in a standoff that goes on for months.

Before one of these combats a beautiful young woman comes to Cuchulain, claiming to be the daughter of a king. She offers herself to him, but he refuses. The woman reveals herself as the Morrigan ("phantom queen"), a sort of Irish Valkyrie who flies over warriors to predict their death, often in the form of a crow. In revenge for the slight, she attacks him in various animal forms on his next day of battle, first as an eel who trips him, then as a wolf who stampedes cattle across the ford, and finally as a red heifer leading the stampede. Cuchulain wounds her in each form and defeats his opponent despite her interference.

In a particularly difficult combat Cuchulain is severely wounded. The god Lugh comes to him to tell him he is his real father. Lugh heals his wounds. When Cuchulain arises, healed, he sees that a troop of boys from Emain Macha has attacked the army of Medb, queen of Connacht, and been slaughtered. Cuchulain goes into his berserker mode:

> Then took place the first rage-spasm of the royal hero Cuchulain, so that he made a terrible, many-shaped, tremendous, unknown thing of himself. His flesh trembled about him like a pole against the torrent or like a rush against the stream, sweeping over every part of him from the top of his head to the soles of his feet. His body whirled within his skin. His feet and shins and knees turned quite around so that they all went behind, while his heels and the flesh of his calves and hams shifted to the front. The muscles of his calves moved around to the front, each huge knot the size of a balled-up fist. The sinews of his head swelled and stood out on his neck, like hills, huge, inestimable, vast, immeasurable, as large as the head of a child one month old.
>
> His face altered into a blaze-red bowl. He sucked in one eye so deep that a crane, with its great beak, could not probe it out and place it on his cheek, and the other sprang forth out on his cheek. His mouth was distorted, like a monster. He opened it so wide that you could see everything inside. His lungs fluttered back in his mouth, in his gullet, and his lower jaw smashed into the upper with the power to kill a lion.

Flakes of fire as large as a ram's fleece reached his mouth from his throat … The loud clap of his heart against his breast was like the yelp of a howling blood-hound or a lion fighting with bears … His hair bristled over his head like branches of a red thorn bush thrust into a gap in a great hedge. If the king's apple tree laden with royal fruit had been shaken around him, scarcely an apple would pass over him and reach the ground, but would have stuck on each single hair as it stood up in his rage.

He attacked the army and killed hundreds, building walls of corpses.

Later the Ulstermen come to the defense of Cooley. At first, Cuchulain stays on the sidelines, recuperating from wounds received in recent encounters, and then he again enters the fray, forcing Medb to retreat. At just this moment, she begins to menstruate. Cuchulain breaks through and captures her as she stops to deal with the situation. Because he does not think it right to kill women, Cuchulain spares Medb and even guards her retreat back to Connacht.

And so ended the cattle raid of Cooley.

## The Loves of Cuchulain

A troublemaker, one Bricriu, incited Cuchulain and two other heroes to compete for the champion's portion at a feast. Cuchulain won every competition, but the other two heroes would not accept the result. **Cu Roi** (ku **ro**-i, "dog of the battlefield"), king of MUNSTER, the southernmost province of Ireland, was one of the judges. He settled the dispute by a test. He visited each hero disguised as a man of hideous appearance. He challenged each hero to behead him on condition that when he returned (!), the man could behead *him*. Each warrior beheads Cu Roi only to see him, to their astonishment, pick up his head and leave. When Cu Roi returned, the other heroes fled and only Cuchulain was brave enough to submit to Cu Roi's ax. Cu Roi spared Cuchulain and he was declared champion. This same story appears in the famous Middle English poem *Sir Gawain and the Green Knight*.

Cu Roi, again in disguise, joins the Ulstermen on a raid against an island (probably the Isle of Man to the east of Ireland). In return for his help, he demands his choice of the spoils. The Ulstermen take a good deal of treasure and abduct the daughter of the king of the island, who is in love with Cuchulain. Cu Roi asks for the princess as his share of the booty. Cuchulain tries to stop him from taking her, but Cu Roi drives Cuchulain into the ground up to his armpits before escaping, taking the princess with him. The princess discovers how to kill Cu Roi and betrays him to Cuchulain. Cuchulain puts Cu Roi to death. Cu Roi's resident bard, enraged at the betrayal of his lord, seizes the princess and leaps off a cliff, killing both of them.

Naturally, Cuchulain had many lovers, but Emer was not jealous until he fell in love with the fairy Fand, wife of Manannan mac Lir (Figure 10.2). Manannan had left her alone, and three evil Fomorians, from the race of ancient spirits, attacked. Cuchulain agreed to help as long as Fand married him. She reluctantly agreed, and then they fell in love.

But their relationship is doomed because Cuchulain is mortal and Fand is a fairy. Still, Emer tries to kill her rival Fand, but when Emer sees the strength of Fand's love for Cuchulain, Emer decides to give up Cuchulain. Moved by Emer's generosity, Fand decides to return to her own husband!

Cuchulain and Emer drink a potion and the whole affair disappears from their memories.

**FIGURE 10.2**  Emer rebukes Cuchulain for falling in love with the fairy Fand, wife of Manannan mac Lir, as shown in this early 1900s illustration by English artist H. R. Miller. Emer, amidst her maids, holds a dagger and points her hand in reproach. Fand sits to the left of Cuchulain, who sits with the fingers of his hands entwined. (Ivy Close Images / Alamy)

## The Death of Cuchulain

Medb conspires with **Lugaid** (**lu**-god), son of Cu Roi, and with the sons of others whom Cuchulain has killed to lure him to his death. Lugaid has three magic spears, and it is prophesied that a king will fall by each of them.

With the first spear he kills Cuchulain's charioteer, king of chariot drivers. With the second he kills Cuchulain's horse, king of horses. With the third he hits Cuchulain, mortally wounding him. Cuchulain ties himself to a standing stone in order to die on his feet (traditionally identified as one still standing at Knockbridge, County Louth, in Ulster). Only when a raven lands on his shoulder do his enemies believe he is dead. Lugaid approaches and cuts off his head, but as he does so a heroic light burns around Cuchulain. In penance, Lugaid cuts off his own hand.

A companion had sworn that if Cuchulain died he would avenge him before sunset. When he hears that Cuchulain is dead, he pursues Lugaid. Because Lugaid has lost a hand, the companion fights him with one hand tucked into his belt, as honor requires, but overwhelms Lugaid after his horse takes a bite out of Lugaid's side. He also kills and beheads the other conspirators.

## OBSERVATIONS: CUCHULAIN AND HISTORY

On May 1, 1169, an army of about six hundred Norman knights landed in Ireland. These Norsemen were originally Vikings from Norway, but came to Ireland mostly from Wales and CORNWALL where they were living. The pope approved the invasion because he wished to reorganize the Irish Church and integrate it into the Roman church. Over the next century, Norman law, written in Latin, gradually replaced the native oral Celtic law.

After the mid-14th century and the Black Death that killed one of every four Europeans, the Norman settlements in Ireland declined. Norman rulers and the native Irish elites had intermarried, although there were laws against assimilation. As English subjects, which the Normans had become, they spoke English, followed English custom, and observed English law. Still, the Norman/English authority in Ireland gradually shrank, then nearly disappeared except for an area around Dublin called the *Pale*. Thus, we say "beyond the pale" as meaning to be in hostile territory or to act unacceptably.

The English Tudor kings in the 16th century reconquered Ireland and consolidated their power during bloody wars in the 17th century. Probably, half the native Irish were killed in these wars. English and Scottish colonists established large plantations, especially in the north.

In 1690, there were two rival claimants to the English, Scottish, and Irish thrones—the Catholic King James and the Protestant King William of Orange, who had deposed James in 1688. William of Orange was not only a nephew of James, but he was married to his daughter Mary! (Hence the College of William and Mary in Virginia, chartered by the king and queen in 1693.) The rivals met at the river Boyne in Ulster, Northern Ireland. William of Orange won the battle and thus insured the continuation of Protestant supremacy in Ireland. The battle is a key part in Ulster Protestant folklore, commemorated today in the Protestant north principally by the Orange men, named after William of Orange.

Ever thereafter the division between the English, Protestant ruling class and the Celtic, Catholic underclass has been viewed in religious terms, though its origins were tribal and linguistic. After the Battle of the Boyne, Roman Catholics and nonconforming Protestant dissenters, for example Presbyterians, were barred from the Irish Parliament and deprived of various civil rights, even to own hereditary property. At this time large numbers of Scottish-Irish Presbyterians emigrated to North America. Because the British dominated the east coast of North America, they traveled to the Ohio Valley, to the Ozarks, and to Georgia, where their descendants live today.

In 1800, the British and Irish parliaments merged to create the United Kingdom of Great Britain and Ireland. The parliament at Westminster in London ruled Ireland directly. In 1840, unusual weather, together with the importation of a deadly potato mold from North America, caused the failure of the ubiquitous Irish potato crop, on which the impoverished Irish subsisted. A great famine ensued in which one million Irish died. Over a million more emigrated to escape the hunger, but these were Irish Catholics, not the Scottish-Irish Presbyterians of earlier times. By 1850, half of all immigration to the United States was from Ireland. Mass emigration became deeply entrenched, and the population continued to decline until 1961, when the population of Ireland slightly increased.

In the late 19th century, Charles Stewart Parnell, who figures in James Joyce's *Portrait of an Artist as a Young Man* (1916), and others campaigned for autonomy within the union of Great Britain, or "Home Rule." Unionists, especially in Ulster, were strongly opposed to Home Rule, which they knew would be dominated by Catholic interests. The failed Easter Rising against the British of 1916 was carried out by followers of Home Rule. The British executed the leaders one by one over seven weeks, a typically British barbarity that utterly changed Great Britain's attitude toward Home Rule. Today all provinces of Ireland, except Ulster, are free of English governance, while the Catholics and the Protestants of the North, still obedient to the crown, live in an uneasy peace.

Curiously, Cuchulain is the hero of both the Catholic Irish nationalists and the Protestant Ulster unionists. Irish nationalists see him as the most important Celtic Irish hero, and therefore important to the whole culture. A bronze sculpture of the dead Cuchulain by Oliver Sheppard, raven on his shoulder, stands in the Dublin General Post Office in commemoration of the Easter Rising of 1916 (Figure 10.3). By contrast, unionists see him as an Ulsterman defending the northern province from enemies to the south. He is depicted in murals in unionist parts of Belfast and in many unionist areas of Northern Ireland.

**FIGURE 10.3**    The death of Cuchulain, by Oliver Sheppard (1865–1941), 1911. He is bound to a stone and a raven alights on his shoulder. He holds a sword in his right hand, and his shield lies at his feet. (Courtesy of An Post, GPO, Dublin)

# WALES

After the Romans withdrew from Wales in the 5th century AD, the southwestern semi-peninsula of Great Britain (see Map 10.2), a distinctive Celtic Welsh culture emerged there, although already Christianized. In Germanic languages, Wales means "foreign" as in *wal*nut, a "foreign nut" (to the Romans). In the 13th century AD, the Norman/English occupied Wales, but the country preserved its Celtic identity. In 1603 Wales was united with England and Scotland to become Great Britain. Still today, as a kind of courtesy, the heir to the British throne is called the Prince of Wales.

The Welsh material is less informative than the Irish about what may have been preChristian belief and practice. There is constant invocation of God and little evidence of pagan cult in the stories from Wales, except in some cases gods seemed to have been downgraded into heroes. Folklore motifs are strong and seem to tie Welsh tales to traditions strong in Europe, especially those surrounding King Arthur and his circle. The earliest Welsh poem, *Culhwch and Olwen* probably goes back to the 10th century AD, and mentions Taliesin as a bard at the court of Arthur (*Taliesin* became the name of the Welsh-American Frank Lloyd Wright's architectural studio in Spring Green, Wisconsin). In fact, nothing whatever is known about King Arthur, who may or may not have lived in the 6th century AD. Poems that survive under the name of Taliesin are much later compilations.

Of far grander scale than *Culhwch and Olwen* is the 11th-century *Four Branches of the Mabinogi*, usually known as the **Mabinogion** after a 19th-century translation by Lady Charlotte Guest (1812–1895). Hers was the first translation into English of the Welsh tales. The meaning of the title is unknown, although it is somehow related to Welsh *mab*, which means "son, boy." Each of the four *Branches* ends with a colophon "thus ends this Branch of the Mabinogi," the *Branches* being related stories told in prose.

## MYTH: PWYLL, PRINCE OF DYFED

The first Branch of the *Mabinogion*, which we will focus on here, tells the story of **Pwyll** (**pow**-el, "wisdom"), his wife **Rhiannon** (**rī**-a-non) ("great queen"), their son Pryderi (pri-**der**-i, "care, anxiety"), and Pwyll's encounter with **Arawen** (ar-a-wen), lord of Annwen, the Welsh underworld.[2]

### Pwyll and Arawen Change Places

Pwyll Pendeuic Dyfed ["prince of Dyfed"] was lord of the seven counties of DYFED. One time while he was at Arbeth, where he had his court, he thought he would go hunting. He thought he would go to hunt in Glyn Cuch. He set out that evening from Arbeth, went a good distance, and there spent the night.

Early next morning, he got up and let loose his dogs in Glyn Cuch. He blew on his horn and mustered the hunt, chasing the dogs and getting away from his companions.

As he was listening for the cry of the pack, he heard the cry of another pack coming to meet his own. There was a clearing in the middle of the wood, like a

[2]For the Welsh texts, cf. Lady Charlotte Guest, *The Mabinogion: The Red Book of Hergest* (London, 1838–1849). See also J. Gantz (trans.), *The Mabinogion* (New York, 1976); S. Davies (trans.), *The Mabinogion* (Oxford, 2007); W. Parker (trans.), *The Four Branches of the Mabinogi* (Dublin, 2007).

smooth plain. Just as his own pack reached the edge of the clearing, a stag burst forth from the other side pursued by the other pack, and in the middle of the field they brought it down. He barely noticed the stag itself because of the color of the pack. He had never seen anything like it. They were a dazzling white with bright red ears.

He came up to his dogs and drove back the pack that had killed the stag. He let his own dogs feast on the stag. While they were feeding, he saw a horseman coming after the pack on an immense gray horse with a hunting horn around his neck and a brown cloth wrapped around him as a hunting cloak.

The horsemen approached, and said, "Lord, I know who you are but I will not greet you."

"Aye," said Pwyll, "perhaps you are so important you don't need to greet me?"

"God knows," he replied, "it is not the dignity of my rank that is holding me back."

"What then, my lord?"

"By God, it's your rudeness and lack of courtesy."

"What discourtesy have I committed?" said Pwyll.

"Why I've never seen a greater discourtesy by a man than driving off a pack which has killed a stag, and then feeding his own dogs on it! That was the discourtesy, and though I won't be exacting revenge, by God I claim a recompense from you to the value of a hundred stags!"

"My lord, if I've offended you, I will redeem your friendship," Pwyll said.

"How will you redeem it?" asked the man.

"As is appropriate to your rank. Who are you?"

"I am a crowned king in my land."

"My Lord," said Pwyll, "well then, good day to you. Which land is that?"

"The land of Annwen. I am Arawen, king of Annwen."

"My Lord, how then might I obtain your friendship?"

"This is how you might obtain it. There is a man whose kingdom borders my kingdom who is forever at war with me. His name is Hafgan king of Annwefen. If you get rid of him—which you can easily do—you will win my friendship."

"I would do that gladly. How?"

"Like this: I will make a strong bond of friendship with you by giving you my place in Annwen. I'll give you the most beautiful woman in the world to sleep with each night. My form and appearance will be upon you so that not the chamber-boy, nor my personal servant, nor anybody else who serves me will know that you are not I. And so it will be until the end of a year from tomorrow, when we will meet again at this very place."

"Very well," Pwyll answered. "Although I'm going to be there until the end of the year, what advice do you have about finding this enemy you speak of?"

"A year from tonight," said Arawen, "the two of us shall meet at the ford. You will be there in my guise. You must give him a single blow: He will not survive it. If he asks you to give him another, don't. No matter how many blows I have given him, he was always able to fight just as well the next day."

"Aye," said Pwyll, "but what about my own country?"

"There will not be a man or a woman in your country who will know that I am you. I will go in your place."

"I see," said Pwyll. "Very well—now I will be on my way."

"You will find no obstacle to your travels until you reach my country. I will guide you to it."

And so Arawen guided Pwyll on his way until he could see the palace and the outlying houses.

"There," he said, "the court and the country is now under your command. Go to the court. Everyone will recognize you. You will soon learn how to behave in the court."

He went inside. There were many bedrooms, halls, and chambers with beautiful decorations. He went to pull off his boots but servants hastened to help him. Everyone greeted him as he approached. Two knights removed his hunting-garb and wrapped him in a garment of gold-brocaded silk. The hall was made ready.

Lo, the household and guests came inside, as exalted and refined as anyone had ever seen. Behind them came the queen, the most beautiful woman in the world. She was wearing a garment of shining gold-brocaded silk. After washing their hands, they sat down at table, the queen on one side and a chieftain (as he thought) on the other.

He began a conversation with the queen. She was most unassuming and genteel in her manner. They drank and ate, they sang and made merry. Of all the courts he had ever seen, this was best for its food and drink, served in golden vessels studded with jewels.

The time came to go to bed, and to bed they went, Pwyll and the queen. The moment they got in bed, he turned his face to the side with his back towards her. He didn't say a single word to her until morning, when they spoke tenderly and with affection. But however fond they might have been during the day, all nights were just the same.

Pwyll passed the year in hunting, singing, dancing, and friendly conversation with his companions until the night of the appointment came. Every man in the country knew of the date, and he went to the appointment along with the nobles of the country. When he came to the ford, a horseman rode up.

He said, "Gentlemen, listen well. Between these two kings is this appointment and between them alone. Each one is a claimant against the other, over land and territory. May the rest stand back and let the contest be between them alone."

At that the two kings closed in on one another, advancing to the middle of the ford. In the first onslaught the king who was in the place of Arawen struck Hafgan on the boss of his shield. It split in half, his armor was broken, and Hafgan went over the back of his horse onto the ground, mortally wounded.

"Lord," said Hafgan, "what right do you have to kill me? I made no claim against you. So why are you putting me to death? But because you've begun, finish it."

"Lord," he replied, "perhaps I would regret doing what I did to you. Find someone else to kill you. I will not kill you."

"My faithful men," said Hafgan, "carry me away from here. My death is upon me. I cannot uphold you any longer."

"And men of mine," said the man who was in the place of Arawen, "make an accounting. Find out who owes me allegiance!"

"Lord, everyone owes you allegiance. There is now no other king in the whole of Annwefen but yourself."

"Yes," he said, "for those who come in peace, they will receive a just reception. For those who do not fall into compliance, there will be force of arms."

Then he received homage from the men. He took possession of the land. By noon the next day both the two kingdoms were in his power. He headed for his meeting in Glyn Cuch. When he arrived, Arawen was waiting. They greeted each other.

"Well," said Arawen, "may God reward you for your friendship. I have heard everything about it."

"Yes," Pwyll said, "when you come to your country you will see all that I have accomplished on your behalf."

"Whatever you have done for me, may God repay you."

Arawen then gave Pwyll Pendeuic Dyfed back his own form, and he recovered his own appearance too. Arawen went towards his court in Annwefen and rejoiced on seeing his followers and his household, having not seen them for so long. Knowing nothing of his absence, however, they were no more surprised at his arrival than before. He spent the day in cheerful merriment, chatting with his wife and noblemen. When it came time to retire, off they went to bed.

He went to the bed and his wife came with him. First they talked, then they made love. She was not used to this, being abstinent for a full year, and she thought, "O God, what has come over him? It has been a full year." She lay in thought for a long time. After that, he woke up and spoke to her three times, but she would not answer him.

"Why won't you speak to me?" he asked.

"I tell you," she replied "for a year I have not spoken even so much as this."

"What do you mean," he said, "we've been talking the whole time."

"Forgive me," she replied, "but for the last year whenever we went to bed you have showed me no affection, nor spoken with me, nor even turned your face towards me. Let alone—making love."

Then Arawen began thinking. "Lord God," he said to himself, "here is a true, a strong friend!"

He said to his wife, "Lady," he said, "You mustn't blame me. I swear to God that I haven't slept with you for a year before last night, nor have I lain here."

And he told her the whole story.

"By God he must be a true friend to you, who warded off temptation and kept his faith with you!"

"I have thought the same," Arawen said.

"I am not surprised," she replied.

Now Pwyll Pendeuic Dyfed came to his country and began asking the noblemen of his realm how things had been during the last year … was his lordship the same as always?

"Lord," they said, "never have you known so much, never have you been more congenial, never were you so generous and never was your rule better than during this year."

"By God," he replied, "it would be better that you thank the man who really was with you during the year. Let me tell you what has happened …"

And Pwyll told them the whole story.

"Aye, Lord," they said, "You should thank God that he has given you this friendship. As for the lordship we had that year, I'm sure it will continue."

"It will still continue, by God."

Ever thereafter a strong friendship grew up between them. They exchanged many gifts, including horses, greyhounds, hawks, and all kinds of treasure. Because of his stay that year in Annwefen, his kingship that had prospered there, and the forging of two kingdoms into one through his tenancy and bravery, ever thereafter he was called Pwyll Penn Annwefen ["lord of Annwefen"] instead of Pwyll Pendeuic Dyfed.

## The Lady on Horseback

Now one time Pwyll Penn Annwefen was holding court in Arbeth, and there a feast was laid out and great hosts of men all around him. After the first course, Pwyll got up to go for a walk. He went to the top of a mound above the court that was called Gorsedd Arbeth.

"My lord," said a member of the court, "it is an odd thing about this mound that when a man of high birth sits upon it, he will depart with one of two things: either wounds or blows, or he will witness a marvel."

"I do not fear wounds or blows. But I would be glad to witness a marvel. I will go to sit on this mound," said Pwyll.

And he went and sat on the mound. As he was seated, he saw a woman on a stately pale white horse, with cloth of shining gold-brocaded silk around her. She was riding along the track that went past the mound. The horse moved at an even, leisurely pace. She drew level with the mound.

"Men," cried Pwyll, "does anyone recognize this lady on horseback?"

"There is no one who recognizes her, my lord," they replied.

"One of you must approach her to find out who she is," he said.

One man got up, but by the time he got to the road the lady had already gone past. He went after her as fast as he could on foot, but the faster he went, the farther away she became. When he saw that following her was useless, he returned to Pwyll and spoke as follows:

"Lord, it is no use trying to follow her on foot."

"Aye," said Pwyll, "go back to the court and take the fastest horse that you can find and go after her."

He found the horse and rode off. He came to smooth open country. He spurred his horse but the harder he spurred, the further away she became. Yet she continued at the same pace at which she began. The horse began to flag, and he returned to Pwyll.

"My lord," he said, "it is useless to follow that lady. There is no horse in the whole land faster than this, but it could not follow her."

"Aye," Pwyll said, "there is magic in this. Let us return to the court."

They returned to the court and there passed the rest of the day. On the next day they got up, but after the first meal of the day Pwyll said, "Let us go now to the top of the mound, the same people as yesterday. And you," he spoke to a retainer, "take the fastest horse you can find."

The retainer did as he was told. They went to the mound with the horse. As they were sitting there, they saw the woman on the same horse, dressed as before, coming up the road.

"Look!" said Pwyll, "here she comes. Get ready, boy, to discover who she is."

"My lord, I'd be very happy to do this," the boy said.

The lady on horseback came up to them. The boy got on his horse, but before he had got settled in the saddle she had already gone past and put a distance between them. Her pace was the same as the day before. He set off at a gallop, supposing he could overtake her. It was no use. He loosed his reins but got no nearer than if he had been on foot. The more he beat his horse, the further away she became, yet her pace was no greater than before.

It was useless to follow her. The boy returned to Pwyll.

"My lord," he said, "you've seen all this horse can do."

"Yes, I've seen," replied Pwyll. "There is no point pursuing her. By God," he continued, "I think she has a message for someone on this plain, if she weren't too stubborn to say what it is. Let's head back to the court."

They went back to the court and spent the evening in song and merriment, just as they pleased.

On the next morning, after the first meal Pwyll said, "Where is the group that went up on the mound yesterday and the day before?"

"Here we are, my Lord," they said.

"Let us go then and sit on the mound. And you," he said to his stable boy, "saddle up my horse and bring him to the path, and bring my spurs too."

The boy did what he was told. They got to the mound, but had not been there long before they saw the lady on horseback, coming along the same path, wearing the same clothes, moving at the same pace.

"Ah, boy, I see the lady on horseback!" said Pwyll. "Bring me my horse."

Pwyll mounted his horse. No sooner had he done so than she passed him by. He chased after her, allowing his horse to go its own lively pace. He supposed that he would catch her on the second or third bound, but no nearer did he get to her than any time before. He spurred his horse as fast as it could go. But he saw that it was useless.

Then Pwyll spoke, saying, "Maiden, for the sake of the man you love best, wait!"

"Of course I'll wait," she said, "but it would have been better for your horse if you had asked me long ago."

The maiden stopped and waited. She drew aside the cloth that covered her face. She looked him in the eye.

"My lady," Pwyll asked, "where do you come from? And where are you going?"

"I am going about my business," she said, "and I am very glad to see you."

"You are just as welcome," he said.

He saw at that moment that the faces of every woman he had ever seen dulled in comparison to this face.

"My lady," he asked, "what is your business?"

"By God, I will tell you," she said. "My chief business was to see you."

"The best business of all, as far as I'm concerned. And will you tell me who you are?"

"I will tell you, my lord," she replied. "I am Rhiannon, daughter of Hyfaidd the Old. I am about to be given to a man against my will. But I do not wish love for any man, because of the love I have for you. I do not want this other man, unless you will refuse me. To find out your answer I have come."

"By God, here is my answer," he replied. "If I were allowed to choose any woman in the world, it is you I would choose."

"If that is your wish, before I am given to this other man, make an appointment with me."

"The sooner the better," said Pwyll. "Wherever you will, make the appointment."

"I will, my lord. One year from now at the court of Hyfaidd the Old," she said. "I will have a feast prepared."

"Gladly," he said. "I'll be there."

"My lord," she said, "farewell, and remember your promise. I must go now."

They parted. He returned to his house. When someone asked him about the maiden and what she said, he would change the subject.

After a year had passed and there came the appointed time, Pwyll decked himself out and went over to the court of Hyfaidd the Old. His arrival was greeted with joy. A great throng met him, rejoicing. The courtiers had made elaborate preparations for his arrival. They had expended all the resources of the court. The hall was prepared, and they went to the tables, Hyfaidd the Old on one side of Pwyll and Rhiannon on the other, and then everyone according to rank. They ate, drank, and made merry.

## The Stranger at the Feast

As they began their after-dinner drinks, a youth with brown hair, tall and with a princely air, wearing brocaded silk, came to the upper part of the hall and greeted Pwyll and his companions.

"God's welcome to you, my friend," said Pwyll, "come, sit down."

"I will not sit down," said the youth. "I am a petitioner, and I will perform my errand."

"Please do so," said Pwyll.

"My lord, I have a request for you. I have come to ask you for it."

"Whatever you ask of me, as far as I am able, it will be yours," said Pwyll.

"Ouch!" said Rhiannon. "Why do you give this answer?"

"That is how he has given it, my lady, in the presence of his nobles," said the youth.

"Well then, friend," said Pwyll, "what do you request?"

"You are about to sleep with the woman whom I love the most. It is to ask for her, along with the foodstuffs that are here, that I have come."

Pwyll fell silent. What answer could he give?

"Be silent as long as you like," said Rhiannon. "Has there ever been a man so slow with his wits as you?"

"My lady," he said, "I didn't know who he was."

"This is the man to whom they wanted to give me against my will," she said. "Gwawl son of Clud ["wall, son of wealth"], a man rich in hosts and lands. Because you have spoken, you must give me to him to avoid all dishonor."

"My lady," he said, "I don't know what you mean. I could never on my life do what you say."

"Give me to him," said Rhiannon, "and I will make it so that he can never have me."

"How will that be?" asked Pwyll.

"I will put a small bag in your hand. Keep it with you safely. He is asking for the feast and the foodstuffs, but they are not under your control. I myself gave the feast to the household, and that will be your answer regarding that. As for myself," she continued, "I will arrange a meeting with him, one year from tonight, to sleep with me. At the end of the year you will be in the orchard up there with this bag and a hundred horsemen. When he is in the middle of his merriment, come inside wearing shabby clothes with the bag in your hand. I will bring it about that whatever food and drink is put inside, the bag will be no more full than before. After so much has been placed in it, Gwawl will ask if your bag will ever be full. You will say it will not be unless a noble lord over many lands will press his feet down on the food in the bag and say, "Enough has been put inside." I will make him go and step on the food in the bag. Then turn the bag over until he goes head over heels inside. Tie a knot on the strings of the bag. Wear a good hunting horn around your neck. When he is tied up in the bag, give a blast on the horn. Let it be a signal to your men. When they hear the horn, they will descend on the court."

"My lord," said Gwawl, "It is time that I receive an answer to my request."

"Whatever you asked for," said Pwyll, "that is under my control, you can have."

"My friend," said Rhiannon, "about the food and the provisions here—these I have given to the men of Dyfed and the household that are here. I cannot allow them to be given away to anyone else. One year from now, however, a feast will be provided in this court for you, my friend, to celebrate your intercourse with me."

## The Invention of "Badger in the Bag"

Gwawl went back home to his country. Pwyll returned to Dyfed. The year passed until it was time for the feast at the court of Hyfaidd the Old. Gwawl son of Clud came to the feast prepared for him, and there was joy at his arrival. As for Pwyll, the Lord of Annwefen, he came to the orchard with a group of a hundred horsemen, just as Rhiannon had commanded him, carrying the bag. Pwyll had clothed himself in dirty rags and put big raggedy boots on his feet. When the after-dinner drinks had begun, he came down into the hall. He crossed to the upper part of the hall and greeted Gwawl and his company of men and women.

"May God bless you," said Gwawl, "and may the welcome of God be upon you."

"My lord," Pwyll replied, "may God repay *you*. I come before you with a request."

"Your request is welcome," Gwawl said "If your request is modest, then I will gladly grant it."

"Modest it is, my lord," he replied. "I ask nothing but relief from starvation. This is the what I ask: to fill this little bag with food."

"That is a humble request," said the other, "and one which you will receive, gladly. Bring him food!" Gwawl commanded.

A large number of courtiers got up and began to fill the bag. Yet however much they stuffed in, it was no more full than before.

"My friend," said Gwawl, "will your bag never be full?"

"By God, it will not," Pwyll replied, "no matter how much you put in there—that is unless a man rich with land, territory, and domains treads with both feet and says, 'enough has been placed herein.' "

"O hero," said Rhiannon, "get up right away and do it!"

"Gladly," he replied.

Gwawl got up and put his two feet into the bag. Pwyll turned the bag so that Gwawl was head over heels in the bag and, quickly closing it, he tied up the strings in a knot. He gave a blast on his hunting horn. At that signal, all his companions fell on the court and seized those who had come with Gwawl and took them prisoner. Pwyll threw off his rags, his old boots, and his shabby garment.

As each one of his companions came into the court, each would strike a blow to the bag and ask, "What is in the bag?"

"A badger," the others would reply.

So they played a game, each one striking a blow with his foot and staff. Thus they made sport of the bag.

As each one came up he would ask, "What game are you playing there?"

"Badger in the Bag" was the reply.

And that was the first time Badger in the Bag was ever played.

"My lord," said the man from the bag, "listen—it is not a fitting death, to be slaughtered in a bag."

"My lord," said Hyfaidd to Pwyll, the lord of the manor, "He speaks truly. You should hear him, that is not a fitting way for this man to die."

"Aye," Pwyll said, "Very well, I agree."

"Here is my advice," said Rhiannon. "We are in a position to give satisfaction to both petitioners and to minstrels. Let us allow Gwawl to give benefice to all on your behalf," she continued, "and establish guarantors against his making a claim against you or pursuing his revenge. That will be punishment enough."

"He will take that gladly!" shouted the man in the bag.

"And gladly I will accept it," replied Pwyll, "on the advice of Hyfaidd and Rhiannon."

"That is our advice," they replied.

"I accept it," said Pwyll. "Who will the guarantors be?"

"We will stand on his behalf," said Hyfaidd, "until his men are free to represent him."

They released Gwawl from the bag and set his men free.

"Now you must take guarantors from Gwawl," said Hyfaidd. "We recognize those taken from him." Hyfaidd then recited the names of the guarantors.

"Formulate the conditions," said Gwawl, "on your own terms."

"Just as Rhiannon formulated them," said Pwyll, "will be fine for me."

The guarantors agreed on those terms.

"Very well, my lord," said Gwawl, "I am injured. I have received serious wounds. I need a bath. With your permission, I will be on my way. I will leave some noblemen in my place who will answer to all who petition you for benefice."

"This is good," Pwyll replied, "if you do just that."

So Gwawl returned to his country.

## The Happiness of Pwyll and Rhiannon

The hall was all arrayed for Pwyll and the host of the court. They came and sat at the tables. As they were seated in the previous year, so they sat down this evening. They ate and drank and when it came time they went off to sleep. Pwyll and Rhiannon went to their chamber, and they passed the night in much mutual pleasure and satisfaction.

On the following morning, at dawn, Rhiannon said to Pwyll, "My lord, get up and begin the indulgence of the minstrels, and don't refuse anyone today what they might ask of you."

"I'll do it gladly," said Pwyll, "both today and every other day, while this feast still lasts."

Pwyll got up and ordered silence for the asking of any petitions the minstrels might have. He granted satisfaction to each of them according to his will and his fancy. And that was done. The feast went on in all abundance, so long as it endured.

When the feast was coming to an end, Pwyll said to Hyfaidd, "My lord, with your blessing, I will be heading off back to Dyfed tomorrow."

"Very well," said Hyfaidd, "may God give you a good ride. And when shall Rhiannon follow?"

"By God," said Pwyll, "we will travel from here together."

"Do you really wish, my lord, to do it this way?"

"In just this way, by God," replied Pwyll.

They set off for Dyfed. They went to the court of Arbeth. A feast was laid out for them. Many noblemen and noble women from the land came to them. Rhiannon bestowed on every one of them a special gift—a broach, a ring, or a valuable stone. They ruled the land in great prosperity for all that year and the next.

## The Penance of Rhiannon

In the third year a heaviness of spirit settled on the men of the land when they saw that the man whom they loved as lord and as foster-brother, Pwyll, had no heir. They summoned him to a meeting in the Precelli mountains in Dyfed.

"My lord," they said, "we know that you are not as old as some men in this land, but we are afraid that the woman you are with will never bear you an heir. You should take another wife who might bear an heir. You will not live for ever and although you may wish to continue the present arrangement, we will not allow it."

"Aye," said Pwyll, "we have been a long time together, and the future is an uncertain thing. Give me this year. We will reconvene a year from now, when I will allow you to judge me."

And so they agreed.

Before the end of the year, a boy was born to Pwyll. He was born in Arbeth. On the night when he was born, six women were brought in to keep watch over the boy and his mother. The women all fell asleep, along with the mother and the baby. They woke up again towards cock crow. When they awoke, they looked for the boy, but he was gone.

"My God," said one of the women, "the boy is lost!"

"Yes," said another, "we would be lucky just to be burned alive because of the boy."

"What shall we do?" asked another of the women.

"I can think of a way out," said the next woman.

"What is that?" asked the others.

"There is a stag-hound bitch here," she explained, "with puppies. Let us kill one of the puppies and smear its blood on Rhiannon's face and hands and leave its bones in front of her. We can accuse her of killing the baby. Against the word of the six of us, her word alone will not stand."

They agreed on this plan.

Towards day, Rhiannon awoke.

"Women," she asked "where is the baby?"

"O Lady," they replied, "Don't you ask us about the boy! We're all bruises and cuts from struggling with you! We have never seen such violence in a woman as in you last night, and struggling with you was no use. It was you that destroyed the baby yourself! Don't ask for him from us."

"O wretched creatures," exclaimed Rhiannon, "for the sake of the Lord God who knows all things, don't put this falsehood onto me! God who knows all things knows that this accusation is untrue. If you are afraid to tell the truth, I will protect you by God."

"God knows," they replied, "we won't suffer harm for anyone in the world!"

"O wretched creatures," said Rhiannon, "you'll come to no harm if you just tell the truth." But despite all she said she could not get the women to change their story.

Pwyll woke up. It was hardly possible to conceal what had happened. The news spread around the country and every nobleman heard it. The noblemen of the land came together and petitioned the king to cast aside his wife because of the terrible atrocity she had committed.

Pwyll replied, "There was never justification for those who wished me to put aside my wife other than that she had born no children. Now she has been with child, so I will not cast her aside. If she has committed a crime, let her take penance."

For her part, Rhiannon summoned her sages and wise men and, once she had decided that it was better to take penance than get involved in a quarrel with the women who were in her chamber, she went about taking her penance. The penance put on her was as follows: She must stay at the court of Arbeth for seven years. There was a block by the gate used to mount horses. She had to sit on it every day telling anyone who came the whole story and offering to carry on her back to the court anyone who desired it. But almost never did anyone allow her to carry them. Thus she passed the rest of the year.

At that time there was a lord, Teyrnon Teweryf Lliant, who ruled over Gwent Ys Coed. He was an excellent man. He had a mare, and nowhere in his realm was there horse or mare as beautiful as she. She would always give birth on the holiday of Beltane—the first of May—yet no one ever knew what happened to the foals.

One night Teyrnon was talking with his wife. "Wife," he said, "it is not right that we allow our mare to foal every year without our getting a single one of them."

"What can we do about it?" she asked.

"Tonight is May 1," he said. "May the vengeance of God fall upon me if I do not find out what is happening to these colts!"

He had the mare brought into the house. He armed himself and began his watch. As night was falling, the mare gave birth to a good-sized foal, perfectly formed, standing up on the spot. Teyrnon admired the sturdiness of the foal. As he was doing this, he heard a loud commotion, then an enormous claw reached through the window and seized the colt by its mane! Teyrnon drew his sword and severed the arm from the elbow down so that most of the arm, together with the colt, fell inside the room beside him.

Then he heard a great scream. He went out the door in the direction of the commotion. He could not see what was going on because of the darkness. He remembered that he had left the door open, so he returned, and by the door—lo and behold!—he saw a small child wrapped in swaddling clothes and a sheet of brocaded silk. He picked up the boy, and saw that he was strong for his age. He fastened the door and went to the chamber where his wife was sleeping.

"My lady," he said, "are you sleeping?"

"No, I'm not, my lord," she said, "I was sleeping and when you came in I woke up."

"Here is a child for you," he said, "if you want him. You have never had one."

"My lord," she exclaimed, "what has happened?"

"Well," said Teyrnon, "it happened like this ..." And he told her the whole story.

"But what kind of clothing is the child wearing?"

"Brocaded silk," he replied.

"Then he is the son of gentlefolk ..." said she. "My lord," she went on, "it would be a pleasure and a comfort to me if that is what you want. I could get the other women to speak for me and say that I had been pregnant."

"I'll gladly support you," he replied.

And so they did. The boy was baptized in the manner that they practiced in those days. They called him Gwri Golden-Hair, for the hair on his head was as yellow as gold.

The child was brought up in court until he was one year old. Before the end of his first year he was walking and was stronger than a three-year old. After another year, he was as strong as a six-year old. Before the end of the fourth year, he was making deals with the stable boys to be allowed to lead the horses down to water.

"My lord," said Teyrnon's wife to him one day, "where is that foal that you saved on the night we got the boy?"

"I put it in the care of the stable boys," he replied, "and asked them to look after it."

"Would it not be good, my lord," she said, "to break it in and give it to the boy? For the night we got the child, the foal was born."

"I will not go against that," replied Teyrnon, "and I will let you give it to him."

"My lord," she said, "May God repay you. I will give it to him."

She gave the horse to the boy. Rhiannon went to the grooms and ordered them to be careful of the horse, and to keep her informed, to tell her when it was to be broken in readiness for the boy.

In the meanwhile, they heard stories about Rhiannon and the penance she served. Teyrnon Teweryf Lliant listened for news and continually made inquiries. He heard many complaints from those who had been to the court about the wretched fate of Rhiannon.

Teyrnon thought about the situation. He looked closely at the boy, realizing that he looked similar in appearance to Pwyll Penn Annwefen, the closest resemblance he had ever seen. He knew very well what Pwyll looked like, for he had been at his court. He grew anxious, thinking how it was wrong to keep the boy when he knew him to be another man's son.

When he got a chance to talk privately with his wife he asked her if they should keep the boy, who was the cause of such punishment to a woman as fine as Rhiannon, as well as surely being the son of Pwyll Penn Annwefen.

Teyrnon's wife agreed to send the boy back. "And three things, my lord, we will get in return: thanks and gratitude for freeing Rhiannon from her penance, thanks from Pwyll for raising the boy, and if the boy becomes a noble man, he will be our foster-son and will always do what he can for us."

The following day Teyrnon equipped himself with two other riders and the boy as the fourth on the mare Teyrnon had given him. They set out to Arbeth. They soon arrived.

As they came towards the court, they saw Rhiannon sitting beside the mounting block. When they came up to her she said, "O Chieftain, go no further than that! I will carry every one of you to the court. And that is my penance for killing him who was my own son, and for his destruction."

"Good woman," replied Teyrnon, "I don't think that any of these people will be going on your back."

"Let him go who wants to," said the boy, "but I myself will not go."

"God knows, friend," said Teyrnon, "we will not go either."

They went into the court, and great joy greeted their arrival. They started in on the feast. Pwyll came back from his rounds in Dyfed. He came into the hall and washed. Pwyll welcomed Teyrnon and they sat down, Teyrnon between Pwyll and Rhiannon and the boy between the two companions of Teyrnon.

When the meal was finished and the drinking began, they chatted. Teyrnon told the whole story about the mare and the boy and how the boy had been in his own charge and the charge of his wife, and how they had raised him.

"Behold your son there, lady!" exclaimed Teyrnon. "Whoever told these lies about you has done you wrong. When I heard of your misery, I thought it wretched. It saddened me. But I think that there is no one here who would not believe this boy to be the son of Pwyll."

"There is no one," they all said, "who is not sure of this!"

"By God," said Rhiannon, "if that is true, I would be freed from my care."

"My lady," said Pendaran Dyfed ["chieftain of Dyfed"] "well did you name the boy "Pryderi" ["care, anxiety"]. It is best for him, Pryderi son of Pwyll Pen Annwefen."

"Let us be sure," said Rhiannon, "that his given name doesn't better suit him."

"What is his name?" asked Pendaran Dyfed.

"Gwri Golden Hair was what we called him."

"Pryderi will be his name," said Pendaran Dyfed. "It is fitting," said Pwyll, "that the boy takes his name from the first word uttered by his mother on hearing the good news about him."

In this way his name was decided.

"Teyrnon, God repay you for raising the boy up until this time. It would be right, if he grows up to be a noble man, that he should repay you."

"My lord," Teyrnon replied, "do not forget the woman who reared him. There is no one in the world who will miss him more. It would be right that he remember me and that woman for what we have done for him."

"By God," said Pwyll, "as long as I am alive I will maintain you and your people as well as I would my own. If he grows to adulthood, it is even more appropriate that he should continue maintaining you than I. And if it is your counsel, and that of these nobles, inasmuch as you have raised him up until now, we will give the boy to Pendaran Dyfed to foster from now on. And both of you will be friends and foster-fathers to him."

"That is good counsel," all agreed.

So the boy was given to Pendaran Dyfed and the noblemen of the country allied themselves with him. Teyrnon Twryf Lliant and his companions set off back to his own country in friendly contentment. The noblemen offered him the most beautiful treasures, the best horses, and the most highly prized dogs. But he did not want anything.

After that each remained in his own land, and Pryderi son of Pwyll Pen Annwefen was brought up with care, in the right way, so that he became the most faultless, the most handsome, and the most accomplished in all noble sports of any in the realm.

Thus they passed one year after the next until the life of Pwyll Penn Annwefen came to an end and he died. And Pryderi ruled the seven counties of Dyfed in prosperity and friendship with his countrymen and with those around him.

After that, he conquered the three counties of Ystrad Twyi and the four counties of Ceredigion: Those seven counties are called Seisyllwch. It came into the mind of Pryderi son of Pwyll Penn Annwefen to take himself a wife. The woman he desired was Cigfa, daughter of Gwynn Gohoyw, son of Gloyw Wallt, son of Casnar Wledic.

And thus ends this branch of the Mabinogion.

## OBSERVATIONS: FOLKTALE MOTIFS IN THE *MABINOGION*

The first Branch of the Mabinogion is really a collection of folktales, ripe with motifs from folklore, from the magical horse that can never be caught, to the virtuous but slandered wife, to the foundling. The Branch opens with a motif sometimes called the "chase of the white stag." Typically it begins with an impulsive desire to hunt. The protagonist is drawn into a wilderness setting where he becomes separated from his companions, often in pursuit of a strange, magical animal. Pwyll's initial offence is to drive off another man's pack, a pack not of this world. Then he fails to recognize a fellow king and show proper respect. Pwyll is in a compromised position: He has offended a powerful being on the border between their domains and must now recompense the other or risk a destructive enmity.

His behavior leads to what folklorists sometimes call the "otherworld sojourn." The purpose of Pwyll's sojourn in the symbolic underworld is to rid Arawen of the rival king Hafgan ("bright as summer") with whom he is locked in an irreconcilable conflict. The motif of shape-shifting turns up in the Arthurian story of the adultery between Uther Pendragon, the father of Arthur transfixed by lust for Igern, wife of the duke of Cornwall. While laying siege to the duke's castle, Uther Pendragon persuades the magician Merlin to transform his appearance into that of the Cornish lord to enable him to gain entry to the castle and have sex with Igern.

In the 14th-century poem *Sir Gawain and the Green Knight*, about two hundred years after the *Mabinogion*, the theme of seduction by an otherworldly hostess plays a central role in a game between Gawain, a young knight of Arthur's court, and the magical Green Knight. The action begins in Arthur's court at the feast of New Year's Eve. A tall, green-skinned knight huge in size and noble in bearing enters carrying an enormous ax. He challenges those seated at board. He will offer someone freedom to strike him as he wills, but in return the other must offer himself one year hence. Gawain, Arthur's nephew, takes up the challenge. He strikes the stranger with his own ax, cutting the Green Knight's head from the shoulders. Then to the horror of all, the Green Knight gets on his feet, picks up his head, and promises to appear at the Green Chapel one year hence. The mysterious knight disappears into the night.

Gawain comes early to the court of the Green Knight, who is not there. A host of the castle warmly greets Gawain. For three days in a row the host goes hunting. During his absence, the knight's wife visits the bedchamber of the young knight and attempts to seduce him. At the end of each day, the Green Knight offers Gawain the trophies he has taken during the day's hunt. Gawain must in return provide the Green Knight with the fruits of his own exploits. He had exchanged a platonic kiss on the cheek with the wife on each day, and so he kisses the knight.

When the year is up, Gawain meets the Green Knight in the Green Chapel—all along he was his host—and because Gawain was pure, he is protected from the full force of the Green Knight's blow, which only scratches his neck.

Combined with the taste for folklore is a kind of nightmarish quality to Welsh myth. For example, the lady on horseback recedes from her pursuers much as in a bad dream. The monster that snatches the foal on Beltane is the embodiment of nightmare. Pwyll and Arawen's exchange of identity, and the substitution of the child for the foal, suggest that you can never be sure of what is real, just as in a dream.

---

## Key Terms

| | | |
|---|---|---|
| Druids 332 | Emain Macha 335 | Cu Roi 345 |
| Ogham 332 | *The Cattle Raid* | Lugaid 346 |
| Cuchulain 333 | *at Cooley* 337 | *Mabinogion* 349 |
| Setanta 333 | Emer 343 | Pwyll 349 |
| Ulster 334 | Scathach 343 | Rhiannon 349 |
| Deichtine 334 | Derbforgaill 343 | Arawen 349 |
| Conchobar 334 | Medb 344 | |

---

## Further Reading

Ellis, P. B., *Celtic Myths and Legends* (New York, 2002).
Green, M. J., *Celtic Myths* (Austin, TX, 1993).
Llywelyn, M., *Red Branch* (New York, 1989). Historical novel about Cuchulain.
Neeson, E., *An Táin: Cuchulain's Saga* (Cork, Ireland, 2004).
Rees, B. and A. Rees. *Celtic Heritage: Ancient Tradition in Ireland and Wales* (New York, 1961).
Rolleston, T. W., *Celtic Myths and Legends* (New York, 1990).
Walton, E. B., Ballantine, *Mabinogion Tetralogy* (New York, 2002).
Yeats, W. B., *The Celtic Twilight: Faerie and Folklore* (1902; reprinted New York, 2004).

# CHAPTER
# 11

# Scandinavian Myth

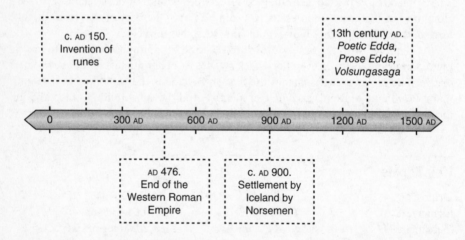

C. AD 150.
Invention of
runes

13th century AD.
*Poetic Edda,
Prose Edda;
Volsungasaga*

0      300 AD      600 AD      900 AD      1200 AD      1500 AD

AD 476.
End of the
Western Roman
Empire

C. AD 900.
Settlement by
Iceland by
Norsemen

The Germanic tribes fall into the east Germans, the west Germans, and—the subject of this chapter—the northern Scandinavians (Map 11). These tribes shared in some cases the same gods, but by no means was there anything like a unified religion or a unified body of myths among them. Principally, in studying the myths of the early Germanic tribes we study the traditions of the Scandinavians, because their stories are the earliest and by far the best preserved.

The importance to us of the traditions of the prehistoric Germans and Scandinavians is clear from the names of the days of our week. Sunday and Monday are the days of *Sun* and *Moon*. Tuesday is the day of *Tyr* (Old English *tiw*), equated by the Romans with Mars (as in French *Mardi* for the second day of the week), but probably once greatest of the Germanic gods; the name is cognate with the root of *Zeus* and *Jupiter*, that is, the Indo-European "shiner." Wednesday is *Wotan's* day, the Germanic form of the Scandinavian **Odin**, the one-eyed chief of the gods,

**MAP 11**   Scandinavia.

ruler over war, poetry, trickery, and wisdom, equated by the Romans with Mercury (hence French *Mercredi* for this day). Thursday is **Thor**'s day, son of Odin, hammer-wielding enemy of the race of the Giants. The Romans equated Thor with Zeus (hence French *Jeudi* for this day). He was also called Donar: In modern German, Thursday is *Donnerstag*. Friday is Freya's day, goddess of fertility (French *Vendredi*, day of Venus). Only our Saturday has a Roman name.

## WRITING AMONG THE NORSEMEN

The northern tribes had an early writing system called **runes** (probably "secret things"), attested from about AD 150 and used side by side with the Latin alphabet for over a thousand years. The use of runes declined radically around AD 1100, but never died out completely; even in modern times there are runic writings (Figure 11.1).

However, what exactly runes were used for remains unclear, but it is unlikely that any narrative myths were preserved in them. Mostly, they were used for magical purposes, to invest an amulet with power. According to the *Havamal* ("Sayings of the High One"), a largely gnomic poem embedded in the 13th century ***Poetic Edda*** (see following poem) giving advice for correct living, proper conduct, and wisdom,

**FIGURE 11.1**    The 9th-century Rok Runestone near Odeshog in southern Sweden, the longest known runic inscription in stone. The text is highly and deliberately obscure, but mentions the emperor Theodoric (who died in AD 526, nine generations before the stone), the Volsung Gunnar, and, in the last line, Thor. Evidently, one Varinn has carved this stone in commemoration of his dead son, whom he may himself have sacrificed. (INTERFOTO / Alamy)

Odin himself received the runes when he hung from a tree for nine days, a sacrifice to himself:[1]

> I [Odin] know that I hung on a windy tree nine long nights,
> wounded with a spear, dedicated to Odin,
> myself to myself, on that tree where no one knows its roots.
> No bread did they give me, nor drink from a horn.
> Downwards I peered. I took up the runes.
> I took them screaming, then fell back from there.

---

[1]For the Scandinavian texts, cf. O. Bray (ed. and trans.), *The Elder or Poetic Edda: Commonly known as Saemund's Edda,* Part 1, *The Mythological Poems* (London, 1908); H. H. Sparling (trans.), *Völsunga Saga: The Story of the Volsungs and Niblungs, with Certain Songs from the Elder Edda* (London, 1923). See also U. Dronke (ed. and trans.), *The Poetic Edda,* vols. I, II (Oxford, 1969, 1997); C. Larrington (trans.), *The Poetic Edda* (Oxford, 1996); P. Terry (trans.), *Poems of the Elder Edda* (Philadelphia, 1990); E. Magnússon and R. G. Finch (ed. and trans.), *The Saga of the Volsungs* (London, 1965); J. L. Byock (trans.), *The Saga of the Volsungs* (New York, 2000).

Francisco de Goya (1746–1828), Saturn Devouring His Children (detail), 1819–1823; oil on plaster transferred to canvas. (Museo del Prado, Madrid; Masterpics / Alamy)

Indian The Transfer of Babes early 19th century Watercolor, opaque watercolor, and gold on paper, Chazen Museum of Art, University of Wisconsin-Madison, Gift of Mr. and Mrs. Earnest C. Watson, 69.28.16

Lindow Man, a bog man discovered in 1984, c. AD 100 (?). (Mike Peel (www.mikepeel.net) http://en.wikipedia .org/wiki/File:Lindow_Man_1.jpg)

Diego Rivera (1886–1957), *The Great City of Tenochtitlan*, 1945. Detail of mural 4.92 × 9.71 m. in the Patio Corridor, Palacio Nacional, Mexico City. (Schalkwijk / Art Resource, NY, © ARS, NY)

A ceremonial platform with seven *moai* statues, dated to around AD 1450. Like almost all *moai*, they look inland, away from the sea. Local legend has it that these *moai* were put up in honor of the seven courageous navigators who first landed on the island. Easter Island, Chile. (Aurbina http://en.wikipedia.org/wiki/File:Moai_Rano_raraku.jpg)

Paul Gauguin (French, 1848–1903), *The Day of the Gods* (*Mahana no Atua*), 1894. Oil on canvas. (Russell Gordon / Alamy)

The death of Minnehaha. Minnehaha was the daughter of an arrow-maker and the wife of Hiawatha. Her name is Siouan for "laughing water," from the waterfall of that name near modern St. Paul, Minnesota. In this Romantic painting, set within a lodge, she lies half draped while ghostly spirits welcome her to the spirit world. Hiawatha holds his head in his hands in sorrow, and a female companion has collapsed against the bier. Oil painting by William de Leftwich Dodge (1867–1935), 1892. (Ivy Close Images / Alamy)

We know about the myths of the northern peoples mainly from two literary sources: the *Poetic Edda* and the *Prose Edda*, from sometime in the 13th century. They are Icelandic texts, written down by the most northwestern of Germanic peoples just at the time of the adoption of Christianity. The language is Old Icelandic, a form of Old Norse, a Germanic dialect. "*Edda*" means "great-grandmother" in Old Icelandic, but how or why it was applied to these books is not known—perhaps to indicate affectionate authority.

The *Poetic Edda* consists of anonymous poems written in a meter with four stresses per line, or with four stresses in one line and two in the next, and one alliteration per line. The lines are grouped into four-line stanzas, but the meter is scarcely recognizable to a modern ear. The ***Prose Edda*** (or *Lesser Edda*) was evidently written by **Snorri Sturluson** (1179–1241), a historian, poet, and politician who was assassinated in his basement at the age of 62. The *Prose Edda* consists of *Gylfaginning* ("the fooling of Gylfi"), a narrative of Norse mythology; the *Skaldskaparmal*, a book of poetic language; and the *Hattatal*, a list of verse forms. Often, items left obscure in the *Poetic Edda* are clarified in the *Prose Edda*.

## THE *POETIC EDDA*

Both Richard Wagner (1813–1883) and J. R. R. Tolkien (1882–1973) were steeped in the *Eddas* and take much from them. Let us here confine ourselves, however, to the poems in the *Poetic Edda*, which can be very opaque and obscure in their meaning, but are powerful poetry on mythical themes.

### "The Giantess's Prophecy"

Odin, wishing to know the future, questions a seeress, who remembers what it was like before the beginning of the world and can foresee what it will be like after the world's destruction. Evidently, the seeress belongs to the race of Giants, whom Odin compels to speak to him through the power of his magic. This poem is called "The Giantess's Prophecy":

Attention I ask from the sacred races,
from Heimdall's sons, both high and low.
You wish, O father of the slain, that I relate
ancient tales I remember of men long ago.

I, born of Giants, remember very well
those who gave me bread in the early days.
Nine worlds I knew, nine Giant women
with mighty roots beneath the earth.

The "sacred races" to which the giantess appeals are the races of humans. **Heimdall** is ordinarily considered to be the guard of the bridge Bifrost, that leads from this world to **Asgard** ("enclosure of the Aesir"), home of the gods, where is **Valhalla**, the hall of the heroes, but here Heimdall is father of humankind—to whom the giantess appeals. When **Ragnarok** comes, the final catastrophic battle between the gods and their enemies, Heimdall will awaken the gods to battle. *Ragnarok* means "fate of the gods," but is confused with *ragnarokkr*, "twilight of the Gods." Thus, *Götterdämmerung*, "twilight of the gods" in modern German, is the title and theme of the fourth opera in Richard Wagner's great *Ring* cycle (*Der Ring des Nibelungen*, 1876; see Perspective 11). "Father of the slain," to whom the giantess will relate her tales, is Odin himself, god of those who die in battle. The "nine worlds" the giantess knew, where those who nourished the giantess lived in the early days, are different levels on the tree **Yggdrasil** (**ig**-dra-sil, "Ygg's horse," Ygg being Odin) that supports the cosmos, whose "mighty roots" go deep into the earth; but it is not clear who the nine Giant women are.

## The Creation of the World

> Young were the years when Ymir lived.
> There was no sea nor cool waves nor sand.
> There was no earth, nor heaven above,
> but a yawning gap [*Ginnungagap*], and no grass to be found.
>
> Then Bur's sons raised up the level land,
> they made Midgard the mighty.
> The sun from the south warmed the earth's stones,
> and the ground grew green with leeks.
>
> The sun, moon's sister, from the south
> cast her right hand over the edge of heaven.
> She did not know where her halls were,
> nor did the stars know their places,
> and the moon did not know his own power.

Now the giantess tells of the origin of things, of the first days. We learn from the *Prose Edda* that **Ymir** is the Giant from whose dismembered parts the world was made. In the beginning was Ymir and a great gap, as in Near Eastern myth. We learn from the *Prose Edda, too,* that the cow Audhumla licked the first god Buri from the primeval ice. Buri's son was Bur, father of Odin and his two brothers, Vili and Ve—"Bur's sons"—who made the world **Midgard**, really "middle enclosure," the abode of humans, Middle Earth (Chart 11.1). Then the warm sun came into being, and vegetation. The moon came into being too, but the moon and the stars have not yet gained their present position.

> Then the gods went to their seats in the assembly,
> the sacred ones, and they held council.
> They named the night and her children,
> they named the morning and the midday,
> afternoon and evening, to reckon the years.
>
> The Aesir met on the plain of Idavoll.
> They built shrines and temples, timbered high.
> They set up forges and they worked the ore.
> They made tongs and fashioned tools.
> They played checkers in the meadows, at peace,
> they did not lack for gold,
> until three girl Giants came,
> mighty and powerful, out of Giantland.

The gods came together and established the regular cycle of day and night that marks the passing of time. The gods met at an unknown place called Idavoll. As in Mesopotamian myth, there are two tribes of gods, the **Aesir** (ā-sir) and, as we will learn, the **Vanir**. The leaders of the Aesir are Odin and his son Thor, whose weapon is the hammer **Mjolnir** (**myol**-nir, "crusher") (see Figure 11.2). The principal Vanir are Njord (ni-**yord**), a fertility-god, and his son and daughter, **Freyr** (**frā**-r) and **Freya** (**frā**-a), the female deity of love and fertility, with many cults throughout Scandinavia and Germany.

At first all was peaceful, and rich, in the land of the Aesir, until the **Giants** came, the enemies of the gods, and threw all into confusion. Sometimes the Giants are said to be hideous in appearance and sometimes very handsome or beautiful. They were the first created beings, even older than the gods. Ymir was a Giant. The Giants live in Giantland. They are not necessarily very large. At Ragnarok, the Giants will lodge

**FIGURE 11.2** This Viking runestone, discovered in a churchyard in Sweden in 1863, probably depicts Odin, Thor, and Freyr. There are two scenes under an arching runic text band that contains three names: Hrothvisl (?), Farbjorn ("far-traveling bear"(?)), and Gunnbjorn ("battle bear"(?)), presumably the dedicators of the stone. The lower panel has three figures who hold, from left to right, a spear, a hammer or club, and a sickle. Because the weapon of Odin was the spear Gungnir, and that of Thor the hammer Mjolnir, and because Freyr is identified with farming (thus the sickle), the figures have been identified as these three gods. A moon may appear behind Freyr, perhaps because of its association with fertility. They wear typical Viking Age clothing, including a cloak and in Odin's case a tasseled conical cap. The upper scene also has three figures. The seated figure holding a spear is probably Odin, the middle figure Thor, and the figure on the left Freyr. A large bird bends its head over Freyr, but it is not known why. The intertwined bands at the bottom of the picture are typical of Viking art. (Statens Historiska Museet, Stockholm; The Art Archive / Alamy)

their final assault on the gods, who though very powerful are by no means immortal and in fact perish at Ragnarok.

Next "The Giantess's Prophecy" gives a long catalogue of the names of dwarves, whom some god (the poem does not say who) made from the blood of the Ymir. Then:

> From the home of the gods came forth three gods,
> mighty and gracious. They found on land
> Ash and Embla, empty of might, empty of fate.
>
> They had no breath, they had no spirit,
> character, nor motion, nor lively hue.
> Breath gave Odin, spirit gave Haenir,
> vital spark gave Lodur and lively hue.

The three gods who come forth are Odin and his brothers Haenir and Lodur. Not much is known of *Haenir*, except that he is said to survive Ragnarok and to return as a god of prophecy. *Lodur* is probably an old name of the trickster-god **Loki**, sometimes said to be one of the Aesir. Loki plays an ambiguous role, sometimes favoring the gods and sometimes opposing them. He is best known for having contrived the death of the beloved god Balder (see "The Death of Balder"). The first humans come from Ash and Embla—that is, ash and elm trees—following a different tradition from that which makes Heimdall the father of all humans, and like the Greek stories in which ancient people descended from ash trees. Here the ash and elm trees are given breath by Odin, heart by Haenir, and life by Loki.

## The World-Tree and the War in Heaven

> I know an ash tree, Yggdrasil by name,
> a high tree, wet with loam.
> From there come the dews that fall in the valleys.
> Always green, it stands over the well of fate.
>
> From there come three girls, deep in wisdom,
> from the lake that stands beneath the tree.
> *Past* is the name of one, *Present* the next—
> they carve on the wood—and *Future* is third.
> Laws they made, and life allotted
> to the sons of men, and set their fates.
>
> The war I remember, the first in the world,
> when the gods struck Gollveig ["gold might"] with spears
> and in One-eye's hall they burned her.
> Three times they burned, and three times she was reborn,
> over and over, yet she is still alive.
>
> Heith ["bright one"] they called her who sought their home.
> The wide-seeing witch, with her magic,
> she bewitched their minds with spells.
> She was a joy to evil women.

At the base of the world-tree, Yggdrasil, is a well. In it live the three **Norns** (*Past, Present, Future*), the female fates, like the Greek fates. They carve runes on wood, making the rules for life and guiding every man's fate. Then there was war in heaven between the two tribes of gods, the Aesir and the Vanir, over the mistreatment of Gollveig ("Gold-Might"). Gollveig is probably a name for Freya, one of the Vanir. "One-eye" is Odin, who sacrificed one of his eyes to gain wisdom. Though they destroyed the goddess three times, she kept returning to life—as in the cycle of nature. Heith—the "wide-seeing witch"—is probably Freya too, who casts her magic spells over the Aesir in Asgard ("their home"), the goddess of witchcraft ("a joy to evil women").

> Then the gods went to their seats in the assembly,
> the sacred ones, and they held council,
> whether the Aesir should give up the tribute,
> or whether all the gods should partake of the sacrifice.

> Odin hurled his spear at the host.
> Then war first came to the world.
> The wall that girdled the Aesir was broken,
> and the savage Vanir trod on the field.

> Then the gods went to their seats in the assembly,
> the sacred ones, and they held council,
> to find who had mixed the air with venom,
> or had given Od's bride to the Giant race.

The war continued, now in a dispute about who should receive the tribute of sacrifice, the Aesir or the Vanir. Odin attacked the Vanir. The Vanir destroyed the wall surrounding Asgard and gained the advantage. Of the Giant Od, who married the Vanir Freya ("Od's bride"), little else is known. Snorri tells in the *Prose Edda* how, when peace was finally achieved between the Aesir and the Vanir, the Aesir employed a Giant as builder of the walls of Asgard. The Giant demanded the sun and moon as his reward and the goddess Freya for his wife, if he finished on time. Loki advised that the gods agree to the deal, but when the Giant made rapid progress, they delayed him by a trick. The enraged Giant then threatened the gods, and Thor killed him with his hammer (Figure 11.3).

## Heimdall's Horn

> In swelling rage Thor rose up.
> Seldom he sat when he heard such things.
> The oaths were broken, the words and promises,
> the mighty pledges they made between them.

> I know of the horn of Heimdall, hidden
> under the radiant, sacred tree.
> Over it there pours from the libation of Father of the Slain [Odin]
> a mighty stream—would you know still more?

**FIGURE 11.3**    Amulet in the form of Thor's hammer Mjolnir. With this weapon Thor defended the gods against the Giants. The decoration at the head of the hammer shows the stark staring eyes associated with Thor. AD 10th century, Viking, silver from Uppland, Sweden. (Statens Historiska Museet, Stockholm, Sweden; Werner Forman / Art Resource, NY)

Alone I sat when the Old One [Odin] sought me,
the terrible one of the Aesir, and he looked in my eyes.
"What have you to ask? Why do you test me?
Odin, I know where your eye is hidden
deep in the famous well of Mimir."
Each morning Odin drinks mead from Father of the Slain's
libation—would you know yet more?

Necklaces I had and rings from the Father of Hosts [Odin].
I received his wise speech, and the rod of divination.
Widely, widely I saw over all the worlds.

Thor was enraged when the oaths were broken with the Giant who rebuilt the walls of Asgard, when the agreement was not fulfilled. Now the Giant seeress singing this song turns from the past to future events. The horn of Heimdall is hidden beneath the tree Yggdrasil, apparently in the well Mimir, if that is what is meant by "libation of Father of the Slain." At Ragnarok Heimdall will blow this horn to wake the gods. Odin gave up one eye to the spirit of the well, Mimir, in return for wisdom. Odin drinks from the well every day. By the repeated question, "Would you know still more?" the seeress, who has received her powers from Odin ("the rod of divination"), addresses Odin directly, asking him whether, now that she has disclosed secrets of the past, he really wishes to know what is fated, what is to come.

## The Death of Balder

From all sides I saw Valkyries assemble,
ready to ride to the ranks of the gods.
Skuld bore the shield, and Skogul rode next,
Gunn, Hild, Gondul, and Spear-Skogul.
Now you have heard the list of the ladies of the general,
the Valkyries ready to ride over the earth.

I saw Balder, the bleeding god,
the son of Odin, his destiny concealed.
There stood grown slender and fair
in the lofty fields, the mistletoe.

From that plant that seemed so slender, so fair
came a harmful shaft that Hoth would hurl.
Balder's brother was soon born.
Odin's son began to fight when one night old.

The **Valkyries** ("choosers of the slain") choose the best warriors and bring them to Valhalla, to prepare for the great war that must come (Figure 11.4). According to the commentary in the *Prose Edda*, **Frigg**, the wife of Odin, demanded of all created things that they swear an oath not to harm **Balder**, the most beautiful and beloved of all the children of Odin. Frigg omitted only the mistletoe because she thought it was too weak ever to cause harm. Thus, it was a sport for the gods to hurl all kinds of weapons at Balder, who could never be harmed. Then the sometimes-evil Loki brought the mistletoe to Balder's blind brother, Hoth, and guided his hand in hurling the twig, thus killing Balder, the first of the great catastrophes soon to overtake the gods. Vali, brother to Balder, was now born to take revenge:

He never washed his hands, nor combed his hair,
until he brought Balder's foe to the funeral pyre.
And in the Swamp-halls Frigg wept
for Valhalla's need—would you know yet more?

I saw one bound with oppressive bonds,
severe bonds made of Vali's guts.
I saw one bound in the wet woods,
a lover of evil. I recognized Loki.
By his side sits Sigyn, nor is glad
to see her mate—would you know yet more?

The "Swamp-halls" are the palace of Odin's wife Frigg in Valhalla. Frigg's "need" is the loss felt for the murdered Balder. For revenge Vali, Balder's brother, bound Loki to a rock with the bowels of his son Narfi, who was torn to pieces by Loki's other son, Vali (not the Vali who is a son of Odin!). Above his head they fastened a serpent whose ghastly venom dripped onto Loki's face. Loki's wife, Sigyn, sat beside him with a basin in which she caught the venom, but when she turned away to empty the basin, the venom again covered his face, and the earth shook with Loki's struggles.

**FIGURE 11.4**   Viking picture stone from Tjangvide, Gotland (in the Baltic Sea, south of Stockholm), AD 9th century, discovered in 1844 on a farm. The picture shows a small man holding a cup on an eight-legged horse greeted by a lady with a drinking horn. Probably, the rider is Odin on his horse Sleipnir, and the woman is a Valkyrie. The hut-like structure in the upper left would be Valhalla. A dead man is above the rider. The man behind the lady appears to carry a bow, and he may be a dead man hunting with his dog. The figure in front of the horse's head is hard to interpret. A damaged runic inscription to the left of the field (not shown) means " . . . raised the stone in memory of Hiorulf, his brother." (Statens Historiska Museet, Stockholm; The Art Archive / Alamy)

## Giantland and the Land of Hel

From the east there pours through poisoned valleys
with swords and daggers the river Slith ["fearful"].
To the north there is a hall in Nithavellir ["dark field"]
made of gold, for those of Sindri's race.
And in Okolnir ["never cool"] stood another hall,
where the Giant Brimir had his beer-hall.

Now the seeress describes the homes of the enemies of the gods. The river Slith is in Giantland; probably, the swords and daggers are ice. "Sindri's race," who dwell in a hall of gold, is the race of dwarves. Brimir (probably Ymir) is the Giant from whose blood the dwarves were made.

I saw a hall standing far from the sun,
on Nastrond ("corpse strand"), and the doors face north.
Venom drops down through the roof vents.
The wall is woven of serpents.

I saw wading through wild rivers
men who foreswore oaths and murderers too,
and seducers of men's wives.
There Nidhogg ["dread biter"] sucks the bodies of the dead
and a wolf tears at the men—would you know yet more?

The seeress now describes the land of the goddess Hel, a daughter of Loki, where the sinful are punished. Nidhogg is a dreadful dragon who constantly gnaws at the roots of Yggdrasil until at Ragnarok the tree finally succumbs. The wolf is presumably **Fenris**, another child of Loki.

## The Fenris Wolf

The gods chained the wolf Fenris with the marvelous chain Gleipnir ("open one"), fashioned by a dwarf out of six things: the noise of a cat's step, the beards of women, the roots of mountains, the nerves of bears, the breath of fishes, and the spittle of birds. To gain the wolf's confidence, the god Tyr placed his right hand in the wolf's mouth, but lost it when Fenris realized that he had been bound. At Ragnarok Fenris will break loose and devour the sun:

The old Giantess sat in Ironwood
in the east, and she bore the brood of Fenris.
A certain one in a monstrous form
will snatch the moon from the sky.

The corpses of doomed men fall,
the house of the gods is red with gore.
Dark grows the sun, and in summer soon
come mighty storms—would you know yet more?

He sat on a hill and plucked his harp,
cheerful Eggther, the Giantess's herdsman.
A cock in Gallows-wood crowed,
that bright red Fjalar.

We do not know who this Giantess is, but her children by Fenris are the wolves Hati and Skoll, the first of whom steals the moon, the second the sun, leaving the world in darkness. Eggther, the (unknown) Giantess's herdsman, seems to be the watchman of the Giants, as Heimdall is of the gods; he is not mentioned elsewhere. The crowing of the cock Fjalar will wake the Giants for the final struggle against the gods at Ragnarok.

## Ragnarok Begins

Then Gold-comb crowed to the Aesir.
He wakens the heroes in Odin's hall.
Another crows beneath the earth,
the rust-red cock at the bars of Hel.

Now Garm howls loud before Gnipahellir ["cliff-cave"],
the fetters will break and the wolf run free.

My wisdom is great. More I can see
of the fate of the gods, mighty in fight.

"Gold-comb" is the cock that wakes the gods and heroes at Ragnarok, as
Fjalar wakes the Giants. The "rust-red cock" wakes the inhabitants of Hel. Garm
is a hellhound who guards the gates of the kingdom of Hel. He will fight and kill
the god Tyr at Ragnarok. Gnipahellir is the entrance to the land of Hel. The wolf
is Fenris.

Brothers will fight and kill each other,
brother and sister will violate their kinship.
It is hard on the earth, adultery rampant,
ax-time, sword-time, shields are cleft,
wind-time, wolf-time, before the fall of the world.
No man will spare another.

The sons of Mim are at play, and fate
is heard in the Giallar-horn.
Heimdall blows loud, the horn is aloft,
Odin speaks with Mim's head.

Yggdrasil shakes, the upright tree,
ancient it groans and the Giant is loose.
All on the road to hell are in terror,
before the kin of Surt swallows it up.

The sons of Mim are unknown, but Mim is probably the same as Mimir, the
spirit of the well of wisdom at the base of Yggdrasil. The Giallar-horn, "shrieking
horn," of Heimdall calls the gods to the last battle. We learn from the *Prose Edda* that
after the war between the Aesir and the Vanir, the Aesir sent Mimir to the Vanir as a
hostage, where his wisdom was evident. The Vanir beheaded him and sent the head
back to the Aesir. Odin embalmed it and through his magic compelled the head to
give good advice. Odin consulted the head at the time of Ragnarok. The "Giant" here
is Fenris. What is swallowed up is unclear, but Surt is a fire-spirit, the Giant who rules
the fiery world called Muspellheim ("flame land"). The "kin of Surt" must therefore be
fire, a poetic circumlocution called in Old Norse poetry a "kenning."

Now Garm howls loud before Gnipahellir,
the fetters will break and the wolf run free.
My wisdom is great. More I can see
of the fate of the gods, mighty in fight.

Hrym comes from the east, his shield held high.
The serpent writhes in Giant rage.
He churns the waves, while the eagle screams
and pale-beaked gnaws the corpses. Naglfar is loose.

Over the sea from the east sails a ship
with Muspell's people, Loki at the helm.
Wild men follow the wolf,
and with them goes the brother of Byleist.

Hrym is a frost-Giant, helmsman of the ship Naglfar. The serpent is the **Midgard Serpent**, a child of Loki. He completely encircles the land. The eagle is the Giant Hresvelg, who sits at the edge of heaven, beating his wings and driving the winds. Naglfar is a ship made of dead men's fingernails that carries the Giants to battle. Muspell is a Giant. The wolf is Fenris, and the brother of Byleist is Loki; nothing else is known of Byleist.

## The Death of Odin

What of the Aesir? What of the elves?
All Giantland groans. The Aesir are in council.
The dwarves roar loudly before their stone door,
the masters of the rocks—would you know yet more?

Surt fares from the south with the harm of branches.
The sun of the battle-gods shines from his sword.
The crags are split, the troll-women wander abroad,
men tread the road to hell, and cloven is the sky.

A second hurt comes to Frigg
when Odin advances to fight the wolf.
And Beli's bright slayer seeks out Surt.
The joy of Frigg must fall.

The "harm of branches" is a kenning for fire, over which Surt is the ruler. The first hurt that came to Frigg was the death of Balder. Now she must see Odin killed by the Fenris wolf. The Vanir Freyr, brother of Freya, killed the Giant Beli with a deer horn—"Beli's bright slayer"—for he had given away his sword to a servant to arrange a marriage with the beautiful Giantess Gerd. Now Freyr must fight, and succumb, to the Giant Surt at Ragnarok. The "joy of Frigg" is Odin.

## Thor and the Serpent

Siegfather's ["father of victory"] mighty son,
Vidar, advances against the Beast of Slaughter.
He stabs Loki's son to the heart.
Thus his father is avenged.

In the air gapes the Earth-girdler.
Against the serpent goes Odin's son.
Its terrible jaws loom above.
The son of Odin must meet the serpent.
Vidar's kin is the death of the wolf.

The glorious son of Odin
advances against the serpent.
In his anger the defender of earth strikes.
All men must flee their homesteads.
Nine steps makes the son of Fjorgyn
with difficulty, from the serpent who is never scorned.

The sun turns black, earth sinks in the sea,
the hot stars whirl from heaven.
The stream rises fiercely into the air,
a high flame plays against the heaven.

Now Garm howls loud before Gnipahellir,
the rope will break, the wolf run free;
My wisdom is great. More I can see
of the fate of the gods, mighty in fight.

Odin is Siegfather, the "father of victory." His son Vidar, the silent god, is
famous for his great shield and strength, which are almost as great as Thor's. He
survives Ragnarok and kills Fenris. The "Beast of Slaughter" is Fenris, Loki's son,
who kills Odin at Ragnarok. The "Earth-girdler" is the Midgard Serpent, abroad in
the water that surrounds the world. Thor is Odin's son, who attacks the Midgard
Serpent. "Vidar's kin is the death of the wolf" means that Vidar's killing of Fenris
is something close to his heart, like a brother. Thor's killing of the serpent is a contest that shakes the world. After killing the serpent, Thor, the son of Fjorgyn, can
barely move ("nine steps" made "with difficulty"). Thor is overcome by the Midgard
Serpent's venomous breath and dies ("The sun turns black . . .). Garm's howling
signals the commencement of Ragnarok, when Fenris runs free (before being killed
by Vidar).

## The World Renewed

But the world will be born anew after Ragnarok:
Now do I see the earth coming up a second time,
rise all green from the waves, earth from the ocean.
The waterfall tumbles, the eagle flies,
hunting fish on the mountain.

The Aesir meet in Ithavol,
they speak of the terrible Earth-girdler.
They call to mind the mighty past
and the ancient runes of the Ruler of Gods.

Again in wondrous beauty once
will golden tables stand in the grass,
which the gods possessed in ancient times.

Without sowing the fields bear fruit,
all ills healed, and Balder returns.
Hod and Balder, lords of slaughter, will dwell together
in the sages' houses—would you know yet more?

Then Hoenir will choose wooden slips for prophecy,
and the sons of the brothers will inhabit
the windy world—would you know yet more?

The "terrible Earth-girdler" is the Midgard Serpent. The "Ruler of the Gods" is Odin. In the Edenic new world a resurrected Balder will return with the brother who killed him, a symbol of the new age of peace. Hoenir, an obscure god, will have the gift of prophecy through manipulation of the runes. The "sons of the brothers" are the gods and "windy world" is heaven.

> I see a hall fairer than the sun,
> thatched with gold, on Gimle it stands.
> There will the noble lords live,
> and take pleasure in all their days.
>
> Then comes from on high, the almighty lord,
> to the judgment place of the gods.
> From below comes the dark dragon,
> the shining serpent, up from Dark-of-the-moon Hills.
> Nidhogg flies over the plain. He bears
> the bodies of men on his wings.
> Now must I sink down.

Gimle is evidently the mountain on which the new hall is built, the home of the happy dead. The "almighty lord" must be Odin, returned to life. Many have suspected Christian influence in the reference to the judgment of the dead, but we cannot be sure of that. There may be something wrong with the text because the "dark dragon" that comes from below belongs to Ragnarok, unless he symbolizes evil in the world, now overcome. Nidhogg is the serpent who gnaws at the world-tree, Yggdrasil. In the last line, the prophetess evidently sinks into the earth or relapses into ordinary form after her shamanic prophecy.

So ends "The Giantess's prophecy."

## OBSERVATIONS: THE NORSE PICTURE OF THE COSMOS

Many of the elements in these powerful myths are familiar from the myths of other peoples. The Midgard Serpent is like the Indian Ananta, except it is malevolent. Thor's killing of the serpent is like Marduk's overwhelming of the dragon Tiamat, except that Thor dies in turn from its venomous breath. The war in heaven between the Aesir and the Vanir is like the war between the demons and the gods in Indian myth, or the Olympians and the Titans or Giants in Greek myth. Ragnarok, the end of the world, is like the periodic dissolution of the world envisioned in Indian myth.

But Scandinavian myth is characterized throughout by a dark pessimism, a notion that it is only a question of time before Heimdall will pick up his horn and blow. The Giants have attacked. Odin is lord of all, but he is a lord of death, presiding over the death of warriors and death in sacrifice. He is one-eyed because he had to give up an eye in order to gain the gift of prophecy. Tiu gave up his hand to the Fenris wolf, that he might be bound, but in the end the wolf will escape and devour the world. All advantage is gained through sacrifice, but the advantage is temporary, only forestalling the inevitable doom that awaits. Yes, the world will be reborn, but the focus is always on its destruction: hardly surprising that these Nordic myths inspired German soldiers dying for the fatherland in the Second World War, certain in their death to be received into the bounteous halls of Valhalla. The infamous battalions of SS troops, responsible for unspeakable crimes during the Second World War, wore two runes on their collars standing for *Schutzstaffel*, "protection staff."

## THE VOLSUNGS

For some reason someone in Iceland decided to write up the story of **Sigurd** the Volsung (the same as the German *Siegfried*) in a prose treatise, called a saga, sometime in the 13th century AD. There are several of these sagas from roughly the same time, contemporary with the *Poetic Edda*. The origin of the prose saga is a puzzle, because ordinarily we associate the stories of heroic behavior with poetry. Probably, the ***Volsungasaga***, "the story of the Volsungs," written in Old Icelandic, a German dialect, is a summary in prose of stories known from now lost poetic sources. Sometimes the saga quotes short passages from these sources.

According to the *Volsungasaga*, there was a son of Odin, Sigi by name, who got into trouble because he killed his host's slave ("thrall"), who had surpassed Sigi in the hunt (Chart 11.1).

To escape the trouble, Sigi traveled across the sea, acquired a kingdom, married, and begot a son called Rerir. Soon the brothers of Sigi's wife's killed Sigi (a prominent theme in Norse myth), but his son Rerir succeeded in taking control of the kingdom. Rerir then put to death his uncles, the brothers of Sigi's wife, for killing his father.

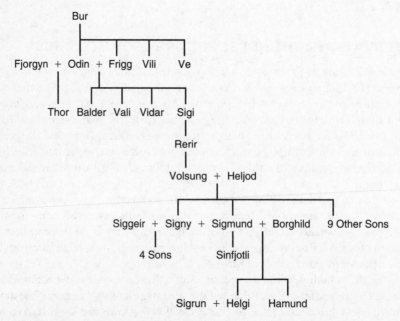

**CHART 11.1**    Odin and his descendants.

Rerir's wife became pregnant, but, after carrying the child for six years (!), she begged that it be cut from her. And so it was. She named the child **Volsung** and then died. Volsung grew up and took over the kingdom. He married Hljod (**hel**-jōd), and fathered ten sons and one daughter. The eldest son was **Sigmund**, the daughter was Signy. A king called Siggeir (the element *sig-* in names means "victory") wished to marry Signy. He came to the hall of the Volsungs for the wedding festival. Suddenly, there appeared at the feast a tall, gray man, with one eye, wearing a cowl that covered his face, and barefoot. He walked to an immense tree that grew at the center of the hall, piercing the ceiling (like Yggdrasil), and plunged his sword into the tree. He said—the stranger is of course Odin—"He who draws this sword from the tree shall receive it as a gift from me, and he shall prove that he has never wielded a better sword than this one."

All of the guests, including King Siggeir, tried to pull the sword from the tree, but could not. Sigmund, however, easily pulled the sword from the tree. Although Siggeir offered three times its weight in gold, Sigmund refused, saying that he would never give up the sword, so obviously meant for him alone, no matter how much gold Siggeir offered.

Siggeir feigned indifference, but announced that he needed to return home. King Volsung should come in three months' time, to make up for the foreshortened feast. And so he did, only to be attacked by Siggeir and his men to get even for the slight of Sigmund in refusing to give up the sword.

King Volsung was killed and his 10 sons taken captive. At their sister Signy's request, the sons were put in stocks instead of being killed outright. On the first night, a she-wolf came and ate the first brother; on the second night, he ate the second brother, and so on, until only Sigmund was left. Signy secretly gave him honey to rub on his face, and in his mouth, and when the she-wolf came, she licked his face and then put her tongue in his mouth. Sigmund bit down on the tongue. The wolf pushed back so hard as to break the stock, then the tongue was pulled from its roots and the she-wolf died.

Sigmund took up residence in a secret underground chamber. King Siggeir thought that all the sons of Volsung were now dead. Signy had borne two sons to Siggeir, but when she sent them to Sigmund as helpmates, they proved frivolous, and at the mother's request, Sigmund killed them. Then she changed shapes with a sorceress and went to Sigmund in the guise of the sorceress and slept with him. Pregnant with the child of her own brother, she gave birth to **Sinfjotli**, whom Sigmund accepted as a secret understudy.

Father trained son (though Sinfjotli did not know that Sigmund was his father) in the arts of rapine and murder. Once they found two men under a spell in a hut, who were allowed only every 10 days to remove their wolf skins. Father and son—Sigmund and Sinfjotli—stole the wolf skins and put them on, but then could not take them off. In this form they killed many, but succeeded in breaking the spell on the 10th day. They removed the skins and burned them.

At last Sinfjotli was fit to accompany Sigmund in avenging the death of King Volsung, Sigmund's father. The two men sneaked into Siggeir's palace and hid among the casks of wine, but one of the two additional children whom Signy had recently borne to King Siggeir discovered them. The young boy told his father about the two men in the room. On Signy's advice Sinfjotli killed the children, then came into the room and threw their corpses at the feet of King Siggeir. A great battle ensued in which many died, and Sigmund and Sinfjotli were taken captive.

To prolong their death Siggeir had a hollow tomb built and the men strapped to either side of a stone divider within it. But Signy managed to smuggle to Sigmund the magical sword that Odin had placed in the tree growing in the court of King Volsung. With it Sigmund cut in two the huge stone divider and then sawed his way out of the tomb. They went into the palace and set it on fire, killing Siggeir and all his retainers. Signy confessed to Sinfjotli and Sigmund that Sinfjotli was really the son of their incestuous union and that she had dedicated everything to taking revenge on her husband Siggeir for his murder of Volsung. Nonetheless, it was a wife's duty to die with her husband. She kissed the two young men good-bye and walked into the burning palace.

Sigmund returned to his kingdom, took control from a usurper, and ruled successfully. He married one Borghild and had two sons, Helgi and Hamund. Helgi grew to be an able man, who led military expeditions at the age of 15 side by side with Sigmund's son Sinfjotli, his half-brother.

One day Helgi went raiding and killed several brave men. At the edge of the forest stood Sigrun, a beautiful woman with her train, the daughter of King Hogni. She was about to be married to Hodbrodd, a man she did not like or want. Helgi promised to kill Hodbrodd. He gathered a large force of men, boarded a ship, and sailed through a storm to Hodbrodd's realm. After a ferocious fight, Helgi was victorious. He married Sigrun and ruled happily ever after in what had been Hodbrodd's kingdom.

Sinfjotli returned home, having earned great distinction for his deeds. He saw a woman whom he desired, but the brother of Borghild, Sigmund's wife and his stepmother, wanted her too. After a great battle Sinfjotli killed the brother. Sigmund offered wergild ("man-money") consisting of much gold to Borghild for his son's killing of her brother. She took the wergild and held a great feast at the funeral. But at the feast she gave Sinfjotli poisoned wine. He fell down dead. Sigmund took up his dead son in his arms and walked to the edge of the fjord. A man was standing there in a small boat. He gave him his son's body and then the boat disappeared (the man was Odin). Sigmund drove out Borghild, who soon died.

Sigmund proved to be the finest king anyone had known, and he ruled for many years. He heard of the beautiful Hjordis (hi-**or**-dis) and wished to marry her. He went to her palace on the understanding that he had not come to fight. There another suitor, King Lyngvi, appeared, but Hjordis chose Sigmund, although he was old. He returned with this bride Hjordis to his own country.

Soon, however, King Lyngvi appeared with a large force, determined to fight. The battle went on for a long time, and Sigmund performed many deeds of slaughter. Then a man appeared to him wearing a slouch hat and a hooded cowl. He was blind in one eye—Odin, again. Sigmund struck the man's spear, but Sigmund's sword—which Odin had once plunged into the tree in the court of King Volsung—broke in two. Sigmund and all his retainers were struck down (Figure 11.5).

Hjordis went to the battlefield and found Sigmund, who still lived. He told her he did not wish to live any longer, but that she was to bear a child who would

**FIGURE 11.5** Many of the symbols on this stone from Gotland from the 8th century AD seem to refer to the cult of Odin. The three interlocking triangles are known as a *valknut*, the "knot of the slain." They are adjacent to an eagle, Odin's bird, in front of a tree from which a man is hanging. Above the tree flies a figure (hard to make out, her head is to the left), probably a Valkyrie. Below the *valknut* are two men, one with a spear, who seem to place a corpse inside a burial mound, or to be sacrificing a prisoner on an altar. Behind, to the right, stand four warriors, three with shields and upraised swords led by a fourth man who holds a large bird of some kind. (Larbro, Gotland (Statens Historiska Museet, Stockholm; sacrificial_scene_on_Hammars_(I).jpg: Berig http://en.wikipedia.org/wiki/File:Sacrificial_scene_on_Hammars_(II).png));

be known throughout the world. She was to take the pieces of his broken sword. When reforged they would make the sword **Gram**, famous in battle. In the meantime, Alf, son of King Hjalprek the Dane, a Viking, landed with a force, and captured the women of Sigmund's court. Hjordis had traded places with her slave, but the truth soon came out, and Alf, admiring her beauty, married her, pregnant as she was with Sigmund's child.

Sigurd was born, destined to be the greatest warrior of ancient times (Chart 11.2).

His foster-father was **Regin** the smith, son of Hreidmar, according to a social custom of adoption among the Norsemen. Regin taught Sigurd sports, chess, and how to read the mysterious runes. Sigurd received a horse from Odin, a child of the

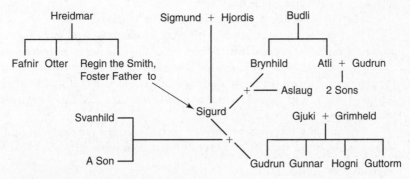

**CHART 11.2** Sigurd, son of Sigmund.

eight-legged Sleipnir (Figure 11.4) named Grani. Regin taunted Sigurd because he had no treasure, but said that a serpent named **Fafnir** guarded a great treasure that he might take. Fafnir, oddly, was Regin's brother. Regin forged Gram from the broken pieces of Sigurd's father Sigmund's sword. So sharp was the blade that Sigurd cut Regin's anvil in half! It cut a puff of wool floating downstream against it right in half!

But first Sigurd had to avenge the death of his father, Sigmund. He gathered many. They went a-Viking across the sea, to the land of the sons of King Lyngvi and his many brothers.

## SIGURD AND FAFNIR

After a ferocious battle, Sigurd killed Lyngvi with Gram and cut his brothers in half. Sigurd returned home rich in the vengeance he had taken for his father's death. The time had come to kill Fafnir and take the treasure, as the 13th-century *Volsungasaga* reports:

> Now Sigurd and Regin rode up the shrubby uncultivated land along that same way where Fafnir crept when he went to the water. They say that the cliff was two hundred feet high along which Fafnir lay when he drank of the water below.
>
> Then Sigurd said, "You said, Regin, that this snake was no greater than other worms, but his tracks are huge."
>
> Regin said, "Make a hole and sit down in it. When the worm comes to the water, strike him to the heart and to death, and thereby win great fame."
>
> But Sigurd said, "What will happen to me if I get in the way of the dragon's blood?"
>
> Regin said, "What's the use in giving you advice if you are afraid of everything? You are little like the Volsungs in stoutness of heart."
>
> Then Sigurd rode over the bushy land, but Regin ran off in fear. Sigurd dug a pit. While he was working an old man with a long beard came up to him and asked what he was doing, and he told him.
>
> Then answered the old man, "You have been given bad advice. You should dig many pits and let the blood run in them. You sit down in one of them, and so thrust the worm through the heart."
>
> Then he vanished.° Sigurd made the pits as he showed.
>
> Now the worm crept down to his place of watering. The earth shook all around him, and he snorted forth poison on all the road before him as he went. Sigurd neither trembled nor was afraid at its roaring. When the worm crept over the pits, Sigurd thrust his sword under its left shoulder so that it sank in up to the hilt. Then up leapt Sigurd from the pit and drew the sword back, and his arm was bloody up to the shoulder.
>
> When that mighty worm saw that he had received the death-wound, he lashed out his head and tail, and everything that was near him was broken to

°*he vanished*: the man is Odin.

pieces. He asked, "Who are you? And who is your father? And what are your kin, that you were so hardy as to bear weapons against me?"

Sigurd answered, "Unknown to men is my kin. I am called a noble beast. Neither have I a father, nor mother, and all alone have I come here."°

Fafnir said, "Whereas you have neither father nor mother, of what wonder were you born? But now, although you will not tell me your name on this my death-day, yet you know well that you are lying."

He answered, "Sigurd am I called, and my father was Sigmund."

Says Fafnir, "Who egged you on to this deed, and why would you be driven to it? Did you never hear that everyone is afraid of me, and of the look of my helmet of terror? You had a good father, O boy with the bright eyes!"

Sigurd answered, "A hardy heart urged me on, and a strong hand, and this sharp sword, which made this deed possible. Rarely is an old man brave who was a coward in his youth."

Fafnir answered, "My speech angers you, but let me say that my gold will bring your downfall."

Sigurd said, "Everyone wants wealth until that day comes, yet every man dies once and for all."

Fafnir said, "You pay my counsel little heed, but be careful of drowning if you travel unwarily over the sea. Stay on the dry land until it is calm."

Then Sigurd said, "Speak, Fafnir, and say, if you know so much, who are the Norns who rule the lot of all mothers' sons?"

Fafnir answers, "There are many Norns, and far apart. Some are kin to the Aesir, and some to the Elves, and some are the daughters of Dvalin."°

Sigurd said, "What do you call the island where Surt and the Aesir mix and mingle the water of the sword?"°

"Oskapt° is that island called," said Fafnir. Then he said, "Regin, my brother, has brought about my end. It gladdens my heart that he will kill you too. Thus it is according to his will."

Again he spoke, "A helmet of terror I showed to the people after I brooded over my brother's inheritance,° and on every side I spewed poison so that none might come near me. I feared no weapon. There were never so many who stood before me that I did not think myself stronger than all. Everyone feared me."

Sigurd answered and said, "Few may gain victory by means of that same cap of terror, for whoever fights among many shall one day learn that no one being is the mightiest of all."

°. . . *alone have I come here*: Sigurd holds back his name because he fears that Fafnir will curse him. °*Dvalin*: a dwarf. °*water of the sword*: at Ragnarok. °*Oskapt*: "the uncreated" °*brother's inheritance*: that is, Otter, the brother of Regin and Fafnir. In another story, when Loki killed Otter, the gods were compelled to cover Otter's skin with gold, the origin of Fafnir's treasure.

Fafnir dies. Sigurd takes possession of the gold.

Thereafter Regin came to Sigurd and said, "Hail, lord and master, a noble victory you have won in the killing of Fafnir. Before, no one dared remain in his path. Your deed of fame will last as long as the world."

Then Regin stared at the ground for a long while and spoke from a gloomy mood. "You have killed my own brother, and scarce may I be called innocent of the deed."

Sigurd took his sword Gram and dried it on the ground. He spoke to Regin: "You went far away when I did this deed. I used this sharp sword with my mighty hand. I had to strive with the might and main of a dragon while you hid in the fields, not knowing if it were earth or heaven."

Regin said, "This snake might have stayed long in his lair if I had not made for you this sharp sword. Otherwise, not you, nor anyone else, would have been successful against him."

Sigurd answered, "In a hard fight the spirit is superior to the sword."

Then Regin said, with great sadness, "You have killed my brother and scarce may I be called innocent of the deed."

Sigurd cut out the heart of the worm with the sword called Ridill.° Regin drank of Fafnir's blood and said, "Do me a favor of little trouble to you. Carry the heart to the fire, and roast it, and give it to me to eat."

Sigurd went and roasted the heart on a spit, and when the blood bubbled out, he put his finger on it to see if it was done. Then he put his finger in his mouth, and lo, when the blood of the heart of the worm touched his tongue, straightway he could understand the voice of birds. He heard the nuthatches chirping in the brush near him, saying, "There you sit, Sigurd, roasting Fafnir's heart for another. You should eat it yourself. Then you would become the wisest man in the world."

And another said, "There lies Regin, who wants to deceive the man who trusts him."

But yet again said a third, "Let him strike off his head and be lord of all that gold."

And once more a fourth spoke and said, "Yes, it would be smart to follow that counsel, then ride to Fafnir's lair and take that mighty treasure that lies there, and then ride over to Hindarfell° where Brynhild sleeps. There he will find great wisdom. Yes, he would be wise to follow your advice and think of his own wellbeing. 'Where wolf's ears are, wolf's teeth are near.' "

Then cried a fifth, "Yea, he is not so wise if he spares him whose brother he has already killed."

At last spoke a sixth, "It would be a wise course if he were to kill Regin and take the treasure!"

Then said Sigurd, "The time has not come when Regin might do me harm. No, one road shall both these brothers travel."

And he drew his sword Gram and cut off Regin's head [Figure 11.6].

°*Ridill*: another sword than Gram. °*Hindarfell*: a mountain.

**FIGURE 11.6**  Sigurd kills the treacherous Regin with his sword, detail from the saga of Sigurd. Viking, AD 12th century. Wood carving from the Hylestad stave church, Setesdal, Norway. (Universitetets Oldsaksamling, University Collections, Oslo, Norway. INTERFOTO / Alamy)

Sigurd goes to Fafnir's lair and takes the gold, loading it onto his horse Grani (Figure 11.7).

## SIGURD AND BRYNHILD

Sigurd rides to Hindarfell and soon sees a great light before him, rising into the heavens. He goes within a rampart of shields and finds a man in armor, asleep. He removes the helmet and finds that it is a woman—**Brynhild** (*bryn*, "mail-coat," *hild*, "battle"), sister to **Atli** (Attila the Hun, AD 406–453) and daughter of Budli (perhaps inspired by a Visigothic princess Brunhilda, who married the French king Sigebert I in 567). He cuts the mail armor from her chest, and she awakens. She is a Valkyrie who had dared to oppose Odin, and Odin has touched her with the thorn of sleep. Brynhild gives Sigurd advice about comportment and behavior. He says he will marry her, and she agrees that she can marry no one else.

**FIGURE 11.7**  Drawing of scenes from the life of Sigurd as engraved on a flat rock close to Ramsund, near Södermanland, Sweden, carved around AD 1000. (1) Sigurd sits naked in front of the fire, cooking the heart of Fafnir for his foster-father, Regin, Fafnir's brother. He touches the heart before it is ready, burns himself, and puts his burned finger into his mouth, thus inadvertently gaining the power to understand the speech of birds. (2) The birds tell Sigurd that Regin is planning to kill him. (3) Instead, Sigurd cuts off Regin's head, his tools lying nearby by which Regin reforged the sword Gram. (4) Regin's horse is loaded with Fafnir's treasure. (5) Sigurd kills Fafnir. (6) Otter, the brother of Regin and Fafnir. The runic inscription reads, "Sigrithr, Alrikr's mother, Ormr's daughter, made this bridge for the soul of Holmgeirr, father of Sigrithr, her husbandman." There are many references to bridges on monuments of this period, either the bridge to the other world or an actual bridge which the family has commissioned (after *Nordisk familjebok*, 1876–1899: http://en.wikipedia.org/wiki/File:Sigurd.svg).

Then Sigurd travels to a large estate, owned by Heimir, who had married Brynhild's sister, Bekkhild (*bekk*, "bench"). Heimir is Brynhild's foster-father, an honorific relation among the early Germans. Soon after Brynhild arrives, and Sigurd sees her—whom of course he already knew—when his hunting hawk alights near her window. He tells the story to a courtier named Alswid:

> Sigurd said, "Good friend, listen to what I have to say. My hawk flew up into a certain tower, and when I went there to get him I saw a beautiful woman. She sat by a needlework of gold in which she portrayed my past deeds, and deeds that are to come."
>
> Alswid said, "You have seen Brynhild, Budli's daughter, the greatest of great women."
>
> "Yes, I see," said Sigurd, "When did she get here?"
>
> Alswid answered, "There was a short interval between your coming and hers."
>
> Sigurd said, "Yes, I learned just a few days ago that she is the best of the world's women."
>
> Alswid said, "Do not pay attention to just one woman, given the sort of man you are. No point in spending all your time lamenting what you cannot have."

"I shall go to meet her," said Sigurd, "and I shall gain her mutual affection and love, and I will give her a gold ring as token of our love."

Alswid answered, "None has ever sat beside her to whom she would give drink. Ever she is minded of war and the winning of renown."

Sigurd said, "I do not know for sure if she will answer me or allow me to sit beside her."

On the next day, Sigurd went to her chamber while Alswid stood outside the bower door, making arrow shafts.

Now Sigurd spoke, "Greetings, my lady. How do you fare?"

She answered, "I do well. My family and my friends are still alive. But who can say what will happen in the end?"

He sat down beside her, and in came four women with great golden beakers filled with the best of wine. They stood before the couple. Then said Brynhild, "That seat is granted to few, except when my father comes."

He answered, "Now it is granted to whoever pleases me."

The room was hung with beautiful tapestries, and the floor was covered with cloth.

Sigurd spoke, "Now it has come to pass even as you promised."

"Do be welcome here!" she said and arose along with the four women. She carried a golden goblet to him and offered him a drink. He stretched out his hand to the goblet and took it, and her hand too. He drew her down beside him and threw his arms around her neck. He kissed her, saying, "You are the most beautiful woman who has ever lived."

But Brynhild replied, "Ah, wiser not to put your trust in a woman. For they always break their promises."

He said, "That day will be happiest when we can enjoy each other."

Brynhild answered, "It is not fated that we should live together. I am a shield-maiden. I wear a helmet like the kings of war. I often help them. Battle is dear to my heart."

Sigurd answered, "Our lives will be most fruitful if we live together. Otherwise this pain in my heart is harder to bear than the stab of a sharp sword."

Brynhild answered, "I must review the hosts of the war kings, but you will wed Gudrun, the daughter of King Gjuki."

Sigurd answered, "No king's daughter shall entrance me! I have no doubts about this. I swear by the gods that I shall have you for my own, or no other woman."

And she said very much the same thing to Sigurd.

Sigurd thanked her for her speech and gave her a gold ring. Now they swore an oath anew, and he went away to his men, and was with them for awhile in great bliss.

Now King Gjuki had three sons, **Gunnar**, Hogni, and Guttorm, and a daughter **Gudrun**. His wife was Grimheld, a ferocious woman with great magical powers (Chart 11.2). Sigurd came to the hall of Gjuki, laden with the gold from the treasure of Fafnir. There he was warmly received. Seeing him as a fine son-in-law, Grimheld, the determined mother of Gudrun, gave Sigurd a draft of forgetfulness during the nightly

## PERSPECTIVE 11

## The *Ring Cycle* of Richard Wagner

Wilhelm Richard Wagner (1813–1883) was a German composer, conductor, and essayist, best known for his operas. Wagner's works are famous for their complex texture, rich harmonies, and the use of leitmotifs—musical themes associated with individual characters, places, or plot elements. The complex interweaving and evolution of leitmotifs illuminates the progression of the drama. Unlike most other composers of opera, Wagner wrote both the music and libretto.

Wagner transformed opera through his concept of the *Gesamtwerk*, the "total work of art" that achieved a synthesis of all visual, musical, and dramatic aspects of the performance. He announced his new ideals in essays published between 1849 and 1852. He built his own opera house in Bayreuth, Bavaria, where his works are still performed. There he made many innovations in theater craft, including darkening the auditorium during performances and placing the huge orchestra in a pit out of view of the audience. Wagner's music is the beginning of modern music because he explored the limits of the traditional tonal system, pointing the way to atonality in 20th-century music.

Wagner realized his concept of *Gesamtwerk* most fully in his four-opera cycle *Der Ring des Nibelungen*, "the ring of the Nibelung," based loosely on Norse and German myth, especially the Old Norse *Poetic Edda* and *Volsungasaga* and the Middle High German *Nibelungenlied*, "song of the Nibelungs." The *Nibelungenlied* is a 12th-century poem rediscovered in 1755 and immediately hailed by German Romantics as the "German national epic." The poem tells of the death of Siegfried (= Norse Sigurd), its principal character.

Wagner worked on the *Ring Cycle* for 26 years (1848–1874). In it he attempted to imitate Athenian drama in which groups of four plays were performed at the Athenian festival of Dionysus. The four plays of the *Ring* are *Das Rheingold* ("the gold of the Rhine," 1854), *Die Walküre* ("The Valkyrie," 1856), *Siegfried*, and *Götterdämmerung* ("Twilight of the Gods," 1869–1874). The plays require about 15 hours of performance over four nights, the only undertaking of such scope today on the world's stages.

The Nibelung of the title is the dwarf Alberich, and the ring is one he makes from the Rhine gold stolen from the Rhine maidens, who live in the Rhine River. In *Das Rheingold* Alberich manufactures the ring, which grants domination over the world. The epic story begins in *Die Walküre* and follows the struggles of gods, heroes, and mythical creatures to take possession of the magic ring, especially the efforts of Wotan (= Norse Odin), chief of the gods. Wotan's grandson Siegfried at last wins control of the ring, as Wotan planned, but he is betrayed and killed. Finally, the Valkyrie Brunhilda (= Norse Brynhild), Siegfried's lover and Wotan's estranged daughter, returns the Ring to the Rhine maidens. At last the gods and their home, Valhalla, are destroyed in the gloomy *Götterdämmerung*.

Wagner's influence on literature and philosophy was significant. Friedrich Nietzsche (1844–1900) was part of Wagner's inner circle during the early 1870s and his first published work, the influential *The Birth of Tragedy* (1872), proposed Wagner's music as the Dionysian rebirth of European culture in opposition to Apollonian rationalist decadence. In the 20th century, W. H. Auden (1907–1973) called Wagner "perhaps the greatest genius that ever lived," while Thomas Mann (1875–1975) and

Marcel Proust (1871–1922) were influenced by Wagner and discussed him in their novels. He figures in some of the works of James Joyce (1882–1941). Wagnerian themes appear in T. S. Eliot's (1888–1965) *The Waste Land* (1922), which contains lines from *Götterdämmerung*. Many of Wagner's concepts, including his speculation about dreams, predate their investigation by Sigmund Freud (1856–1939). Some film scores have utilized Wagnerian themes, for example Francis Ford Coppola's *Apocalypse Now* (1979), which features the "Ride of the Valkyries." Adolf Hitler (1889–1945) greatly admired Wagner's music and saw in his operas his own vision for the German nation. Because of Wagner's antisemitism (he wrote against "Jewish music"), the performance of his music in Israel has been a source of controversy.

J. R. R. Tolkien's *The Lord of the Rings* (1937–1949) appears to borrow elements from *Der Ring des Nibelungen*, though Tolkien said that "both rings were round, and there the resemblance ceases." Tolkien and Wagner drew on the same source material, including the *Volsungasaga* and the *Poetic Edda*. But Tolkien does seem indebted to Wagner, for example in having the ring give its owner mastery of the world; in the ring's inherently evil nature; in its corrupting influence on the minds of its possessors; and in the need for the ring's destruction in order to redeem the world. Both rings are cursed and return to their first owner. Bilbo finds the Ring while heading to the abode of the dragon Smaug; Siegfried takes the Ring from Fafnir's hoard. Wagner's and Tolkien's dragons both watch over a hoard they stole from the dwarves. Gandalf resembles the Wanderer (Wotan in disguise), who wears a gray cloak and great hat and uses his spear as a staff. The Eye of Sauron looks like Wotan's missing eye, which he lost in order to obtain the world's knowledge.

carousing. Suddenly, Sigurd forgot about Brynhild completely. He saw that Gudrun was attractive, and after two and one half years at the castle, he married her. They lived like one grand family, going forth in the day and killing the sons of kings and taking their wealth for booty.

Grimheld then complained that her son Gunnar had everything but a wife. He should ask Brynhild to marry him, she said, and Sigurd would accompany him. When they arrived at Brynhild's chamber, they found it encircled by a ring of fire. Gunnar's horse would not cross it, and even Grani, which Sigurd loaned to Gunnar, would not cross it. Then the two men changed shape, a magical trick they had learned from Grimheld. Grani responded to Sigurd who thus crossed the fire, but in the form of Gunnar:

> When Sigurd had passed through the fire, he came to a lovely dwelling where sat Brynhild.
> She asked, "Who is it?"
> Then he named himself Gunnar, son of Gjuki, and said, "You are awarded to me as my wife by the good will and word of your father Budli and your foster-father Heimir. I have ridden through the flame of your fire, according to your requirement."
> "I do not know," she said, "how to answer you."

Sigurd stood up straight and leaning on the hilt of his sword he said, "I shall pay a generous marriage settlement of gold and other precious things in exchange for your hand."

She answered in a dark mood from her seat, where she sat like a swan on a wave, with a sword in her hand and a helmet on her head, clad in mail. "O Gunnar, speak not to me of such things unless you are the first and the best of all men, and you will kill all those who ask for my hand, if you have the heart for it. I have been in battle with the king of Gardariki° and my weapons were stained with crimson blood. I still yearn for such things."

He answered, "Yes, surely you have accomplished many great deeds. But remember your oath, when you swore you would go with the man who crossed the fire."

She admitted that he spoke the truth. Heeding his words, she arose and received him. He stayed there three nights in one bed together, but he took the sword Gram and laid it between them. She asked why he laid it there, and he answered that he must in this way wed his wife, or else die.°

Then she took off the ring that Sigurd had given her before and gave it to him, and Sigurd (disguised as Gunnar) gave her another ring from Fafnir's hoard.

Thereafter, Sigurd rode away through the same fire to his friends, and he and Gunnar changed appearances again. They rode into Hlymdale and reported how it had gone with them.

That same day Brynhild went home to her foster-father Heimir and told him, whom she trusted, that a king had come to her. "And he rode through my flaming fire, and said he had come to seek my hand, and he called himself Gunnar. But I said that only Sigurd might have done such a deed, with whom I swore an oath on the mountain. He is my first husband."

Heimir said that there was nothing to do but accept what had happened.

Brynhild said, "Aslaug, my daughter by Sigurd, shall be raised here with you."°

Now the kings went home, but Brynhild went to her father. Grimheld welcomed the kings appropriately, and thanked Sigurd for his fellowship. A great feast was held, to which many were invited. Budli the king came with his daughter Brynhild, and his son Atli, and for many days did the feast endure. At the feast Gunnar was wedded to Brynhild. When it came to an end, once more Sigurd remembered all the oaths that he swore to Brynhild, but he did not let this be known. Brynhild and Gunnar sat together at the entertainment and drank good wine.

°*Gardariki*: "the kingdom of cities," probably referring to a chain of Norse forts in Russia. °... *or else die*: the implication is that he did not sleep with her because he wished to preserve her virginity for Gunnar; but see below. °...*here with you*: apparently, Sigurd had slept with Brynhild when they first met on the mountain.

One day while bathing in the river Brynhild taunted Gudrun about who had the best husband, saying that Gunnar was better than Sigurd because he had crossed the ring of fire. Gudrun replied by telling her the truth, which somehow she knew, that it was *Sigurd* who crossed the fire in Gunnar's shape. To prove it Gudrun showed Brynhild the very ring that Sigurd had given Brynhild in her chamber, that Brynhild gave to the man she *thought* was Gunnar, and that Sigurd had given to Gudrun!

Now Brynhild sank into a ferocity of hatred against Sigurd for his treachery and in fact the whole world. She went to her bed and would not rise. Gunnar went in to her, and Brynhild said to him:

"What did you do with that ring that I gave you, the one which my father King Budli gave me at our last parting,° when you and your father King Gjuki came to my father and threatened fire and the sword unless you had me to wife? At that time my father led me apart and asked me whom I had chosen of those who had come. I prayed that I might defend the land and be chief over the third part of his men. But my father gave me two choices, either to wed the man he chose, or lose his goodwill. He said that his friendship would be better than his wrath. I wondered if I should bow to his will, or kill many a man. It seemed to me that it was pointless to strive with my father. Thus I promised to wed whoever rode the horse Grani through my flaming fire, and whoever killed those men whom I called on him to kill. *Sigurd* rode through the fire because he had the courage to do so. He slew the dragon Fafnir, and Regin, and five kings besides.

"But you, Gunnar, have done nothing of the kind, pale like a corpse. You are no king and no champion. I made a vow to my father that I would love only the noblest man alive. This is none other than Sigurd. I have broken my oath. I have brought it to nothing because he is none of mine, and for this cause I shall bring about your death. And a great reward of evil things do I have for Grimheld, your mother, as her reward. Never, I know, has there lived a woman more evil or more base."

Gunnar answered so that few might hear him. "Many a vile word you have spoken! You are an evil-hearted woman. You revile a woman, my mother, far better than you. Never would she be so discontent, nor has she tormented the dead, or murdered anyone. She lives her life well, praised of all."

Brynhild answered, "I have had no secret meetings, nor committed any crimes. Yet I would gladly kill you."

And thereupon would she have killed Gunnar, but his brother Hogni placed her in chains.

Gunnar said, "I don't want her to lie in chains."

Then she said, "Don't be concerned about that! For never again will you see me happy in your hall, never drinking or at the chess board, never speaking words of kindness, never embroider the fair cloths with gold, never give you good counsel. Ah, my sorrow of heart, that I might not take Sigurd to me!"

Then she sat up and struck her needlework, ripping it apart. She opened the doors of her chamber so that far away the wailings of her sorrow might be heard. There was great mourning and lamentation heard throughout the stronghold.

°*at our last parting*: but Sigurd, not King Budli, gave it to her at their meeting in Brynhild's chamber; Brynhild is dissembling because she does not want to say that she received the ring from Sigurd as a pledge of their love.

Sigurd speaks to Brynhild, assuring her of his undying love, but she spurns him rudely. She goes to Gunnar and says that Sigurd must die, or else she will leave him.

Gunnar regrets to kill a friend, and also he has sworn an oath to Sigurd, as did his brother Hogni. But the third son of Budli, Guttorm, did not swear the oath. Through persuasion and magic they coerce Guttorm to perform the deed.

At first Guttorm was afraid, but while Sigurd slept Guttorm sneaked in and stabbed him. Sigurd awoke and threw his sword Gram at Guttorm, cutting him neatly in half. While dying, Sigurd swore to Gudrun, who lies beside him, that he had never touched Brynhild (when he slept with a sword between them . . . but he slept with her earlier, hence the child). He dies in Gudrun's bloody arms:

> Now was the dead corpse of Sigurd arrayed according to ancient tradition, and a high pyre was raised. When it was fully kindled, they laid on it the dead corpse of Sigurd, the bane of Fafnir, and his three-year old son° whom Brynhild had put to death, and Guttorm too. And when the pyre was all ablaze, Brynhild went upon it and told her chambermaids to take the gold that she wanted them to have. And so she died, burned by the side of Sigurd. Thus their days of life came to an end.

> °*three-year old son*: by Gudrun.

Gudrun, devastated by Sigurd's death, traveled to a castle in Denmark. Her mother Grimheld, learning where she was, came with a great entourage. She informed Gudrun that now she must marry Atli, the brother of Brynhild, and Grimheld promised her great wealth and lands in return for accepting the match. Gudrun had no choice. She journeyed to Atli's castle and there married him in a match sure to turn sour.

Now King Atli wondered where the treasure of gold was that Fafnir had once guarded and how he might get his hands on it. The gold was surely in the possession of Gunnar and Hogni, he thought, so the king invited them to a great banquet, although Gudrun, suspecting treachery, had warned them not to come.

When the party arrived, Atli and his men immediately attacked them. After a ferocious battle in which many of Atli's allies were killed, Gunnar and Hogni were taken captive. Atli cut out Hogni's heart and showed it to Gunnar, saying that this would be his fate unless he told him where the gold was hidden. Still he would not talk, and so Atli imprisoned him in a pit filled with snakes. Gudrun sneaked in a lyre, however, which Gunnar played so beautifully that all the snakes fell asleep, except one particularly hideous serpent who crawled under Gunnar's shirt and bit him to death.

A great funeral feast was held both for Atli's men and Gudrun's brothers Gunnar and Hogni:

> But Gudrun did not forget her sorrow. She brooded on how she might work some mighty shame against the king. At nightfall she took her sons by King Atli as they played about the floor. The youths were downcast and asked what she would do with them.

> "Ask me not," she said. "You shall die, the both of you!"

> Then they answered, "You may do with your children what you wish, nor shall anyone stop you. But shame there is in this deed."

> For all that she cut their throats.

When the king asked where his sons were, Gudrun answered, "I will tell you, and gladden your heart by telling. You caused me a great sorrow in the killing of my brothers. Now see what I have done. You have lost your sons. Their skulls are beakers on the table. You have yourself drunk their blood blended with the wine. I have taken their hearts and roasted them on a spit and you have eaten them."

King Atli answered, "You are a grim woman for murdering your sons and giving me their flesh to eat! Little time there is between one evil deed and the next!"

Gudrun said, "My heart is set on doing to you the greatest shame as I am able. No punishment can be cruel enough for such a king as you are."

Later, when Atli was stupefied with drink, a surviving son of Hogni and Gudrun stabbed him to death. Gudrun attempted suicide by drowning, but the sea carried her to the fortress of a King Jonakr, who married her. She bore him three children. When a previous daughter by Sigurd named Svanhild committed adultery with her husband's son, her husband had her trampled to death by horses. Gudrun's sons by King Jonakr avenged Svanhild's death, but they themselves were killed.

And so ends the story of Volsungs!

## OBSERVATIONS: THE SAGA OF THE VOLSUNGS

The Norse sagas come from a time when violence was a way of life. To be excellent was to be more violent than your neighbors, to kill and maim a path to status and glory. The stories are filled with treachery and honor, made possible through magical devices: the sword of Sigmund, the shape-shifting of Gunnar and Sigurd, the fire that surrounds Brynhild. A main scene in the story of Sigurd the Volsung is the slaying of a dragon, but not a trace remains of the cosmogonic meaning of such a deed that we find in Near Eastern myth. The dragon simply guards a great treasure of the sort that every Viking longed for in his endless raids.

Animals and humans slip in and out in a curious tangle. Regin is human, but one brother is an otter and the other a dragon. We are never sure why Regin wishes to kill Sigurd, for Regin made it possible for Sigurd to kill his brother Fafnir. Regin is of course a smith, a class both feared and despised and closely associated with magical practices. In Norse society, as in primitive societies, the smith was the man who made the weapons that did the killing that earned one status. His means were secretive and dangerous.

We saw the same shape-shifting in the Irish story of Pwyll and Anwen, but there the purpose was to eliminate a dangerous enemy. Here the motif supports the romantic encounter that makes clear Sigurd's virtue, but in the end proves his undoing. Brynhild, said to be a Valkyrie, is a surprising character in her preference for martial exploits; otherwise, little is made of her association with the Valkyries, dread spirits who appeared in battle to select those who would die. Of course in a sense she selects Sigurd to die, and she is truly furious in her love and dedication.

Over the entire saga of the Volsungs hangs the specter of Odin and his cult of death and dying. He stabs the magic sword into the tree and then breaks the sword when Sigmund's time has come. Regin mends the sword, only to die by means of it. Brynhild has somehow offended Odin, but serves his ends in arranging for the death of Sigurd and his children. Gudrun is no better, in serving up a drink of blood in the skulls of her own children. All is darkness and blood, revenge, and the lust for gold. Scant wonder that one day the Fenris wolf will one day escape its bonds and the world will collapse in chaos and fire.

## Key Terms

| | | |
|---|---|---|
| Odin 364 | Aesir 369 | Sigurd 380 |
| Thor 365 | Vanir 369 | *Volsungasaga 380* |
| runes 365 | Mjolnir 369 | Volsung 381 |
| *Poetic Edda 365* | Freyr 369 | Sigmund 381 |
| *Prose Edda 367* | Freya 369 | Sinfjotli 381 |
| Snorri Sturluson 367 | Giants 369 | Gram 383 |
| Heimdall 367 | Loki 370 | Regin 383 |
| Asgard 367 | Norns 371 | Fafnir 384 |
| Valhalla 367 | Valkyries 373 | Brynhild 387 |
| Ragnarok 367 | Frigg 373 | Atli 387 |
| Yggdrasil 368 | Balder 373 | Gunnar 389 |
| Ymir 368 | Fenris 375 | Gudrun 389 |
| Midgard 368 | Midgard Serpent 377 | |

## Further Reading

Crossley-Holland, K., *The Norse Myths* (New York, 1981).
Davidson, H. R. E., *Gods and Myths of Northern Europe* (New York, 1965).
Faulkes, A., trans., *Edda* (New York, 1987).
Lindow, J., *Norse Mythology: A Guide to Gods, Heroes, Rituals, and Belief* (Oxford, 2002).
Page, R. I., *Norse Myths* (Austin, TX, 1990).
Young, J. I., *The Prose Edda: Tales from Norse Mythology* (Berkeley, CA. 1954).

# The Myths of Mexico

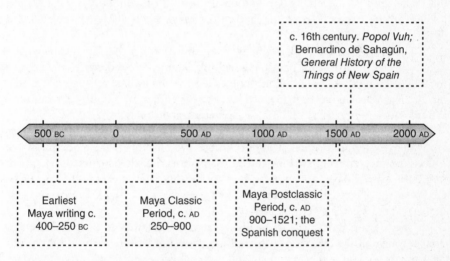

c. 16th century. *Popol Vuh;*
Bernardino de Sahagún,
*General History of the
Things of New Spain*

500 BC     0     500 AD     1000 AD     1500 AD     2000 AD

Earliest
Maya writing c.
400–250 BC

Maya Classic
Period, c. AD
250–900

Maya Postclassic
Period, c. AD
900–1521; the
Spanish conquest

The Maya of Yucatan were the most highly developed of the peoples who occupied the American continent before the arrival of Europeans. As far as we can tell, Maya civilization was a wholly native development, without traceable influence from the Old World. The surest proof is found in the unique nature of American art, the result of countless centuries of isolation. American language, arithmetic, and methods of time reckoning, too, bear no resemblance to other systems, European or Asiatic. This is not surprising, because the inhabitants of the Americas were separated from the Old World for tens of thousands of years.

Furthermore, nearly all the cultivated food-plants found on the continent at the period of the discovery were totally different from those known to the Old World. Maize, cocoa, tobacco, the tomato, the potato, and chilies were new to the European conquerors. Absent were virtually all domestic animals that had made Old World civilizations possible—the horse, camel, donkey, cow, sheep, goat, pig, chickens—eloquent proof of the prolonged isolation that the American continent underwent after its original settlement by humans. This settlement took place at an unknown time, but is constantly being pushed back by new discoveries, certainly to 30,000 BC and perhaps even to 80,000 BC, when the Bering Strait formed a land bridge connecting Asia and America. Because of its very long separation from the Old World, human development in the New World has always served as a kind of test case to determine what is essentially human instead of what is essentially cultural.

## MAYA CIVILIZATION

The Maya civilization had the only known American system of writing, although the Aztecs developed a kind of picture writing accompanied by occasional phonetic elements in names. We cannot say when writing originated in the New World, but evidently some time before the Classic Period, c. AD 250 to AD 900, when Maya centers reached their highest development. A vigorous Maya culture continued throughout the Postclassic Period after c. AD 900 until the Spanish conquest in AD 1521. At its peak in the Classic Period, the land of the Maya was a densely populated and dynamic society.

The Maya civilization shares many features with other Mesoamerican civilizations, especially maize as the basis of agriculture. Women ground maize into a coarse meal by rubbing it with a grinding stone called a *mano* against a flat stone called a *metate*. The Mesoamericans made tortillas from the corn meal. Additional crops were avocados, beans, squash, sweet potatoes, tomatoes, and chilies.

Such institutions as writing and the calendar did not originate with the Maya, but with a mysterious people called the OLMECS, who lived near the modern town of VERACRUZ. However, both writing and the calendar reached their highest development under the Maya. Maya influence can be found in the modern states of HONDURAS, GUATEMALA, BELIZE, and northern EL SALVADOR as far as central MEXICO, especially in the YUCATAN peninsula (Map 12).

The Maya peoples have never disappeared. Today, they form sizable populations throughout the Maya area with a distinctive set of traditions and beliefs resulting from the merger of preColumbian and postconquest Spanish culture. Many Maya languages are spoken as primary languages today.

The Maya territory encompasses a vast and varied landscape, from the mountainous regions of the MAYA HIGHLANDS to the arid plains of northern Yucatan. Climate can vary tremendously. Low-lying areas are particularly susceptible to the hurricanes and tropical storms that frequent the CARIBBEAN. The Maya have inhabited this territory from time immemorial. Recent discoveries of Maya occupation in Belize, including monumental structures, are carbon dated to around 2600 BC. The Maya calendar commences on a date equivalent to August 11, 3114 BC.

The Classic Period (c. 250–c. 900 AD) witnessed the peak of large-scale construction and urbanism, monumental inscriptions, and high intellectual and artistic development, particularly in the southern lowlands where the Maya developed intensive agriculture and numerous independent city-states with such major ceremonial centers as TIKAL, PALENQUE, COPAN, and UXMAL. The most notable monuments are the stepped pyramids they built to serve their cult of human sacrifice. A priest held the victims' arms and legs while the priest, often under the influence of psychotropic

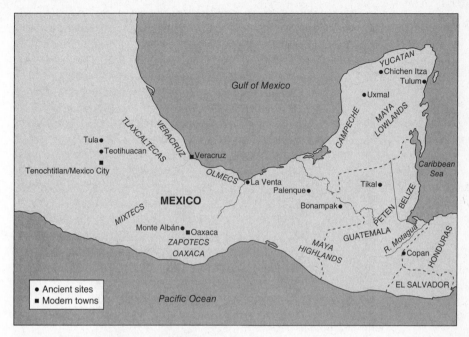

**MAP 12**    Mesoamerica.

drugs, cut open the victim's chest and tore out his living heart as an offering to the god. The body was then thrown down the steps of the temple, roasted, and eaten, at least in part (Figure 12.1; cf. Figure 12.9).

Other important archaeological remains include the palaces of the kings and carved stone slabs that depict rulers along with written texts describing their genealogy, military victories, and other accomplishments (Figure 12.2).

For unknown reasons the Maya centers declined during the 8th and 9th centuries AD and were abandoned shortly thereafter. Monumental inscriptions and large-scale architectural construction came to an end, although during the succeeding Postclassic Period, from the 10th to the early 16th century, the Maya cities of the northern lowlands in Yucatan continued to flourish until conquered by the Spanish in lengthy and difficult campaigns. Unlike the Aztec and Inca empires, there was no single Maya political center that, once overthrown, would end resistance from the indigenous peoples. Instead, the forces of the conquistadors needed to subdue the numerous independent Maya centers one by one, many of which put up a fierce resistance. The conquest was not complete until 1697.

A typical Classic Maya center was headed by a hereditary ruler. Such kingdoms were usually no more than a local center of power with several lesser towns, although there were greater kingdoms that controlled larger territories. The royal household, and especially the person of the king, was central. None of the Classic Maya cities shows evidence of economic specialization and commerce on the scale of Aztec **TENOCHTITLAN** (later to become Mexico City). Instead, Maya cities were enormous

**FIGURE 12.1**    Mayan ruins at Tikal in Guatemala, so-called Temple I or the Temple of the Jaguar. The human victims were thrown down the steps after their hearts were cut out in the building at the top. (Lee Dalton / Alamy)

royal households, the locales of the administrative and ritual activities of the royal court where privileged nobles could approach the holy ruler. There aesthetic values were formulated and aesthetic items consumed. The fall of a royal court would cause the inevitable "death" of the associated settlement.

At the heart of the Maya city were large plazas surrounded by the most important governmental and religious buildings: the royal acropolis, great pyramid temples, and usually a ball court. Enclosed on two sides by stepped ramps, the ball court was shaped like a capital "I" and was found in all but the smallest of Maya centers.

Careful attention was placed on the orientation of temples in accordance with Maya interpretation of the orbits of the heavenly bodies. The Maya were keen astronomers and had mapped out the phases of celestial objects, especially the moon and Venus. Inscriptions reveal them working with sums up to the hundreds of millions and with dates of enormous range. Their charts of the movements of the moon and planets are equal or superior to those of any other civilization working with the naked eye. Immediately outside of this ritual center were the structures of lesser nobles, smaller temples, and individual shrines. Outside of the urban core were the modest homes of the common people.

**FIGURE 12.2**    A Mayan stela in the main court at Copan, Honduras. The figure of the local ruler is elaborately dressed in feathers and ornaments. Men excavate nearby. (© Robert Harding Picture Library Ltd / Alamy)

Without draft animals, metal tools, and even pulleys, Maya architecture required abundant manpower. All stone for Maya structures was taken from local quarries. They most often used limestone, which remained pliable enough to be worked with stone tools while being quarried. Limestone hardened only when removed from the quarry. For the common Maya houses, wooden poles, adobe, and thatch were the primary materials. They did not understand the true arch and used corbelling instead—overlapping stones so that the gap gradually closes.

Palaces were large and often highly decorated, set close to a city center to house the elite (Figure 12.3). The most important religious temples sat atop the towering Maya pyramids. Sometimes the pyramids contained tombs. As they were often the only structure in a Maya city to exceed the height of the surrounding jungle, the roof decorations atop the temples were carved with representations of rulers that could be seen from great distances.

**FIGURE 12.3** The "governor's palace" at Uxmal, Yucatan, Mexico, c. AD 900. Individual rooms open off a platform reached by a steep staircase. The superstructure is decorated with elaborate carvings. (Peter M. Wilson / Alamy)

## MAYA WRITING

The Roman Catholic Church and Spanish government officials systematically destroyed Maya texts, thinking them diabolic, and with the texts they destroyed knowledge of Maya writing. The modern decipherment of Maya writing has been a long and laborious process because of the extraordinary, or maddening, complexity of the system. Some elements were first deciphered in the late 19th and early 20th century, mostly having to do with numbers, the calendar, and astronomy. Major breakthroughs came in the 1950s to 1970s.

Now partly deciphered, the Maya writing system proves to have been a combination of syllabic symbols and logograms: Logograms are signs that refer to words but have no phonetic value in themselves (like 1, 2, 3), like Chinese signs. The writing is most often classified as a logosyllabic writing, in which syllabic signs play a significant role. Mesopotamian cuneiform and Egyptian hieroglyphs were logosyllabic systems. It is the only writing system of the preColumbian New World that represented to some extent the spoken language of the community. In total, the script has more than a thousand different glyphs, although many are variations of the same sign. The earliest inscriptions date to 250–400 BC, but the writing was used until the arrival of Europeans in the 16th century. Although the early Spanish conquistadors tell of individuals who could read and write the script, all knowledge of it was lost within a few generations.

In excess of 10,000 individual texts in the native Maya script have been recovered, mostly inscribed on stone monuments, lintels, stelae, and ceramic pottery. The Maya also produced texts painted on a form of paper made from tree-bark. The paper was bound as a single continuous sheet folded into pages of equal width, like a concertina (see Figure 12.4). Shortly after the conquest, all codices that could be found were ordered burned by zealous Spanish priests, notably Bishop Diego de Landa (1524–1579) in 1561. Only three Maya codices survive and a few pages from a fourth found in a cave in the 1970s.

**FIGURE 12.4**   Page from the Dresden codex, a Maya book of the 11th or 12th century of the Yucatecan Maya in CHICHEN ITZA. The Maya codex is believed to be a copy of an original text of some three- or four-hundred years earlier. It is the earliest known book written in the Americas. It is an astronomical text showing a section of a season of 260 days. Each picture is a day, its name and number given in the Maya glyphs written above the figure. From the top left: a human-headed serpent; a jaguar; an armed warrior; a god; Quetzalcoatl ferrying a woman; an eagle biting a serpent; Quetzalcoatl again, holding a war-ax; a god; a god sitting in a shrine. It is eight inches high and eleven feet long. (Royal Library at Dresden, Germany; The Print Collector / Alamy)

Most surviving preColumbian Maya writing are from stelae and other stone inscriptions, many of which were abandoned before the Spanish arrived. The inscriptions on the stelae mainly record the dynasties and wars of the sites' rulers. Much of the remainder of Maya writing is found on funeral pottery.

Scribes held a prominent position in Maya courts. Maya art often depicts rulers with trappings indicating they were scribes or at least able to write. Many burials of rulers have been found together with such writing tools as shell or clay inkpots. But literacy was surely not widespread beyond the elite classes. Unfortunately, the surviving codices and stone inscriptions do not record any myths, but are mostly of an astronomical nature.

## MYTH: *POPOL VUH*

A single Maya document survives that reports Maya myth, called the ***Popol Vuh,*** "Book of the Community," "Book of Counsel," or more properly "Book of the Mat," from a Postclassic kingdom in Guatemala's western highlands, a tribe called the Quiché (**kē**-chä) Maya. "Mat" is as we say "throne," referring to highest ruler. The book was written in the early 18th century by a Dominican priest named Francisco Ximenez, but sank into obscurity until a full version was published in 1941. Ximenez's book is apparently based on a much earlier 16th-century phonetic transcription of an oral recitation, although no trace of this book has been found. Ximenez's book is written in alphabetic characters but in the Maya language and, in a parallel text, in Spanish.

The first part of the extremely strange *Popol Vuh* consists of two stories: (1) a narration of the failure of the gods to create earthly beings who will adore, obey, and sustain them; (2) the story of how two mysterious twins, **Hunahpu** (wann-a-pwa) and **Xbalanque** (sha-ba-**lan**-kä), destroy an arrogant demonic bird, **Vucub Caquix** (**vo**-kob **ka**-kwish, "seven macaw," the name of a day), and his two sons, **Zipacna** (sip-**ak**-na) and **Cabracan** (kab-**ra**-kan), who refused to adore; obey; and sustain their creators (Chart 12).

The first story of the first part opens with a description of what it was like before the creation began. In the sea, surrounded with light, hidden under green feathers, was **Gucumatz** (**gwa**-kwa-mats) (the same as the Aztec **Quetzalcoatl** (ket-zal-co-**at**-el,

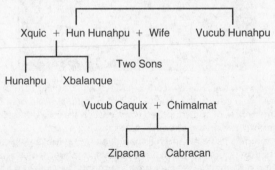

**CHART 12**   Genealogies in the *Popol Vuh.*

"plumed serpent") and his consort Tepeu. In the sky was Heart of Heaven. Then came the word, like a lightning bolt ripping through the sky and penetrating the waters, fertilizing the mind of Gucumatz and Tepeu. Then the creator couple said, "Let it be done," and the earth emerged from the sea, plants put forth shoots, wild animals came to be. The gods made three unsuccessful attempts to create humankind: first out of animals, then out of mud, and finally out of wood. The descendants of the wooden men are today's monkeys.

In the second story of the first part of the *Popol Vuh*, the demonic Vucub Caquix had two sons, Zipacna and Cabracan, both of whom made the earth shake as they burrowed under mountains. The hero twins Hunahpu and Xbalanque, whose origin we only learn later (see below), go out hunting. They shoot Vucub Caquix in the jaw with a blowgun while he is in a tree eating fruit. Angered, Vucub Caquix tears off Hunahpu's arm. To recover the arm, the twins team up with an elderly couple, pose as dentists, go to Vucub Caquix's house, and dupe him into letting them pull his teeth and replace them with white corn kernels. Vucub Caquix no longer looks like a lord with his white corn kernel teeth and loses everyone's respect. He dies in poverty, along with his wife. Hunahpu recovers his arm.

Then the hero twins set out to kill Zipacna, a son of Vucub Caquix, who has himself just finished killing four-hundred young men. Zipacna had feigned death when the four-hundred men tried to kill him by having him dig a hole in the ground, then planting a pole on top of him. Zipacna escaped. While the four-hundred young men celebrated his death, Zipacna crushed them all and the four-hundred young men became stars in the sky. The hero twins make a crab that kills Zipacna. Next, the hero twins poison a bird with white earth. When Cabracan, the other son of Vucub Caquix, eats the bird, he dies.

In the second section of the *Popol Vuh*, we learn about the brothers **Hun Hunahpu** ("one Hunahpu," the name of a day) and **Vucub Hunahpu** ("seven Hunahpu," also the name of a day). The story goes back in time here because Hun Hunahpu is the father of the hero twins Hunahpu and Xbalanque (it is confusing that the father is Hun Hunahpu and the son is Hunahpu!).

Hun Hunahpu and his wife have two sons (later, Hun Hunahpu and another woman, **Xquic** (**shē**-kik), "Mrs. Blood," are the parents of the hero twins Hunahpu and Xbalanque). Hun Hunahpu teams up every day with his bachelor brother Vucub Hunahpu to play the ball game against his sons. The noise of their ball game annoys the lords of Hell (= **Xibalba**, shi-**bal**-ba), who summon Hun Hunahpu and Vucub Hunahpu to come down into Hell and play ball.

The Hunahpu brothers go down to Hell and after a series of tortures are sacrificed and buried. On the spot where the brothers are buried, a tree springs up, loaded with skulls for fruit. Among the fruit is the head of Hun Hunahpu.

Along comes Xquic, daughter of one of the lords of Hell. She reaches up to pick one of the fruits and the skull of Hun Hunahpu spits in her hand, making her pregnant with the hero twins Hunahpu and Xbalanque.

When the pregnancy becomes obvious, her father orders four messengers to take Xquic out into the woods, sacrifice her, and bring back her heart for burning. Xquic talks the messengers into letting her live, so they bring back a false heart in a gourd. Xquic goes up to the earth where she gives birth to the hero twins Hunahpu and Xbalanque.

Here are selections from the early portions of the long *Popol Vuh*, which begins with a description of the creation of the world.[1]

## The Maya Creation of the World

In the beginning all was suspended, there was calm, silence, no motion, quiet, and the whole sky was empty. Here is the account of the beginning. There were no humans, animals, birds, fishes, crabs, trees, rocks, caves, arroyos, grasslands, nor forest. There was only sky.

The earth had not yet appeared, only the calm expanse of the sea and the expanse of the sky. Nothing had been made. There was nothing to make a sound, nothing to move or shake, or make a noise in the sky. Nothing was standing. There was only the calm sea, placid, tranquil. Nothing had come into existence.

There was only silence in the night, in the dark. Only the creator, the maker, those who give birth, *Tepeu* and *Gucumatz* were in the water, surrounded by light. Because they were obscured by green and blue feathers, they were called Gucumatz.° They were wise, sage. This is how the sky existed and the *Heart of Heaven*, the name of God.

Then the word came. Tepeu and Gucumatz came together in the darkness, in the night, and they spoke with one another. They talked things over, they discussed things, they deliberated. They came to an agreement and brought together their words and their thoughts.

While they thus meditated, it seemed that at first light they should bring forth humans. Thus they planned the creation, the growth of trees and bushes, the beginning of life, the creation of humans. Thus the Heart of Heaven, who is called *Huracan*, arranged it in the dark and in the night. The first is called *Caculha Huracan*, the second is called *Chipi Caculha*, the third is called *Raxa Caculha*. These three are the Heart of Heaven.

Tepeu and Gucumatz came together and they discussed about life and light, how they would bring about the dawn, and who would provide food and sustenance. Let it be done. Let the empty space be filled. Let the waters pull back and make a space. Let the solid earth appear. Let it be done.

°*Gucumatz*: the Maya Quetzalcoatl (also called Kukulcan), a serpent with feathers that moves in the water.

[1]For the Mexican texts, cf. Recinos, A. (trans.), *Popol vuh : las antiguas historias de Quiché* (México City, 1947); A. Recinos, D. Goetz, and S. G. Morley (trans. and eds.), *Popol Vuh: The Sacred Book of the Ancient Quiché Maya* (Tulsa, 1950); Bernardino de Sahagún, J. O. Anderson and C. E. Dibble (trans.), *Florentine Codex: General History of the Things of New Spain* (Salt Lake City, 1950–82), See also L. Spence, *The Myths of Mexico and Peru* (London, 1913); D. Tedlock, *Popol Vuh: The Definitive Edition of* The Mayan Book of The Dawn of Life *and* The Glories of Gods and Kings (New York, 1996); A. J. Christenson, *Popol Vuh: The Sacred Book of the Maya: The Great Classic of Central American Spirituality* (Tulsa, 2007); M. Leon-Portilla and E. Shorris. *In the Language of Kings* (New York, 2001).

Chapter 12 • The Myths of Mexico **407**

So they spoke. Let there be light and dawn in the sky and on the earth. There shall be no glory in our creation until we have made man, until man is formed. So they spoke.

Then they made the earth. In truth, they created the earth. Let there be earth, they said, and straightaway there was earth. The creation was like a mist, like a cloud, like a cloud of dust. The mountains came out of the water and rapidly grew. It was a miracle, an act of magic, the formation of the valleys and the mountains. Immediately the cypress groves and the pine trees grew on the surface of the earth.

Gucumatz was filled with joy. He said, "Your coming has been fruitful, Heart of Heaven, and you O Calculha Huracan, and you O Chipi Caculha, and you O Raxa Caculha!"

"We will finish the work, the creation," they answered.

Then the earth was made, the mountains, the valleys, the streams of water that ran between the hills. For the water was separated when the high mountains appeared. And so the earth was made, formed by the Heart of Heaven, the *Heart of Earth*, as are called those who first made it fruitful when the sky was suspended and the earth still hidden in the water. Thus they perfected the work, after thinking about it and meditating on it.

Then they made the small animals of the forest, protectors of the woods, the spirits in the mountains, deer, birds, mountain lions, jaguars, snakes, the protectors of the bush.

Then those who give birth° asked, "Should there be only silence in the forest, under the vines? There should be somebody to guard them."

Thus they spoke in their meditations. Immediately were made the deer and the birds. Straightaway they made homes for the deer and the birds. "You deer shall sleep in the fields beside the rivers and the arroyos. You shall be in the thicket and in the pasture. You shall become many in the forest. You will walk on your four feet. So it may be done."

Thus they spoke. Then they found homes for the birds both great and small. "You will live in the trees and among the vines. You shall make your nests there. You will multiply. You will increase in the branches of the trees and in the vines." This is what they told the deer and the birds. They did what they were told and they found their homes and nests.

°*those who give birth*: apparently the Heart of Heaven and the Heart of Earth working together.

## The Creation of Humans

When they had finished making the four-footed animals and the birds, their creator and maker and those who give birth said, "Speak, cry, tweet, sing out, speak every one according to what kind you are."

Thus they spoke to the deer, birds, mountain lions, jaguars, and serpents.

"Speak our names, praise us who are your mother and father. Call forth to Calculha Huracan, Chipi Caculha, Raxa Caculha, the Heart of Heaven, the Heart of Earth, the creator, the maker, those who give birth. Speak, call to us, adore us," they said.

Still, they could not make them speak like men. They hissed, they screamed, they cackled. They could not form words. Each made its own kind of scream.

When the creator and the maker saw how they could not talk to each other, they said, "They cannot say our names, their creators and makers. This is not good," said those who give birth.

Those who give birth said to the creatures, "Because you cannot talk, we will change you. We have changed our minds. You shall have your food, pasture, homes, nests. They shall be the arroyos and the forests because you cannot adore us and invoke us. There must be those who adore us. We shall make other beings obedient to us. You must accept your destiny: Your flesh will be torn in pieces. It will be this way. This is your lot."

Thus they spoke, revealing their will to the animals great and small that crawl on the face of the earth.

But they wanted to give them another chance. They wanted to make another attempt. They wanted all living things to adore them. Yet they could not understand each other's speech. They succeeded in nothing and could do nothing. Thus they were sacrificed. The animals on the earth were condemned to be killed and to be eaten.

They needed to try again to make men, the creator, the maker, those who give birth.

"Let us try again. Dawn is near. Let us make him who shall nourish and maintain us. What do we need to do to be remembered on earth? We have tried with our first creation, our first creatures, but we were unable to make them praise and adore us. Let us try once again to make obedient, respectful creatures who will nourish and maintain us." So they spoke.

They began the creation and formation. They made man's flesh of earth and mud. They saw that it was not good. The flesh melted away. It was soft, it did not move, it had no strength, it fell down, went limp, could not move its head. Its face fell to the side. Its sight was blurred. It could not turn around. At first it spoke, but it had no mind. It soaked up the water and could not stand.

The creator and the maker said, "Let us try once more. Our creatures cannot walk, they cannot multiply. Let us think about this," they said.

They broke up and destroyed their work, their creation. They said, "What shall we do to make it perfect so that our worshipers, those who call on us, will succeed?"

So they spoke when again they conferred. And instantly they made the figure of wood. They looked like men, they talked like men, they populated the surface of the earth. They were there, they reproduced, they had daughters, they had sons, these wooden figures. But they had no souls, they had no minds, they were unaware of their creator, of their maker. They walked around on all fours, aimlessly. They did not remember the Heart of Heaven. They fell from favor. It was only a test, an attempt at man.

At first they spoke, but there was no expression on their faces. Their feet and hands were without strength. They had no blood. There was no moisture, nor flesh. Their cheeks were dry, their feet and hands were dry, their flesh was yellow. They did not think of their creator, their maker, those who had made them and took care of them.

These were the first humans who existed in large numbers on the face of the earth.

Immediately they destroyed, broke up, ruined, and killed the wooden figures. The Heart of Heaven sent forth a great flood that fell on the heads of the wooden creatures . . . A heavy pitch fell from the sky. They gouged out their eyes. They cut off their heads. They devoured their flesh. They broke and mangled their bones and nerves and ground and crumbled their bones. This was to punish them because they did not think of their mother, their father, the Heart of Heaven called Huracan. And for this reason the face of the earth was darkened and a black rain fell day and night.

Thus was the ruin of the humans who had been created and formed, the humans made to be destroyed, the mouths and faces of them mangled. The monkeys that now live in the forest are their descendants, all that remains because their flesh was made of wood by the creator and maker. That is why monkeys look like humans, a generation of humans that were created but were only wooden figures.

## The Death of Vucub Caquix

Clouds covered the earth. It was twilight. There was still no sun. There was a creature called Vucub Caquix who took pride in his power.

There was earth, there was sky, but you could not see the faces of the sun and moon. Vucub Caquix said, "They are clear examples of the people who were drowned. They are like supernatural beings.° I will be greater than all the creatures created and formed. I am the sun, the light, the moon," he declared. "My glory is magnificent. Because of me men shall walk, they shall conquer. My eyes are made of silver. They are bright, they shine like precious stones, like emeralds. My teeth shine like perfect stones, like the face of the sky. My nose shines like the moon. My throne is made of silver. The face of the earth is filled with light when I rise from my throne. I am the sun, I am the moon. I shine for all mankind. Thus it will be because I see very far."

Thus Vucub Caquix spoke. But he was not really the sun. He was only proud because of his feathers and because of his riches. He could see only to the horizon. He could not see the whole world.

The face of the sun had not yet appeared, nor the face of the moon, nor the stars. Dawn had not yet come. But Vucub Caquix became vain as if he were the sun and the moon because the light of the sun and moon had hot yet shown itself. Vucub Caquix wanted only to exalt himself, to hold dominion over all. All this happened when the flood came and overwhelmed the wooden people.

---

°*supernatural beings*: apparently the monkey people.

Now is the story of how Vucub Caquix was defeated, how he died, how man was made by the creator and the maker. Here is the beginning of the defeat and ruin of Vucub Caquix brought about by the two young men. The first was called Hunahpu and the second Xbalanque. Really, they were gods. When they saw how the vainglorious one had brought harm and planned yet to do more harm to the presence of the Heart of Heaven, the young men said, "This is not a good thing, when man still does not live on earth. We shall try to shoot Vucub Caquix with our blowgun when he is eating. We shall shoot him and make him sick. That will be an end to his riches, his jade, his valuable metals, his emeralds, those jewels of which he is so proud. So it will be for all men because they must not become vain because of their power and their riches."

Vucub Caquix had two sons. The first was called Zipacna and second was Cabracan. Their mother was called Chimalmat, the wife of Vucub Caquix.

Zipacna played ball with the large mountains that Zipacna created in a single night. Cabracan moved the mountains and made the mountains tremble both great and small. Thus did the sons of Vucub Caquix proclaim their pride.

"Listen, I am the sun," said Vucub Caquix.

"I am the one who made the earth," said Zipacna.

"I am the one who shook the sky and made the earth shake," said Cabracan.

Thus did the sons of Vucub Caquix follow the example of their father's pretended greatness. All this seemed evil to the young twin heroes. Neither the first mother nor the first father had yet been made. For this reason the young men decided to kill Vucub Caquix and his sons.

Now comes the story of how the two youths shot their blowguns at Vucub Caquix and how each of those who had become arrogant was destroyed. Vucub Caquix had a large fruit tree and he ate its fruit. Every day he climbed to the top of the tree. Hunahpu and Xbalanque saw that this fruit was his food. They hid themselves at the bottom of the tree, among the leaves. Vucub Caquix came to eat. Instantly Hunahpu struck him with his blowgun in the jaw. Screaming, he fell to the earth from the top of the tree.

Hunahpu ran up to overpower him, but Vucub Caquix took hold of his arm and wrenched it away, bent it back to the shoulder. Thus Vucub Caquix tore out Hunahpu's arm. Carrying the arm, Vucub Caquix went home and arrived there nursing his jaw.

"What has happened to you, my lord?" asked his wife Chimalmat.

"What else but those two demons shot me with blowguns and knocked out my jaw? For that reason my teeth are loose and cause me great pain. But I have brought his arm, to put it on the fire. Let it hang there over the fire. These demons will come looking for it." Thus spoke Vucub Caquix and hung up the arm of Hunahpu.

After thinking it over, Hunahpu and Xbalanque went to talk with an old man with white hair and an old woman, both of them very old and bent . . . The youths said to the old woman and the old man, "Come with us to Vucub Caquix's house to get our arm. We will come after you, and you shall say, 'These are our grandchildren. Their mother and father are dead. So they follow us everywhere when we beg for alms. The only thing we know is how to remove the worm from the teeth.' Vucub Caquix will think we are just boys. We will be there to advise you," said the two youths.

"Very well," said the old man and the old woman.

They started out for the house of Vucub Caquix. They found him sitting on his throne. The old woman and the old man walked ahead, followed by the two boys. So they arrived at the house of the lord who was screaming because his tooth hurt him so much.

When Vucub Caquix saw the old man and the old woman and the boys with them, he said, "Where do you come from, grandparents?"

"We come looking for something to eat, honorable sir," they replied.

"And what do you eat? Are those not your sons?"

"O no, sir. They are our grandsons. We are sorry for them. What we obtain, we share with them, sir," answered the old man and the old woman.

In the meanwhile the lord was suffering terribly from the pain in his tooth. It was with difficulty that he spoke.

"I earnestly beg you to have pity on me. What can you do? What can you cure?" the lord asked them.

The old ones answered, "O sir, we only take the worm from the teeth, we cure the eyes, and we set broken bones."

"I see. Well, cure my teeth then, which make me suffer day and night. Because of them, and because of my eyes, I cannot rest, I cannot sleep. This is because two demons shot me with a pellet from their blowgun. I cannot eat. Pity me, tighten my teeth with your hands."

"Very well, sir. You suffer because of a worm. We can pull these bad teeth and put others in their place."

"Well, it is not good that you pull my teeth. It is because of them that I am a lord. My greatest decorations are my teeth and eyes."

"We will put others of ground bone in their place." But in fact the ground bone was only grains of white corn.

"Very well, pull them then. Come, give me some relief," he answered.

Then they pulled out Vucub Caquix's teeth. In their place they put the grains of white corn, which shone in his mouth. Straightaway his features drooped. He no longer had the appearance of a lord. They removed the rest of his teeth, which shone like pearls in his mouth. Finally they cured Vucub Caquix's eyes by piercing the pupils. Then they took all his riches.

But Vucub Caquix felt nothing any more. He only watched as on the advice of Hunahpu and Xbalanque they took all the things of which he had been so proud.

Then Vucub Caquix died, and Hunahpu got back his arm. His wife died too, Chimalmat. In this way Vucub Caquix lost his wealth. The old man and old woman took all the emeralds and precious stones that had been his great pride on earth. The old woman and the old man who did this were miraculous beings. Recovering the arm of Hunahpu, they restored it to its rightful place. It was only to cause the death of Vucub Caquix that they had done this because it seemed wrong to them that he was so arrogant. Then the two youths went on, having in this fashion carried out the orders of the Heart of Heaven.

## Zipacna Kills the Four-Hundred Boys

Now we tell the story of what Zipacna did, son of Vucub Caquix.

"I have created the mountains," said Zipacna.

Zipacna was taking a bath at the edge of a river. Four-hundred youths came past, dragging a log for their house. The four hundred had just cut down a large tree to make the central pole of their house. Zipacna approached the four-hundred youths. He said, "What are you doing, boys?"

"We cannot lift this log and carry it on our shoulders," they said.

"I will carry it," said Zipacna. "Where does it go? What is it for?"

"It is to be the central pole of our house," they said.

"All right," Zipacna answered. Lifting the pole, he put in on his shoulders and carried it to the entrance of the house of the four-hundred boys.

"Now stay with us," they said. "Do you have a father or mother?"

"I have neither," said Zipacna.

"Then we will hire you tomorrow to get another log to support our house."

"That is good," answered Zipacna.

The four-hundred boys talked together. They said, "How shall we kill this boy? It is not good that he has lifted the log all by himself. Let us make a big hole and push him into it. 'Go down, take the earth from the pit,' we will tell him. When he stoops to go down into the pit, we will let the large log fall on him. He will die there in the pit."

So spoke the four-hundred boys. Then they dug a large, deep pit. They called Zipacna. "We like you a lot. Go and dig out the dirt. We cannot reach the bottom of the pit," they said.

"All right," Zipacna answered. He went into the pit.

Calling down to him as he dug the dirt, they said, "Have you gone very deep yet?"

"Yes," he answered, digging in the pit. But the pit he dug was to save himself from the danger. Zipacna knew they wanted to kill him, so when he dug the pit he made a second hole in one side.

"How far have you gone?" the four-hundred boys called down.

"I am still digging," Zipacna said. "I will call to you when I have finished digging," Zipacna said from the bottom of the pit. But he was not digging his grave. He was opening another pit to save himself.

At last Zipacna called up to them. But when he called, he was already in the second pit.

"Come and take away the dirt that I have dug at the bottom of the pit," he said. "I have made it very deep. Do you hear my call? Your calls, your words repeat like an echo—once, twice, and so I hear very well where you are." Thus Zipacna called from the pit where he was hidden, shouting from the depths.

Then the boys threw in the great log. It fell quickly with a thud to the bottom of the pit.

"Do not speak! Let us wait until we hear his dying screams," they said to each other in whispers, each one covering his mouth as the log fell, making a lot of noise. Zipacna spoke then, crying out, but he only called once when the log fell to the bottom.

"How well we have succeeded! He is dead," said the boys. "If he had gone on doing what he began, we would have perished, because he already had interfered with us, the four-hundred boys."

Joyfully they said, "Now we must make our *chicha*° within three days. When three days are passed, we will drink to the construction of our new house, we, the four-hundred boys."

Then they said, "We will look tomorrow and the day after tomorrow to see if the ants come out of the earth when the body smells and begins to rot. Then we will become calm and drink our *chicha*," they said.

From his pit Zipacna heard all that they said. Later, on the second day, a multitude of ants came, back and forth, gathering under the log. Some had Zipacna's hair in their mouths, others carried his fingernails.

When the four-hundred boys saw this, they said, "That devil has died. Look how the ants have gathered. They come by the hordes, some with hair, the others with fingernails. Look what we have accomplished!" Thus they spoke to one another.

But Zipacna was very much alive. He had cut his hair and gnawed off his fingernails to give them to the ants.

And so the four-hundred boys believed that he was dead. On the third day they began the orgy. All of the boys got drunk. Being drunk, the four hundred knew nothing. Zipacna let the house fall on their heads, killing all of them. Not even one or two of the four hundred survived. Zipacna killed them, the son of Vucub Caquix. Thus the four-hundred boys died. It is said that they became the Pleiades, but who knows.

°*chicha*: an intoxicating drink made from maize.

## The Twins Overcome Zipacna, Son of Vucub Caquix

Now comes the story of how the two boys Hunahpu and Xbalanque killed Zipacna.

The boys were enraged on account of the four hundred killed by Zipacna. His daily food was fish and crabs, which he hunted at the river's bank. During the day he hunted for food; at night he carried mountains on his back.

From the leaf of a forest plant Hunahpu and Xbalanque made a figure to look like a large crab. With a leaf they made the crab's stomach. The claws they made of smaller leaves. For the back, they used a rock. They put the crab at the bottom of a cave in a huge mountain. Then the boys went to Zipacna at the edge of the river.

"Where are you going?" they asked him.

"I'm going nowhere," Zipacna said. "I am looking for food, boys."

"And what is your food?"

"I eat fish and crabs. But I have not found any here. I have not eaten for two days. I am dying of hunger," Zipacna said to Hunahpu and Xbalanque.

"Over there in the bottom of the ravine is a crab, a big one, and you should eat it. It bit us when we tried to catch it so we are afraid. We wouldn't catch it for anything," said Hunahpu and Xbalanque.

"O boy! Come and show me, boys," Zipacna pleaded.

"We do not want to do that. You go by yourself. You won't get lost. Follow the riverbank and you will come to the foot of a large mountain. It is making noise there at bottom of the ravine. You only have to go there," said Hunahpu and Xbalanque.

"O poor me, won't you come with me, boys? Come, show it to me. There are many birds you can shoot with your blowguns. I know where to find them," said Zipacna.

His humility convinced the boys. They asked, "But can you really catch him? It is only for your sake that we go back there. We are not going to try to capture the crab again because it bit us when we were crawling into the cave. Then we were afraid to crawl in. Still, we almost caught it. It is best if you crawl in," they said.

"Very well," said Zipacna.

They went with him. They came to the bottom of the ravine. There, stretched on his back, was the crab. His shell was bright red. There also in the bottom of the ravine was the boys' trick.

"Great!" said Zipacna happily. "I wish it were in my mouth already!" He was really dying of hunger. He wanted to crawl in. He wanted to enter, but the crab began to climb up. Zipacna came out right away, and the boys asked, "Did you get it?"

"No, I didn't, because he was climbing up. I almost caught him. Maybe it would be best if I went in from above."

Then he entered from above, but when he was almost inside, with only the bottoms of his feet showing, the great hill began to slide. It fell slowly on his chest. Zipacna never came back. He was changed into stone. Thus Hunahpu and Xbalanque defeated Zipacna, who was the older of the sons of Vucub Caquix. According to ancient legend, he was the one who made the mountains. At the foot of the hill he was overcome. Only by a miracle was he overcome, the second of the arrogant ones. One was left, whose story we now tell.

## The Twins Overcome Cabracan, Son of Vucub Caquix

The third of the arrogant ones was Cabracan, the second son of Vucub Caquix.

"I demolish mountains," he said.

But Hunahpu and Xbalanque also overcame Cabracan. Caculha Huracan, Chipi Caculha, and Raxa Caculha° spoke to Hunahpu and Xbalanque and said, "May the second son of Vucub Caquix also be overcome. We wish this because it is not good what they do on earth, always reveling in their glory, greatness, and power. We cannot allow it. Lure him to where the sun rises," said Huracan to the two young men.

"Very well, honored sir," they said. "What we see is not right. Do you not exist, you who are at peace, Heart of Heaven?" the boys said as they listened to the command of Huracan.

°Caculha Huracan, Chipi Caculha, and Raxa Caculha: each is one-third of Huracan, the Heart of Heaven; apparently Huracan is "God."

In the meanwhile, Cabracan busied himself with shaking the mountains. Even with a gentle tap, the mountains opened, both great and small. It was easy to find Cabracan and the boys asked, "Where are you going, young man?"

"Nowhere," he answered. "I am moving the mountains. I am leveling them to the ground forever." Cabracan asked Hunahpu and Xbalanque, "How have you come here? I do not know who you are. What are your names?"

"We have no names," they answered. "We are merely shooters of blowguns and hunters with bird traps on the mountains. We are poor. We have nothing, young man. We walk over the mountains great and small, young man. We have just now seen a large mountain, there where you can see the pink sky. It rises very high and overlooks the tops of the hills. We have not been able to catch even one or two birds on it, young man. Is it true that you can level all the mountains?" Hunahpu and Xbalanque asked Cabracan.

"Where is this mountain of which you speak? I will demolish it. Where did you see it?"

"It is over there, where the sun rises," said Hunahpu and Xbalanque.

"Very well, show me the road," he said to the two young men.

"O no," they answered. "We will take you between us, one at the left and the other at your right. We have our blowguns. If there are any birds, we can shoot them."

Thus they set out merrily, trying their blowguns. But when they shot them, they did not use clay pellets in the tube, but knocked down the birds with a puff of air, which surprised Cabracan. The boys built a fire and placed the birds on it to roast. They rubbed one of the birds with chalk. They covered it with a white earth.

"We will give him this, to whet his appetite with the odor that emanates from it. We will ruin him with this bird of ours. As we cover this bird with earth, thus will we bring him down to earth and bury him in it. Great will be the wisdom of a created being, fashioned when it is dawn, when there is light," said the boys.

Meanwhile the birds were roasting. They turned a golden brown. The juice dripping from them made a delicious odor. Cabracan wanted very much to eat them. His mouth was watering. He yawned. The saliva and spit drooled down because of the delicious smell that the birds gave off.

He asked, "What is that you are eating? The smell is great. Give me a piece," Cabracan said to them.

They gave a bird to Cabracan. This bird would be his ruin. When he finished, they set out toward the east where the large mountain was. Already Cabracan's legs and hands weakened. He had no strength because of the earth with which the bird had been rubbed. He could do nothing to the mountains. He could not level them.

The boys tied him up. They tied his hands behind him. They tied his neck and his feet together. They threw him to the ground. They buried him. Thus was Cabracan overcome by Hunahpu and Xbalanque. You could never tell all the things that they accomplished on earth.

## The Birth of Hunahpu and Xbalanque

Now comes the story of how Hunahpu and Xbalanque were born, having told the story of how Vucub Caquix and Zipacna and Cabracan were destroyed. We will tell the name of the father of Hunahpu and Xbalanque, though we shall not tell of his origin nor the history of the birth of Hunahpu and Xbalanque. We will only tell the half of it, only part of the history of his father.

The story goes like this . . .

We now hear the genealogy of Hun Hunahpu, the father of the twins, and of his brother Vucub Hunahpu (see Chart 12). Hun Hunahpu had two sons, Vucub Hunahpu had none. The two brothers Hun Hunahpu and Vucub Hunahpu did nothing all day but play at dice and, together with the sons of Hun Hunahpu, the ball game. They made so much racket that the lords of the Xibalba, the underworld, were disturbed. The lords coveted the leather pads, the gloves, and the crown and masks that were their playing gear:

"Go and tell Hun Hunahpu and Vucub Hunahpu that they must come. Say, 'Come with us. The lords say that you must come.' They must come here to play ball with us so that we shall be happy. Really they amaze us. They must come," said the lords. "And tell them to bring their playing gear, their rings, their gloves, and their rubber balls too," said the lords. "Tell them to come quickly," they told the messengers of the underworld, who were owls . . .

The owls soon arrived, bringing their message to the court where Hun Hunahpu and Vucub Hunahpu were playing ball . . .

"Very well, we will go," said the young men. "Only wait for us. We want to say goodbye to our mother."

They went straight home and said to their mother, for their father was dead, "We are going, our mother, but only for a little while. The messengers of the lords of the underworld have come to take us. 'They must come,' they said . . ."

Hun Hunahpu and Vucub Hunahpu went right away. The messengers showed them the road. Thus they descended to Xibalba by some very steep stairs. They descended until they came to the bank of a river. They crossed it. They crossed the rivers that flow among the thorn trees. There were many such trees, but they passed through without being hurt.

They came to the bank of a river of blood. They crossed it without drinking its water. They only went to the bank and so they were not overcome. They went until they came to where four roads join. There at the crossroads they were overcome.

One of the four roads was red, another black, another white, and another yellow. The black road said, "You must take me because I am the way of the master." Thus spoke the road.

From this point on they were overcome. They were taken on the road to Xibalba. When they arrived at the council room of the lords of Xibalba, they had already lost the match.

The first ones seated there were figures of wood, arranged by the men of Xibalba. The brothers greeted the figures first, but they did not answer. The lords of Xibalba burst out laughing because they took for granted the defeat of Hun Hunahpu and Vucub Hunahpu. They went on laughing.

The lords said, "Very well, you have come. Tomorrow you will prepare the mask, your rings, and your gloves. Come and sit down on our bench," they said. But the bench that they offered was of hot stone. When they sat down, they were burned. They squirmed on the bench. If they had not stood up, they would have burned their bottoms.

Again, the lords of Xibalba burst out laughing. They were dying of laughter. They laughed so much that they felt pain in their stomach, in their blood, in their bones.

"Go now to that house," they said. "There you will get sticks of fat pine and a cigar. There you shall sleep."

Immediately they arrived at the House of Gloom. There was only darkness. Meanwhile the lords of Xibalba discussed what they should do.

"Let us sacrifice them tomorrow. Let them die quickly, quickly, so that we can have their playing gear," said the lords of Xibalba.

Hun Hunahpu and Vucub Hunahpu burn the pine sticks, though they are told not to. Then the punishments of the underworld are described: the House of Gloom, where there is only darkness; the House of Cold, where an unbearable wind blows; the House of Jaguars, where jaguars constantly stalk about; the House of Bats; the House of Knives, in which knives constantly grate against each other. But Hun Hunahpu and Vucub Hunahpu do not enter these houses. Instead the lords of Xibalba call them forth:

"Where are my cigars? Where are my sticks of fat pine that I gave you?"

"They are all gone," the two youths replied.

"Well, today shall be the end of your days. Now you shall die. You shall be destroyed. We will break you into pieces. Your faces will stay hidden. You will be sacrificed," said the lords of the underworld.

Right then they sacrificed them. They buried them. Before burying them, they cut off the head of Hun Hunahpu and buried the older brother together with the younger.

"Take the head and put it in that tree beside the road," said the lords.

Once the head was put in the tree, instantly the tree, which had never born fruit, was covered with fruit. The tree is the one that we now call the "head of Hun Hunahpu."

The lords looked in amazement at the fruit on the tree. The round fruit was everywhere, but they could not recognize the head of Hun Hunahpu because it was exactly like the other fruit. Thus it seemed to all the people of Xibalba when they looked at it. The tree seemed miraculous because of what happened when they put Hun Hunahpu's head in its branches.

The lords said, "Let no one come to pick this fruit. Let no one come and sit under this tree." And so the lords of Xibalba resolved to keep everyone away.

## Xquic Tricks the Lords of Xibalba

But a young girl named Xquic (**shē**-kik) heard the story of the fruit tree. Apparently Xquic lives in the underworld. She goes to the tree and the skull speaks to her, saying that all the fruit are skulls. She reaches up to take the fruit when a few drops of spittle fall into her palm that instantly disappear. The skull orders her to go to the upper world, where she will not die. But she returns home, and six months later her father notices that she is pregnant. When he tells the lords of Xibalba, they say:

> "Command her to tell the truth about her pregnancy. If she refuses to speak, punish her. Take her far from here and sacrifice her."
>
> "Very well, honorable lords," the father answered. He questioned his daughter. "Whose child do you bear, my daughter?"
>
> She answered, "I have no child, father. I have not yet known a man."
>
> "Very well," he said. "You are nothing but a whore. Take her and sacrifice her. Bring me her heart in a gourd and return this very day before the lords," he said to the messengers, who were owls.
>
> The owls took the gourd and set out with the young girl in their arms. They took a knife of flint with which to sacrifice her.
>
> She said, "It cannot be that you will kill me, O messengers, because I bear no disgrace in my belly. I became pregnant when I went to look at the head of Hun Hunahpu. You must not sacrifice me, O messenger!" she said turning to them.
>
> "Well, what shall we put in place of your heart? Your father told us, 'Bring the heart, return before the lords, do your duty, bring it in the gourd, put the heart in the bottom of the gourd.' Did he not speak so? What shall we put in the gourd? We wish not to kill you," said the messengers.
>
> "Very well. My heart does not belong to them. This is not your home. You must not allow them to force you to kill me. Later the real criminals will be at your mercy. The blood, and only the blood, shall be there, and be given to them. My heart will not be burned before them. Gather what comes from this tree," said the young girl.
>
> The red sap gushing forth from the tree fell into the gourd. With it they made a ball that glistened and formed into the shape of a heart. The tree gave forth sap like blood with the appearance of real blood. Then the blood, or rather the sap of the tree, clotted and formed a bright coating inside the gourd like clotted blood. The tree glowed at the device of the young girl. Once it was called the red tree, but since then it has taken the name Blood Tree because its sap is called "blood."
>
> "On earth you will be beloved and you shall have all that belongs to you," the girl said to the owls.

The messengers present the false heart to the lords. The lords place the heart on the coals, where it gives forth a sweet fragrance. The girl goes to the upper world, to the mother of Hun Hunahpu and Vucub Hunahpu, and announces that she is her daughter-in-law. Her sons are not dead, but live in the children about to come forth. Presently she gives birth to Hunahpu and Xbalanque.

## The Rest of the Story

The older half-brothers of the hero twins (having the same father, Hun Hunahpu) envy the hero twins Hunahpu and Xbalanque and try to kill them with ants and this-tles, but the hero twins survive (see Chart 12). Once grown, the hero twins trick their half-brothers into climbing a tree, where they are turned into monkeys.

Next we learn about the hero twins as cultivators of maize. Then they go to Xibalba, to Hell. The lords of Xibalba put the twins to a series of tests, putting them in various "houses," the very houses that Hun Hunahpu and Vucub Hunahpu, the father and uncle of the twins, had refused to enter. Between houses, the twins play ball with the lords of Hell, always winning or tying with them. Then the lords of Hell set up a contest where the twins are supposed to jump four times over a bonfire without getting burned. The twins deliberately jump into the fire and die, but soon afterward they arise miraculously and re-appear as old men. They present themselves disguised first as dancers, then as magicians. They kill a dog and restore it to life, then they kill themselves and are resurrected.

Seeing this, the envious lords of Hell ask to be sacrificed and brought back to life. The twins sacrifice them, but do not restore them to life. The twins give a farewell speech and are lifted into the sky to become the sun and the moon.

So much for the first story of the second part of the *Popol Vuh*.

In the second story of the second part of *Popol Vuh* the first true humans ap-pear. The first four men were made this time from corn dough. Heart of Heaven blows mist into their eyes so that they can only see what is close, thus checking their desire to become gods. Then the first four women are created as wives for the first four men.

They all speak the same language. They receive their god, Tohil, the great god of the Quiché Maya. They have no fire, and by this time they can no longer understand one another. Tohil gives them fire. At first Tohil wants only blood—"Bleed your ears, prick your elbows, this will be your thanks to god." Later, after he has given the Maya fire, he de-mands their hearts also. Symbolic wounding is not enough; death is the perfect offering.

We learn of the ultimate victory of Tohil, who operated on the lords of the earth through priests who began abducting men from the outlying tribes for sacrifice to Tohil. Gucumatz (the feathered serpent) raises the Quiché Mayans to their greatest peak of power. Gucumatz could foresee things. He could change himself into different animals. He instituted an elaborate ritual of fasting and other rites of abstinence.

The *Popol Vuh* ends with the genealogies of the tribes of the Quiché Maya.

## OBSERVATIONS: THE *POPOL VUH*

In this very strange tale various themes keep recurring. Vucub Caquix is a creator god who pretends more than he can do; hence, he must die and make way for legiti-mate creator-gods. His power is based on vanity, and when he loses its inspiration—his beautiful teeth and his wealth—he becomes as nothing. His sons are no better. Zipacna's and Cabracan's real power is only to destroy, first the four-hundred boys, then mountains, which Cabracan routinely demolishes.

Brothers here function as a single hero in duplicate; they are indistinguishable. They represent the power in male friendship. Constantly they are killed and brought back to life, notably in the ball game that the twin heroes play with the lords of Death.

The Houses in the land of death are a projection of all the terrors that faced the Maya: cold, fire, dangerous animals, weapons. But death is only the other side of life, and necessary if there is to be life. When Hun Hunahpu's head is cut off and placed in a tree, instantly the tree bears rich fruit. But all the fruit are skulls. One skull dribbles spittle into Xquic's hand, and she becomes pregnant with the children of Hun Hunahpu. Xquic lives in the underworld and is Death herself—hence she will never die. When she goes into the upper world and bears the twin heroes, she becomes life, mother of the hero twins. The sap of the tree becomes the blood of her heart because all are the same. The sap and the spittle, wet things, are the life, and the sacrificed blood is the source of life.

Mixed up with these myths of the resurrected life through blood sacrifice are many folktale motifs and etiologies (for example, why the sap of a tree is called "blood"). Virtually absent is the amorous content so predominant in most of the myths we have so far studied. Love is no motive for behavior in the myths of the Maya.

## THE AZTECS

The glory days of the Maya were in the distant past when the Spaniards came to Mexico in the early 16th century. Then the **Aztec** people had emerged as by far the dominant power in central Mexico. The Aztecs fashioned the largest preColumbian empire ever, stretching from the Pacific Ocean to the Gulf of Mexico. Their power reached far south into Mesoamerica, conquering towns as far as Guatemala. The empire reached its maximum extent just prior to the arrival of the Spanish conquistadors led by **Hernán Cortés** (1485–1547), who toppled it by allying with the traditional enemies of the Aztecs.

The Aztecs spoke a **Nahuatl** language, completely unrelated to Mayan. Aztec is the Nahuatl word for "people from Aztlan," the "place of reeds," a mythical place somewhere in the north. Their migration into the valley of Mexico points to a northern origin, where they lived in a place "by the water," though no one knows where that might be. The term Aztec may refer broadly to the cultural patterns common for all Nahuatl-speaking peoples of what is called the Late Postclassic Period in Mesoamerica, c. AD 1250–1521.

Aztec culture had rich and complex mythical and religious traditions. Their architectural and artistic accomplishments were also quite remarkable. Sometime around AD 1345 one group of Nahuatl speakers founded the city of TENOCHTITLAN on islands in Lake Texcoco. In 1521, in the most widely known episode in the Spanish colonization of the Americas, Cortés conquered Tenochtitlan and overcame the Aztec empire led by **Montezuma**. Subsequently the Spanish founded the new settlement of Mexico City on the site of the ruined Aztec capital.

Aztec culture and history is known principally through such archaeological evidence as that of the renowned Templo Mayor, the "Great Temple," in Mexico City, and from 14 codices, books made of folding pages similar in appearance to the surviving Maya codices. The Aztecs employed a system of "writing" in which events, persons, and ideas were recorded by means of drawings and colored sketches (but not by phonetic symbols). These were executed on paper made from the agave plant, or were painted on the skins of animals. By these means not only Nahua history and myths were passed on from one generation to the next, but also the transactions of daily life.

Other important sources of information are eyewitness accounts by the Spanish conquistadors, including Hernán Cortés himself, and from 16th- and 17th-century descriptions of Aztec culture and history written by Spanish clergymen and literate Aztecs in the Spanish or Nahuatl language. By far the most important example of such a record, and our source for most of what we know about Aztec myth, is the massive so-called Florentine Codex (because it is kept in Florence), or *Historia general de las cosas de Nueva España* ("General History of the Things of New Spain"), compiled by the Franciscan monk **Bernardino de Sahagún** (1499–1590). Sahagún was fluent in Nahuatl and attempted to learn from Aztec informants about native myth and religion. He taught Aztecs to write the original Nahuatl accounts using the Latin alphabet. Fearing his countrymen, the Spanish authorities, Sahagún maintained the anonymity of his informants and wrote a heavily censored version in Spanish. Unfortunately the manuscript of the *General History of the Things of New Spain* was lost for centuries and the Nahuatl original was not fully translated until the 20th century.

As with other Mesoamerican societies, the basic social organization depended on a rigorous division into nobles and commoners. The Aztecs also shared a complex of religious beliefs and practices, including most of the pantheon, and a complex calendrical system of 365 days intercalated with a second calendar of 260 days. The Aztecs of Tenochtitlan especially venerated **Huitzilopochtli** (wēt-zil-o-**pok**-tlē), personification of the sun and of war; **Tlaloc** (**tlā**-lok), god of rain; and Quetzalcoatl, the bringer of culture (the same as the Maya Gucumatz or Kukulcan).

The Aztec empire was a "tribute empire" based in Tenochtitlan, that is, the Aztecs did not interfere in local affairs as long as tribute payments were made. The empire never commanded territory by imposing military garrisons in conquered provinces, like the Romans, but controlled client states through marriage alliances with friendly rulers. The empire extended its control through trade and military conquest. Client states depended on the imperial center for the acquisition of luxury goods.

The Nahua peoples began to migrate into Mesoamerica from northern Mexico in the 6th century AD. During the Postclassic Period they rose to power at such sites as TULA (modern Tollan) about 25 miles northeast of Tenochtitlan/Mexico City, where they were known as the **Toltecs**.

Expelled from Tula, Huitzilopochtli, according to the myth, directed the wanderers to found a city on the site where they saw an eagle perched on a fruit-bearing cactus devouring a snake. In AD 1325 the Aztecs saw just such a sight on a small swampy island in Lake Texcoco. There they founded Tenochtitlan. Today this event is pictured on the Mexican flag.

The city plan was based on a symmetrical layout that divided the city into four city sections. The houses of the poorer classes were made of adobe with thatched roofs, but those of the nobility were built of a red porous stone quarried nearby, usually one story high with flat roofs, many covered with flowers. The city was interlaced with canals useful for transportation. Probably two hundred thousand Aztecs lived in Tenochtitlan at the time of the conquest, or seven hundred thousand including the surrounding islands and shores.

The Aztecs constructed twin temples in the center of the city, one to Huitzilopochtli, the war-god, and one to Tlaloc, the rain-god (Figure 12.5). This was

**FIGURE 12.5**   Reconstruction of the central square in Tenochtitlan, c. AD 1400. 19th century drawing. To the left, the double *El Templo Mayor*, dedicated to Huitzilopochtli and Tlaloc, surrounded by ceremonial structures. The temple stood where today stands the cathedral of Mexico City, constructed of its stones. (INTERFOTO / Alamy Images)

the Great Temple (*el Templo Mayor*). The enclosing walls of the building were 4,800 feet in circumference, decorated by carvings of intertwined reptiles (Figure 12.6).

The mass of the structure was composed of a mixture of rubble, clay, and earth, covered with carefully worked stone slabs cemented together and coated with a hard gypsum. A flight of 340 steps led to the upper platform on which were raised two three-storied towers. Statues of the gods stood in these structures and the stones of sacrifice. In the sanctuaries, say the conquistadors who entered them, human blood was spattered everywhere. The Great Temple of Huitzilopochtli/Tlaloc was surrounded by 40 smaller temples. In one were collected the grisly relics of the countless victims to the Aztec war-god. The Spanish conquerors counted 136,000 human skulls (Figure 12.7)!

Hernán Cortés arrived at the gates of Tenochtitlan on November 8, 1519, allied with the Nahuatl-speaking Tlaxcalans, ferocious enemies of the Aztecs. Apparently at first thinking that Cortés was the god Quetzalcoatl returned, the "plumed serpent," the Aztecs soon realized that he was no such thing. In June 1520 hostilities broke out, culminating in the Spanish massacre of the natives in the Great Temple and the death of Montezuma at the hands of his own people. The Spaniards fled, then in spring of 1521 returned to lay siege to Tenochtitlan, a battle that ended with the destruction of the city.

**FIGURE 12.6**    A stone serpent head guards the foot of the main staircase of the Great Temple (*El Templo Mayor*), discovered in 1974 during excavations for an electrical project beneath the central square in Mexico City. (John Mitchell / Alamy)

**FIGURE 12.7**    Skull rack found in modern times at the base of the ruins of *El Templo Mayor*, carved into stone in imitation of real racks with real skulls. (Danita Delimont / Alamy)

## PERSPECTIVE 12.1

### Diego Rivera

Diego María de la Concepción Juan Nepomuceno Estanislao de la Rivera y Barrientos Acosta y Rodríguez (1886–1957) was a prominent Mexican painter born in Guanajuato in the central highlands of Mexico. His large paintings on walls in fresco helped establish the Mexican Mural Renaissance. Between 1922 and 1953, Rivera painted murals in Mexico City, Cuernavaca, San Francisco, Detroit, and New York City. In 1931, a retrospective exhibition of his works was held at the Museum of Modern Art in New York City. He was one of the foremost painters of modern times.

Born to a well-to-do family, Rivera was descended on his mother's side from Jews who had converted to Roman Catholicism and on his father's side from Spanish nobility. After he arrived in Europe in 1907, Rivera went to Paris to live and work with the great gathering of artists in Montparnasse, where his friend Amedeo Modigliani painted his portrait in 1914. Paris was witnessing the beginning of cubism by Pablo Picasso and Georges Braque, a school that Rivera enthusiastically embraced.

In 1920, Rivera left France and traveled through Italy studying its art, including Renaissance frescoes. He returned to Mexico in 1921 and became involved in the government-sponsored Mexican mural program. In January 1922, he painted his first

**PERSPECTIVE FIGURE 12.1**   Diego Rivera (1886–1957), *The Great City of Tenochtitlan*, 1945. Detail of mural 4.92 × 9.71 m. in the Patio Corridor, Palacio Nacional, Mexico City. (Schalkwijk / Art Resource, NY, © ARS, NY)

significant mural, *Creation*. His murals dealt with Mexican society and reflected the country's 1910 Revolution. Rivera developed his own native style based on large, simplified figures and bold colors with an Aztec influence.

His art, similar to the Mayan steles, always tells stories. Rivera's radical communist political beliefs, and his attacks on the church and clergy, made him a controversial figure even in communist circles. The Russian revolutionary Leon Trotsky lived with Rivera and his wife Frida Kahlo, also a famous painter, for several months while Trotsky was exiled in Mexico. During the McCarthy era of the 1950s, somebody placed a large sign outside of a building in Detroit where Rivera was working declaring that, while the murals had merit, their politics was "detestable."

In this picture of Tenochtitlan, painted in 1945, you can see the twin temples to Huitzilopochtli and Tlaloc in the upper right (Perspective Figure 12.1). In the center-right the Aztec king sits in majestic calm, holding a fan, apparently regarding a beautiful Aztec maiden with a white headdress at the left of the picture. To the immediate right hand of the maid stands a priest, with a feather headdress, holding the bloody arm of a sacrificial victim, while the canals and the streets teem with the life of the city. Rivera was an atheist and saw all religion as evil, including the religion of the Aztecs.

In spite of the destruction of the Aztec empire, most Mesoamerican cultures were intact after the fall of Tenochtitlan. The freedom from Aztec domination was considered a good thing by most outlying peoples. In 1520–1521, an outbreak of smallpox swept through the population of Tenochtitlan, killing as many as half the population (Figure 12.8). In the next 60 years the indigenous population of the Valley of Mexico declined by more than 80 percent. All over North America, and soon South America, European diseases decimated the native populations. Some estimates indicate the mortality rate as high as 95 percent. There has never been a destruction of peoples like it.

The accounts of the conquistadors, faced by an utterly alien civilization, are hard to interpret. Cortés's letters to Charles I of Spain are a valuable firsthand account, but one letter is lost and the others were censored prior to publication. In any case, Cortés was not writing a dispassionate account but justifying his actions and to some extent exaggerating his success and downplaying his failures. Bernal Díaz del Castillo accompanied Cortés, and he later wrote a book called *The Discovery and Conquest of Mexico*. In his book, Bernal Díaz del Castillo describes the events leading up to the conquest of Mexico, including horrific accounts of human sacrifice and cannibalism.

Veneration of Huitzilopochtli, the personification of the sun and of war, was central to the religious, social, and political activity of the Aztecs. Huitzilopochtli was little known outside Tenochtitlan. The Aztecs believed that much of their culture derived from the ancient Toltecs (Nahua "craftsmen of the highest order"), whose culture flourished between AD 800–1000, but they confused Toltec influence with that of the builders of the astonishing, far more ancient pyramid complex 30 miles northeast of Tenochtitlan at Teotihuacan (c. 200 BC–c. AD 700, te-o-ti-wa-**kan**). The name is Nahua for "birthplace of the gods," but in fact the ethnic

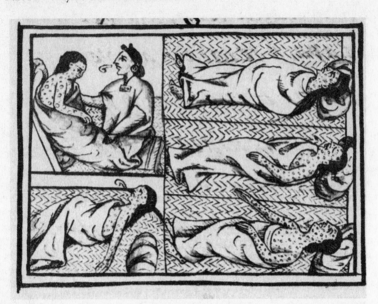

**FIGURE 12.8**   Aztec Indians with smallpox contracted from the Spaniards, ministered to by a medicine man. The sign coming from the mouths of the men on the left symbolize speech. Illustration from Father Bernardino de Sahagún's 16th-century treatise, *General History of the Things of New Spain* (the "Florentine Codex"). (The Granger Collection, NYC)

affinities of the builders of Teotihuacan are unknown, and we cannot be sure of their relationship to the Aztecs. The builders of Teotihuacan are a great mystery.

While human sacrifice was practiced throughout Mesoamerica, the Aztecs brought this practice to an unprecedented level. For the reconsecration of Great Temple of Tenochtitlan in AD 1487, the Aztecs sacrificed 84,400 prisoners over the course of four days (Figure 12.9)! Accounts by the Tlaxcaltecas, the primary enemy of the Aztecs at the time of the conquest, show that at least some of them considered it an honor to be sacrificed. In one legend, a warrior freed by the Aztecs returned of his own free will to die in ritual sacrifice.

## MYTH: THE BIRTH OF HUITZILOPOCHTLI

Huitzilopochtli was the war-god of the Aztecs; it was he who showed them the vision of where to build the city of Tenochtitlan. His name means "hummingbird to the left," because the god wore the feathers of the hummingbird on his left leg. According to the myth reported by Bernardino de Sahagún, near the Toltec city of Tula (modern Tollan), there lived a pious widow called **Coatlicue** (co-a-tel-ē-kwā) who every day went to a nearby hill to pray to the gods:

> While occupied in her devotions one day, Coatlicue was surprised by a small ball of brilliantly colored feathers that fell on her. She was pleased by the bright variety of its colors and placed it against her breasts, intending

**FIGURE 12.9**    Aztec human sacrifice. The priest cuts out the victim's heart
with a flint knife, then casts the body down the steps of the pyramid. A second
priest holds the prisoner pinned to the altar from below. Seven other priests stand
at the base of the pyramid, ready to consume parts of the sacrifice. From the
Codex Magliabecchiano, 16th century AD. (Museo Nazionale, Florence, Italy,
(World History Archive / Alamy)

to offer it to the sun-god. Sometime afterwards she learned that she was
to become the mother of another child. Her four-hundred sons, hearing of
this, rained abuse upon her, being incited to humiliate her in every way by
their one sister.

Coatlicue went about in fear and anxiety, but the spirit of her unborn infant came and spoke to her and encouraged her, soothing her troubled heart.
Her sons, however, were resolved to wipe out what they considered an insult to
their race by the death of their mother. They deliberated with one another in the
best way to kill her. They dressed themselves in war gear and arranged their hair
as if they were going into battle.

But one of them relented and confessed the treacherous plan of his brothers to the still unborn Huitzilopochtli, who replied, "O brother, pay close attention to what I say. I know full well what is about to happen."

The other brothers went to find their mother. At their head marched their
sister. They were armed to the teeth and carried bundles of darts with which
they intended to kill the luckless Coatlicue.

The one brother climbed the mountain to tell Huitzilopochtli that his
brothers were approaching to kill their mother.

"Mark well where they are," replied the infant god. "How far have they
got to?"

"To Tzompantitlan," responded the brother.

Later on Huitzilopochtli asked, "Where are they now?"

"At Coaxalco," was the reply.

Once more Huitzilopochtli asked to what point his enemies had advanced. "They are now at Petlac," the brother replied.

After a little while the one brother informed Huitzilopochtli that his three-hundred ninety-nine brothers were at hand under the leadership of their sole sister. They cut off their mother's head at the very instant that Huitzilopochtli was born, flourishing a shield and a spear colored blue [Figure 12.10]. Huitzilopochtli was painted and on his head was a plume, and his left leg was covered with feathers.

**FIGURE 12.10**    Coatlicue, "she of the skirt of snakes," goddess of the earth, of life and death. Dual serpents emerge from her head, which her sons cut off. Serpents also emerge from her severed arms, and she wears a skirt of serpents. She wears a necklace of hands and hearts and the head of jaguar. Aztec, Late Postclassic Period, 16th century. (Mexico Nacional de Antropologia, Mexico City; JTB Media Creation, Inc. / Alamy)

Huitzilopochtli shattered his sister with a flash of serpentine lightning and then pursued the brothers. He chased them four times around the mountain. They did not attempt to defend themselves, but fled for their lives. Many perished in the waters of a nearby lake, to which they rushed desperately. All were killed except for a few who surrendered their arms.

Bernardino de Sahagún, *General History of the Things of New Spain*

Huitzilopochtli goes on to become a great god for the Aztecs, identified with the powers of the sun.

## MYTH: THE PLOT OF TEZCATLIPOCA AGAINST QUETZALCOATL

Perhaps the greatest god in the eyes of the Aztecs was Quetzalcoatl, the "feathered serpent" according to his name, a flying reptile who marks the boundaries between earth and sky. He is the same as the Mayan Gucumatz and Kukulcan. Quetzalcoatl was no simple god, but functioned in many realms. He was related to gods of the wind, of the planet Venus, of dawn, of merchants, and of arts and crafts. He was the patron of learning. He was a creator-god: He created man. He was often represented as a serpent, sometimes with a feather collar, but he also had anthropomorphic forms (Figure 12.11).

Quetzalcoatl was thought to be an actual ruler of the city of Tula northeast of Mexico City at some early time, but we cannot disentangle history from myth. In any event during his reign, according to Bernardino de Sahagún, maize was plentiful, calabashes—a kind of gourd from which vessels were made—were thick, and cotton grew in every color without having to be dyed. Birds of rich plumage filled the air with their song. Gold, silver, and precious stones were abundant. In the reign of Quetzalcoatl, long ago, there was peace and plenty for all men. One day he would come again.

**FIGURE 12.11**    Statue of Quetzalcoatl, the Plumed Serpent. (National Museum of Anthropology, Chapultepec Park, Mexico City, Mexico; Travelpix / Alamy)

## PERSPECTIVE 12.2

## The Plumed Serpent of D. H. Lawrence

The British author D. H. Lawrence (1885–1930), who wrote the infamous and scandalous *Lady Chatterley's Lover* (1928, published in Italy), was at the top of his game after the success of his novels *Sons and Lovers* (1913), *The Rainbow* (1915; impounded by the British police for obscenity), and *Women in Love* (1920), works that represent an extended reflection on the dehumanizing effects of modernity and industrialization. In his books Lawrence endorsed emotional health and vitality, spontaneity, human sexuality, and the free reign of instinct. After travels in Europe, Asia, and Australia, Lawrence and his wife Frieda (a distant relative of the World War I flying ace Manfred von Richthofen, the "Red Baron"), arrived in the United States in September, 1922. He retired to the mountains of Taos, New Mexico, north of Santa Fe. In 1924, in exchange for the manuscript of *Sons and Lovers,* the Lawrences acquired the 160-acre Kiowa Ranch.

Lawrence stayed in New Mexico for two years, with extended visits to Mexico. There he worked on his novel *The Plumed Serpent,* whose original title was *Quetzalcoatl.* The novel is set during the Mexican Revolution. Tourists are viewing a bullfight in Mexico City. One of them, Kate Leslie, is disgusted by the spectacle. She meets Don Cipriano, an Oxford-educated, pure-blood Zapotec Indian and an army general. She is attracted to him. She meets his friend, an intellectual landowner of Spanish descent named Don Ramon. She travels to a small town beside a lake. It turns out that Ramon and Cipriano are leaders in a revival of preChristian cult, into whose practices Kate is drawn.

In the novel Lawrence refashions the myth of Quetzalcoatl to fit his own idiosyncratic views on sex and on the roles of men and women, according to his theory of gender. Don Ramon and Don Cipriano wish to raise up the downtrodden Mexican populace through their new cult of Quetzalcoatl. They write and distribute hymns of the new Quetzalcoatl, which men read aloud while drumming and dancing to a frenzy after dark in the plazas.

Don Ramon explains his purpose: "Quetzalcoatl is just a living word for these people, no more. All I want them to do is to find the beginnings of the way to their own manhood, their own womanhood. Men are not yet men in full, and women are not yet women. They are all half and half, incoherent, part horrible, part pathetic, part good creatures . . . But these people don't assert any righteousness of their own, these Mexican people of ours. That makes me think that grace is still with them. And so, having got hold of some kind of clue to my own whole manhood, it is part of me now to try with them."

After viciously attacking the Mexican Catholic Church for the devastation it has visited on the Mexican people, Don Ramon enters the local church, removes all the statues of Jesus, Mary, and the saints, and ceremonially burns them while singing the *Quetzalcoatl Hymn:* "Goodbye Jesus and Mary, hello Quetzalcoatl." Don Ramon sees himself as the resurrected Quetzalcoatl, and Don Cipriano sees himself as the resurrected Huitzilopochtli, god of war, in the new pantheon of Mexico.

After D. H. Lawrence's death in Italy in 1930, his wife returned his bones to the ranch outside Taos, New Mexico, and placed them in a small chapel, where you can visit them today. The ranch, now called the D. H. Lawrence Ranch and a writer's retreat, is owned by the University of New Mexico and is open to the public.

Envious of the success of the god and his people, the Toltecs, three wicked black magicians plot his downfall, the gods Huitzilopochtli, **Tezcatlipoca** (tez-ka-tel-i-**pok**-a), and Tlacahuepan (tla-ka-**wē**-pan). They place evil enchantments on the city of Tula. Tezcatlipoca takes the lead in the conspiracy.

Tezcatlipoca is one of the four sons of Ometeotl (om-ē-tē-**o**-tel), an Aztec creator-god. Tezcatlipoca is associated with a wide range of concepts including the night sky, the night winds, hurricanes, the north, the earth, obsidian, enmity, discord, rulership, divination, temptation, jaguars, sorcery, beauty, war, and strife. His name means "smoking mirror," alluding to his connection with obsidian, the material from which mirrors were made in Mesoamerica, used for shamanic rituals.

Disguised as an aged man with white hair, Tezcatlipoca presented himself at the palace of Quetzalcoatl, where he says to the servants tending him:

> "Please present me to your master the king. I wish to speak with him."
>
> The servants advised him to withdraw, for Quetzalcoatl was feeling ill and could see no one. Tezcatlipoca requested the servants, however, to tell the god that he was waiting outside. They did so, and at last he gained admittance.
>
> On entering the chamber of Quetzalcoatl the wily Tezcatlipoca pretended much sympathy for the suffering god-king.
>
> "How are you, my son?" he asked. "I have brought you a drug which you should drink and which will put an end to your sickness."
>
> "You are welcome, old man," replied Quetzalcoatl. "I have known for many days that you would come. I am exceedingly indisposed. The sickness affects my entire system and I can use neither my hands nor feet."
>
> Tezcatlipoca assured him that if he took the medicine that he had brought he would immediately experience a great improvement in health. Quetzalcoatl drank the potion, and in fact right away felt much revived. The cunning Tezcatlipoca pressed another and still another cup of the potion upon him, and as it was nothing but pulque,° the wine of the country, Quetzalcoatl quickly became intoxicated and became as wax in the hands of his adversary.
>
> Tezcatlipoca now took the form of an Indian named Toueyo and went to the palace of a chief of the Toltecs. The chief's daughter was so attractive that many wished to marry her, but her father refused her hand to all of them. The princess, beholding the false Toueyo passing her father's palace, whose penis was exposed, fell deeply in love with him, and so tumultuous was her passion that she became seriously ill. Her father, hearing of her illness, went to her apartments and asked her servants the cause of her illness. They told him that it was caused by the girl's sudden passion for the Indian who had recently come that way. The father at once gave orders that Toueyo be arrested. He was hauled before the chief.
>
> "Where do you come from?" the chief asked his prisoner, who wore almost no clothing.

°*pulque*: an intoxicating drink made from the maguey cactus.

"Lord, I am a stranger, and I have come here to sell green paint," replied Tezcatlipoca.

"Why are you dressed like this? Why do you not wear a cloak?" asked the chief.

"My lord, I follow the custom of my country," replied Tezcatlipoca.

"You with your exposed penis have inspired a passion in the breast of my daughter," said the chief. "What should be done to you for disgracing me like this?"

"Kill me. I don't care," said the cunning Tezcatlipoca.

"No," replied the chief, "for if I kill you my daughter will die of longing. Go to her and say that she may wed you and be happy."

Now the marriage of Toueyo to the chief's daughter aroused much discontent among the Toltecs. They murmured among themselves, "Why did the chief give his daughter to this Toueyo?" The chief, hearing of these murmurings, resolved to distract the attention of the Toltecs by making war upon the neighboring state of Coatepec.

The Toltecs assembled, armed for the fight, and having arrived at the country of Coatepec they placed Toueyo in ambush with his men, hoping he would be killed. But Toueyo and his men killed a large number of the enemy and caused them to flee.

The chief celebrated the victory with a great party. The plumes of a knight were placed on Toueyo's head and his body was painted red and yellow, an honor reserved for those distinguished in battle.

Tezcatlipoca's next step was to announce a great feast in Tula, to which everybody for miles around was invited. Great crowds assembled and danced and sang in the city to the sound of the drum. Tezcatlipoca sang to them and forced them to accompany the rhythm of his song with their feet. Faster and faster the people danced until the pace became so furious that they were driven to madness, lost their footing, and tumbled pell-mell down a ravine and were changed into rocks. Others, attempting to cross a stone bridge, fell into the water below and were changed into stones.

On another occasion Tezcatlipoca presented himself as a valiant warrior and invited all the inhabitants of Tula and its surrounding territory to come to a flower garden. When they had assembled there, he attacked them with a hoe and killed a large number. Others in a panic crushed their comrades to death.

Tezcatlipoca and Tlacahuepan on still another occasion went to the market place of Tula. Tezcatlipoca showed an infant on the palm of his hand. He caused the image to dance and to perform many amusing capers. This infant was in reality Huitzilopochtli. At the sight the Toltecs crowded together to get a better view, and many were crushed to death.

So enraged were the Toltecs at what had happened that, on the advice of Tlacahuepan, they killed both Tezcatlipoca and Huitzilopochtli. The bodies of the dead gods gave forth a pernicious stench and thousands of Toltecs died of disease. The god Tlacahuepan advised them to cast out the bodies before worse befell them, but when they tried to cast them out they found that their weight was so great that they could not move them. Hundreds wound cords round the corpses, but the strands broke and those who pulled on them fell and died suddenly, tumbling on top of one another and suffocating those on whom they collapsed.

## MYTH: THE JOURNEY TO TLAPALLAN

The Toltecs were so tormented by the enchantments of Tezcatlipoca that it was soon obvious to them that their luck was running out and that the end of their empire was at hand. Quetzalcoatl, disturbed at the turn of affairs, decided to leave Tula and go to the country of Tlapallan, his mythical place of origin, perhaps in the north. He had come from there when he first came on his civilizing mission to Mexico. He burned all the houses that he had built and buried his treasure of gold and precious stones in the deep valleys between the mountains. He changed the cacao trees into mesquite, and he ordered all the birds of rich plumage and song to quit the valley of Tula and to follow him to a distance of more than three hundred miles:

> On the road from Tula he discovered a great tree. There he rested and requested his servants to hand him a mirror. Looking at himself in the polished surface, he exclaimed, "I am old!"
>
> Proceeding on his way accompanied by musicians playing the flute, he walked until fatigue overcame him. He sat down on a stone, on which he left the imprint of his hands. This place is called Temacpalco ["impress of the hands"].
>
> At a place called Coaapan he was met by the Nahua gods, who were hostile to him and to the Toltecs.
>
> "Where are you going?" they asked. "Why do you leave your capital?"
>
> "I go to Tlapallan," replied Quetzalcoatl, "where I came from."
>
> "Why?" persisted the enchanters.
>
> "My father the sun has called me there," replied Quetzalcoatl.
>
> "Go, then," they said, "but leave us the secret of your art, the secret of casting silver, of working in precious stones and woods, of painting, of feather-working, and other matters."
>
> But Quetzalcoatl refused and cast all his treasures into the fountain of Cozcaapa ["water of precious stones"]. At Cochtan he was met by another enchanter, who asked him where he was going. On learning his destination, they offered him a draught of liquor. When he tasted the drink, Quetzalcoatl was overcome with sleep.
>
> Continuing his journey in the morning, the god passed between a volcano and the Sierra Nevada ["mountain of snow"], where all the servants who accompanied him died of cold. He very much regretted this misfortune and wept, lamenting their fate with bitter tears and mournful songs. On reaching the summit of the mountain, he slid to the base. When he arrived at the seashore, he embarked on a raft of serpents and was wafted away toward the land of Tlapallan.
>
> Bernardino de Sahagún, *General History of the Things of New Spain*

Other accounts state that the king cast himself on a funeral pyre and was consumed and that the ashes flew upward and were changed into birds of brilliant plumage. His heart also soared into the sky and became the morning star. Thus they bestowed upon him the title "Lord of the Dawn." When he died he was invisible for four days. For eight days he wandered in the underworld, after which the morning star appeared, when he achieved resurrection and ascended his throne as a god.

It is widely believed that the arrival of Cortés was seen as the return of Quetzalcoatl from Tlapallan, a white man with a beard, once again to institute a reign of peace and wealth on the earth. But there are no native accounts to support this interpretation, which depends principally on a letter that Cortés wrote to Charles I of Spain. Because the letters of Cortés are filled with posturing and self-justification, it is impossible to know if the Aztecs actually saw him in this way.

As for Tezcatlipoca, he was one of the great Aztec gods. His priests far surpassed in power the priesthoods of the other Mexican gods. To him is credited the invention of many of the practices of civilization. The other gods were worshiped for some special purpose, but the worship of Tezcatlipoca was regarded as compulsory and to some extent as a safeguard against the destruction of the universe, which the Nahua thought Tezcatlipoca might one day cause.

On the day of a great festival to Tezcatlipoca a young man was sacrificed, who for the previous year had been carefully nurtured. The boy was selected from among the best war captives of that year. His body was perfect, without blemish. He assumed the name, the clothing, and the attributes of Tezcatlipoca himself. All the people regarded him with awe, regarding him as the god's earthly representative. He rested during the day and came forth only at night to wander the roads armed with the arrow and shield of the god. Thus he symbolized the wind-god's dominance over the night-bound highways. He carried Tezcatlipoca's whistle with which he made a noise like the wind through the streets. Small bells were attached to his arms and legs. Many servants followed, and he periodically rested on stone seats made ready along the highway. He had sexual access to four beautiful maidens of high birth, with whom he passed the time in pleasant amusement. The men of high station entertained him at table as the earthly representative of Tezcatlipoca. His last days were a constant round of feasting and pleasure.

At last the fatal day arrived. The boy said good-bye to the girls. He was carried to the temple. When he reached the summit, the high priest received him. The priest made the boy one with the god whom he represented, Tezcatlipoca, by tearing his heart out on the stone of sacrifice.

## OBSERVATIONS: THE MYTHS OF MEXICO

We can only be puzzled by the myths of ancient Mexico. They are strange in their bewildering accounts of transformations, treacheries, and seemingly unmotivated schemes, but over all lingers the profound conviction that in order for the world to prosper, there must be sacrifice, especially human sacrifice. We may forget that the same thinking underlies St. Paul's doctrine in the Christian New Testament of the atonement, that for an angry, vengeful God to be satisfied, the blood of his own son must be shed. Such a doctrine hardly corresponds to Jesus' teaching that the essence of God is love, but corresponds very well with notions that divine power is inherently hostile and unfriendly to human concerns.

The Aztecs and the Maya carried this thinking very far: If God is pleased by the destruction of property, then he will be very pleased by the destruction of many thousand human beings. He will gladly drink their blood, and we will gladly offer it. Never is there the notion that death is the end in the Mexican vision, but death is only the beginning, the prelude to resurrection and life. In the blood is the life, the nurturing fluid, and the hope of the future.

## Key Terms

Tenochtitlan *399*
*Popol Vuh 404*
Hunahpu *404*
Xbalanque *404*
Vucub Caquix *404*
Zipacna *404*
Cabracan *404*
Gucumatz *404*

Quetzalcoatl *404*
Hun Hunahpu *405*
Vucub Hunahpu *405*
Xquic *405*
Xibalba *405*
Aztec *420*
Hernán Cortés *420*
Nahuatl *420*

Montezuma *420*
Bernardino de
  Sahagún *421*
Huitzilopochtli *421*
Tlaloc *421*
Toltecs *421*
Coatlicue *426*
Tezcatlipoca *431*

## Further Reading

Coe, M. D., *The Maya*, 7th ed. (London, 2005).
Freidel, D., and L. Schele, *A Forest of Kings: The Untold Story of the Ancient Maya* (New York, 1992).
Miller, M., and K. Taube, *An Illustrated Dictionary of the Gods and Symbols of Ancient Mexico and the Maya* (London, 1997).
Taube, K., *Aztec and Maya Myths* (Austin, TX, 1993).
Sharer, R., and L. Traxler, *The Ancient Maya*, 6th ed. (Stanford, CA, 2005).

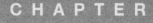

# CHAPTER

# 13

# Oceanic Myth

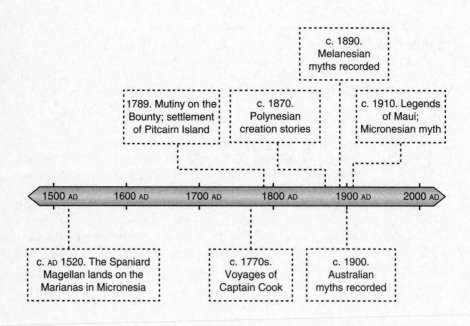

c. 1890.
Melanesian
myths recorded

1789. Mutiny on the
Bounty; settlement
of Pitcairn Island

c. 1870.
Polynesian
creation stories

c. 1910. Legends
of Maui;
Micronesian myth

1500 AD    1600 AD    1700 AD    1800 AD    1900 AD    2000 AD

c. AD 1520. The Spaniard
Magellan lands on the
Marianas in Micronesia

c. 1770s.
Voyages of
Captain Cook

c. 1900.
Australian
myths recorded

The southeast Asian land mass slips beneath the sea in a great southeastern diaspora, creating first the smallest continent, Australia, then large islands—New Guinea, the largest island in the world, but also Indonesia, the Philippines, Taiwan—then small or tiny islands all the way to Easter Island, 1,500 miles from Pitcairn Island, the closest landfall, and 2,500 miles from South America. Except for the large islands, most of Oceania consists of thousands of volcanic islands and coral atolls, with small human populations. Rainfall can be abundant, but the paradise early explorers imagined

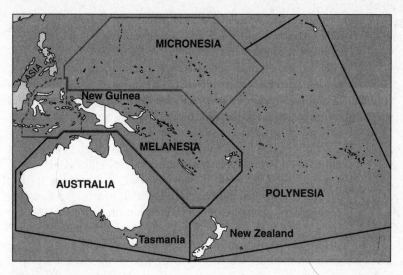

**MAP 13.1** Oceania.

was in reality a precarious dependence on a limited source of food and territory for expansion. Even continental Australia is one-third arid, uninhabitable desert.

In primordial times, different races emigrated from mainland southeast Asia across these great expanses of sea, but speaking very generally it makes sense to speak of four categories of Oceania: the *Polynesians, Micronesians, Melanesians*, and *Australians* who all had distinctive myths (see Map 13.1).

Immigrants into Australia and southern New Guinea were dark skinned with frizzy hair. Immigrants to the north, genetically distinct from the southerners, were lighter skinned with straight dark hair. The northerners—the Polynesians, Micronesians, the northern Melanesians—at some time acquired agriculture in combination with the raising of pigs, dogs, and chickens, but this Neolithic revolution bypassed Australia and portions of New Guinea. At the time of European contact in the late 18th century, Australian aborigines, sometimes said to be the most primitive peoples on earth, were nomads without stone tools who had not advanced beyond a clan organization and did not recognize the connection between sexual intercourse and pregnancy.

## EUROPEAN CONTACT

European exploration and settlement of Oceania began in the 16th century, beginning with Spanish landings and shipwrecks in the MARIANAS ISLANDS (Map 13.4) east of the Philippines (in Micronesia). Rivalry between European colonial powers, opportunities for trade, and the institution of Christian missions inspired further European exploration and settlement. The British were the dominant colonial power, establishing permanent colonies in what would become Australia and New Zealand. Today the populations of each are predominantly of European descent. New Caledonia (in Melanesia), Hawaii (in Polynesia), Easter Island (in Polynesia), and Guam (in

Micronesia) also have significant European populations. In general, Europeans have become the principal ethnic group in Oceania, both numerically and culturally.

When Ferdinand Magellan (Portuguese, 1480–1521) crossed the Pacific in 1519–1522, he made no landfall until he reached the Marianas in northern Micronesia. Alvaro Mendaña (Spanish, 1541–1596) by contrast left a trail of blood in his explorations. In 1595 when he raised the most holy cross on the Marquesas Islands in French Polynesia he murdered two hundred of the inhabitants. In the following two centuries islands were discovered, then lost, until in the 1770s Captain James Cook (British, 1728–1779) zig-zagged in three voyages through the Pacific, searching for a great south land (Australia) of which he had heard rumors, and fixed the position of most of the islands.

Those Europeans who followed came in pursuit of wealth or the spiritual en-lightenment of the natives. They introduced disease and firearms, and enslaved the population for work in the sugar fields of Fiji and Hawaii, and in the copper mines of Chile. The change in Oceanic life was sudden, drastic, and permanent. In the "black drive" in TASMANIA (Map 13.1), the large island south of Australia, the British settlers marched in a line across the island, literally driving all the native inhabitants into the sea. On Easter Island in the 1870s, 1,000 laborers were rounded up for work in the guano deposits in Chile. There most died, and when a few returned they brought with them smallpox, reducing the island population to 600. By the end of the 19th century the preservers of the old culture had died or converted to Christianity. Statues of gods and spirits were systematically destroyed, so that very little material culture survives from before European contact.

## THE STUDY OF OCEANIC MYTH

As a result of the extraordinary diversity of Oceanic peoples, and their lack of unity in any political sense, and poor communications between the archipelagos, and the absence of a system of writing, and the European depredations, we are faced with a situation in study-ing their myths somewhat similar to that in North and South America and very differ-ent from the ancient world. Our information is never expressed in a native literary form, although in some cases attempts were made to record the native languages in Roman al-phabetic characters. Really, we have reports of scattered European ethnologists mostly from the late 19th and early 20th centuries, whose investigations were of a scientific na-ture. These ethnologists, who included sometimes highly distinguished theorists and an-thropologists, would talk to individuals in this or that community and record their tales. Elsewhere in this book we have sought literary examples, to show how a certain people told a story, but this procedure is scarcely possible with Oceanic myth. Most tales record-ed are local and individual, and manifold, so that it is hard to speak of, say, "Polynesian myth." Nonetheless, certain aspects do emerge about which we can generalize.

## THE MYTHS OF POLYNESIA

**Polynesia** forms a kind of triangle in the Pacific Ocean (Map 13.2). At the lower right-hand corner is **EASTER ISLAND**, 2,500 miles west of South America and 1,500 miles east of its nearest neighbor, **PITCAIRN ISLAND**, which was peopled in 1789 by survivors of the mutiny on the *Bounty* and Tahitian women; it is called Pitcairn after Robert

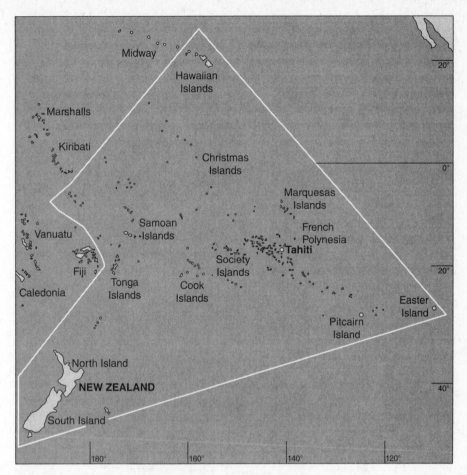

**MAP 13.2**  Polynesia.

Pitcairn, the midshipman on the British ship that sighted the island in 1767. Easter Island receives its name from its discovery by a Dutch explorer on Easter Sunday, 1722. At the lower left-hand corner is NEW ZEALAND, consisting of NORTH ISLAND and SOUTH ISLAND. The name *New Zealand* originated with Dutch cartographers, who called the islands Nova Zeelandia after the Dutch province of Zeeland. British explorer James Cook subsequently anglicized the name to New Zealand.

At the left center are the SAMOAN ISLANDS and the TONGA ISLANDS. In the center are the SOCIETY ISLANDS, apparently named after the Royal Society who commissioned the British expedition there, and the COOK ISLANDS, named after Captain Cook, who made the first accurate maps of the South Seas. At the right middle of the triangle is FRENCH POLYNESIA, where French is spoken, including the largest island TAHITI. At the top of the triangle are the HAWAIIAN ISLANDS, which James Cook called the Sandwich Islands after his sponsor the Earl of Sandwich. They sweep upward to the northwest from the big islands in a great arc 1,500 miles long. All these peoples speak Polynesian languages, although often they are mutually unintelligible.

## PERSPECTIVE 13.1

### The Statues of Easter Island

The 887 Easter Island statues have become world-renowned since first being sighted by Europeans in the early 18th century, taking their place with the Egyptian pyramids, Greek temples, and the Great Wall of China as monuments to the human spirit (Perspective Figure 13.1).

Unlike the Egyptians, Greeks, and Chinese, however, the Polynesian islanders left no written records to explain them. An Easter Island script called Rongorongo, surviving on 21 wooden tablets, has never been deciphered. The script was probably inspired by European writing because examples seem to date after European contact. In any event, although anthropologists have studied the statues extensively for well over a century, it remains a matter for speculation about how they were made, when they were made, and why.

Called *moai* in Polynesian, these stone monoliths seem to have been carved between AD 1100 and 1680. Probably *moai* represent deified ancestors. Although commonly called "Easter Island heads," the statues are really complete torsos. The figures kneel on bent knees with their hands over their stomachs. Some upright *moai* have become buried up to their necks by the shifting soils. They have heavy

**PERSPECTIVE FIGURE 13.1**    A ceremonial platform with seven *moai* statues, dated to around AD 1450. Like almost all *moai*, they look inland, away from the sea. Local legend has it that these *moai* were put up in honor of the seven courageous navigators who first landed on the island. Easter Island, Chile. (Aurbina http://en.wikipedia.org/wiki/File:Moai_Rano_raraku.jpg)

brows, long noses, protruding lips, and oblong ears. The jaw lines stand out against a shortened neck. The backs generally are not carved, but sometimes have a girdle motif on the buttocks and lower back. The tallest of the *moai* is almost 33 feet high and weighs 75 tons; the heaviest is shorter but weighs 86 tons. One unfinished sculpture, if completed, would have been approximately 70 feet tall with a weight of 270 tons! It is altogether unclear how the statues were transported, especially since there are no trees on Easter Island that could have served as sledges (but maybe once there were).

Most *moai* were carved out of a compressed, easily worked solidified volcanic ash found at a single site on the island inside an extinct volcano. The native island-ers who carved them used only stone hand chisels, which can still be found in the quarry. Only a quarter of the statues were set up on stone platforms around the island's perimeter, facing inland across clan lands. Nearly half remain in the quarry near the volcano. The rest lie elsewhere on the island, probably on their way to final locations.

Most *moai* were standing when Europeans first visited the island in the early 18th century, but all were later toppled during local conflicts. The last standing statues were reported in 1838 by a French naval officer. *Moai* were usually toppled forward to have their faces hidden, often so that their necks were broken. Today, about 50 *moai* have been re-erected, and a few are in museums around the world.

Polynesia is Greek for "many islands." The people who inhabited, or still inhab-it, these islands seem to be a blending of several waves of immigration, bringing rel-atively fair-skinned peoples from the Indonesian area (or still farther west) eastward through Melanesia ("black islands") into the Pacific. There have been at least two such great waves, probably more, during which the Polynesians to some extent mixed with the dark-skinned people of Melanesia in transit. Nonetheless the genome of modern Polynesians is different from the genome of most Melanesians.

## Myth: Polynesian Creation Myths

On New Zealand the native people are the **Maori**, who seem to have come to the is-land from the east in the 14th century; but an earlier population lived there, about whom we know very little. The Maori were, one might say, cultural leaders among the Polynesians, who told a tale about the origin of things from an initial chaos that bears striking resemblances to tales told in the ancient Near East. From this initial chaos an evolutionary descent led to the present world order.

Overlooking the countless local variations, in the beginning there was only **Po**, a void or chaos. There was no light, heat, or sound, or form, or motion. Faint stirrings gradually began in the darkness, moanings and whisperings, and then, as at early dawn, light appeared and grew until there was a full day. Next came heat and moisture, from whose interaction came substance and form, ever more con-crete, until a solid earth and an overarching sky took shape. Many have thought that this rather rarefied conception of a self-evolving cosmos might derive from early Polynesian contact with the religion of India, perhaps in Indonesia around the

1st century AD. This is of course possible. An example recorded among the Maori of New Zealand reads:[1]

From the conception the increase.
From the increase the swelling.
From the swelling the thought.
From the thought the remembrance.
From the remembrance the consciousness, the desire.
The word became fruitful.
It dwelt with the feeble glimmering.
It brought forth night,
the great night, the long night,
the lowest night, the loftiest night,
the thick night, the night to be felt,
the night touched, the night unseen,
the night following on,
the night ending in death.
From the nothing, the begetting.
From the nothing, the increase.
From the nothing, the abundance,
the power of increasing, the living breath.
It dwelled with the empty space.
It produced the atmosphere above us,
the atmosphere that floats above the earth,
the great solid place above us.
The spread-out space dwelled with the early dawn.
Then the moon sprang forth.
The atmosphere above dwelled with the glowing sky.
Immediately was produced the sun.
They were thrown up above as the chief eyes of sky.

---

[1]For the Oceanic texts, cf. R. Taylor, *Te Ika a Maui, or New Zealand and Its Inhabitants, Illustrating the Manners, Customs, Mythology, Religion, Rites, Songs, Proverbs, Fables and Language of the Natives, Together with the Geology, Natural History, Productions and Climate of the Country; Its State as Regards Christianity*, 2nd edition (London, 1870); A. Fornander, *An Account of the Polynesian Race; Its Origins and Migrations*, vol. 1 (London, 1880); G. Grey, *Polynesian Mythology and Ancient Traditional History of the New Zealand Race, as Furnished by Their Priests and Chiefs* (London, 1855); E. Shortland, *Maori Religion and Mythology, with Translations of Traditions* (London, 1882); G. Turner, *Nineteen Years in Polynesia* (London, 1861); W. D. Westervelt, *Legends of Maui, A Demi-God of Polynesia* (London, 1910); R. H. Codrington, *The Melanesians: Studies in Their Anthropology and Folk-Lore* (Oxford, 1891); J. Meier, *Mythen und Erzählungen der Küstenbewohner der Gazellehalbinsel* (Münster, 1909); J. S. Suas, "Mythes et légendes des indigènes des Nouvelles Hebrides," in *Anthropos*, vol. 6 (1911), vol. 7 (1912); J. Meier, "Mythen und Sagen der Admiralitätsinsulaner," in *Anthropos*, vol. 2 (1907); M. Girschner, "Die Karolineninsel Namoluk und ihrer Bewohner," in *Baessler Archiv*, vol. 2 (1912); K. L. Parker, *Australian Legendary Tales* (London, 1896); W. Dunlop, "Australian Folk-Lore Stories," in *Journal of the (Royal) Anthropological Institute of Great Britain and Ireland*, vol. 38 (1899). See also, R. B. Dixon, *Oceanic Mythology, Mythology of All Races*, ed. L. H. Gray, vol. 9 (Boston, 1916); P. Rascher, "Die Sulka: ein Beitrag zur Ethnographie von Neu-Pommern," in *Archiv für Anthropolgie*, vol. 29 (1904); K. Strehlow, "Mythen, Sagen und Märchen des Aranda-Stammes in Zentral-Australien," in *Veröffentlichungen aus dem städtischen Völker-Museum, Frankfurt am Main*, vol. 1, part I (1907).

Then the sky became light, the early dawn, the early day,
the midday, the blaze of day from the sky.
The sky that floats above the earth
dwelled with Hawaiki.°

°*Hawaiki*: the Polynesian underworld.

The successive stages in the development of the cosmos are personified and each
is regarded as the offspring of the preceding.

According to another Maori tale on New Zealand the primordial beings were
Father Sky, often called **Rangi** or something similar, and Mother Earth, whose name
in many places was **Papa**. Rangi and Papa were locked in an eternal embrace, very
like Uranus and Gaea in the Greek myth. From them came all features and nature, all
gods, and at last man himself (Figure 13.1).

At first there was no place for their offspring to go. For a long time the gods lived
in darkness, but at last they determined to lift Rangi on high, to separate Sky from
Earth. **Tane** (**ta**-ne), god of forests, at last succeeds in making the separation:

Darkness then rested upon the heaven and upon the earth, and they still cleaved
together, for they had not yet been rent apart. The children they had begotten

**FIGURE 13.1** Carving from the front of a storehouse depicting the Maori gods, Rangi
or Father Sky and Papa or Mother Earth, as a couple copulating on top of Po, or chaos. In
Maori myth they were finally separated from their embrace only by the intervention of
Tane, god of the forests. The children of Rangi and Papa are shown as three heads in the
carving. New Zealand, Maori, 18th century, wood. Otago Museum, Dunedin, New Zealand.
(Sergey Komarov-Kohl / Alamy)

were always thinking among themselves what might be the difference between darkness and light. They knew that beings had multiplied and increased, and yet light had never broken upon them, but it was always dark.

At last the beings who were begotten by Sky and Earth, worn out by the continued darkness, consulted among themselves, saying, "Let us now determine what we should do with Rangi and Papa, whether it would be better to kill them or to rend them apart."

Then spoke Tu-matauenga, the fiercest of the children of Sky and Earth, "It is well, let us kill them."

Then spoke Tane-mahuta, the father of forests and of all things that inhabit them or that are constructed from trees, "No, not so. It is better to tear them apart and to let the sky stand far above us and the earth lie under our feet. Let the sky become a stranger to us, but the earth remain as close to us as our nursing mother."

The brothers all consented to this proposal with the exception of Tawhirima-tea, the father of winds and storms. Fearing that his kingdom was about to be overthrown, he grieved greatly at the thought of his parents being torn apart. Five of the brothers willingly consented to the separation of their parents, but this one would not agree to it.

Their plans having been agreed on, lo, Rongo, the god and father of the cultivated food of man, rose up that he might rend apart the heavens and the earth. He struggled but he could not rend them apart.

Lo, next Tangaroa, the god and father of fish and reptiles rose up to rend apart the heavens and the earth. But he could not rend them apart.

Lo, next Haumia-tikitiki, the god and father of the food of humans that springs up without cultivation, rose up and struggled, but ineffectually.

Lo, then, Tu, the god and father of fierce human beings, rose up and struggled, but he too failed in his efforts.

Then, at last, slowly rose up Tane, the god and father of forests, of birds, and of insects, and he struggled with his parents.

In vain he strove to rend them apart with his hands and arms. Lo, he pauses, his head now firmly planted on his mother the earth, his feet raised up and resting against his father the sky. He strained his back and limbs with a mighty effort. Now were rent apart Rangi and Papa. With cries and groans they shrieked aloud, "Why are you thus killing your parents? Why do you commit so dreadful a crime as to kill us, as to rend your parents apart?"

But Tane did not pause. He regarded not their shrieks and cries. Far, far beneath him he pressed down the earth. Far, far above him, he thrust up the sky.

Up to this time, the vast Sky has ever remained separated from his spouse the Earth. Yet their mutual love continues—the soft warm sighs of her loving bosom still ever rise up to him, ascending from the woody mountains and valleys, and men call these mists. And the vast Sky, as he mourns through the long nights his separation from his beloved, drops frequent tears upon her bosom, and men, seeing these, called them drops of dew.

Many other accounts have been collected telling of the origins of all things. The thoughts of the Polynesian people in regard to origins by no means present a uniform type. Nonetheless, the creation is normally attributed to a single power, or they see Sky/ Earth as progenitors of an evolutionary sequence. The Polynesians had a highly developed social structure, with status determined by genealogy: One was important because one's ancestors had been important. In the case of the chiefs, a divine descent was claimed. The genealogical explanation of origins flattered this means of achieving status.

## Myth: The Polynesian Creation of Humans

Some Polynesian myths told how the creator-god made the first man and his consort of clay or mud. Another type of story told how the creator first made a female, then had intercourse with her to produce human beings. In a Maori version from New Zealand, it is not the creator-god himself, Rangi, but his son Tane who wishes to have intercourse with the first female, Papa, in this case his own mother:

> Some time after this Tane desired to have his mother Papa for his wife. But Papa said, "Do not incline towards me, for only evil will come of it. Go to your ancestor Mumuhango." So Tane took Mumuhango to wife, who brought forth the *totara*-tree.°
>
> Tane returned to his mother dissatisfied, and his mother said, "Go to your ancestor the Mountain Maid [Hine-tu-a-maunga]." So Tane took the Mountain Maid to wife, who conceived, but did not bring forth a child. Her offspring was the rusty water of mountains, and the monster reptiles common to mountains.
>
> Tane was displeased and returned to his mother. Papa said to him, "Go to your ancestor Ranga-hore." So Tane went and took that female for a wife, who brought forth stone.
>
> This greatly displeased Tane, who again went back to Papa. Then Papa said, "Go to your ancestor the Tender One [Ngaore]." Tane took the Tender One to wife. And the Tender One gave birth to the *toetoe*.°
>
> Tane returned to his mother in displeasure. She next advised him, "Go to your ancestor Pakoti." Tane did as he was bid, but Pakoti only brought forth *phormium tenax*° [*harekeke*].
>
> Tane had a great many other wives at his mother's bidding, but none of them pleased him, and his heart was greatly troubled, because no child was born to give birth to humans. He thus addressed his mother: "Old lady, there will never be any progeny for me." Thereupon Papa said, "Go to your ancestor, Ocean, who is grumbling there in the distance. When you reach the beach at Kurawaka, gather up the earth in the form of humans."
>
> So Tane went and scraped up the earth at Kurawaka. He gathered up the earth, the body was formed, and then the head, and the arms, then he joined on the legs and patted down the surface of the belly so as to give the form of humans. And when he had done this, he returned to his mother, and said, "The whole body of humans is finished." Then he named this female form the Earth-formed Maid [Hine-ahu-one].
>
> Tane took the Earth-formed Maid to wife. She first gave birth to Tiki-tohua— the egg of a bird from which have sprung all the birds of the air. After that, Tiki-kapakapa was born, a female. Then first was born for Tane a human child.

°*totara-tree*: a medium to large tree native to New Zealand. °*toetoe*: a species of rush-like grass. °*phormium tenax*: a flax-like evergreen perennial plant native to New Zealand.

Another type of myth of the origin of humans describes them as emerging from a preexistent form, often a worm. According to a tale told in Samoa, after Tangaloa had created the world by casting down a rock from heaven and had sent earth and creeping plants to cover it and give it shade, these vines died. From the worms that killed them, or into which their rotting stalks were changed, humans emerged:

> When the heavens alone were inhabited and the earth covered over with water, Tangaloa sent down his daughter in the form of a snipe to search for a resting-place. After flying about for a long time, she found a rock partially above the surface of the water. Turi went up and told her father that she had found but a single spot on which she could rest.
>
> Tangaloa sent her down again to visit the place. She went to and fro repeatedly, and every time she went up she reported that the dry surface extended on all sides. Tangaloa sent down his daughter with some earth and a creeping plant, for all was barren rock.
>
> She continued to visit the earth and return to the skies. On the next visit, the plant was spreading. On the next time, it was withered and decomposing. On the next visit, it swarmed with worms. And the next time, the worms had become men and women!

## Myth: Legends of Maui

Of all the Polynesian myths, the best known are those that recount the deeds and adventures of **Maui** (**mow**-ē), after whom is named the large Hawaiian island. Maui was the Heracles of Polynesia. He snared the sun. He pulled up islands from the ocean depths. He lifted the sky into its present position and smoothed its arched surface with his stone adze. Maui was one of the Polynesian demigods. His parents belonged to a family of supernatural beings. He himself was possessed of supernatural powers and made use of all manner of enchantments. In New Zealand Maui was said to have assisted other gods in the creation of man. Nevertheless Maui was very human. He lived in thatched houses, had wives and children, and was scolded by the women for not properly supporting his household.

Almost every group had its own version of these tales, but usually Maui is described as one of a series of brothers, the number varying from three to six. His father is variously named, but his mother is usually Hina. Maui is usually the youngest child, as in folktales generally. The older brothers are stupid or forgetful, while Maui, the hero, is clever or mischievous. Thus the older brothers used spears without barbs and eel-pots without trap-doors and wondered why they were not catching anything, but the youngest brother invented the barb on the spear and the trap-door for the eel-pot and succeeded where they failed.

In New Zealand Maui is said to have been an abortion, which his mother Hina wrapped up in her apron and either abandoned in the bush or threw into the sea. Although thus deserted, Maui survived, tended by supernatural beings and reared to manhood. Maui was determined to seek out his parents and brothers. He came upon his brothers while they were playing a spear-throwing game. After the brothers had hurled their spears, Maui asked if he could throw. As he did so he shouted his name, but the others at once said that he had no right to be called Maui. He asked them to summon their mother to decide. When Hina came, she declared that he was no child of hers and asked that he leave. Maui asked her to remember that which she had cast away. Hina mother recognized him, and he became her favorite child.

Of the many exploits of Maui three are most widely reported: fishing up the land, snaring the sun, and the quest of fire.

## Myth: Maui Fishes up the Land

According to the New Zealand Maori version, Maui was so mischievous that his brothers refused to have anything to do with him. Thrown on his own resources, Maui determined to make a hook that would catch something worthwhile. Maui had an ancestress to whom it was the duty of the older brothers to carry food, but they neglected her and ate it themselves. Maui offered to take their place, but when he came to his ancestress, he found her sick. One half of her body was already dead. He wrenched off her lower jaw, made a fish-hook, and returned home. But still the brothers would not allow him to come fishing with them, although he pleaded and pleaded.

Maui could change his shape and had deceived his brothers before through this power. Now again:

> Maui went out to the canoe and concealed himself as an insect in the bottom of the boat so that when the early morning light crept over the waters and his brothers pushed the canoe into the surf they could not see him. They were glad that Maui did not appear and paddled away over the waters.
>
> They fished all day and all night. On the morning of the next day, out from the fish in the bottom of the boat came their troublesome brother.
>
> They had caught many fine fish and were satisfied and intended to paddle homeward, but their younger brother pleaded with them to go out, far out, to the deeper seas and permit him to cast his hook. He said he wanted larger and better fish than any they had caught.
>
> So they paddled to their outermost fishing grounds, but this did not satisfy Maui. He sang:
>
> *Farther out on the waters,*
> *O! my brothers,*
> *I seek the great fish of the sea.*
>
> It was easier to work for him than to argue, so far out in the sea they went. The homeland disappeared from view. They could see only the outstretching waste of waters. Maui urged them out still farther. Then he drew his magic hook from under his loincloth. The brothers wondered what he was going to do for bait when he struck his nose a mighty blow until the blood gushed forth. When this blood became clotted, he fastened it on his hook and let it down into the deep sea.
>
> Down went the hook to the very bottom and caught the underworld. It was a mighty fish and the brothers paddled with all their might and main as Maui pulled in the line. It was hard rowing against the power that held the hook down in the depths of the sea, but the brothers had become enthusiastic over Maui's large fish and were generous in their strenuous endeavors.

Every muscle was strained and every paddle held strongly against the sea, so that not an inch should be lost. There was no sudden leaping and darting to and fro, no "give" to the line, no "tremble" as when a great fish shakes itself in impotent wrath when held captive by a hook. It was simply a struggle of tense muscle against an immensely heavy dead weight. To the brothers there came slowly the feeling that Maui was in one of his strange moods and that something beyond their former experiences with their tricky brother was coming to pass.

One of the brothers glanced backward and with a scream of intense terror he dropped his paddle. The others also looked. Then each caught his paddle and with frantic exertion tried to force the canoe onward. Deep down in the heavy waters they pushed their paddles. Out of the great seas the black, ragged head of a large island was rising like a fish. It seemed to be chasing them through the boiling surf. In a little while the water became shallow around them, and their canoe finally rested on a black beach.

Maui for some reason left his brothers, telling them not to try to cut up this great fish. But the unwise brothers thought they would fill the canoe with part of this strange thing that they had caught. They began to cut up the back and put huge slices into their canoe. But the great fish—the island—shook under the blows and with a mighty earthquake tossed up the boat of the brothers, destroying the canoe. As they struggled in the waters, the great fish ate them up. The island came up more and more from the waters, but the deep gashes made by Maui's brothers did not heal. They became the mountains and valleys, stretching from sea to sea.

In some versions the land hauled up was Tonga in western Polynesia; in others, it was New Zealand in southwestern Polynesia, which some Maori call the "Fish of Maui."

## Myth: Maui Snares the Sun

According to a Hawaiian legend, Maui's mother Hina was much troubled by the shortness of the day caused by the rapid movement of the sun, making it impossible to dry properly the sheets of *tapa*—made from a beaten inner bark—used for clothing. Therefore the hero resolved to cut off the legs of the sun so that he could not travel so fast:

After studying the path of the sun, Maui returned to his mother Hina and told her that he would go and cut off the legs of the sun so that he could not run so fast.

His mother said, "Are you strong enough for this work?"

He said, "Yes."

Then Hina gave him fifteen strands of well-twisted fiber and told him to go to his grandmother, who lived in the great crater of Haleakala, for the rest of the things needed in his struggle with the sun. She said, "You must climb the mountain to the place where a large *wiliwili* tree is standing. There you will find the place where the sun stops to eat cooked bananas prepared by your grandmother. Stay there until a rooster crows three times. Then watch your grandmother go out to make a fire and put on food. You had better take her bananas. She will look for them and find you and ask who you are. Tell her you belong to Hina."

When she had taught him all these things, he went up the mountain to the place Hina had directed. There was a large *wiliwili* tree. Here he waited for the rooster to crow. When the rooster had crowed three times, the grandmother came out with a bunch of bananas to cook for the sun. She took off the upper part of the bunch and laid it down. Maui immediately snatched it away. In a moment she turned to pick it up, but could not find it. She was angry and cried out, "Where are the bananas of the sun?"

Then she took off another part of the bunch, and Maui stole that too. Thus he did until all the bunches had been taken away. She was almost blind and could not detect him by sight, so she sniffed all around her until she detected the smell of a man.

She asked, "Who are you? To whom do you belong?"

Maui replied, "I belong to Hina."

"Why have you come?"

Maui told her, "I have come to kill the sun. He goes so fast that he never dries the *tapa* Hina has beaten out."

The old woman gave a magic stone for a battle ax and one more rope. She taught him how to catch the sun, saying, "Make a place to hide here by this large *wiliwili* tree. When the first leg of the sun comes up, catch it with your first rope, and so on until you have used all your ropes. Fasten them to the tree, then take the stone ax to strike the body of the sun."

Maui dug a hole among the roots of the tree and concealed himself. Soon the first ray of light—the first leg of the sun—came up along the mountain side. Maui threw his rope and caught it. One by one the legs of the sun came over the edge of the crater's rim and were caught. Only one long leg was still hanging down the side of the mountain. It was hard for the sun to move that leg. It shook and trembled and tried hard to come up. At last it crept over the edge and was caught by Maui with the rope his grandmother had given him.

When the sun saw that his sixteen long legs were held fast in the ropes, he began to go back down the mountain side into the sea. Then Maui tied the ropes fast to the tree and pulled until the body of the sun came up again. Brave Maui caught his magic stone club or ax and began to strike and wound the sun, until he cried, "Give me my life."

Maui said, "If you live, you may be a traitor. Perhaps I had better kill you."

But the sun begged for life. After they had talked a while, they agreed that there should be a regular motion in the journey of the sun. There should be longer days. Half the time he might go quickly as in the wintertime, but the other half he must move slowly as in summer. Thus men dwelling on the earth would be blessed.

## Myth: Maui Goes in Quest of Fire

A third great exploit accredited to Maui is the fire-quest. Fire distinguishes the human life from that of the beast, and its possession is in many myths throughout the world attributed to a trickster, who takes fire from the gods. The Hawaiian story of finding fire is one of the least marvelous of all the myths about Maui:

Hina, Maui's mother, wanted fish. One early morning Maui saw that the great storm waves of the sea had died down and the fishing grounds could be easily reached. He awakened his brothers and with them hastened to the beach. This was at Kaupo on the island of Maui. Out into the gray shadows of the dawn they paddled.

When they were far from shore they began to fish. But Maui, looking toward land, saw a fire on the mountainside.

"Look," he cried. "There is a fire burning. Whose can this fire be?"

"Whose in fact?" his brothers replied.

"Let us hurry to the shore and cook our food," said one of the brothers.

They decided that they had better catch some fish to cook before they returned. Therefore in the morning, before the hot sun drove the fish deep down to the dark recesses of the sea, they fished until a bountiful supply lay in the bottom of the canoe.

When they came to land, Maui leaped out and ran up the mountainside to get the fire. For a long, long time they had been without fire. The great volcano Haleakala above them had become extinct, and they had lost the coals they had tried to keep alive. They had eaten fruits and uncooked roots and the shellfish broken from the reef and sometimes the great raw fish from far out in the ocean. But now they hoped to gain living fire and cooked food.

But when Maui rushed up toward the cloudy pillar of smoke he saw a family of birds scratching the fire out. Their work was finished, and they flew away just as he reached the place.

Maui and his brothers watched for fire day after day but the birds, the curly-tailed Alae,° made no fire. Finally the brothers went fishing once more, but when they looked toward the mountain again they saw flames and smoke. Thus it happened to them again and again.

Maui proposed to his brothers that they go fishing, leaving him to watch the birds. But the Alae counted the fishermen and refused to build a fire for the hidden one who was watching them. They said among themselves, "Three are in the boat, and we know not where the other one is. We will make no fire today."

So the experiment failed again and again. If one or two stayed behind, or if all waited on the land, there would be no fire, but the dawn that saw the four brothers in the boat saw also the fire on the land.

Finally Maui rolled some *tapa* cloth together and stuck it up in one end of the canoe so that it looked like a man. He then concealed himself near the haunt of the Alae while his brothers went out fishing. The birds counted the figures in the boat and then started to build a heap of wood for the fire.

Maui was impatient and just as the old Alae began to select sticks with which to make the flames, he leaped swiftly out and caught her and held her prisoner. He forgot for a moment that he wanted the secret of fire-making. In his anger against the wise bird his first impulse was to taunt her and then kill her for hiding the secret of fire.

°*Alae*: a kind of mudhen.

But the Alae cried out, "If you are the death of me, my secret will perish also and you cannot have fire."

Maui then promised to spare her life if she would tell him what to do.

Then came the contest of wits. The bird told Maui to rub the stalks of water plants together. He guarded the bird and tried the plants. Water instead of fire ran out of the twisted stems. Then she told him to rub reeds together, but they bent and broke and did not make fire. He twisted her neck until she was half dead, then she cried out, "I have hidden the fire in a green stick."

Maui worked hard, but not a spark of fire appeared. Again he caught his prisoner by the head and wrung her neck, and she named a kind of dry wood. Maui rubbed the sticks together, but they only became warm. He resumed his neck-twisting and repeated it again and again until the mudhen was almost dead and Maui had tried tree after tree. At last Maui found fire.

Then as the flames rose, he said, "There is one more thing to rub." He took a fire stick and rubbed the top of the head of his prisoner until the feathers fell off and the raw flesh appeared. Thus the Hawaiian mudhen and her descendants have ever since had bald heads, and the Hawaiians have had the secret of fire-making.

In New Zealand a completely different version is told of the theft of fire. Maui and his brothers lived with their mother Hina, but every morning she disappeared before they awoke. Nobody knew where she went. Determining to solve the mystery, Maui stopped up every chink and cranny in the house, thus preventing the morning light from coming in so that his mother overslept. Maui, waking in time, saw Hina leave the house, pull up a clump of reeds or grass, and disappear down the opening. Disguising himself as a bird, he flew down the hole to the world below, where he revealed himself to his mother and demanded food.

However, Hina had no fire. Maui volunteered to bring it from the house of his ancestor Mafuike, an old woman who was the owner and guardian of fire. He begged a brand from Mafuike, but she gave him one of her fingers in which fire was concealed. When out of sight, he quenched it in a stream and returned for more. Mafuike gave him another finger, but he extinguished it in a similar manner and in this way got from her all her fingers and toes except the last, with which, in anger, she set the world afire.

Maui fled the flames, which threatened to consume everything. He called upon rain, snow, and hail to aid him, and they put out the conflagration and saved the world. The last of the fire fell into various trees, which since then have preserved the germ of fire, which can be called forth by friction.

## Myth: Maui Raises the Sky

Maui's home was for long enveloped by darkness. The heavens had fallen down, or, rather, had not yet been separated from the earth. The skies pressed so closely and heavily on the earth that when the plants tried to grow, all the leaves were flattened out. Thus the leaves have remained flat through all the days of humankind. The plants lifted the sky inch by inch until men were able to crawl about between the heavens and the earth, and thus pass from place to place and visit one another. Then, as told in Hawaii:

After a long time, Maui came to a woman and said, "Give me a drink from your gourd calabash, and I will push the heavens higher."

The woman handed the gourd to him. When Maui had taken a deep drink, he braced himself against the clouds and lifted them to the height of the trees. Again he hoisted the sky and carried it to the tops of the mountains. Then with great exertion he thrust it upwards once more and pressed it to the place it now occupies. Nevertheless dark clouds many times hang low along the eastern slope of Maui's great mountain—Haleakala—and descend in heavy rains upon the hill Kauwiki. But they dare not stay, or Maui the strong will come and hurl them so far away that they cannot come back again.

A man who had been watching the process of lifting the sky ridiculed Maui for attempting such a difficult task. When the clouds rested on the tops of the mountains, Maui turned to punish his critic. The man had fled to the other side of the island, but Maui rapidly pursued and finally caught him on the seacoast, not many miles north of the town now known as Lahaina. After a brief struggle, the man was changed into a great black rock that can be seen by any traveler.

## Myth: The Death of Maui

On New Zealand the Maori uniquely told of Maui's attempt to secure immortality for humankind.

Maui returned to his parents, and when he had been with them for some time, his father said to him one day, "O my son, I have heard from your mother and others that you are very courageous and that you have succeeded in all feats that you have undertaken in your own country, whether small or great. But now that you have arrived in your father's country, you will, perhaps, be at last overcome."

Then Maui asked him, "What do you mean, what things are there that I can be vanquished by?"

And his father answered, "You can be overcome by your great ancestress, by Great Hina of the Night,° whom you may see flashing, if you look, and opening and shutting there where the horizon meets the sky."

And Maui replied, "Put aside such idle thoughts and let us both fearlessly seek whether men are to die or live forever."

And his father said, "My child, there has been an ill omen for us. When I was baptizing you, I omitted a portion of the correct prayers, and this I know will be the cause of your perishing."

Then Maui asked his father, "What is my ancestress Great Hina of the Night like?"

And he answered, "What you see yonder shining so brightly red are her eyes, and her teeth are as sharp and hard as pieces of volcanic glass. Her body is

°*Hina of the Night:* not Maui's mother.

like that of man, and as for the pupils of her eyes, they are jasper. And her hair is like tangles of long seaweed, and her mouth is like a barracuda's."

Then his son answered him, "Do you think her strength is as great as that of the Sun, who consumes man, and the earth, and the very waters by the fierceness of his heat? But I laid hold of the Sun, and now he goes slowly."

And his father answered him, "That is all very true, O my last born, and the strength of my old age. Well then, be bold, go and visit your great ancestress who flashes so fiercely there where the edge of the horizon meets the sky."

Hardly had Maui concluded this conversation with his father before the young hero went forth to look for companions to accompany him on this enterprise. There came to him as companions the small robin, the large robin, the thrush, the yellow-hammer, and every kind of little bird, and these all assembled together, and they all started with Maui in the evening and arrived at the dwelling of Great Hina of the Night. They found her fast asleep.

Then Maui addressed them all, and said, "My little friends, now if you see me creep into this old chieftainess, do not laugh at what you see. No, no, do not I pray you, but when I have got altogether inside her, and just as I am coming out of her mouth, then you may shout with laughter if you please."

And his little friends, frightened at what they saw, replied, "O sir, you will certainly be killed."

And he answered them, "If you burst out laughing at me as soon as I get inside her, you will wake her up, and she will certainly kill me at once, but if you do not laugh until I am quite inside her, and am on the point of coming out of her mouth, I shall live, and Great Hina of the Night will die."

And his little friends answered, "Go on then, brave sir, but please take good care of yourself."

Then the young hero started off and twisted the strings of his weapon tight round his wrist. He went into the house and stripped off his clothes. The skin on his hips looked mottled and as beautiful as that of a mackerel from the tattoo marks cut on it. He entered the old chieftainess.

The little birds now screwed up their tiny cheeks, trying to suppress their laughter. At last the little Tiwakawaka could no longer keep it in and laughed out loud with its merry cheerful note. This woke the old woman up. She opened her eyes, started up, and so killed Maui.

Maui had wished that man might not die forever, and so he said to Hina,° the moon, "Let death be very short—that is, let man die and live again, and live on forever." Whereupon Hina replied, "Let death be very long, that man may sigh and sorrow." Maui again said, "Let man die and live again, as you, the moon, die and live again." But Hina said, "No, let man die and become like soil, and never rise to life again." And so it was.

°*Hina*: still another Hina, not Maui's mother.

## PERSPECTIVE 13.2

## Paul Gauguin in Tahiti

Eugène-Henri-Paul Gauguin (1848–1903), born in Paris, was one of the leading French paint-ers of the postimpressionist period. The son of a French journalist and a Peruvian Creole, he was brought up in Lima, Peru, joined the merchant navy in 1865, and in 1872 began a suc-cessful career as a stockbroker in Paris. He married a Danish woman and had five children. Gauguin's attitudes to art were deeply influenced by his witnessing the first impressionist exhibition in 1874, and he himself exhibited in exhibitions of 1880, 1881, and 1882.

In 1883–1884 the bank that employed him fell into difficulties, allowing Gauguin to paint every day. He settled for a while in Rouen, France, then joined his wife and children in Denmark, then returned to Paris before going to paint in Pont-Aven in Brittany in northwestern France, a resort for artists. In Pont-Aven he adopted a more independent style that had little in common with the other Impressionists.

In 1891 Gauguin organized an exhibition to finance an excursion to places where he could live on "ecstasy, calmness, and art." He sailed to the tropics to escape European civilization and "everything that is artificial and conventional." In Polynesian Tahiti Gauguin discovered primitive art with its flat forms and violent colors, as for example in *The Day of the Gods* (Perspective Figure 13.2).

**PERSPECTIVE FIGURE 13.2**   Paul Gauguin (French, 1848–1903), *The Day of the Gods* (*Mahana no Atua*), 1894. Oil on canvas. (Russell Gordon / Alamy)

Set in a Tahitian landscape by the sea, the composition is divided into three horizontal bands. In the top band, Polynesian women perform a ritual near a monumental sculpture, derived not from the local religion but from photographs of reliefs on a Buddhist temple complex in Java, far to the east. In the middle band, three figures, arranged symmetrically, stand against a field of pink earth. The woman in the center reflects the sculpture at the top. The lower band evokes the brilliant contrasting hues reflected in the water.

Gauguin sought in his art a new way of life that is more primitive, more earnest, more real. His break from a solid middle-class world, his abandonment of family, children, and job, and his refusal to accept easy glory and gain distinguished Gauguin's life and personality. He accepted the myth of the noble savage, the notion that in a state of nature, unfettered by civilization and its oppressive laws, unhampered by a corrupt religion and its dogmas, humans are essentially good.

Like his friend Vincent van Gogh, with whom he spent nine weeks painting in southern France in 1888, Paul Gauguin experienced bouts of depression. At one time he attempted suicide. In 1903, in a disagreement with the government in the MARQUESAS ISLANDS (Map 13.2), he was sentenced to three months in prison. There he died at age 54, his body ruined by syphilis and a life of dissolute behavior.

# THE MYTHS OF MELANESIA

Geographically, **Melanesia** falls into two parts: NEW GUINEA with the smaller adjacent islands forming one part, and the long series of islands lying to the north and east, from the ADMIRALTY ISLANDS to NEW CALEDONIA and FIJI, constituting the other (Map 13.3).

The population of Melanesia is highly complex, being composed of a number of different racial types. By far the largest island is New Guinea, divided today into west and east. Western New Guinea is called the province of **PAPUA** and belongs to the nation state of Indonesia. The eastern portion is called **PAPUA NEW GUINEA** and acknowledges the queen of England as sovereign.

We can recognize at least three racial group in New Guinea. First, confined to the more inaccessible parts, are a number of very dark-skinned tribes, but we know little about them. Second, most of the population of the interior of New Guinea, and of portions of other islands, are known as Papuan, but we know little about their myths. The third type occupies much of southeastern New Guinea, together with part of its northern and northwestern coasts, and forms the majority of the inhabitants of the islands reaching from the Admiralty Islands to Fiji. In general, they are called Melanesians.

From this third group come most of myths that we can study.

## Myth: The Origin of Man

Striking is the absence in Melanesia of myths describing the origin of the world. The earth is regarded as having always existed in much the same form as it is today. A variety of stories were told, however, about the creation of man, including in the NEW HEBRIDES (now the nation of VANUATU) that he was made of mud. The New Hebrides was the colonial name for an island group east of New Britain, colonized by both the British and French in the 18th century shortly after Captain James Cook visited the

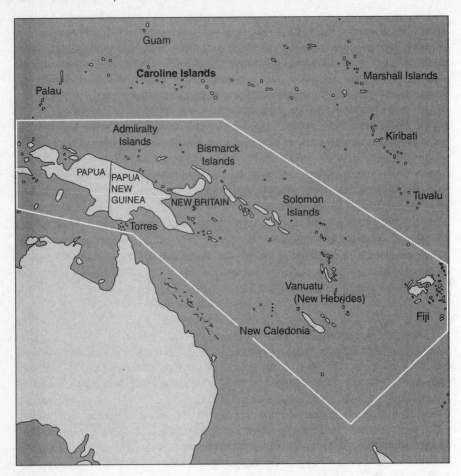

**MAP 13.3**  Melanesia.

islands. The islands were uniquely ruled by the French and British working together, until they gained their independence as Vanuatu:

> Takaro° made from mud ten figures of men. When they were finished, he breathed upon them, breathed upon their eyes, their ears, their mouths, their hands, their feet, and thus the images became alive.
>
> But all the people he had made were men and Takaro was not satisfied, so he told them to light a fire and cook some food. When they had done so, he ordered them to stand still and he threw at one of them a fruit, and lo! one of the men was changed into a woman. Then Takaro ordered the woman to go and stay by herself in the house. After a while, he sent one of the nine men to her to ask for fire, and she greeted him as her elder brother. A second was sent to ask for water, and she greeted him as her younger brother. And so one after another, she greeted them as relatives, all but the last, and him she called her husband.
>
> So Takaro said to him, "Take her as your wife, and you two shall live together."

°*Takaro*: a creator-god.

## Myth: The Origin of Races

One anthropologist reports a myth that accounts for the racial divide in New Guinea:

> To-Kabinana, the first brother, said to To-Karvuvu, the second brother, "Get two light-colored coconuts. One of them you must hide, then bring the other to me."
>
> To-Karvuvu, however, did not obey, but got one light and one dark nut, and having hidden the dark nut he brought the light-colored one to his brother. He tied it to the stern of his canoe and sat down in the bow. He paddled out to sea. He paid no attention to the noise that the nut made as it struck against the sides of his canoe nor did he look around. Soon the coconut turned into a handsome woman, who sat on the stern of the canoe and steered, while To-Kabinana paddled.
>
> When he came back to land, his brother fell in love with the woman and wished her as his wife, but To-Kabinana refused and said that they would now make another woman. Accordingly, To-Karvuvu brought the other coconut, but when his brother saw that it was dark colored, he upbraided To-Karvuvu and said, "You are indeed a stupid fellow. You have brought misery upon our mortal race. From now on, we shall be divided into two classes, into you and us."
>
> Then they tied the coconut to the stern of the canoe and paddled away as before. The nut turned into a black-skinned woman. When they had returned to shore, To-Kabinana said, "Alas, you have only ruined our mortal race. If all of us were only light of skin, we should not die. Now, however, this dark-skinned woman will produce one group, and the light-skinned woman another, and the light-skinned men shall marry the dark-skinned women, and the dark-skinned men shall marry the light-skinned women."
>
> And so To-Kabinana divided humankind into two classes.

## Myth: The Melanesian Origin of Fire

Once all food was eaten raw, but many myths told of the discovery of fire. A version from the admiralty islands runs as follows:

> The daughter of Ulimgau went into the forest. A serpent saw her and said, "Come!" and the woman replied, "Who would have you for a husband? You are a serpent. I will not marry you."
>
> But he replied, "My body is in fact that of a serpent, but my speech is that of a man. Come!"
>
> And the woman went and married him, and after a time she bore a boy and a girl, and her serpent-husband put her away and said, "Go, I will take care of them and give them food."
>
> And the serpent fed the children and they grew. And one day they were hungry, and the serpent said to them, "Do you go and catch fish." And they caught fish and brought them to their father. And he said, "Cook the fish."
>
> And they replied, "The sun has not yet risen."
>
> By and by the sun rose and warmed the fish with its rays, and they ate the food still raw and bloody. Then the serpent said to them, "You two are spirits,

for you eat your food raw. Perhaps you will eat me. You, girl, stay, and you, boy, crawl into my belly."

The boy was afraid and said, "What shall I do?"

But his father said to him, "Go," and he crept into the serpent's belly. And the serpent said to him, "Take the fire and bring it out to your sister. Come out and gather coconuts and yams and taro and bananas."

So the boy crept out again, bringing the fire from the belly of the serpent. And then having brought the food, the boy and girl lit a fire with the brand which the boy had secured and cooked the food. And when they had eaten, the serpent said to them, "Is my kind of food or your kind of food the better?" And they answered, "Your food is good, ours is bad."

## Myth: The Wise and the Foolish Brothers

A noteworthy feature of Melanesian mythology is tales of two brothers, one of whom is wise and benevolent, while the other is foolish and malicious. The opposition is clear in a story from the New Hebrides. In this story the brothers are named **Meragbuto** and **Tagaro**:

One day Meragbuto saw Tagaro, who had just oiled his hair with coconut oil, and admiring the effect greatly, asked how this result had been produced. Tagaro, asked him if he had any hens, and when Meragbuto answered that he had many, Tagaro said, "Well, when they have roosted in the trees, do you go and sit under a tree and anoint yourself with the ointment which they will throw down to you."

Meragbuto carried out the instructions exactly and rubbed not only his hair, but his whole body with the excrement of the fowls. On the following day he went proudly to a festival, but as soon as he approached every one ran away, crying out at the intolerable odor. Only then did Meragbuto realize that he had been tricked, and washed himself in the sea.

Another time Tagaro placed a taboo on all coconuts so that no one should eat them, but Meragbuto paid no attention to this prohibition, eating and eating until he had devoured nearly all of them. Thereupon Tagaro took a small coconut, scraped out half the meat, and leaving the rest in the shell, sat down to await the coming of Meragbuto, who soon appeared. Seeing the coconut, he asked Tagaro if it was his.

"Yes," said Tagaro, "if you are hungry, eat it, but only on condition that you eat it all." So Meragbuto sat down and scraped the remainder of the nut and ate it, but though he scraped and scraped, more was always left, and so he continued eating all day.

At night Meragbuto said to Tagaro, "My cousin, I can't eat any more, my stomach pains me."

But Tagaro answered, "No. I put a taboo on the coconuts and you disregarded it. Now you must eat it all."

So Meragbuto continued to eat until finally he burst and died. If he had not perished, there would have been no more coconuts, for he would have devoured them all.

At last Tagaro determined to destroy Meragbuto utterly.

Accordingly he said, "Let us each build a house."

This they did, but Tagaro secretly dug a deep pit in the floor of his house and covered it over with leaves and earth, after which he said to Meragbuto, "Come, set fire to my house so that I and my wife and children may be burned and die. Thus you will become the sole chief."

So Meragbuto came and set fire to Tagaro's house and then went to his own and lay down and slept. Tagaro and his family, however, quickly crawled into the pit that he had prepared, and so they escaped death. When the house had burned, they came up out of their hiding-place and sat down among the ashes. After a time Meragbuto awoke, and saying, "Perhaps my meat is cooked," he went to where Tagaro's house had been, thinking to find his victims roasted. Utterly amazed to see Tagaro and his family safe and sound, he asked how this had happened. Tagaro replied that the flames had not harmed him at all.

"Good!" said Meragbuto. "When it is night, do you come and set fire to my house and burn me also." So Tagaro set fire to Meragbuto's house, but when the flames began to burn him, Meragbuto cried out, "My cousin! It hurts me. I am dying."

Tagaro, however, replied, "No, you will not die. It was just that way in my case. Bear it bravely. It will soon be over." And so it was, for Meragbuto was burned up and entirely destroyed.

## Myth: Melanesian Myths of Cannibalism

The South Sea islanders, as many native peoples throughout the world, were cannibals. Cannibalism was either practiced as revenge against an enemy, or in order to acquire the qualities of the dead man, or as a ritual. The Fiji Islands in Melanesia (see Map 13.3) were once called the Cannibal Islands. Although in reality cannibalism could be a pious ritual act, in the myths cannibals are always the bad guys, even ogres. As told by the Sulka, a Papuan tribe of New Britain, one of these stories runs as follows:

Once there was a cannibal and his wife who had killed and eaten a great many persons so that, fearing that they should all be destroyed, the people resolved to abandon their village and seek safety in flight. Accordingly they prepared their canoes, loaded all their property on board, and made ready to leave.

But Tamus, one of the women of the village, was pregnant, so the others refused to take her with them, saying that she would only be a burden upon the journey. She swam after them and clung to the stern of one of the canoes, but they beat her off, compelling her to return to the deserted village and to live there alone.

In due time she bore a son, and when he grew up a little she would leave him in her hut while she went out to get food, warning him not to talk or laugh, or the cannibals might hear and come and eat him.

One day his mother left him a *dracaena* plant as a plaything, and when she was gone he said to himself, "What shall I make out of this, my brother or my cousin?" Then he held the *dracaena* behind him, and presently it turned into a boy, with whom he played and talked.

Resolving to conceal the presence of his new friend, Pupal, from his mother, he said to her on her return, "Mother, I want to make a partition in our house. Then you can live on one side, and I will live on the other," and this he did, concealing Pupal in his portion of the house.

From time to time his mother thought that she heard her son talking to someone and was surprised at the quantity of food and drink he required, but though she often asked him if he was alone, he always declared that he was. At last one day she discovered Pupal and learned how he had come from the *dracaena*. She was glad that her son now had a companion, and all three lived happily together.

Mother Tamus was, however, more than ever afraid that the cannibals would hear sounds, and suspecting the presence of people in the deserted village, would come to eat them, but the two boys reassured her, saying, "Have no fear. We shall kill them if they dare to come."

Accordingly, making themselves shields and spears, they practiced marksmanship and also erected a slippery barricade around the house so that it would be difficult to climb. When they had completed their preparations, they set up a swing near the house. While they were swinging they called out to the cannibals, "Where are you? We are here, come and eat us."

The cannibals heard, and one said to the other, "Don't you hear someone calling us over there? Who can it be, for we have eaten all of them."

So they set out for the village to see what could have made the noise, the two boys being ready in hiding. When the cannibals tried to climb the barricade, they slipped and fell. The boys rushed out and killed them both after a hard fight. The children then called to the boy's mother, who was greatly terrified, and when she came and saw both the cannibals dead, she built a fire. They cut up the bodies and burned them, saving only the breasts of the ogress. These Tamus put in a coconut shell, and setting it afloat on the sea said, "Go to the people who ran away from here, and if they ask, 'Have the cannibals killed Tamus, and are these her breasts?'—then remain floating. But if they say, 'Has Tamus borne a son and has he killed the cannibals, and are these the breasts of the ogress?'—then sink!"

The coconut shell floated away at once and by and by came to the new village built by the people who had fled years before. All occurred as Tamus had foreseen, and through the aid of the coconut shell and its contents the people learned the truth. When they discovered the death of the cannibals, they were overjoyed and set out at once for their old home, but just as they were about to land, Pupal and Tamus's son attacked them, and Tamus said, "You abandoned my mother and cast her away. Now, you shall not come back." After a while, however, he relented and allowed the people to land, and all lived together again happily and safely in their old home.

Another cannibal story is told in the New Hebrides: (Figure 13.2)

There was once a cannibal named Taso who came one day upon the sister of Qatu and killed her, but did not eat her because she was pregnant. So he abandoned her body in a thicket, and there, though their mother was dead, twin boys

**FIGURE 13.2**    A cannibal tribesman in New Guinea. On the rack beside him he has reconstructed and dressed the victim he has earlier devoured. One arm of the decorated skeleton is draped over the rack. (Presselect / Alamy)

were born. They found rainwater collected in dead leaves and shoots of plants that they could eat. Thus they lived, and when they grew old enough to walk, they wandered about in the forest. One day they found a sow belonging to their uncle Qatu. He came daily to give it food, but when he had gone, the boys would eat part of the sow's provisions. Thus they grew, and their skins and hair were fair.

Qatu wondered why his sow did not become fat, and laying in wait discovered the twins and caught them. But when they told him who they were, he welcomed them as his nephews and took them home with him. After they grew bigger, he made little bows of palm fronds for them, and when they could shoot lizards, he broke the bows, giving them larger ones with which they brought down greater game. Thus he trained them until they were grown up and could shoot anything.

When they were young men, Qatu told them about Taso and how he had murdered their mother, warning them to be careful, in case Taso should catch them. The twins, however, were determined to kill the cannibal, so they set a taboo on a banana tree belonging to them and said to their uncle, "If our bunch of bananas begins to ripen at the top and ripens downwards, you will know that Taso has killed us. But if it begins to ripen at the bottom and ripens upwards, we shall have killed him."

So they set off to kill Taso, but when they came to his house, he had gone to the beach to sharpen his teeth and only his mother was at home. Accordingly they went and sat in the men's house to wait for him. Lighting a fire in the oven, they roasted some yams and heated stones in the blaze. Thereupon Taso's mother sang a song, telling him that there were two men in the men's house and that there would be good food for him and for her. So the cannibal quickly returned from the shore, and as he came he moved his head from side to side, striking the trees so that they went crashing down.

When he reached the men's house, he climbed over the door rail, but the boys immediately threw at him all the hot rocks from the oven and knocked him down. With their clubs they beat him until he was dead. Then they killed his mother and set fire to the house over them and went away.

Now Qatu, hearing the popping of the bamboos as the house burned, said, "Alas, Taso has probably burned the boys!" Hastening to see what had happened, however, he met them on the way and heard from them that they had killed Taso and had revenged their mother whom Taso had slain.

## THE MYTHS OF MICRONESIA

The largest island in **Micronesia**, "land of small islands," is tiny GUAM, the southernmost of the MARIANA ISLANDS, today a U.S. territory (Map 13.4). Discovered by Ferdinand Magellan in 1521 on the first circumnavigation of the planet, Guam was

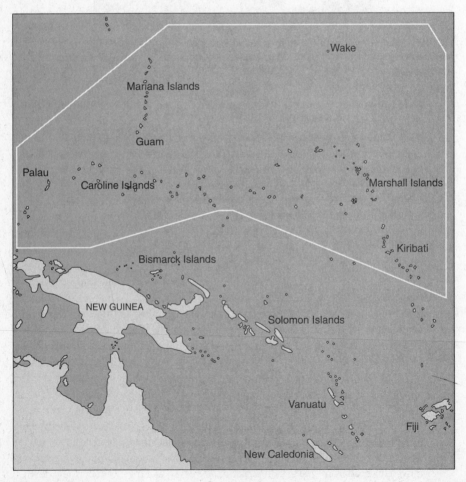

**MAP 13.4**  Micronesia.

ceded to the United States by Spain in 1898. During the two and one half years of Japanese occupation, the native people were subject to systematic rape, beheadings, and the usual Japanese atrocities until recaptured by the United States in 1944. The inhabitants of Micronesia are a mixture of Melanesians, Filipinos, and Polynesians (Figure 13.3).

Of all the islands of the Pacific, Micronesia offers the poorest store of mythic material, not so much because they did not tell stories, but because little attempt was made to gather and record them.

## Myth: The Exploits of Olofat

South of Guam are the about 500 tiny CAROLINE ISLANDS, named after the Spanish king Charles II in 1686 (Figure 13.4). Long a possession of Spain, the Carolines are today independent. An important story recovered from the Carolines tells of the

**FIGURE 13.3**    Indigenous young females in the Caroline Islands in traditional dress. Ifalik Island, Yap Caroline Islands, Federated States of Micronesia. (Douglas Peebles Photography / Alamy)

**FIGURE 13.4**    Rock Island, PALAU, Micronesia. Palau is one of the most recent (1994) and the smallest of all nations, consisting of a cluster of islands in the westernmost Caroline Islands. On one of these, Peleliu, was fought in 1944 a horrific battle in which more than 2,000 Americans and 10,000 Japanese died. (Douglas Peebles Photography / Alamy)

exploits of **Olofat**, the eldest son of Luk, the highest god. He appears as a mischievous, almost malicious person who stands in marked contrast to his brother or brothers, who are beneficent. The great trickster, he always survives attempts to exterminate him:

> Olofat saw that one of his brothers was better than he and also more beautiful, and at this he became angry. Looking down from the sky-world and seeing two boys who had caught a couple of sharks, with which they were playing in a fishpond, he descended to earth and gave the sharks teeth so that they bit the hands of the children. When the boys ran home crying with pain and told their troubles to their mother, Ligoapup, sister of Olofat, she asked them if they had seen any one about. They said that they had and that he was more handsome than any man whom they had ever beheld.
>
> Knowing this must be her brother Olofat, Ligoapup asked her sons where he was, and they answered, "Close by the sea." She then told them to go and get the man and bring him to her, but when they reached the place where they had left him, they found only an old, gray-haired man, covered with dirt. Returning to their mother, they informed her that the man whom they had seen was no longer there. She told them to go back and bring whomever they might find.
>
> Accordingly they set off, but this time they saw only a heap of excrement in place of a man. And so once more they went home to their mother, who told them to return a third time. Obeying her, they questioned the filth, saying,

"Are you Olofat? For if you are, you must come to our mother." Whereupon the pile of excrement turned into a handsome man who accompanied them to Ligoapup.

She said to him, "Why are you such a deceiver?"

And Olofat replied, "How so?"

And she said, "First, you turned yourself into a dirty old man and then into a pile of filth."

"I am afraid of my father," answered Olofat.

"Yes," said Ligoapup, "you are afraid because you gave teeth to the shark."

Then Olofat replied, "I am angry at Luk, for he created my brother handsomer than I am, and with greater power. I shall give teeth to all the sharks in order that they may eat men whenever canoes tip over."

When Luk, who was in the sky-world, became aware of these things, he said to his wife, "It would be well if Olofat came back to heaven, because he is only doing evil on earth." And his wife, Ino-a-eman, said, "I think so, too. Otherwise he will destroy mankind, for he is an evil being."

Accordingly Luk ordered the people of the sky-world to build a great house, and when it was finished he commanded that a feast be announced. He had a large fish basket prepared in which they placed Olofat and sank him in the sea. After five nights, when they thought he would be dead, two men went in a canoe and hauled up the basket, but behold! it contained only a multitude of great fish. Olofat had slipped away and seated himself in a canoe near by.

The men asked him, "Who are you?" And he replied, "I am Olofat. Come here, and I will help you to put the fish into your boat." Taking one fish after the other, he handed them to the men, but in so doing he removed all the flesh of the fish and gave the men merely the empty skins. For himself he kept nothing but the smallest ones.

And when the people said, "Why is it that you take only the little fish?"

Olofat replied, "Give Luk all the big ones. I am quite satisfied with the little ones."

Then the people brought the catch to Luk, who asked them, "Where is the fish basket? Who took the fish out?" When they replied, "Olofat did that, but he has again placed the basket in the sea." Luk said, "Has he then taken no fish for himself?" To which they answered, "Only the very smallest ones."

Luk now ordered all sorts of food to be prepared for the feast and commanded that the fishes should be cooked. And when all were gathered in the house, while Olofat sat at the entrance, Luk said, "Let everyone now eat. Let the food be divided, and let each receive his share." Nevertheless, Olofat refused to receive any. And when the guests took up the fish, lo! there were only the empty skins, and within was nothing, so that they had to content themselves with fruit.

Olofat, however, ate his own fish. But Luk said, "See, we have nothing, whereas Olofat is able to eat his own fish and is still not finished with them."

Thereupon he became very angry and sent word to Thunder to destroy Olofat. But because Thunder lived in a house at a distance, Luk said, "Take Thunder some food." So one of the gods took some of the viands, but Olofat, snatching them from him, himself carried them to Thunder.

On arriving at the house, he called out, "O Thunder, I bring food." Now Thunder had found a white hen and, coming out, he thundered. Though Luk cried, "Kill him," and though Thunder blazed, Olofat merely placed his hand before his eyes. Nevertheless, Thunder followed him and thundered again and again behind him. From under his mantle Olofat took some coconut milk that he had brought with him. Sprinkling it on Thunder, he quenched the lightning. After this he seized Thunder and bore him back to his own home.

When Olofat had returned to the feast house, Luk said, "Why has the man not been killed?" Olofat again took his place by the door while Luk ordered another of the gods to take food to Anulap.° Thereupon Olofat stood up and walked along behind the one who carried the food and he took the provisions away from him, saying, "I myself will take the food to Anulap."

So he went to the god and said, "Here are provisions for you." Then he turned about and came back to the great assembly house, whereupon Luk said to Anulap, "Why have you not killed the man?" Then Anulap took his great hook, which was fastened to a strong rope, and throwing it at Olofat, he caught him around the neck. But Olofat quickly seized a mussel shell and cut the rope, after which he hastened to the house of Anulap, where he sat down on the threshold. When Anulap saw him, he seized his club to strike Olofat, but as he stretched it out, Olofat changed himself into a wooden mortar.

Thereupon Anulap called, "Where is Olofat?" and his wife said, "He must have run away." They lay down and slept. After all this Luk said, "We can do nothing with Olofat. I believe he cannot die. Go and tell the people to come in the morning to make a porch for the house."

When the people had come and asked how they should construct the porch, Luk said, "Go to the forest and bring great tree-trunks." And when this was done, and the tree trunks were laid by the house, Luk commanded, "Now, go and fetch Olofat."

Olofat came and said, "I shall go, too."

But Luk replied, "You must help us to build the porch. You must make three holes in the ground, two shallow and one deep, and in these the tree trunks must be set."

Accordingly Olofat dug three holes, but in each of them he made an excavation at one side, after which Luk asked, "Olofat, are you ready yet?" Thereupon Olofat, taking a nut and a stone, hid them in his girdle, and Luk said, "Now set the tree-trunks in the holes." In obedience to this, three men seized the upper end while Olofat grasped the lower part, and they pushed Olofat so that he fell into the hole, only to creep quickly into the space that he had made on the side. Not knowing this, however, they then raised the tree-trunk high, and dropping it into the hole, the men made it firm with earth and stone. All now believed that Olofat had been caught under the great post and had been crushed to death.

Olofat, however, sat in his hole on the side, and being hungry five nights later he cracked the nut with the stone that he had brought with him and ate it. Ants came, and taking the fragments that had fallen to the ground, they carried the food along the trunk to the surface, going in long rows. The man who sat in the house above, seeing this, said to his wife, "Olofat is dead, for the ants are bringing up parts of his body." But when Olofat heard the speech of the man, he

°*Anulap*: a god of fishermen.

turned himself into an ant and crept with the others up the post. Having climbed high, he allowed himself to drop upon the body of the man, who pushed the ant off so that it fell to the ground, where it was immediately changed into Olofat.

As soon as the people saw him, they sprang up in fear, and Olofat said, "What are you talking about?" When Luk beheld him, he said, "We have tried in every possible way to kill you, but it seems that you cannot die. Bring me Samenkoaner."°

After Samenkoaner had come and sat down, Luk asked him, "How is it that Olofat cannot die? Can you kill him?" To this Samenkoaner replied, "No, not even if I thought about it for a whole night long, could I find a means, for he is older than I."

Luk said, "But I do not wish that he should destroy all men upon the earth." And so Rat, Luk's sister, advised that they should burn Olofat. Accordingly they made a great fire, to which they brought Olofat. But he had with him a roll of coconut fiber, and when Luk ordered them to throw him into the flames, he crept through the roll and came out safely on the other side of the fire.

Then Luk said, "Rat, we have tried everything to kill him, but in vain," and Rat answered, "He cannot die, so make him the lord of all who are evil and deceitful."

°*Samenkoaner*: a younger brother of Olofat.

Strikingly, Olofat plays the same trick with the hole and post as does Zipacna in the Mesoamerican story (Chapter 12), but no connection is possible. Thus can folktale motifs appear independently in different world myths.

## THE MYTHS OF AUSTRALIA

The continent of Australia ("the southern land") is not only by far the largest landmass of Oceania, but presents in its physical characteristics a sharp contrast to the remainder of the region. Only a small portion of its great extent possesses a tropical environment. The whole interior and most of its western area are a vast and almost waterless desert. Instead of life being easy and the food supply sufficient, as in the tropical islands, the quest for food required most of the energies of its inhabitants. In the desert the summer heat is furious, while on the elevated plateaus and in the mountains of the southeast there is heavy snow in winter with intense cold. The forests of eucalyptus, acacia, and oak offer little shade, in sharp contrast to the dense growths of the tropics. The animal life is highly peculiar, with many marsupials and great ostrich-like birds. Moreover, Australia is isolated from the remainder of the whole area. Only in the extreme north does it closely approach any of the surrounding lands.

The native peoples of Australia are as distinctive as the continent's physical features, climate, plant life, and animal life (Figure 13.5). Isolated for at least 40,000 years from the rest of the world until discovered by the Dutch in 1606, Australian culture was among the least developed in the world. At the time of contact with the Europeans, the natives were ignorant of chipped stone tools, agriculture, pottery-making, techniques

**FIGURE 13.5**  Australian aborigine. New South Wales, 1998. (Giovanni Mereghetti / Alamy)

of navigation, and the use of domestic animals (except the dog). They made crude baskets out of reeds. They ate nuts and berries, where available, and anything that moved, including insect larvae, a staple of their diet. Their social organization, however, was complex with an elaborate religious ceremonial.

Today the aborigines number about 2 percent of the population of 22 million. They are divided into around four hundred separate groups, each with a different language. There is scarcely a common culture, except that the stories they tell are said to have taken place in the "Dreamtime," a mythical era before the present (Figure 13.6).

Each group has its own stories, so that all of Australian myth is pretty much local. No distinction is drawn between things spiritual, ideal, and mental, and things material, nor is there any distinction made between the sacred and the profane. All life's meaning arises out of the eternal, ever-present Dreaming.

Knowledge of Australian myth is comparatively meager. The rapid extinction of a large portion of the population before adequate observations were made, mostly through disease, leaves little more than fragments available. Myths of the origin of the world are largely lacking. The existence of the earth and sky seems to have been assumed, and apart from certain special mountains, rocks, rivers, and other natural features, no account is given of their origin.

**FIGURE 13.6**    Aboriginal painting depicting a woman perhaps giving birth and various spirit beings. Such illustrations are difficult to date and to interpret. Aboriginal Painting in Kakadu National Park, Australia, Northern Territory. (Blickwinkel / Alamy)

## Myth: The Australian Origin of Humankind

On the origin of humankind, however, several views are offered. The various clans had totemic ancestors who "came up out of the ground," some in human and some in animal shapes. They traveled around the country leaving offspring here and there by unions with women of the people (whose origin is not described). Eventually they journeyed beyond the confines of the territory known to a particular tribe, or went down into the ground again, or became transformed into a rock, tree, or some other natural feature of the landscape.

For example, according to one story a Kangaroo Man arose out of the ground as a child and was found by a woman belonging to the Lizard clan, who gave it milk. Every day she went to gather berries for her husband, who was a Wild Turkey Man, and every day she gave milk to the kangaroo child. When he grew larger, he ran away and met a number of Iguana Women, who tried to fight him with lightning. After killing and eating them, he traveled on and met a man from the Wren totem, whom he also killed. Then he climbed a hill, scratching the sand with his fingers as he went and traveling on all fours. He came to the camp of some Rain Women. They offered him food, but he grew angry when they would not yield to his sexual demands, refused to eat the food, and threw it away. Whereupon the women killed him, after which he disappeared into the ground.

The **Arunta** tribe in central Australia told how there were in the western sky two self-existent beings of whose origin nothing is stated. From their lofty position they saw far to the east a number of *Inapertwa*, rudimentary human beings or incomplete men. These *Inapertwa* were of various shapes and lived along the edges of the sea:

> They had no distinct limbs or organs of sight, hearing, or smell, and did not eat food, and presented the appearance of human beings all doubled up into a rounded mass in which just the outline of the different parts of the body could be vaguely seen. The two sky-beings came down, therefore, from the sky and armed with large stone knives, set to work to make these amorphous objects into men.
>
> First of all the arms were released, then the fingers were added by making four clefts at the end of each arm; then legs and toes were added in the same way. The figure could now stand. After this the nose was added and the nostrils bored with the fingers. A cut with the knife made the mouth. A slit on each side separated the upper and lower eyelids, hidden behind which the eyes were already present. Another stroke or two completed the body and thus, out of the *Inapertwa*, men and women were formed.

## Myth: The Origin of the Moon

In New South Wales—on the central east coast—was told a story about the origin of the moon:

> The moon was an old man, very fat and lazy, who lived with two young men who were his relatives. They aided him and did most of the hunting, but because he treated them very badly, taking for himself all the choice portions of meat and giving them only what was left, after a while they decided that they could no longer stand it and decided to leave.
>
> In camp they were accustomed to sit or lie behind him, and because he could not easily turn over, he would from time to time call to them to see if they were there. When their plans were ready they started off, secretly instructing some rubbish, which they left behind, to answer if the old man called.
>
> After they had traveled some distance, they were fortunate enough to kill an emu.° Taking the bird with them to a large flat rock, they prepared to cook

°*emu*: the largest Australian bird, similar and related to the African ostrich.

and eat it, but when the food was about ready, they remembered that emu flesh was taboo to them as young men. They could not have it until they received some at the hands of an older man.

They therefore decided on a stratagem. They called out to the old man, who for the first time realized their absence. He hastened toward them, but before he got there they caused the rock on which they were to grow tall so that he could not reach them. When he had come, they showed him the emu. He at once demanded that they throw some of the meat to him, so they tossed down a piece of the fat. He did not like the fat and hurled it back at them. Thus the taboo was broken, for they had received emu flesh at his hands.

Because the moon wished to ascend to them, they told him to get a sapling and lean it against the rock so that he might climb it. But while he went to find it, they caused the rock to grow still higher, so that his pole was not long enough to reach the top. Accordingly, he went again, and this time brought a stick that was long enough. He started to climb up, carrying his two dogs with him. His hands, however, were greasy from handling the emu fat, and when he was near the top, the two boys twisted and shook the stick so that the old man lost his hold and fell to the ground, his two dogs being killed and his back so injured that he had to walk bent over. For this reason the new moon has a bent back when it appears each month.

## Myth: The Australian Origin of Fire

As to the origin of fire, a tribe near Melbourne in southern Australia reports that once two women were cutting a tree to find ants that they could eat when they were attacked by snakes. The women fought them for some time, but at last one of them broke her fighting stick. Fire came out of the end of it and the crow, seizing the stick, flew away with it. Pursued by two men, the crow let the fire fall, thus starting a conflagration. These two men rose to the sky as stars. They told all the people to be careful not to lose fire now that they had it, but after a time they let it go out, and humankind was again fireless while snakes covered the world (Figure 13.7).

At length one of the men sent his sister Karakarook down from the sky to guard the women. She went about everywhere with a great stick, killing snakes, but in killing one her stick broke and fire came from it. The crow once more seized the stick and flew away with it. The two men who had followed him before descended from the sky, and going to the high mountain where the crow had hidden the fire, brought it back again safely to humankind.

Karakarook, the sister, had told the women to examine carefully her broken stick from which the fire had come and never to lose the secret. One of those who had rescued the fire from the crow took the men to a mountain where grew the proper sort of wood to make fire-sticks and showed them how to make and use them, so that ever afterward they should have fire whenever they needed it.

## Myth: How the Curlew Got Red Legs

Tales that explain the origin of the individual habits, markings, or cries of animals and other living creatures are as typical, on the whole, for Australia as are the Maui myths for Polynesia or the wise and foolish brothers for Melanesia. A large proportion of the Australian myths belongs to this class, which are usually rather local in character.

For example, in southern Australia the story is told how the curlew got its red legs:

One day the hawk, the mother of Ouyan, the curlew, said to the curlew, "Go out and get an emu for us. You are a man and a hunter and must go and get food for us and not stay in camp like a woman."

Accordingly Ouyan took his spears and went off, but being unable to find an emu, and fearing the jeers of the women, he cut some flesh from his own legs and carried it home, telling his mother that he had gone far and seen little game but that he had brought something and that there would be enough for all. So the women cooked the flesh and ate it. Afterward they were quite ill.

The next day Ouyan went off again and being unsuccessful as before, he brought back another piece of his flesh. But this time the women were suspicious, and thinking that the meat was unlike that of the emu, they determined to see what Ouyan did on the following day. Thus they found how he got the meat, and when he returned as usual and then went to lie down, saying that he was tired, they rushed up and pulling off the covering that he had drawn over himself, disclosed his legs all raw and bleeding.

They upbraided him for his laziness and evil tricks and beat him, after which his mother said, "You shall have no more flesh on your legs hereafter, and they shall be red and skinny forever." So Ouyan crawled away and became a curlew, and these birds cry all night, "Bou-you-gwai-gwai! Bou-you-gwai-gwai!" which means, "O my poor red legs! O my poor red legs!"

## Myth: Australian Myths of Cannibalism

Stories about cannibals are common, as was cannibalism in fact. A tale from central Australia runs:

Two old men, who were brothers, were traveling with a young man who was their nephew, but because the old men were cannibals and planned to kill and eat the young man, one of them hid himself in a cave while the other sat down near by. Meanwhile the young man went off to hunt and drove much game down from the hill, all of which ran into the cave where one of the old men was hidden. The other cannibal then called to his nephew to go in and kill the game, which he did, partly by blows and partly by suffocating the animals with thick smoke from a fire built at the mouth of the cave. After this the old man asked the young man to enter again and drag out the game, and while he was doing so the cannibal who had concealed himself rushed from his hiding-place and tried to kill the boy.

The latter dodged him, however, and crept out, telling his other uncle that there was a man in the cave who had tried to murder him. The old deceiver stoutly denied this. Going in, he whispered to his accomplice that he must hide himself elsewhere for a while until their nephew had grown up, or the nephew might kill them both. The boy heard them talking and asked who was there. The old man declared that there was no one else in the cave and that he was only speaking to an old wallaby,° which he dragged out as he came.

°*wallaby:* a small kangaroo.

The boy, however, did not believe it. The one who had been hidden in the cave came out secretly and concealed himself in another cave. After a while the same drama was enacted as before, but this time the boy was determined to destroy both cannibals. Accordingly, when the old man who was hidden in the cave struck at him, he again induced the other to enter. Piling up a great quantity of grass before the opening and setting fire to it, the nephew smothered them both to death. After they were dead, they ascended to the sky, where they may still be seen as stars.

A second cannibal tale from southern Australia goes like this:

The members of a certain tribe began to decrease one by one, and hunters and women who went far from camp failed to return, until at last only one family was left. Determining to find out how all their kinsmen had perished, and leaving their old father to take care of the women, the sons set out. After traveling for some distance they met an old man carrying a hollow log, who asked them to aid him to get a bandicoot° out of it. They feared trickery, however, and refused to put their hands into the log, thrusting in a stick instead. Their suspicions were justified, for out came a great snake with a head at each end of its body.

Taking their sticks, they cut the reptile in two and thus made them as we see them today. Then they killed the old man. Continuing on their way, they came to his hut where were piles of bones of the people whom he had killed. Going farther, they reached a lake by which grew a tree. In the tree was a beautiful woman who invited the men to climb up to her. Before they did so, they noticed that the lake was filled with the remains of human bodies, for the woman was a cannibal and enticed men to ascend the tree that she might kill and eat them. Resolved to punish her for her misdeeds, they climbed up with care and pushed her into the lake, where she was drowned.

°*bandicoot*: a small chipmunk-like marsupial.

## OBSERVATIONS: THE MYTHS OF OCEANIA

A prominent type of tale in Oceania recounts the origin of the totemic ancestors by coming up out of the ground and their wanderings and activities as instructors in ceremonial and social usages. Relatively absent are tales relating to heroes, except for Maui among the Polynesians. Most mythical persons are associated with limited groups of people, the common property of the tribe. Animal stories are most abundant, and a few cosmogonic tales refer to the creation of the world, but there is little interest in the doings of gods, or even a clear category for "gods." Rather, humans have supernatural powers, or can turn into animals or objects, but so can they in real life in which every shaman, and many others, have these powers. Gods, humans, animals, things—they are all part of a continuum where differences are lost.

A large proportion of the myths have originated within the region in which they now occur, or are the outgrowth of imported elements that have been so profoundly modified that the original sources are obscured. Striking are the resemblances between Oceanic and Native American myth (Chapter 14), but there is no evidence for migrations between Oceania and America or vice versa. We have already commented on the similarity between the trickery of Olofat and the Mesoamerican Zipacna. Everywhere is the dominance of folktale and stories of the trickster's defeat of his enemies, often members of his own family. The purpose is not so much to explain the world, as to give an entertaining account of it.

## Key Terms

| | | |
|---|---|---|
| Polynesia 438 | Rangi 443 | Papua New Guinea 455 |
| Easter Island 438 | Papa 443 | Meragbuto 458 |
| New Zealand 439 | Tane 443 | Tagaro 458 |
| Tahiti 439 | Maui 446 | Micronesia 462 |
| Maori 441 | Melanesia 455 | Olofat 464 |
| Po 441 | Papua 455 | Arunta 470 |

## Further Reading

Dixon, R. B., *Oceanic Mythology* (http://www.sacred-texts.com/pac/om/index.htm, 1916).

Poignant, R., *Oceanic Mythology: The Myths of Polynesia, Micronesia, Melanesia, Australia* (New York, 1967).

Schmitz, C. A., *Oceanic Art: Myth, Man and Images in the South Seas* (New York, 1972).

# Myths of the North American Indians

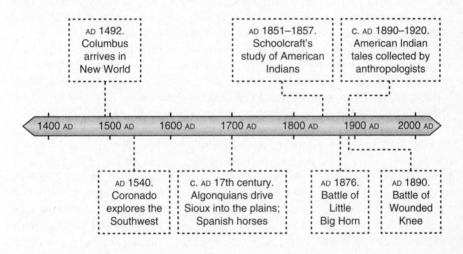

As we have seen, the American Indians came over the Bering Land Bridge at some unknown, but very early, time. They belong to a different human race than the Chinese, but must have been in conflict with them in primordial times. When Columbus first came into contact with the native peoples of the Americas, he thought he was in India, hence the name "Indians" for the native people.[1] The American Indian spread over both continents and remained without contact with the old world for a long, long time. We have already explored developments in the valleys of Mexico (Chapter 12). Tribes north of Mexico pursued a rather different course, never evolving

---

[1] A politically correct term is *Native Americans*, but it is rejected by the Indian peoples themselves, who have been called *Indians* for four hundred years. *Native Americans* would also include the Polynesian Hawaiian islanders and the Eskimos, peoples racially and culturally distinct from the American Indians.

the sort of tribute-empires found in Mexico, based on the ritual of human sacrifice, although some tribes were cannibals. Their intimate contact with northern Europeans, who came to the New World to found utopian communities, was very different from their contacts with the Spaniards, who came to loot, murder, exploit, and convert to the Roman Catholic Church. No tribal people has been more studied than the North American Indian.

## AMERICAN INDIAN CULTURE

The North American Indian lived in a wide variety of environments, from the cold, rainy northwest to the gorgeous valleys of California; from the desert southwest to the wind-riven high plains; from the eastern woodlands to the hot and luscious south. So rich in natural resources—salmon and whales—was the northwest that the wealthy Indians who lived there never resorted to agriculture. Nor did the Indians of California, who lived from acorns, from which the bitter acids were leached through pounding and repeated immersion in water, and from deer. There was no agriculture in California, today one of the richest agricultural areas in the world. In the Southwest, by contrast, the city-dwelling peoples there either dry-farmed maize or, in southern Arizona, used irrigation agriculture. Really, the Southwest cultures were the northernmost extension of the Central American maize culture practiced by the Maya and Aztecs.

Agriculture was also practiced in the southeast, probably historically the most advanced of the Indian cultures but almost unknown today because of the early destruction of these peoples through European disease: smallpox, measles, and chicken pox, which had also decimated the Aztecs. The first explorers of the southeast described the area as teeming with its Indian population; by the 17th century it was a desert (Figure 14.1).

In 1832 Prince Maximilian of Wied visited the prosperous and populous Mandan Indians who lived on the banks of the upper Missouri River in Montana; in 1835, 95 percent of the population had perished from smallpox. In the Northeast, Indian culture remained alive because the Indians could to some extent back off from the Europeans by withdrawing into Canada and across the Great Lakes.

In the 17th century, as the southeastern Indians disappeared, the OJIBWA, or Chippewa, Indians, migrated across the Great Lakes under European pressure. They were speakers of Algonquin languages, a language family. They drove most of the Siouan-speakers out of northern Wisconsin. The Algonquin speakers remain in the northern Great Lakes today, while the Siouan-speakers crossed into the Dakotas and became the famous SIOUX Indians of the 19th century.

In precontact times, the plains Indians lived along the waterways of the Missouri and its tributaries. The women farmed squash and maize while the males hunted. When these peoples acquired horses from the Spanish in the 17th century, these Indians gave up agriculture and hunted buffalo across the plains, living in highly portable skin huts. In the development of culture, they went backward, creating a romantic and nomadic way of life based on horse-theft and horse-breeding. The government of the United States fought long and hard against these ferocious warriors until the Battle of Wounded Knee in 1890 ended the Indian wars.

In general Indian religion was fetishism, the honoring of power objects, although most tribes had a vague tradition of the Great Spirit that ruled over all. Sometimes this Great Spirit was thought to be the sun. The male, who lived for war and the hunt, kept

*Great Mortality among the Indians.*

**FIGURE 14.1**   "Great mortality among the Indians," referring to the smallpox epidemic among the Wampanoags of Massachusetts during the 1600s. Hand-colored woodcut of a 19th-century reproduction of an earlier illustration. (North Wind Picture Archives / Alamy)

his fetishes in a "medicine" pouch to which he reverted in times of trouble. Many tribes adopted a totem, usually an animal, that embodied the welfare of the tribe, but there are no gods as such, no divine beings to whom one might offer prayer or sacrifice. The world, however, was filled with spirits of every conceivable kind. In the southwest a religion of the spirits that live in nature, worshiped in ritual dance, was developed that still exists today. The well-known kachina dolls of the HOPI Indians of Arizona and the Pueblo Indians of New Mexico represent such spirits (Figure 14.2). The individual may hope to communicate with a protective spirit whose presence can be discovered in a vision quest, through self-torture and starvation.

Marriage was always matrilocal—the husband went to live with the wife's relatives—so the accumulation of centralized power was difficult, and in fact never took place. The five tribes of the IROQUOIS of upstate New York came together in a confederacy in the 16th century, but in no sense did the native peoples ever evolve a state that might oppose European aggression. State-formation was impossible without a system of writing, and although a kind of writing with a limited range developed among the Maya (and, long after contact, among the CHEROKEE: see below), no form of writing ever appeared among the precontact North American Indians. For this reason when we study their myths, we are always dependent on European collectors who impose their own expectations on the stories.

A pioneer in the collecting of North American tales was **Henry Rowe Schoolcraft** (1793–1864), who discovered the source of the Mississippi and was the first U.S. Indian agent, in Sault Sainte Marie ("cataract of Saint Mary") between Lake Huron and Lake

**FIGURE 14.2**   A Hopi kachina doll. As spirits of the invisible life forces, kachinas were impersonated during masked ceremonies between the winter solstice and July, their main purpose being to bring rain for the spring crops. However, a kachina can represent almost anything, from an ancestor to a location, a meteorological phenomenon, a heavenly body, quality, or concept. There are more than four hundred different kachinas. (Photo by Author)

Superior, the oldest European settlement in the Midwest. His first wife was part Ojibwa (Chippewa), and from her he learned Ojibwa and many of the stories he told. Between 1851 and 1857 appeared Schoolcraft's *Historical and Statistical Information Respecting the Indian Tribes of the United States*, where he tells these stories, the source of Henry Wadsworth Longfellow's (1807–1882) *Song of Hiawatha* (see Perspective 14). Since Schoolcraft, many workers in the field, especially under the direction of Franz Boaz (1858–1952), the founder of American anthropology, have recorded hundreds of tales from dozens of tribes.

## MYTH: HOPI CREATION

True cosmogonies are very rare in North American Indian myth. There are one or two from California and the following story from the southwestern **Hopi**, who live today in villages spread out across the northern part of Arizona on a remote reservation entirely surrounded by the much larger Navajo reservation, the largest in the country (Map 14). The Hopi number about 7,000. Though their name means "the peaceful people," they have waged constant war against the marauding and seminomadic Navajo. Agriculture is an important part of Hopi culture. Their village of Old Oraibi is the oldest continuously inhabited village within the territory of the United States, founded before AD 1100.

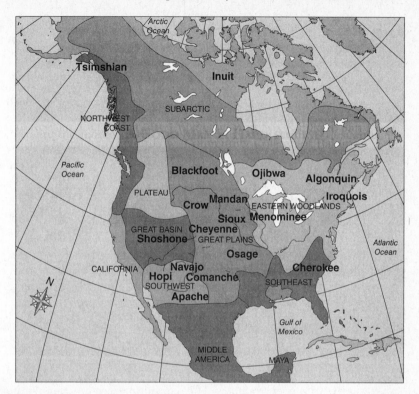

**MAP 14**    North American Indian tribes.

The Hopi were first contacted by the Spanish General Francisco Vasquez de Coronado in 1540, searching for the reportedly fabulously wealthy seven cities of Cibola. Catholic friars attempted to convert the Hopi to Christianity, with limited success. In 1680 in the great pueblo revolt the Spanish were expelled and never returned to the Hopi pueblos. Today the Hopi maintain their ancient religion of ritual dance based on a seasonal cycle. The Hopi kachina dolls represent spirits in this religion (see Figure 14.2). The Hopi are also well known for their beautiful pottery, with ancient roots, and their exquisite silver jewelry.

The Hopi have a story about the origin of the world and the people that are in it, centering on Hard Being Woman and the creator **Spider Woman**:[2]

A very long time ago there was nothing but water. In the East, Hard Being Woman, the spirit of all hard substances, lived in the ocean. Her house was a

---

[2]For North American Indians texts, cf. H. R. Voth, *The Traditions of the Hopi* (New York, 1905); J. Mooney, *Annual Report of the Bureau of American Ethnology,* 1897–1898, Part I (1900); F. Boaz, *Annual Report of the Bureau of American Ethnology,* vols. 6, 31 (1884, 1916); H. H. St. Clair, *Journal of American Folk-Lore,* vol. 22 (1909); W. J. Hoffman, *Report of the Bureau of American Ethnology,* vol. 14 (1896); S. C. Simms, *Field Museum: Anthropological Series* 2, No. 19 (1903); F. G. Speck, *Memoirs of the Geological Survey of Canada: Anthropological Series,* vol. 9 (1916); C. Wissler, and D. C. Duvall, *Anthropological Papers of the American Museum of Natural History,* vol. 2, No. 6 (1908); G. A. Dorsey, *Field Museum: Anthropological Series,* vol. 7, No. 22 (1905); J. Curtin, *Seneca Indian Myths* (New York, 1922; reprinted 2008).

kiva° like the kivas of the Hopi of today. To the ladder leading into the kiva usually was tied the skin of a gray fox and one of a yellow fox. Another Hard Being Woman lived in the ocean in the West in a similar kiva, but to her ladder was attached a turtle-shell rattle.

The Sun also existed at that time. Shortly before rising in the East, the Sun would dress up in the skin of the gray fox, whereupon it would begin to dawn—the so-called "white dawn" of the Hopi. After a little while the Sun would take off the gray skin and put on the yellow fox skin, whereupon the bright dawn of the morning would appear—the so-called "yellow dawn" of the Hopi. The Sun would then rise, that is, emerge from an opening in the north end of the kiva in which Hard Being Woman lived. When arriving in the West again, the sun would first announce his arrival by fastening the rattle on the top of the ladder, then he would enter the kiva, pass through an opening in the north end of the kiva, and continue his course eastward under the water, and so forth.

Eventually these two spirits° caused dry land to appear in the midst of the water. The waters receded eastward and westward. The Sun passing over this dry land constantly took notice of the fact that no living being of any kind could be seen anywhere, and mentioned this fact to the two spirits. So the Hard Being Woman of the West sent word through the Sun to the Hard Being Woman in the East to come over to her because she wanted to discuss this matter.

The Hard Being Woman of the East complied with this request and proceeded to the West over a rainbow. After consulting each other on this point, the two concluded that they would create a little bird. So the spirit of the East made a wren of clay, and covered it up with a piece of native cloth. Hereupon they sang a song over it, and after a little while the little bird showed signs of life.

Removing the cloth, a live bird came forth, saying, "Why do you want me so quickly?"

"Yes," they said, "we want you to fly all over this dry place and see whether you can find anything living."

They thought that as the Sun always passed over the middle of the earth, he might have failed to notice any living beings that might exist in the North or the South. So the little wren flew all over the earth, but upon its return reported that no living being existed anywhere. Tradition says, however, that by this time Spider Woman lived somewhere in the southwest, at the edge of the water, also in a kiva, but the little bird had failed to notice this.

Hereupon the spirit of the West proceeded to make very many birds of different kinds and shape, placing them again under the same cover under which the wren had been brought to life. They again sang a song over them. Presently, the birds began to move under the cover. The spirit removed the cover and found under it all kinds of birds and fowls.

---

°*kiva*: an underground site for ceremonial activity. °*two spirits*: Hard Being Woman of the East and Hard Being Woman of the West.

"Why do you want us so quickly?" they asked.

"Yes, we want you to inhabit this world."

Hereupon the two spirits taught every kind of bird the sound that it should make, and the birds scattered out in all directions.

Hereupon the Hard Being Woman of the West made all different kinds of animals out of clay, and they were brought to life in the same manner as the birds. The animals also asked the same question, "Why do you want us so quickly?"

"We want you to inhabit this earth," was the reply given them, whereupon their creators taught the animals their different sounds or languages, after which they proceeded forth to inhabit the different parts of the earth.

The spirits now concluded that they would create humans. The spirit of the East made of clay first a woman and then a man,° who were brought to life in exactly the same manner as the birds and animals before them. The woman and the man asked the same question, and were told that they should live upon this earth and should understand everything. Hereupon the Hard Being Woman of the East made two tablets of some hard substance, whether stone or clay tradition does not say, and drew upon them with a wooden stick certain characters. She handed these tablets to the newly created man and woman. They looked at them, but did not know what they meant. So the spirit of the East rubbed first the palms of the woman, and then the palms of the man, with the palms of her own hands. They were enlightened so that they understood the writing on the tablets. Hereupon the spirits taught the man and woman a language.°

After the spirits had taught the man and woman language, the goddess of the East took them out of the kiva and led them over a rainbow to her home in the East. There they stayed four days, after which Hard Being Woman of the East told them to go now and select for themselves some place and live there. The two went forth, saying that they would travel around a while. Wherever they found a good field, they would remain.

Finding a nice place at last, the man and the woman built a small, simple house, similar to the old houses of the Hopi. Soon the Hard Being Woman of the West began to think of the matter again and said to herself, "This is still not the way that things should be. We are not done yet," and communicated her thoughts to the Hard Being Woman of the East.

By this time Spider Woman had heard about all this, and she decided to get ahead of the Hard Being Woman of the West and the Hard Being Woman of the East by also creating some beings. So she also made a man and woman of clay, covered them up, sang over them, and brought to life her handiwork. But these two proved to be Spaniards. She taught them the Spanish language, also giving them similar tablets and imparting knowledge to them by rubbing their hands in the same manner as the woman of the East had done with the white men.

°*and then a man*: these are the "white men," as we later learn. °*a language*: because the white men can read and write, which the Hopi could not do.

Hereupon she created two burros, which she gave to the Spanish man and woman. The Spaniards settled down close by. After this, Spider Woman continued to create people in the same manner as she had created the Spaniards, always a man and a woman, giving a different language to each pair.° But all at once she found that she had forgotten to create a woman for a certain man, and that is the reason why now there are always some single men.

Spider Woman continued creating people in the same manner, giving new languages as the pairs were formed. Then she found that she had failed to create a man for a certain woman, in other words there was one more woman than there were men.

"Oh my!" said Spider Woman, "How is this?" and then addressing the single woman she said, "There is a single man somewhere who went away from here. You try to find him and if he accepts you, you live with him. If not, both of you will have to remain single. You do the best you can about that."

The two finally found each other, and the woman said, "Where shall we live?"

The man answered, "Why here, anywhere. We shall remain together."

So he went to work and built a house for them where they lived. But soon they started to quarrel with each other.

"I want to live here alone," the woman said. "I can prepare food for myself."

"Yes, but who will get the wood for you? Who will work the fields?" the man said. "We had better remain together."

They made up with each other, but peace did not last. They soon quarreled again, separated for a while, came together again, separated again, and so forth. If these people had not lived in that way, all the Hopi would now live in peace, but others learned it from them. That is the reason why there is so much contention between men and their wives. These were the kind of people that Spider Woman had created.

The Hard Being Woman of the West heard about this situation and began to meditate on it. Soon she called the spirit from the East to come over again.

"I do not want to live here alone," the spirit of the West said. "I also want some good people to live here." So she also created a number of other people, but always a man and his wife. They were created in the same way as the spirit of the East had created hers. They lived in the West. But wherever the people that Spider Woman had created came in contact with these good people, there was trouble.

People at that time led a nomadic life, living mostly on game. Wherever they found rabbits or antelope or deer they would kill the game and eat it. This led to many disagreements among the people.

Finally, the Woman of the West said to her people, "You remain here. I am going to live, after this, in the midst of the ocean in the West. When you want anything from me, you pray to me there." Her people regretted this very much, but she left them. The Hard Being Woman of the East did exactly the same thing, and that is why at the present day the places where these two live are never seen.

---

°*to each pair*: presumably including the Hopi.

Those Hopi who now want something from them deposit their prayer offerings in the village. When they say their wishes and prayers, they think of those two who live in the far distance, who the Hopi believe still remember them.

But the Spanish were angry at Hard Being Woman,° and two of them took their guns and proceeded to the abiding place of the spirit. The Spaniards are very skillful, and they found a way to get there. When they arrived at the house of Hard Being Woman, she at once guessed what they intended.

"You have come to kill me," said Hard Being Woman. "Don't do that, Lay down your weapons and I will show you something. I am not going to harm you."

They laid down their arms, whereupon she went to the rear end of the kiva and brought out a white lump like a stone and laid it before the two men, asking them to lift it up. One tried, but could not lift it, and what was worse, his hands stuck to the stone. The other man tried to help him, but his hands also stuck to the stone. Thus they were both prisoners.

Hereupon Hard Being Woman took the two guns and said, "These do not amount to anything." She rubbed them between her hands until they became powder.

Hard Being Woman then said to the Spaniards, "You people ought to live in peace with one another. You people of Spider Woman know many things, and the people whom we have made also know many things, but different. You ought not to quarrel about these things, but learn from one another. If one has or knows a good thing, he should exchange it with others for other good things that they know and have. If you will agree to this I will release you."

They said they did agree and that they would no more try to kill the spirit. Then Spider Woman went to the rear end of the kiva where she disappeared through an opening in the floor, from where she exerted a secret influence upon the stone and thus released the two men. They departed, but Hard Being Woman did not fully trust them, thinking that they would return. But they never did.

°*Hard Being Woman*: again considered as a single spirit, not split into the duality of West and East.

Kivas are found in ancient ruins as old as AD 1000 and still exist today, found in all the Hopi villages. The kiva is a large underground chamber, usually circular, and reached by a ladder in the center. The kiva is emblematic of the world, and as we see from this story actually precedes the creation. It has openings through which life can emerge.

In the Hopi story there are three creator spirits, Hard Being Woman of the West and East and Spider Woman. Hard Being Woman of the West and East made living things, beginning with the white man. Spider Woman's creations were, however, troublesome—she made the Spanish—and the source of all later difficulties between men and women. Hard Being Woman (of the East and West) appears to have created the Hopi subsequent to the white man, though the story is not explicit about their creation.

The story postdates European contact with its reference to writing—taken to be the language of the white man—and to the Spanish. Writing is the source of the power of the white man and of the Spanish (distinguished from the white men), along with their guns. In the end the troublesome Spaniards attempt to attack Hard Being Woman because they are hostile to native religions, but the story advises that there are good in all things and that peoples should live with one another in peace. The expulsion of the troublesome Spanish may refer to the Pueblo revolt of 1680 when the Spanish were driven from the Hopi villages. Although expected to return, they never did, and still today the Hopi live according to their traditional religion.

## MYTH: RAVEN, BRINGER OF ABUNDANCE

A **Tsimshian** story from the northwest also has some cosmogonic elements. The Tsimshians ("inside the Skeena River") are a northwest tribe in British Columbia and Alaska. Like all Northwest coastal peoples, they lived from the abundant sea life, especially salmon, in permanent towns of large longhouses. They speak an isolated language, unrelated to any other language family. Extended families lived all in the same building, made from cedar house posts and panels.

In the following story about **Raven** little distinction is made between animal and human actors: Such is typical of Indian tales. Raven is a culture hero, bringing fruit to the land and fish to the waters (Figure 14.3):

**FIGURE 14.3**   Raven, Northwest Indian painting on the exterior of a long house. In a typically abstract design, the "eye" on the right-hand wing echoes the bird's eye, while the design on the left-hand wing echoes the beak. (Don Paulson / Alamy)

At one time the whole world was covered with darkness. At the southern point of Queen Charlotte Islands there was a town in which the animals lived. Its name was Kungalas.

A chief and his wife were living there, and with them a boy, Raven, their only child, whom his parents loved very much. Therefore his father tried to keep him out of danger. He built for his son a bed above his own in the rear of his large house. He washed him regularly, and the boy grew up to be a youth.

When Raven was quite large, the youth became ill, and it was not long before he died. The hearts of his parents were very sad. They cried on account of their beloved child. The chief invited his tribe, and all the animal people went to the chief's house and entered. Then the chief ordered the child's body to be laid out, and he said, "Take out his intestines."

His attendants laid out the body of the chief's child, took out the intestines, burned them at the rear of the chief's house, and placed the body on the bed that his father had built for his son. The chief and his wife wailed every morning under the corpse of their dead son, and his tribe cried with them. They did so every day after the young man's death.

One morning before daylight came, the chief's wife went again to wail. She arose, and looked up to where Raven was lying. There she saw a youth, bright as fire, lying where the body of their son had been. She called her husband, and said to him, "Our beloved child has come back to life."

The chief got up and went to the foot of the ladder that reached to the place where the body had been. He went up to his son and said, "Is it you, my beloved son? Is it you?" Then the shining youth said, "Yes, it is I." Suddenly gladness touched the hearts of the parents.

The tribe entered again to console their chief and his wife. When the people entered, they were much surprised to see the shining youth there. He spoke to them. "Heaven was much annoyed by your constant wailing, so he sent me down to comfort your minds." The chief's tribe was very glad because the prince lived again among them. His parents loved Raven more than ever.

The shining youth ate very little. He stayed there a long time and he did not eat at all. He only chewed a little fat, but he did not eat any. The chief had two great slaves—a miserable man and his wife. The great slaves were called Mouth-at-Each-End. Every morning they brought all kinds of food into the house. One day, when they came in from where they had been, they brought a large cut of whale meat. They threw it on the fire and ate it. They did this every time they came back from hunting. Then the chief's wife tried to give food to Raven who had come back to life, but he declined it and lived without food.

The chief's wife was very anxious to give her son something to eat. She was afraid that her son would die again. On the following day the shining youth took a walk to refresh himself. As soon as he had gone out, the chief went up the ladder to where he thought his son had his bed. Behold, there was the corpse of his own son! Nevertheless he loved his new child.

One day the chief and his wife went out to visit the tribe, and the two great slaves entered, carrying a large piece of whale meat. They threw the whale fat into the fire and ate of it. Then the shining youth came toward them and questioned the two great slaves, asking, "What makes you so hungry?"

The two great slaves replied, "We are hungry because we have eaten scabs from our shin bones."

Therefore the shining youth said to them, "Do you like what you eat?"

The slave man said, "Yes, my dear!"

The prince replied, "I will also try the scabs you speak about."

Then the slave woman said, "No, my dear! Don't desire to be as we are."

The prince repeated, "I will just taste it and spit it out again."

The male slave cut off a small piece of whale meat and put in a small scab. Then the female slave scolded her husband for what he was doing. "O bad man! What have you been doing to the poor prince?" The shining prince took up the piece of meat with the scab in it, put it into his mouth, tasted it, and spat it out again.

Then he went back to his bed. When the chief and his wife came back from their visit, the prince said to his mother, "Mother, I am very hungry."

The chief's wife said at once, "O, dear, is it true, is it true?"

She ordered her slaves to feed her beloved son with rich food. The slaves prepared rich food, and Raven ate it all. Again he was very hungry and ate everything, and the slaves gave him more to eat than before.

He did so for several days, and soon all the provisions in his father's house were at an end. Then the prince went to every house of his father's people and ate the provisions that were in their houses. This was because he had tasted the scabs of Mouth-at-Each-End.

Now the provisions were all used up. The chief knew that the provisions of his tribe were almost exhausted. Therefore the chief felt sad and ashamed on account of what his son had done, for he had devoured almost all the provisions of his tribe.

The chief invited all the people in and said, "I will send my child away before he eats all our provisions and we lack food."

Then all the people agreed to what the chief had said. As soon as they had all agreed, the chief called his son. He told him to sit down in the rear of the house. As soon as he sat down there, the chief spoke to his son and said, "My dear son, I shall send you away inland and to the other side of the ocean."

He gave his son a small round stone and a raven blanket and a dried sea-lion bladder filled with all kinds of berries.

The chief said to his son, "When you fly across the ocean and feel weary, drop this round stone on the sea, and you shall find rest on it, and when you reach the mainland, scatter the various kinds of fruit all over the land. And also scatter the salmon roe in all the rivers and streams, and also the trout roe, so that you may not lack food as long as you live in this world."

Then he started off. His father named him "Giant."

Raven comes from another world, where all is darkness. He is a resurrected being, but a danger to the community when he acquires an insatiable hunger, something the Tsimshian would understand too well. The burning of his entrails is a normal treatment of the dead (at one time the human entrails were in fact eaten). When resurrected, he is a being of light in a lightless world. He acquires his insatiable hunger when he eats the dried blood of the slaves: In this way he is "brought down," but because of his hunger, he is sent away. Often in Indian myth the pebble that Raven carries grows into the whole world, but here it seems to be only a resting place for Raven. When he arrives at the mainland—that is, in this world—Raven causes the fruits to grow and the rivers to be filled with salmon and fish, the staple diet of the Tsimshian. Raven is the source of all abundance. The power of Raven is "gigantic."

## MYTH: SEDNA, MISTRESS OF THE UNDERWORLD

The Eskimo, in Canada called the **INUIT**, are not Indians, but have separate racial origins and speak a language unrelated to any Indian language. Their origin is mysterious, but from time immemorial they have lived close to the Arctic Circle in Siberia, Alaska, Canada, and Greenland. Although they are not Indians, Eskimo stories resemble Indian stories. The Inuit had a story that told of the origin of whales and seals, in which the woman **Sedna** became the ruler of the dead:

> Once upon a time there lived on a solitary shore an Inuit with his daughter Sedna. His wife had been dead for some time and the two led a quiet life. Sedna grew up to be a handsome girl and the youths came from all around to sue for her hand, but none of them could touch her proud heart.
>
> Finally, at the breaking up of the ice in the spring a seagull flew from over the ice and wooed Sedna with enticing song. "Come to me," it said. "Come into the land of the birds, where there is never hunger, where my tent is made of the most beautiful skins. You shall rest on soft bearskins. My fellows, the seagulls, will bring you all your heart desires. Their feathers will clothe you. Your lamp shall always be filled with oil, your pot with meat."
>
> Sedna could not long resist such wooing, and they went together over the vast sea. When at last they reached the country of the seagull, after a long and hard journey, Sedna discovered that her spouse had shamefully deceived her. Her new home was not built of beautiful pelts, but was covered with wretched fish skins, full of holes, that gave free entrance to wind and snow. Instead of soft reindeer skins her bed was made of hard walrus hides and she had to live on miserable fish, which the birds brought her. Too soon she discovered that she had thrown away her opportunities when in her foolish pride she had rejected the Inuit youths.
>
> In her woe she sang, "Aye, O father, if you knew how wretched I am you would come to me, and we would hurry away in your boat over the waters. The birds look unkindly upon me, a stranger. Cold winds roar about my bed. They give me only miserable food. O come and take me back home."
>
> When a year had passed and the sea was again stirred by warmer winds, the father left his country to visit Sedna. His daughter greeted him joyfully and besought him to take her back home. The father, hearing of the outrages done to his daughter, determined upon revenge. He killed the seagull, took Sedna into his boat, and they quickly left the country which had brought so much sorrow to Sedna. When the other seagulls came home and found their companion dead and his wife gone, they all flew away in search of the fugitives. They were very sad over the death of their poor murdered comrade and continue to mourn and cry until this day.

Having flown a short distance they discerned the boat and stirred up a heavy storm. The sea rose in immense waves that threatened the pair with destruction. In this mortal peril the father determined to offer Sedna to the birds and flung her overboard. She clung to the edge of the boat with a death grip. The cruel father then took a knife and cut off the first joints of her fingers. Falling into the sea they were transformed into whales, the nails turning into whalebone. Sedna held on to the boat more tightly. The second finger joints fell under the sharp knife and swam away as seals. When the father cut off the stumps of the fingers, they became ground seals.

In the meanwhile the storm subsided, for the seagulls thought Sedna was drowned. The father then allowed her to come into the boat again. But from that time she cherished a deadly hatred against him and swore bitter revenge. After they got ashore, she called her dogs and let them gnaw off the feet and hands of her father while he was asleep. Upon this he cursed himself, his daughter, and the dogs that had maimed him. The earth opened and swallowed the hut, the father, the daughter, and the dogs. They have since lived in the land of Adlivun, of which Sedna is the mistress.

The story is etiological to explain the origin of whales and seals, and of how Sedna became ruler of the dead. The marriage between a human and an animal—in this case a seagull—is common in such tales. Sedna rules over the spirits of animals and the souls of the dead in Adlivun, usually described as a frozen wasteland, where she reigns with her wicked father—the mistress and master of the dead. Adlivun ("those beneath us") refers to both the spirits of the departed who reside in the underworld and the underworld itself, located beneath the land and the sea. The souls are purified there in preparation for travel to the Land of the Moon, where they find eternal rest and peace.

## MYTH: THE RELEASE OF THE WILD ANIMALS

The COMANCHE were a powerful tribe of eastern New Mexico, West Texas, and Oklahoma. They had broken from the SHOSHONE, a dialect of whose language they spoke, around 1700 AD. They were probably the greatest light cavalry ever known, whose devastating power was only broken by disease in the mid-19th century. The famous Texas Rangers were founded in order to resist their unrelenting attacks on white settlements.

Otherwise the Comanche were similar to other plains tribes, except they owned far more horses. They lived with their horses and were so often on raids that few children were born. Hence the Comanche resorted to the capture of children and of women. The celebrated Comanche chief Quanah Parker (c. 1845–c. 1911) was the son of a European American woman, a captive named Cynthia Ann Parker.

When not raiding, the Comanche depended on the buffalo and told a story about how the trickster **Coyote** released buffalo onto the plains:

Long ago two persons owned all the buffalo. They were an old woman and her young cousin. They kept them penned up in the mountains so that they could not get out.

Coyote came to the people. He summoned the Indians to a council. "That old woman will not give us anything. When we go over there, we will plan how to release the buffalo."

They all moved near the buffalo enclosure.

"After four nights," said Coyote, "we will hold a council as to how we can release the buffalo. A very small animal shall go to where the old woman and her cousin draw water. When the child gets water, it will take the animal to his home for a pet. The old woman will object, but the child will like the animal so much that it will begin to cry and will be allowed to keep it. The animal will run off at daybreak, and the buffalo will burst out of their pen and run away."

The first animal they sent failed. Then they sent the Kill-dee [a small bird]. When the boy went for water, he found the Kill-dee and took it home.

"Look here!" he said to the old woman, "This animal of mine is very good."

The old woman replied, "O, it is good for nothing! There is nothing living on the earth that is not a rascal or schemer." The child paid no attention to her. "Take it back where you got it," said the woman. He obeyed.

The people held another council.

"Well, she has got the better of these two. They have failed," said Coyote, "but that makes no difference. Perhaps we will release the buffalo; perhaps we will fail. This is the third time now. We will send a small animal over there. If the old woman agrees to take it, it will liberate those buffalo. It is a great schemer."

So they sent the third animal. Coyote said, "If she rejects this one, we shall surely be unable to liberate the game."

The animal went to the spring and was picked up by the boy, who took a great liking to it. "Look here! What a nice pet I have!"

The old woman replied, "O, how foolish you are! It is good for nothing. All the animals in the world are schemers. I'll kill it with a club."

The boy took it in his arms and ran away crying. He thought too much of his pet. "No! This animal is too small," he cried.

When the animal had not returned by nightfall, Coyote went among the people, saying, "Well, this animal has not returned yet. I dare say the old woman has consented to keep it. Don't be uneasy, our buffalo will be freed." Then he told all the people to get ready just at daybreak. "Our buffalo will be released. Do all of you mount your horses."

In the meantime the animal, following its instructions, slipped over to the buffalo pen and began to howl. The buffalo heard it and were terrified. They ran towards the gate, broke it down, and escaped. The old woman, hearing the noise, woke up.

The child asked, "Where is my pet?" He did not find it.

The old woman said, "I told you so. Now you see the animal is bad, it has deprived us of our game."

She vainly tried to hold the buffalo back. At daybreak all the Indians got on their horses, for they had confidence in Coyote. Thus the buffalo came to live on this earth. Coyote was a great schemer.

Once upon a time there were no buffalo on the plains; then there were plenty of buffalo. This is because they were released from their trap in the mountains. Coyote did it through a trick: Coyote is the clever culture bearer, the figure who made things the way they are.

## MYTH: LODGE-BOY AND THROWN-AWAY

As in other traditions, many stories told of a child born in a special way who did extraordinary things. This following tale about Lodge-Boy and Thrown-Away was collected from the CROW Indians (or Absaroka, "children of the large-beaked bird"), a Siouan-speaking people who live in the Yellowstone River valley of Montana. The Crow long warred against the Dakota (Sioux), although they spoke a Siouan language. In the Indian Wars they allied with the U.S. Cavalry and often served as scouts. George Armstrong Custer's (1839–1876) scout Curly was Crow. For their service to the U.S. government they were awarded a large reservation near Billings, Montana, where they live today (Figure 14.4).

Iron Bull,
Mountain Crow Chief and Wife

**FIGURE 14.4**   Iron Bull and wife, c. 1880, from the Crow tribe. The wife wears a typical dress decorated with elks' teeth. Crow men normally wore their hair brushed back severely from their foreheads in a kind of wave. This man wears fetishes in his hair and a fine war shirt decorated by strips made of woven porcupine quills with a typically Crow-decorated front panel and a fringe made of ermine tails. His moccasins have a long fringe attached to the rear so as to obscure his footprints as he walks. (Paris Pierce / Alamy)

Once upon a time there lived a couple. The woman was pregnant. The man went hunting one day, and in his absence a certain wicked woman named Red Woman came to the tipi and killed his wife and cut her open and found boy twins. She threw one behind the tipi curtain and the other she threw into a spring. She then put a stick inside the woman and stuck one end in the ground, to give her the appearance of a live person, and burned her upper lip, giving her the appearance of someone laughing.

When her husband came home, tired from carrying the deer he had killed, he saw his wife standing near the door of the tipi looking as though she were laughing at him, and he said, "I am tired and hungry, why do you laugh at me?" and he pushed her. As she fell backwards, her stomach opened. He caught hold of her and discovered that she was dead. He knew at once that Red Woman had killed his wife.

While the man was eating supper alone one night, a voice said, "Father, give me some of your supper." As no one was in sight, he resumed eating and again the voice asked for supper. The man said, "Whoever you are, you may come and eat with me, for I am poor and alone." A young boy came from behind the curtain. He said that his name was Thrown-behind-the-Curtain.

During the day, while the man went hunting, the boy stayed home. One day the boy said, "Father, make me two bows and the arrows." His father asked him why he wanted two bows. The boy said, "I want them to use one, then the other." His father made them for him, but surmised the boy had other reasons and decided he would watch the boy. One day, earlier than usual, he left his tipi and hid on a hill overlooking his tipi, and while there, he saw two boys of about the same age shooting arrows.

That evening when he returned home, he asked his son, "Is there not another little boy of your age around here?" His son said, "Yes, and he lives in the spring." His father said, "You should bring him out and make him live with us." The son said, "I cannot make him because he has sharp teeth like an otter, but if you will make me a suit of rawhide, I will try and catch him."

One day, preparations were made to catch the boy. The father said, "I will stay here in the tipi and you tell him I have gone out." So Thrown-behind-the-Curtain said to Thrown-in-the-Spring, "Come out and play arrows." Thrown-in-the-Spring came out just a little and said, "I smell something." Thrown-behind-the-Curtain said, "No, you don't, my father is not home."

Persuaded, Thrown-in-the-Spring came out and both boys began to play. While they were playing, Thrown-behind-the-Curtain disputed a point of their game, and as Thrown-in-the-Spring stooped over to see how close his arrow came, Thrown-behind-the-Curtain grabbed him from behind and held his arms close to his sides. Thrown-in-the-Spring turned and attempted to bite the other boy, but his teeth could not penetrate the rawhide suit. The father came to the assistance of Thrown-behind-the-Curtain and the water of the spring rushed out to help Thrown-in-the-Spring. But Thrown-in-the-Spring was dragged to a high hill where the water could not reach him, and there they burned incense under his nose, and he became human.

The three of them lived together.

One day one of the boys said, "Let us go and wake up mother." They went to the mother's grave and one said, "Mother, your stone pot is dropping," and she moved. The other boy said, "Mother, your hide dresser is falling," and she sat up. Then one of them said, "Mother, your bone crusher is falling," and she began to arrange her hair, which had begun to fall off. The mother said, "I have been asleep a long time." She accompanied the boys home.

The boys were forbidden by their father to go to the river bend above their tipi, for an old woman lived there who had a boiling pot. Every time she saw a living object, she tilted the kettle toward it and the object was drawn into the pot and boiled for her to eat. The boys went one day to see the old woman. They found her asleep and they stole up and got her pot and awakened the old woman and said to her, "Grandmother, why do you have this here?" at the same time tilting the pot towards her so that she was drowned in it and was boiled to death. They took the pot home and gave it to their mother for her own protection.

Their father told them not to disobey him again and said, "There is something over the hill I do not want you to go near." They were very anxious to find out what this thing was, and they went over to the hill. As they poked their heads over the hilltop, the thing began to draw in air and the boys were drawn in also. As they went in, they saw people and animals, some dead and others dying. The thing proved to be an immense serpent like an alligator.

One of the boys touched the kidneys of the thing and asked what they were. The serpent said, "That is my medicine, do not touch it." And the boy reached up and touched its heart and asked what it was, and the serpent grunted and said, "This is where I make my plans." One of the boys said, "You make plans, do you?" He cut the heart off and it died. They made their escape by cutting between the ribs and liberated the living ones. They took a piece of the heart home to their father.

After the father had administered another scolding, he told the boys not to go near the three trees standing in a triangular-shaped piece of ground, for if anything went under them they would bend to the ground suddenly, killing everything in their way. One day the boys went towards these trees, running swiftly and then stopped suddenly near the trees, which bent down violently and struck the ground without hitting them. They jumped over the trees, breaking the branches and the trees could not rise after the branches were broken.

Once more the boys were scolded and told not to go near a tipi over the hill. It was inhabited by snakes that would approach anyone asleep and enter his body through the rectum. Again the boys did as they were told not to do and went to the tipi, and the snakes invited them in. They went in and carried flat pieces of stone with them. As they sat down they placed the flat pieces of stone under their rectums.

After they had been in the tipi a short while, the snakes began putting their heads over the poles around the fireplace and the snakes began to relate stories. One of them said, "When there is a drizzling rain, and when we are under cover, it is nice to sleep." One of the boys said, "When we are lying down under the pine trees and the wind blows softly through them and has a weird sound, it is nice to sleep."

All but one of the snakes went to sleep. That one tried to enter the rectum of each of the boys but failed on account of the flat stones. The boys killed all of the other snakes except that one, and they took that one and rubbed its head against the side of a cliff. That is the reason why snakes have flattened heads.

Again the boys were scolded by their father, who said, "There is a man living on the steep-cut bank, with deep water under it, and if you go near it he will push you over the bank into the water for his father in the water to eat."

The boys went to the place, but before going, they fixed their headdresses with dried grass. Upon their arrival at the edge of the bank, one said to the other, "Just as he is about to push you over, lie down quickly." The man suddenly rushed out from his hiding place to push the boys over, and just as he was about to do it, the boys threw themselves quickly upon the ground. The man went over their heads, pulling their headdress with him, and his father in the water ate him.

Upon the boys' return, and after telling what they had done, their father scolded them and told them, "There is a man who wears moccasins of fire, and when he wants anything, he goes around it and it is burned up." The boys ascertained where this man lived and stole upon him one day when he was sleeping under a tree, and each one of the boys took off a moccasin and put it on. They awoke him and ran about him and he was burned and went up in smoke. They took the moccasins home.

Their father told them that something would yet happen to them, for they had killed so many bad things. One day while walking the valley they were lifted from the earth. After traveling in mid air for some time, they were placed on top of a peak in a rough high mountain with a big lake surrounding it. The Thunder Bird said to them, "I want you to kill a long otter that lives in the lake [Figure 14.5]. He eats all the young ones that I produce and I cannot make him stop."

**FIGURE 14.5**   The Thunder Bird, petroglyph of unknown date in Washington State Park, Missouri. The Thunder Bird is one of the few mythical elements we can securely identify in prehistoric American Indian carvings. (Harel Stanton / Alamy)

The boys began to make arrows, and they gathered dry pine sticks and began to heat rocks, and the long otter came towards them. As it opened its mouth
the boys shot arrows into it. As that did not stop it from drawing nearer, they
threw the hot rocks down its throat, and it curled up and died. They were taken
up and carried through the air and gently placed upon the ground near their
homes, where they lived for many years.

The story is based on the folktale prohibition, "Whatever you do, don't . . ." Of
course the boys, whose birth is miraculous, undertake all the forbidden exploits and
are always successful, even bringing their dead mother back to life. They, too, are tricksters, defying death. Constantly they turn the powers of their adversaries against them:
turning the pot against the old woman, being swallowed by the serpent only to cut out
its heart from within, breaking the branches of the deadly trees, enchanting the snakes
with their own spell, feeding the lurking man to his own father, burning the man who
burns with his own moccasins, and feeding hot stones to the voracious otter. Because
they depend on their own intuitions and abilities and ignore the dangers that face them,
doing what they are told not to, they are always successful: That is the moral of the tale.

## MYTH: THE BEAR-WOMAN

A good example of animals becoming human and humans becoming animals, sometimes
by putting on a skin—of bear, eagle, or deer—is this **BLACKFOOT** tale of the bear-woman,
which also explains the origin of the Big Dipper in the sky. The Blackfoot (so-called
because they painted the soles of their moccasins black) were a buffalo-hunting people
who live in what is today Glacier National Park, and further north in Canada. They spoke
an **Algonquian** language, like the Ojibwa (Chippewa). They were fine horsemen and
fierce warriors, enemies of the Crow and the Sioux (Figure 14.6):

Once there was a young woman with many suitors, but she refused to marry.
She had seven brothers and one little sister. Their mother had been dead many
years, and they had no relatives, but lived alone with their father. Every day the
brothers went out hunting with their father.

It seems that the young woman had a bear for her lover and, as she did not
want any one to know this, she would meet him when she went out after wood.
She always went after wood as soon as her father and brothers went out to hunt,
leaving her little sister alone in the lodge. As soon as she was out of sight in the
brush, she would run to the place where the bear lived.

As the little sister grew older, she began to be curious as to why her older
sister spent so much time getting wood. One day she followed her. She saw the
young woman meet the bear and saw that they were lovers. When she found this
out, she ran home as quickly as she could, and when her father returned she told
him what she had seen. When he heard the story he said, "So, my older daughter
has a bear for a husband. Now I know why she does not want to marry."

Then he went about the camp, telling all his people that they had a bear
for a brother-in-law, and that he wished all the men to go out with him to kill
this bear. So they went, found the bear, and killed him.

**FIGURE 14.6**   Blackfoot rider, color engraving, watercolor by Karl Bodmer (1809–1893), 1833, from Maximilian von Wied (1772–1867), *Travels in the Interior of North America During the Years 1832–1834*. Bodmer was trained in European art schools. His representations of American Indians are the most celebrated of all, made mostly in the Mandan village on the upper Missouri where Maximilian and Bodmer spent the winter of 1833. Here the warrior wears two eagle feathers in his hair and turns on his horse to a companion. He wears a deerskin shirt decorated with beaded strips and decorated deerskin leggings. On his back he carries a quiver with a bow, supported by a quilled band across his chest. He carries a flintlock rifle and powder horn. A rifle scabbard lies against the horse's flank, an Appaloosa he would have acquired by theft or trade from the Nez Perce Indians across the Bitterroot Mountains to the west (in Idaho), who bred these horses. His saddle is equipped with stirrups, a device learned from the white man. (INTERFOTO / Alamy)

When the young woman found out what had been done, and that her little sister had told on her, she was very angry. She scolded her little sister vigorously, then ordered her to go out to the dead bear and bring some flesh from his paws. The little sister began to cry, and said she was afraid to go out of the lodge, because a dog with young pups had tried to bite her.

"O, do not be afraid!" said the young woman. "I will paint your face like that of a bear, with black marks across the eyes and at the corners of the mouth. Then no one will touch you." So she went for the meat.

Now the older sister was a powerful medicine-woman. She could tan hides in a new way. She could take up a hide, strike it four times with her skin-scraper, and it would be tanned.

The little sister had a younger brother that she carried on her back. Because their mother was dead, she took care of him. One day the little sister said to the older sister, "Now you be a bear and we will go out into the brush to play." The older sister agreed to this, but said, "Little sister, you must not touch me over my kidneys."

So the big sister acted as a bear, and they played in the brush. While they were playing, the little sister forgot what she had been told, and touched her older sister in the wrong place. At once she turned into a real bear, ran into the camp, and killed many of the people. After she had killed a large number, she turned back into her former self. When the little sister saw the older run away as a real bear, she became frightened, took up her little brother, and ran into their lodge. Here they waited, badly frightened, but were very glad to see their older sister return after a time as her true self.

Now the older brothers were out hunting, as usual. As the little sister was going down for water with her little brother on her back, she met her six brothers returning. The brothers noted how quiet and deserted the camp seemed to be. So they said to their little sister, "Where are all our people?"

The little sister explained how she and her sister were playing when the older sister turned into a bear, ran through the camp, and killed many people. She told her brothers that they were in great danger, as their sister would surely kill them when they came home. So the six brothers decided to go into the brush. One of them had killed a jackrabbit. He said to the little sister, "You take this rabbit home with you. When it is dark, we will scatter prickly pears all around the lodge, except in one place. When you come out, you must look for that place and pass through."

When the little sister came back to the lodge, the older sister said, "Where have you been all this time?"

"O, my little brother dirtied himself and I had to clean him," replied the little sister.

"Where did you get that rabbit?" she asked.

"I killed it with a sharp stick," said the little sister.

"That is a lie. Let me see you do it," said the older sister.

Then the little sister took up a stick lying near her, threw it at the rabbit, and it stuck in the wound in his body. "Well, all right," said the older sister.

The little sister dressed the rabbit and cooked it. She offered some of it to her older sister, but she refused so the little sister and her brother ate all of it. When the older sister saw that the rabbit had been eaten, she became very angry and said, "Now I have a mind to kill you."

The little sister arose quickly, took her little brother on her back, and said, "I am going out to look for wood." As she went out, she followed the narrow trail through the prickly pears and met her six brothers in the brush. They decided to leave the country and started off as fast as they could go.

The older sister, being a powerful medicine-woman, knew at once what they were doing. She became very angry and turned herself into a bear to pursue them. Soon she was about to overtake them, when one of the boys tried his power. He took a little water in the hollow of his hand and sprinkled it around. At once it became a great lake between them and the bear. The children hurried on while the bear had to go around the lake.

After a while the bear caught up with them again, when another brother threw a porcupine tail [a hairbrush] on the ground. This became a great thicket, but the bear forced its way through, and again overtook the children. This time they all climbed a high tree. The bear came to the foot of the tree, and, looking up at them, said, "Now I shall kill you all."

She took a stick from the ground, threw it into the tree and knocked down four of the brothers. While she was doing this, a little bird flew around the tree, calling out to the children, "Shoot her in the head! Shoot her in the head!" One of the boys shot an arrow into the head of the bear, and at once she fell dead. Then they came down from the tree.

Now the four brothers were dead. The little brother took an arrow, shot it straight up into the air, and when it fell one of the dead brothers came to life. This he repeated until all were alive again.

Then they held a council, and said to each other, "Where shall we go? Our people have all been killed, and we are a long way from home. We have no relatives living in the world." Finally they decided that they preferred to live in the sky. The little brother said, "Shut your eyes." As they did so, they all went up.

Now you can see them every night. The little brother is the North Star. The six brothers and the little sister are seen in the Great Dipper. The little sister and oldest brother are in a line with the North Star, the little sister being nearest it because she used to carry her little brother on her back. The other brothers are arranged in order of their age, beginning with the oldest. This is how the seven stars [of the Great Bear, the Big Dipper] came to be.

## MYTH: THE TRICKSTER'S GREAT FALL AND HIS REVENGE

To the Indians of the plains, Coyote was the trickster, but in the central woodlands of Wisconsin it was **Manabozho** (cf. Perspective 14).

### PERSPECTIVE 14

### Longfellow's *Hiawatha*

Henry Wadsworth Longfellow (1807–1882) was an American poet and teacher. He was the author of "Paul Revere's Ride," *The Song of Hiawatha*, and *Evangeline*, and the first American to translate Dante Alighieri's *The Divine Comedy*. At one time his poems were a staple of American education.

Longfellow was born in Portland, Maine. His maternal grandfather was an officer in the Revolutionary War and a member of Congress. Longfellow attended Bowdoin College where he met Nathaniel Hawthorne (1804–1864), and the two men became lifelong friends. After a tour of Europe, Longfellow became a professor at Bowdoin, then at Harvard. His first major poetry collections were published in 1839 and 1841. Longfellow withdrew from teaching in 1854 in order to concentrate on his writing. He lived the rest of his life in Cambridge, Massachusetts, in a house that had once been the headquarters of George Washington.

Longfellow's first wife died in 1835 from a miscarriage after four years of marriage. His second wife burned to death in 1861 when her dress caught fire from hot sealing wax. Devastated by her death, Longfellow resorted to laudanum and ether to relieve his sorrow. He worried he would go insane and begged "not to be sent to an asylum."

Longfellow wrote lyric poems known for their musicality that often presented stories from myth and legend. The swiftness with which American readers embraced Longfellow was without precedent in the United States. By 1874, he was earning $3,000 a poem! He was popular in Europe too: His poetry was translated into Italian, French, and German. Ten thousand copies of "The Courtship of Miles Standish" sold in London in one day. In 1884, Longfellow became the first nonBritish writer to receive a bust in the Poet's Corner of Westminster Abbey in London, the only American ever so honored.

*The Song of Hiawatha* was published in 1855. Two years later it had sold 50,000 copies. Longfellow described it as "this Indian Edda." Written in trochaic tetrameter, supposedly on the model of Finnish epic, it features an American Indian hero. It is loosely based on the legends of the Ojibwa described by Henry Rowe Schoolcraft.

Hiawatha (also known as Ayenwatha or Aiionwatha) was a founder of the Iroquois confederacy in the 15th or 16th century, but there is no connection, apart from the name, between Longfellow's hero and the historical Iroquois chief, about whom little real is known, except that he sponsored the unification of the Iroquois peoples. In feeling and overall conception Longfellow's poem is a product of American Romantic literature, not a representation of American Indian oral tradition.

Longfellow at first intended to follow Schoolcraft and call his hero Manabozho, the Ojibwa trickster, but decided on Hiawatha, who was not in fact "another name for the same personage," as Longfellow put it (Schoolcraft had made the same mistake). Longfellow set *The Song of Hiawatha* along the shore of Lake Superior favored by the Manabozho stories. Because of the poem, the name *Hiawatha* has been applied to everything from towns to an Amtrak train to a telephone company in the upper Great Lakes, although this is the land of the Ojibwa, not the Iroquois.

The *Song* tells the story of Hiawatha and his courtship of the princess Minnehaha. In the poem, she dies of "Famine and the Fever," causing Hiawatha great sorrow (Perspective Figure 14). A selection of 94 lines was and still is anthologized under the title "Hiawatha's Childhood," which begins with the famous lines:

By the shores of Gitche Gumee,

By the shining Big-Sea-Water,

Stood the wigwam of Nokomis,

Daughter of the Moon, Nokomis.

Dark behind it rose the forest,

Rose the black and gloomy pine-trees,

Rose the firs with cones upon them;

Bright before it beat the water,

Beat the clear and sunny water,

Beat the shining Big-Sea-Water.

There the wrinkled old Nokomis

nursed the little Hiawatha,

Rocked him in his linden cradle,

bedded soft in moss and rushes,

**PERSPECTIVE FIGURE 14**   The death of Minnehaha. Minnehaha was the daughter of an arrow-maker and the wife of Hiawatha. Her name is Siouan for "laughing water," from the waterfall of that name near modern St. Paul, Minnesota. In this Romantic painting, set within a lodge, she lies half draped while ghostly spirits welcome her to the spirit world. Hiawatha holds his head in his hands in sorrow, and a female companion has collapsed against the bier. Oil painting by William de Leftwich Dodge (1867–1935), 1892. (Ivy Close Images / Alamy)

> Safely bound with reindeer sinews;
> stilled his fretful wail by saying,
> "Hush! the Naked Bear will hear thee!"
> Lulled him into slumber, singing,
> "Ewa-yea! my little owlet!
> Who is this, that lights the wigwam?
> With his great eyes lights the wigwam?
> Ewa-yea! my little owlet!"
> Many things Nokomis taught him
> of the stars that shine in heaven;
> Showed him Ishkoodah, the comet,
> Ishkoodah, with fiery tresses;
> Showed the Death-Dance of the spirits,
> warriors with their plumes and war-clubs,
> Flaring far away to northward
> in the frosty nights of winter;

Showed the broad white road in heaven,

pathway of the ghosts, the shadows,

Running straight across the heavens,

crowded with the ghosts, the shadows.

At the door on summer evenings,

sat the little Hiawatha;

Heard the whispering of the Pine-trees,

heard the lapping of the water,

Sounds of music, words of wonder;

"Minne-wawa!" said the pine-trees,

"Mudway-aushka!" said the water.

The poem closes when a birch bark canoe approaches Hiawatha's village. In the canoe is "the Priest of Prayer, the Pale-face," that is, a Jesuit priest. Hiawatha welcomes him happily, and the "Black-Robe chief."

Told his message to the people,

Told the purport of his mission,

Told them of the Virgin Mary,

And her blessed Son, the Saviour.

Hiawatha and the chiefs accept the priest's message, Hiawatha bids farewell to Nokomis and all the others, telling them:

"But my guests I leave behind me.

Listen to their words of wisdom,

Listen to the truth they tell you."

He gives his approval to the Christian missionaries, then paddles his canoe into the sunset.

In *Hiawatha,* Longfellow presents his own vision of a sentimental view of the past together with the Indian as noble savage. The poem almost immediately inspired parodies, and continues to do so today. In 1856 appeared *The Song of Milkanwatha: Translated from the Original Feejee,* by "Marc Antony Henderson" (really George A. Strong, 1832–1912), published by "Tickell and Grinne." An example:

In one hand Peek-Week, the squirrel,

in the other hand the blow-gun—

Fearful instrument, the blow-gun;

And Marcosset and Sumpunkin,

Kissed him, 'cause he killed the squirrel,

'Cause it was a rather big one.

From the squirrel-skin, Marcosset

Made some mittens for our hero,

Mittens with the fur-side inside,

With the fur-side next his fingers

So's to keep the hand warm inside;

That was why she put the fur-side—
Why she put the fur-side, inside.

In 1941 the Warner Brothers cartoon "Hiawatha's Rabbit Hunt," starring Bugs Bunny and a tiny Hiawatha, was nominated—unsuccessfully—for an Academy Award.

The following tale was collected from the **MENOMINEE**, who live today northeast of Oshkosh, Wisconsin. Their name means "people of the wild rice" in Algonquian, to which general language family they belong, along with the Fox, Kickapoo, and Ojibwa (Chippewa). Wild rice, which they collected in birch bark canoes, was a principle source of food, along with deer, bear, and fish. The Menominee seem to be indigenous to Michigan and Wisconsin:

Once while Buzzard was soaring away through the air he saw Manabozho walking along. He flew a little toward the ground with his wings outspread and heard Manabozho say, "Buzzard, you must be very happy up there where you can soar through the air and see what is transpiring in the world beneath. Take me on your back so that I may ascend with you and see how it appears down here from where you live."

The Buzzard came down, and said, "Manabozho, get on my back and I will take you up into the sky to let you see how the world appears from my abode."

Manabozho approached the Buzzard, but seeing how smooth his back appeared said, "Buzzard, I am afraid you will let me slide from your back, so you must be careful not to sweep around too rapidly, so I can keep my place on your back."

The Buzzard told Manabozho that he would be careful, although the bird was determined to play a trick on him if possible. Manabozho mounted the Buzzard and held on to his feathers as well as he could. The Buzzard took a short run, leaped from the ground, spread his wings and rose into the air. Manabozho felt rather timid as the Buzzard swept through the air and, as he circled around, his body leaned so much that Manabozho could scarcely retain his position, and he was afraid of slipping off.

Presently, as Manabozho was looking down on the broad earth below, Buzzard made a sharp curve to one side so that his body leaned more than ever. Manabozho, losing his grasp, slipped off and dropped to earth like an arrow. He struck the ground with such force as to knock him senseless. Buzzard returned to his place in the sky, but hovered around to see what would become of Manabozho.

Manabozho lay a long time like one dead. When he recovered, he saw something close to him and apparently staring him in the face. He could not at first recognize it, but when he put his hands against the object he found that it was his own buttocks, because he had been all doubled up. He arose and prepared to go on his way when he espied Buzzard above him, laughing at his trick.

Manabozho then said, "Buzzard, you have played a trick on me by letting me fall, but as I am more powerful than you. I shall revenge myself." Buzzard replied, "No, Manabozho, you will not do anything of the kind, because you cannot deceive me. I shall watch you."

Manabozho kept on and Buzzard, not noticing anything peculiar in the movements of Manabozho, flew on his way through the air. Manabozho then decided to transform himself into a dead deer, because he knew that Buzzard had chosen to live off dead animals and fish. Manabozho then went to a place visible from a great distance and from many directions, where he laid himself down and changed himself into the carcass of a deer. Soon the various birds and beasts and crawling things that subsist on such food began to congregate about the dead deer. Buzzard saw the birds flying toward the place where the body lay, and joined them. He flew around several times to see if it was Manabozho trying to deceive him, then thought to himself, "No, that is not Manabozho. It is truly a dead deer."

He approached the body and began to pick a hole into the fleshy part of the thigh. Deeper and deeper into the flesh Buzzard picked until his head and neck was buried each time he reached in to pluck the fat from the intestines. Without warning, while Buzzard had his head completely hidden in the carcass of the deer, the deer jumped up and pinched together his flesh, firmly grasping the head and neck of the Buzzard.

Manabozho said, "Aha! Buzzard, I did catch you after all, as I told you I would. Now pull out your head."

Buzzard with great difficulty withdrew his head from the cavity in which it had been enclosed, but the feathers were all pulled off, leaving his scalp and neck covered with nothing but red skin. Manabozho said to the bird, "Thus do I punish you for your deceit. Henceforth you will go through the world without feathers on your head and neck and you shall always stink because of the food you will be obliged to eat."

That is why the buzzard is such a bad-smelling fellow, and why his head and neck are featherless.

Indian stories often end in this way, "and that is why . . ." but such etiological tags are mostly tacked on. In this case, however, the etiology is the point of the story. Why does the buzzard have a naked head? Because . . .

## MYTH: THE GIRLS ENTICED TO THE SKY

In North American Indian myth the notion is common that you can reach the other world through a hole in the sky. The **Ojibwa** (meaning unknown), who told this story, lived originally around Sault Saint Marie, but later moved south and west and today live in Michigan, Wisconsin, Minnesota, and southern Canada (Figure 14.7). Known for their birch bark canoes, they speak an Algonquian language and hence are related to the Cheyenne, Blackfoot, and Menominee. They are today the third largest Indian group in the United States (after the Cherokee and Navajo), numbering about 150,000:

At the time of which my story speaks people were camping just as we are here. In the wintertime they used birch bark wigwams. All the animals could then talk together. Two girls, who were very foolish, talked foolishly and were in no respect like the other girls of their tribe. They made their bed out-of-doors and slept right out under the stars. The very fact that they slept outside during the winter proves how foolish they were.

**FIGURE 14.7**   Ojibwa chief Strong Wind, painting by George Catlin (1796–1872), 1845, oil on canvas. On his head Strong Wind wears a "roach," a decoration made of porcupine hair. A "roach spreader" holds the roach in place and supports an eagle feather to indicate the warrior's valor. He wears elaborate earrings and three necklace pendants, one a seashell and the other two metal images usually of American presidents called "peace medals," given to prominent Indians. The painting of a hand on the face is unusual. George Catlin made a famous series of paintings of American Indians, many from the Mandan village on the upper Missouri, which he visited in 1834 one year after Maximilian von Wied. One year later, most of the Mandans were dead from smallpox. Catlin toured with these paintings on the East Coast and in London, but in the end went bankrupt. Most of the paintings are today in the Smithsonian and in the Indian museum in Cody, Wyoming. Catlin gave his name to "catlinite," the red stone from which the plains Indians made their pipe bowls. (Smithsonian Institution, Washington. DC; INTERFOTO / Alamy)

One of these girls asked the other, "With what star would you like to sleep, the white one or the red one?"

The other girl answered, "I'd like to sleep with the red star."

"O, that's all right," said the first one, "I would like to sleep with the white star. He's the younger. The red is the older."

Then the two girls fell asleep. When they awoke, they found themselves in another world, the star world. There were four of them there, the two girls and the two stars who had become men. The white star was very, very old and was gray-headed, while the younger was red-headed. He was the red star. The girls stayed a long time in this star world, and the one who had chosen the white star was very sorry, for he was so old.

There was an old woman up in this world who sat over a hole in the sky, and, whenever she moved, she showed them the hole and said, "That's where you came from." They looked down through and saw their people playing below. The girls grew very sorry and very homesick.

One evening, near sunset, the old woman moved a little way from the hole. The younger girl heard the noise of the shamans down below. When it was almost daylight, the old woman sat over the hole again, and the noise of shamans stopped. It was her spirit that made the noise. She was the guardian of the shamans.

One morning the old woman told the girls, "If you want to go down where you came from, we will let you down, but get to work and gather roots to make a string-made rope, twisted. The two of you make coils of rope as high as your heads when you are sitting. Two coils will be enough."

The girls worked for days until they had accomplished this. They made plenty of rope and tied it to a big basket. They then got into the basket, and the people of the star world lowered them down.

They descended right into Eagle's nest, but the people above thought the girls were on the ground and stopped lowering them. They were obliged to stay in the nest because they could do nothing to help themselves.

Said one, "We'll have to stay here until someone comes to get us." Bear passed by. The girls cried out, "Bear, come and get us. You are going to get married sometime. Now is your chance!"

Bear thought, "They are not very good-looking women." He pretended to climb up and then said, "I can't climb up any further." And he went away, for the girls didn't suit him.

Next came Lynx. The girls cried out again, "Lynx, come up and get us. You will go after women some day!" Lynx answered, "I can't, for I have no claws," and he went away.

Then an ugly-looking man, Wolverine, passed and the girls spoke to him. "Hey, Wolverine, come and get us." Wolverine started to climb up, for he thought it a very fortunate thing to have these women and was very glad. When he reached them, they placed their hair ribbons in the nest. Wolverine agreed to take one girl at a time, so he took the first one down and went back for the next. Then Wolverine went away with his two wives and enjoyed himself greatly, as he was ugly and nobody else would have him.

They went far into the woods, and then they sat down and began to talk. "O!" cried one of the girls, "I forgot my hair ribbon."

Wolverine said, "I will run back for it," and he started off to get the hair ribbons. Then the girls hid and told the trees, whenever Wolverine should come back and whistle for them, to answer him by whistling.

Wolverine soon returned and began to whistle for his wives, and the trees all around him whistled in answer. Wolverine, realizing that he had been tricked, gave up the search and departed very angry.

## MYTH: THE MAN-EATING WIFE

The **Iroquois**, "the people of the long house" because they lived in longhouses much as the Northwest Indians, were known for having formed a powerful political organization probably in the 16th century, called the Five Nations or the Iroquois League and consisting of the closely related Mohawk, Oneida, Onondaga, Cayuga, and Seneca nations (see Perspective 14, Figure 14.8).

RED JACKET,
A SENECA WAR CHIEF.

**FIGURE 14.8**   Red Jacket, a Seneca War Chief, c. 1750–c. 1830. He wears a large peace medal. Portrait painted in 1828 by Charles B. King (1785–1862). (Lebrecht Music and Arts Photo Library / Alamy)

The League still exists today. They live in upstate New York west of the Hudson River. They were enemies of the Algonquian tribes, who lived in New England. In the 17th century, armed by the Dutch, they exterminated some Algonquian tribes (for example, the Mohicans) and drove others across the Great Lakes, where they live today as the Ojibwa Indians. The Iroquois were related to the Cherokee, who spoke an Iroquoian language but seem to have migrated to the southeast sometime before contact with Europeans. The Iroquois sided with the British during the Revolutionary War and suffered considerably from the American victory.

Iroquois economy was based on some farming, but they were hunter-gatherers too. Occasionally they practiced cannibalism, like the Oceanic peoples and the inhabitants of central America. They told a story about a cannibal woman:

A man and a woman lived by themselves in a clearing in the forest. The man hunted while the woman raised beans and corn.

One day, when the woman sat in front of the fire baking an ash cake,° a large spark flew out and burned her. She rubbed the spot with her finger, and when it began to blister she wet her finger in her mouth and rubbed the blister. In this way she got the taste of her own flesh, and she liked it.

She took a flint knife, cut out the burnt piece of flesh and ate it. The taste was so agreeable that she took a coal of fire, burned another place on her arm,

°*ash cake*: a lump of bread cooked directly on the coals.

cut out the flesh and ate it. The desire grew upon her and she kept burning and eating herself till she had eaten all the flesh she could reach on her arms and legs.

The man had a dog that was wise and was his friend. The dog sat by the fire and watched the woman. When she was about half through eating herself, she said to him, "You had better go and tell your friend to run away and to take you with him. If he doesn't hurry off, I shall eat both of you."

The dog ran as fast as he could and when he came to where the man was hunting, he told him what had happened, that his wife had become a man-eater and was going to eat herself and then eat them.

The man and the dog started off. The dog's legs were short and he couldn't run fast, so the man put him in a hollow tree and commanded him to become punk.° The dog was willing, for he wanted his master to save himself.

The man went on as fast as he could till he came to a river with high banks. By the river sat an old man.

"Grandfather," said the man, "I am in great trouble. Put me across the river. Save me, my wife is following me and she wants to kill and eat me."

"I know she is following you," said the old man, "but she is still a long way off. I will put you across but first you must bring me a basketful of fish from my fish pond."

The man went for the fish. The pond was enclosed. On the bank was a basket with a handle. The man caught a large number of fish, filled the basket, and carried it to the old man, who cooked the fish and then said, "Sit down and eat with me."

They ate together, then the old man said, "Now you must bring me a basketful of groundnuts."°

The man ran to the old man's garden, dug up the groundnuts as quickly as possible and carried them to him. After he had cooked and eaten the groundnuts, he said, "Now I will put you across the river."

He lay down at the edge of the water and, leaning on his elbows, stretched his neck to the opposite bank and called out, "Walk across on my neck, but be careful. I am not as strong as I used to be."

The man walked over carefully, then the old man bade him goodbye, saying, "Far off in the west you will come to a large bark house. That house belongs to your three aunts. They will help you."

In the meanwhile the man's wife took a stick and, pushing the marrow out of her bones, ate it. She filled her bones with pebbles and the pebbles rattled as she moved. Every little while she stopped eating and danced and when she heard the stones rattle in her legs and arms, she said, "Oh, that sounds good!"

The woman devoured everything in the cabin, meat, bread, skins, everything that could be eaten, and when there was nothing left she started off to find her husband.

---

°*punk*: soft crumbly wood used as tinder. °*groundnuts*: a North American vine of the pea family that bears clusters of fragrant flowers and yields a sweet edible tuber.

She came upon his tracks and followed them. Once in a while she stopped and danced and listened with delight to the rattle of the pebbles in her bones. Then she went on again.

When she came to the bank of the river and saw the old ferryman, she screamed to him, "Old man, come and put me across the river. I am following my husband. Be quick!"

The fisherman turned slowly toward her, and said, "I can't put you across. There is no crossing for a woman who is chasing her husband to catch and eat him."

But the woman urged and begged till at last the old man said, "I'll put you across, but first you must bring me a basketful of fish and dig me a basketful of groundnuts."

She brought the fish and the groundnuts, but when they were cooked she wouldn't eat with the old man. She would eat nothing now but human flesh.

After the old man had eaten the fish and the groundnuts he stretched his neck across the river but in the form of a horse's neck, very narrow and arching. The woman was angry, and asked, "How do you think I am going to walk on that?"

"You can do as you like," answered he. "I am old. I can't make my neck flat. It would break. As it is, you must walk carefully."

No matter how the woman raged, she had to stay where she was or cross on the arched neck. At last she started, picking her steps and scolding as she went.

The water was deep and full of terrible creatures. When the woman reached the middle of the river, the old man, angry because she scolded, jerked his neck. She fell into the water and instantly was seized and devoured, all except her stomach, which floated down the river and past the house of the three aunts. The woman's life was in her stomach.

The aunts were watching, for their nephew had been at the house and they had promised to help him. They caught the stomach, chopped it up and killed it.

And so the man escaped the terrible cannibal wife!

## MYTH: THE FATAL SWING

Some Indian stories turn on the jealousies, and sexual attraction, between family members living in close proximity and sleeping in the same tent. One such story tells of the passion of a mother-in-law for her son-in-law (as in the Greek story of Hippolytus). As often in Indian tales, the dead are brought back to life, to the sorrow of the living. The story is OSAGE, a Siouan-language tribe that originated in the Ohio River valley in present-day Kentucky. After years of war with invading Iroquois, the Osage migrated west of the Mississippi River to present-day Arkansas, Missouri, Kansas, and Oklahoma by the mid-17th century. At their height in the early 18th century, the Osages were the dominant power between the Missouri and the Red River, now the border between Texas and Oklahoma.

Once there was a man living by the big water. He was a deer hunter. He would go out and kill wild turkeys and bring them in. Finally, his mother-in-law fell in love with him. There was a swing by the water, and the old woman and her daughter would swing across it and back. After a while, the old woman partially cut the rope, so that it would break.

While the husband was out hunting one day the old woman said to her daughter, "Let us go to the swing and have some fun." The old woman got in first and swung across the water and back. Then the girl got in the swing and she swung across all right, but when she was halfway back, the rope broke in two and the girl fell into the water and was drowned.

The old woman went home and got supper for her son-in-law. The man came in just at dark, and he missed his wife and said, "Mother-in-law, where is my wife?" The old woman said, "She has gone to the swing and has not yet returned."

The old woman began to prepare supper for her son-in-law. The man said, "Do not give me any supper." So he started to cry.

The old woman said, "Do not cry. She is dead and we cannot help it. I will take care of the baby. Your wife is drowned, so she is lost entirely."

The man cut off his hair and threw his leggings away and his shirt, and he mourned for his wife. He would go out and stay a week at a time without eating. He became very poor. Finally he said he was going off to stay several days, that he could not help thinking of his wife. He went off and stayed several days, and when he came home he would cry all the time.

One time, when he was out mourning, a rain and thunderstorm came up and lightning struck all around the tree he was sitting under. He went back home and saw his baby, but stayed out of his sight.

Again he went out, and it rained and thundered, and he went up by a big tree and lightning struck a tree near by him. Lightning left him a club and said, "Man, I came here to tell you about your wife for whom you are mourning. You do not know where she is or how she came to be missing. That old woman drowned her in the big water. The old woman broke the rope, and the girl is drowned in the big water. This club you must keep in a safe place. I was sent here to you, and I will help you get your wife back, and you must not be afraid of the big water. Go ahead and try to get her and on the fourth day you will get her all right."

The man went to the big water, and he saw his wife out in the water, and she said, "I cannot get to you. I am tied here with chains. I am going to come up four times." The next time she came out halfway. She said, "Bring me the baby, and I will let her nurse." So the man took the baby to her mother and let her nurse. The woman said, "They are pulling me, and I must go. But the next time you must get me."

So she came out the third time up to her knees. The man took the baby to her and let it nurse again. The woman said, "I have got to go back. They are pulling me by the chains. I must go, but the next time will be the last. I want you to try your best to get me."

The man said, "I am going to get you, without doubt." The woman came out the fourth time and the man hit the chain with the club. It seemed as though lightning struck it, and broke it. He got his wife.

So they went home, and the old woman said, "My daughter, you have got home."

But the woman said not a word. Then the man heated an arrow red hot and put it through the old woman's ears. So they killed the woman.

## MYTH: CHEROKEE ORIGIN OF FIRE

The **Cherokee**, who lived in the southeast United States, were known as one of the "five civilized tribes" because at an early time they adopted Anglo-American dress and ways of life. In 1838 many were moved to Indian Territory, present-day Okalahoma, by Andrew Jackson in the "Trail of Tears." They are today the most numerous of all Indian tribes, numbering around 300,000.

**Sequoyah** (c. 1767–c. 1843), a Cherokee mixed blood whose English name was George Guess, was a silversmith who in 1821 invented the Cherokee syllabary, making reading and writing in the Cherokee language possible. As far as we know this is the only time that a member of an illiterate people independently created an effective writing system (Figure 14.9). After much labor and experimentation, he came up with system of 86 syllabic characters, some of which were Roman letters that he obtained from a spelling book, but there is no relationship between their sounds in English and in Cherokee. Sequoyah spoke no English, only Cherokee. In 1825 the Cherokee Nation officially adopted the writing system. From 1828 to 1834 writers and editors used Sequoia's syllabary to print the *Cherokee Phoenix*, the first newspaper of the Cherokee Nation, with text in English and Cherokee.

But Cherokee myths were never preserved in Sequoia's syllabary. For them we must depend on the collections of ethnographers. The Cherokee told a story about the origin of fire:

> In the beginning there was no fire, and the world was cold until the Thunders sent their lightning and put fire into the bottom of a hollow sycamore tree that grew on an island. The animals knew it was there, because they could see the smoke coming out at the top, but they could not get to it on account of the water. They held a council to decide what to do. This was a long time ago.
>
> Every animal that could fly or swim was anxious to go after the fire. Raven offered, and because he was so large and strong they thought he could surely do the work, so he was sent first. He flew high and far across the water and alighted on the sycamore tree, but while he was wondering what to do next, the heat scorched all his feathers black, and he was frightened and came back without the fire.
>
> Little Screech-owl volunteered to go, and reached the place safely, but while he was looking down into the hollow tree a blast of hot air came up and nearly burned out his eyes. He managed to fly home as best he could, but it was a long time before he could see well and his eyes are red to this day.
>
> Then Hooting Owl and Horned Owl went, but by the time they got to the hollow tree the fire was burning so fiercely that the smoke nearly blinded them, and the ashes carried up by the wind made white rings about their eyes. They had to come home again without the fire, but with all their rubbing they were never able to get rid of the white rings.
>
> Now no more of the birds would venture out, and so the little Black Racer snake said he would go through the water and bring back some fire.
>
> He swam across to the island and crawled through the grass to the tree and went in by a small hole at the bottom. The heat and smoke were too much

SE-QUO-YAH,

INVENTOR OF THE CHEROKEE ALPHABET.

**FIGURE 14.9**    Sequoia and his syllabary. He wears European dress, wears a peace medal, and smokes a pipe. Portrait painted in 1828 by Charles B. King (1785–1862). (Lebrecht Music and Arts Photo Library / Alamy)

for him, too, and after dodging about blindly over the hot ashes until he was almost on fire himself he managed by good luck to get out again of the same hole, but his body had been scorched black, and he has ever since had the habit of darting and doubling on his track as if trying to escape from close quarters.

He came back, and great Blacksnake, "The Climber," offered to go for fire. He swam over to the island and climbed up the tree on the outside, as the black-snake always does, but when he put his head down into the hole, the smoke choked him so that he fell into the burning stump. Before he could climb out again he was completely black.

Now they held another council, for still there was no fire and the world was cold, but birds, snakes, and four-footed animals all had some excuse for not going. In reality they were all afraid to venture near the burning sycamore.

At last Water Spider said she would go. This is not the water spider that looks like a mosquito, but the other one, with black downy hair and red stripes on her body. She can run on top of the water or dive to the bottom, so there would be no trouble to get over to the island, but the question was, How could she bring back the fire?

"I'll manage that," said Water Spider. She spun a thread from her body and wove it into a bowl, which she fastened on her back. Then she crossed over to the island and through the grass to where the fire was still burning. She put one little coal of fire into her bowl and came back with it, and ever since we have had fire, and Water Spider still keeps her bowl.

The story is not so much about the origin of fire as the origin of the various qualities of animals, for which many etiologies are given.

## OBSERVATIONS: THE STORIES OF THE NORTH AMERICAN INDIANS

In the stories of the North American Indians there are no gods, no demons, and no heroes. Animals act just like humans and slip back and forth between the animal and human world, as in a children's movie in which the animals all talk and act like humans while still observing their animal nature. There is scarcely any distinction made between animals and humans, except that animals are stronger and more clever. Humans readily have sexual adventures with animals. Spirits are everywhere, and humans easily slip into the spirit world to become a bringer of abundance (Raven) or ruler of the spirits of the dead (Sedna). Humans are easily brought back to life (the Bear-Woman, the Fatal Swing). The characters constantly play tricks on one another to make the world the way it is, as Coyote brings the buffalo onto the plains by tricking their keeper or Manabozho tricks the buzzard so that its head is now hairless.

There is never a moral judgment against violence, but characters are violent against one another when opportunity presents itself. Only success counts and the power that success confers.

## Key Terms

| | | |
|---|---|---|
| Henry Rowe Schoolcraft 477 | Sedna 487 | Menominee 501 |
| Hopi 478 | Comanche 488 | Ojibwa 502 |
| Spider Woman 479 | Coyote 488 | Iroquois 504 |
| Tsimshian 484 | Crow 490 | Osage 507 |
| Raven 484 | Blackfoot 494 | Cherokee 509 |
| Inuit 487 | Algonquian 494 | Sequoyah 509 |
| | Manabozho 497 | |

## Further Reading

Dove, M., *Coyote Stories* (New York, 1990).
Edmonds, M., and E. E. Clark, *Voices of the Winds: Native American Legends* (New York, 2009).
Erdoes, R., and A. Ortiz, *American Indian Myths and Legends* (New York, 1985).
Erdoes, R., and A. Ortiz, *American Indian Trickster Tales* (New York, 1999).
Thompson, S., *Tales of the North American Indians* (Bloomington, IN, 1967; reprinted 2009).

CHAPTER

15

# African Myth

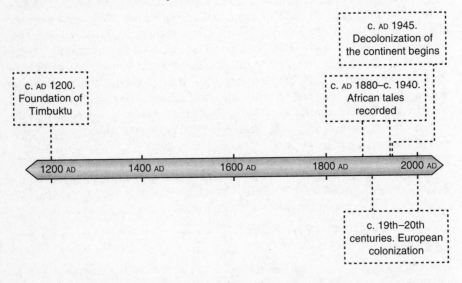

c. AD 1945.
Decolonization of
the continent begins

c. AD 1200.
Foundation of
Timbuktu

c. AD 1880–c. 1940.
African tales
recorded

1200 AD    1400 AD    1600 AD    1800 AD    2000 AD

c. 19th–20th
centuries. European
colonization

Africa, a word of unknown meaning, is the world's second-largest continent and, after Asia, the second most populous, covering 20 percent of the total land area of the planet (Map 15). With a billion people, Africa contains 15 percent of the world's population. To the north lies the MEDITERRANEAN SEA, to the southeast the INDIAN OCEAN, and to the west the ATLANTIC OCEAN. Today the continent has around 55 states, including MADAGASCAR. Africa straddles the equator and encompasses numerous climate zones. It is the only continent to stretch from the northern temperate to southern temperate zones. On dubious evidence, it is claimed to be the oldest inhabited part of the world. We cannot be sure of such claims, but certainly in early times dark-skinned peoples were driven out of EGYPT and up the Nile. There, because of the spreading Sahara desert, these peoples were isolated from cultural developments in the rest of the world, especially in the Near East, including Egypt, which is culturally and historically part of the Near East, not Africa.

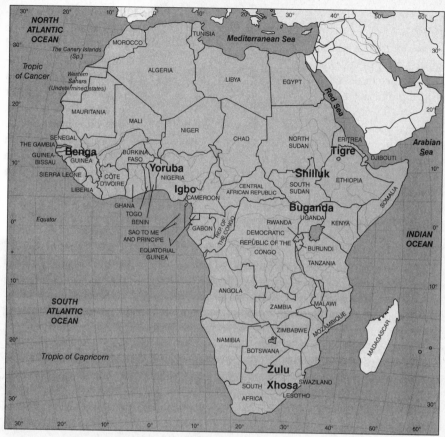

**MAP 15**   African tribes and places mentioned in this chapter.

## AFRICAN HISTORY

There is a strong division between the light-skinned inhabitants of the north of the continent, who speak Afro-Asiatic languages and are today Islamic (see Chapter 3, Egyptian Myth), and the dark-skinned, subSaharan peoples, who speak unrelated languages, and mostly follow native religions or Christianity. The subSaharan peoples spread virtually to the southern tip of Africa. There they remained unmolested by outsiders until modern times. Although centers of power developed especially in Nigeria and Central Africa, based on trade, Africans always retained a tribal social structure. Like the North American Indians, they had no system of writing, on which the modern state depends. Domestic cattle appeared at an early time, perhaps by 6000 BC, and may have preceded the development of agriculture in some regions. Still today many African tribes depend on cattle solely for their survival.

During the Middle Ages, Islam did cross the Maghreb, "the Arab West"—western North Africa—and the Sahel, "the coast," a sort of plain separating the Sahara desert from the southern savannas, or grasslands with trees that do not form a canopy. The Sahel extends all the way from the Atlantic Ocean to the Red Sea. The Muslims established

an important center of culture at Timbuktu, founded in t~~
ern West African nation of MALI. From the late 15th cent~~
Arabs captured large numbers of slaves from West, Centra~~
shipped them overseas, mostly to the Americas. European c~~
ceeded apace in the late 19th and early 20th centuries until~~
divided principally between France, Portugal, and the United K~~
extent by Germany and Italy. After the Second World War the~~
creating the modern map of Africa consisting of independent stat~~

The history of subSaharan Africa before European coloniza~~
because of the lack of written sources, though some progress ca~~
oral history, linguistics, and archaeology. In this chapter we will~~
subSaharan myth.

## CONDITIONS OF PERFORMANCE

Because no system of writing evolved among African peoples, all inform      we have
about African myth comes from the reports of local tales, almost always by nonAfri-
cans. Usually, these were published in alphabetic writing in the later 19th and early
20th centuries (although some are being collected even today). They are based, sometimes loosely, on actual performance of stories by native storytellers. The people would
gather at night around a campfire, and the teller of tales would hold forth before them,
sometimes in groups of 10 or 15. The storyteller is sometimes female. Written versions represent very poorly the experience of the storyteller and the audience, because
such stories were illustrated by exaggerated facial gestures, changes in tone of voice,
bodily gestures, and sometimes dance and song. The audience would often interrupt
the speaker, or respond in some way to the story being told. The reader of such oral
tales needs imagination to see the intent of the storyteller, who weaves in elements of
folklore and contemporary society in order to entertain his audience.

## MYTH: CREATION IN UGANDA

Buganda is the kingdom of the BAGANDA (or Ganda) people, the largest kingdom
in present-day UGANDA with about six million people. The Baganda, unlike many
African communities, has shown little interest in cattle-raising, but depends for its
economy on agriculture, especially in modern times the growing of bananas. The
name Uganda, Swahili for Buganda, was adopted by British officials in 1894 when they
established the Uganda Protectorate, centered in Buganda [Figure 15.1].

There are few stories in African myth about the creation of the world, but the
Baganda told a story about **Kintu**, the first man, and **Nambi**, the first woman:[1]

> Kintu was the first man. When he came from the unknown, he found nothing in
> Uganda—no food, no water, no animals, nothing but a blank. He had a cow with
> him, and when he was hungry he drank her milk.

---

[1]For the African texts, cf. H. Johnston, *The Uganda Protectorate*, vol. 2 (London, 1904); E. Littmann, *Publications of the Princeton Expedition to Abyssinia* (Leiden, 1910); E. Dayrell, *Folk Stories From Southern Nigeria*; R. H. Nassau, *Where Animals Talk* (Boston, 1912); G. M. Theal, *A Selection from the Traditional Tales Current among the People Living on the Eastern Border of the Cape Colony* (London, 1886); D. Westermann, *The Shilluk People, Their Language and Folklore* (Philadelphia, 1912); A. Werner, *Myths and Legends of the Bantu* (New York, 1933).

**FIGURE 15.1**   King Mutesa of Uganda, 1864, from the journal of John Speke (1827–1864), discoverer of the headwaters of the Nile. He wears a loose robe and carries a spear and is accompanied by a dog. Behind is a large thatched hut, the home of the king, protected by a guard. (North Wind Picture Archives / Alamy)

One day as he roamed about searching for something, he saw two girls just dropping down from Mugulu ["Heaven"]. He stopped. The girls also stopped a long way off. They were Mugulu's daughters, Nambi and her sister.

The girls were much surprised, and Nambi said, "Sister, look at the two things over there [that is, Kintu and the cow]. What can they be?"

The sister looked, but said nothing.

Nambi continued, "We never saw anything like them before. Just go down and see what brings things like these to such a place as the earth."

"How can I?" replied the sister. "Look at those horns!"

"O, I don't mean that one. Try the other."

The sister then advanced a little way, and when Kintu saw her coming he also advanced to meet her, whereupon the sister ran back to Nambi and they both prepared for flight. Kintu, however, did not continue the pursuit, but returned to the cow.

After some time Nambi and her sister decided to come close to Kintu, and when a hundred paces only separated them, Nambi spoke to him:

"Who are you?"

"I am Kintu."

"And what is that?" pointing to the cow.

"That is my cow."

Nambi and her sister withdrew to consider whether this could possibly be true. They soon returned and asked, "We have never seen anything like you before. Where did you come from?"

"I do not know."

Kintu at this point milked some milk on to the palm of his left hand and drank it.

"What do you do that for?" asked Nambi.

"That's my food," replied Kintu.

"We see no water here. What do you drink?"

"I drink milk."

The girls then withdrew for another conference. Nambi confided to her sister that she believed this was a man—nothing else could do such extraordinary things.

They returned to Kintu and submitted their decision, and Kintu said, "Yes, I am a man."

Nambi then told him all about themselves and suggested that he should accompany them to Mugulu. Kintu agreed on condition that they also take his cow. This they declined to do and disappeared.

As soon as they arrived, they told Mugulu that they had found a man and a cow.

"Where?" asked Mugulu.

"On the earth."

"Not a real man, surely?" and Mugulu smiled as if he did not believe them, but they suspected he knew all the time.

"O yes, a real man. We know he is a real man because he wants food, and when he is hungry he drags on the udder of his cow and squeezes out white juice, which he drinks."

"I will make inquiries."

"He is very nice," said Nambi, "and I want to bring him up here. May I go and get him?"

"Leave the matter to me," said Mugulu, and the girls withdrew.

As soon as they had gone, Mugulu called his sons and said, "Go to the earth and test this story about a real man being there. Nambi says she saw a wild man and a cow and that the man drank the cow's juice. Fetch the cow."

The boys prepared to start at once.

"Wait a bit," said Mugulu. "I don't want the man. He will probably die when he sees you. Bring the cow only."

The boys arrived near Kintu's resting place. He was asleep. They took the cow and carried her off. When Kintu awoke, he did not see the cow, but just then he did not start in search of her because he supposed she had only wandered a short distance. Soon he got hungry and tried to find the cow, but in vain. He ultimately decided that the girls must have come back and stolen her, and he was very angry and hungry. He used many words not of peace. He sat down and pointed his nails and sharpened his teeth, but there was no one to fight with. He peeled the bark off a tree and sucked it, and thus he fed himself.

Next day Nambi saw Kintu's cow as the boys arrived, and she exclaimed, "You have stolen Kintu's cow! That cow was his food and drink. Now what has he to eat? I like Kintu, if you do not. I shall go down tomorrow, and if he is not dead I will bring him up here." And she went and found Kintu.

"So they have taken away your cow?"

"Yes."

"And what have you been eating since?"

"I have been sucking the bark of a tree."

"Did you really do that?"

"What else was there to do?"

"Well, come with me to Mugulu, and you shall have your cow given back to you."

They went. Kintu, when he arrived, saw a vast multitude of people and plenty of bananas and fowls and goats and sheep—in fact, everything was there in plenty. And the boys, when they saw Nambi arrive with Kintu, said, "Let us tell our father Mugulu," and they went and told him, and Mugulu said, "Go and tell my chiefs to build a big house without a door for the stranger Kintu."

The house was built, and Kintu went into it.

Mugulu then gave the following lavish order: "My people, go and cook ten thousand dishes of food, and roast ten thousand cows, and fill ten thousand vessels with beer, and give it to the stranger. If he is a real man, he will eat it, if not, then—the penalty is death."

The food was prepared and taken to Kintu's house. Because there was no door, the crowd put their shoulders to one side of the house and raised it up off the ground and put the food inside. They told Kintu that if he did not finish it all at a meal the result would be death. They let down the side of the house again and waited outside.

Kintu surveyed the mass of food with dismay and then started to walk round it, muttering his feelings to himself. As he went round the heap, his foot slipped into a hole, and on examination he found that it was the opening of a cavern.

"Ha, ha!" said he, "this cave has a good appetite. Let me feed it." He took the ten thousand measures of beer and spilled them in, laying the empty vessels on one side. Then the ten thousand carcasses of roast cows were pitched into the cavern, and lastly the food from the ten thousand baskets. Then he called to the people outside, after he had closed the hole, "Haven't you got a little more food out there?"

"No," they replied. "Did we not give you enough?"

"Well, I suppose I must do with it, if you have nothing more cooked."

"Have you finished it all?"

"Yes, yes. Come and take away the empty dishes."

The crowd raised the side wall of the house, came inside, and asked Kintu whether he really had eaten all the food. He assured them that he had, and they cried out together, "Then it is a man indeed!"

They went straight to Mugulu and told him that the stranger had finished his meal and asked for more. Mugulu at first thought this statement to be a lie, but on consideration he believed it. He pondered for a moment, then taking up a copper ax he said to his chiefs, "Take this to Kintu. Tell him I want material for a fire. Tell him that Mugulu is old and cold and that Mugulu does not burn wood for a fire. Tell him I want stones, and tell him that he must cut up rocks with this copper ax and fetch the pieces and light me a fire. If he does so, then he may claim his cow. He may also have Nambi, and he can return to the earth."

The chiefs went to Kintu and told him that Mugulu wanted a fire made of stones, and that he must chop a rock with the copper ax.

Kintu suspected there was something wrong, but he said not a word. He put the ax on his shoulder and went out before they allowed the wall of Kintu's house to drop to the ground. He walked straight to a big rock, stood in front of it, placed the head of the ax on the rock, and rested his chin on the tip of the handle.

"It does not seem easy to cut," said he to the ax.

"It is easy enough to me," replied the ax. "Just strike and see."

Kintu struck the rock, and it splintered in all directions. He picked up the pieces of rock, went straight to Mugulu and said, "Here's your firewood, Mugulu. Do you want any more?"

Mugulu said, "This is marvelous! Go back to your house. It only remains now for you to find your cow," and Kintu went away.

Next morning the chiefs were called before Mugulu and he said, "Take this bucket to Kintu and tell him to fetch water. Tell him that Mugulu does not drink anything but dew and if he is a man he is to fetch it quickly."

Kintu received the bucket and the message. Again he suspected there was something wrong, and he spoke words to himself, but nothing aloud. He took the bucket and went out and he set it down on the grass, and he said to the bucket, "This does not seem very easy."

The bucket replied, "It is easy enough for me." When Kintu looked down he saw that the bucket was full of dew. He took it to Mugulu and said, "Here's your drinking water, Mugulu. Do you want any more?"

Mugulu said, "This is marvelous. Kintu, you are a wonder. I am now satisfied that you are a man indeed, and it only remains for you to get your cow. Whoever took Kintu's cow let him restore it."

"Your own sons stole my cow," said Kintu.

"If so," replied Mugulu, "drive all the cows here and let Kintu pick out his cow if she is amongst them."

Ten thousand cows were brought in a herd. Kintu stood near the herd in great perplexity, lost in thought. A hornet came and sat on Kintu's shoulder, and as Kintu gave no heed the hornet prepared his sting and drove it home.

Kintu struck at the hornet and missed him, and the hornet said, "Don't strike, I'm your friend."

"You have just bit me," replied Kintu.

"It wasn't a bite. Listen. You can never pick out your cow in all that herd. Just you wait until I fly out and sit on the shoulder of a cow. That's yours. Mark her."

The herd of ten thousand cows was driven past, but the hornet did not move. Kintu said aloud, "My cow is not amongst them."

Mugulu then ordered another herd to be brought, numbering twice as many cows as the last herd. But the hornet did not move, and Kintu said aloud, "My cow is not amongst them."

The herdsmen drove the cows away and another herd was brought, and the hornet flew off and sat on the shoulder of a cow. Kintu went forward and marked her. "That's mine," said he to Mugulu. The hornet then flew to another, a young cow, and Kintu went forward and marked her, and said, "That also is mine." The hornet flew to a third, and Kintu went forward and marked this one also, and said, "That is mine also."

Mugulu said, "Quite correct. Your cow has had two calves since she arrived in heaven. You are a wonder, Kintu. Take your cows, and take Nambi also, and go back to the earth. Wait a bit."

Here Mugulu called his servants and said to them, "Go to my store and fetch one banana plant, one potato, one bean, one Indian corn, one ground nut, and one hen."

The things were brought, and Mugulu then addressed Kintu and Nambi. "Take these things with you. You may want them." Then addressing Kintu he said, "I must tell you that Nambi has a brother named Warumbe ["Disease" or "Death"]. He is mad and ruthless. At this moment he is not here, so you had better start quickly before he returns. If he sees you he may wish to go with you, and you are certain to quarrel."

Then to Nambi, "Here is some millet to feed the hen on the road down. If you forget anything, don't come back to fetch it. That is all. You may go."

Kintu and Nambi started, and when they were some distance on the journey Nambi suddenly remembered that it was time to feed the hen. She asked Kintu for the millet, but it was nowhere to be found, and now it was clear they had forgotten it in the hurry of departure.

"I shall return and fetch it," said Kintu.

"No, no, you must not. Warumbe will have returned, and he will probably wish to accompany us. I don't want him, and you had better not return."

"But the hen is hungry, and we must feed it."

"Yes, it is," assented Nambi.

Nambi remained where she was, and Kintu returned to Mugulu and explained that he had forgotten the millet. Mugulu was very angry at his having returned, and Warumbe, who just then arrived, asked, "Where is Nambi?"

"She is gone to the earth with Kintu."

"Then I must come too," said Warumbe.

After some hesitation Kintu agreed to this, and they returned together to Nambi.

Nambi then objected to Warumbe accompanying them, but he insisted, and finally it was agreed that he should come for a time and stay with Nambi and Kintu.

They all three proceeded and reached the earth at a place called Magongo in Uganda and they rested. Then the woman planted the banana and the Indian corn, the bean and the ground nut, and there was a plentiful crop. In the course of time three children were born, and Warumbe claimed one of them.

"Let me have this one," said he to Kintu. "You have still two remaining."

"O, I cannot spare one of these, but later on, perhaps, I may be able to spare one."

Years passed by and many more children were born, and Warumbe again begged Kintu to give him one. Kintu went round to all the children with the object of selecting one for Warumbe, and he finally returned and said, "Warumbe, I cannot spare you one just yet. Later on, perhaps, I may be able to do so."

"When you had three you said the same thing. Now you have many and still refuse to give me one. Mark you, I shall now kill them all. Not today, not tomorrow, not this year, not next year, but one by one I shall claim them all."

Next day one child died, and Kintu charged Warumbe with the deed. The next day again another died, and the next day again another. At last Kintu proposed to return to Mugulu and tell him how Warumbe was killing all his children.

Kintu accordingly went to Mugulu and explained matters. Mugulu replied that he had expected it. His original plan was that Kintu and Warumbe should not have met. He told him that Warumbe was a madman, and that trouble would come of it, yet Kintu returned for the millet against the orders of Mugulu. This was the consequence.

"However," continued Mugulu, "I shall see what can be done." And with that he called his son Kaikuzi ["Digger"] and said to him, "Go down and try to bring me back Warumbe."

Kintu and Kaikuzi started off together, and when they arrived were greeted by Nambi. She explained that in his absence Warumbe had killed several more of her sons. Kaikuzi called up Warumbe, and said, "Why are you killing all these children?"

"I wanted one child badly to help me cook my food. I begged Kintu to give me one. He refused. Now I shall kill them every one."

"Mugulu is angry, and he sent me down to recall you."

"I decline to leave here," said Warumbe.

"You are only a small man in comparison to me. I shall fetch you by force," said Kaikuzi.

With this they grappled, and a savage contest ensued. After a while Warumbe slipped from Kaikuzi's grasp and ran into a hole in the ground. Kaikuzi started to dig him out with his fingers and succeeded in reaching him, but Warumbe dived still deeper into the earth. Kaikuzi tried to dig him out again. He had almost caught him when Warumbe sunk still further into the ground.

"I'm tired now," said Kaikuzi to Kintu. "I will remain a few days, and have another try to catch him."

Kaikuzi then issued an order that there were to be two days' silence in the earth, and that Warumbe would come out of the ground to see what it meant. The people were ordered to lay in two days' provisions, and firewood and water, and not to go out of doors to feed goats or cattle. This having been done, Kaikuzi went into the ground to catch Warumbe. He pursued him for two days, and he forced Warumbe out at a place called Tanda. At this place there were some children feeding goats. When they saw Warumbe they cried out, and the spell was broken, and Warumbe returned again into the earth. Directly afterwards Kaikuzi appeared at the same place and asked why the children had broken the silence. He was angry and disappointed, and he said to Kintu that the people had broken his order, and that he would concern himself no further with the recalling of Warumbe.

"I am tired now," said Kaikuzi.

"Never mind him," replied Kintu, "let Warumbe remain because you cannot expel him. You may now go back to Mugulu."

Kaikuzi returned to Mugulu, and explained the whole circumstances. "Very well," said Mugulu, "let Warumbe remain there."

And Warumbe did remain.

In this story the first man is a trickster, one of the most common types in African folktale as it is in North American Indian myth. Kintu is known to be a man because he drinks milk, and only men do that. When **Mugulu** steals his cow, he takes away his sustenance; Kintu must eat the bark from trees. Kintu goes to heaven, where there is plenty to eat: bananas, cows, goats, and sheep, and other good things. Mugulu will not return the cow unless Kintu can pass several tests, impossible in themselves: to eat vast quantities of food; to chop stone with a soft copper ax, then to make a fire with the stones; to fill a pot with dew; and to identify the cow among thousands. The clever ruse of pouring the food in a pit, the help provided by the magic ax and pot, then the magical helper in the form of a wasp—by these devices Kintu tricks Mugulu and passes the test. Such impossible tasks, accomplished by magical means, are common in folklore throughout the world.

At last he receives the cow and Nambi as reward, but because he disobeys and returns for the millet, Death accompanies Kintu to the earth. Hence Kintu's children die, the common lot of earthly folk. The Digger attempts to remove Death by pursuing him into his realm beneath the earth, but is unsuccessful. Thus, there is Death is the world that Kintu and Nambi made, the Adam and Eve of Ugandan myth.

## MYTH: THE TALE OF ABUNAWAS

The **Tigre** are an Islamic nomadic people who live in the northern, western, and coastal lowlands of Eritrea and parts of eastern Sudan. There are about 800,000 speakers of Tigre. In Eritrea, they inhabit the central and northern plateau and the Red Sea shores. Arabic script is traditionally used to write Tigre, at least among Muslims.

In a Tigre tale the trickster is demoted from the first man to just a clever fellow, who made a fool of an old man. Appealing to the old man's greed, at first **Abunawas** wins the old man's loaded camel, then frustrates the old man's efforts to find him through the trick of the false name. In the end Abunawas wins the king's reward, through being honest at the right time—when the pay is good:

Abunawas had a well and also a young goat. Around his well he had stuck goat's horns in the ground, but the points of the horns were above ground.

Now there was a man traveling who was leading a loaded camel, and he turned aside to the well of Abunawas to drink water. When Abunawas saw the man coming to him with his camel, he put the goat in the well. When the camel-driver arrived, he and Abunawas greeted each other.

The stranger said to Abunawas, "Let me drink!"

Abunawas said, "Very well," and went down into the well to draw water. And first he pulled up the goat and brought it out. After that he let the stranger drink.

When the stranger had drunk, he asked Abunawas, "This goat which you have brought out of the well, where did you find it?"

Abunawas replied, "These horns which you see around the well, are all goats. Every day if I pull out two of them, a goat comes out of this well."

The man was very much astonished and he entreated Abunawas, saying, "Give me your well and you take my camel with his load."

Abunawas answered, "This is my place which is of great profit to me. But for your sake—what shall I do? Take it then!"

And the man said to Abunawas, "What is your name?"

And Abunawas answered, "My name is Nargusfen."° Thereupon said Abunawas to the man, "Now then, of these horns pull out two every day and at once a goat will come out for you. Today, however, do not pull out any of them, for I have pulled out two of them before and brought out this goat."

And the man said, "All right."

Abunawas took the loaded camel and went to his village. The next morning the man pulled out two of the horns, but the horns came out by themselves. Nor looking into the well did he find anything. And saying, "What is this?" he pondered a great deal.

And every day he said, "Today, even today I shall find it," and he pulled out all the horns. Thereupon he thought in his heart, "Nargusfen has cheated me. And now I better go and find him."

So he set out to seek Nargusfen. And when he came to a village he asked the people, "Do you know Nargusfen?" And the people of the village replied, "Dance here!"

And gathering around him they clapped their hands. But the man was very much afraid and terrified because they made fun of him. And again, when he went into another village and inquired, these other people also did the same to him as the first. The man was about to go crazy. But afterwards the chief of the village asked him, saying, "What kind of a man are you? And what do you wish to say?"

And the man told him all that had happened to him. The chief sent word and asked, "Who is it that cheated this man?" But all the people said, "We do not know."

Thereupon the chief took an oath, saying, "I shall give some money to him who has done this, if he says to me, "It is I."

And Abunawas said to him, "It is I who have done this!" So the chief gave him money, but the camel with his load he turned over to his owner.

And all the people were astonished at the doings of Abunawas!

°*Nargusfen:* Nargusfen sounds something like the Arabic for "Where shall we dance?"

We saw already in the *Odyssey* the folkloristic trick of the false name, whereby Odysseus tricks the Cyclops, recorded nearly 3,000 years earlier!

## MYTH: HARE

The Uncle Remus stories depend on African archetypes. For example, the story of the "Tar-baby" is known to Bantu-speaking tribes south of LAKE VICTORIA, in ANGOLA, and in the lower CONGO (Perspective 15).

### PERSPECTIVE 15
### Joel Chandler Harris and Uncle Remus

Joel Chandler Harris (1845–1908) was an American journalist, fiction writer, and folk-lorist best known for his collection of Uncle Remus stories. Harris was born in Eaton-ton, Georgia, where he served as an apprentice on a plantation during his teenage years. He spent most of his adult life in Atlanta working as an associate editor at the *Atlanta Constitution*. As an editor and journalist Harris stressed regional and racial rec-onciliation during the Reconstruction era.

While at the plantation as a youngster, Harris spent hundreds of hours in the slave quarters, and his background as an illegitimate, red-headed son of an Irish im-migrant made him sympathetic to the slaves' condition. He absorbed the stories, language, and inflections of the African-American storytellers that later became the inspiration for his Uncle Remus tales. Brer ("brother") Rabbit seems to be based on the folklore trickster Hare in YORUBA tales that slaves had brought from Africa (though some see the influence of Cherokee stories too). The Yoruba live in NIGERIA in West Africa and were frequently enslaved.

*Uncle Remus: His Songs and His Sayings* was published in 1880, consisting of 34 plantation fables. The stories, mostly collected directly from African-American oral storytellers, were revolutionary in their use of dialect, animals that talk, and landscape. Hundreds of newspapers reviewed the book, an immediate bestseller. Harris traveled to Washington and met Theodore Roosevelt, who said, "Presidents may come and presidents may go, but Uncle Remus stays put. Georgia has done a great many things for the Union, but she has never done more than when she gave Mr. Joel Chandler Harris to American literature."

Remus's stories feature a trickster hero called Brer Rabbit, who uses his wits against hardship, though his efforts do not always succeed. Brer Rabbit is accom-panied by friends and enemies alike: Brer Fox, Brer Bear, Brer Terrapin, and Brer Wolf. Harris published nine books of Uncle Remus stories. The tales, 185 in total, became immensely popular among white readers in the North and South. Few outside of the South had ever heard such accents as those spoken in the tales, and no one had ever seen the dialect recorded in print. Mark Twain noted in 1883, "in the matter of writing the Negro dialect, he is the only master the country has produced." The Uncle Remus tales have since been translated into more than 40 languages.

Beatrix Potter illustrated eight scenes from the Uncle Remus stories between 1893 and 1896, and she borrowed language from the Uncle Remus stories, like "cottontail," "puddle-duck," and "lippity-clippity" into her own work. Mark Twain admired Harris's use of dialect and borrowed turns of phrase in many of his works, especially the Adventures of Huckleberry Finn (1885). A. A. Milne borrowed diction, plot, and narrative structure from several Brer Rabbit stories, for example, "Pooh Goes Visiting" and "Heyo, House!" In 1946, the Walt Disney Company produced a film based on Uncle Remus called *Song of the South*. The film earned two Academy Awards and "Zip-A-Dee-Doo-Dah," still a popular song, won the award for best original song.

Harris's best-known story is of "Brer Rabbit and the Tar-Baby" in which, for once, the trickster is himself the victim of a trick:

"Didn't the fox never catch the rabbit, Uncle Remus?" asked the little boy the next evening.

"He come mighty nigh it, honey, sho's you born—Brer Fox did. One day atter Brer Rabbit fool 'im wid dat calamus root,° Brer Fox went ter wuk en got 'im some tar, en mix it wid some turkentime, en fix up a contrapshun w'at he call a Tar-Baby, en he tuck dish yer Tar-Baby en he sot 'er° in de big road, en den he lay off in de bushes fer to see what de news wuz gwine ter be. En he didn't hatter wait long, nudder, kaze bimeby here come Brer Rabbit pacin' down de road—lippity-clippity, clippity-lippity—dez ez sassy ez a jay-bird. Brer Fox, he lay low. Brer Rabbit come prancin' 'long twel he spy de Tar-Baby, en den he fotch up on his behime legs like he wuz 'stonished. De Tar-Baby, she sot dar, she did, en Brer Fox, he lay low.

" 'Mawnin'!' sez Brer Rabbit, sezee—'nice wedder dis mawnin,' 'sezee.

"Tar-Baby ain't sayin' nuthin,' en Brer Fox he lay low.

" 'How duz yo' sym'tums seem ter segashuate°?' sez Brer Rabbit, sezee.

"Brer Fox, he wink his eye slow, en lay low, en de Tar-Baby, she ain't sayin' nuthin.'

" 'How you come on, den? Is you deaf?' sez Brer Rabbit, sezee. 'Kaze if you is, I kin holler louder,' sezee.

"Tar-Baby stay still, en Brer Fox, he lay low.

" 'You er stuck up, dat's w'at you is,' says Brer Rabbit, sezee, 'en I'm gwine ter kyore° you, dat's w'at I'm a gwine ter do,' sezee.

"Brer Fox, he sorter chuckle in his stummick, he did, but Tar-Baby ain't sayin' nothin.'

" 'I'm gwine ter larn you how ter talk ter 'spectubble folks ef hit's de las' ack,' sez Brer Rabbit, sezee. 'Ef you don't take off dat hat en tell me howdy, I'm gwine ter bus' you wide open,' sezee.

"Tar-Baby stay still, en Brer Fox, he lay low.

"Brer Rabbit keep on axin' 'im, en de Tar-Baby, she keep on sayin' nothin', twel present'y Brer Rabbit draw back wid his fis', he did, en blip he tuck 'er side 'er de head. Right dar's whar he broke his merlasses jug. His fis' stuck, en he can't pull loose. De tar hilt 'im. But Tar-Baby, she stay still, en Brer Fox, he lay low.

---

°*calamus root*: "sweet flag," a tall wetland plant. °*sot 'er*: "set her" °*segashuate*: African-American vernacular for "sagaciating." "How do you sagaciate?" means "How are you?" "sym'tums" is "symptoms." °*kyore*: "cure."

" 'Ef you don't lemme loose, I'll knock you agin,' sez Brer Rabbit, sezee, en wid dat he fotch 'er a wipe wid de udder han', en dat stuck. Tar-Baby, she ain'y sayin' nuthin', en Brer Fox, he lay low (Perspective Figure 15).

" 'Tu'n me loose, fo' I kick de natal° stuffin' outen you,' sez Brer Rabbit, sezee, but de Tar-Baby, she ain't sayin' nuthin'. She des hilt on, en de Brer Rabbit lose de use er his feet in de same way. Brer Fox, he lay low. Den Brer Rabbit squall out dat ef de Tar-Baby don't tu'n 'im loose he butt 'er cranksided.° En den he butted, en his head got stuck. Den Brer Fox, he sa'ntered fort', lookin' dez ez innercent ez wunner yo' mammy's mockin'-birds.

" 'Howdy, Brer Rabbit,' sez Brer Fox, sezee. 'You look sorter stuck up dis mawnin',' sezee, en den he rolled on de groun', en laft en laft twel he couldn't laff no mo.' 'I speck you'll take dinner wid me dis time, Brer Rabbit. I done laid in some calamus root, en I ain't gwineter take no skuse,' sez Brer Fox, sezee."

Here Uncle Remus paused, and drew a two-pound yam out of the ashes.

"Did the fox eat the rabbit?" asked the little boy to whom the story had been told.

"Dat's all de fur de tale goes," replied the old man. "He mout, an den agin he moutent. Some say Judge B'ar come 'long en loosed 'im—some say he didn't. I hear Miss Sally callin'. You better run 'long."

°*natal*: "natural." °*cranksided*: "lopsided."

**PERSPECTIVE FIGURE 15** Brer Rabbit gets stuck in the Tar-Baby, illustration from the 1895 version of Joel Chandler Harris's *Uncle Remus: His Songs and His Sayings* by A. B. Frost. (http://en.wikipedia.org/wiki/File:Brer_Rabbit_and_the_Tar_Baby.jpg)

Brer Rabbit is known in these traditions as Hare, as in following story told by the **Yoruba** in Nigeria, where they today number about 40 million people:

Once upon a time there was a terrible drought over all the country. No rain had fallen for many months and the animals were all dying of thirst. All the pools and watercourses were dried up. So Lion called the beasts together to the dry bed of a river and suggested that they should all stamp on the sand to see whether they could not bring out some water.

Elephant began and stamped his hardest, but produced no result except a choking cloud of dust. Then Rhinoceros tried, with no better success. Then Buffalo. Then the rest in turn—still nothing but dust, dust! At the beginning of the proceedings Elephant had sent for Hare, but he said, "I don't want to come."

Now there was no one left but Tortoise, whom they all had overlooked on account of his insignificance. He came forward and began to stamp. The onlookers laughed and jeered. But, behold before long there appeared a damp spot in the riverbed. And Rhinoceros, enraged that a little thing like that should succeed where he had failed, tossed him up and dashed him against a rock so that his shell was broken into a hundred pieces. While he sat, picking up the fragments and painfully sticking them together, the rhinoceros went on stamping, but the damp sand quickly disappeared, and clouds of dust arose, as before. The others repeated their vain efforts, till at last Elephant said, "Let Tortoise come and try." Before he had been at work more than a few minutes the water gushed out and filled the well, which had gradually been excavated by their combined efforts.

The animals then passed a unanimous resolution that Hare, who had refused to share in the work, should not be allowed to take any of the water. Knowing his character, they assumed that he would try to do so, and agreed to take turns in keeping watch over the well.

Hyena took the first watch, and after an hour or two saw Hare coming along with two calabashes,° one empty and one full of honey. He called out a greeting to Hyena, was answered, and asked him what he was doing there. Hyena replied, "I am guarding the well because of you so you may not drink water here."

"O," said Hare, "I don't want any of your water. It is muddy and bitter. I have much nicer water here."

Hyena, his curiosity roused, asked to taste the wonderful water, and Hare handed him a stalk of grass which he had dipped in the honey. "Oh, indeed, it is sweet! Just let me have some more!"

"I can't do that unless you let me tie you up to the tree. This water is strong enough to knock you over if you are not tied."

Hyena had so great a longing for the sweet drink that he readily consented. Hare tied him up so tightly that he could not move, went on to the well, and filled his calabash. Then he jumped in, splashed about to his heart's content, and finally departed laughing.

In the morning the animals came and found Hyena tied to the tree. "Why Hyena, who has done this to you?"

°*calabashes*: a gourd used as vessel.

"A great host of strong men came in the middle of the night, seized me, and tied me up."

Lion said, "No such thing! Of course it was Hare, all by himself."

Lion took his turn at watching that night, but, strange to say, he fell a victim to the same trick. Unable to resist the lure of the honey, he was ignominiously tied to the tree.

There they found him next morning and Hyena, true to his nature, sneered, "So it was many men who tied you up, Lion?" Lion replied, with quiet dignity, "You need not talk. He would be too much for any of us."

Elephant then volunteered to keep watch, but with no better success. Then the rest of the animals, each in his turn, only to be defeated by one trick or another.

At last Tortoise came forward, saying, "I am going to catch that one who is in the habit of binding people!" The others began to jeer: "Nonsense! Seeing how he has outwitted us, the elders, what can you do, a little one like you?" But Elephant took his part and said that he should be allowed to try.

Tortoise then smeared his shell all over with bird-lime, plunged into the well, and sat quite still at the bottom. When Hare came along that night and saw no watcher he sang out, "Hallo! Hallo! the well! Is there no one here?" Receiving no answer, he said, "They're afraid of me. I've beaten them all! Now for the water!"

He sat down beside the well, ate his honey, and filled both his gourds before starting to bathe. Then he stepped into the water and found both his feet caught. He cried out, "Who are you? I don't want your water. Mine is sweet. Let me go and you can try it."

But there was no answer. He struggled. He put down one hand to free himself. He put down the other. He was caught fast. There was no help for it. There he had to stay till the animals came in the morning. And when they saw him they said, "Now, indeed, Hare has been shown up!"

So they carried him to Lion for judgment, and Lion said, "Why did you first disobey and afterwards steal the water?"

Hare made no attempt to plead his cause, but said, "just tie me up, and I shall die!"

Lion ordered him to be bound, but Hare made one more suggestion. "Don't tie me with coconut-rope, but with green banana-fiber. Then if you throw me out in the sun I shall die very quickly."

They did so, and after awhile, when they heard the banana-fiber cracking as it dried up in the heat, they began to get suspicious, and someone said to Lion that Hare would surely break his bonds. Hare heard him and groaned out, as though at his last gasp, "Let me alone. I'm just going to die!"

So he lay still for another hour, and then suddenly stretched himself. The banana-fiber gave way, and he was off before they could recover from their astonishment. They started in pursuit, but he outran them all, and they were nearly giving up despair when they saw him on the top of a distant anthill, apparently waiting for them to come up.

When they got within earshot he called out, "I'm off! You're fools, all of you!" and disappeared into a hole in the side of the anthill. The animals hastened up and formed a circle round the hill, while Elephant came forward and thrust his trunk into the hole. After groping about for a while he seized Hare by the ear, and Hare cried, "That's a leaf you've got hold of. You've not caught me!" Elephant let go and tried again, this time seizing Hare's leg. "O-o-o-o-o! He's got hold of a root." Again Elephant let go, and Hare slipped out of his reach into the depths of the burrow.

The animals grew tired of waiting, and, leaving Elephant to watch the ant-hill, they went to fetch hoes so that they might dig out Hare. While they were gone Hare, disguising his voice, called out to Elephant, "You who are watching the burrow open your eyes wide and keep them fixed on this hole so that Hare may not get past without your seeing him!"

Elephant unsuspectingly obeyed, and Hare, sitting just inside the entrance, kicked up a cloud of sand into his eyes and dashed out past him. Elephant, blinded and in pain, was quite unaware of his escape and kept on watching the hole till the other animals came back. They asked if Hare was still there. "He may be, but he has thrown sand into my eyes." They fell to digging, and, of course, found nothing.

Meanwhile Hare had gone away into the bush, plaited his hair in the latest fashion, plastered it with wax taken from a wild bees' nest, and whitened his face with clay, so that he was quite unrecognizable. Then he strolled casually past the place where the animals were at work, asked what they were doing, and offered to help. He was given a hoe, which he used with such vigor that it soon came off the handle. He asked Giraffe for the loan of his leg, used it as the handle of his hoe, and speedily broke it, whereupon he shouted, "I'm Hare!" and, fled, taking refuge in another anthill, which had more than one entrance.

They started to dig. He escaped through the second hole, which they had not noticed, disguised himself afresh, and came back as before. This time, when his hoe came off the handle, he asked Elephant to let him hammer it in on his head, and he did it with such good will that he soon killed him. He ran away once more, shouting insults as he went, and the animals, having lost their two principal leaders, returned home, weary and discouraged.

Hare then went on his way quite happily, till, some time later, he met Lioness, who seized him and was about to kill him. But he pleaded so eloquently for his life, assuring her that he could make himself very useful if she would let him be her servant, that at last she relented and took him home to her den. Next day, when she went out to hunt, she left him in charge of her ten cubs. While she was gone Hare took the cubs down to the stream to play and suggested that they should wrestle. He wrestled with one of them, threw it, and twisted its neck as they lay on the ground.

Returning to the cave with the others, he skinned and ate the dead one at the first convenient opportunity. In the evening the mother came home and, staying outside the cave, told Hare to bring the children out for her to nurse. He brought one, and when she told him to bring the rest he objected, saying it was better to bring them out one by one. Having suckled the first, she handed it back, and he brought her the remaining eight, taking the last twice over.

Next day he did the same, bringing out the last cub three times, and so deceived the mother into thinking she had suckled the whole ten. This went on until he had eaten all but one, which he brought out ten times. When it came to the tenth time Lioness noticed that the cub refused to suck. Hare explained that it had not been well all day, and Lioness was satisfied and only told him to take good care of it.

As soon as she was gone next day he killed, skinned, and ate the last cub, and, taking the other skins from the place where he had hidden them, set out on his travels. Towards evening he came to the village of the baboons, and found them playing with teetotums.° He went and sat down in the usual place for strangers, and when some of them came to greet him said, "I have brought beautiful skins to sell. Does anyone want to buy them?" The baboons crowded round, admiring the skins, and all ten were soon disposed of. They then returned to their game, and Hare sat watching them. Presently he said, "You are not playing right. Shall I show you how?" They handed him a teetotum and he began to spin it, singing all the time, "We have eaten Lion's children on the quiet!"

They listened attentively and then said, "Let us learn this song." So he taught them the words and they practiced for the rest of the evening. After that he shared their meal, and was given a hut to sleep in.

In the morning he was off before it was light, and made his way back to Lions' den, where he found Lioness distractedly searching for her missing cubs. On the way he had been careful to roll in the mud and get himself well scratched by the thorny bushes so that he presented a most disorderly appearance.

On seeing her he set up a dismal wail. "O! O! Some wild beasts came yesterday and carried off your children. They were too much for me. I could do nothing. See how they knocked me about and wounded me! But I followed them, and I can show you where they live. If you come with me you will be able to kill them all. But you had better let me tie you up in a bundle of grass and put some beans just inside and I will carry you and tell them that I have brought a load of beans. They have the skins of your children, whom I saw them eating."

Lioness agreed, and, having tied her up, Hare started with his load. Arriving at the village, he laid it down in the place for strangers. The baboons were so intent on their game that they hardly noticed him at first, and Lioness could hear them singing with all their might, "We have eaten Lion's children on the quiet."

After a while they came up and greeted Hare, and he said that he had brought them a load of beans in return for their hospitality of the day before. He loosened one end of the bundle to show them the beans, and then eagerly accepted their invitation to join in the game. By the time it was once more in full swing, Lioness had worked herself free and sprang on the nearest baboon, bearing him to the ground. The others tried to escape, but Hare had run round to the gate of the enclosure, closed it, and fastened the bar. Then began a murder grim and great. Not one of the baboons was left alive, and when Hare had brought

---

°*teetotums*: a kind of top made of a piece of gourd shell with a splinter of wood stuck through it.

out the skins of the poor cubs and laid them before Lioness, she knew for a certainty that she had but done justice, and was duly grateful to Hare. He, however, thought it just as well not to remain in her neighborhood, so took his leave and resumed his wanderings.

Many other stories are told of Hare's trickery, but one tells of his end:

Hare went one day to call on his friend Cock, and found him asleep with his head under his wing. Hare had never seen him in this position before, and never thought of doubting the hens' word when they informed him that their husband was in the habit of taking off his head and giving it to the herd-boys to carry with them to the pasture.

"Since you were born have you ever seen a man have his head cut off and for it to go to pasture, while the man himself stayed at home in the village?"

And Hare said, "Never! But when those herd-boys come, will he get up again?"

And those women said, "Just wait and see!"

At last, when the herd-boys arrived, their mother said, "Just rouse your father there where he is sleeping." Cock, when aroused, welcomed his guest, and they sat talking till dinner was ready, and still conversed during the meal. Hare was anxious to know how it was done, and Cock told him it was quite easy, "if you think you would like to do it." Hare confidently accepted the explanation, and they parted, having agreed that Cock should return the visit next day.

Hare was so greatly excited that he began to talk of his wonderful experience as soon as he reached his home. "That person the fowl is a clever fellow. He has just shown me his clever device of cutting off the head till, on your being hit, you see, you become alive again. Well, tomorrow I intend to show you all this device!"

Next morning he told his boys what to do. They hesitated, but he insisted, and when they were ready to go out with the cattle they cut off his head, bored the ears, and put a string through them to carry it more conveniently. The women picked up the body and laid it on the bed, trusting, in spite of appearances, to his assurance that he was not dead.

By and by his friend arrived, and, not seeing him, inquired for him. The women showed him the body lying on the bed. He was struck with consternation, and, let us hope, with remorse.

"But my friend is a simpleton indeed!" They said, "Is not this device derived from you?" But he turned a deaf ear to this hint and only insisted that Hare was a simpleton. He thought, however, he would wait and see whether, after all, he did get up. The boys came home when the sun went down. They struck their father, as he had told them, but he did not get up. And the children burst out crying. And the mothers of the family cried. And folks sat a-mourning. And all the people that heard of it were amazed at his death.

"Such a clever man! And for him to have met with his death through such a trifling thing!"

That was Hare's epitaph.

## MYTH: THE STORY OF THE CANNIBAL MOTHER
## AND HER CHILDREN

The **Xhosa** (kho-sa) people are speakers of Bantu languages living in southeast South Africa (Figure 15.2). Xhosa-speaking peoples are divided into several tribes with related but distinct heritages. There are about eight million Xhosa today. Xhosa is South Africa's second most common indigenous language after Zulu, to which Xhosa is closely related. Among its features, the Xhosa language famously has 15 click sounds.

In the late 18th-century Afrikaners—that is, Dutch colonists—migrating outward from Cape Town came into conflict with Xhosa pastoralists around the eastern cape. Following more than 20 years of intermittent conflict, in 1812 the British finally forced the Xhosas to migrate eastward. Then in the following years many Xhosa-speaking clans were pushed back west by the powerful Zulus, where they reside today, making up about 18 percent of the population of South Africa.

Like the Mexicans, the North American Indians, and the peoples of Oceania, the Xhosa practiced cannibalism, about which they told a story:

There was once a man and a woman who had two children, a son and a daughter. These children lived with their grandfather. Their mother was a cannibal, but not their father.

One day they said to their grandfather, "We have been long with you. We should like very much to go and see our parents."

Their grandfather said, "Ho! will you be able to come back? Don't you know your mother is a cannibal?"

After a time he consented. He said, "You must leave at such a time that you may arrive there in the evening so that your mother may not see you, only your father."

**FIGURE 15.2** A woman of the Xhosa tribe smoking a pipe. Her face is smeared with ash. South Africa near Pretoria. (Frans Lemmens / Alamy)

The boy's name was Hinazinci. He said: "Let us go now, my sister."

They started when the sun was set. When they arrived at their father's house, they listened outside to find out if their mother was there. They heard the voice of their father only, so they called to him. He came out, and when he saw them he was sorry, and said, "Why did you come here, my dear children? Don't you know your mother is a cannibal? "

Just then they heard a noise like thunder. It was the coming of their mother. Their father took them inside and put them in a dark corner where he covered them with skins. Their mother came in with an animal and the body of a man. She stood and said, "There's something here. What a nice smell it has!"

She said to her husband, "Sohinazinci, what have you to tell me about this nice smell that is in my house? You must tell me whether my children are here."

Her husband answered, "What are you dreaming about? They are not here."

She went to the corner where they were and took the skins away. When she saw them, she said, "My children, I am very sorry that you are here, because I must eat people."

She cooked for them and their father the animal she had brought home and the dead man for herself. After they had eaten, she went out.

Then their father Sohinazinci said to them, "When we lie down to sleep, you must be watchful. You will hear a dancing of people, a roaring of wild beasts, and a barking of dogs in your mother's stomach. You will know by that that she is sleeping, and you must then rise at once and get away."

They lay down, but the man and the children only pretended to go to sleep. They were listening for those sounds. After a while they heard a dancing of people, a roaring of wild beasts, and a barking of dogs. Then their father shook them, and said they must go while their mother was sleeping. They bade their father farewell and crept out quietly so that their mother might not hear them.

At midnight the woman woke up, and when she found the children were gone, she took her ax and went after them. They were already a long way on their journey when they saw her following them. They were so tired that they could not run.

When she was near them, the boy said to the girl, "My sister, sing your melodious song. Perhaps when she hears it she will be sorry and go home without hurting us."

The girl replied, "She will not listen to anything now, because she is in want of meat."

Hinazinci said, "Try, my sister. It may not be in vain."

So she sang her song, and when the cannibal heard it, she ran backwards to her own house. There she fell upon her husband and wanted to cut him with the ax. Her husband caught hold of her arm, and said, "Ho! if you put me to death who will be your husband?"

Then she left him and ran after the children again.

They were near their grandfather's village and were very weak when their mother overtook them. The girl fell down and the cannibal caught her and swallowed her. She then ran after the boy. He fell just at the entrance of his grandfather's house, and she picked him up and swallowed him also. She found only the old people and the children of the village at home, all the others being at work in the gardens. She ate all the people that were at home and also all the cattle that were there.

Towards evening she left to go to her own home. There was a deep valley in the way, and when she came to it she saw a very beautiful bird. As she approached it, the bird got bigger and bigger, until at last when she was very near it, it was as big as a native hut.

Then the bird began to sing its song. The woman looked at it and said to herself, "I shall take this bird home to my husband."

The bird continued its song, and sang, "I am a pretty bird of the valley, you come to make a disturbance at my place."

The bird came slowly towards her, still singing its song. When they met, the bird took the ax from the woman and still sang the same song.

The cannibal began to be afraid. She said to the bird, "Give me my ax. I do not wish for your flesh now."

The bird tore one of her arms off.

She said, "I am going away now. Give me what is mine."

The bird would not listen to her, but continued its song. She said again, "Give me my ax and let me go. My husband at home is very hungry. I want to go and cook food for him."

The bird sang more loudly than before and tore one of her legs off. She fell down and cried out, "My master, I am in a hurry to go home. I do not want anything that is yours."

She saw that she was in danger. She said to the bird again, "You don't know how to sing your song nicely. Let me go and I will sing it for you."

The bird opened its wings wide and tore open her stomach. Many people came forth, most of them alive, but some were dead. As they came forth she caught them and swallowed them again. The two children were alive, and they ran away. At last the woman died.

There was great rejoicing in that country. The children returned to their grandfather and the people came there and made them rulers of the country because it was through them that the cannibal was brought to death. The girl was afterwards married to a son of the great chief, and Hinazinci had for his wife the daughter of that great one.

## MYTH: THE DISOBEDIENT DAUGHTER WHO MARRIED A SKULL

Nigeria in West Africa is the most populous state in modern Africa and the eighth most populous state in the world. It is named from the Niger River, which flows down the center of the country. The **IGBO** people who live in its southeastern corner are one of the most numerous ethnic groups in Africa. They are an agricultural people heavily dependent on the growing of yams. The largest nearby city is Calabar. They were heavily enslaved during the slave trade (Igbo may mean "slave"), and many African-Americans are of Igbo descent. Many of the tribal practices, including the word *Ju Ju*—a fetish imbued with power—are still preserved in New World (Figure 15.3).

The Igbo tell the following story about **Afiong**, a girl who through vanity ended up marrying death. The theme is familiar in world folklore (for example, in the Inuit

**FIGURE 15.3**   Igbo fetish. Such fetishes are considered responsible for the health, prosperity, and general well being of the people and the productivity of field and stream. They are kept in special houses where they are revered, then during festivals and ceremonies are brought out and paraded through the villages. Wood, covered with a yellow clay. (Peter Horree / Alamy)

story of Sedna, Chapter 14). But *Ju Ju* and magic brought her back to life, having learned that it is best to obey one's parents after all:

> Effiong Edem was a native of Calabar. He had a very fine daughter, whose name was Afiong. All the young men in the country wanted to marry her on account of her beauty but she refused all offers of marriage in spite of repeated entreaties from her parents. She was very vain, and said she would only marry the best-looking man in the country, who would have to be young and strong, and capable of loving her properly. Most of the men her parents wanted her to marry, although they were rich, were old and ugly, so the girl continued to disobey her parents, at which they were much aggrieved.
>
> The Skull who lived in the spirit land heard of the beauty of this Calabar virgin and thought he would like to possess her, so he went about amongst his friends and borrowed different parts of the body from them, all of the best. From one he got a good head, another lent him a body, a third gave him strong arms, and a fourth lent him a fine pair of legs. At last he was complete, a very perfect specimen of manhood.

He then left spirit land and went to the Calabar market where he saw Afiong and admired her very much. About this time Afiong heard that a very fine man had been seen in the market who was better-looking than any of the natives. She went to the market at once, and when she saw the Skull in his borrowed beauty, she fell in love with him and invited him to her house. The Skull was delighted and went home with her. On his arrival he was introduced by the girl to her parents. Immediately he asked their consent to marry their daughter. At first they refused, as they did not wish her to marry a stranger, but at last they agreed.

The Skull lived with Afiong for two days in her parents' house and then said he wished to take his wife back to his country, which was far off. To this the girl readily agreed, as he was such a fine man, but her parents tried to persuade her not to go. However, being very headstrong, she made up her mind to go, and they started off together.

After they had been gone a few days the father consulted his *Ju Ju* man, who by casting lots very soon discovered that his daughter's husband belonged to the spirit land and that she would surely be killed. They therefore all mourned her as dead.

After walking for several days, Afiong and the Skull crossed the border between the spirit land and the human country. As soon as they set foot in spirit land, first of all one man came to the Skull and demanded his legs, then another his head, and the next his body, and so on until in a few minutes the Skull was left by itself in all its natural ugliness. At this the girl was very frightened and wanted to return home, but the Skull would not allow this and ordered her to go with him.

When they arrived at the Skull's house they found his mother, who was a very old woman quite incapable of doing any work, who could only creep about. Afiong tried her best to help her and cooked her food and brought water and firewood for the old woman. The old creature was very grateful for these attentions and soon became quite fond of Afiong.

One day the old woman told Afiong that she was very sorry for her, but all the people in the spirit land were cannibals. When they heard there was a human being in their country, they would come down and kill her and eat her. The Skull's mother then hid Afiong, and because Afiong had looked after her so well, she promised she would send her back to her country as soon as possible, providing that she promised for the future to obey her parents. This Afiong readily consented to do.

The old woman sent for the Spider, who was a very clever hairdresser, and made him dress Afiong's hair in the latest fashion. She also presented her with anklets and other things on account of her kindness. She then made a *Ju Ju* and called the winds to come and convey Afiong to her home. At first a violent tornado came, with thunder, lightning and rain, but the Skull's mother sent him away as unsuitable. The next wind to come was a gentle breeze, so she told the breeze to carry Afiong to her mother's house and said good-bye to her. Very soon afterwards the breeze deposited Afiong outside her home and left her there.

When the parents saw their daughter, they were very glad, for they had for some months given her up as lost. The father spread soft animals' skins on the ground from where his daughter was standing all the way to the house, so that her feet should not be soiled. Afiong then walked to the house, and her father called all the young girls who belonged to Afiong's company to come and dance, and the feasting and dancing was kept up for eight days and nights.

When the rejoicing was over, the father reported what had happened to the head chief of the town. The chief then passed a law that parents should never allow their daughters to marry strangers who came from a far country. Then the father told his daughter to marry a friend of his, and she willingly consented and lived with him for many years and had many children.

The story enforces the moral order—one should obey one's parents, especially in the matter of marriage; they know best!

## MYTH: THE MAGIC DRUM

BENGA people are an African ethnic group, members of the Bantu group, who are indigenous to GUINEA and GAMBIA (see Map 15). Their indigenous language is Benga (Figure 15.4). The following story collected from the Benga about the Golden Age when all was harmony explains why turtles live only in water and leopards on the land, and also turns on the trickster ancestor of the turtles:

In the ancient days, humankind and all the tribes of the animals lived together in one country. They built their towns, and they dwelt together in one place.

**FIGURE 15.4**   Reliquary mask from Gambia made of copper inlaid with silver strips. Such masks are worn in rituals to arouse the attention of the ancestors. (The Art Archive / Alamy)

In the country of King Maseni, Turtle and Leopard lived in the same town, the one at one end of the street, and the other at the other end.

Leopard married two women. Turtle also had two.

It happened that a time of famine came, and a very great hunger fell on the tribes who lived in that whole region of country. So, King Maseni issued a law to the effect that "any person who shall be found having a piece of food, that person shall he brought to me."° And he appointed police as watchmen to look after the whole region.

The famine increased. People sat down hopelessly and died of hunger just as, even today, hunger destroys the poor, not only of Africa, but also in White Man's Land. As the days passed, people continued sitting in their hopelessness.

One day, Turtle, whose name was Kudu, went out early, going, going, and entering into the jungles, to seek for his special food, mushrooms. He had said to his wife, "I am going to stroll on the beach off down toward the south."

As he journeyed and journeyed, he came to a river. It was a large one, several hundred feet in width. There he saw a coconut tree growing on the riverbank. When he reached the foot of the tree and looked up at its top, he discovered that it was full of very many nuts. He said to himself, "I'm going up there to gather nuts, for hunger has seized me."

He laid aside his traveling-bag, leaving it on the ground, and at once climbed the tree, expecting to gather many of the nuts. He plucked two and threw them to the ground. Plucking another, and attempting to throw it, it slipped from his hand and fell into the stream running below.

Then he exclaimed, "I've come here in hunger and does my coconut fall into the water to be lost?" He said to himself, "I'll leave here and drop into the water and follow the nut."

So he plunged down, splash! into the water. He dove down to where the nut had sunk to get it. And he was carried away by the current.

Following the nut where the current had carried it he came to the landing place of a strange town where there was a large house. People were in it, and other people were outside playing. They called to him. From the house he heard a voice, saying, "Take me! take me! take me!" (It was a Drum that spoke.)

At the landing place there was a woman washing a child. The woman said to him, "What is it that brought you here? And, Kudu, where are you going?"

He replied, "There is great hunger in our town. So on my way I came seeking for my mushrooms. Then it was that I saw a coconut tree and I climbed it, for I am hungry and have nothing to eat. I threw down the nuts. One fell into the river. I followed it and I came here."

Then the woman said, "Now then, you are saved." And she added, "Kudu! Go to that house over there. You will see a thing there. That thing is a Drum. Start and go at once to where the Drums are."

Others people called out to him, "There are many such things there. But the kind that you will see that says, 'Take me! take me!' do not take it. But, the Drum that is silent and does not speak, but only echoes, 'wo-wo-wo' without

---

°*to me*: that is, for the equal distribution of the food.

any real words, you must take it. Carry it with you and tie it to that coconut tree. Then you must say to the Drum, 'Ngama! Speak as they told you!'"

So, Turtle went on, and on, to the house and took the Drum and, carrying it, came back to the riverbank where the woman was. She said to him, "You must first try to learn how to use it. Beat it!" He beat it. And a table appeared with all kinds of food! And when he had eaten, he said to the Drum, "Put it back!" And the table disappeared.

He carried the Drum with him clear back to the foot of the coconut tree. He tied it with a rattan to the tree and then said to the Drum, "Ngama!° Do as they said!" Instantly, the Drum set out a long table and put on all sorts of food. Turtle felt very glad and happy for the abundance of food. So he ate and ate and was satisfied.

Again he said, "Ngama! Do as they said!" And Drum took back the table and the food up the tree, leaving a little food at the foot, and then came back to the hand of Turtle. He put this little food in his traveling-bag and gathered from the ground the coconuts he had left lying there in the morning and started to go back to his town.

He stopped at a spot a short distance in the rear of the town. So delighted was he with his Drum that he tested it again. He stood it up and with the palm of his hand struck it, tomu!° A table at once stood there with all kinds of food. Again he ate and also filled his traveling bag. Then he said to a tree that was standing near by, "Bend down!" It bowed down, and he tied the Drum to its branch and went off into the town. The coconuts and the mushrooms he handed to his women and children.

After he had entered his house, his chief wife said to him, "Where have you been all this long while since the morning?" He replied evasively, "I went wandering clear down to the beach to gather coconuts. And this day I saw a very fine thing. You, my wife, shall see it!" Then he drew out the food from the bag, potatoes and rice and beef. And he said, "While we eat this food, no one must show any of it to Nja." So, the two of them and his other wife and their family of children ate.

Soon day darkened, and they all went to sleep. Soon another day began to break. At daybreak, Turtle started to go off to the place where the Drum was. When he got there, he went to the tree and said to the Drum, "Ngama! Do as they said!" The Drum came rapidly down to the ground and put out the table all covered with food. Turtle took a part and ate and was satisfied. Then he also filled the bag. Then he said to the Drum, "Do as you did!" And Drum took back the things and went up the tree.

On another day, at daybreak, he went to the tree and did the same thing.

On another day, as he was going, his eldest son, curious to find out where his father obtained so much food, secretly followed him. Turtle went to where the Drum was. The child hid himself and stood still. He heard his father say to the tree, "Bend!" And its top bent down. The child saw the whole thing as Turtle took the Drum, stood it up, and with the palm of his hand, struck it,

---

°*Ngama*: an exclamation. °*tomu*: Here the singer will strike a drum that he holds.

tomu! saying, "Do as you have been told to do!" At once a table stood prepared at which Turtle sat down and ate. And when he had finished, saying, "Tree! bend down," it bent over for Drum to be tied to it. He returned Drum to the branch and the tree stood erect.

On other days, Turtle came to the tree and did the same way, eating and returning to his house, on all such occasions, bringing food for his family. One day, the son, who had seen how to do all these things, came to the tree, and said to it, "Bow down." It bowed and he did as his father had done. So Drum spread the table. The child ate and finished eating. Then he said to Drum, "Put them away!" And the table disappeared.

Then he took up the Drum, but instead of fastening it to the tree secretly carried it to town to his own house. Privately he went to call his brothers and his father's women and other members of the family. When they had come together in his house, at his command, the Drum did as usual, and they ate. And when he said to the Drum, "Put away the things!" it put them away.

Turtle came that day from the forest where he had been searching for the much-favored mushrooms for his family. He said to himself, "Before going into the town, I will first go to the tree to eat."

As he approached the tree, when only a short distance from it, the tree was standing as usual but the Drum was not there! He exclaimed, "Truly, now, what is this joke of the tree?" As he neared the foot of the tree, still there was no Drum to be seen! He said to the tree, "Bow down!" There was no response! He passed on to the town, took his ax and returned at once to the tree, in anger saying, "Unless you want me to cut you down, bend!" The tree stood still.

Turtle began at once with his ax chopping, Ko! Ko! The tree fell, toppling to the ground, tomu! He said to it, "You! Produce the drum or I will cut you in pieces!" He split the tree all into pieces but he did not see Drum. He returned to the town and, as he went, he walked anxiously, saying to himself, "Who has done this thing?"

When he reached his house, he was so displeased that he would not speak. Then his eldest son came to him and said, "O! my father! Why is it that you are silent and do not speak? What have you done in the forest? What is it?"

He replied, "I don't want to talk."

The son said, "Ah! my father! You were satisfied when you used to come and eat and you brought us mushrooms. I am the one who took the Drum."

Turtle said to him, "My child, now bring out to us the Drum." He brought it out of an inner room. Then Turtle and the son called together all their people privately and assembled them in the house. They commanded the Drum. It did as it usually did. They ate.

Their little children took their scraps of potatoes and meat of wild animals and, in their excitement, forgot orders and went out eating their food in the open street. Other children saw them and begged of them. They gave to them. Among them were children of Leopard, who went and showed the meat to their father.

All of sudden Leopard came to the house of Turtle and found him and his family feasting. Leopard said, "Ah! Chum! You have done me evil. You are eating and I and my family are dying from hunger!"

Turtle replied, "Yes, not today, but tomorrow you shall eat." So, Leopard returned to his house.

After that, the day darkened. And they all went to lie down in sleep. Then, the next day broke.

Early in the morning, Turtle, out in the street, announced, "From my house to Nja's there will be no strolling into the forest today. Today, only food."

Turtle then went off by himself to the coconut tree, where he had secretly carried the Drum during the night. When he got to the foot of the tree, he wanted to see if its power had been lost by the use of it in his town. So, he gave the usual orders and they were as usual obeyed.

Turtle then went off with Drum, carrying it openly on his shoulder, into the town, and directly to the house of Leopard and said to him, "Call all your people! Let them come!" They all came into the house and the people of Turtle also. He gave the usual commands. At once, Drum produced an abundance of food and a table for it. So, they all ate and were satisfied. And Drum took back the table to itself.

Drum remained in the house of Leopard for about two weeks. Then it ended its supply of food, being displeased at Leopard's rough treatment of it, and there was no more food. Leopard went to Turtle and told him, "Drum has no more food. Go, and get another." Turtle was provoked at the abuse of his Drum, but he took it and hung it up in his house.

At this time, the watchmen heard of the supply of food at Leopard's house and they asked him about it. He denied having any. They asked him, "Where then did you get this food which we saw your children eating?" He said, "From the children of Kudu."

The officers went at once to King Maseni and reported, "We saw a person who has food."

He inquired, "Who is he?"

They replied, "Kudu."

The king ordered, "Go and summon Kudu."

They went and told Turtle, "The king summons you."

Turtle asked, "What have I done to the king? Since the king and I have been living in this country, he has not summoned me."

Nevertheless he obeyed and journeyed to the king's house. The king said to him, "You are keeping food, while all the tribes are dying of hunger? You! bring all those foods!"

Turtle replied, "Please excuse me! I will not come again today with them. But, tomorrow, you must call for all the tribes."

The next morning the king had his bell rung and an order announced, "Any person whatever, old or young, come to eat!" The whole community assembled at the king's house. Turtle also came from his town, holding his Drum in his hand. The distant members of that tribe (not knowing and not having heard what the Drum had been doing) twitted him, "Is it for a dance?"

Entering into the king's house, Turtle stood up the Drum. With his palm he struck it, ve! saying, "Let every kind of food appear!" It appeared. The town was like a table, covered with every variety of food. The entire community ate and were satisfied, and they dispersed. Turtle took the Drum and journeyed back to his town. He spoke to his hungry family, "Come!" They came. They struck the Drum. It was motionless and nothing came from it! They struck it again. Silent! The Drum was indignant at having been used by other hands than those of Turtle. So, they sat down with hunger.

The next day, Turtle went rapidly off to the coconut tree, climbed it, gathered two nuts, threw one into the river, dropped into the stream, and followed the nut as he had done before. He came as before to that landing place and to the woman and told her about the failure of the Drum. She told him that she knew of it and directed him to go and take another.

He went on to that house, and to those people. And they, as before, asked him, "Kudu! Where are you going?"

He replied, "You know I have come to take my coconut."

But they said, "No! leave the nut and take a Drum."

And, as before, they advised him to take a silent one. So he came to the house of drums. These called to him, "Take me! take me!" Then, he thought to himself, "Yes! I'll take one of those Drums that talk. Perhaps they will have even better things than the other." So, he took one, and came out of the house, and told those people, "I have taken. And now for my journey".

He started from the landing place and on up the river to the foot of the coco tree. He tied the Drum to the tree with a cord, as before, set it up, and gave it a slap, ve! And a table stood there! He said, "Ngama! do as you usually do!" Instantly, there were thrown down on the table, mbwa! whips instead of food.

Turtle, surprised, said, "As usual!" The Drum picked up one of the whips and beat Turtle, ve! He cried out with pain and said to the Drum, "But, now do also as you do. Take these things away." And Drum returned the table and whips to itself. Turtle regretfully said to himself, "Those people told me not to take a Drum that talked but my heart deceived me."

However, a plan occurred to him by which to obtain a revenge on Leopard and the king for the trouble he had been put to.

So taking up the Drum he came to his own town and went at once to the house of Leopard, to whom he said, "Tomorrow come with your people and mine to the town of King Maseni."

Leopard rejoiced at the thought, "This is the Drum of food!"

Then Turtle journeyed to the king's town and said, "I have found food according to your order. Call the people tomorrow."

In the morning, the king's bell was rung and his people, accompanied by those of Turtle and Leopard, came to his house. Turtle privately spoke to his own people, "No one of you must follow me into the house. Remain outside of the window."

Turtle said to the king, "The food of today must be eaten only inside of your house." So, the king's people, with those of Leopard, entered into the house. There, Turtle said, "We shall eat this food only if all the doors and windows are fastened." So they were fastened (excepting one which Turtle kept open near himself).

Then, the Drum was sounded, and Turtle commanded it, "Do as you have said," the tables appeared. But, instead of food, were whips. The people wondered, "Ah! what do these mean? Where do they come from?"

Turtle stationed himself by the open window and commanded the Drum, "As usual!" Instantly the whips flew about the room, lashing everybody, even the king, and especially Leopard. The thrashing was great, and Leopard and his people were crying with pain. Their bodies were injured, being covered with cuts.

But Turtle had promptly jumped out of the window. And, standing outside, he ordered, "Ngama! do as you do!" And the whips and tables returned to it, and the whipping ceased. But, Turtle knew that the angry crowd would try to seize and kill him. So taking advantage of the confusion in the house, he and his people fled to the water of the river and scattered, hiding among the logs and roots in the stream. As he was disappearing, Leopard shouted after him, "You and I shall not see each other! If we do, it will be you who will be killed!"

It is a common feature in African stories, as in Native American tales, for inanimate objects and animals to talk like humans. There is never enough food in Benga society, so a magical way of finding food is what everybody wants. The object that cries out, "Take me, take me," always brings ill consequence in African stores, whereas the silent object brings good fortune. When the trickster Turtle understands this, he turns the tables on the king and all his men by appealing to their greed, also a common theme.

And that's why turtles live in the water!

## MYTH: NYIKANG AND THE SUN

The **SHILLUK** are the third-largest minority ethnic group of the newly created (2011) Republic of Southern Sudan, after the Dinka and the Nuer. Southern Sudan is bordered by the Republic of Northern Sudan to the north, ETHIOPIA to the east, KENYA and Uganda to the southeast, the DEMOCRATIC REPUBLIC OF THE CONGO to the west, and the CENTRAL AFRICAN REPUBLIC to the southwest. The world's longest river, the Nile, divides the country between east and west sides. Like most Nilotic groups, cattle-raising forms a large part of their economy, although agriculture and fishing are significant. Most Shilluk are sedentary, led by a king considered to be divine who traces his lineage back to the culture hero **Nyikang**. When the king is well, the people are well. There are castes of royals, nobles, commoners, and slaves (Figure 15.5).

The following tale tells the story of Nyikang and how once he fought the sun, which retreated to the sky to escape him. Then he founded the Shilluk people:

In ancient times the people came to the country Kerau, this is the country into which Nyikang came. Here they separated, he and his brother Duwat.

Duwat said, "Nyikang, where are you going?"

He replied, "I am going to that place there."

Again he said, "Nyikang, look behind!"

And Nyikang turned round and looked back, and he saw a stick for planting yams, which Duwat had thrown to him. When Nyikang came back to take it, he asked, "What is that?"

Duwat replied, "Go, that is a thing with which to dig the ground of your village."

And Nyikang came and sat down in the country of Turo. This is the country of his son Dak.

Dak used to sit on the ashes of the village and to play the *torn* [a stringed instrument]. But his uncles, the brothers of Nyikang, said, "Is the country to be ruled by Dak alone?" They were jealous of him.

**FIGURE 15.5**   Shilluk warriors armed with sharpened sticks as spears. Southern Sudan, Africa, 1936. (The Print Collector / Alamy)

His uncles went to sharpen their spears. But it was told to Dak, "Your uncles are going to kill you!"

Then Nyikang went to get a fetish. He hewed it and made hands for it so that it looked like the statue of a man. Dak went and sat down in the same place again and began playing his instrument. His uncles came and stabbed him—that is, the statue. Dak went into his enclosure unhurt.

Nyikang came and said, "My son has been killed by his uncles." His uncles were afraid, saying, "Let every man stay at home four days. When four days have passed, we may mourn him."

The morning after four days were gone, all the people came to mourn. There were a great many. Suddenly Dak came out from his enclosure and went to dance the *mado* dance. When his uncles saw this, they ran away, and the mourning was finished.

Nyikang said, "I will go!"

And he came and went along a river, a certain river called Faloko. And the people settled on this river. Here the cow ran away, the cow of Nyikang, because of her calves. Her calves used to be speared by Nyikang.°

°*Nyikang*: when Nyikang came to a new place, he killed a calf.

The cow went and came to the country of the sun. And Ojul ["gray hawk"] went to search for her. He found the cow among the cows of the sun. He said, "I am searching for a cow."

Garo, the son of the sun, said, "Man, what do you search for?"

He replied, "I search for a cow!"

He asked, "What cow?"

Ojul said, "The cow of Nyikang."

Garo asked, "Where has it come from?"

He answered, "From the country of Nyikang."

Garo replied, "No, never! Here is no cow of Nyikang."

He, Ojul, turned back and told Nyikang, "Nyikang, we have found the cow! Among the cows of a certain man. He is very tall, just like Dak. On his hands he has silver bracelets."

Nyikang said, "Raise an army, and find the cow!"

Dak went and attacked Garo. He threw him on the ground. He cut off his hands, pulled the bracelets off them, and chased the enemy's army. He came to the sun. But there the army of Nyikang was chased, and it was utterly destroyed. Then Nyikang himself came. He took an adze and aimed it towards the sun. He hit the sun and it returned to the sky. Nyikang went and took the bracelet. With it he touched the dead of his army and they returned to life.

The people came. They came to the head of a river. There they arose and approached the junction of the river in boats. They found the river full of sudd.°

Nyikang said, "Where does this come from? What shall we do?"

Their way was barred. Then Obogo° arose saying, "Nyikang, I have finished eating. Spear me under the sudd!"

He said again, "Nyikang, thus I shall part asunder the sudd and if you come to any place where the sudd is, you just follow after it."

So Obogo was stabbed under the sudd and the sudd broke asunder, so they came to their place together with the sudd.

He settled with his people in Achyete-guok but he found the country occupied by the white people. Therefore the people returned to this side of the river. They settled at the head of the Pijo. Dak passed on to Wij-Palo. The army went home, scattered because the war was finished.

He, Nyikang, built the following villages: Nyelwal, Pepwojo, Adele, Ted go, Palo. The people went on and built Wau, Onshore, Pe Nyikang Otego, Aurea, Moro, Or Yang. These are the villages of Nyikang.

Nyikang went saying,° "Ah, there are still Shilluks left!"

Then Dak ruled. He went away.° After him his son Odak ruled. He went away while hunting game. The people were perplexed and they said, "What is that?"

Nyikang returned° saying, "Bring a cow that we may make a bier."

°sudd: a floating mass of vegetation that often obstructs navigation in tropical rivers; Sudan is named from the great bog in southern Sudan. °Obogo: "albino," hence white, dead: evidently a reference to human sacrifice to appease the sudd. °went saying: he died, and these were his last words. ° went away: that is, he died. °returned: he came back to life.

When that was finished, Duwat ruled after him. When he had finished, Bwoch ruled after him. After him Dokot ruled, then Tugo, then Okwon, then Kudit, then Nyakwacho.

All kings are descended from Nyikang, a culture hero and founder. Nyikang led the people to Kerau, where they now live. He taught them how to plant yams, which he had learned from his brother. In the early days, he foiled a plot to kill his son Dak and exterminate his line, perhaps a piece of oral history. Cattle are central to the Shilluk and we learn that Nyikang's own cow had escaped to the land of the sun. But Nyikang's son Dak recovered it by killing the son of the sun, Garo. He forced the sun to take its position in the sky. When Nyikang's army was destroyed, he brought it back to life through magic. He overcame the forces of the *sudd*, which makes travel on the river impossible, through human sacrifice. The story must postdate European colonization because Nyikang was unable to settle where the white man lived. After Nyikang died, his son ruled, then his son, then his son, and so forth. The spirit of Nyikang is thought to indwell each king, for he "returned." He is the intermediary between the people and divinity.

This is a story of origins, telling of the first time when the world, and the people, came into existence and occupied their present place in the world. In the Nilotic tribes of the Sudan, status is determined by ancestry, and this story establishes the ancestry, power, and prestige of the living king.

## OBSERVATIONS: AFRICAN MYTH

Many have noticed the similarities between African, Oceanic, and American Indian myths. In none of these traditions are gods and demons strongly defined, unlike in the myths of many other peoples. These stories are filled with talking animals and talking objects that act like humans. There is no distinction between the human world and the animal world. There is little interest in such grand themes as the origin of the world or the origin of evil, but an emphasis on the trickster who secures his advantage by cleverness and deceit, qualities highly valued by the societies that told these stories.

## Key Terms

| | | |
|---|---|---|
| Baganda *514* | Abunawas *521* | Afiong *533* |
| Kintu *514* | Yoruba *526* | Benga *536* |
| Nambi *514* | Xhosa *531* | Shilluk *542* |
| Mugulu *521* | Igbo *533* | Nyikang *542* |
| Tigre *521* | *Ju Ju 533* | |

## Further Reading

Arnott, K., *African Myths and Legends* (Oxford, UK, 1990).
Belcher, S., *African Myths of Origin* (New York, 2006).
Parrinder, E. G., *African Mythology* (New York, 1998).
Scheub, H., *The African Storyteller: Stories from African Oral Traditions* (Dubuque, IA, 1998).

CHAPTER

# 16

# Theories of Myth Interpretation

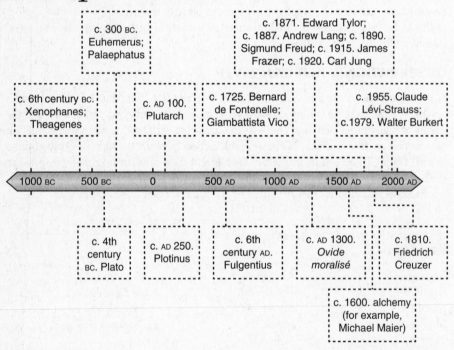

c. 300 BC. Euhemerus; Palaephatus

c. 1871. Edward Tylor; c. 1887. Andrew Lang; c. 1890. Sigmund Freud; c. 1915. James Frazer; c. 1920. Carl Jung

c. 6th century BC. Xenophanes; Theagenes

c. AD 100. Plutarch

c. 1725. Bernard de Fontenelle; Giambattista Vico

c. 1955. Claude Lévi-Strauss; c.1979. Walter Burkert

1000 BC     500 BC     0     500 AD     1000 AD     1500 AD     2000 AD

c. 4th century BC. Plato

c. AD 250. Plotinus

c. 6th century AD. Fulgentius

c. AD 1300. *Ovide moralisé*

c. 1810. Friedrich Creuzer

c. 1600. alchemy (for example, Michael Maier)

There are no facts; only interpretations.

—FRIEDRICH NIETZSCHE *(1844–1900)*

*Where Do Myths Come* from? What do these stories, some handed down from the unknown past, often bizarre or mysterious, signify? Disturbed by the irrational and often immoral content of their traditional tales, Greek intellectuals were the first to pose these questions already in ancient times, initiating a long tradition of theoretical inquiry into the nature and meaning of myth. The investigation into the meaning of myth is a wholly Greek, and subsequently European, undertaking; no other people has shown the slightest interest in "what myths mean."

Some ancient Greeks rejected the traditional stories completely, giving rise to our notion of "myth" as an untruthful account, but others developed elaborate theories to show that myths contain profound truths, despite their initial implausibility. Such theories enjoy a broad appeal in the modern world, for example, in the popular writings of Joseph Campbell (1904–1987). This tradition was developed further in the medieval period and the Renaissance. In the modern era, with the development of new fields of inquiry, the factual or philosophic truth of myth has ceased to be the only question considered. Anthropologists, for example, are concerned with the social function of myth, and psychologists develop theories about the emotional needs that myth reflects and satisfies. In the following pages we trace some of the major phases in the history of the interpretation of myth from ancient Greek to modern times.

## GREEK THEORIES

Through their **rationalism** the Greeks, assisted by the radical technology of the Greek alphabet, were the first people to become fully self-conscious and critical of their own traditions. The inquiry was closely bound up with Greek philosophy, which began partly in speculation about the nature of myth, then developed into a system of reasoning about causes and effects and about the nature of things that was independent of traditional—that is, mythical—explanations. The Greek philosophers wanted to reduce dependence on explanations that used the anthropomorphic categories of Greek religion so prominent in Greek traditional tales. They criticized the traditional stories for their implausible and irrational details or immoral content. Already in the 6th century BC **Xenophanes** (ksen-**of**-a-nēz) of Colophon (in Asia Minor) complained of the ethical weakness of the Olympians, insisting that popular notions about the gods must be wrong (*fragment*, 21 B 14–16, Diels-Krans):

> In my opinion mortals have created their gods with the dress and voice and appearance of mortals. If cattle and horses had hands and wanted to draw or carve as men do, the cattle would show their gods in the form of cattle and horses would show them as horses, with the same form and appearance as their own. The Ethiopians say that their gods have snub noses and black skins, while the Thracians say that theirs have blue eyes and red hair.

And (*fragment*, 21 B 23, Diels-Krans):

> One god is greatest among gods and men, but his appearance and thought are nothing like ours.

Xenophanes, who lived about two hundred years after Homer, questions the very existence of the gods that populate Greek myth and, by implication, attacks the truth of the traditional tales cherished by the Greeks as their cultural heritage.

Plato, a friend of Socrates and founder of the immensely influential Academy during the 4th century BC in Athens, criticized such tales even more severely. He thought that the irrational stories of Homer and other poets had a corrupting influence because they presented to the untutored mind a false image of reality. In his ideal state, described in the *Republic*, Plato banned the poets and their lying tales. On the other hand, Plato was aware that some important truths lie beyond the grasp of human reason. In fact the burden of his philosophy was to demonstrate the existence of timeless eternal realities that lie behind the transient and changing surface of the everyday world, realities Plato called "Ideas" or "Forms" (Greek *eidos* = "shape"), hence our word *idealism*, belief in values not apparent in the material world.

Although opposing traditional Greek myth, Plato considered mythlike stories to be an appropriate vehicle for giving expression to these truths. So he wrote his own "myths," dealing especially with the soul's fate after death, but also with the nature of being and of the perfect political order. As we have seen in Chapter 1 (Perspective 1), The "Myth of Atlantis," a wealthy powerful city on an island that disappeared beneath the sea, was Plato's invention.

Other Greek thinkers went beyond Plato, asserting that even the traditional myths Plato had criticized so vigorously could be seen to contain a kernel of philosophical or historical truth. The task, they thought, was to interpret the myths so that this kernel would come to light. Despite their bizarre or immoral content, the traditional stories meant something other than what they appeared at first glance to mean. There was no need to dismiss myths as errors, containing nothing that need be taken seriously. They must be allegories, the Greeks argued, stories that look like one thing on the surface but are really something else inside.

**Allegory** is a Greek word that means "saying something in a different way" or "saying something different from what appears to be said." In allegorizing myth, the story is translated from its initial frame of reference into another that is more acceptable. For example, the Greek story of the nymph Daphnê's transformation into a laurel tree to escape the clutches of Apollo can be explained as an allegory about chastity. The story does not mean that a girl, pursued by Apollo, literally was changed into a tree but that abstinence from sexual intercourse can, at least for a woman, be desirable. Allegory is closely related to **symbolism**, "something put together with something else," because in both allegory and symbolism one thing points to and brings another thing to mind. Thus Daphnê can be interpreted as a symbol of virginity.

The allegorical or symbolic meaning found in a story depended entirely on the frame of reference that the ancient interpreter believed to be true. Because Greek philosophers were concerned primarily with "the truth" in such fields as cosmology, history, and—as in the case of Daphnê—morality, the meanings they found in myth generally originated in these spheres.

## Physical Allegory

Theagenes (thē-**aj**-e-nēz), who lived in southern Italy during the later 6th century BC, is said to have been the first to use the allegorical method. None of his writing survives, but later commentators say that he explained mythical accounts of battle among the gods as representing conflicts among natural forces. In Theagenes' cosmology, dry is opposite to wet, hot to cold; water extinguishes fire, fire evaporates water. Such natural oppositions, Theagenes thought, must be embodied in Homer's story in the *Iliad* (20.54 ff.) of Apollo who, armed with his arrows, faces Poseidon: Apollo stands for fire, Poseidon for water. The mythical conflict of the two gods is the allegorical expression of a basic cosmological principle concerning the opposition of fire and water. Other allegorists did not hesitate to apply allegory in psychological interpretations as well, making Athena personify rational thought; Ares, irrational violence; Aphrodite, desire; and Hermes, reason.

During the Hellenistic Period (after 323 BC) when Greek culture had become world culture, thanks to the conquests of Alexander the Great, Stoic philosophers refined physical allegory into a powerful tool that could be applied to any myth. For example, they argued that the Greek creation myths contained profound truths about the origin of the universe. The story of Uranus' castration by sickle was explained as meaning that the original creative element of the universe, "fiery air" (= Uranus), begot its offspring spontaneously without the assistance of sexual union. Likewise, the Stoics identified Cronus with *chronos* = "time," and his role in creation was interpreted to mean that all things were begotten by time. The children of Cronus are the ages, and the story that Cronus devoured them means that "time consumes the ages." The story that Zeus overthrew Cronus and bound him in the underworld means that time, although great in extent, is nonetheless limited.

The interpretation of Cronus as *chronos* illustrates how the Stoics used **etymology**, speculation about "the true meaning of a word," to reinforce allegory. They believed that the meaning of a word or name can reveal the meaning of a myth. The famous biographer Plutarch (c. AD 50–c. 125) offers another example. He interprets the story of Demeter and Persephonê as an allegory conveying an important insight about life after death. In the story Hades, brother of Zeus, snatched Persephonê to make her his wife. Demeter's mourning caused infertility in the world, but in the end Persephonê is permitted to spend part of the time among the living.

According to Plutarch, Demeter is the earth, Hades the shadow cast by the earth, and Persephonê the moon, which reflects the light of the sun. He proves this by reminding us that Persephonê's other name, *Korê*, means in Greek not only "girl," but also "pupil of the eye." As the eye (*korê* = "pupil") acts like a mirror reflecting little images of objects, so does the moon reflect the light of the sun. *Korê*, or pupil/Persephonê, is the moon, and the story of Persephonê's descent into the underworld and subsequent return refers to the waxing and waning of the moon, when the moon slips in and out of the shadow of the earth, Hades' realm. By extension, the story of Persephonê's descent and return means that after losing their bodies at death, human beings exist as souls and minds in Hades. If they are blameless, however, they may subsequently escape to the sun as pure minds. By adding a philosophical meaning, Plutarch's physical allegory turns the myth into a vehicle for deeper truth.

The etymologies offered by the Stoics, which depended on similarity in sound, must have seemed reasonable in a society in which myth was still part of the living, aural language. In reality, their etymologies were often quite fantastic because the science of linguistics was unknown in the ancient world. We now know that the name Cronus is etymologically unrelated to the word *chronos*. But through this false etymology arose the common picture of Father Time as the Grim Reaper, an old man carrying a sickle, because C(h)ronus/Time castrated his father with a sickle.

Roman writers who followed the Stoic philosophy also used Latin etymologies to interpret myths. For example, they argued that Juno (corresponding to Hera in Greek myth) was really air because the Greek (and Latin) word for air (*aêr, aura*) sounded like *Hera*. This etymology was supported by the belief that air lay just beneath the aether, or upper atmosphere, symbolized in myth by Jupiter. The position of air (= Juno) just beneath aether (= Jupiter, Juno's mate) was the true meaning of the story that Jupiter united with Juno in sexual embrace.

These physical allegorical interpretations attempted to explain a cultural inheritance from a distant, preliterate past in light of sophisticated philosophical thought about forces in nature. The allegorists had no notion that myths arose at different times and in different cultural conditions and for different reasons (a mistake easy to make!) and of course they knew nothing about nonGreek myth. Their explanations permitted the allegorists to maintain the respectability of the traditional tales, which might otherwise be rejected because of their patent factual errors or offensive moral content. In addition to protecting the decency and social utility of traditional stories, physical allegory was a philosophically respectable way of bringing to light hidden, even mysterious truths about the world.

## Historical Allegory: Euhemerism

Allegorical interpretation of myth goes back to the 6th century BC, but about 300 BC the Greek mythographer Euhemerus (yū-hēm-er-us) offered a new approach, suggesting myth revealed historical rather than cosmological truth. Euhemerus wrote a book describing a journey to three fabulously wealthy islands in the Indian Ocean. On the main island, Panchaea (modeled after Plato's Atlantis), Euhemerus said that he had found a golden column on which was inscribed the history of the reigns of early human kings. This alleged history suggested a very different interpretation of Greek myth.

First to rule, according to Euhemerus' story, was Uranus, so called because he was learned in the study of the heavens. From union with his human wife, Hestia, Uranus begot the Titans and Cronus. The column gave further information about Uranus' successors, Cronus, Zeus, and their families. The war in heaven and Cronus' swallowing his children were explained as recollections of palace intrigues. During his reign, according to the column, Zeus traveled the earth teaching the arts of civilized life, banning such reprehensible religious practices as cannibalism, and founding temples. According to the story, he actually lived for a while on Mount Olympus, then, at the end of a long life, Zeus retired to Crete, died, and was buried there. That is why the Cretans spoke of "the tomb of Zeus."

Although Euhemerus' story of the inscribed column is a fiction, his underlying theory is quite plausible and enters many modern interpretations of myth. By asserting that gods were in origin great men, so respected or feared that they were worshiped after death, he attempted to explain myth as a form of early history. From his book comes the modern term **euhemerism**, the thesis that gods once were humans.

Many features of the Greek mythical tradition lent themselves to explanation along these lines. After all, the gods were organized in a family on Olympus, and they looked and acted like Greek aristocrats. As for such deified heroes as Heracles, everyone always thought them to be real men anyway, who had actually lived, founded cities, and done great deeds.

Euhemerus' thesis derived convenient support from the politics of Hellenistic monarchs, especially in Egypt, who presented themselves to their peoples as gods incarnate and who included the native gods in their dynastic genealogies. The deification of dead rulers made more plausible the notion that great humans of the past had, with the passage of time, become more than human. Behind myth lay history.

An approach closely related to that of Euhemerus is found in a handbook on myth called *On Incredible Things*, of which an excerpt survives, written by one Palaephatus (pal-ē-fat-us), a contemporary of Euhemerus. Palaephatus' special contribution was to explain myths as originating from a misunderstanding of language. For example, the Greeks told a story about Actaeon, who espied Artemis while she was bathing. She turned him into a stag, and he was torn apart by his own dogs. According to Palaephatus, Actaeon really was a man ruined by spending too much money on his hunting dogs. The myth arose when neighborhood gossip began to tell of how "poor Actaeon is being devoured by his dogs." The interpretation of myth as a "disease of language" was to undergo a surprisingly successful renaissance in the theories of the German-born, Oxford scholar Max Müller in the 19th century AD (see later in this chapter).

## Moral Allegory

The interpretation of myth as a system of advice on good and bad behavior, or moral allegory, was more highly developed than physical or historical allegory. We have already seen a crude example of it in the explanation of the story of Apollo and Daphnê as exhorting young women to remain chaste. So the winged-demon Harpies who rob Phineus, a king in the story of the Argonauts, of his food are really prostitutes who ruin young men through their high fees. In the myth of the Judgment of Paris a Trojan prince must choose who is most beautiful among Athena, Hera, and Aphrodite; he chooses Aphrodite, receives Helen as his prize, and so causes the Trojan war. Really, according to moral allegory, the goddesses represent three kinds of life: the active (Hera); the contemplative (Athena); and the amorous (Aphrodite), among which every man (Paris) must choose.

## PERSPECTIVE 16
### Apuleius' Allegory of Cupid and Psychê

Sometimes allegory is an interpretation that the listener or reader teases out of the story, suggesting, for example, that the marriage of Zeus/Jupiter and Hera/Juno really refers to the upper air that lies upon the lower. At other times, the allegory appears to have been consciously in the mind of the storyteller.

The philosopher Apuleius of Madaura in North Africa (mid-2nd century AD) included one such story, a folktale much beloved in Europe after the Middle Ages, in a long Latin prose novel titled the *Metamorphoses*, but usually called the *Golden Ass*. The story, told by an old woman to comfort a girl kidnapped by robbers, tells of the love between Cupid (= Greek Eros), "sexual desire," and Psychê (sī-kē), "soul," a Greek word almost as vague as the English.

Psychê was the youngest and most beautiful of three sisters, so beautiful that she aroused the jealousy of Venus. No one dared court her for fear of the goddess, and her father consulted an oracle, who ordered him to dress her as if for marriage, but then to expose her on a cliff to a winged monster of whom even Zeus was afraid. A wind picked up Psychê, left alone, and bore her to a garden of a beautiful palace.

A delicious meal was placed before her and heavenly music played, although she could see no one. She went to bed and in the black of night awoke to realize that someone was in bed with her. Her lover warned her that she must never see him or she would lose him forever. He visited her night after blissful night, but she never saw him by day (Perspective Figure 16).

Reluctantly, he allowed her to have her sisters visit her. Fiercely jealous, they persuaded Psychê to kill her husband, who, they insisted, was the monster of whom the oracle had spoken.

Psychê therefore armed herself with a knife, lit a lamp, and entered her bedroom. So surprised was she to see the handsome, sleeping young man with wings that she let a drop of hot oil fall on him. Cupid—for it was he—leaped up, flew to the top of a tree, and bade poor Psychê farewell. The girl rushed off in despair to one of her sisters, told her the whole story, and added that her husband had announced that he much preferred the sister. The vain woman ran to a cliff and jumped off, expecting to be borne up by the wind, but was dashed to bits on the rocks below. The same thing happened with the second sister.

Cupid, tormented by the hot oil, could not protect Psychê from the anger of his mother, Venus, who, aided by her servants Convention, Worry, and Gloom, beat

**PERSPECTIVE FIGURE 16**    "Cupid and Psychê," by Francois-Edouard Picot (1786–1868). The winged god leaves the beautiful girl after a night of love-making. Oil on canvas, 1817. (Louvre, Paris; Réunion des Musées Nationaux / Peter Barritt / Alamy)

and tormented the girl. According to a folklore pattern that we have seen many times in this book, she was forced to sort a heap of mixed seeds in one night; she succeeded when a swarm of ants came to her aid. She had to bring golden wool from a flock of man-eating sheep by a river; friendly reeds plucked it for her. She had to bring Venus water from a stream that burst from a precipice; the eagle of Zeus himself fetched it. Finally, she had to go down to Hades to bring back in a box a day's supply of Persephonê's beauty ointment—a journey beset with traps laid by Venus. The girl evaded all these and obtained the box. Although forbidden, she opened it, hoping to make herself beautiful and win back Cupid. At once she fell into a profound sleep.

Cupid had by now recovered. He found Psychê, awakened her with a prick of his arrows, and appealed to Zeus to let him have his beloved. Zeus consented, Venus was appeased, they had a grand marriage feast, and Psychê became immortal.

The story contains many motifs familiar from modern folktales: the jealous sisters, like those of Cinderella; and miraculous assistance at an impossible task, like that of the dwarf who spun Rapunzel's gold. Like many of the stories of the Grimm brothers, an old serving-woman tells this tale too. On the other hand, the frame is that of an intentional allegory—a story with a further meaning obvious from the names of the characters: the longing of Soul (Psychê) for union with Desire (Cupid), who must overcome hindrances set up by Convention, Worry, and Gloom.

Such interpretations, like those of the physical and historical allegorists, fail to preserve myth, whatever the intentions of their practitioners, for they remove the charm of the original story and replace it with a truism or historical or physical incident. An intellectual movement linked loosely to Platonism dealt with myth more positively and gently.

In the final centuries of the pagan era (AD 200–500), a school known as **Neoplatonism** revived and developed many of Plato's theories and became the major philosophic movement of the day. Neoplatonists, like their founder, Plato, believed in a higher dimension of reality beyond the limits of time and space, where perfection and absolute truth—that which is always and everywhere the same—could be found. This higher world is accessible to us through our minds, if they are freed from our bodies and senses. The material universe, by contrast, yields only an inferior knowledge based on sense perception, at best imperfect and ultimately false because everything in the material world is always changing.

Yet this material world is somewhat modeled after the perfect rational world, having features that symbolize the eternal blueprint. Thus transient physical beauty, such as a sunset, symbolizes eternal beauty. In the same way, say the Neoplatonists, myths give us hints about the moral world beyond. Neoplatonism lends itself to allegory, although of a kind that does not reduce myth to literal fact but expands it into a vehicle for discovering profound truths, usually moral, about a higher domain hidden behind appearance.

Plotinus (c. 204–c. 270), the founder of Neoplatonism in the 3rd century AD, held that myth describes timeless realities in the form of temporal events. He saw a correspondence between the sequence

- **Uranus**
- **Cronus**
- **Zeus**

and the three great principles of reality:

- **Unity** (unchanging, the same in all parts = Uranus)
- **Intellect** (unchanging, but plural = Cronus)
- **Soul** (plural and subject to change and motion = Zeus)

Plotinus' student Porphyry (c. AD 234–305) produced an extremely complex interpretation of Homer's description of the cave of the nymphs on Ithaca, where Odysseus hides his treasure after returning from his wanderings (*Odyssey*, 13.102–112). The cave, he argues, represents the universe because it is generated from matter and is natural; the nymphs, as spirits of water, represent the ceaseless flow of events within time; the looms of stone on which they weave represent souls descending to incarnation, as the flesh is woven on the bones (the stones of the body). The moral truths are obvious: The material world, including our bodies, is an illusion and unworthy of our aspiration.

The increasing interest of Neoplatonists in such allegories reflects an effort to rehabilitate myth and to establish its value for revealing higher truths in the face of the growing threat from Christianity. In the end Christianity swallowed Neoplatonism. St. Augustine (AD 354–430) began as a dualist (believer in the Persian principal of two opposed principles), became a Neoplatonist, and ended as one of the greatest of Christian theologians.

## MEDIEVAL AND RENAISSANCE THEORIES

Platonic modes of thinking exerted powerful influence on early Christian theology. Both myth itself and the various methods devised for interpreting it were part of the cultural heritage taken over by the Christian church. Although some church fathers rejected allegory on the ground that it was a way of holding onto pagan myth, most found allegorical interpretations a legitimate way to interpret pagan myth, especially when a moral encouraging righteous conduct could be found within the tale.

The allegorical method whereby moral meanings were drawn from old stories was also applied extensively to the Bible. For example, the frankly erotic content of the *Song of Solomon*, which tells of sexual love between a man and a woman, was explained as an allegory of God's love for the church (in fact the poem descends from secular Egyptian love poetry). Euhemerism was a useful method of analysis for the Christians because it served to justify the authority of the church by proving that pagan religion was idolatry, just as Christians and Jews had always maintained.

The ancient methods of interpretation lived on, but direct acquaintance with classical culture and its literature declined drastically, especially in the Latin-speaking West. The Greek myths were now known principally through handbooks, which became increasingly important and elaborate. One of the most influential was the *Mythologies* of Fulgentius (ful-**jen**-shus), a North African Christian of the 6th century AD. On reading his account of some god, the reader would find a succinct entry that included both the facts of the story and a moral based on an allegorical interpretation. Fulgentius gives the allegorical interpretation of the Judgment of Paris mentioned earlier.

Such material reappeared in other handbooks over the next centuries and for a long time made up the basic source of myths available in the West. Interpretation had become more complex and important than the myths themselves, whose telling might consist of little more than a few key details. Allegory continued to focus on acceptable moral meanings.

*Ovide moralisé* ("Ovid Moralized"), a text originally in French that went through many versions from AD 1300 on, listed interpretations of the often racy myths retold in Ovid's poetry. The story of Daphnê transformed into a laurel tree to escape the lustful Apollo is explained as an allegory for the moral that chastity, like the laurel, remains as cool as a river and always blooms, but never bears fruit. We may also understand the story as a botanical allegory (the warmth of the sun, Apollo, when combined with water, Daphnê, makes the laurel flourish) or even a medical allegory (chased by a rapist, she dies from exhaustion under a laurel tree). Such interpretations reached a wider public through Christian sermons, which could use Odysseus' encounter with the Sirens, for example, as an object lesson of the temptations posed by pleasure during a Christian's voyage through life.

Part of the renewed emphasis given to classical culture at the time of the Renaissance came from interest in Platonism. The Platonic conviction that myth contains profound symbolic truth concerning higher spiritual realms was highly attractive to Christian culture and led to a vogue for even more elaborate allegory that combined pagan and Christian elements. Repeating arguments made earlier by the Neoplatonists, whom they admired, students of classical myth during the Renaissance maintained that bizarre, shocking features were actually the surest sign of truth in a myth. Only those who earnestly sought the truth would delve beneath the repulsive surface appearances to penetrate to the deeper riches hidden beneath.

For example, Hesiod's description of the birth of Aphrodite is a raw, even brutal account, beginning with a son's mutilation of his father's genitals. The foam that gathers around the genitals suggests to Hesiod the false etymology for Aphrodite's name as "foam-goddess" (because Greek *aphros* = "foam"), but the image is taken from actual intercourse. From these gory events and viscous fluids emerged a figure that is in appearance the opposite: lovely and lithesome, the object of desire. Yet within remains the blood and the foam, a woman's deceptive nature, occluded by the irresistible sweetness of always destructive passion.

From the same story Botticelli (c. 1445–c. 1510), a master artist of the 15th century, drew an entirely different lesson (Figure 16.1).

Botticelli was a member of the circle of the rich and powerful Lorenzo de Medici's (1449–1492) Platonic Academy of Philosophy, whose guiding genius was Marsilio Ficino (1433–1499), an eminent Greek scholar. Ficino, following the Neoplatonists of the 3rd to 6th centuries AD, taught that the universe was a hierarchy of descending spheres reaching from the oneness of God through angelic spheres to our own world of base matter. Before birth, the human soul (= Botticelli's Venus) was perfect and lived in the angelic spheres, then was caught at birth in the dark material world (the cloak in Botticelli's painting). Only through God's love, as expressed in the beauty of creation, could the soul regain its original perfection and be saved from vile matter. Through the contemplation of beauty (Botticelli's beautiful picture of the birth of Venus), the soul could perceive the abstract beauty behind the material expression, which would then restore the soul to its spiritual nature. Art, then, serves a philosophical function.

**FIGURE 16.1**   The birth of Venus, by Sandro Botticelli (1445–1510), c. 1485. (Classic Image / Alamy)

The medieval and Renaissance alchemists, who believed that knowledge of nature's secrets would allow them to transform common metals into gold or silver, found a different kind of truth in classical myth, reviving in new form Greek physical allegory. Accepting Neoplatonic theories about the relationship between matter and spirit, they put allegorical interpretation of myth to use in their description of secret physical processes. The figure of Hermes (= Mercury), for example, was taken to be a ready-made allegory of chemical facts about the element mercury.

In the alchemical work *Atalanta Fugiens* ("Atalanta Running Away") published in 1617, Michael Maier (1568–1622) provided his text with pictures and a musical score, "so that your eyes and ears may take in the emblems, but your reason searches out the hidden signs." Both text and pictures treat the mythical tradition as a treasure trove of alchemical allegory. In the famous myth of Oedipus, the hapless hero, a found-ling from Corinth, goes to the oracle at Delphi to inquire about his birth and is told that he is destined to kill his father and marry his mother. Returning, he kills a bully at a crossroads, then goes to Thebes, to avoid any contact with his mother. A dangerous sphinx oppresses the city, but Oedipus destroys it by answering a riddle. He marries the widowed queen. Only later does he discover that the man he killed at the cross-roads was his father and the woman he marries his own mother. On discovering the truth, he blinds himself (Figure 16.2).

In the myth of the swift-runner Atalanta, she defeats all contestants for her hand, then suspends their heads from her door. The hero Hippomenes casts golden apples before her and, when she stoops to retrieve them, wins the race and her hand. According to Maier, Atalanta is the "volatile" mercury that "flees" and her suitor Hippomenes is the sulfur that overcomes her, that is, effects a chemical reaction. The golden apples are another ingredient retarding the process.

EMBLEMA XXXIX. *De secretis Naturæ.* 165

Oedypus Sphynge superata & trucidato Lajo patre
matrem ducit in uxorem.

E PIGRAMMA XXXIX.

S *Phyngem ænigmatico Thebis sermone timendam*
   *Oedypus ad propriam torserat arte necem:*
*Quæsitum est cui mane pedes sint bis duo, luce*
   *Sed mediâ bini, tres ubi vesper adest.*
*Victor abhinc Lajum nolentem cedere cædit,*
   *Ducit & uxorem quæ sibi mater erat.*    X 3    BA-

**FIGURE 16.2** Oedipus in *Atalanta Fugiens* by Michael Maier (1617). The story of Oedipus was interpreted as an alchemical allegory. In clockwise order beginning at the top: the snaky-tailed sphinx besieges Thebes; Oedipus meets his mother Jocasta; and Oedipus kills his father Laius. In the foreground is the riddle of the three ages, really about the laws of nature: The triangle on the old man's (= Old Age) forehead is body/soul/spirit; the hemisphere on the mature man (= Maturity) is the moon; and the square on the baby (= Childhood) is the four elements. At the left the sphinx is about to leap from a cliff in despair at Oedipus' answering the riddle. The Latin poetic text means

> While Thebes lies quaking in dread of the riddling monster's enigma,
> Oedipus cleverly twists the Sphinx's word to its doom.
> The creature had asked, "Who, pray, has twice two legs in the morning,
> at noonday only a pair; eventide sets him on three?" ["man" is the answer, who
> walks on all fours as an infant, on two feet as an adult, and uses a cane in old age]
> Oedipus, puffed up in triumph, bids Laius, "Get out of my way!"
> kills him, then takes as his wife she who had given him birth.

Along with such specialized esoteric texts, handbooks continued to provide basic information for artists or writers along with interpretations. Greek myth had virtually become a language for talking about timeless truths, and in the 17th century the theory that pagan myth was a distorted version of biblical history reemerged with vigor. Scholars gathered evidence intended to show that many details in Homer were muddled versions of events in the Old Testament. The siege of Troy was explained as a recasting of Joshua's attack on Jericho. Odysseus' wanderings reflected those of the patriarchs.

## THEORIES OF THE ENLIGHTENMENT

Such interpretations fell under serious attack in the 18th century as part of the profound cultural revolution called the **Enlightenment**. As the institutional power of the church waned in response to political and social changes in Europe, everything traditional was subject to reexamination, usually with a notable lack of sympathy. Because few things were so traditional as myth, the authority of mythical accounts (including the Bible) and the value of allegory for preserving their worth were increasingly questioned.

The book of Bernard de Fontenelle (1657–1757) *De l'origine des fables*, "Concerning the Origin of Fables" (1724), is a monument of the radical change in attitude taking place, initially in France, and paved the way for many of the central themes of the Enlightenment. Fontenelle laid down new principles for dealing with myth. Instead of seeking deep, esoteric truths, he saw that myth was rooted in the ignorance of humans living at earlier stages of cultural development. Fontenelle shifted the emphasis of theory from interpreting myth (that is, Greek myth) to explaining the origin of myth, which, he asserts, develops in savagery and ignorance. Some scholars date the modern meaning of *myth* as a fanciful tale, or the notion that it exists as a discrete category at all, to Fontenelle's writings.

Information about the cultures of the American Indians, the peoples of the South Seas, the Africans, and other preliterate peoples coming in from missionaries or colonial administrators—which form a large part of this book—was a source for Fontenelle's theories. Such information justified his distinguishing the "primitive" mind from the enlightened and his finding of parallels between the "primitive" cultures of his day and that of the early Greeks. For example, Sedna in the Eskimo story becomes mistress of the underworld, just as does Persephone in the Greek myth. Greek myth, too, he assumed, was the product of a "primitive" mode of thought. This radical, new, and dramatic approach, taking as its premise the notion of progressive evolutionary development away from an earlier condition of savagery to present conditions of civilization, was destined to shape Western thought for the coming centuries and still has great power today.

The Italian Giambattista Vico (jom-ba-tēs-ta vē-kō) (1668–1744), sometimes regarded as the first modern historian (*Scienza nuova*, "New Science," 1725), accepted this evolutionary approach to the understanding of the past. History, he thought, was the study of the origin and unfolding of human society and institutions. (His contemporaries regarded history as the biographies of great men or the record of the unfolding of God's will.) Vico argued that history moves in great cycles, each of which has three phases, the same in every cycle but modified by new circumstances and developments.

The first phase in each cycle is the Age of Gods. In our own cycle, this was the period immediately after the Flood. In the Age of Gods, human activity is limited to a struggle for physical survival. People live close to nature, whose power they understand only as a display of anger by a mighty god. From this phase comes the image of God and of gods as terrible and wrathful beings and what we have called divine myth. In the next phase, the Age of Heroes, nature becomes separated from humankind. Emerging social institutions are connected with personified gods and heroes about whom stories are told. From the Age of Heroes descend what we have called legends. The third and last stage (we live in one now) is the Age of Man, in which reason replaces instinctive imagination and passion. Philosophy arises in this phase.

Vico's theory is one of the earliest of many efforts to understand myth as part of an all-embracing history of thought. Allegory, in his view, deals only with particular myths. What was really needed, Vico thought, was to discover a principle of myth itself in human consciousness. Myth originated in the earlier phases of culture, when humankind's thinking was highly concrete. At that time language, originally monosyllabic and versified, expressed a poetry and ritual more powerful than any we know today, a direct representation of reality. This is why myth is so personal and dramatic, so disconcerting to those who live in the "rational" Age of Man.

By recognizing that ways of thinking change fundamentally, Vico avoided two common pitfalls associated with evolutionary schemes: He did not simply idealize preliterate culture, and he recognized that earlier forms of understanding, which cannot be fully grasped by the standards of rational thought, are valid in their own terms.

## THEORIES OF THE 19TH AND 20TH CENTURIES

### Romantic Theories

Although there have been many disagreements in emphasis, approaches to myth since the Enlightenment have either used an evolutionary perspective, which assumes that myths are the relics of savagery, or have studied myth with the methods of the social sciences, which assume that myth reflects ways of thinking different from our own. Both approaches are closely related, and their effect is to reduce myth to a cultural relic. However, the counterview of myth as valid and understandable in its own terms, which did not entirely disappear at the time of the Enlightenment, surfaced again in the Romantic movement during the late 18th and early 19th centuries.

**Romanticism** was a reaction against what many saw as the arrogance, superficiality, and outright blindness of the Enlightenment. Opposing the Enlightenment's confident rationalism, the Romantics saw the emotional side of experience as most distinctively human: intense feeling, awareness of powerful but obscure forces, abnormal states, and a direct intuitive relationship to nature. Whereas thinkers of the Enlightenment attacked myth as a product of primitive mental and emotional states, the Romantics returned to myth as a vehicle for regaining lost truths. Such ideals were expressed mostly in poetry, painting, and music, but ambitious philosophical theories, especially in Germany, argued for the timeless truth of myth and for its continuing vital role in the modern world.

An explanation of how this could be, that myth embodies timeless truths, was given by Friedrich Creuzer (1771–1858) in his long book (in German) *Symbolism and Mythology of the Ancient Peoples, Especially the Greeks* (1810). Creuzer studied recently discovered material on the myths of ancient India and interpreted all myth, in

Neoplatonic fashion, as a set of symbols for universal truths. Indian religious texts, he argued, contained an ancient revelation of absolute truth. For example, Brahma as sole creator of the universe is a revelation of the truth of monotheism. As the Aryans—that is, the Indo-Europeans—spread from their homeland, the once pristine truth became obscure, preserved only in symbolic forms by a priestly elite, refracted like white light broken into various colors by a lens. The different mythologies of the Indo-European peoples are those colors, each expressing in its own idiom a truth that was originally, Creuzer thought, symbolized visually by means of hieroglyphs like those of Egypt.

Creuzer considered myth to be a way of dealing with absolute, infinite truth in finite narrative form. Whereas truth is rational and abstract, myth is dramatic and concrete. For example, the golden rope by which Zeus could suspend sea and earth if he chose (*Iliad*, 8.18–19) symbolizes the divine energy that supports the world. This is the same cosmic energy described as a thread of pearls in the Sanskrit classic *Bhagavad Gita*, "Song of the Blessed One." Each mythic image—the golden rope and the string of pearls—descends ultimately from a single primordial revelation to humankind of truth about the nature of reality.

Another imaginative, partly Romantic theory was advanced by **Johann Bachofen** (1815–1887; *Das Mutterrecht*, "Mother Right," 1861), a student of Roman law who noticed that women enjoyed considerable status in some ancient legal and social systems. All modern theories of a matriarchal phase in early human social development go back to Bachofen, who concluded that the patriarchal authority, which has dominated all present-day societies, was preceded by a stage during which women exercised great influence in their capacity as mothers.

Much of his evidence for this claim came from classical myth, which he considered to contain hidden truths about early human social structure. According to Bachofen's explanation, the earliest nomadic hunting phase was lawless, represented in myth by Aphrodite, who is unbridled lust. In this phase women were victims of violence. In a later phase, represented by Demeter, the institutions of agriculture and marriage were introduced, and values clustering around the mother encouraged peace and feelings of communal affection. On the other hand, the aggressive potential in woman's nature was reflected in myths about the Amazons.

Although Bachofen described favorably the early "mother right," he recognized a third, and higher, Apollonian phase, represented by Rome. Here the older, more primitive communal mother right was overthrown, and authority was invested in law that embodied the higher values of patriarchy, individuality, and rationality. His scheme, which influenced later Marxist theory, combined speculation about a happier, maternal past with a typically evolutionary pattern that moved through earthly and lunar phases to the present solar triumph of the patriarchal principle.

Friedrich Engels (1820–1895), one of the founding fathers of modern communism, took Bachofen's position in his book *The Origin of the Family, Private Property, and the State* (1883). Before the evolution of the state and the family, women ruled society and were free to have intercourse with whomever they pleased, so that no son ever knew his father. The eminent Russian folklorist Vladimir Propp (1895–1970), writing under the Soviet regime, pointed out that such was the situation of Oedipus: The myth must therefore be a historical reminiscence of the shift from a matriarchal to a patriarchal organization of society.

According to Propp, the shepherds in the Greek legend, who transported the foundling Oedipus to the wild and then to city of Corinth, stand for the foster-parents who in a primitive matriarchy cared for the children. Oedipus' age-mates, who questioned his birth, reflect some early collective, before the evolution of the family. Such teaching, about a primordial primitive matriarchy replaced by an enlightened patriarchy, is still official doctrine in the communist People's Republic of China.

## Anthropological Theories

The flood of information about newly discovered cultures pouring into Europe from colonial outposts and journeys of exploration did seem to support the view that myth is a symptom of intellectual backwardness, and students of myth formulated many variations on the concept of "primitive" societies and "primitive" ways of thinking by which myth could be understood. During the second half of the 19th century, the process of integrating diverse data into general theories of development was further encouraged by Charles Darwin's theory of biological evolution advanced in *The Origin of Species* (1859). From such studies emerged what is now called anthropology.

One of the most influential of these formulations was advanced by British anthropologist Edward Tylor (1832–1917), who presented his theory of universal cultural evolution proceeding through several stages in *Primitive Culture* (1871). Tylor explained the "quaint fancies and wild legends of the lower tribes" in terms of an original stage that he called "animistic." Animism is the belief that everything has a soul. Myth and religion, which are natural consequences of such a belief, do not ultimately come from inherently poetic language, as Vico thought. Instead, myth is a mistaken science or philosophy, rooted in fear or ignorance but designed to explain natural phenomena.

Other theories were advanced about the primitive state through which all human societies must pass. The model for the evolution of human societies was drawn from the biological evolution a species. Thus societies that represent earlier stages can exist, although only in isolated backwaters, at the same time as more evolved societies. Technologically primitive communities still intact in Australia or Africa, and practices and beliefs of European peasants, were found to be similar. For example, both operated on the assumption of the reality and efficacy of magic, and were devoted to the power of fetishes.

British author Andrew Lang (1844–1912; *Myth, Literature, and Religion*, 1887) popularized his general approach. Trained as a classicist in Greek and Latin, he was a prolific essayist, historian, poet, sportswriter, and critic, one of the leading intellectuals of his day. His retelling of traditional stories in the *Blue Fairy Book* and others, which he published with his wife, are still popular among children.

Deeply affected by the interest in evolution, he at first accepted Tylor's laws of cultural development, but as he examined the evidence more critically, he came to believe that there must have been more than a single pattern of development. Myth was indeed, as Tylor maintained, a protoscientific effort at explanation, but the primitive stage of culture was not always a time of confused theories about natural forces. Faced with examples of what seemed to be ethical monotheism among "savages," Lang argued that monotheism must in some cases have actually preceded animism and polytheistic myth, into which it subsequently degenerated. For example, the animistic religions of North America still preserved a notion of the Great Spirits that somehow stood behind all phenomena.

To most scholars, then, myth essentially reflected an early, clumsy effort to do what science later did better: explain why things are the way they are. **Sir James Frazer** (1854–1941), a classical scholar and one of the founders of modern anthropology, accepted the validity of social evolution as an explanation with universal application. With immense industry Frazer gathered evidence from all over the world, from American Indians, from Africans, from Melanesians, as scientific evidence from which decisive conclusions about the meaning of myth could be drawn.

Frazer's celebrated book, *The Golden Bough*, is often ranked as one of the most influential works of modern times. It began as two volumes published in 1890 and reached 12 volumes in the 1911–1915 edition. Frazer started by inquiring into the ancient tradition that a "King of the Wood" at Aricia, a village near Rome, ruled over a grove sacred to the Italic god Virbius. If a runaway slave came into the wood and broke a branch, a golden bough, from a sacred oak, the priest was compelled to fight the man, hence the title of Frazer's book (no connection, apparently, with the golden bough in Vergil's story of Aeneas' descent into the underworld: Chapter 6). If the priest was killed, the slave became the new priest. The priests of Virbius were always runaway slaves and always killed their predecessors.

Frazer searched the world over for evidence of his thesis that the story of the golden bough is a late survival of a primordial human social and religious institution in which the King of the Wood embodied and ensured the fertility of the realm. For example, Mexican myths are based on the conviction that human sacrifice is the basis for all fertility. When his waning power threatened the well-being of the people, the king had to be killed and a young, vital successor placed on the throne. The king must die that the people might live. As embodiment of a "corn" (that is, wheat) or fertility-god, his life and death represent the fundamental vitality of nature. The story of Osiris, for example, is a mythical projection of this pattern.

On the basis of this hypothetical primordial rite, Frazer attempted to account for much that we find in myths and religions worldwide. An elaborate system of taboos hemmed in the king's life. If he broke a taboo, his ability to help his people would diminish. Here, Frazer argued, is the origin of the dos and don'ts in every religion and of the many violated taboos in myth. Because the old king must die, many myths tell of the death of kings and gods. These stories, he thought, arose as explanations for real rituals in which a king actually was killed. The origin of myth is thus closely tied to religious ritual. This is the **ritual theory of myth**.

Frazer's understanding of myth as a secondary elaboration of ritual exerted considerable influence. Like others influenced by evolutionary thought, Frazer wanted to formulate a comprehensive theory of cultural development. To that end he replaced Tylor's "animism" with "magic," understood as a mechanical operation used by primitive peoples as part of a ritual to coerce impersonal natural or supernatural forces to obey human wishes.

When humans realized that magic was often ineffective, religion was born. The propitiation of quasihuman gods replaced coercion through magic. Science, in turn, was destined to replace religion. Myth is associated especially with the religious phase of development because myth is characterized by a belief in personal forces that act in stories, whereas science and magic are concerned with impersonal forces.

The concept of progress preoccupied Europeans of the late 19th century. Especially in England, progress was considered a change for the better and, in fact, implicit in the principle of evolution. Like writers on myth during the Enlightenment, Frazer ignored the possibility that change may not always bring improvement. Frazer himself did no fieldwork. He integrated into his master scheme a vast body of data, often carelessly gathered, and manipulated it to fit his theory.

In the 20th century, anthropological method was much improved by Bronislaw Malinowski (1884–1942; *Magic, Science, and Religion*, 1948), who was born in Poland but pursued his career chiefly in England. Influenced by French sociological thought, his own theory was based directly on fieldwork carried out between 1914 and 1918 among the Trobriand Islanders, a Melanesian people of a remote island complex northeast of New Guinea. Objecting to the evolutionary understanding of myth as protoscience, Malinowski held that its purpose was to serve as a "charter," a justification for the way things are. This is the **charter theory of myth**.

For example, a story might be told to justify someone's ownership of a certain part of the island—because that is where his ancestors sprang from the ground. According to Malinowski, myths justify and validate economic, political, social, and religious realities. We should not explain myth according to hypothetical patterns of cultural evolution at all, but from its social function, from how myth helps to deal with the practical problems of living. Malinowski usually is considered the founder of *functionalism*, the notion that the function of a practice determines the form it takes.

## Linguistic Theories

The science of Indo-European linguistics, which made great advances in the 19th century, was the basis for another allegorical approach to myth in theories advanced by **Max Müller** (1823–1900), the leading Sanskrit scholar of his day and a vigorous rival of Andrew Lang. Müller, a German-born Oxford don, saw in nearly every myth, whether about heroes or gods, an allegory of the struggle between sunlight and darkness. Hence this method of interpretation is called **solar mythology**.

Müller's theory, like others inspired by evolutionary thought and the rapid growth of science, sought to understand myth as the effort of early peoples to explain prominent natural phenomena, such as storms or celestial bodies, but Müller's theory was unusually influential because of the linguistic support he provided for the central role assigned to the sun.

In the fairly obscure Greek story of Endymion and Selenê, Endymion was a handsome youth whom Selenê ("moon") saw as he lay sleeping in a cave. She fell deeply in love with him and bore him many children. The two were separated when Zeus allowed Endymion to choose anything he wanted: He chose to sleep forever, never growing old. Because the Greek *endyein* originally meant "to dive," the name *Endymion* at first simply described the sun's setting ("diving") in the sea. The original meaning of *endyein* faded and was misunderstood to refer to a person, Endymion ("Diver"). The mythical story of the love of Selenê and Endymion, then, began with the words "Selenê embraces Endymion," that is, "Moon embraces Diver," which in the metaphorical "primitive" expression of early peoples was a way of saying "the sun is setting and the moon is rising."

Max Müller combined ancient physical allegory with the theories of Palaephatus about the distortion of language. Myth, he thought, begins through a "disease of language" whereby the original meaning of language, especially in observations about solar phenomena, was gradually misunderstood and reinterpreted. Müller and his followers were able in this way to argue that bloody death in myth was really the red-streaked sunset, that Odysseus' imprisonment in a cave was the waxing and waning year, and that Achilles' destruction of his enemies was really the splendid sun breaking through the clouds. King Midas and his golden touch was the sun gilding everything it touches.

Müller did attempt to furnish a theoretical explanation for shifts in the meaning of the names of mythical figures. In this he differed from his many predecessors in the long history of allegory, who simply proclaimed, without justification, the truth of whatever came to their minds. Still, Müller and his followers found the sun in everything. Like many ambitious theories of myth, this one began to refute itself. Andrew Lang wittily parodied the theory in a learned article that proved, by Müller's methods, that Müller had never existed, but was himself a solar myth!

"Solar mythology" arose under the influence of one of the great intellectual discoveries of modern times, that most European languages (except Basque, Finnish, Hungarian, and Estonian) and many others spoken as far east as central India (including Armenian, Iranian, and Sanskrit, but not the Semitic languages) and even in China are descended from the hypothetical parent-language called protoIndo-European. The discovery usually is credited to Sir William Jones (1746–1794), chief justice of India, founder of the Royal Asiatic Society, presented in a lecture in 1786. If it is possible to elucidate the origin and inner structure of modern European languages by comparing them with Greek, Latin, and Sanskrit, it should also be possible, according to the supporters of **Indo-European comparative mythology**, to elucidate European myths in the same way and to discover essential patterns and original meanings of myth.

For example, the Romans told a story about Mucius Scaevola ("Lefty"), who deliberately burned off his right hand to demonstrate Roman bravery to an enemy king. The Norsemen, Indo-European speakers like the Romans, told a story about the war-god Tiu (hence "Tuesday"), whose right hand the wolf Fenris bit off, an enemy of the present order of creation. While the wolf was biting off Tiu's hand, Tiu bound the distracted wolf by an unbreakable chain. We could thus infer the existence of an original Indo-European story about a man who sacrificed his hand for the good of all. This story becomes a patriotic tale among the Romans, who emphasized civic duty, but among the Norsemen, concerned with the opposition between the cosmic forces of order and chaos, it became a tale of temporary world redemption (one day the Fenris Wolf will escape its bonds and the world will end).

Indo-European comparative mythologists maintain that myths accompany language as language is passed on. They seek a common "grammar" or inner structure in the stories, which ought also to reveal something characteristic of Indo-European social traditions. In the mid-20th century the French scholar Georges Dumézil (1898–1986) refined this sort of interpretation by correlating three hypothetical original classes in Indo-European society with the roles played by certain deities in Indo-European myth. These classes are rulers and priests, warriors, and food producers, corresponding for example, in Norse myth to Odin as the patron of priests and magicians; to Thor as the sponsor of warriors; and to Freyr as the overseer of fertility and farming.

Take the Greek story of the Judgment of Paris. Why does Hera attempt to bribe Paris with an offer of royal power, while Athena offers him military glory and Aphrodite offers him Helen? Because the three choices represent the three fundamental activities in Indo-European society: Hera stands for royal authority, the ruling class; Athena stands for the warrior class; and Aphrodite, who sponsors reproduction and sustenance, represents the food producers. We might expect Demeter to represent sustenance, however, because Aphrodite's concerns are preeminently with human sexuality; furthermore, Aphrodite is a goddess of Semitic origin. But Dumézil must accept the story as it is given. In fact, the theory works poorly with Greek material.

## Psychological Theories

New fields of study of the past century inspired corresponding new theories of myth. Sociology and anthropology led to functionalism; linguistics led to Indo-European comparative mythology. Psychology, too, has brought with it both a key myth—the story of Oedipus—and a variety of new psychological theories.

At the time when anthropological approaches were developing, **Sigmund Freud** (1856–1939) advanced a view of myth based on the individual rather than on society. Myth, he thought, was a by-product of personal psychological forces. Freud's theories of myth began with his thinking about the dreams of individuals. The mind of a sleeper works by different rules from the mind of the wakeful, although dream symbols can correlate with things in the waking world. Freud formulated rules by which translation from everyday reality to symbolism in dreams takes place.

For example, *condensation* occurs when several things from the waking world are fused together in a dream, perhaps with disturbing effect. *Displacement* occurs when something in a dream stands for something quite different in the waking world, even its opposite, as when an enemy represents a lover whom the sleeper does not entirely trust. Condensation and displacement are necessary to the dreamer because the true thought is morally or emotionally repugnant to the waking consciousness. Because the thought is still there, however, it must be dealt with, and the mind releases tension by dealing with the problem indirectly. Dreams are symptoms of psychological tensions that can affect the waking world of those suffering from mental disease, from neuroses.

How do the dreams of individuals result in myths, which belong to a whole people? They do, Freud thought, because myths are the collective and recurrent dreams of the race. An example in myth of dream condensation would be the mythical Centaurs or Sirens, made up of two separate beings fused together. An example in myth of dream displacement would be the upward anatomical shift of a woman's pubic region to create the terrible face of Medusa.

Freud also held that neuroses and their symbolic expression in dreams go back to the infant's experience of his or her personal sexuality. He emphasized the **Oedipus complex**, first set forth in *The Interpretation of Dreams* (1899). From this story Sigmund Freud developed his notion that adult male psychology arises from the infant boy's sexual attraction to his mother and his hostility and jealousy toward his father.

Freud did not seek the origins of the legend in social history, as had the Soviet folklorist Vladimir Propp, but in the incest dreams of his patients, which he took to represent suppressed desires of childhood. The son wishes sexual contact with his mother, from whose breasts he feeds and in whose warm body he is daily encompassed. He resents the father's sexual demands on the mother, which remove him from her embrace. He wants to kill the father, that he might have the mother to himself. Only by overcoming such hidden, taboo, and obviously unspoken desires might one become an adult, Freud thought.

The myth of Oedipus, then, emerges from primeval dreams. To make his point Freud ignored inconvenient parts of the legend, above all the story that at the end of his life Oedipus may even have been taken up by the gods. Freud also ignores Oedipus' exposure as an infant and his great intelligence. Critics of Freud starkly complain that Freud's true intentions in his fantasies about human psychology were to denigrate human nature, to reduce it to raw and amoral animal impulse, a vision much in favor at the end of the 19th century. Like Oedipus, Freud says, we live in ignorance of our inner wishes that are so repugnant to morality, which Nature has forced upon us, but when we see them clearly, we seek to close our eyes. Freud was little interested in explaining the Oedipus story itself.

In Freudian interpretation, stories that describe heroes slaying dragons and marrying maidens are really forms of the Oedipus complex because they echo the son's repressed desire to kill his father (= the dragon) and have sexual intercourse with his mother (= the maid). Cronus castrated Uranus because sons want to deprive their fathers of sexual power, and they fear the same treatment from their own sons in turn. Mythical kings and queens represent parents; sharp weapons are the male sexual organ, and caves, rooms, and houses symbolize the mother's containing womb. The imagery of myths can therefore be translated into sexual imagery, often in specifically anatomical ways.

Freud saw myths as arising among a race in the way that dreams arise in the individual, but he also argued that individual psychological development repeats the psychological history of the whole race. Sometime before Freud embryologists had developed the notion that "ontogeny recapitulates phylogeny"—the development of the individual goes through the same stages as that of the race. This is an adaptation of evolutionary thinking. The individual's dreams reflect the same primitive mode of consciousness that we find in myth, which are collective dreams preserved from the primitive childhood of the race.

His theory is yet another that connects the mythical with the primitive and the irrational, an approach common since the Enlightenment. A Freudian reading of myth is allegory in yet another guise, translating mythical patterns and events into psychological patterns and events. But like Max Müller, and unlike earlier interpreters, Freud explained not merely how but also why shifts occur from one meaning to another.

Freud's associate **Carl Jung** (yunk, 1875–1961) continued to explore the notion of an unconscious part of human nature. Like Freud, Jung discerned a complex symbolism that both conceals the unconscious and, to the psychiatrist, furnishes access to it. Jung did not believe, however, that the symbolism of the unconscious mind was predominantly sexual in nature, nor even that dream symbolism ultimately belonged to the individual.

Jung's theory resembles Eastern religious teachings in some respects. For him the consciousness of the individual is like a bay or an inlet on a great ocean of psychic activity, which he called the **collective unconscious** (Freud had implied as much, with his notion of racial dreaming). Into the bay swim, from time to time, great beings that inhabit the deep. These are the *archetypes* (a Greek term also used by Neoplatonists), timeless recurrent images on which our emotional world and our myths are built.

Certain groups of archetypes may dominate the consciousness of entire cultures for periods of time. Jung spoke of such different archetypes as the Wise Old Man, the Earth Mother, and the Divine Child. Jung considered the *mandala*, a perfectly symmetrical, geometric visual figure used for focusing the consciousness in Buddhist meditation, to be an emblem of the total psychological integration that each person seeks and that myth reflects. In this sense myth can never be discarded from human life. Whether we know it or not, we live out myths in our own lives, a notion Joseph Campbell, deeply influence by Jung, popularized in many books, especially *The Hero with a Thousand Faces* (New York, 1968).

Another follower of Jung, Erich Neumann (1905–1960), used Jung's method to explain the common myth of the dragon-combat. The myth, he argued, symbolizes the breaking away of an individual's consciousness from the great collective unconscious of the world. The dragon represents the collective unconscious, always trying to swallow the hero, who symbolizes individual consciousness. The collective unconscious is also represented by the Great Mother-goddess, the mother of all things, a recurrent type in myth and in the history of religion. Although she is the source of individual consciousness and of life itself, she threatens to swallow her own progeny.

For this reason, evil female forces—monsters like Tiamat—threaten the male hero. At some point the monster may actually swallow the hero (as the whale swallowed Jonah), but defeat is always temporary. The hero's ultimate victory over the dragon represents the emergence of personal identity, the victory of the individual consciousness over the threatening collective unconscious. The hero's reward—princess or treasure—represents the devouring collective unconscious in a tamed-down form, defeated, and now made fecund. The combat myth is really a description of an individual's psychological destiny.

## Structuralist Theories

A highly influential theory of myth interpretation is **structuralism**, especially as propounded by French anthropologist **Claude Lévi-Strauss** (1908–2009). Meaning in a traditional story is not conveyed by the content, he maintained, but by the structural relations behind the content. In this most rationalistic and abstract of theories, the meaning of myth is its pure form.

Structural relations often are so subtle that they can be made clear only by means of diagrams, charts, and formulas, which resemble mathematical formulas. The meaning of a story, then, is independent of any particular telling of it, residing ultimately in all possible variants of the story taken together. Far from confining himself to "traditional tales," Lévi-Strauss declared that even the interpretation of a myth is to be considered part of the myth, including Lévi-Strauss' own analyses, which are simply additional variants!

Lévi-Strauss finds the origin of myth in the principle that "mythical thought always works from the awareness of oppositions toward their progressive mediation." Humans perceive the world in terms of sharp, intolerable dualities: hot and cold, bitter and sweet, raw and cooked, alive and dead. Because by nature we cannot tolerate opposition for which intermediaries do not exist, we bridge perceived contradictions by telling stories.

For example, the story of Cronus fathering his children but refusing to allow them to be born, and of Uranus' son Cronus swallowing his children after they were born, mediate between the opposites of birth and death. The irreconcilable opposites are brought together by telling a story in which the same creature both generates and consumes his progeny. The story in *Gilgamesh* of a man who went to the land of the dead and returned brings together the irreconcilable opposites of life and death: Although life and death are opposites, in myth we can tell how a man journeyed to the land of the dead and returned. There are many such stories in myths from around the world. Our binary perception of reality derives, Lévi-Strauss thought, from the binary physical structure of our brains, which is supposed to make consciousness possible. Because of this binary structure, we can never be fully and finally reconciled with perceived oppositions—hence the dynamic quality of myth.

In 1955, Lévi-Strauss offered a celebrated interpretation of the myth of Oedipus. Despite its obscurity, his reading of the myth has attracted widespread comment. According to Lévi-Strauss, the myth has no message. It expresses the perception of irreconcilable claims about human origins. The Thebans claimed to be autochthonous, "sprung from the earth." Thus Oedipus, "swollen-footed," is so called because creatures who spring from the earth have something wrong with their feet. On the other hand, the Thebans obviously sprang from their mothers' wombs, and Oedipus is certainly born from Jocasta. Therefore the myth of Oedipus is alleged to bridge, through story, what cannot be bridged through logic.

Lévi-Strauss' interpretations are difficult to assess, in part because of the obscurity of his expression. He summarizes his argument about the myth of Oedipus in this way: "Overvaluation of blood relations is to their undervaluation as the attempt to escape autochthony is to the impossibility of succeeding in it."

It is also hard to know when we have found the true structure of a myth because different possibilities for analysis so often exist. As an anthropologist, Lévi-Strauss worked principally among South American Indians, through whose myths he wanted not only to discover the deep concerns, fears, and ambitions of these peoples but to lay open the inner workings of the whole human mind. In this he follows the ancient tradition of commentators wanting to prove that secrets about human nature and human destiny are hidden in traditional tales. More specifically, Lévi-Strauss echoed the Neoplatonists' program of discovering behind the stuff of myth an abstract pattern or code that explains the very nature of things.

In spite of its limitations, Lévi-Strauss' structural method of interpretation has had considerable exploratory power because it brings out hitherto unnoticed facets of myth by bringing together whole systems of myth and, beyond that, by relating myth to broader aspects of culture. A group of Lévi-Strauss' French followers has followed up the method for Greek myth, especially J.-P. Vernant (1914–2007), Pierre Vidal-Naquet (1930–2006), and Marcel Detienne (b. 1935). These authors, together with Claude Lévi-Strauss himself, are often called the **Paris school of myth criticism**.

We can take as an example of their method their treatment of the Greek pantheon. The usual way of studying the pantheon is to examine each god in isolation, speculating on his or her origin and saying something about associated myths and rituals. According to J.-P. Vernant, however, we can never understand any one god in isolation, any more than a single word; one must seek the "syntax," the complicated interrelations that bind together all the gods in myth. Only then can we understand the conceptual universe of the Greeks.

For example, the traveler Pausanias noted that on the base of Phidias' statue of Zeus in Olympia were linked the images of Hestia and Hermes. Why? Because, according to Vernant, Hestia and Hermes embody the contrary but complementary aspects of the Greeks' apprehension of space. Hestia is the fixed point, the hearth at the center of the household and of the city; Hermes represents transition, movement, change, the connecting link between oppositions.

Greek social life echoes the same polarity. As Hestia is to Hermes, so is woman to man: The woman stays at home, while the man travels abroad, conducts business, and wages war. Neither Hestia nor Hermes, then, can be understood in isolation because they constitute opposite poles of a single concept. To us the word *space* represents this single concept, but the Greeks, who lacked this abstract expression, represented the same notion by the different but complementary activities of Hestia and Hermes. (In fact, several words in Greek do roughly correspond to our *space*.)

By selecting and linking apparently disparate items taken from all aspects of culture, structuralist interpretations attempt to detect the rules shaping myth. The complexity of the enterprise points to both its possibilities and its hazards. Interplay between details and larger patterns yields fascinating insights, but the objectivity and significance of what emerges are a persistent difficulty. The universal claims of structuralist theory, professing as it does to be based on the very laws of human thought, permit it to be applied practically everywhere but encourage criticism on the familiar ground of attempting too much.

## Contextual Approaches

The German scholar Walter Burkert (b. 1931) well describes such weakness in his book *Structure and History in Greek Mythology and Ritual* (1979), which has had strong influence. Burkert accepts the importance of structure in the study of myth, agreeing that the very identity of a tale is maintained by a structure of sense within it. The existence of this constant, partly invisible, internal structure makes it possible for us to say that Homer's story of Oedipus, in which he does not blind himself and stays in Thebes, and Sophocles' story, in which he blinds himself and leaves the city, are both "the myth of Oedipus," despite their differences. However, Burkert opposes Lévi-Strauss' indifference to changing cultural and historical conditions, which constantly impart different collective meanings to a myth. Cultural and historical context must always be taken into account, Burkert insists.

Reviving in part the ritual theory of myth, Burkert argues that the structures that inform myth reflect biological or cultural **programs of action**. An example of a cultural program of action can be found in the hunting practices of Paleolithic man. Forced to kill his prey in order to survive but feeling a close relationship with and affection for animals, the hunter assuages his feelings of guilt through various ceremonies. After killing an animal, he makes a mock restoration by setting up its bones.

This program of action can explain details in the myth of the hunter Actaeon, who was turned into a stag by Artemis, a goddess of hunting, and torn to pieces by his own dogs. The story reflects a prehistoric ritual in which real animals were hunted by men in animal disguise. Thus the dogs are personified in the mythical tradition to the extent of being given individual names. In one version of this myth, the dogs' grief-stricken howling at Actaeon's death is brought to an end when the Centaur Chiron makes an image of Actaeon, which the dogs mistake for their slain master. This making of the image of the slain man/animal, in Burkert's view, reflects the very old ritual reconstruction of the dead animal by the guilt-ridden hunter, actually practiced by tribal peoples.

Surely, Greek myth does preserve many ritual elements, including, no doubt, some drawn from Paleolithic hunting practice, and Burkert's remarks on religion and myth are always enlightening. However, his thesis that Greek sacrificial ritual, and the myths that reflect it, derive from ancient hunting practice leaves unexplained why Greek sacrificial ritual nearly always used domestic animals, not wild animals captured for the purpose. His conviction that ancient hunters felt "guilty" about killing their prey is also open to criticism. Although hunters undoubtedly respect their prey, we usually think of guilt as an emotion arising from violating the social mores; killing animals did not violate the mores of Paleolithic hunters. No doubt one reason that ancient hunters reconstructed their slain prey was to ensure, through magic, that there might be still more animals to kill.

Feminist critics may also apply a contextual approach, using myth to cast light on underlying social realities related to gender or show how myths may actually construct reality. Thus the myth of Demeter and Persephonê explained to Greek women their expected roles in marriage, childbearing, and religious cult, making such roles seem intrinsic and natural.

The contextual approach to myth is complex, making use of insights from structural, historical, and comparative methods and appealing broadly to what we know about human biology, the history of religion, language, and anthropology.

## CONCLUSION: THE STUDY OF MYTH

What are we to make of this long development, the history of the interpretation of myths, of which we have here given only brief highlights? We must be impressed by the abiding fascination that myths have exercised over the human mind. But what validity do these systems of interpreting myth have for our understanding of myth, if by "understanding" we mean placing something in a larger and more familiar context?

The ancient Greek theorists, puzzled by the strangeness of traditions taken from a preliterate and prephilosophic past, attempted to explain their own myths by assimilating them to "correct" models of reality as created by philosophy. They saw in myths allegories for philosophic descriptions of the physical world or, in euhemerism, a source for historical reconstruction of the human past, or a set of examples for how one should behave. Later methods have worked much the same way, adapting myths to new models of reality as they emerged from Christian to modern times. The scientific model of reality, which has increasingly dominated thought since the Enlightenment and especially since the 19th century, is only the latest in a long line of such models. Although the 19th-century theory of myth as a "disease of language" centering on natural phenomena was encouraged by scientific linguistics, it is remarkably similar to the interpretation proposed by Palaephatus in 300 BC. Modern psychological theories, especially those of Jung and Lévi-Strauss and Joseph Campbell, offer explanations that in important ways repeat and refine approaches used by much earlier interpreters who sought in myth allegories of spiritual and psychological truths.

The strength of science lies in defining ideas precisely and treating them within strictly controlled guidelines. The power of humanistic studies, on the other hand, lies in their concern with the capacity of humans, as symbol-making beings, to create alternative worlds. Myth is one such alternative world, and the interpretation of myth is another. Each is an expression of the same human capacity.

Historically, the interpretation of myth is fully as important as myth itself and in fact occurs on a far grander scale. The interchangeable use of the words *myth* (the story itself) and *mythology* (reflection on myth) in English usage unintentionally points to this critical confusion, a fact recognized by structuralists when they suggest that interpretations of myths are only the addition of new myths to old. If myth embodies the tensions, values, and intellectual currents of the society that produces it, myth interpretation embodies those currents no less faithfully. A sketch of the history of myth interpretation turns out to be a sketch of the history of ideas. In the history of myth interpretation we can watch and study ever-changing intellectual fashions in relation to an unchanging body of material.

The grand theorizers about myth like to pick out this or that story, this or that figure, make impressive observations, and then speak as if their conclusions were applicable to all myths from all times and all places. But myths are so different from one another, and even our definition of myth so vague and controversial, that any universal explanation is bound to be arbitrary and to serve the theoretical interests of the definer. The history of the interpretation of myth richly demonstrates this fact. With careful selection any theory will work well in particular instances, elucidating minor points with astonishing clarity. Applied to the next myth, the theory may be unable to deal plausibly with even obvious features.

Myth taken together is too complex, too many-faceted, to be explained by a single theory, as is fully recognized in the contextual approach, which we have favored throughout this book. The complexity of myth is bound up with the complexity of human consciousness itself and with the special role that the Greeks, the inventors of the alphabet, played in the transition from an oral traditional culture to one that was alphabetic and self-critical. To understand myth, we must make use of insights offered by different schools of interpretation. No one method of analysis will dissolve the endless mysteries of myth.

## Key Terms

rationalism 547
Xenophanes 547
allegory 548
symbolism 548
etymology 549
euhemerism 550
Neoplatonism 553
Enlightenment 558
Romanticism 559

Johann Bachofen 560
Sir James Frazer 562
ritual theory of myth 562
charter theory of myth 563
Max Müller 563
solar mythology 563
Indo-European
comparative
mythology 564

Sigmund Freud 565
Oedipus complex 565
Carl Jung 566
collective unconscious 566
structuralism 567
Claude Lévi-Strauss 567
Paris school of myth
criticism 568
programs of action 569

# Further Reading

## GENERAL

Czapo, E., *Theories of Mythology* (Oxford, UK, 2005).
Buxton, R., ed., *From Myth to Reason* (Oxford, UK, 1999).
Dundes, A., ed., *Sacred Narrative: Readings in the Theory of Myth* (Berkeley, CA, 1984).
Kirk, G. S., *The Nature of Greek Myths* (New York, 1974).
Segal, R. A., ed., *Literary Criticism and Myth*, 6 vols. (New York, 1996).

## GREEK THEORIES

Guthrie, W. K. C., *The Greek Philosophers, from Thales to Aristotle* (New York, 1960).
Kirk, G. S., and J. E. Raven, *The Presocratic Philosophers: A Critical History with a Selection of Texts* (Cambridge, UK, 1962).

## MEDIEVAL AND RENAISSANCE THEORIES

Allen, S. H., ed., et al., *Survival of the Gods: Classical Mythology in Medieval Art* (Providence, RI, 1987).
Bush, D., *Mythology and the Renaissance Tradition in English Poetry* (Minneapolis, MN, 1932; reprinted New York, 1963).
Seznec, J., *The Survival of the Pagan Gods: The Mythological Tradition and Its Place in Renaissance Humanism* (New York, 1953; reprinted Princeton, NJ, 1994).

## THEORIES OF THE ENLIGHTENMENT

Marsak, L. M., trans. and ed., *The Achievement of Bernard le Bovier de Fontenelle* (New York, 1970).

## ROMANTIC THEORIES

Kamenetsky, C., *The Brothers Grimm and Their Critics, Folktales and the Quest for Meaning* (Athens, OH, 1992).

## ANTHROPOLOGICAL THEORIES

Ackerman, R., *The Myth and Ritual School: J. G. Frazer and the Cambridge Ritualists* (New York, 1991).
Fontenrose, J., *The Ritual Theory of Myth* (Berkeley, CA, 1966; reprinted 1971).
Frazer, J. G., *The New Golden Bough*, ed. T. Gaster (New York, 1959).
Malinowski, B., *Magic, Science, and Religion, and Other Essays* (New York, 1948; reprinted Prospect Heights, IL, 1992).
Vickery, J. B., *The Literary Impact of The Golden Bough* (Princeton, NJ, 1973).

## LINGUISTIC THEORIES

Puhvel, J., *Comparative Mythology* (Baltimore, MD, 1987; reprinted 1989).

## PSYCHOLOGICAL THEORIES

Jung, C. G., et al., *Man and His Symbols* (New York, 1968).

_____, and K. Kerényi, *Essays on a Science of Mythology: The Myth of the Divine Child and the Mysteries of Eleusis* (Princeton, NJ, 1993).

Neumann, E., *The Origins and History of Consciousness*, trans. R. F. C. Hull (Princeton, NJ, 1954; reprinted 1970).

## STRUCTURALISM

Detienne, M., *The Creation of Mythology*, trans. M. Cook (Chicago, 1986).

Gordon, R. L., ed., *Myth, Religion and Society. Structuralist Essays by M. Detienne, L. Gernet, J.-P. Vernant and P. Vidal-Naquet* (Cambridge, UK, 1981).

Leach, E., *Claude Lévi-Strauss*, rev. ed. (New York, 1974; reprinted Chicago, 1989).

Lévi-Strauss, C., *The Raw and the Cooked*, trans. J. and D. Weightman (Chicago, 1980).

Propp, V., *Morphology of the Folktale*, 2nd ed. (Austin, TX, 1968; Russian original, 1928).

Vernant, J.-P., *Myth and Society in Ancient Greece*, trans. J. Lloyd (New York, 1990).

## CONTEXTUAL APPROACHES

Burkert, W., *Structure and History in Greek Mythology and Ritual* (Berkeley, CA, 1979).

_____, *Homo Necans: The Anthropology of Ancient Greek Sacrificial Ritual and Myth* (Berkeley, CA., 1983: German original 1972).

Dowden, K., *The Uses of Greek Mythology* (London, 1992).

Powell, B. B., *Classical* Myth, 7th ed (Upper Saddle River, NJ, 2011).

_____, *A Short Introduction to Classical Myth* (Upper Saddle River, NJ, 2002).

# INDEX

Page numbers followed by "f" indicate content in figures.